GARIBALDI

GARIBALDI

INVENTION OF A HERO

LUCY RIALL

YALE UNIVERSITY PRESS
NEW HAVEN AND LONDON

For information about this and other Yale University Press publications, please contact:

US Office: sales.press@yale.edu   yalebooks.com
Europe Office: sales@yaleup.co.uk   www.yaleup.co.uk

Set in Minion by MATS Typesetters, Southend-on-Sea, Essex
Printed in Great Britain by St Edmundsbury Press Ltd, Bury St Edmunds

Library of Congress Cataloging-in-Publication Data

Riall, Lucy, 1962–
    Garibaldi: invention of a hero/Lucy Riall.
       p. cm.
    Includes bibliographical references and index.
    ISBN 978–0–300–11212–2 (alk. paper)
    1. Garibaldi, Giuseppe, 1807–1882. 2. Garibaldi, Giuseppe, 1807–1882—Influence. 3. Garibaldi, Giuseppe, 1807–1882—Public opinion. 4. Generals—Italy—Biography. 5. Statesmen—Italy—Biography. 6. Italy—History—1849–1870. 7. Italy—History—1870–1914. I. Title.
    DG552.8.G2R514 2007
    945'.083092—dc22
    [B]
                                                                                    2006032507

A catalogue record for this book is available from the British Library.

10 9 8 7 6 5 4 3 2 1

A Ciccio

CONTENTS

ILLUSTRATIONS AND MAPS

ILLUSTRATIONS

MAPS

ACKNOWLEDGEMENTS

I wish to thank the following organisations for their generosity in funding the research on which this book is based: the Leverhulme Trust, the British Academy, the University of London Central Research Fund, and Birkbeck College Faculty of Arts Research Fund. I am also grateful to the staff of the Archivio di Stato and the Archivio Comunale, Palermo; the Istituto per la Storia del Risorgimento Italiano, Rome; the Museo del Risorgimento, Milan; and the National Archives, London. My thanks also to the librarians of the Società Siciliana per la Storia Patria, Palermo; the Biblioteca di Storia Moderna e Contemporanea, Rome; the Biblioteca Nazionale, Florence; the Museo del Risorgimento, Genoa; the Fondazione Giangiacomo Feltrinelli, Milan; the Staatsbibliothek and the Ibero-Amerikanisches Institut, Berlin; the Bibliothèque Nationale de France; the New York Public Library; the University of London Library; Birkbeck College Library (especially Aubrey Greenwood); and the British Library.

I owe a very real debt to my colleagues in the School of History, Classics and Archaeology at Birkbeck College for providing me with an intellectually stimulating and socially relaxing environment in which I could think about, and carry out the research for, this book. They were also kind enough to allow me long stretches of leave so that I could write it. I would like to thank John Arnold, Joanna Bourke, Filippo de Vivo, Catherine Edwards, David Feldman, Marybeth Hamilton, Daniel Pick, Jan Rüger, Chandak Sengoopta, Julian Swann and Frank Trentmann for answering all my questions and requests for information. As well as providing much-needed scholarly advice, Sean Brady, Emma Dench and Naoko Shimazu were a great source of personal encouragement; Sean Brady was also kind enough to read the entire manuscript and encouraged me to clarify many points and avoid as many errors. My thanks also to Jon Wilson for his help with the illustrations.

A long series of discussions with Alberto Banti, Paul Ginsborg, Stephen Gundle, Brian Hamnett, Maurizio Isabella, David Laven, Adrian Lyttelton and Silvana Patriarca helped me to formulate the questions and ideas on which the book is based. Stephen Gundle, Silvana Patriarca and John Foot read and made very valuable comments on the manuscript. Colin Barr was an obliging source of information on Irish Catholics and Garibaldi, and let me see the letters of Paul Cullen that he is editing for publication. Nicola Miller and David Rock helped me with the South American material; Rohan McWilliam advised me on British popular politics; Axel Körner told me about popular theatre; Derek Beales helped me understand nineteenth-century British Protestantism; and Patrizia di Bello did the same for nineteenth-century photography. Marta Bonsanti chased a number of hard-to-find references in Italy and Christopher Duggan answered questions about Crispi. None of the above is responsible for my errors, but I am grateful to all of them for their advice. I want especially to thank Denis Mack Smith, who gave me the contents of his Garibaldi library at the beginning of my research, and who has been a very generous supporter of my version of the Garibaldi legend.

One of the pleasures of writing a book about a figure of international popular renown has been the contacts which I have been able to make with other scholars. Much of the material in this book has been tried out on audiences in seminars, conference papers and lectures at the University of Cambridge, the University of Oxford, the Institute of Historical Research London, the British Academy, Columbia University, Princeton University, Vanderbilt University, Wofford College, the British School at Rome, the University of Pisa, the Ecole Normale Supérieure, Paris, and the Freie Universität, Berlin. The final result has benefited considerably from all their comments and criticisms. My thanks to Gilles Pécout at the Ecole Normale Supérieure and to Oliver Janz at the Freie Universität for arranging for me to spend longer periods of time as a visiting professor at both institutions and for their patient advice and encouragement. I hope that at least some of my enjoyment and appreciation of these broader cultural opportunities is conveyed in what follows.

It is a truism that writing a book is a strange and solitary, if satisfying, experience, and this one has been no exception. So I am very happy to thank all my friends for their help and support during some not always easy times. Both my parents died before I finished the book but it owes a great deal to my father's fair-mindedness and my mother's passionate enthusiasm. For their generous hospitality during overseas research trips, I would like to thank Annliese Nef, Cesare Garaffa, Marliese Eckau, Christian Garaffa, Maria Luisa Garaffa and Marilyn Nicoud; and I must add a special thank-you to Elena Pezzini, Rosa di Liberto and Sergio Aiosa for their company and conversation during the long Palermo evenings after the libraries closed. George and Fernanda Herford were an unfailing source of spport and friendship, while Matthew Brettler and Sarah Garaghan were never far from the other end of a telephone line. Andrew Hudders gave me a place to stay in New York, and has followed attentively the book's progress in London, Palermo and Berlin. The biggest thank-you must go to my husband, Francesco Filangeri. He took many of the photographs for the illustrations in this volume, and was an informative and lively guide through the wealth of visual material on Garibaldi. More generally, his advice, comments, criticisms and humour all proved indispensable, and I hope that the book is a sufficient expression of my love and appreciation.

INTRODUCTION

I have seen to-day the face of Garibaldi; and now all the devotion of his friends is made as clear as day to me. You have only to look into his face, and you feel that there is, perhaps, the one man in the world in whose service you would, taking your heart in your hand, follow blindfold to death.
(Harriet Meuricoffre, Naples, August 1860)[1]

An exemplary life

The life of Giuseppe Garibaldi (1807–82) spanned the defining events and places of the nineteenth century. He was born in Nice, at that time under Napoleonic rule, and spent much of his youth travelling as a merchant sailor through the Mediterranean from Nice to the Black Sea and back again. It was through travel that he acquired a political awareness, mainly through encounters with French political exiles and with Italian revolutionary conspirators. He became a follower of the Italian nationalist, Giuseppe Mazzini, and embraced republican nationalism. In 1834, involvement with an abortive 'Young Italy' uprising in Genoa against the Piedmontese government obliged him to leave Europe altogether, and he was to spend much of the formative period of his life (from twenty-eight to forty years of age) in South America. South America was where Garibaldi first began to get a name for himself. By the early 1840s, newspaper reports had already begun to speak of Garibaldi as a romantic 'bandit leader' and to tell of (and often condemn) his adventures in Brazil and of his formation of an 'Italian Legion of Montevideo' to defend liberal Uruguay against the aggression of Buenos Aires. Garibaldi then won international fame during the 1848–9 revolutions in Italy. Returning to Italy from South America to fight for the revolution, he helped mastermind the heroic, if doomed, defence of the Roman Republic against the French army sent to restore the Pope in the summer of 1849. His last-ditch attempt to march north to save the besieged Venetian Republic, his daring exploits in eluding the enemy when all was lost and the tragic death *en route* of his pregnant wife Anita added to the growing legend surrounding Garibaldi.

During the early 1850s, already a celebrity and increasingly pursued by journalists and assorted admirers, Garibaldi went once more into exile and into a form of political retirement. He spent almost two years living quietly among the Italian community in Staten Island, New York, and then travelled again as a merchant sailor to central America and around the Pacific Ocean to China and the Philippines. In 1854 he returned to Nice via England and settled in a new home on the isolated island of Caprera off the northern coast of Sardinia. In the more liberal climate of Italian politics from the mid-1850s onwards, he seemed to abandon his republican convictions and to distance himself from Mazzini; he came gradually out of retirement to form close links with the Piedmontese government – with the Piedmontese prime minister Cavour, with his Italian moderate liberal colleagues and with the king of Piedmont, Vittorio Emanuele II. He appeared to endorse the 'Piedmontese' or monarchical formula for Italian unification. In 1859, he even became a general in the Piedmontese army, and led a volunteer army into the 'Second War of Independence' against Austria. Yet in 1860, in what was probably his greatest triumph, he defied Cavour and the king of Piedmont to head an expedition of a 'Thousand' volunteers, which sailed across the Mediterranean from Quarto near Genoa to Marsala in Western Sicily in order, as he put it, to help his 'brothers in danger',[2] or in an attempt to save a revolution in Sicily from certain defeat. These dramatic actions completely overturned the status quo in Italy and in Europe as a whole. The surprising success of Garibaldi's expedition led in under six months to, successively, the collapse of the Bourbon monarchy of the Two Sicilies, the overthrow of papal power in central Italy and the creation of an Italian nation state, with Vittorio Emanuele II of Piedmont as its monarch.

After 1860, while ostensibly a national hero, Garibaldi became increasingly alienated from the Piedmontese 'solution' and from monarchical Italy. He moved ever further to the left, towards socialism and extreme anti-clericalism. He organised two disastrous attempts (in 1862 and 1867), in the face of official opposition, to seize Rome from the Pope and make it the capital of Italy. But he also participated in the 1866 war on the government side against Austria, after which Italy gained control of Venetia. He embarked on a triumphant tour of England in 1864. In 1870, already an old and sick man, and in an emotional, if largely futile, attempt to help defend the nascent French Republic against the German Empire, Europe's new superpower, he organised a final expedition of volunteers to fight in the Franco-Prussian war. The rest of his life was spent in partial seclusion with his family at home in Caprera, a seclusion interrupted by sporadic forays into public life. Even before his death in 1882 Caprera had become a place of pilgrimage, with a large and dedicated band of followers and enthusiasts seeking to pay homage to Garibaldi. Only two months before his death, and so incapacitated by arthritis that he could rarely leave his bed and had to be carried in a specially designed chair, he had set out on a tour of southern Italy, and came to Sicily once more, this time to commemorate the 600th anniversary of the revolt known as the Sicilian Vespers.[3]

From relatively humble beginnings, Garibaldi became one of the most popular and enduring political heroes of the nineteenth-century world. His appeal transcended social classes and his fame crossed national frontiers. Indeed, as a revolutionary 'outsider' with little, if any, official backing, and as a political leader who was in power for less than six months in his entire political career, he was the first to achieve a truly worldwide fame, and to reach a mass audience via the new technologies of mass communication. Lithographers and photographers produced countless images of Garibaldi, stressing variously the hero's strength, bravery, endurance, virility, humanity, kindness, saintliness and spirit of adventure. His name sold newspapers and books in London, Paris, Berlin and New York, as well as in Italy, and both journalists and their readers revelled in his exploits. He was hated as much by the Church and traditionalists as he was loved by the young and excluded. Young men volunteered to fight alongside him and middle-class women rushed to get close to him. As head of the 1860 revolution in Sicily, he was said to be 'worshipped' by peasants 'as a mythical hero'[4] and had children 'held up towards him as before a saviour'.[5] Hailed on a visit in 1864 as 'the greatest man by whom England has ever been visited', Garibaldi's arrival in London 'resulted in such a scene as can hardly be witnessed twice in a lifetime'.[6] He attracted vast and enthusiastic crowds, pubs were named after him, and souvenirs and replicas were produced on a huge scale. As recounted in countless cheap biographies and reproduced in innumerable illustrations, his life had all the ingredients to make him famous and popular among the nineteenth-century reading public. He was a general who triumphed against terrible odds, a dignified leader who cared for the common man, and a romantic figure who had experienced his full share of personal suffering, loneliness and hardship. His striking appearance – his good looks and flamboyant clothes – made him an instantly recognisable figure, while his simple manner and austere lifestyle reinforced the seductive appeal of a hero unspoilt by his cult status.

After his death in 1882, Garibaldi became the subject of an offical cult. This cult was part of a concerted attempt by the Italian government, and especially by Francesco Crispi, the dominant political figure of the time, to create Italy's 'Risorgimento' (the 'national resurgence', c. 1792–c. 1870) as a 'place of memory', as well as to give Italians a political education which would compete with and replace the traditional loyalites and teachings of the Catholic Church and old regime states.[7] National ceremonies such as the burial of King Vittorio Emanuele II's body in 1878 in the Pantheon in Rome and the national pilgrimage in 1884 to his tomb;[8] annual commemorative events such as Constitution Day;[9] huge choreographed parades to celebrate anniversaries like that of 20 September (the date of the breach of Rome's Porta Pia by the Italian government in 1870);[10] and the creation of new public spaces such as museums of the Risorgimento[11] and monuments (most famously the *Vittoriano* in Rome):[12] all these were intended to confirm the status of the Risorgimento as Italy's foundation story and to create a 'civic religion' which would sacralise the secular state and create a common sense of national and political belonging.[13] And, since their purpose was to lend legitimacy to the government, such memorials and anniversaries sought to create and reinforce a particular memory of the Risorgimento. They invariably stressed the unifying, and satisfactory, nature of the monarchical solution to the Risorgimento, and told of the common aims of its protagonists and the heroic, disinterested actions of its leaders.

Control of the posthumous memory of Garibaldi was central to this secular yet monarchical vision of Italian national identity. Official efforts concentrated on creating a conciliatory cult of national heroes, which was to turn the old rivals Garibaldi, Vittorio Emanuele II, Cavour and Mazzini into lifelong allies, and which venerated them alongside a medley of other famous Italians such as Dante Alighieri, Christopher Columbus, Giordano Bruno and Ugo Foscolo.[14] During the twenty years after his death, monuments were raised to Garibaldi all over Italy. Whether on horseback or on foot, sword in hand or pointing toward future glory, Garibaldi replaced princes, saints, and even sometimes the Madonna herself as the subject of public representations in squares all over Italy.[15] Garibaldi was to become a secular saint, a symbol of Italian unity. At the inauguration of the Turin monument to Garibaldi in 1887, the official orator, Tommaso Villa, spoke passionately to the assembled crowds of Garibaldi's saintly qualities, of his virtue and dedication to the nation, and of his role as a symbol of national unity.[16] The importance of Garibaldi to the government, and especially to its leader, Crispi, was clear in Rome, where the monument to Garibaldi was said to be the largest of its kind ever built in Europe and took almost ten years to complete (see figure 1 opposite). The unveiling of the vast equestrian statue on the Janiculum hill, the site of Garibaldi's famous defence of the Roman Republic in 1849, was timed to coincide in 1895 with the extended celebrations for the 25th anniversary of the Italian government's seizure of Rome from the Pope, and Crispi used the occasion openly to attack the Church, to claim that the destruction of the Pope's temporal power was divinely ordained 'just has it had been the will of the Almighty that Italy . . . should be restored to unity'.[17]

1   Monument to Garibaldi on the Janiculum hill in Rome (1895).

The image of Garibaldi as a sacred symbol of secular Italy was promoted
relentlessly, and not just by the central government. Municipal councils across
Italy, with far fewer resources at their disposal but still keen to contribute to
the creation of new commemorative spaces, embarked on a programme of
renaming main streets and squares after Garibaldi. Marble plaques were fixed
to buildings, to honour where Garibaldi had been – where he had slept, fought,
thought and spoken – and to conserve this memory for future generations.[18]
In the twenty or more years after his death, continuing public enthusiasm for
the cult of Garibaldi was reflected in the proliferation of patriotic pamphlets
and other ephemera (calendars, flyers, postcards, china figures) both on the
occasion of his death and to commemorate various anniversaries thereafter.[19]
It can also be traced in the growth of a large market of generally left-wing
readers for Garibaldian literature, which included major biographies, personal
memoirs, novels, plays and poetry. Many, especially Risorgimento veterans
and those involved in radical and left-wing politics, kept up an active commitment to Garibaldi and to *garibaldinismo*.[20]

Far from diminishing the cult of Garibaldi, the rise of a new, more strident
nationalism in Italy in the years before the First World War, together with a

creeping disaffection with the ideals of Italian liberalism, simply added to
Garibaldi's mythical status. The writer and activist Gabriele D'Annunzio
recast Garibaldi as a futurist hero, an 'Omnipotent Leader [*Duce*]'[21] and
fearless warrior whose patriotic example would lead Italians to sacrifice
themselves for the nationalist cause. Encouraged equally by the 1907
celebrations for the centenary of his birth, Garibaldi's name was invoked to
claim 'unredeemed' Italy (*l'Italia irredenta*, namely, the Trentino and Trieste)
and then to justify intervention in the First World War. During the war itself,
Garibaldi's grandsons organised a volunteer legion to help defend France
against German aggression – to fight for Italy's 'sister nation' against 'the
German hordes' – and two of them, Bruno and Costanzo, died on the front at
Argonne.[22] This use of Garibaldi to (re)associate militarism with national
unity led, in turn, to his appropriation by Mussolini's Fascists, who were
seeking to co-opt the Risorgimento and rewrite it as their own foundation
story. An attempt was made to 'Fascistise' Garibaldi by stressing continuities
between his and Mussolini's actions (red shirts and black shirts; the marches
on Rome). In a parallel process driven by another of Garibaldi's grandsons, the
Fascist enthusiast Ezio Garibaldi, a new season of Garibaldi publications got
under way, which produced scholarly editions of his writings, the re-issuing of
biographies and volunteers' memoirs and the journal *Camicia Rossa*. A high
point was reached in 1932, the 50th anniversary of Garibaldi's death. Official
celebrations were personally directed by Mussolini and included school
holidays, an exhibition of relics in Rome, and the inauguration of a monument
to Garibaldi's first wife, Anita, on the Janiculum hill, along with the
ceremonial transfer of her ashes from a cemetery in Genoa to the monument
in Rome.[23] In the mid-1930s, the first professorial chairs in Risorgimento
history were established at Italian universities, and in 1934 Blasetti's film *1860*,
about the expedition of Garibaldi's Thousand to Sicily, appeared on Italian
screens.[24]

Fascism was not, however, the last word on Garibaldi and the Garibaldian
cult. Also during the 1930s, the opposition to Fascism sought to combat the
aggressive nationalism of the Fascist regime by reinvoking Garibaldi as the
symbol of popular liberation and internationalism. Agitating against
Mussolini's intervention on the side of Franco in the Spanish Civil War, Carlo
Rosselli, leader of the new Action Party, proclaimed 'today in Spain, tomorrow
in Italy'. Volunteers for Spain were organised into groups called 'Garibaldi
brigades', and these fought with the Republican Popular Front against Franco
and his supporters. The 'second Risorgimento' (1943–5) also saw communist
Garibaldi brigades fight in the Resistance in Italy and Yugoslavia.[25]

Thereafter, during the early years of the Italian Republic, Garibaldi found
his place again as a founding father of democracy, and was incorporated into

a revised republican 'religion' which linked the new myth of the Resistance and anti-Fascism to the Risorgimento.[26] Garibaldi became a unifying and consensual figure, and in the long decades of Christian Democrat rule after 1948 his extreme anti-clericalism tended to be erased from public view. He was remembered every year on Republic Day (2 June, the date of the referendum which created the Republic, coincidentally also the date of Garibaldi's death), with its symbols and rituals referring explicitly to Risorgimento iconography, and he was commemorated further in a series of centenaries – in 1949 (for the Roman Republic of 1849); in 1959–60 (for national unification in 1859–60); and 1982 (the centenary of his death). During the 1980s, two of Italy's most prominent politicians – the leader of the republican party, Giovanni Spadolini, and the leader of the socialist party, Bettino Craxi – vied with each other to re-propose Garibaldi according to their own idealised images as, respectively, a symbol of republican virtue and a founder of Italian socialism.[27]

Craxi was an intensely controversial figure who was later disgraced in the *mani pulite* scandals of the early 1990s and forced to flee Italy to avoid arrest. Not surprisingly, his part in celebrating and promoting Garibaldi was the kiss of death for the Garibaldi cult as a 'place of memory' for the Italian people. But, in any case, the power of the cult to evoke a popular response had been in decline from the Second World War onwards. It is unlikely that the efforts to revive Garibaldi and other Risorgimento heroes in the aftermath of Fascism and Italy's military collapse in 1943 were ever that successful; instead, Garibaldi shared the more general fate of patriotic tropes and symbols, which lost much of their mobilising force in the post-war period.

Indeed, it is hard to escape the conclusion that, by the end of the war, the cult of Garibaldi had run its course. For almost a hundred years, Garibaldi had been used as an 'exemplary life', held up as the physical embodiment of a series of values and truths with which Italians should identify and so construct a sense of national community.[28] Yet the effort to turn Garibaldi into a genuinely consensual national symbol in the cold war period reduced his life to a succession of apolitical banalities, depriving it of precisely those unusual and unsettling aspects which had given his figure such an emotional charge. Thus, as personal links with the nineteenth century receded with the passing of generations, Garibaldi's role as the symbol of Italian identity was reduced to a list of received values – unity, virtue, patriotism, military courage – whose repetition in public debate failed to mask its emptiness as national rhetoric. Even Garibaldi's dress, appearance and heroic gestures, hitherto considered among his most captivating features, seemed increasingly ridiculous, appropriate perhaps for school textbooks but embarrassing if taken seriously by adults. Finally, in the early 1960s, a new generation which cared little about either the Risorgimento or its ideals produced a new political symbolism and an entirely different set of heroes. In global consciousness, the place of Garibaldi, it may be argued, was taken by Che Guevara, a figure of a rather different order, who nonetheless shared with the 'hero of two worlds' some important characteristics, notably a taste for guerrilla war, revolution rather than government, an internationalist outlook and a striking personal appearance.

Garibaldi and the historians

In terms of their relationship to Garibaldi, historians were, for once, at the forefront of popular trends. Most of them had lost interest in him as early as the 1950s, if not some time before. Previously, historians had embraced the nationalist legend of Garibaldi, and indeed had contributed significantly to the creation of a national past for Italy through histories and biographies which glorified Garibaldi's contribution to Italian unification.[29] But after the Second World War, with the experience of dictatorship an all too powerful memory, historians throughout Europe began strenuously to resist the hagiography of 'Great Men' and their role in history.[30] Alberto Mario Ghisalberti, head of Rome's Istituto per la Storia del Risorgimento Italiano (Institute for the History of the Italian Risorgimento), and Emilia Morelli, first the secretary and then Ghisalberti's successor at the Institute, who together controlled the official academic approach to the Risorgimento from the mid-1930s until the late 1980s, took a decidedly unheroic line on Garibaldi. Ghisalberti went against prevailing orthodoxy to emphasise the contribution of Mazzini to the achievement of national unity in 1860–1 and downplayed the importance of Garibaldi.[31] He also broke with the practice of Risorgimento historiography and challenged the celebration of its principal protagonists (Vittorio Emanuele II, Cavour, Garibaldi and Mazzini) to focus on lesser-known figures and activists, 'to search for', as he put it, 'the contribution of *so many humble heroes* to the solid and durable construction of a new Italy'.[32] In a series of articles written for the *Giornale d'Italia* in 1949 to commemorate the centenary exhibition on the Roman Republic, Ghisalberti called for attention to be focused on 'minor figures of the Risorgimento', on 'lesser-known personalities and aspects',[33] on important, but neglected figures such as Pietro Roselli, whose actions in defence of the 1849 republic had, as Ghisalberti put it, been overshadowed by the 'gigantic figure of the man from Nice'.[34]

Ghisalberti and Morelli also concentrated their efforts on accumulating and cataloguing vast quantities of historical documents relating to the Risorgimento in their institute's archive in Rome. This emphasis on archival research – and thus exclusively on what was knowable from the original sources – represented in itself a departure from nationalist traditions of Risorgimento narrative, where it had long been held inappropriate, in the words of one Italian prime minister, Giovanni Giolitti, to let 'beautiful historical legends be discredited by historical criticism'.[35] It gave rise to a more prosaic and critical attitude to the Risorgimento. Henceforth, scholarly interest in, for instance, the 1849 Roman Republic moved away from the dramatic and heroic actions of Garibaldi and his men, and towards both the daily details of government and the mistakes of its political leaders, including Garibaldi.[36] This approach, with the huge amount of new archival material which became available to historians in the post-war period, found its way also into post-war biographies of Garibaldi, where the stress was increasingly on Garibaldi the man, politician and/or general, rather than on Garibaldi 'the hero' *per se*. Nonetheless it is worth noting that historians were still reluctant really to 'speak badly of Garibaldi' (*parlar male di Garibaldi*); the new biographies remained essentially within the old nationalist historiographical tradition. So this new research did not manage to shake the consensus on, and thus revitalise interest in, Garibaldi as a historical figure.[37]

In 1949, as the celebrations for the centenary of the Roman Republic got under way, Antonio Gramsci's notebooks on the Italian Risorgimento were published for the first time.[38] These notebooks, part of a huge collection of writings produced by the communist theorist and activist while in a Fascist prison, outlined a radically different, Marxist interpretation of Italian unification and its consequences. Gramsci found the origins of the Fascist dictatorship in the weaknesses of the Risorgimento and the Italian state which it had created. He defined the Risorgimento as a failed social revolution, where capitalism had failed to emerge from the ruins of feudalism and the bourgeoisie had been unable to defeat the nobility; Italy was thus unfit for liberalism and instead a kind of 'bastard', and inherently unstable, political system was created, without an effective opposition and based on a mixture of coercion, corruption and incompetence.[39] Gramsci's notebooks gave a huge stimulus to historical debate in Italy. By the 1950s, indeed, the pre-eminent position of the Institute for Risorgimento History and the control of Ghisalberti and Morelli over Risorgimento research were being vigorously challenged by a group of Marxist historians – often based at the Istituto Gramsci in Rome, a few streets away from the home of the Institute for Risorgimento History – who outlined an alternative view. Marxist historians found in the Risorgimento evidence of 'passive revolution', repressed class conflict and political betrayal. They stressed the frustration of popular aspiration, denied the primacy of politics and questioned the assumption that Risorgimento history, as outlined by Ghisalberti *et al.*, was ideologically objective and 'value-free'.[40]

The bitter controversy generated by this challenge still did little to spark new debate about Garibaldi. On the one hand, Ghisalberti and Morelli came to insist on more respect for Garibaldi and the 'Risorgimento myth',[41] while on the other, Marxist historians suggested that the role played in Italian unification by human action, and especially by Risorgimento heroes such as Garibaldi, had simply been overstated. At the same time, Marxist historians refused to exonerate Risorgimento leaders from responsibility for what had gone wrong. Gramsci always insisted that the failure of Italian unification was really the fault of its leaders: despite their rhetoric, Mazzinians had never organised themselves as a mass-mobilising revolutionary vanguard since they were secretly frightened of popular, especially peasant, revolution. Garibaldi had 'a relationship of personal subordination' to Cavour and his moderate liberal party, and instead of forging an 'organic and coherent' link with the masses he had preferred to lead a paternalistic and superficial movement, 'the political equivalent of gypsy bands and nomads'.[42] Nor was this the end of Garibaldi's now harsh treatment at the hands of historians. The arrival in Italy towards the end of the 1970s of the 'new social history' with its emphasis on the view from below, and on structures and trends rather than on political action, accelerated the move away from the study of politics and political leaders like Garibaldi. The effect was to create a growing sense among historians of modern Italy that Garibaldi, along with the Risorgimento itself, was 'old hat'. The history of the Risorgimento was said to be dominated by an elitist and conservative historical approach which favoured 'great men' over 'labouring men' (and women), and the actions of these men was felt to be much less relevant to an understanding of contemporary Italy than were, for example, the experience of Fascism or the policies of post-war politicians.[43]

There has, of course, been a recent revival of interest in the Risorgimento and nineteenth-century Italian nationalism. Much new research has followed the lead given some years ago by scholars like Ernest Gellner, Eric Hobsbawm and Benedict Anderson, who have encouraged us to look at national identity not as ancient or inevitable but as something modern, and as the deliberate, and largely artificial, creation of a new bourgeois elite.[44] As a result, historians have turned back to studying the idea and images of the Italian nation, but this time in the hope of understanding (rather than either glorifying or decrying) the bases, appeal and impact of nationalism and nationalist movements in Italy, and as a means of redefining their own relationship to a complex historiographical tradition which itself has its origins in the Risorgimento.[45]

Looking at the early decades of the Risorgimento (the 1790s to around the 1830s), and primarily at cultural developments rather than political conflict, Alberto Banti has argued for the existence of a Risorgimento 'canon'. He points to the key role played by around forty texts (novels, poems, histories, paintings and operas) in producing the symbols, metaphors and images which Italian nationalists made their own, and on which Italian nationalism based its appeal. Crucially, Banti suggests that the idea of an Italian resurgence was primarily the result of a cultural elaboration, that it became immensely popular quite quickly (if only among an educated elite) and that this cultural movement ultimately accounts for the willingness of young Italian men to become revolutionaries and, if necessary, die on the barricades. According to Banti, this cultural movement brought about political change: writing, painting or singing about Italy became, in the repressive political climate of post-Napoleonic government, a substitute, basis and impetus for political action.[46]

Banti's culturalist approach is paralleled, but to an extent also counter-balanced and contradicted, by research into Italian nationalism after national unification. Here historians have looked at how Italy's leaders sought to 'make Italians', and at political attempts, such as those made by Francesco Crispi, which were described above, to construct a sense of national belonging based on the language, symbols and rituals produced during the Risorgimento. In contrast to Banti, however, most have argued that these post-unification attempts to create an Italian national identity were not only politically driven and imposed from above, but were also unconvincing and ineffective. Research had shown that most national commemorations and monuments did not impact upon the collective imagination and, if anything, served to focus attention on the weaknesses and divisions within the Italian nation.[47]

What scholarly attention has been paid to Garibaldi in this new research has concentrated on his role as a place of memory, and particularly on the official cult of Garibaldi, which was created after his death and lasted into the twentieth century. We now know a great deal about the manifestations and manipulations of the official cult, from Crispi through Mussolini to Bettino Craxi, and how it changed over time. We are familiar with the people who constructed, supported, paid for or opposed the cult.[48] We have become especially accustomed to hearing of its shortcomings and failures. We know about radical and socialist attempts to protest against Garibaldi's appropriation by the monarchists[49] and about the struggles between Mussolini and Garibaldi's grandson, Ezio, over the precise codification of political meaning in the 50th anniversary commemorations of Garibaldi's death.[50] Thanks to the work of Maurice Agulhon, we have also been informed of the rise and fall of the myth of Garibaldi in France, and the controversies surrounding it, and we know something about the myth of Garibaldi elsewhere as well.[51] More recent studies have either remained within the reverential tradition of older biographies, or have focused on lesser-known aspects of his political career, or on his role in the international circulation of republican ideas.[52]

Yet, quite remarkably, we still understand rather little about the popularity of Garibaldi in his own lifetime. This lacuna reflects our more general ignorance, in terms of current research, about how Italian nationalism changed during the climactic years of national unification: that is, between the early 1840s and 1860s. Currently, we have only the vaguest sense of what must have happened to transform a patriotic literary canon espoused by an intellectual elite in the early years of the nineteenth century into a nationalist orthodoxy available to be used (rather unsuccessfully, as it turns out) as a political justification for the Italian nation state in the 1880s and thereafter. Recent research on Italian nationalism leaves the critical moments of political action and political transformation largely out of the equation. In particular, it ignores the role of Mazzinian and democratic activists in producing and synthesising an idea of the Italian nation, which was also a blueprint (successful or not) for political action.

Thanks to the efforts of previous generations of historians, we are familiar with every last detail of Garibaldi's colourful life. But we don't really know how he became so famous and why his contemporaries considered his life to be politically significant and emotionally moving. We have hardly thought at all about what message his fame was meant to convey and to whom, or about the political or cultural impact of Garibaldi's celebrity. What part, if any, Garibaldi himself played in creating, promoting and popularising the cult which surrounded him has rarely been considered. Garibaldi, as one historian has remarked, 'precisely because of the suffocating rhetoric which has overwhelmed him', still remains 'largely unknown'.[53]

Rethinking Garibaldi

There is a long tradition in Italian politics, dating back to the Risorgimento, of portraying Garibaldi as honest and honourable but also as personally foolish and politically inept. This image served his opponents in obvious ways. By allowing Garibaldi a role as a moral symbol while denying him one as a thinker and strategist, it helped to neutralise his presence as an effective leader or representative of a genuine movement: Garibaldi had charm, it was said, but should not be taken too seriously.[54] Yet this image, cast in a more positive light, worked equally in Garibaldi's favour and was promoted by the democratic left. It enhanced his status as a genuinely popular figure. Unlike Cavour, Mazzini and most other Risorgimento leaders, Garibaldi could be portrayed as 'of the people': uneducated, unsophisticated, with a plain upbringing and modest demeanour. Garibaldi's apparent sincerity also distinguished him effectively from the compromises of public life, and preserved him from the accusations of self-serving cynicism which damaged so many of his contemporaries and successors on the Italian political scene then and later. Most crucially perhaps, his conspicuous simplicity helped maintain a distance between his political presence and the emotional response to it; his own lack of calculation made the cult of Garibaldi seem spontaneous and, hence, much more genuine and more powerful.

Promoted by his opponents and supporters, and whether presented as a defect or a virtue, this image of Garibaldi as a humble hero has proved remarkably enduring. With very few exceptions, it has prevented historians from ever considering that he might have played a serious part in creating himself as a political celebrity.[55] However, my research suggests that this view of Garibaldi is unsustainable. As a political leader, Garibaldi was not especially foolish or inept, although the prevailing, elitist rules of public life may have made him seem uneducated and unworldly. He read a lot and wrote copiously, was an expert (if self-taught) in navigation, agriculture and warfare, and had travelled very widely, from a very early age. Moreover, from his South American days onwards, Garibaldi worked closely with other nationalist leaders to promote himself and seek publicity for the Italian cause. Any careful analysis of his public persona taken as a whole – his speeches, his memoirs, his novels and poetry, his clothes, his appearance and the photographs of it, his actions on the battlefield, his behaviour in parliament, his lifestyle on Caprera – must surely conclude that here was a man who understood very well the impact of his presence and knew how to protect and manipulate it to achieve the desired effect. It seems clear, in other words, as I will seek to show, that Garibaldi's celebrity was the result of a political and rhetorical strategy.[56] How this strategy worked both in structure and content, what its purpose was, and what impact it had, are the major concerns of this book.

The heroic narrative of Italian unification, and especially the climactic events between the 1848–9 revolutions and Garibaldi's expedition to Sicily, captivated most contemporaries. And, at least until the last years of Fascist rule, the same narrative obscured historical hindsight in Italy and elsewhere. For example, both nineteenth-century English liberals and the great English liberal historian George Macaulay Trevelyan, writing in the early 1900s, saw the Risorgimento as a kind of 'latter-day morality tale', a battle between good (the Italians) and bad (the Austrian Empire; the Papacy) and with the satisfaction of a happy ending, where virtue seemed to triumph with the unification of Italy.[57] Yet, however biased or inaccurate this tale may seem to us, it would be a mistake entirely to ignore it, since it provides us with a key to understanding Risorgimento politics. The moral engagement of British liberals with Italian unification should be seen as the reflection of a successful, and enduring, Risorgimento myth or, to follow Anthony Smith's definition, a nationalist narrative of 'cultural-ideological' descent which sought to recreate, and identify itself with, the 'heroic spirit (and the heroes)' of a 'past golden age'.[58] Equally, the creation of this Risorgimento myth was the outcome of a sophisticated propaganda exercise organised by Italy's nationalist leaders and aimed outside as well as inside Italy, which presented their struggle for political liberty as a concluding stage in Italy's national story. Put simply, the conviction that Italian unification was morally just and historically grounded, and the contrary view of Austria and the Papacy as irretreivably retrograde and undeniably evil, may have been a misrepresentation, an illusion or an outright untruth, but it had an undeniable rhetorical and mobilising force, which was at least partly the effect of a careful political strategy.[59] Indeed, so successful was this political strategy that to this day it still conditions our understanding of, and our response to, the Risorgimento and its protagonists.

Garibaldi was crucial to this strategy. The deliberate creation of a cult of Garibaldi meant that his military successes were not just applauded and admired, they also became a symbol of all that was justifiable (virtuous, inevitable) about the Italian cause. Hence, the heroic cult of Garibaldi was used to represent and spread the Italian nationalist myth at home and abroad. The fame of Garibaldi brought material support – men and money – for the wars of Italian unification and helped to make them victorious. So the cult served to focus, integrate and mobilise public support for the political myth of the Italian nation and to legitimise Italian nationalism as a political movement. As a symbol of the Italian nation, the cult of Garibaldi was supposed to transform the way people imagined their rulers and thought about politics; his heroic leadership was part of a broader attempt to create new rituals and promote a political language, and to make persuasive the nationalist vision of the future and the past.[60] After unification, the cult of Garibaldi was used in different attempts to create and reinforce a collective national identity, or a sense of political belonging which could accompany the new legal definitions of the state's relationship with society and would bind people emotionally to their new rulers.[61] The great interest to us of a man like Garibaldi is that his fame, and the use which was made of it, allows us to ask general questions about how political heroes are made and what purpose they serve as collective symbols of a political idea.

As a political leader, Garibaldi seems to conform very closely to the ideal type of 'charismatic' authority defined by Max Weber as a 'certain quality of an individual personality by virtue of which he is considered extraordinary and treated as endowed with supernatural, superhuman, or at least specifically exceptional powers or qualities', and on the basis of which he is recognised by others as a leader.[62] Weber's analysis of charismatic authority has been immensely influential, notably in studies of the twentieth-century dictators, and is extremely useful in helping us to understand the general social and political conditions under which charismatic authority can develop, and the mechanisms of its operation. Other scholars have pointed to a 'widespread disposition to attribute charismatic propensities to ordinary secular roles', or for any form of 'central authority' to acquire an 'inherent sacredness' or charisma; they suggest that Weber's analysis can offer broader insights into the relationship between political power and its symbolic representation.[63] The association of Garibaldi, in various textual and visual representations, with 'extraordinariness'; with divine and/or sacred qualities, magical powers and physical prowess, are all suggestive of the charismatic properties of his public persona.[64] So, in this book, I follow Weber in treating the cult of Garibaldi as an example of charismatic authority, and I also seek to explain the political and symbolic purpose which it served.

However, my emphasis is more strictly historical and, as such, rather different from the more general sociological interests of Weber. In particular, I seek to analyse and explain the specific means by which Garibaldi's charisma was created and promoted; in other words, I am interested in how, when and why Garibaldi became 'extraordinary' and a charismatic leader in the eyes of a general public. I argue that the cult of Garibaldi was part of a process of political and cultural modernisation, and especially that its reach and impact were made possible by huge improvements in mass communication. It is also worth remembering that the public's perception of Garibaldi as an extra-ordinary and exceptional individual preceded the general success of the Italian nationalist movement. Although the nationalist victories in Italy gave an enormous boost to his fame, he remained, for the most part, as (if not more) effective as an alternative political symbol, or as a symbol which represented political opposition and aversion.[65] In effect, what makes a study of Garibaldi especially interesting and important is that, unlike most successful charismatic leaders of the nineteenth and twentieth centuries in Europe, he was not (or was hardly ever) in power. His success allows us to examine the process, generally neglected by scholars of both charismatic leadership and modern political symbolism, whereby radical movements invent new rituals and symbols, and use these both to delegitimise established authority and to make believable their claim to be the genuine governing elite.[66]

The present study seeks to go beyond both the hagiography of traditional histories and the neglect characteristic of more recent research on Garibaldi. Rather than either celebrating or deflating the heroic cult of Garibaldi, my work engages directly with the cult and its manifestations. My aim is to explore the political motives for the creation of a Garibaldi cult, the political message which it embodied and popularised and the forms of its public representation. But rather than looking at the official cult of Garibaldi after 1882, this study

concentrates on his own lifetime and on his own activity, and on the period of
his major political engagement and popularity between the mid-1840s and the
1870s. My focus, in other words, is on Garibaldi the symbol of revolutionary
nationalism rather on the posthumous Garibaldi, an official symbol of the
Italian state. Since Garibaldi must be understood as an international celebrity
as well as a nationalist hero, my research also takes in the view of Garibaldi
offered by the press in London, Paris, Berlin, New York and Buenos Aires. At
the same time, I place great emphasis on Garibaldi's experiences in Sicily. The
reason for doing so is that this brief period (May to October 1860) was the only
time he enjoyed political power. It was also the absolute high point of his
national and international fame. Lastly, I consider anti-Garibaldi rhetoric,
especially attempts by the Church to enter into, and combat, the nationalist
discourse, and I also look at how both Garibaldi and his public dealt with his
political failures and his old age.

Garibaldi's life has always been told as a coherent and ordered narrative,
with a series of minor adventures leading to a heroic climax and a gradual
retirement thereafter. In so far as it uses a chronological approach, this book is
no exception. On a purely practical level, it is difficult to make sense of
Garibaldi's long career without reference to his own life cycle and the changing
political times he lived through and participated in. Nevertheless, my analysis
places equal weight on the conscious creation and diffusion of a biography of
Garibaldi and on the literary construction of an exemplary life for political
purposes. The life of Garibaldi must be considered through the study of two
different narratives, each with its own timing and logic: the first being the
highs and lows of Garibaldi's political career and military engagements; the
second, the refashioning of this career as a public spectacle representing a
series of political and moral imperatives (or the creation of a 'myth' of
Garibaldi as part of his personality cult). In the latter case, his life story could
be made up and it had more than one author. His biography was in fact the
product of several authors (including Garibaldi himself) whose stories could
conflict with each other and escape into the realms of fiction and fantasy, and
where the dominant motif was as much entertainment, dramatic appeal and
literary convention as biographical truth.

Weber was clear that charismatic authority was inherently unstable, prone
both to 'routinisation' and to challenge and failure.[67] Most studies of
twentieth-century leader cults have found a stark distinction between image
and reality, or a huge gulf between a 'script' which cast these leaders as popular
heroes and an entirely different political truth, which was about constructing
an apparatus of power and 'stupefying the masses'. Recently, even British
Fascism has been recast as a 'spectacular' failure, whose electoral and ideological bankruptcy contrasts with its energetic marketing of megalomania.[68] In

the case of Garibaldi, all these contrasts are much less vivid. First, the Garibaldi cult was surprisingly resistant to attempts at institutionalisation, at least during his lifetime and for a while thereafter. Second, although part of his heroic image was, as I have just stressed, an elaborate construction, based on novelistic fantasy and dramatic invention, part of it was also based on his military accomplishments and undeniable physical presence. In this sense, the life lived and the life imagined were dependent on each other; to give just one example, the events of 1859–60 provide an effective climax to both. The moment of Garibaldi's greatest military and political successes also offered a chance to rewrite Garibaldi's life story, and to revisit and recast his previous adventures as a precursor to this triumph. And during the political failures which followed, the memory of 1860 could be used to give a glorious, melancholic and persuasive rationale to Garibaldi's actions. Garibaldi, in other words, was not just a 'sign', he was also 'lived existence'.[69] If Garibaldi's greatness has significance for historians, it should lie precisely in this combination of invention and reality, or this mixture of literary elaboration and concrete achievement, and in our attempt to explore and understand it.

If it is a mistake neatly to separate Garibaldi's political and military successes from the stories told about them, it is equally imposssible to ignore their public impact and reception. My study will also be concerned with the response to Garibaldi: with the formation of a liberal public keen on Garibaldi and with the need to keep this public informed, well-read and satisfied with the stories told about him. One of the general concerns of this book is to make visible the complex dialogue which developed in the middle of the nineteenth century – thanks largely to new technologies and to increased education and wealth – between political leaders, journalists and the public over the production and control of information, and over the kind of language and symbols used to represent the public sphere. Perhaps especially, a study of the cult of Garibaldi bears out Geoff Eley's point about the existence of diverse and competing publics, rather than a single, liberal model, and about the increasingly 'democratic resonance' and radical character of the public sphere in the nineteenth century.[70] I will also argue that Garibaldi was genuinely 'popular', in that his appeal stretched beyond an elite intellectual readership and reached a broader literate public through cheap and easily accessible textual and visual media. Most of the sources which I have used to study the cult of Garibaldi are those of romantic low literature, a literature which was commercially successful, characterised by increasingly standardised forms and which created a new and popular, if by no means mass, reading culture.[71] It was this culture which formed Garibaldi's public.

Modern political heroes, like the nationalist movements with which they are identified, are often treated as political inventions imposed from above on a passive population. I will suggest instead that, while there was a great deal about Garibaldi's appeal which was planned by political leaders, his definition and creation as a political hero was still a largely collaborative effort, involving audience participation as well as directions from the stage.[72] The public's enthusiasm for Garibaldi reflected a broader contemporary appetite for romantic heroes and adventure stories, and Garibaldi modelled his political image to fit this popular demand. The task of Garibaldi was not only to make Italy, he had also to make Italy convincing. How he did so, and whether he fully succeeded, will be discussed in the chapters which follow.

CHAPTER 1

NATION AND RISORGIMENTO

Mazzini and 'Young Italy'

In 1843, the Italian nationalist leader Giuseppe Mazzini wrote from his exile in London to another Italian exile in Uruguay: 'Garibaldi is a man who will be of use to the country when it is time for action'.[1] His correspondent was Giovanni Battista Cuneo, who was a journalist and a Ligurian like Mazzini, and who, like Mazzini and Garibaldi himself, had been forced to flee Italy in the early 1830s as a result of his involvement in political conspiracies against the Piedmontese government. Such transatlantic contacts between Mazzini and Cuneo tell us much about the ambitions of Mazzini and the role he envisaged for Garibaldi. They were part of a political strategy which he had developed over the previous decade, and reflected the network he had built up, incorporating exiles, activists, writers and sympathisers in Europe and the Americas, as well as conspirators within Italy itself.

Mazzini was the founder and head of what he claimed to be an immense revolutionary organisation called 'Young Italy' (*Giovine Italia*), of which Cuneo and Garibaldi were both members. He had established Young Italy in Marseille in 1831, after the failure of a series of uprisings against the conservative governments in central Italy. These uprisings had discredited the Carbonari secret society (to which Mazzini had belonged) and other revolutionary secret societies, and had shown both their conspiratorial methods and their dependence on French leadership to be misguided.[2] The new movement – Young Italy – which Mazzini proposed aimed to be quite different from the secret societies. It was based on youth because only the young, Mazzini believed, were uncompromised by the failure of the old sectarian organisations and their practices inherited from the French Revolution; the young had no memory of that revolution and were instead the bearers of a new, romantic spirit and culture. Only they could carry out the task of democratic renewal and national 'resurrection' which Mazzini envisaged for Italy.[3]

The goal of Mazzini was nothing less than the creation of a new society based on the Saint-Simonian principles of association, progress and religious faith.[4] However, unlike Saint-Simon, he made Italy, not France, the leader of the new age: 'It is in Italy that the European knot must be untied. To Italy belongs the high office of emancipation; Italy will fulfill its civilizing mission.'[5] His mission for Italy in Europe was expressed succinctly in a letter written to a sympathiser in 1846: 'Twice we have given moral Unity to Europe; and I have faith in God that we will give it . . . a third time.'[6] Mazzini's new religion of 'Humanity' was also to be achieved through a political revolution which would introduce a concrete set of changes. In an early draft of the statutes and instructions for the organisation, Mazzini set out five political, religious and social aims:

1. One republic, undivided across the whole territory of Italy, independent, united and free. 2. The destruction of the entire upper hierarchy of the clergy and the introduction of a simple parish system. 3. The abolition of all aristocracy and every privilege which is not the result of the eternal law of capacity and action. 4. An unlimited encouragement of public education. 5. The most explicit declaration of the rights of man and the citizen.[7]

Young Italy was to adopt the slogan 'Unity, Independence, Liberty', and the establishment of a unitary republic in Italy was to be the signal for a general revolution, marking the end of monarchy, aristocracy and clerical privilege across Europe.

Mazzini's republican and democratic vision for Italy represented a fusion of romantic socialist and Jacobin ideas. In fact, Mazzini admitted that the ideas behind Young Italy were not especially original but were simply intended to realise and apply to Italy 'truths that today are diffused throughout Europe'.[8] Mazzini's early strategies were equally derivative. They were influenced as much by the old Italian Jacobin, Buonarotti, as they were by his desire to distinguish the new movement from, and supplant, Buonarotti's methods.[9] And it is worth remembering that for Mazzini and his followers the *risorgimento* ('resurgence') of Italy was a call for immediate military action. To become a nation, Italians had to fight. The new foundation story for the 'Third Rome' was to be based on political freedom and military success: Italians would become an example to the rest of the world of military heroism as well as civic virtue.

Military planning was central both to Mazzini's thinking and to disagreements with him. Debates about strategy revolved around two difficult questions: how to overcome the indifference of the mostly rural population – how, in other words, to involve the Italian people militarily in their own emancipation – and how the revolution could defend itself against the unquestionably superior forces of Austria and its allies. Mazzini's general answer was that Italians would liberate themselves, and specifically that the selfless heroism of a few activists could inspire the Italian people to rise and throw off the Austrian yoke. The link to, and the creation of, the people – no longer mere individuals but now the *popolo* associated as a nation – would be entrusted to a recognisably Jacobin figure: a 'genius', 'a prophetic actor of the future destinies of nations and of humanity', a 'spark of God', and a thinker and activist capable of expressing and embodying the unity and 'brotherhood' of humanity.[10] In this way, the revolution would encompass an elite and a mass 'moment'. As Mazzini conceived of it initially, it would start off as an urban uprising led by the elite conspirators of Young Italy, but would continue as a rural war or *guerra per bande*, with the people organised into guerrilla bands in the countryside.[11]

As one of Mazzini's biographers remarks, Young Italy was part secret society and part modern political party. It was a secret society in so far as it relied on conspiratorial methods and the leadership of 'an inner core of true believers', but it was also modern in that it 'called out to the people'.[12] In practice, Mazzini relied heavily on the dedication and enthusiasm of his (mostly young, mostly educated) followers and on their readiness to die for Italy. The 'general instruction for the brothers of Young Italy', which members – including Garibaldi – swore when they joined, resembles the oaths sworn by members of secret societies in its appeal to a sense of religious truth and belonging. A lengthy preamble stated the rationale for Young Italy as 'the brotherhood of Italians believing in a law of *progress* and *duty* . . . convinced that Italy is destined to be a nation', while it defined the territory of Italy as the peninsula 'between the sea to the south and the upper circle of the Alps to the north' and the islands 'declared as Italian in the talk of native inhabitants'. The preamble further declared Young Italy's aims to be 'republican and unitary' by nature, history and destiny: republican because 'all the men of a nation are destined . . . to be free, equal and brothers; and the republican institution is the only one which assures them this future – because sovereignty resides essentially in the nation'; and unitary because 'without unity there is no nation . . . no force . . . because the entire logic of Italian civilisation has for centuries . . . tended towards unity'.

Furthermore, in swearing loyalty to Young Italy, members swore loyalty not only to Italy but to everything the nation could feasibly be identified with: God, the (national) saints and martyrs, family (brothers, mothers and children), a sense of place and history, and a sense of duty, morality and sacrifice for the community. Thus, members swore:

In the name of God and Italy, [i]n the name of all the martyrs of the holy Italian cause, fallen under the blows of foreign and domestic tyranny . . .

[and] for the duties that tie me to the land where God has placed me, and to the brothers that God has given me – for the love, innate in every man, for the places where my mother was born and where my children will live – for the hate, innate in every man, for evil, injustice, usurpation, arbitrary power ... for the memory of past glory – for the knowledge of present humiliation – for the tears of Italian mothers – for sons who have died on the scaffold, in prisons, in exile – for the misery of millions.

They also promised to dedicate themselves (*'di consecrarmi'*) for ever to the cause of Italy *'united, independent, free, republican'* and to 'promote' by all possible means, 'by word, writings, action, [and] the education of my brothers', the values and association of Young Italy.[13]

Mazzini's use of religious and romantic language can easily confuse the reader today, but the essential point here is that Young Italy was a revolutionary organisation, and that Mazzini's 'general instruction' seeks to be both political rhetoric – in that it seeks to encourage and inspire believers – and a concrete statement of political realities. The long preamble states the existence of Italy ('destined to be a nation') and delineates its physical borders, hence justifying the actions of Young Italy; the invocation gives its members a common history, experience and identity ('for the memory of past glory – for the knowledge of present humiliation') and places a special emphasis on sacrifice and martyrdom for the community; while the pledge offers them a goal (Italy *'united, independent, free, republican'*) and all the means – words, action, education – to achieve it. Like his Jacobin predecessors, Mazzini sought not just to overthrow the existing government but to transform the way Europeans (led by the Italians) thought, talked and behaved politically. And, perhaps even more than the Jacobins, Mazzini sought to achieve this revolution as much by an appeal to religious dedication and emotional belonging as by a call to reason and recourse to armed conflict. Young Italy was a secular religion. As Emilio Gentile has remarked, Young Italy 'was an apostolate, revolutionary action devoted to the "religion of martyrdom" and leading to the resurrection of a "new Italy"'.[14]

The idea of the nation

Mazzini's invocation of religion and history, and his reliance on the selfless dedication (even until death) of young men, also reflected his perception of the problems which Italian nationalists faced in making visible and convincing their idea of the Italian nation. Scholars of nationalism and nationalist movements have long disagreed about whether modern nations are built on pre-existing 'ethnies' or whether they are merely the product of modernisation, either as the accompaniment to urbanisation and industrialisation or as a conscious invention of new political elites in the last three decades of the nineteenth century.[15] However, if we look more closely at how Italian national identity was formed, this debate appears to be somewhat misconceived. What Alberto Banti has called the 'national–patriotic discourse' in Risorgimento Italy seems neither to have been invented *ex nuovo* nor to be based on an existing ethnic or political identity. Instead, the national–patriotic discourse simply 'manipulated', 'transposed' and 'modelled itself on' an existing set of symbols, metaphors and rituals.[16] It is equally clear that although Italy did not exist politically in any sense before the middle of the nineteenth century, quite a strong sense of cultural *italianità* (Italian-ness) did exist among a small educated elite in the seventeenth and eighteenth centuries, and was expressed in their scientific interests, in their associational life – in courts, salons, academies and opera houses – and in literature and the visual arts.[17] Indeed, as Raymond Grew tells us, '[e]ducated Italians took delight in their common culture: the Latin classics; Dante, and all the Italian poets after him; five centuries of paintings and sculptures recognized as Italian, and music that was admired and imitated across Europe. Culture ranked with geography . . . as a marker of Italian identity.'[18]

However, this elite culture was profoundly affected by the French invasions and occupations of Italy which took place between 1792 and 1815. The French Revolution and Napoleonic wars represent a watershed in the politics of the Italian peninsula: the ensuing upheavals shook the legitimacy of the *ancien régime* states; upset the already delicate relations between state, Church and nobility; brutally modernised and centralised the administration of power; and repeatedly altered Italy's internal and external frontiers. The revolution in government brought about social change in that a new generation and a new class of men, with new ideas and values, came to fill important positions in public administration and the army.[19] Perhaps most significantly for our understanding of the rise of nationalism in Italy was the experience of the short-lived Jacobin Republics (1797–9), which sought to transform the way people thought about politics. The Jacobins introduced new political symbols and rituals and a new language of politics, and encouraged new forms of political engagement and belonging. And although many intellectuals denounced the revolution, they did embrace some of its principles, and the arrival of the French gave an enormous stimulus to intellectual life, especially in cities like Milan, which saw the establishment of forty journals between 1796 and 1799.[20] Most of all, the old elite language of *italianità* proved receptive to the introduction of a new political vocabulary of revolution, which had words like 'nation' and '*patria*' (fatherland) at its core.[21]

In short, Italian national identity was derived from the culture of the eighteenth-century elite, but this culture was first transformed by the French Revolution and then by Napoleon. Restoration Italy did the rest. The revolutionary period was followed by a public backlash after the return of Italy's *ancien régime* rulers in 1814–15 as part of a general settlement created by the Congress of Vienna, which restored (most of) Italy's internal frontiers and placed the whole peninsula within an Austrian, and thus conservative, sphere of influence. The anti-revolutionary backlash sought to punish and 'purge' those who had supported the revolution and to repress its symbols – to outlaw the use of revolutionary images, rituals and language – as well as to cancel some (although by no means all) of its political ideas and administrative legacy.[22] Political discussions of *italianità*, associated with the vocabulary of revolution, were stifled by government censors. But since the censors in Restoration Italy were concerned with an ostensibly political threat, they largely failed to notice and control the growing popularity of the idea of Italy in the arts: in poetry, novels, opera, histories and painting. In fact, under the influence of the romantic movement, whose arrival in Italy was announced by Mme de Staël in 1816, studying Italy's past, painting Italian subjects and writing and singing about Italy became highly fashionable.[23]

Italian romanticism is usually seen as less interesting than its English or German counterparts. It is said to be largely derivative of the romantic movement in northern Europe; to represent less of a break with the eighteenth-century Enlightenment; and to have developed in Italy only when it was already past its peak elsewhere. For our purposes, however, the artistic merits of Italian romanticism are less important than its impact and reception, and here it is worth noting that romanticism in Italy was less conservatively inclined and had a broader reach than romanticism elsewhere. Partly because it was more consensual, romanticism in Italy was able to incorporate both a strongly religious dimension and progressive eighteenth-century ideas. This consensus meant that while Italian romantics united around what they called the 'modernisation' of Italian literature and rejected the rigid conservatism of the academy, they could do this without denying the weight of their own history and culture. They spoke of the need for art and literature to reach the people and of a literary, linguistic and artistic tradition which was specifically 'Southern' and had its roots in the medieval period. In this way, Italian romantics could openly engage with problems of the present while embracing specific aspects of their 'national' past. [24]

In post-revolutionary Italy, the concern with Italy's past probably owes as much to this new culture of romanticism as it does to previous narratives of *italianità*. Banti suggests that the romantic literary and artistic forms through which *italianità* was expressed in Restoration Italy meant that it reached a far wider audience than a 'cold and remote work of [political] analysis' might have done.[25] For example, the historical adventure novel was something of a publishing phenomenon in the 1820s and 1830s. Walter Scott's medieval romance, *Ivanhoe*, was published in nine separate editions between 1822 and 1854, and Italy produced its own version of this genre, most notably with the novels of Alessandro Manzoni, Domenico Guerrazzi and Massimo d'Azeglio.[26] Generally, through the works of such writers, as well as the poetry of Foscolo and Leopardi, the operas of Rossini, Bellini and Verdi and the paintings of Hayez, the idea of Italy met with public acclaim and touched a chord in public emotions. In this way, the conservatism and censorship of Restoration Italy can be said to have indirectly stimulated the growth of a Risorgimento culture. It helped to introduce future Italian patriots to an Italian nation whose appeal was all the more powerful because it was first heard in romantic novels, paintings or song.

The central argument of Alberto Banti's work is that the Risorgimento texts produced by romantic writers and artists in Restoration Italy created the symbols, images and metaphors which Italian nationalists like Mazzini were then able to make their own. Hence, the national–patriotic discourse gave shape to the political struggles of the Risorgimento and offered an identity to united Italy. According to Banti, this discourse used a number of key themes which were common to all Risorgimento texts and are repeated in the political rhetoric of all Italian nationalists: the nation is conceived as a voluntary pact amongst a free and equal fraternity, and is also a natural and organic community, an extended family and a shared historical identity. The nation is, in other words, envisaged as a community established by bonds of nature, affection and history. For example, in *L'assedio di Firenze*, a historical novel about the end of the Florentine Republic in 1530 and the final defeat of Italian independence and liberty, Guerrazzi describes the fatherland as the place which 'first gives you life and the air that you breathe and the light which you see and the love of your father and mother'.[27] Yet, as Guerrazzi's novel makes clear, the fatherland is under threat, and Italy's more recent past must be written as a story of decadence, foreign oppression and internal division. Hence, another common theme of Risorgimento narratives is suffering and danger – a hero betrayed, a virgin dishonoured, a land oppressed by foreign tyranny – and with this threat comes an equal emphasis on the redemptive power of courage, rebellion and martyrdom.

One of the most popular of all Risorgimento narratives was the Sicilian Vespers. This popular rising in Palermo against the French in 1282 was studied by two historians (Nicolini in 1831; Amari in 1842), was painted no less than three times by Hayez (in 1822, 1835 and 1844–6), and was the subject of an opera by Verdi in 1853. For Amari, who was Sicilian, the outbreak of the revolt – when a Frenchman was killed with a single blow for insulting the honour of a Sicilian woman on her way to church – 'restored Grecian virtue to the people of Palermo, and the latter to the whole island'. 'Our people', Amari maintained in a specific reference to the Vespers as a national foundation story and in an attempt to make Sicily part of an Italian narrative, 'proudly preserves until today the memories of that ancient fierce virtue.' The broader significance of the Vespers was that it could be depicted as the first successful fight for national independence against foreign oppression (although it is also worth pointing out that Amari, Hayez and Verdi all had problems with the undeniable presence of mob violence in the ensuing massacre of Frenchmen).[28] The exceptional resonance of the Sicilian Vespers was due to its potent combination of Risorgimento themes: of sexual aggression perpetrated by a foreign oppressor as well as courage in upholding and defending the honour of the national community, represented here by the threat to a 'pure' woman.

In Risorgimento narratives like the Sicilian Vespers, these themes of foreign aggression, defiance in the face of oppression, and redemption are represented and played out in the actions of individual characters or protagonists. They are the main means by which the reader is drawn into and identifies with the plot and they are responsible for driving the plot – or their adventure – forward. The most important of these protagonists is the hero. According to Mario Praz, romanticism produced a new kind of rebel hero, a unique and memorable individual who rejects the dictates and constrictions of society to remain true to his own belief in freedom and justice, and who is prepared to sacrifice his happiness and even his life for these convictions.[29] This hero takes his place in the romantic novel, especially in the historical adventure novels favoured by Italian romantic writers, as a brave and intensely physical individual: 'prodigies of courage and endurance, unnatural to us, are natural to him . . . the hero is a leader . . . [with] authority, passions and powers of expression far greater than ours'.[30] But the hero can also be the 'perfect knight', who embodies older, chivalric ideals of loyalty, sobriety and perseverance.[31] Thus, in Risorgimento narratives, the hero is a virile man and an attractive lover, and a courageous soldier who is ready to lead his community against the enemy; he is also an honourable man who is prepared to die to defend his principles, and in fact he is nearly always destined for a dramatic death which will save and 'redeem' the community. As we will see in the next chapter, this idealised Italian, a brave, virile and honourable hero, finds a seemingly real-life counterpart in the figure of Garibaldi.

Two other protagonists are central to Risorgimento narratives. The villain betrays his community and the hero to the foreign oppressor for glory and/or for money: he thereby 'collaborates' in the decline and humiliation of the community. The heroine – who represents in some sense the quest or prize of the historical adventure – is a convinced patriot, a virtuous mother, a sister and/or a lover, whose honour and sexual purity are threatened by the villain or the foreign oppressor, and sometimes by both at the same time. The relationship between the hero and heroine introduces the themes of romantic love and/or family attachment, giving the hero the opportunity to appear gentle, kind and sensitive to us rather than merely fearless and violent.[32] This relationship and its opposite – the evil designs of the villain or foreigner on the virtuous heroine – bring sex into the plot, a device which clearly attracted audiences, if the success of the Sicilian Vespers is anything to go by. At the same time, what Alberto Banti calls 'this figurative triad of the national narrative' (hero, villain, heroine) evokes the gospels and relies heavily on religious references. Thus, the hero can equally be seen as a Christ figure who fights and sacrifices himself for a holy cause. Moreover, like Christ, his actions and his suffering save the community from dishonour and show the way to resurrection (or *risorgimento*), while the villain is a Judas figure whose betrayal of the community drives the plot forward.[33]

The Vespers, and the use of similar episodes in Italy's past, point us to what is perhaps one of the most powerful and constant of all Risorgimento themes, which is that of war and the culture of war. The plot of almost all Risorgimento narratives involves a battle or series of battles, and the hero is usually a military man. In Guerrazzi's *L'assedio di Firenze*, the hero is the real-life military leader, Francesco Ferruccio, 'the valiant Ferruccio' who fights to the death with a tiny army to defend Florentine (and Italian) liberty and independence against Imperial and Papal agression. In D'Azeglio's *Ettore Fieramosca, ossia la disfida di Barletta* ('Hector Fieramosca or the challenge of Barletta'), the young patriotic hero, Fieramosca, leads a duel between thirteen French and thirteen Italians to defend Italian honour against the accusation that Italian soldiers are only good 'for intrigue and betrayal' and are 'the worst soldiers who ever put foot in a stirrup and wore a breastplate'. But the Italians win the day and return to Barletta, to be welcomed as heroes by the local population.[34]

There is, of course, nothing unusual about the emphasis on war in Italian adventure stories. The history provided in the novels of Scott, Dumas and other contemporary non-Italian writers is almost invariably a history of war, armed struggle and violence.[35] It is nevertheless worth remembering, since the Risorgimento and Risorgimento rhetoric are not often associated with militarism. Indeed, as a foundation story for the Italian nation, war is an extremely ambivalent one: it is as much, if not more, a narrative of defeat, of 'battles lost', as a story of military success.[36] Yet, war is important since it provides the basic plot of most Risorgimento narratives; it ties together the themes of oppression, resistance to oppression and redemption even in defeat, and it produces one of the crucial ingredients of popular success: identification with, and exaltation of, the valiant hero who defends national honour. Equally, war provides Risorgimento culture with a crucial – and otherwise largely absent – link to political rhetoric. In a tradition which goes back to Machiavelli, the story of battles lost is associated with the corruption of Italy's rulers, while military victories – such as the 'challenge' at Barletta – are linked to the selfless heroism of individuals or small groups acting on their own initiative, usually without (or despite) government intervention.[37]

If Banti is correct in locating the origins of a national–patriotic discourse in Italy in pre-existing narratives – such as the story of Christ or well-known military episodes in Italy's history – then the great achievement of Italian writers and artists in this period was to respond to the challenge of romanticism by creating a more popular Italian literature, which recast these stories in an individual and heroic vein, and which linked their plot lines of love, sex, religion and violence to new ideas of community, association, independence and liberty. Yet this romantic vision of Italy had no immediate political objective. An Italy that was past was imagined by the romantics, and was imagined in suggestive and emotive ways, but in the post-revolutionary climate of Restoration Italy there were few obvious signs of Italy's present existence. Many (although not all) romantic intellectuals were far from interested in politics, preferring to adopt a more melancholy or nostalgic attitude towards political questions. And however passionate the readers of romantic novels were about these stories and their heroes, they were still part of a tiny and restricted – if admittedly expanding – section of the population, who were actually able to read Italian.[38] In this respect, the Restoration censors were not wrong to ignore romanticism. For the rest, Italy was precisely what the Austrian chancellor, Prince Metternich, described it as – 'a geographical expression'. It had 'no national traditions of sacred monarchy',[39] no secular symbols of national 'belonging', a language which was written and spoken by few, and a past which, while it could be reassigned by romantics to celebrate a cultural *italianità*, was equally, if not more, credible as a narrative of 'division and weakness and mutual enmity'.[40]

Risorgimento

It was in his conception of this problem of credibility, and in his answer to it, that Mazzini's political genius lies. Banti argues convincingly that the popularity and diffusion of the national–patriotic discourse was due to its manipulation of religious and historical tropes – to its 'capacity to evoke remembered echoes, known images [and] values already recognised'[41] – and to its expression in broad, popular genres such as novels and opera. But, as an explanation for the rise of a political movement in Italy after 1830, this is surely to confuse the meaning of the nation with the nation as a cause: it is to reintroduce the nation and a sense of national belonging as the causal explanation for the rise of nationalist movements. Thus, while the 'culturalist' explanation of Banti tells us much about how the idea of the nation was created in Restoration Italy and what it meant to contemporaries, it tends to neglect the crucial part played by political activists in extracting political meaning from, and manipulating and popularising, this cultural manifestation. It was Mazzini who transformed the idea of Italy expressed so powerfully in literature into an equally powerful political ideology. Mazzini perceived, brought out and added a political dimension to Italian romanticism and tied the romantic idea of Italy to a political mixture of Jacobinism and romantic socialism. It was he and his followers who made the connection between the nation as a romantic cultural identity and nationalism as a democratic political movement. It was they, in turn, who dedicated all their practical energies and resources to promoting this ideology to as wide an audience as possible, and sought to construct a successful political organisation around it.

To understand Mazzini's strategy, and the role he envisaged in it for Garibaldi, we must also appreciate that he faced an uphill struggle. He had to make this link between the romantic, nostalgic idea of Italy and his volunteerist Jacobin ideal of political engagement effective, persuasive and generally accepted. Probably the clearest expression of Mazzini's understanding of the difficulties involved was his insistence on the unity of 'thought and action'. He always argued that the revolution needed intellectuals who produced art and literature as much as soldiers who fought wars, and that the revolution in thought and revolutionary action should be part of the same moment. For Mazzini, art and literature reflected politics. Cultural decline had followed the extinction of republican freedom in Italy; renewed creativity would follow its revival.[42] But writers, according to Mazzini, had also to be 'the advance guard of liberty'.[43] He took pains to encourage political engagement in artists and writers, and was himself a (politically engaged) critic and writer before he became a political activist; in fact, his earliest public interventions were in support of Italian romanticism. Throughout his life he acted as an art critic and literary reviewer, writing in English, French and Italian, partly for money but also to maintain a political dimension in cultural debate. Mazzinians, and those influenced by Mazzini, also experimented with new and popular literary forms, such as the historical novel and the autobiography–memoir. Others painted or wrote music, poetry and songs.[44] Even Mazzini's most political writings were suffused with a romantic aesthetic: as we have seen, the political 'general instruction' appealed to the family, to the past and to God, and used a language borrowed entirely from Manzoni and Guerrazzi.

On a more immediately political level, writing was part of a broad focus on the educative action of intellectuals in creating the *popolo* and indicates Mazzini's firm belief in the power of journalism and publishing. For Mazzini, the press with its power to persuade public opinion was a key tool in the realisation of the Italian nation; as Galante Garrone puts it, 'to move and enlighten people . . . [was] to provoke thoughts and actions'.[45] Mazzini called the press 'the arbiter of nations' ('the ink of the wise is a match for the sword of the strong')[46] and 'our only hope'. Journalism was 'a power; and even the only power in modern times; because it speaks and insists . . . it speaks to all the classes; it discusses all questions; it touches all the chords which move in the human soul . . . it is for the intellect what steam is for industry'.[47] Almost from the start (from 1832), Young Italy had a newspaper – *La Giovine Italia* – and Mazzini spared no effort in producing it, and in smuggling it past the censors and into Italy. He also encouraged the publication of other journals, newspapers and pamphlets by exiles in France and Switzerland.[48] In his own long political career Mazzini acted as, variously, a founder, director, editor, collaborator, correspondent, printer, copy-editor and shipping agent in the world of journalism.[49]

It is in this emphasis on the press and cultural production that Young Italy most resembles a modern political party, and here Mazzini can justifiably lay a claim to genuine political innovation. Moreover, Mazzini's interest in public opinion reached past the sphere of cultural production strictly defined, and involved the use of politics itself – especially insurrection – as symbolic action. Mazzini's insistence on insurrection, his apparently blind faith that a few conspirators would inspire a general revolutionary conflagration, has long been considered his real undoing, and in a sense it was, since the constant lack of popular uprisings and the brutal effectiveness of Austrian repression led to disillusionment and widespread defection among Mazzini's followers. However, these insurrections must be understood as part of a broader political strategy. If we take just one example – the disastrous 1844 insurrection of the Bandiera brothers – this strategy becomes quite clear. Defying widespread criticism of his role, Mazzini came out fighting and published a series of articles on 'martyrs of Italian liberty', with the Bandieras in first place. For Mazzini, their willingness to die, and – as he insisted – to die calmly and happily was the sign of 'God fermenting in the heart of a great people'. Men like the Bandiera brothers, Mazzini wrote, 'are Apostles; their tomb is an Altar. It matters little that they have not succeeded. The Appeal of Martyrdom is brother to the Angel of Victory.'[50] They were proof that Italy existed.

The endless litany of botched uprisings organised by Mazzini did not simply illustrate poor military planning and implementation (which it undoubtedly did). It may even be a mistake to see the risings as revolutions, in the sense of rapid regime change. These uprisings were, to borrow a phrase from Sudhir

Hazareesingh, 'not so much goal-driven as expressive';[51] they were equally – and sometimes even primarily – successful symbolic events. As a political romantic, Mazzini believed that death could be heroic, and heroic failure a form of success. A failed insurrection was not futile; it could – and indeed did – reveal Austrian repression to the Italians and, equally importantly, to the rest of the world. It was still a chance to appeal to the public imagination, to assert physically the existence of a political Italy; it was an occasion for speeches, proclamations and demonstrations and an opportunity to create heroes and martyrs. A failed insurrection could also be the opening salvo in a more general and prolonged assault on public opinion, involving letters to and articles in the press, the production of commemorative books and pamphlets, and, to act as a reminder some time later, the publication of personal memoirs by those caught up in the action or those who had suffered prison and exile for their convictions.

Conclusion

Mazzini was denounced by Metternich as the most dangerous man in Europe, while his erstwhile associate, the novelist and activist Guerrazzi, described Mazzini as a man 'who disturbed the sleep of kings and terrified the great powers of Europe'. His British friend Carlyle said he never saw a more 'beautiful person . . . with his soft flashing eyes, and face full of intelligence'.[52] A contentious figure in his own lifetime, Mazzini has often been judged a failure by historians, an idealist who organised doomed insurrections or a cynic who must bear his share of the responsibility for the failure of the democratic movement in Italy and the conservative turn of Italian and European politics from the late 1850s onwards.[53] Even those historians who don't condemn him admit he is a difficult figure to judge, 'hard to classify ideologically and politically', with a life 'full of ironies and paradoxes', who 'worked on the minds of men rather than through the more easily studied means of politics, diplomacy or military conquest'.[54] Yet these strong reactions to Mazzini, and the confusion about his achievements, point us directly to his motives and the real nature of his success. He was in exile almost all his adult life and had hardly any money at his disposal; he was at the head of government only once, in Rome in 1849, for a very brief period, and was under attack from his opponents from the outset. His achievement lies in having provoked such robust responses and in having established such fame, notoriety and affection for himself, on the basis of so little.

To attain his ultimate goal of transforming European politics on the basis of progress and the association of humanity, Mazzini placed great hope in the militant and military enthusiasm of youth, and he had equal confidence in the persuasive power of writing, education and example. All of Mazzini's activities can be seen as an expression of his belief in the unity of thought and action. As the next chapter will show, his contacts, networks and personal friendships; the use of newspapers, letters to newspapers and pamphlets; his own appearance, behaviour and lifestyle and those of his followers; and the organisation of conspiracies, uprisings and expeditions, even those doomed to failure – all of these were a means of publicising his political mission for Italy, of giving Italy a new foundation story and of creating a new language of politics with the 'republic' and 'nation' as its main forms of identification. It is in the context of this task to promote Italy by every means possible, of the uphill struggle to make the romantic idea of Italy visible, convincing and successful politically, that Mazzini's comment about Garibaldi with which we began this chapter can best be understood.

CHAPTER 2

IN SEARCH OF GARIBALDI

London calling

At the time of his 1843 letter to Cuneo about Garibaldi, Mazzini had been in exile from Italy for a decade. Young Italy had been more or less wiped out in Piedmont and elsewhere after the failure of a series of conspiracies which Mazzini had organised in Genoa in 1833 and 1834. In the harsh crackdown which ensued, most of his followers – including Cuneo and Garibaldi – had been forced to flee Genoa, while conditions became so difficult for Mazzini in Marseille that he had to leave for Geneva in 1833. In Geneva he founded a new organisation, 'Young Europe', to encourage and assist national revolutions throughout Europe and beyond. But while this new association partly restored his standing in revolutionary circles it also attracted the attention of the police, so that soon he was forced to go underground to avoid arrest and eventually had to leave Switzerland too. He chose this time to go to London, arriving there in 1837 in time for Queen Victoria's coronation, and was immediately shocked by the dirt, the fog and the expense of the city as well as by the drunken behaviour of its inhabitants. Yet London was to be his home for virtually all of the rest of his life.[1]

Apart from the daily and very real material difficulties which he had to deal with in London, Mazzini had severe problems on the political front too. Revolution seemed very far away. The conservative regimes in Restoration Italy had generally never been stronger or enjoyed more stability, and many were in the process of introducing administrative reform. Moderate liberals in northern and central Italy, soon to become the great rivals of Mazzini in presenting an alternative vision to conservatism, were already starting to voice their opposition to his republicanism and to his 'absurd' unitary vision for Italy. Mazzini's own networks were in disarray. He faced criticism of his tactics from within his own movement, notably from the fellow conspirator Nicola Fabrizi who, from his place of exile in Malta, sought to organise an autonomous *legione italica* which would lead a guerrilla movement and would have its base far from Mazzini, in southern Italy. Fabrizi focused especially on Sicily, where a cholera outbreak in 1837 had provoked widespread popular disturbances, but Mazzini feared Sicilian separatism, and suggested that the Sicilian rebels would break free from Naples and had no interest in uniting Italy.[2]

All these difficulties are worth stressing because Mazzini, while temporarily depressed, was ultimately undaunted. In 1840, he reorganised and relaunched Young Italy from London. This political organisation reaffirmed his romantic belief in the revolutionary potential of the younger generation, but this time he placed more emphasis on education and made a particular appeal to women and to workers. Workers had their own newspaper, *Apostolato Popolare*, most of which Mazzini wrote himself and managed to circulate in the United States and North Africa as well as throughout Europe. Mazzini also raised a public subscription to set up a free school in Hatton Garden in Holborn for the families of Italian migrants.[3] He continued to be involved with conspiracies in Italy. In 1844 he initially encouraged the disastrous mutiny and expedition planned by Attilio and Emilio Bandiera, two Venetian officers in the Austrian navy, arguing that it was 'better [to] act and fail than do absolutely nothing' and that their actions would offer Europe proof of the dedication and courage of Italians.[4] Perhaps especially important were the lasting friendships he forged with British writers and radicals. Thomas and Jane Carlyle helped to introduce him to London literary circles, where he met Dickens, Browning and the romantic poet Samuel Rogers, and his close friendship with the Carlyles, with the family of the radical lawyer William Ashurst and with Ashurst's son-in-law James Stansfeld did much to sustain Mazzini personally while in exile. Moreover, it was these friendships which served both to revitalise his own ideas and tactics and, in the longer term, to mobilise British liberal opinion in favour of the Italian national cause.[5]

It is hard to over-emphasise the importance of the British experience for Mazzini's fame, political strategy and contacts. Long before the 1848–9 revolutions made household names of Mazzini, Garibaldi and other Italian and European revolutionaries, London life had helped Mazzini to develop his own image as a nationalist hero and selfless martyr of the revolution. He had always been an admirer of Byron, and might have been imagining either himself or an idealised Mazzinian follower when in 1840 he wrote in the *Monthly Chronicle* of Byron's genius 'as a man and a poet': 'He never deserted our cause: he never betrayed a single human sympathy. Lonely and unhappy since childhood . . . slandered . . . beset by pecuniary problems; forced to leave his country . . . without friends . . .'[6] And while Mazzini could not hope to emulate Byron's flamboyance or overt sexuality, he still cultivated an air of romantic intensity and passionate dedication by living a life of extreme frugality, dressing always in black (because in mourning for his country), never marrying and displaying a general (if by many accounts false) indifference to sexual passion. He worked all night, lived on coffee and cigars and gave away what little money he earned or was sent by his mother; 'money is shit' he told his mother in 1843.[7] This pose seemingly held a strong fascination for the middle-class radical men and (perhaps especially) women whom Mazzini was assiduous in cultivating.

Britain, and London in particular, confirmed Mazzini's belief in the power of publicity, and especially the press, in politics. By the early 1840s, Mazzini had established a distinct public profile in London. His contacts with the Carlyles gave him the chance to publish articles on politics and literature in journals like *The Westminster Review*, and he gained additional publicity and made more useful contacts through his activities at the Italian school in Hatton Garden. Even the disastrous expedition of the Bandiera brothers in the end worked in his favour. Although he was blamed when the brothers were captured in Calabria and executed, it later emerged that his letters had been intercepted by the British government and passed on to the government in Vienna. The huge public and parliamentary outcry which resulted gave free publicity to Italian nationalism and to Mazzini in particular. Thomas Carlyle wrote a letter to *The Times* extolling Mazzini's 'genius and virtue' and his 'sterling veracity, humanity, and nobleness of mind'; Mazzini, he stated, was one 'of those rare men . . . who are worthy to be called martyr souls, who, in silence, piously in their daily life, understand and practice what is meant by that'.[8] Pictures were sold of Mazzini all over London and Mazzini published an article praising the Bandieras' 'martyrdom' in *The People's Journal*.

Mazzini arrived in England at the height of Chartist agitation, and he was profoundly affected by it and by the whole popular radical tradition in British politics. His new interest in working-class politics, expressed in the reorganisation of Young Italy, clearly reflects the influence of Chartist associational life.[9] He was especially struck by how Chartists successfully encouraged, and made political use of, popular involvement in radical issues. During the 1840s, the Chartist press produced newspapers, periodicals and works of fiction, and these grew increasingly in number and circulation.[10] The behaviour of Chartist leaders – their use of new print media, of visual images and artefacts, and of clothing and appearance(s) to promote themselves (and what James Vernon calls the 'insatiable appetite' of the British public for such leaders and heroes) – was arguably crucial in developing Mazzini's understanding of personality and the use of theatre and performance in popular politics.[11] At the opposite end of the political spectrum, he would have been equally aware of the promotion of Queen Victoria through popular publishing – through newspapers and the visual image – as a populist monarch.[12] (I discuss these developments in more detail in Chapter 5.)

Mazzini's interest in Garibaldi as a potential Italian nationalist hero must be traced in part to his experiences of the British press and British politics: to his awareness of the successful publicity strategies of British radical leaders and the use of the press to promote political issues and endorse the prevailing cult of personality in politics. On a more immediate level, his interest in Garibaldi can be linked to a series of new political contacts. The renewal of Chartist contacts with, and commitment to, European radicalism confirmed Mazzini's own belief in the potential of international revolutionary networks, and he came increasingly to use London's role as the centre of European political emigration to meet and often make long-term friendships with Hungarian, Polish and Russian exiles as well as with other Italians.[13] In 1847, he helped to found the People's International League, based on a loose network of liberal reformers, Nonconformists, working-class radicals and foreign exiles. Its purpose was to mobilise British public opinion in favour of radical and nationalist causes in Europe.[14]

Equally, Mazzini began to establish contact with exiles and sympathisers beyond Europe. He was in contact with some Young Italy exiles among emigrant circles in New York. He also struck up a correspondence with the Christian Alliance in the United States, an organisation of Protestant missionaries who were sympathetic both to Mazzini's anti-clerical stance and to his use of religious language. Particularly useful in the longer term was the relationship which developed between Mazzini and the American writer, Margaret Fuller, a prominent member of the Transcendentalists of New England, who came to London in 1846.[15] When she decided to go on to Italy later that year, Mazzini wrote her a letter of introduction, describing her as 'the rarest of women for her love and active sympathy for everything which is beautiful, great and holy, and, thus, for our Italy' and encouraging followers also to 'convert' her travelling companions, two prominent anti-slavery campaigners from the USA, to the Italian cause.[16] In fact, Fuller met and married a Mazzinian sympathiser, the Marchese Ossoli, during her Italian journey.

Perhaps especially significant were the contacts which Mazzini established with Italian migrant workers and political exiles in South America. These contacts were important because Young Italy had continued to recruit in the coastal towns of Brazil and the Rio de la Plata during the otherwise lean period of the late 1830s. By the early 1840s Young Italy in South America had a leadership, newspapers and something approaching a mass movement.[17] It was here that a group of young and militant enthusiasts, based in Rio de Janeiro and in the Uruguayan capital, Montevideo, formed around the journalistic and organisational activities of Cuneo and another prominent member of Young Italy in South America, Luigi Rossetti. Many were also involved in the naval and military exploits led by Garibaldi. And it was for this group – young, active and, as journalists and soldiers, the living expression of Mazzini's concept of the unity of 'thought and action' – that Mazzini began to make great plans.

A South American romance

After the abortive Young Italy uprisings of 1833–4 in Genoa, both Cuneo and Garibaldi had gone into exile. Giovanni Battista Cuneo, who was one of Garibaldi's political mentors during his years in South America, arrived there earlier than Garibaldi, in 1834, and quickly became involved in exile politics. In typical Mazzinian fashion, he immediately established a local branch of Young Italy and a newspaper (also called *Young Italy*) in Rio de Janeiro. Moving to Montevideo, he made a series of influential contacts with the so-called 'generation of 1837'. These young literary and political exiles, men such as Juan Bautista Alberdi, Esteban Echeverría, and Bartolomé Mitre along with another celebrated exile, Domingo Faustino Sarmiento (based in Chile), had been forced out of Buenos Aires by the dictator Rosas and had begun to mount a propaganda assault on the Rosas regime through novels, poetry and journalism. They were also greatly influenced by Mazzinian ideas and language and originally called themselves 'the Association of the Young Argentine Generation'.[18]

Thanks in part to this connection with the generation of 1837, and working with them to produce politicially engaged journalism, Cuneo became increasingly active as a writer and publisher.[19] He collaborated on the papers *El Iniciador* and *O Povo*, the latter being the paper of the rebel Rio Grande republic engaged in a war of independence with the Brazilian empire, initially edited by Luigi Rossetti. In 1841, he founded and edited in Montevideo the free weekly newspaper *L'Italiano*, aimed at Italian workers. During the height of the war between Uruguay and Buenos Aires, in which both Cuneo and Garibaldi played an important part, Cuneo published another free paper, *Il Legionario Italiano*, which had as its mast head 'Liberty, Equality, Independence, Unity, Humanity'. The paper quickly became a mouthpiece for Mazzinian ideas in Montevideo.

Garibaldi, who arrived in Rio at the age of twenty-eight some two years after Cuneo, had a career which was at first much less remarkable. In fact, despite the efforts of his biographers to suggest otherwise, there had been little in his early life to indicate anything unusual about Garibaldi. Its peripatetic nature (he was a merchant seaman) and his shady political activities seem all too typical of this post-revolutionary generation, to which both Cuneo and Mazzini also belonged. Nor was there anything especially surprising about his

association with the Young Italy uprisings in Genoa: Genoa was a hotbed of
political conspiracy, and conspiracy provided an outlet for many disaffected
young men during this period. Although Garibaldi had apparently been
recruited for Young Italy (perhaps by Cuneo) in the Black Sea port of
Taganrog in 1833, arguably just as important an influence on his political
development was his encounter earlier in the same year with a group of Saint-
Simonian exiles, and especially with their leader Emile Barrault, whom he
transported by ship from Marseille to Turkey. During the long journey, he
talked with Barrault, and Barrault gave him a book, the *Nouveau christianisme*
by Saint-Simon, which Garibaldi kept with him all his life.[20] It is possible that
the ideas of the romantic socialists – their confidence in the benefits of
technological progress; their spiritualism and especially the faith in a new
religion of 'Humanity'; the idea of community based on affective ties; a belief
in female emancipation; a non-monogamous attitude to sex and the rejection
of marriage – had as strong an impact on Garibaldi's political convictions, if
not stronger, as the later nationalist elaborations of Mazzini.[21]

Garibaldi's motives for going to Rio de Janeiro in the summer of 1835 are
not entirely clear. We know that he had found himself in a very precarious
position. As a sailor in the Piedmontese navy, he had been placed under a
sentence of death for having conspired against the king in the 1833–4
uprising, and during much of 1834 and the first half of 1835 he had been
forced to lead a kind of twilight existence under a false name in Marseille, and
had survived by travelling as a merchant seaman to Odessa and to Tunis. In
1835 he had apparently been entrusted with a political mission by Luigi
Canessa, a maverick Mazzinian activist in Marseille, to carry out in South
America. But his decision to leave Marseille may simply have been connected
to the terrible cholera epidemic there or to general disillusionment at the
prospects of revolution in Europe. Whatever the reasons, Garibaldi was given
a warm welcome by the revolutionary exiles in Rio and he quickly made
friends with Cuneo, Rossetti and others.[22] However, he went on to pursue the
fairly typical life of an Italian migrant, taking up his earlier career as a
merchant seaman, and trading along the coast between Rio and Montevideo
in a fishing boat. Then in 1837, and 'tired', as he put it, of leading 'an existence
so useless to our country' and convinced of a 'greater destiny',[23] he abandoned
commercial life to become a 'corsair' for the Rio Grande rebels, and with his
boat *Mazzini* and an assorted crew started to attack Brazilian shipping.[24] At
this stage, however, there were still few, if any, signs of the fame that was to
come.

Garibaldi spent four tough years of fighting on land and at sea, during which
he was taken prisoner and tortured, suffered a tragic shipwreck, and met and
eloped with his first wife, Anita. As the Rio Grande wars petered out into a

bloody guerrilla conflict, Garibaldi decided to move to Montevideo, where there was a more vibrant community of Italian exiles and migrants (some 6,000 Italians out of a population of 42,000, as well as 10,000 French and 3,000 Spaniards), including Cuneo and Francesco Anzani.[25] Garibaldi left for Montevideo with his family in April 1841 and marched overland with 900 head of cattle to sell in the city; but none of the cattle survived the journey, so he was obliged to eke out an impoverished existence as a mathematics teacher and salesman. Despite these inauspicious beginnings, Garibaldi soon began to do well in Montevideo, and became involved with the complex and prolonged war between the government of Uruguay, led by General Fructuoso Rivera, and the Argentine Confederation, under the dictatorship of Juan Manuel de Rosas (see map 1 on page 40).

This war lasted for over twelve years, and from 1842 involved the blockade and then siege of Montevideo by the Argentine Confederation; the siege itself was organised by the deposed Uruguayan president General Oribe, who had gone over to the Argentine side. The conflict was more significant than the Rio Grande wars, in that it had consequences for international trade and specifically damaged the commercial interests of both Great Britain and France. In 1845, Britain and France organised a joint naval intervention to prevent the Argentine conquest of Uruguay by blockading Buenos Aires.[26] The conflict was also much more newsworthy than the Rio Grande wars. Propaganda, of which the Argentine dictator Rosas was a well-known master,[27] played a major part in the war, with both the liberal Uruguayans and the Rosistas seeking to persuade the British and the French that trading interests would be better served by their winning the war. Both sides conducted lengthy press campaigns in the foreign language newspapers of the Rio de la Plata as well as in the national newspapers of London and Paris.[28] After the Anglo-French intervention, the Argentine government sought to present itself as the victim of foreign aggression,[29] while Uruguay, helped by its series of talented writers, represented the war as a great liberal cause, 'pitting a weak and increasingly defenceless state against a powerful Argentine adversary in a desperate fight for survival'. Thus, the defence of Montevideo came to symbolise 'in the European mind the virtues of nationalist struggle and political progress'.[30]

The Uruguayan government first placed Garibaldi in command of a naval squadron. This squadron was sent up the Paraná river right through Argentine territory, in a daring attempt to bring supplies to the besieged province of Corrientes and cut off Argentine trade with Paraguay. However, and perhaps not surprisingly, this expedition ended in failure and Garibaldi was forced to burn all his ships and escape with the surviving crews. In 1843, Garibaldi raised enough money by public subscription to build up a new naval force with

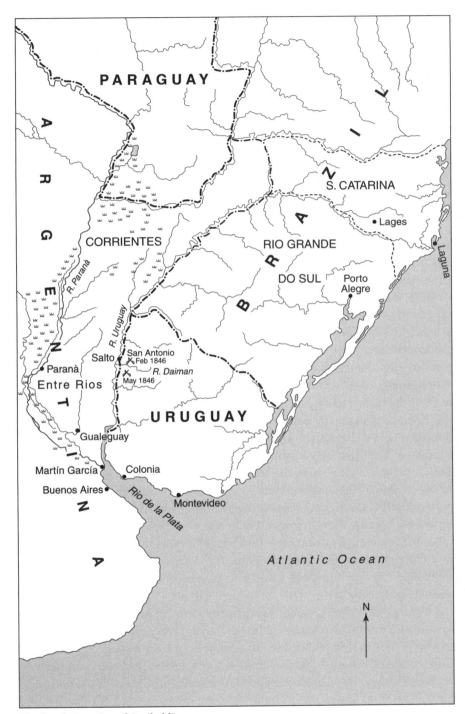

The South America of Garibaldi

which he attempted to disrupt Argentine shipping in the River Plate area. He intensified these activities after 1845 when, as commander of the Uruguayan fleet, he began to work with the Anglo-French naval forces, and he helped them to capture the Uruguayan port of Colonia and the island of Martín García. Also in 1843, Garibaldi decided to continue the fight on land and he organised an Italian Legion of volunteers to help in the military defence of Montevideo. This force of around 600 men was modelled on the much larger French Legion set up for the same purpose, and which had its own newspaper, *Le Patriote Français*. Initially, the Italian Legion met with a mixed reception and had equivocal results. Its members were accused of cowardice after one engagement, of brutality after another, and of deserting and going over to Rosas' forces when they reached enemy lines. However, all this changed in February 1846, when Garibaldi and his men stood firm against a much larger enemy force at San Antonio del Salto and won a celebrated victory. Salto marks the real change in Garibaldi's fortunes. It was after Salto that Garibaldi became famous and a political and military actor in his own right. A special issue of *Il Legionario Italiano* was published which was entirely dedicated to the heroism of Garibaldi and his men; it included letters from Garibaldi, official decrees and a poem, and presented the battle as an emblematic moment in Italy's recovery of past glory.[31] It was only after Salto that Mazzini and the Mazzinian press back in Europe began to take a more active interest in Garibaldi and his men.[32]

Garibaldi's life and experiences in South America are among the least known and most mythologised of his entire career. Certain episodes – Garibaldi's torture when a prisoner at Gualeguay; his meeting with his first wife Anita; Anita's own flight from the enemy while, variously, pregnant or with Garibaldi's infant son in her arms; the battles of the Italian Legion in defence of Montevideo – have achieved a kind of canonical status. However, much of what we know about Garibaldi's activities in the service of the Rio Grande rebels we know from Garibaldi himself, from his memoirs written in the 1850s, and these are not always reliable. Although his years in Uruguay are better documented, here too it is difficult to penetrate both the mythology produced by the war itself, of the celebration of Montevideo as the 'New Troy' and of Garibaldi as the defender of Uruguayan freedom,[33] and the use subsequently made of it by nationalist propagandists back in Italy. So it is hard to establish with any certainty the real nature and scale of his military achievements in these years.

A recent study based on British government sources has suggested that, on their own, Garibaldi and his men 'achieved very little' in *La Defensa* of Montevideo. Contemporary British reports referred to him not as a hero but as an adventurer, and they complained specifically about his habit of seizing and requisitioning private shipping, which disrupted trade and arguably prolonged the war. Although Garibaldi was popular with the civilian population, especially in the countryside where the humane conduct of his soldiers seemed to compare favourably with the brutality of the Argentine troops, he made himself unpopular with some sections of the government in Montevideo for his 'maritime misdemeanours' and general refusal to obey orders. The Uruguayan leader, Rivera, was told that Garibaldi had 'scandalously plundered Colonia and Gualeguaychú' in 1845, and that his actions would 'greatly discredit' their cause. Some Montevidean leaders also viewed Garibaldi with suspicion as a 'foreigner' whose powerful position threatened Uruguayan independence. Indeed, it was said to be 'the general dislike evinced on the part of all at having an Italian at the head of the garrison and at having the town completely under the foreign mercenaries' which forced his resignation as the commander of the Uruguayan navy in July 1847.[34] All this suggests that Garibaldi's negative reputation in Buenos Aires as a dangerous 'adventurer' was not entirely unjustified.

Nevertheless, Garibaldi's experiences in these years were crucial for his own personal and political development; especially important were the revolutionary contacts and ideals he developed there. It was in Rio de Janeiro that he first joined the Freemasons, a significant front organisation for Young Italy in South America,[35] and a crucial political network for much of the rest of his life. What was to become an enduring belief in biographical writing and journalism as an extension of political action may owe as much to Garibaldi's direct contacts with men like Mitre of the Argentine generation of 1837, or to his knowledge of the work of Domingo Sarmiento, as it did to the arguably more indirect influence of Mazzinian journalism.[36] It was also during the years in Rio Grande that Garibaldi met his first wife, Anita, a person by all accounts as adventurous, courageous and unconventional as he, and who remained in most respects his female ideal for the rest of his life.[37] Garibaldi made other important friends in Rio Grande and in Uruguay. Some of them, like Rossetti, died early (in 1840), but others – like Cuneo, Francesco Anzani and Livio Zambeccari – stayed with him much longer; all these friends came to represent a vision of fraternal friendship and male 'virility' which influenced his own behaviour and which he used as a political model in his later political writings and speeches.

Anzani (who died in 1848 returning to Italy with Garibaldi) was an older revolutionary and an exile from the revolutions of 1821. Before fighting for the Rio Grande rebels, where he met Garibaldi, Anzani had already fought as a volunteer in the Greek war of independence and in the Portuguese civil war, and he became a key influence on Garibaldi's military thinking. He helped him organise the Italian Legion of Montevideo, and was responsible for maintaining discipline and order in the ranks.[38] Another Italian exile who did much to encourage and influence Garibaldi's political and military career was the intellectual and *carbonaro* Zambeccari. In the late 1830s he was the chief propagandist for the Rio Grande rebels.[39] He was also the initial point of contact between Garibaldi and the Rio Grande president, Bento Gonçalves da Silva, a prominent republican whom one historian has described as 'a copybook romantic leader and popular hero . . . a fine horseman, picturesque in dress, enthusiastically followed by his men', and who, in turn, did much to influence and encourage Garibaldi's political activities.[40] For the rest of his life, Garibaldi maintained friendly contacts with the Uruguayan leader, Joaquín Suárez. Suárez invited Garibaldi to return to Montevideo in the 1850s and, at the moment of Garibaldi's greatest triumph in 1860, wrote to congratulate him and to acknowledge the great contribution he had made to 'the independence of my country'.[41]

Garibaldi was much taken by the land and the people of South America. In his memoirs, he romanticised the life of the pampas and was especially enthused by what he saw as the 'independent' life of its gaucho inhabitants. Described as a 'white savage, divorced from society', the gaucho was a 'mounted nomad' and an important figure on the early nineteenth-century South American pampas. The antithesis of urban, cultured society, the gaucho refused settled work or occupation and rejected family, home and respectability.[42] It may be that Garibaldi saw in gaucho society a kind of embodiment of his romantic socialist ideas. According to Guerzoni, Garibaldi's friend and biographer, Garibaldi always admired the gaucho as the 'ideal type' of free man. Indeed, Guerzoni writes, Garibaldi brought back from South America the 'beliefs' and 'personal habits and clothes' of the 'corsairs, soldiers, sailors and cattle ranchers' he met there: 'The Garibaldi who came back to Italy in 1848 was . . . a gaucho . . . Time and the habits of civility would partially change him . . . but a gaucho he fundamentally remained all his life.'[43] The restlessness and poverty of Garibaldi's daily life during the South American years display features of the gaucho. Gaucho values, together with romantic socialist beliefs, may also help to explain his (for the time) scandalous relationship with his wife Anita, who was an eighteen-year-old married woman when he met her, whom he more or less seized from her home and ran off with, and whom he married only in 1842, two years after the birth of their first child.[44]

Some of Garibaldi's political ideas, most notably his lasting belief in the virtue of dictatorships – if only in time of war and for a limited period – were derived from his observations of politics and the conduct of war in South America. Many of the battles over the political forms of nation-building and the struggles between conservatives and liberals which Garibaldi was to become involved in on his return to Italy, he first encountered in republican circles in Montevideo.[45] He seems equally to have been affected by the public or theatrical aspects of Rio de la Plata politics, arguably in much the same way as Mazzini was affected by the Chartists in Britain. Here too the gauchos would seem to have been important, in that many features of their rebellious and violent culture were adopted and adapted as a political style by leaders such as the Argentinian dictator Rosas.[46] John Lynch tells us that while Rosas did little to help the gauchos in social terms and punished any signs of crime and rebellion with astonishing rapidity and cruelty, he still 'identified culturally with the gaucho', in part as a means of representing the interests of the interior provinces against those of the liberal, more European-oriented elites of Buenos Aires. Rosas was noted for his horsemanship, went about dressed as a gaucho and his idea of a joke when out riding was to throw a lasso around a man's neck and drag him along the ground. He also encouraged the extensive use of brutal rituals and employed a language of politics 'which was charged with violence and designed to terrorize'.[47] Aspects of gaucho behaviour were adopted by Garibaldi, although for very different purposes to those of Rosas. Many of the elements of Garibaldi's public persona which were to captivate Europeans in 1848 and 1849 – his physical strength, his long hair and beard, his 'poncho' and brightly coloured clothes, as well as his displays of horsemanship, daring gestures and eccentric manners – were clearly fashioned during his years in South America. These characteristics were copied directly from the gaucho militias with – and against – whom Garibaldi fought. They may also have been adopted by him as a public means of challenging and subverting Rosista propaganda, of giving Rosas' violent populist style a revolutionary and democratic 'twist' by directing it to liberal and humanitarian ends.

South America was crucial for Garibaldi in a more practical sense still, for it was in Rio Grande and Uruguay that he learnt how to fight. As it turned out, the kinds of battles he fought in South America – commanding untrained men of mixed background and capabilities; fighting against an enemy superior in number and resources; relying on mobility and surprise to gain advantage – were to prove invaluable when he returned to Italy, as was his newly acquired ability to ride a horse. Perhaps most notably of all, Garibaldi seems to have discovered in himself at this time the qualities of an inspiring and talented leader of men. His letters regarding the conduct of war in Montevideo reveal a professionalism and knowledge of military tactics which are surprising in someone hitherto entirely untrained.[48] Even allowing, moreover, for the inevitable hyperbole of newspaper reports and of retrospective accounts designed to exalt his exceptional bravery, Garibaldi appears to have been increasingly entrusted in South America with leading what he called – not without irony – 'chivalrous enterprises' (as he wrote to Cuneo after the Paraná expedition: 'Never mind! These chivalrous enterprises always come down to me').[49] Such daring missions, whether they failed (as with the Paraná expedition) or succeeded (as with the conflict at San Antonio del Salto), relied on the energy, enthusiasm and stamina of the men and their leader, and were designed to confuse and demoralise the enemy by their sheer audacity and their displays of individual courage. They also did much to publicise the Uruguayan liberal cause to the national and international press.

It was in South America, in other words, that Garibaldi discovered his true vocation – not as a (failed) merchant sailor nor as an (outlawed) political conspirator, but as a soldier hero.[50] His military experiences confirmed and clarified his core political ideals, especially his basic commitment to fighting oppression and upholding liberty and independence wherever he felt it was threatened. The Italian Legion of Montevideo was a concrete expression of Garibaldi's belief in the capacity of young, enthusiastic volunteers, rather than professional or paid soldiers (mercenaries), to act as the military vanguard and living symbol of a political idea.[51] Garibaldi sought to identify war and soldiering with a higher moral cause. He told his men to expect no material reward for their courage or sacrifice; he publicly rejected all promotions and pecuniary rewards for himself, and after the victory at San Antonio del Salto he refused the rank of general and the offer of land, and made sure his officers did the same. As a result, he acquired the reputation – never to leave him – of a 'disinterested individual', as well known for his poverty as for his courage, and remembered for his kind manners and quiet voice as much as for his passionate gestures.[52]

With the help of Cuneo's journalism, the heroism of Garibaldi and the Italian Legion as a whole was identified with *italianità*. The Italian Legion of Montevideo became a powerful symbol of national pride and belonging. As a result of military success, Italian nationalists in both South America and Europe were able to use the legion as proof that Italians could fight courageously; and the legion's refusal to accept rewards was used to show the moral superiority of Italians, especially *vis-à-vis* the French (although they were the accepted leaders of revolutionary action, the French Legion of Montevideo had received land and money in return for their efforts). The flag of the Italian Legion drew an explicit parallel between military virtue and national identity. It depicted an exploding volcano on a black background, with the black representing mourning for the enslaved fatherland, and the volcano (Vesuvius) the patriotic fervour and eternal flame of the legionaries themselves.[53] The legionaries wore red shirts, said to be a 'job lot' from a slaughterhouse,[54] but also effective on a symbolic level: as another means of subverting Rosista propaganda (Rosista federalists used red as their colour), and to affirm the association of red with liberty, republicanism and the French Revolution. For all these reasons, the exploits of the Italian Legion in Montevideo and of their leader came increasingly to be identified with the vision of a 'resurrected' – virtuous, virile and militant – Italian nation.

'Man of genius'

Garibaldi was at this time in the full vigour of manhood [a British naval officer in Montevideo later recalled], with a firm well-built frame which sat his horse like a centaur. He wore his hair and beard long; they were then of a dark brown colour, with a reddish tint in the latter. His countenance was remarkable for its serenity, and the lips pressed close together denoted a strong will, whilst his eyes were steadfast and piercing in their gaze. In stature he was of medium height, and was altogether the *beau ideal* of a chief of irregular troops. His scarlet tunic fitted loosely to the body, and round its collar were tied the two ends of a gaudy handkerchief . . . His cavalry sword-belt confined the dress to the waist, and in his saddle holsters were a pair of pistols. On his head was the same description of black felt hat and feather as worn by all his corps.[55]

It was in Uruguay that Garibaldi developed a conspicuous and perhaps exceptional personal allure. His friend Anzani was among the first to record Garibaldi's appeal, writing enthusiastically not only of his 'decisiveness', 'courage' and 'patriotic love' as a soldier but also of his capacity to win the affection ('*simpatia*') of the Montevideans.[56] Much of this attraction seems to have been due to his striking physical presence. On the one hand, Garibaldi is described as strong and physically imposing: he wears flamboyant clothes, and has abundant facial hair and flowing locks, piercing eyes (of indeterminate colour, perhaps light brown but often said to be blue), and a robust, athletic body. On the other, his bearing is graceful and 'serene'; and the earliest portraits of him show a man with a kind and pleasant face, and blue eyes.[57] He is a virile 'white savage' with a gentlemanly countenance, and it is perhaps this combination of strength and mildness, a combination so popular in the romantic literary hero, which best explains his immediate physical attraction.

Equally importantly, Garibaldi's allure transferred to the broader public sphere. In Uruguay, Garibaldi developed a clear talent for attracting publicity. Yet although both *Il Legionario Italiano* and *El Naçional*, the Montevidean liberal paper, made a hero out of him, a great deal of the publicity was negative. The Rosas propaganda machine emphasised Garibaldi's activities as a corsair during the Rio Grande years and his continuing attacks on foreign shipping, and he was depicted as a dangerous, undisciplined and voracious mercenary.

He was accused variously in the Rosista press of being a 'cruel and greedy adventurer', 'a vile adventurer' and 'an unknown adventurer, come . . . to this land to pursue his personal profit'. He was also described as a 'bandit' and a bucaneer, an 'Italian pirate', a '*gringo* pirate', a 'savage Unitarian [liberal] thirsting for gold and blood'. After the battle for Colonia, he was accused of leading his 'cruel' and 'wicked' Italians to commit 'atrocities' and acts of religious sacrilege; during the taking of Salto he was said to have set an example in the looting: 'With his band of marauders he ran from one habitation to another of the unfortunate families . . . whence he robbed with his own hands their money and jewels. He afterwards ordered a general pillage.'[58] When two members of the Italian Legion deserted to Oribe (Rosas' ally in Montevideo), Rosista papers in both Buenos Aires and Montevideo published their statements which made personal accusations against Garibaldi. Garibaldi, they declared, was 'immoral' and 'corrupted'; a spendthrift who never paid his debts and a 'pirate' who had forcibly abducted another man's wife 'whom he afterwards married in Montevideo'.[59] Moreover, this negative press spread back to Europe, so that the London *Times* (quoting a Buenos Aires paper) mentioned Garibaldi's 'piratical depredations' in January 1845. In 1846 the Paris *Journal des Débats* published an article accusing the Italians in Montevideo of 'robberies' and 'atrocities', and the *Restauracion* of Lisbon described his men as bandits: 'Condottieri . . . [who] eating, drinking and playing the fruits of their plunder at dice, brought to mind an epoch fortunately forgotten in Europe'.[60]

Yet these accusations did little to harm the growing reputation of Garibaldi and his men. Above all, Mazzini caught on quickly to Garibaldi's potential both as a military leader and as what he called 'a *moral influence*' in Italy, and was seemingly unperturbed by the prevailing press hostility.[61] Cuneo first mentioned Garibaldi to Mazzini in April 1841,[62] and by the autumn of 1842 Mazzini was already expressing high hopes, describing Garibaldi as 'Genoese, young and an exile from Italy for the affairs of '33' and 'extolled, as a man of genius, by *El Naçional*'.[63] Mazzini had been enthused by the Paraná expedition and *El Naçional*'s coverage of it as a heroic defeat.[64] It mattered not to him that Garibaldi had failed and lost all his boats; what was important was the heroic nature of the defence – '[h]e defended a difficult position for I don't know how many days against seven boats, with him having two' – and, he said, 'Garibaldi is all that is talked about' in the region.[65] As the siege of Montevideo persisted without hope of relief, Mazzini wrote to his mother that the news was good. 'Our Italian Legion and Garibaldi produce wonders: the Italians are loved and respected by the population as saviours of the city. The Italian national cause is as loved there as it could be here with us. I would so like you to see the newspapers of the city.'[66]

From the outset, in fact, Mazzini was concerned to promote Garibaldi's standing in Italy and Europe and to create closer links with Garibaldi and his followers. He asked his friend Giuseppe Lamberti to circulate news about Garibaldi in Paris,[67] and he published reports about Garibaldi's activities in his London-based *Apostolato Popolare*. '[W]e name him [Garibaldi] with pride to our brothers,' the paper told its readers, 'because we are sure that he considers his career in South America to be merely the apprenticeship for the Italian war which one day will call him back to Europe.'[68] Mazzini directly encouraged Garibaldi to expect 'greater destinies than dying in London or Montevideo' and asked Cuneo to tell all the legionaries 'that the men who knew how to risk their lives for liberty in a foreign country, must die in their own land'.[69]

In January 1846 Mazzini decided openly to combat the attacks in the French press on Garibaldi and the Italian Legion. Mazzini published a letter in the London *Times* along with two documents: one from the Uruguayan leader Rivera offering land to Garibaldi and the legion, and a reply from Garibaldi rejecting the offer and declaring that 'it is the duty of all free men to fight the battles of freedom, wherever tyranny threatens its cause'. Mazzini was careful to add that the French Legion had accepted 'a donation of the same nature as the one declined by my countrymen', and that when Rivera's letter was read to the Italian Legion, 'there arose from the ranks one unanimous cry, "We are no hirelings – we are no Swiss"' (i.e. the legions were volunteers, not mercenaries). In July of the same year, Mazzini translated his letter to *The Times* into French and gave it a new introduction. Republishing it as a pamphlet, he circulated it among the various exile circles in Europe and attempted to smuggle it directly into Italy as well.[70]

Both the publicity drive in Europe and Mazzini's contacts with the Young Italians in Montevideo intensified after Garibaldi's victory in San Antonio del Salto in February 1846. The fact that Garibaldi had once again rejected all rewards seems to have been as important to Mazzini as the fact of the victory itself. As he wrote enthusiastically to his mother: 'physical courage and virtue, everything that I admire is in this man, and that I would like my compatriots to admire'.[71] Mazzini had also received a copy of the text of Garibaldi's letter rejecting rewards in which Garibaldi stated, 'as the Head of the Italian Legion, all that I can have deserved by way of recompense, I donate to the wounded and to the families of the dead. Not only the benefits, but the honours too, would weigh on my soul, if bought with so much Italian blood.'[72] Mazzini and his supporters were clearly enthused by the language and content of this letter, and they were to make great use of it in the months that followed. Mazzini wrote immediately to Lamberti in Paris, enclosing a copy of Garibaldi's letter rejecting all rewards and commenting 'it is a fine moral act on Garibaldi's part, and it would be useful to create a name for him in Italy'. He asked Lamberti to circulate the letter in France and to send copies to two Mazzinian writers: Augusto Vecchi and Filippo de Boni, who was publishing a new Mazzinian journal, *Così la penso*, from exile in Switzerland.[73]

This time, Mazzini's propaganda efforts had a much broader impact than hitherto. This was because the political climate in Italy was itself changing. During the early 1840s, public opinion had been mobilised in favour of Italian nationalism by a series of works written by prominent moderate liberals, and notably by the publication of Vincenzo Gioberti's *Del primato morale e civile degli italiani* ('On the moral and civil primacy of Italians') in 1843 and by Cesare Balbo's *Delle speranze d'Italia* ('The hopes of Italy') in 1844. In June 1846, a new pope, Pius IX, was elected and he created something of a media frenzy with a few liberal reforms and an apparent endorsement of the (moderate) nationalist cause.[74] Although Mazzini was no friend of the monarchically inclined moderates or of the Pope, he was quite prepared to take advantage of this swing in public opinion, or, as he put it in a letter to Cuneo, to try to 'insinuate something National in the demonstrations [in favour of the Pope]' and to turn popular hopes into an expression of anti-Austrianism when, as he believed would happen, the Austrians put a stop to the Pope's reforms.[75]

For once, Mazzini was swimming with the political tide. A strong indication of the increasingly nationalist direction of opinion was offered by the Scientific Congress in Genoa in September 1846, where nationalist sentiments were openly expressed and, for the first time in Italy, linked openly to the figure of Garibaldi. There, one of the participants, Odoardo Turchetti, made a speech calling for aid for the victims of an earthquake in Lucca. At the end of the speech he suggested that a book honouring the efforts of the Italian Legion in Montevideo led by the '*prode* [valiant] *genovese Garibaldi*' be produced and its profits given to the earthquake victims.[76] The book, *Documenti storici intorno ad alcuni fatti d'arme degl'italiani in Montevideo* (essentially, a collection of the letters offering rewards to Garibaldi and his rejection of them) was produced and circulated legally. The author was Cesare Laugier de Bellecour, a soldier–writer known for his popular melodramas which always had the same hero, a brave, selfless and patriotic soldier, at the centre of the action; and he wrote that he wanted in the book to show 'that the ancient valour of the Italic people is not dead'.[77] A Bolognese newspaper, *Il Felsineo*, published glowing reports of the battle of San Antonio del Salto, stressing the extraordinary welcome given to the legionaries by the women of Salto and publishing the decree of the Montevidean government praising the combatants (this information was said to be supplied by Felice Foresti, a Mazzinian agent in New York). The left-liberal Turinese paper, *Letture di Famiglia*, published an article about Garibaldi under the title 'Italians who bring renown to the fatherland in foreign lands' and described him as a 'renowned Italian who [is] renewing the examples of ancient heroism'. These papers too were able to circulate legally without government censorship (and the article in *Letture di Famiglia* was published in another paper, *L'Eco*, a month later).[78]

Nor was the clandestine press quiet on the subject of Garibaldi. The Mazzinian journalist Filippo de Boni published a long article in his Lugano-based monthly, *Così la penso*, in which he decried the lack of public interest in the sacrifices made by the Italian Legion of Montevideo. He attributed it to the fate of Italy more generally – to the fact that 'Italians have no fatherland constituted as a nation, [and] because for certain governments the blood of exiles and generous men is not human blood'. Hoping to inspire his readers with their 'noble and worthy examples of military virtue', he gave a detailed account – complete with documents – of the Italian Legion, stressing the victory at Salto and the offer and rejection of honours, and exalting Garibaldi as 'a man resolute in his generosity, a man of courage and intelligence, capable of great deeds, and for this freely elected by the legionaries as their colonel'.[79]

An even clearer sign of the changing climate of public opinion, and of the role it created for Garibaldi, was given by the establishment of a national subscription in Italy in October 1846 as a tribute to Garibaldi and his men. This subscription – the brainchild of two Florentine radicals, Carlo Fenzi and Cesare della Ripa – asked for donations (the amount fixed was very low) to give a sword of honour to Garibaldi, a gold medal to Anzani, and silver medals to all the legionaries. Fenzi and Della Ripa wrote a circular asking for donations in which they specifically mentioned the legion's 'noble refusal' to accept rewards for their actions, and the heroic efforts of Garibaldi and Anzani. 'The whole world', they wrote, 'should know of Italy's recognition of the actions of its children'; these 'brave brothers' should know that they are in 'the thoughts of their distant Fatherland' and be encouraged to 'ever greater and more high-minded deeds'.[80] The Paris-based Mazzinian, Lamberti, announcing the opening of the subscription in France, stated that it would be the means of publicising 'the name of our brave Italians and the tyrannical injustices of governments', as well as 'tacitly protesting against the slumber of Italians'.[81] The subscription for Garibaldi and his legion met with huge success. Lamberti collected signatures in Paris, Mazzini did the same in London and so did De Boni in Switzerland. In Italy itself, it had an enormous impact.[82] Collections were permitted in the Two Sicilies, the Papal States and Tuscany, while in Piedmont, King Carlo Alberto was persuaded by the prominent moderate liberal, Massimo d'Azeglio, personally to authorise the subscription. It was signed by well-known liberals and nationalists from all over Italy (names included Carlo Poerio, Carlo Pisacane, Quintino Sella and Cristina di Belgioioso) and by December, only two months after the opening of the subscription, it had been signed by thousands of people and the desired sum of money had been collected.[83]

The publicity campaign for Garibaldi was not confined to Europe or to the political sphere. Also in 1846, a novel was published in New York in which Garibaldi had a walk-on part. The book, *Dolores*, which describes itself as a 'historical novel', was written by a Danish poet, Paul Harro-Harring, who had been a friend of Mazzini during his Swiss exile and, since he had acted as a contact and courier of letters and newspapers between Mazzini and the South American exiles in 1841 and 1842, would have met Garibaldi, Cuneo and other Young Italians.[84] *Dolores* is set in the South American wars in which Garibaldi played a part. Although it was a vehicle for the author's anti-clerical, feminist, republican and Mazzinian ideas, it was also something of a commercial success, since it went into three editions in New York and London and was translated into Swedish and German (although not Italian). Harro-Harring's character Barigaldi is the commander of a Baltimore schooner called *Mazzini*; he is said to be 'an Italian bandit . . . a famous fellow' known for his 'daring heroism'.[85] Yet long scenes underline his gentlemanly qualities and his calm and good humour even when talking to the stereotypically idiotic Irishman, Patrick Gentleboy. The novel also offers us a physical picture of Barigaldi – a 'notorious' bandit but equally easy to recognise 'as belonging to the higher classes of the social world':

> The lengthened form of his face, his pale complexion, sharply defined and somewhat curved nose, well formed lips, and deep set, dark eyes, with an expressive glance, black hair, and the peculiarly sonorous sound of a clear breast voice, all marked him as an Italian. He was dressed in a simple, dark blue uniform, armed with sword and pistols, and wearing on his head a marine hat, in the form of a shallop . . . which displayed the same green, red, and white cockade, that he had worn in Savoy.

When Barigaldi catches sight of his friend Ormur, he greets him by pressing him to his breast, 'while the eyes of both appeared to become moist, and their lips to quiver with the emotions that pervaded their manly hearts'.[86] Barigaldi is here an archetypal Italian patriot: a man whose face, voice and clothes all 'marked him' as Italian, and a romantic bandit hero ('armed with swords and pistols') who is distinguished, sexual and sensitive all at the same time.

During 1847, Mazzinians and journalists sympathetic to Mazzini were able to take advantage of the relaxation of press censorship in the Papal States, Tuscany and Piedmont to write even more openly and explicitly about Garibaldi.[87] In April, Mazzini wrote to Cuneo asking him for a 'short historical outline' of the legion, 'from its formation onwards, with the fine deeds . . .

without great words, and documented as much as possible'.[88] In the event, Cuneo went further and published the most complete and detailed account of Garibaldi and the legion to date, which ran across seven issues of the radical paper *Il Corriere Livornese* during July and August 1847.[89] Cuneo's account followed the already standard lines established by Mazzini and produced by De Boni and others in the previous year. It was richly illustrated with (the now usual) documents and claimed to recount all details of the war in Montevideo, 'as they happened, without altering any aspect of them'. In common with the previous descriptions of Garibaldi and his men, Cuneo made much of the accusations that Garibaldi was a 'mercenary' and 'adventurer'. He commented that 'the foreigner, ever in search of new opportunties to heap abuse on our fatherland, invents new scoops, by altering the facts, and spreads the news'. Announcing that such 'a terrible insult has made me shake with rage', he confided that it was this insult which had inspired him to write the present account. He insisted that he sought only to defend Garibaldi and that Italians should be proud of Garibaldi's achievements and the achievements of his 'slandered brothers' in the legion.[90] Once again, the main proof of 'the moral qualities of this unusual man' and of the 'noble and lofty character' of Garibaldi lay, for Cuneo, in his exceptional courage and qualities as a leader and in his rejection of all rewards. Hopelessly outnumbered at San Antonio, Garibaldi encouraged his men by telling them 'above all to remember the honour of Italy', to which his men replied 'with one voice': 'we will fight to win, or die, Colonel'. Faced with a counter-attack, Garibaldi rallied his men 'with his voice and with example', and fought with such enthusiasm and fury as to scare off the enemy. Like earlier writers, Cuneo also stressed the fame of the legionaries in Uruguay: they were welcomed as heroes returning to Salto, the wounded were tended to by the 'gentle sex', and public ceremonies were held to honour their accomplishments.[91]

Throughout 1847, press interest in Garibaldi showed few signs of abating. In May, London's *Times*, which was hostile to the liberals in Uruguay and hence to Garibaldi, and in 1846 had declined to publish a second letter from Mazzini detailing the events of San Antonio del Salto, now mentioned his 'brilliant victory' there and described him as 'brave and single-minded'.[92] Again, in London, a non-Mazzinian Italian exile, the journalist Antonio Gallenga, wrote an anti-Austrian tract which found space to express faith in Garibaldi's potential as a military leader.[93] In the same year, the Turin-based liberal publisher Lorenzo Valerio began to produce regular features about Garibaldi in his papers, *Letture di Famiglia* and *La Concordia*, and these continued to appear during early 1848.[94] *La Concordia* began a regular pattern of publishing letters from Garibaldi himself. After he had received his sword of honour, Garibaldi wrote to Valerio that he would always treasure it, adding

– and again here he established what would become a popular theme – that he had never expected any reward for his deeds, and all his men were pleased and surprised by the 'applause' given to 'our small efforts'. Garibaldi thanked and praised the musician Giuseppe Bertoldi for his 'robust poem', published as a pamphlet that year in Lugano.[95] Bertoldi's pamphlet, *Alla legione italiana in Montevideo ed al colonnello Giuseppe Garibaldi*, was published by Valerio, and had included a description of the public subscription for Garibaldi and various letters about his activities in Uruguay. The poem itself – a 'hymn' – of the same title likened Garibaldi to David conquering the giant with stones and a sling, and to George Washington, and it looked forward to 'the glorious day' when Garibaldi would lead the people against the 'oppression' of the 'barbarians' (i.e. against Austrian rule). It was a minor publishing success, with repeat orders for the pamphlet coming in from at least one bookshop, and it was sold in Bologna and Florence as well as Turin.[96]

Somewhat more prosaic, but arguably more significant in its connections and impact, was the article published in October 1847 about Garibaldi in a moderate liberal Florentine paper, *La Patria*, owned by Baron Ricasoli. The author, Stanislao Bentivoglio, was the brother-in-law of the official French envoy to Uruguay, Count Walewski, and he had personally met Garibaldi in Montevideo. Bentivoglio explicitly identified his pleasure at an Italy 'risen again to new life' with Garibaldi, 'who there with his brave companions puts on such a fine display of Italian valour'. Reflecting his perhaps more moderate leanings, Bentivoglio stressed Garibaldi's commitment to order as much as his courage and leadership: 'Garibaldi bravely fights enemies much greater in number than he, he represses internal uprisings with equal vigour, he punishes wicked men who are ever ready for disorder and strife, and he rouses with energetic words or just by his presence the spirits of those who otherwise would have been crushed by such a long and exhausting war.' And he too looked forward to the day when Garibaldi returned 'to his friends and the Fatherland', commenting that then the sword of honour given to him by the Italians 'would be in his hands a pitiless weapon against our enemies'.[97]

Mazzini was not slow to realise the potential of this broadening of public interest in Garibaldi, and sought to turn it to his advantage. In 1847 he wrote to Cuneo and to another exile in Montevideo, Giacomo Medici, about sending a painting of Garibaldi to Europe, which he planned to have lithographed and circulated to raise money for a newly launched National Fund which, among other projects, would help Garibaldi and his men return to Europe.[98] A painting by Gaetano Gallino, the same Italian artist in Montevideo who had designed the flag of the Italian Legion, was produced and lithographed in 1848 by a Turin-based company called Doyen. The lithograph depicts Garibaldi as a romantic, exotic figure, half turned towards the viewer. Although his hands

2 Portrait of Garibaldi published in *Il Mondo Illustrato*, 1848. This portrait, of which many versions exist, was the first picture of Garibaldi to be published in Europe and was produced before he arrived in Italy in June 1848.

rest on a sabre, there the orthodox military references stop; he wears a long cloak over one shoulder and a loose dark 'blouse' with full sleeves, his hair is flowing and shoulder length and he has a full beard and sloping, sensuous eyes.[99] A similar lithograph was produced by the same company in the same year as *Giuseppe Garibaldi di Genova* (this time he wears a large, sloping beret, and a white open shirt tied with a tassel), to accompany the text of Bertoldi's hymn to the Italian Legion.[100] The same lithograph – a slightly altered copy signed 'Delangle' – was also published in the newly launched illustrated magazine, *Il Mondo Illustrato*, of Turin in February 1848 (see figure 2 opposite).[101] By early 1848, in effect, engraved portraits of Garibaldi had begun to circulate in northern Italy.

However, Mazzini did not have things entirely his own way, and Garibaldi proved more difficult to control than he had expected. In January 1847 Mazzini expressed genuine alarm and irritation at the rumours that Garibaldi and Anzani were planning to organise a military expedition from Montevideo to Italy ('What a misfortune . . . for our affairs! So, it's possible to lose your head in this way!'). By November, however, he had decided to make their plans his own, and wrote to Felice Foresti in New York to ask him for help in transporting Garibaldi and a thousand men to Italy and in supplying them with firearms (he mentioned buying them some of the new Colt revolvers). Garibaldi, Mazzini told Foresti, 'is really an exceptional man for us': those who met him confirmed his 'unusual abilities', and in Italy his name 'has begun to carry weight'.[102] In the end, Garibaldi only set sail for Italy from Montevideo in April 1848, with sixty-three of his legionaries and a dying Francesco Anzani. His wife and children had left for Europe before him, as had his colleague from the Italian Legion, Giacomo Medici, destined for London to make contact with Mazzini.

The return of the South American exiles to Italy was strictly supervised by Mazzini, and was the result of his strategy to hold them in readiness to fight and die for Italy when he felt the political and military moment was right. But by late 1847 it had already become difficult to hold Garibaldi back. Garibaldi was disillusioned with developments in Montevideo and anxious to return home. He was particularly enthused by the election of the 'liberal' pope, Pius IX, in Italy and, unlike Mazzini, believed that he represented a new oppor-tunity for Italy. Indeed, in October Garibaldi and Anzani – convinced, as they put it, that a man 'had arisen in the breast of our Fatherland' who understood the 'needs of the century' – had written a letter to the papal representative in Rio offering the military services of their legion to the Pope.[103] In December, the first newspapers arrived in Montevideo giving details of the reforms taking place in Italy, and a celebration was held by the Italian community in Montevideo. Garibaldi and the officers of the legion led a torchlit procession through the streets, to the sound of musical bands and revolutionary and patriotic songs. Just days before his departure for Italy, Garibaldi would probably also have heard the news from Italy that a popular revolution had occured in Palermo, which had overthrown the rule of the king of Naples.[104]

Conclusion

The early fame of Garibaldi was the result of a deliberate strategy conceived by Mazzini and enthusiastically endorsed by his followers, including Garibaldi himself. As a national hero, Garibaldi represents a triumph for Mazzini's insistence on the unity of thought and action. His fame was the result of cultural elaboration and military accomplishment, and its purpose was to inspire and publicise political engagement in word and in deed. Especially worthy of comment are the various 'fits' between the first accounts of Garibaldi and the Risorgimento narratives discussed in the previous chapter: Garibaldi provides a concrete and symbolic link between the nation as cultural identity and nationalism as a revolutionary political movement, and there are striking similarities between the way Garibaldi is described and the qualities of a Risorgimento literary hero. Like the Risorgimento hero, Garibaldi is virile and attractive: he smoulders in long hair and flowing clothes. He is of a 'noble and lofty character', personally modest yet rebellious, and defiant in the face of defeat; and he is exceptionally courageous and daring when it comes to upholding moral principles and defending the honour of the community. Equally, in these early accounts Garibaldi is always, and is perhaps above all, a soldier, a military hero who shows the way forward to the glorious day when Italy will rise again to a new life. Garibaldi can perhaps best be understood as a kind of Italian fusion (or bricolage)[105] of Walter Scott hero and Mazzinian genius, of eclectic borrowings from romantic sensibilities and militant Jacobinism.

It is vital to note that, especially in the accounts written by Mazzinians like Cuneo and De Boni, Garibaldi does not stand alone. Like the imaginary/ historical heroes of Risorgimento novels and paintings, Garibaldi embodies the romantic idea of the nation; thus, he is part of a free and equal fraternity, and he is tied to his 'brothers' in the Italian Legion as much by feeling as by disinterested virtue.[106] Garibaldi's greatness lies not only in his capacity for 'great deeds' but also in his qualities as a leader. It is his leadership of those 'brave brothers' who have 'freely elected' him as their colonel, and whom he encourages by his own example and with his own voice, that is repeatedly stressed in these narratives. Moreover, all the legionaries fight as bravely as he, and are just as prepared to die for the honour of Italy. They too are the heroes of San Antonio del Salto, cared for by the 'gentle sex'; and when, after the battle, in a clear public gesture which is underlined in all these accounts, Garibaldi dedicates his honours to the dead and wounded of the legion, he downplays his own contribution and emphasises the religious and romantic virtues of martyrdom. So, if Garibaldi represents the elaboration of an Italian ideal of heroism which takes its inspiration from a romanticised past, the Italian Legion also represents a new political ideal – that of fraternity and sacrifice for fraternity – derived from Jacobinism and the French Revolution. In this way, Garibaldi's legionaries are a voluntary 'band of brothers', whose association and actions provide a model for the new national community envisaged by Mazzini and his followers.

Perhaps the most interesting feature of all, and common to nearly all early accounts, is the juxtaposition of the squalid insults 'heaped' on Garibaldi and his legion by foreigners and the enemies of Italy with the marvellous truth revealed by Italian patriots and honest journalists. The starting point for the texts discussed above is broadly the same: the accusation of 'mercenary', 'adventurer' or 'bandit' and/or the public's ignorance of the glorious exploits of Italy's exiled 'children' far away from the fatherland. These allegations serve to throw into sharper relief the magnificent true story of the legion, true because the letters of those involved and reports about them reveal the full extent of their selflessness, bravery and heroism in serving a just cause. The structure of these accounts is remarkable for its closeness to Risorgimento narrative, and specifically to its stages of decadence, rebellion, death and redemption. As we saw with D'Azeglio's novel, *Ettore Fieramosca* (see page 27), attacks by foreigners on the independence and honour of Italy were a particular theme in Risorgimento texts, as was the refusal by a few heroes to accept this insult to national pride. This suggests that the story of Garibaldi in South America would have been easily recognised and provoked an emotional response in many readers, and that a clear attempt is being made to identify the political/military actions of Garibaldi and his men with the general *risorgimento* of Italy. Thus, in the narrative structure and in the use of familiar themes, we see the creation of a story for Garibaldi and his legion which both resembles those found in the popular novels, poems and paintings of the period and aspires to be a more general foundation story for the new Italian polity.

In a very short period of time – between early 1846 and late 1847 – Garibaldi became a symbol of the 'new' Italy, a resurgent Italy no longer just imagined but being brought to life. That Italy's Restoration governments were forced to tolerate the circulation of such dangerous political rhetoric about a revolutionary hero gives us some idea of his popularity, or of the almost irresistible tide of public opinion running in his favour. Enthusiasm for Garibaldi was now shared by scientists, diplomats and artists as well as by the group of dedicated Mazzinians who were his original friends and promoters. During this period, in other words, Garibaldi became a sign as well as a lived existence. His life became as important for what it could symbolise and provoke imaginatively as for what he could achieve materially. Although not all aspects of Garibaldi's public personality were evident, a number of key features were already in place when he set sail for Italy in April 1848. Perhaps most noteworthy is the remarkably successful – because convincing – combination of moral rectitude and personal bravery (Mazzini's 'physical courage and virtue', quoted above), personal qualities which were, in turn, identified with an idealised general concept of *italianità*. Just as interesting, however, is the extent to which his ideas and image were formed by experiences away from Italy. Garibaldi's knowledge of French socialism and South American politics were as central to his political formation as were his encounters with the Mazzinians. His defiantly exotic and sensual physical appearance could hardly have differed more from the austere image carefully cultivated by Mazzini for himself while in London. In this respect, Garibaldi's persona, and the strong responses to it, point to his cultivation of a different, more physical political aesthetic, which was to have a broad international appeal.

Nevertheless, the fame of Garibaldi was tied to the making of a specifically Italian public opinion in the years immediately before and after the election of the 'liberal' pope, Pius IX, in 1846. His fame contributed to and was helped by this broader development. By the end of 1847, Garibaldi had become a well-known personality in liberal–nationalist circles in Italy. His character and actions had been created and recorded, and these formed part of a new narrative which Italians could tell themselves about themselves, or hold up as an example for others to aspire to. Thus, the two or so years before the outbreak of revolution in 1848 saw the first fashionings of a cult of Garibaldi. The building blocks of a story were laid; a story which, by its power to move, entertain and inspire, helped to create a stronger, more persuasive and arguably more political sense of an Italian national community.

CHAPTER 3

REVOLUTION

The age of the hero

The early fame of Garibaldi was a Mazzinian creation, and its success was tied up with immediate political events. More precisely, the growing political cult of Garibaldi reflected and assisted the rapidly changing nature of Italian politics and public opinion in the early to mid-1840s. These changes then combined with economic hardship and social transformation to produce a general revolutionary conflagration in 1848 and 1849. Yet like the revolutions themselves, which were the product of a long-term crisis and extended rapidly across Europe, the pace at which Garibaldi's popularity grew and spread cannot be understood as a short-term or purely Italian phenomenon. Rather, the development of a Garibaldi cult was part of a longer European tradition of heroes and hero worship, a tradition which had a clear, and deliberate, political purpose. This tradition is worth looking at briefly as it helps us to understand both the success of Garibaldi and the radical aspects of his image.

The fact that Garibaldi 'worked' as a political hero was due to an existing public familiarity with such figures. Equally, he had to fit in with, or otherwise appeal to, public expectations. By the time Garibaldi emerged on the political scene in the early 1840s, the European public's familiarity with political heroes was already of quite long standing: as with much else in mid-nineteenth-century revolutionary politics, it dated back to the French Revolution. The French Revolution had provoked, and thus had to face, a symbolic as well as a material vacuum at the centre of power. In particular, the initial desacralisa-tion and the ultimate destruction of the monarchy through the creation of a republic and execution of the king – the 'father' of the French 'family' – had led to a crisis in the representation of power, spelling the apparent ruin of paternal and religious symbols of royal authority and the end of deference as the basis for political obedience.[1] Power, in the words of François Furet, 'had lost its moorings' and 'was perceived by everyone as vacant'.[2] French revolutionary leaders had responded to this vacuum by seeking to establish both an alternative revolutionary discourse of power based on fraternity and a new 'iconological rubric' which would represent the Republic and help create a different sense of political community. This task was not easy, and it was undermined by the persistence in the popular imagination of the traditional symbols of power, by the absence of any clear personification of the abstract ideal of 'Republic', and by the sheer scale of the challenge which revolutionaries had set themselves – 'to mobilise, engage and galvanise the masses' with the second revolution of 1792 and the coming of war during the same year.[3]

In the effort to overcome the difficulties of creating a new political symbolism to reach and inspire the whole of French society, the whole of society had become the object of a symbolic reinvention. The clothes people wore and the way they behaved, as well as the structure of their lives (consumer goods, currency, the calendar), became a sign of revolutionary belonging and 'a field of political struggle' between government and people.[4] Revolutionary festivals sought to create and transmit a new tradition, and to transform and transfer in people's imagination the sacrality of the old regime on to the Republic.[5] The Greek hero Hercules, the personification of physical strength and courage, was made an emblem of the Republic; the lion, a traditional symbol of power, was recast to represent popular sovereignty; and an invented and idealised woman in a Phrygian cap – 'Marianne' – became first the representation of liberty and later of the Republic in general.[6] Politics became an instrument for reshaping society and sought to absorb and control all aspects of culture. The Revolution, to quote Furet again, 'ushered in a world where mental representations of power governed all actions, and where a network of signs completely dominated political life'.[7]

One of the most evident, and perhaps the most enduring, of the 'signs' of mass politics was the creation and use of personality cults. Jacobin cults are generally associated with the attempt both to replace the symbols and rituals of Catholicism and to appropriate them for the new religion of the fatherland. Leaders introduced new ceremonies and a revolutionary liturgy, and they promoted a cult of 'patriot saints', most famously with the commemoration and funeral of the assassinated leader Marat and the celebration of the boy-hero Bara, executed in the Vendée by counter-revolutionaries for refusing to shout *Vive le roi*.[8] Such 'martyrs for liberty' were heroes of the Revolution in much the same way as religious martyrs can be seen as heroes of God. Hence, the purpose of such cults was to encourage an emotional identification with, and popular allegiance to, the patriot saint and, through him, to the source of his greatness – the Republic itself. Yet it is unlikely that these cults were especially successful in supplanting traditional religion. Although Marat was a great *sans-culotte* hero, there is little evidence that people attributed therapeutic or other sacralising powers to him, and in so far as the various ceremonies in his honour did lead to his sanctification in the popular imagination, they may also have encouraged a resurgence in religious feeling and an affirmation of Catholic rituals.[9]

Nevertheless, the promotion of these cults in revolutionary France served to popularise an ideal of the heroic individual which was tied to a new political aesthetic drawn from neo-classicism. In the famous paintings by Jacques-Louis David, *Marat at his Last Breath* (1793) and *The Death of Bara* (1793), the political virtue of Marat and Bara – their selfless heroism as a model for political engagement – was associated with an aesthetic ideal of antique Greek art and a political ideal of freedom enjoyed by the Greek states in antiquity. Beauty was identified with freedom, and personified by a virtuous, and either dead or dying, male hero. It was in this way that the male hero – physically beautiful, morally virtuous, personally courageous and, until Napoleon, never living – came to be a powerful political symbol both for the revolution and for the heirs of the revolution.[10]

David's paintings of Marat and Bara are part of a much larger body of work which celebrated male heroes in antiquity (the Horaces; Socrates; Brutus), and especially the ideals of male beauty and male companionship.[11] In the earlier part of his career, his artistic production coincided with, and contributed to, a broader Jacobin cult of antiquity, where the virtues of republican Rome were promoted as a model of political behaviour and personal morality as well as of artistic taste. Here antiquity reinforced a cult of Great Men and marginalised other forms of identity. With the breakdown of court and aristocratic culture in France, the men of the revolution self-consciously 'manufactured ... classical identities for themselves' and identified with the heroes of classical times; they adopted a 'Stoic' role – a physical demeanour of dignity, reserve and authenticity – so as to personify personally and physically the individual 'classical' virtues which were held to be at the basis of public life.[12] Equally, neo-classicism – whether as personal role-playing or as artistic style – reinforced a prevailing tendency to exclude women and the feminine as active protagonists in the revolution. On both a symbolic and material level, women were confined to the family and to a restricted 'feminine' domain of sensibility and emotion; in revolutionary mythology, according to Dorinda Outram, 'women react, relate, perceive, involve; men cling to the heroic *moments* and *postures* of personification'.[13] Moreover, in the novels and paintings of the Jacobin period, as well as in government legislation and the legal system, the traditional family (not just the father, but also wives and, to a lesser extent, sisters) was sacrificed or, at best, ignored and subordinated for the sake of the Republic. The Republic was represented as an alternative family, a voluntary act of belonging to a non-hierarchical fellowship of men. Thus, the patriarchal family was replaced by a voluntary fraternity or a 'band of brothers'. These brothers, in revolutionary discourse, were the heroes of the revolution: 'romantic heroes willing to fight for virtue and the triumph of the republic . . . prepared to become martyrs for their cause . . . [whose] chief reward was their sense of solidarity with their brothers', and who reached true heroic status only with death.[14]

Napoleon marks a development of, and a change of direction in, revolutionary symbolism, in much the same way as he does with revolutionary politics more generally. Under the Jacobins, revolutionary heroes (ancient or modern) personified abstract virtues such as courage, dignity and selfless service to the Republic, which were meant to inspire and encourage popular emulation. With Napoleon, however, revolutionary symbolism had a more simple purpose: it was used to glorify his personal power and enhance the process of his self-legitimation. The cult of the hero was no longer identified with a collective ideal but became a purpose in itself. Art became a tool in Napoleonic propaganda. Neo-classicism ceased to have an educative function and was appropriated and recast as a decorative and architectural style which recalled the florid opulence of imperial Rome; and history – ancient Rome, along with the Merovingian and Carolingian monarchies and Renaissance painting – was 'plundered' for sources to represent Napoleonic power. Napoleon himself posed as a man of literature and learning, a patron of the arts as well as a fierce warrior and tireless ruler.[15] He became a classical hero: cold, reserved but with a great inner strength.[16] The pantheon of dead republican brothers was reduced to one living 'Great Man'.

The fusion of authoritarian and traditional symbols of power with those of revolution, and its concentration into one living ruler (the 'Emperor'), filled the symbolic vacancy caused by the French Revolution. Although foreshadowed in many ways by the aesthetic ideals and totalitising practices of Jacobinism, Napoleon's shift towards authoritarianism and dictatorship is generally seen as definitive, marking a decisive rightward turn in the symbols and rituals of mass politics. Focusing specifically on Germany, George Mosse traces a general ideal of 'heroic manhood' derived from neo-classicism back to the revolutionary and Napoleonic period, through the nineteenth century and forward to the authoritarian regimes of the twentieth century. He argues that an unchanging and public representation of masculinity as beautiful, courageous and self-controlled was established during the French Revolution and came to be adopted or 'co-opted' by political movements thereafter, and especially by nationalist movements, as 'one means of . . . [their] self-representation'.[17] Thus, post-revolutionary nationalist movements came to use an idealised man – a Greek youth, a beautiful athlete – as a symbol of the nation. Moreover, through the experience of war, first the national wars of the early nineteenth century and then the total wars of the twentieth, masculinity became ever more identified with a military aesthetic and military values. 'The modern warrior now joined the Greek youth and the athlete as a model of masculinity', and the military virtues of death and sacrifice became central both to the masculine stereotype and to images of the nation itself.[18]

This trope of masculinity as used by nationalist movements in the nineteenth century (and beyond) was generally regarded as a positive stereotype – 'a motor that drove the nation and society at large'[19] – but actually worked to constrain and to exclude. Mosse says that it enforced middle-class notions of sexual respectability and restraint, and may even have served to de-sexualise the male body: 'The nation protected the ideal of beauty from the lower passions of man and helped transform it into a symbol of self-control and purity'.[20] At the same time, the association of masculinity and nation with war and soldiering helped to make war more seductive and the nation more aggressive. If fraternity could be expressed by volunteering (or being conscripted) to fight for the fatherland – by being part of the arms-bearing brotherhood of citizens – then the idea of the fatherland in continental Europe was increasingly shaped by military values and images. The image of the soldier also changed. No longer was it enough to obey and be brave: the soldier had to sacrifice himself for the nation. Both in France, as we have seen, and in Prussia during the wars of liberation, a myth was created of the patriotic hero choosing freely to die for his country and, in so doing, being elevated to the status of martyr and immortalised.[21] Equally, in the long term, the identi-fication of war with sacrifice and heroism, and with nation, can explain why nationalists should have become the main advocates of a much more belligerent and chauvinistic masculinity in the decades after the French Revolution.[22]

When Mazzini's friend Thomas Carlyle bemoaned the devaluation of heroes in contemporary society – the lack of opportunities for 'Able-man' and the absence of 'Hero-worship' – he inadvertently betrayed his culture's obsession with them.[23] The nineteenth century became the age of the hero. Fictional heroes like Ivanhoe, D'Artagnan and Ettore Fieramosca captured the imagination of the nineteenth-century reader, and literary geniuses as diverse as Lord Byron and Dante Alighieri jostled for the attention of the public. Whether remembered or imagined as with the Jacobins, or borrowed and elaborated as in the person of Napoleon, the cult of the hero became a central part of nineteenth-century nationalism and was celebrated in monuments, paintings, poetry, novels and history all over Europe and the Americas. Napoleon survived defeat, exile and death to become a symbol of France and a far more genuinely popular figure than in his own lifetime. The cult of the hero also spread to Britain, one of Napoleon's fiercest opponents, and was expressed in the ongoing public enthusiasm for military heroes like Nelson and Wellington, and liberal and radical heroes such as Daniel O'Connell, William Gladstone, and the Chartist leaders Ernest Jones and Feargus O'Connor. From the 1830s onwards, it is also possible to talk of a cult of political celebrity, where figures like Queen Victoria and Napoleon III were actively produced and promoted using the new technologies of print media.[24]

Throughout the nineteenth century, the political purpose of the hero remained broadly that of the French Revolution: to personify a political idea, to embody an elite or collective movement, and/or to sacralise a regime. In particular, nationalist heroes seemed to give voice to the nation, and they lent credibility to claims for the existence of national communities and the genuineness of nationalist feeling. It was precisely in this way that Garibaldi embodied and legitimised the claims of Risorgimento Italy, and he was fashioned explicitly for this purpose. Indeed, he probably represents the most complete expression of 'heroic masculinity' allied with nationalism in all of nineteenth-century politics.

However, the example of Garibaldi is also significant because it suggests real problems with the model outlined by Mosse. Garibaldi points us to a tradition in democratic thought which directly challenged the authoritarian symbolism of Napoleon. Thus, Saint-Simonians admired Napoleon, but they also argued that in removing himself from society – by posing as a great man and saviour – he had become less effective: a hero did not have to be a 'great man' responsible for exceptional deeds. Historians in post-revolutionary France – Guizot, Thierry, Michelet – as well as many democrats, such as Louis Blanc, took pains to question the idea of an exceptional individual, and argued that greatness resided just as much in a capacity to identify with the hopes and action of the people.[25] As Thierry put it, 'the essential aim of [my] history is to contemplate the destiny of peoples, and not that of certain famous men, to recount the adventures of social life, and not those of individual life'. For Michelet, genius was 'the people', and the new identity was one of collectivity. 'How I need to clasp hold of the *patrie*,' he wrote, 'to know and love France more and more!'[26]

This critique of the authoritarian hero should also remind us of an older, American and republican, tradition of hero worship, where the hero was a man like Washington, uncomfortable with power, and imagined as 'a symbol of people's aspirations' rather than being venerated for his own achievements.[27] Crucially, this critique of the exceptional individual was taken up by another republican, Mazzini. Mazzini challenged what he saw as the primacy given to the '*individual*' (his emphasis) in nineteenth-century thought and in an essay, 'On the works of Thomas Carlyle (genius and tendencies)', he publicly criticised his friend's belief that '[t]he nationality of Italy is the glory of having produced Dante and Christopher Columbus; the nationality of Germany that of having given birth to Luther, to Goethe'. He insisted that these men 'were only the interpreters or prophets' of national thought: they were 'of the people, who alone are its depositary'. Thus, for Mazzini, the hero – or what he called 'genius' – was a democrat, whose function was to perceive and represent the collectivity, and he protested 'in the name of the democratic spirit of the age' against the 'great man' thesis:

> History is not the biography of great men . . . The great men of the earth are but the marking stones on the road of humanity: they are the priests of its religion . . . There is yet something greater, more divinely mysterious, than all the great men – and that is the earth which bears them, the human race which includes them, the thought of God which stirs within them, and which the whole human race collectively can alone accomplish . . . The inspiration of genius belongs one half to heaven, the other to the crowds of common mortals from whose life it springs.[28]

Like the Jacobins before them, Mazzinian nationalists were convinced that politics held the key to cultural transformation – in this case, to 'making Italians'. But their task differed from that of both the Jacobins and Napoleon in a number of ways. First, they were not in power, but mostly outside or excluded from it. Second, they were democrats and were part of a moment of democratic politics in the middle decades of the nineteenth century when mass politics was a revolutionary idea and where its signs were those of opposition and rebellion. Thus, the function of the hero was to include and to liberate, and to defy the prevailing status quo. Moreover, if we look at political culture and taste in mid-nineteenth-century Europe, what is immediately striking is not so much the presence of neo-classicism as the influence of romanticism. In the Italian case, it is especially worth remembering that neo-classicism (or simply 'classicism') was seen as part of a cosmopolitan tradition against which romantics specifically and vocally identified themselves; Italian romantics looked instead to the very different ideals, traditions and images of medievalism for inspiration.[29] For politically engaged romantics, including Mazzini, classicism was also a discredited movement as a result of its association with Napoleon and thus with an older, now superseded, political epoch. And whatever the importance of classical Rome as a symbol of Italian 'primacy', its precise meaning was equivocal as a result of the inevitable confusion between its republican and imperial pasts. For all these reasons, Risorgimento nationalists preferred to refer to the medieval past and to its far clearer associations with political independence, freedom and community.[30]

Although there are many artistic continuities between classicism and romanticism,[31] it is also important to stress the break and conflict between the two traditions. This means that there are strong distinctions as well as continuities between the neo-classical and the romantic hero. The romantic hero was a rebel like Byron; he could also be melancholic, transgressive and even criminal.[32] The bandit was an especially common, and not necessarily negative, hero-figure in many romantic dramas and novels, from Schiller's *The Robbers* (1791) to the novels of Walter Scott, and beyond. The bandit–hero is often a good man pushed outside the law, who scorns rational civilisation for the passions and energy of nature. Rob Roy MacGregor, the eponymous hero of one of Scott's most popular stories, has an appearance which is 'wild, irregular, and . . . unearthly'; he is described as an 'outlawed robber' and a 'celebrated freebooter', a 'kind and gentle' man and loving husband but with 'ideas of morality' which 'were those of an Arab chief'.[33] His 'commanding' wife, the cruel 'virago' Helen, fights with him, and teaches his young sons to do the same. Moreover, Rob Roy rejects the offer to be reconciled with the law because he cannot leave his native land: 'the heather that I have trod upon when living, must bloom ower me when I am dead – my heart would sink, and my arm would shrink and wither like fern in the frost, were I to lose sight of my native hills; nor has the world a scene that would console me for the loss of the rocks and cairns'. Nor can he leave his wife, he adds: she will never leave the Highlands and he cannot bear the 'heartbreak' of being separated from her.[34]

Adrian Lyttelton argues that romantic critics of the classical tradition in Italy proposed 'the dethronement of the hero or central figure' and his replacement by secondary figures who would emphasise the popular and collective dimension of historical events.[35] And while the hero had eventually to be retained 'for full dramatic impact' in romantic narratives, his character and resonance changed. The Italian romantic hero personified an idealised Italian past; he was firmly based in a national time and space, and his function was to be part of, and to inspire, the collectivity. Instead of being 'an exemplar of timeless virtue and dignity' who suppressed all domestic and affective ties for the public good, the Italian romantic hero's qualities were, like those of Rob Roy MacGregor, 'grounded in feeling'. In line with popular taste, he was driven by passion and enthusiasm; he was adored by, and adoring of, women, and his love for his family was the basis for the love for his country. He had always a private, family reason for action as well as a patriotic one.[36] When it came, the clash between family and 'fatherland' was no longer resolved decisively in favour of the latter, but was instead shown as an agonising and poignant choice with uncertain outcome. [37] All this served to define the appeal of the romantic hero as a specifically 'Italian' figure, a hero who was democratic and of, or with, the people, and who was more passionate, sensitive and sexual – indeed, more feminine – than his neo-classical counterpart.

This is not to suggest that there was no trace of the neo-classical hero in Garibaldi or that the tendency towards authoritarianism identified by Mosse is entirely mistaken. Rather, it is to argue against the idea of a straightforward or uncontested political and cultural continuum between the symbols of the French Revolution and Napoleon and the totalitarian cults of the twentieth-century dictators. Like political concepts, the meaning of symbols can alter while their outward (linguistic or visual) structure remains the same.[38] Heroes too have their history, and what they signified changed and was subject to challenge. In the course of the nineteenth century, Napoleon himself went from 'saviour' to 'black legend' (and back again) and from dictator to a liberal and to a romantic hero.[39] At the same time, as Lyttelton shows, which symbols and narratives were chosen to construct the nation had a real political signficance. They could be 'the terrain of a vigorous contest' between political rivals, their meanings could be challenged and could alter over time, and control over their interpretation was essential for 'conveying the desired national message'. And it mattered who or what 'was cast as the protagonist of the story', and at what time.[40]

The promotion of Garibaldi as a national hero during the 1840s should be seen as part of a political struggle to personify and popularise a specific vision of national community. This vision was tied not so much to an authoritarian and exclusive form of mass politics as to an inclusive, democratic ideal of liberty and fraternity. To support this vision, Italian democrats not only had to identify themselves with romanticism, they also had to appropriate the revolutionary symbolism of the Jacobins, and to challenge and subvert the conservative legacy of Napoleon. How these struggles related to Garibaldi, and how the cult of Garibaldi was fashioned and elaborated during the moments of democratic initiative and political power during the 1848–9 revolutions, is the subject of the rest of this chapter.

The return of the hero

The January revolution in Palermo, which Garibaldi might have heard about as he left Montevideo, was the start of an extraordinary spring. The revolutions which followed were the result of a deep and prolonged economic crisis, which had begun in 1845 with the failure of the potato crop in much of Europe. With the bad grain harvest in 1846, Europe's rural population faced near or real famine conditions, which in turn caused rising prices and food shortages in the towns and cities and produced a downturn in the business cycle, together with a crisis in the banking sector. In part, the symptom of larger structural changes in European society, such as industrialisation, the commercialisation of agriculture and the expansion of cities, the general economic depression, placed the social, financial and political structures of Europe under an intolerable strain. Open criticism by a disaffected middle class and the growth of opposition movements across Europe (the banquet campaign against Louis-Philippe in France; radical and constitutional agitation in the German states; the explosion of public opinion in Italy) challenged and undermined the legitimacy of most European states. Popular riots and demonstrations in early 1848 then delivered them an evidently devastating *coup de grâce*.

Starting with the revolt in Palermo, governments crumbled and rulers succumbed to revolution across Europe. The Sicilian revolt spread to the mainland and a constitution was proclaimed in Naples. In February, both the king of Piedmont and the Grand Duke of Tuscany were forced to grant constitutions and, in March, there were successful popular revolts against Austrian rule in the cities of Milan and Venice, while in Rome the Pope granted a constitution for the Papal States. Nationalism appeared in the ascendant when the king of Piedmont, Carlo Alberto, declared war on Austria and crossed the frontier into Lombardy on 23 March, supported by a seemingly united coalition of the Pope, Leopold II of Tuscany and Ferdinando II of Naples. Between March and July 1848, around 300 volunteer corps were organised all over Italy to help in the fight against Austria; this was a striking indication of patriotic feeling and engagement among young men, albeit largely from the urban and educated classes.[41]

These events in Italy encouraged, and were encouraged by, revolts in France, Germany and the Habsburg Empire, and were paralleled in Chartist agitation in Britain and, the following year, a Young Irelander uprising in Ireland. In February 1848, a republic was proclaimed in Paris; this was followed by street fighting in Berlin and Vienna, and nationalist demonstrations in Zagreb, Prague, Cracow and Budapest. Rulers – including Louis-Philippe in France and the Austrian chancellor Prince Metternich – fled their capitals; the king of Prussia promised a constitution; and liberal governments were formed in the south German states. Discussions began in Frankfurt for the formation of a popularly elected German national assembly. By the time Garibaldi set out for Italy in April, the revolution had already taken a more radical turn, with a republican uprising in Baden, riots in Paris and moves toward separatist rule in Sicily and in the Habsburg Empire.[42]

So it seemed that Garibaldi's arrival in Italy could hardly have been better timed. It had been predicted and heralded well in advance by the Turin paper *La Concordia*, which was owned by the moderate radical Lorenzo Valerio and was already supportive of Garibaldi. On 6 March the paper had announced the arrival of his family in Nice and indicated that 'the intrepid warrior' himself was soon to arrive in Rome. On 10 March Garibaldi was said to have left Montevideo; on 27 March a position was said to have been offered him in the Piedmontese army; and on 13 April he was apparently at sea with twenty-five men and making for Civitavecchia, a port to the north of Rome.[43] Although none of this, other than the arrival of his family in Nice, was true, it helped to sustain an air of excitement about the 'valiant' hero's imminent arrival.

Garibaldi finally arrived in Italy on 21 June, landing at his birthplace, Nice (until 1860 part of Piedmontese territory), having learnt at Alicante the news of revolution. The welcome was so enthusiastic that all the passengers on board his ship, *La Speranza*, were able to ignore the two-week quarantine regulations and come ashore at once. 'Since he is a native of this city', the governor-general of Nice reported to the capital, Turin, 'and his arrival had been eagerly awaited for over a month, a quantity of people gathered at the port to see him' and to welcome him back to the 'fatherland'. A Milan paper, *Il 22 Marzo*, noted their arrival by describing for its readers the appearance of Garibaldi and his men: 'their uniform is rather beautiful (red blouse with green patterns; white trousers); they are armed and parade with great skill; they are chosen men who can serve as a nucleus to form an excellent regiment'.[44] Mazzini's new daily newspaper, *L'Italia del Popolo* of Milan, greeted Garibaldi with the words: 'another brave man has joined the brave men who are defending the fatherland'; he had come, the paper told its readers, for:

> the final duel between the House of Austria and of Italy; between civilisation and barbarism, between liberty and tyranny . . . thus, Garibaldi is among us; with him is his companion Anzani; and he is followed by a hundred courageous and expert fighting men . . . We therefore salute with brotherly love the brave, the long-awaited Garibaldi, and we wish him new glory, for his glory is our glory, and is Italian glory.[45]

All Italian nationalists, it seemed, expected great things of Garibaldi.

From Nice, Garibaldi raised around a hundred extra volunteers and after a week he moved on to Genoa, where his arrival was again the occasion for nationalist demonstrations and he again recruited more men. Both his speech from the York hotel to the inhabitants of Nice and his speech at the National Club in Milan were reported and republished by *La Concordia* on 23 June, 29 June, 1 July and 6 July; the democratic paper *Il Pensiero Italiano* of Genova and the moderate *La Patria* of Florence also published his Milan speech on 4 July and 7 July, respectively. In these speeches, Garibaldi endorsed the war of Carlo

Alberto, the Piedmontese king, and declared himself ready to renounce his republicanism in favour of uniting all their forces: '[t]he great, the only question at this moment is the expulsion of the foreigner, and the war of independence'.[46] After Genoa, Garibaldi went to the Piedmontese army's front line just outside Mantua, determined to meet with the king and offer him his services and those of his men. His movements from there to the War Office in Turin, and then back to Milan in mid-July, were again reported and celebrated by *La Concordia*, which drew attention to his popularity and to his 'sweetly austere and martial appearance'; the paper also expressed a hope that Garibaldi would be 'quickly, and without bureaucratic cares and delays' given a mission which was 'worthy of him'.[47]

In fact, Garibaldi had got himself into trouble almost immediately. The republican groups who had led the famous *Cinque Giornate* (five-day uprising) in Milan against the Austrians were far from convinced by Carlo Alberto's decision to enter their war, ostensibly on their side. Even Mazzini himself, who had arrived in Italy on 7 April to a 'triumphal progress' from the frontier to Milan, had fallen foul of the republican leaders Ferrari and Cattaneo when he had attempted to mediate between them and the Piedmontese monarchists for the sake of Italian unity.[48] Cattaneo and Ferrari were in favour of a federal Italy, and told Mazzini that they feared Piedmontese ambitions in Lombardy more than Austrian rule; when Mazzini called them 'municipalists', Cattaneo accused him of 'selling out'.[49] By May, however, Mazzini had been outmanoeuvred by the Piedmontese king and his ministers, and so was infuriated by Garibaldi's speeches and actions in their favour. 'Garibaldi is another disappointment', he told his mother; his decision to join forces with the regular army meant 'he will no longer be the Garib[aldi] that Italy loved and admired'.[50] But Garibaldi was soon to be disappointed too. He was obstructed in his efforts at every turn by Carlo Alberto's generals, and, although he was eventually appointed a general by the Milan administration, he was confined to an office organising the call-up of volunteers. He then caught malaria, and was forced to stay in bed for several days.[51]

The difficulties which Garibaldi encountered upon returning to Italy reflected serious problems with the revolution itself, and specifically with the military campaign in northern Italy. Apart from anti-Austrian feeling, there was little common ground and even less love lost between moderate liberals and republicans in Milan, and thus between those who sought an alliance (or union) with monarchical Piedmont and those who refused to consider the possibility. The republicans were of course sharply divided between unitarians (like Mazzini) and federalists (like Cattaneo and Ferrari). In reality, neither side had the support of the countryside, and both were more or less dependent on the military power of Piedmont. Yet King Carlo Alberto's ambitions in

Lombardy were dynastic more than nationalist, and his Italian coalition soon fell apart when the Pope pulled out at the end of April, refusing to countenance war against Austria, another Catholic state. Moreover, Piedmont was no match for Austria. As David Laven has remarked, the initial defeat of the Habsburg army in Lombardy and Venetia was 'illusory'; it masked the strength of Austria's strategic position within the famous Quadrilateral fortresses of Mantua, Peschiera, Verona and Legnano, the resilience of the conservative coalition behind Austria, and the weakness and divisions within the Italian camp.[52] All of this was amply demonstrated in the crushing defeat suffered by the Piedmontese army at Custoza on 24 July. Carlo Alberto initially fell back on Milan. But when the news arrived in the city of the Salasco armistice, in which he had agreed to abandon Lombardy and Venetia to the Austrians, the king's headquarters were besieged by indignant crowds and he was forced to flee to Turin, amid accusations of cowardice and general public derision.[53]

It was of course entirely characteristic that both Mazzini and the other republicans – including Garibaldi – saw this disaster as an opportunity. No sooner had the news arrived of the defeat at Custoza than the republicans in Milan settled their differences and formed a committee of public safety to defend the city. Mazzini issued a call 'to young men' to volunteer to defend the revolution, and it was published in a special supplement to his newspaper, *L'Italia del Popolo*, at the end of July.[54] Garibaldi too launched an appeal to youth to fight for Italy ('[r]ush forward: gather round me: Italy needs ten, twenty thousand volunteers . . . We will show Italy, Europe, that we want victory and we will have it').[55] He established a new volunteer battalion, the Italian Battalion of Death, with the slogan 'COMPLETE INDEPENDENCE OR DEATH'.[56] At the end of July, he marched to Bergamo with around 1,500 men to help in the defence of Brescia, 'acclaimed', according to *L'Italia del Popolo*, 'by the joyful cries of all Milan'.

> Today the Italian man rises as one; strengthened by danger itself, he will rebaptise himself in battle; who wants to win, will win . . . The serene fearlessness of their leader [Garibaldi], whose name is so dear to all of Italy because it represents Italian honour across the ocean, will inspire faith in victory; obeying his military prowess we will have victory . . . Follow him with confidence, oh Lombards; gather round him in every place, blessing and expanding the holy legion of Garibaldi.[57]

From Bergamo, where he was joined by around another 1,500 men and by his comrade from South America, Giacomo Medici, and Mazzini himself, Garibaldi headed for Como. Mazzini had decided to join the fighting as an ordinary soldier, but he was unable to stand the physical pace and soon left for

Lugano. Garibaldi and a (dwindling) band of men spent the next three weeks moving between Varese and the area around Lake Maggiore, acting as guerrilla fighters and attempting to disrupt the Austrian advance as much as possible. Early on, Garibaldi seized two boats in Arona, which allowed him and his men to move easily around the lake and avoid capture. They also came out on top in their first encounter with the enemy (a Croat unit) at Luino on 15 August, and succeeded in occupying Varese for two days, but they were subsequently caught at the small town of Morazzone, and forced to disperse and retreat across the border into Switzerland. And although Garibaldi was keen to organise new guerrilla incursions into Italy, he was dissuaded from doing so by Medici, who was planning a larger (but eventually abortive) campaign against the Austrian forces with Mazzini.[58]

In military terms, the Lake Maggiore campaign was a failure. It may not have been helped by the fact that Garibaldi was sick with malaria for much of the time – 'very dejected and discouraged and rather ill', as one government official who saw him put it[59] – or by the unresolved tensions over military strategy between Garibaldi, on the one hand, and Medici and Mazzini, on the other. Yet it is hard to escape the conclusion that, as a military action, Garibaldi's Lake Maggiore campaign was entirely unwinnable. Why, then, did he pursue it? The desire to embarrass the Piedmontese government by breaking the armistice with Austria should not be discounted, nor should the plan to disrupt the progress of the Austrian army via surprise appearances and rapid manoeuvres and by generally making a nuisance of themselves. In both aims, moreover, Garibaldi was quite successful, if the correspondence between Austrian and between Piedmontese officials is anything to go by.[60] But perhaps a comment made about Mazzini in an anonymous report to the Austrians provides the real key to understanding what they were all up to. Mazzini, according to the anonymous writer, 'knows that the war cannot bring any great success, but his idea is to attract the attention of Europe and to get sympathy for the Republic and for the relentless struggle for freedom'.[61] In other words, Garibaldi's action in Lake Maggiore was part of an ongoing drive to win support for the struggle through his own valiant example. By remaining as much as possible in the public eye, he hoped to promote and diffuse revolutionary and nationalist propaganda.

Arriving in Lugano in early August, Mazzini issued a proclamation 'to Italians', with the memorable opening sentence: 'The royal war is over; the war of the people begins.' It was published as a sixteen-page pamphlet, first in Lugano and then in Italy; extracts were subsequently published in various newspapers including the *Corriere Mercantile* and the *Corriere Livornese*. He also published a shorter 'Protest', first as a flyer in Lugano and then in a series of newspapers.[62] With an eye on the wider world, he published a series of articles on 'Parties and affairs in Italy' in the London *Spectator*, in which he argued that both monarchs and moderates had betrayed their claims to leadership in Italy and that the republicans were the only true leaders, capable of enacting and inspiring feats of self-sacrifice and heroism.[63] At his temporary headquarters at Castelletto Ticino, just south of Lake Maggiore, on 13 August Garibaldi also issued a 'Protest' to 'Italians', which began with Mazzini's slogan 'God and the People'. Rejecting the 'humiliating agreements' signed by a king who kept his crown 'through cowardice and misdeed' and affirming that 'the People doesn't want any more tricks', Garibaldi swore that his army would fight 'without pause and like lions the holy war, the war of Italian Independence'.[64] Both this, and an earlier manifesto issued at Bergamo, were printed and clearly intended for mass circulation; the Castelletto appeal was apparently taken with Garibaldi into action, was posted on walls as the army passed through built-up areas and made news in Tuscany and Rome, as well as falling into the hands of the Austrians.[65]

Although at the time the claims of Mazzini and Garibaldi may have seemed like wishful thinking, in retrospect they mark a turning-point in the revolution. Along with the decision of Venice to resist Austrian attack and the Bologna riots of 8 August, the action in Lake Maggiore and the Ticino meant that the democratic movement gained the initiative from the moderate liberals, who had always been frightened of the mass protests and uprisings in Italian cities and who had no response to Carlo Alberto's hasty abandonment of Lombardy. Instead, the democrats embraced the collapse of the Piedmontese front and the defection of the Pope, and they took advantage of the vacuum left by the royal retreat to introduce a new language based on 'people' and 'nation' into Italian political discourse. Moreover, this initiative produced practical results. Disturbances in Livorno in October resulted in the formation of a democratic government in Tuscany, and a month later in Rome popular militancy culminated in the assassination of the moderate minister, Pellegrino Rossi, after which a panic-stricken Pius IX fled to the safety of Gaeta in Neapolitan territory. During the weeks that followed, popular elections for a Roman constituent assembly were called, and democrats of all types, including talented pro-Mazzinian propagandists like Piero Ceroni, Antonio Torricelli and Filippo de Boni, moved to Rome.[66]

Garibaldi's own fame grew considerably during the summer and autumn of 1848. While his main concern was military – raising and deploying an army of young volunteers – his speeches and proclamations at this time are an interesting reflection of both nationalist rhetoric in 1848 and his own place within it. On the one hand, Garibaldi sought to project to his audience an ideal of selfless service to a nation in danger and to identify himself with a model of humble and disinterested virtue, whose heroic example could nevertheless inspire others:

He who speaks these words to you has fought as best he could to honour the
Italian name in far-off shores; he has rushed with a handful of valiant
companions from Montevideo so that he too can help the fatherland in
victory, and to die on Italian soil. He has faith in you; young men, will you
have faith in him?[67]

On the other hand, he offered an extraordinarily eclectic image of national
belonging, which was seemingly conceived to be both as compelling and as
inclusive as possible. Perhaps the best example of Garibaldian bricolage is the
proclamation issued in Bergamo on 3 August, in which he appealed to Italy's
classical and medieval past, to religion, martyrdom and betrayal, to military
aggression and hatred of the foreigner (the 'cowardly German'), to sex, the
family and local pride in order to encourage the youth of Bergamo to join him:

> When Rome had barbarians at the gate . . . it sent its Legions to Spain, to
> Africa, and they made them march past the besiegers so as to scorn them . . .
> Look, for God's sake, at your babies, who expect from you a life as free
> people, to your women, to your virgins . . . I hope that my words, however
> weak, will be listened to: that the generous people of the city, of the towns,
> of the valleys and the mountains will repeat the echo of the Italian crusade,
> of the wiping-out of the foreigner; everyone, looking around himself, will
> find an arm, a tool to defend the beautiful land which has nourished him
> and brought him up.[68]

Finally, Garibaldi added, in an explicit reference to what was a central episode
for historians, poets, musicians and painters during the Risorgimento, and was
especially important for Lombardy: 'Bergamo will be the Pontida of the
present generation and God will bring us to Legnano.' (Pontida was the place
where the Lombard cities made an alliance against Emperor Frederick
Barbarossa in 1167, and the battle of Legnano in 1176 resulted in a famous
victory for the Lombard League over Frederick.)[69]

Of course, we can have little idea of the effect of this rhetoric on Garibaldi's
audience. It seems that any initial rush to volunteer in Milan ran out of steam
in the mountains; by all accounts, the people of the Varesotto were unenthusi-
astic about his campaign and, even where they cheered his progress, were
reluctant actually to join him.[70] Yet there is no doubt about his growing
reputation. When Garibaldi arrived back in the Italian Riviera at the beginning
of September, *La Concordia* greeted his return as a hero: it reported that he had
been reunited with his wife and children and was 'physically exhausted'; that
'[h]e tells of the exploits of his legion with a moderation and sincerity which
has no equal'; and that Garibaldi's 'strong constitution and even more his

indomnitable spirit will win out and soon he will go back into battle'.[71] Earlier, the governor-general of Nice had asked Turin for instructions about letting Garibaldi return to his home town. The governor was concerned about the effect of Garibaldi's presence on the mood of the people; indeed his popularity was such, the governor worried, that either a refusal to allow him entry or a decision to permit his return would be likely to lead to serious disorder.[72]

Towards the end of September, as his health recovered, Garibaldi decided to travel to Genoa and to make contact with the democratic clubs there. His journey was punctuated by halts at San Remo, Oneglia and Savona: these were occasions for Garibaldi to make speeches and for public festivities held in his honour, and his appearances were reported as major events in *La Concordia* and in *Il Pensiero Italiano*.[73] In San Remo, Garibaldi was formally greeted by the mayor and by the French and Spanish vice-consuls (the latter had him to stay in his home). He enjoyed a guard of honour throughout the night, courtesy of the mayor, was serenaded at 9 p.m. by the municipal band and was given lunch the next day, again by the mayor and the officers of the Civic Guard. Yet although the crowd was equally enthusiastic, there was evidently some confusion about what Garibaldi represented. On his way to the Spanish vice-consul's house, he was pursued by an excited crowd shouting '*Viva Garibaldi. Evviva Pio IX. Evviva l'independenza italiana*'. After the 9 p.m. serenade, when Garibaldi came out to speak to his public, he was greeted by cries of '*Viva Garibaldi. Viva Pio IX. Viva Carlo Alberto.*'[74] The reaction of the crowd to Garibaldi suggests that if, as Mazzini had proclaimed, the war of the people was under way, the traditional presence of royalty and religion was still very much at hand.

The Third Rome

The revolutions of 1848–9 have generally not been favourably judged by historians. As Jonathan Sperber tells us, '[g]entle mockery, open sarcasm and hostile contempt have frequently set the tone for narrative and evaluation'. The political movements of 1848–9 are treated as too poetic and too romantic, or simply too incompetent, to be taken seriously, or at any rate to be compared 'to the real business of 1789 and 1917'.[75] In this way, the failure of the 1848–9 revolutions – the practical reversals suffered as a result of internal divisions, military weakness and conservative counter-attack between the summer of 1848 and the summer of 1849 – has tended to overshadow its more lasting achievement in politicising the people.

In fact, during the eighteen or so months of revolution, a 'new space opened up for political activity in Europe'.[76] Parliaments provided a forum for public debate and for political alignment (and realignment) at the centre of power, and this change also affected society. Petitions offered a means of dialogue between people and the politicians, and the establishment of political clubs, both in capital cities and in regional and local centres, allowed for wide-ranging discussions on a regular basis and the formation of new associational networks. The revolution saw the affirmation of more traditional forms of mass political expression, such as riots and popular festivals, as well as the emergence of more orderly 'modern' events like mass meetings and demonstrations. The revolutionary events themselves generated a new political culture. Representing, celebrating, denigrating or just reporting the revolution became central to the whole political process, and with the end of censorship and the arrival of new technologies – notably the electric telegraph and cheaper printing machines – there was an information revolution, expressed in the proliferation of newspapers and a popular press. None of this, moreover, was confined to the major cities. Research on France, in particular, has shown how far the politics of rural life and in the periphery were affected by revolutionary events. So, far from being a failure, it seems that the revolution should best be seen 'as a pioneering venture in mass political mobilization'.[77]

Events in Italy bear out this interpretation. Although research is relatively sketchy, it is evident that the Italian revolutions were preceded and accompanied by newspapers and pamphlets, and marked by popular demonstrations and the establishment of political clubs.[78] During the spring and summer of 1849, a great deal of this general political activity came to be centred on Rome, which had been in a state of political flux for some time, and where a republic was declared in February. Indeed, from the moment of the first constitutional changes in the spring of 1848, the unfolding events were discussed, written about, celebrated and opposed by men and by women, not just in Rome but also in cities, towns and villages throughout the Papal States, and not just in formal meetings and on special occasions but in taverns, osterie, cafés, piazzas and the street as well.[79] Newspapers, periodicals and pamphlets of every kind proliferated. Mainstream papers assumed a crucial function as 'a tool of organisation and propulsion in public life and as a centre of association for the currents which faced each other in political life';[80] others were deliberately ephemeral, openly satirical or concerned with purely local or material issues.[81]

During late 1848 and early 1849, and especially after the declaration of a republic in February, the radicals gained control in Rome and political mobilisation intensified. The politicial clamp-down in the republican stronghold of Genoa and in Lombardy–Venetia (outside the republican enclave in the city of Venice), the increasing strength of reaction in the Kingdom of the Two Sicilies, and the second resounding defeat of the Piedmontese army by the Austrians, at Novara in March 1849, led to increased political interest in Rome and cemented its real importance for the nationalist cause. Mazzinian activists and propagandists moved to Rome from northern Italy because they saw an opportunity there, and because political activity had simply become too difficult at home. Many went first to Tuscany, but the radical government there was lukewarm about their unitarian plans, so sooner or later they all moved on to Rome. The elections in Rome for a proposed Italian constituent assembly in January 1849 also helped endorse the Mazzinians and Mazzinian policies, and Mazzini himself arrived in Rome on 5 March and attempted to become its temporary dictator.[82] He was joined by a large and important group of sympathisers (including famous names of the future like Saffi, Pisacane, Nicotera, Bertani, Belgioioso, Medici, Mameli, and Garibaldi himself). Other non-Mazzinians arrived later, notably a group of 600 Lombard volunteers led by a veteran of the *Cinque Giornate* in Milan, Luciano Manara. For all these reasons, by the spring of 1849 Rome had become the main focus of nationalist aspirations in the Italian peninsula as well as the basis for republican experiments.

Yet Rome had an importance all of its own, 'a mystical significance' which represented a particular political challenge to the revolutionaries in 1849.[83] As the capital of Roman Catholicism, it had an unrivalled symbolic role as the capital of (almost) all Italians, and this was recognised by Mazzini in his appeal to 'the Third Rome' of 'the people' (after the 'Rome of the Caesars' and the 'Rome of the Popes'). The problem, however, was the same one which had faced the Jacobins in the 1790s: how to replace the religion of the Pope and the Catholic Church with the new religion of humanity and the nation as the source of popular identity, and how to do this without offending or alienating a deeply religious and Catholic population. Nor was this task made any easier by the pervasiveness of papal symbols and Catholic rituals in the city of Rome and throughout the papal territories, or by the existence of a tradition which linked Catholicism to a sense and expressions of national belonging.[84] And although, by the middle of the nineteenth century, Rome had become a dusty and declining backwater, surpassed by the size of Naples, the growth of Milan and the sophistication of Florence, it had an immense cosmopolitan significance, with a powerful resonance for foreigners as both religious centre and 'cradle of civilisation'.[85] Its fame assured international attention, and this attention was both an opportunity – to win publicity and support for the nationalist struggle – and a danger, as the republic was physically isolated and could easily attract hostile intervention from foreign powers. Finally, there is evidence that many Roman political leaders – notably Pietro Sterbini – resented the intrusion of Mazzini and his unitarian ideas into their revolution. The assembly initially refused his bid to be an emergency dictator; they also disliked some of his domestic policies and not everyone endorsed his plans for union with the other Italian republics.[86]

The importance of Rome on both a practical and a symbolic level for a whole series of opposing groups and governments guaranteed a bitter struggle for its future. Although Mazzini soon succeeded in gaining power in Rome, as one of a triumvirate with Carlo Armellini and Aurelio Saffi, criticism of him continued and his position was insecure in every other way. That Mazzini was fully aware of his own isolation is indicated by his repeated attempts not to offend religious sensibilities: the republican constitution declared Catholicism to be the official religion, the Pope's spiritual authority was guaranteed and Mazzini himself attended Easter Sunday mass at St Peter's. He encouraged popular support for the government by introducing a series of social reforms – the confiscation and redistribution of church property; the lowering of taxes; new schools for the poor – as well as abolishing the death penalty, censorship and the monopoly of ecclesiastical courts. Mazzini also revived his newspaper, *L'Italia del Popolo*, as a tool of propaganda. In late April, he helped organise a huge republican festival in and around the ancient Roman monuments, which culminated in the illumination of the Colosseum with the colours of the tricolour flag.[87]

Yet it is uncertain whether any of these measures were particularly successful. Research has shown that this short experience of republican government and its downfall marks a crucial stage in the politics of the Papal States, in that it led to the decline of traditional deference to authority and challenged popular affection for the Pope. It also marked a definitive break between the Italian nationalist movement and the Catholic world.[88] Yet it is much less likely that the republican government succeeded in transferring the dwindling loyalty to papal government to itself or to the national idea.[89] In any case, the government faced a far more serious external threat to its existence. In a response to the Pope's appeal for international aid, Austria, Spain, Naples and France sent armies to intervene against the Roman Republic. The most dangerous of these – a 12,000-strong French expeditionary force led by General Oudinot – was allowed to land unopposed at Civitavecchia, some forty miles north of Rome, towards the end of April. Confident, according to the famous phrase of one French envoy, that 'the Italians do not fight [*les Italiens ne se battent pas*]', i.e. they were too cowardly to fight, they proceeded to march on the capital, expecting to take it without too much resistance.[90]

Once again, however, this negative turn of events was seized on by Mazzini as a propaganda opportunity for the Italian revolution. The French had sought to present their intervention as a mediation between the Pope and the Republic, but Mazzini successfully presented it as an unprovoked attack. It is notable how many foreign writers in Rome got to see Mazzini at this time, and were confided in by him, probably for publicity purposes. Already in April, Mazzini had revealed his strategy to the English poet, Arthur Clough, to the effect that:

he expects foreign intervention in the end, and of course thinks it likely enough that the Romana Repubblica will fall. Still he is convinced that the separation of the temporal and spiritual power is a thing to be, and that to restore the Pope as before will merely breed perpetual disquiet, conspiracies, assassinations &c.; and he thinks it possible the Great Powers may perceive this in time.[91]

The American writer Margaret Fuller saw Mazzini more than once, and during the fighting he also took time to see the artist, William Wetmore Story, and told him that he 'wished that America could give the Republic its sympathy and adhesion'.[92] When Oudinot's forces tried to enter Rome on the morning of 30 April and met with resistance organised by Garibaldi, Mazzini found a moment to write to an English contact, Emilie Hawkes: 'We fight bravely. The cannon is roaring but, as true as I am living, we shall conquer them or die in a manner that will honour Rome for ever.'[93] On the same day, following the defeat of the French by Garibaldi's forces, he wrote a proclamation telling the Roman people '[o]ur honour is safe. God and our guns will do the rest. Energy and order. You are worthy of your fathers.'[94] Although by June it had become clear that there was no chance of saving the Roman Republic, Mazzini called on the people of Rome to fight on: for able-bodied males to rush to the front lines; for women and children to help the wounded; for civilians to donate their weapons to the army; and for republican orators to take to the streets 'to arouse the people'.[95] By making it last so long, he helped to establish the defence of the Roman Republic as 'the most significant and moving scene of the Risorgimento'.[96] Since, moreover, this action took place in Rome, he was able to convey his message to a wide national and international audience, and guarantee as much attention in the press for their resistance to 'counter-revolution' as for the contemporaneous struggles in Hungary, Baden and Bavaria.[97]

In May 1849, the future Italian prime minister (and long-term enemy of Mazzini), Camillo Benso di Cavour, expressed his pleasure at being well away from the news, in his country house outside Turin, since 'here at least I will not hear the praises sung about the Mazzinians ... by the radicals because of the defeat imposed on the French'.[98] In fact, during June there was a popular demonstration in Turin with crowds shouting '*Viva Garibaldi, Viva la repubblica romana*'.[99] Outside Italy too, the public was preoccupied by the action in Rome. In France, George Sand wrote a series of letters in which she exalted the heroism and sacrifice of the defenders of Rome; these letters show that she was entirely convinced by the political significance and the romantic symbolism of the events. 'Rome makes me ill,' she wrote to Pierre Bocage on 7 July, 'yet Mazzini writes me letters as great and calm as heaven itself. There are still heroes and saints in the world.' Later in the same month, she wrote directly to Mazzini:

you have thought and acted well in all things. You have done well to uphold honour until the very last . . . All that you have sought for and accomplished is just. The whole world feels it, even those wretches who believe in nothing, and the whole world will say so in a loud voice when the time comes . . . national communities will not perish. They will overcome this collapse, so we should be patient; do not cry over those who are dead, do not complain about those who must still die.[100]

Public opinion turned strongly against the Pope. Margaret Fuller, trapped in Rome by the siege with her husband, and now an openly Mazzinian activist, wrote a series of letters to the readers of the *New York Daily Tribune* in May. She predicted that, '[s]hould guns and bayonets replace the Pope on the throne, he will find its foundations, once deep as modern civilization, now so undermined that it falls with the least awkward movement.'[101] Inspired in part by Fuller and the generally negative press reporting, American poets like Henry Tuckerman and John Greenleaf Whittier wrote verses condemning the Pope, where previously they had praised him. For Tuckerman, Pius IX was the 'skeleton at Freedom's feast'; for Whittier, he was 'the Nero of our times'.[102] Even the Rome correspondent of *The Times* of London, which at this time was consistently hostile to the republicans in Italy, pointed out that the French attack on Rome, and its initial failure, had 'so excited the minds of the people, particularly the young, that, where one was ready to serve, and risk his life for the Republic, there are a dozen eager to do so now'. Since the Pope was seen as 'the instigator' of the attack, 'the odium has fallen on him':

> It has . . . united the people to oppose him in a manner no other event could have done, and I and my friends found many who had declared themselves his staunch supporters, now strenuously upholding the Republic and resolute against a return to priestly domination . . . so far as Rome is concerned, and the Pope's cause depends on it, I regard it as utterly lost.[103]

In Paris after the fall of the Roman Republic, the performance of *Roma* at the Theatre Porte-Saint-Martin,[104] which was meant to be a spectacular show celebrating Pius IX and the French intervention, was interrupted by jeering crowds. The audience transformed the play into a pro-republican demonstration. According to one observer, the Tuscan exile Montanelli:

> Pius IX was applauded for as long as he remained a liberal. The French entering Rome in triumph were hissed at in a terrible way. Oudinot was supposed to ride in on his horse, but the storm of hissing was so great that

they had to lower the curtain. Every word uttered by the triumvirate was applauded. Garibaldi appeared. They had done everything to make him look ridiculous. But the applause which greeted him was completely deafening.[105]

At a certain point, the audience started to chant 'Down with the Jesuits! Long live the Roman Republic, long live Mazzini and Garibaldi!', after which they broke into a spontaneous rendition of 'All Peoples Are Brothers', the popular hymn of the socialist 'poet laureate', Pierre Dupont. So great was the fear of popular disorder in Paris as a result of these performances that the (liberal) Minister of the Interior closed the play down after only four days.[106] But the news of the play reached French-occupied Rome, where one observer noted that at the mention of the Roman triumvirate and popular struggle the Parisian theatre had erupted into 'frenetic applause and songs'.[107]

The 'man of the occasion'

Like many other Italian democrats, Garibaldi had spent an unsuccessful winter trying to be of use to the revolution. In October 1848, he had irritated everybody by deciding to leave Genoa, where both Mazzini and Mazzini's protegé, Goffredo Mameli (the author of the future Italian national anthem, 'Fratelli d'Italia'), had great plans for him. Instead Garibaldi set sail for Sicily with his wife, Anita, and seventy-two volunteers to fight in the resistance to the Bourbon reconquest of the island. 'What things men are!' Mameli exclaimed to Mazzini: 'And I thought you judged Garibaldi too severely!'[108]

This tension with Mazzini and other Mazzinians was to persist during the months that followed and throughout the siege of Rome. Pausing for supplies in Livorno, Garibaldi was persuaded to remain in Tuscany, and spent much of the autumn and early winter in Tuscany and Emilia–Romagna trying – and failing – to leave for Venice in order to help Daniele Manin fight the Austrians. In the January elections for the Roman constituent assembly, he was elected a deputy for the region of Macerata, and travelled to Rome to tell the assembly they should immediately declare a republic. He was reproached by Sterbini for his lack of parliamentary experience, and then sent off to Rieti to organise more volunteers.[109] Although he was consistently welcomed by republican groups and public receptions were arranged everywhere in his honour, the various delays caused by other republican leaders combined with a severe attack of rheumatism to cause Garibaldi great frustration and bad humour. In March 1849, he wrote to the Minister of War in Rome that his legionaries were 'trembling with impatience' to fight all invaders,[110] but he is more likely to have been referring to himself. On 19 April, he wrote to his wife Anita to express his disdain for 'this hermaphrodite generation of Italians': 'so often have I tried to make them worthy of you, little though they deserve it . . . I am ashamed to belong to a family which contains so many cowards.'[111]

Yet, as Garibaldi himself anticipated in the same correspondence, the coming struggle for Rome would 'redeem' them all. 'Italy has never had such hope as now', he told Anita only three days later; 'Rome has been and will be worthy of its ancient glories', he wrote to her after the first day's fighting on 30 April.[112] Garibaldi's famous victory over the greatly superior French force on 30 April was due to the same elements of surprise and enthusiasm which had served him so well in Uruguay. It helped that the French were expecting to enter Rome without resistance. During initial hand-to-hand fighting on the Gianicolo hill, Garibaldi's men were pushed back, but the French recruits were then alarmed and put to flight by a massive bayonet charge led by Garibaldi himself, on horseback, reportedly holding a sabre high in the air. Despite being wounded in the fighting, Garibaldi wanted to chase and destroy the retreating French army, but was prevented by Mazzini, who was at the time seeking an agreement with the radical groups in Paris to stop the fighting.[113] Instead Garibaldi was ordered to leave Rome with his legionaries and Manara's volunteers to meet an attack from the Neapolitan army. Once again, this time at Palestrina, he dispersed a much larger force using the tactics of prolonged close combat followed by a rapid cavalry and infantry charge. He then won a second victory at Velletri on 19 May. Here too, however, the engagements were marked by disagreement over tactics between Garibaldi and the government in Rome, and with Mazzini in particular.

The second, doomed phase of the defence of Rome opened with the surprise attack on Rome ordered by Oudinot on the night of 2 June. After Oudinot's forces captured the vital strategic heights around the Villa Corsini, Garibaldi counter-attacked, but at the end of an entire day of prolonged and bloody fighting, and with heavy loss of life, he was obliged to admit defeat and retreat. Although it was clear at the time that the battle of 3 June 'sealed the fate of Rome',[114] the volunteers fought on for another desperate month, while Oudinot tried to bombard the city into submission. Finally, on 30 June, after one more assault by the French on the city walls, Garibaldi ('[w]rapped in his cloak, sweating profusely and covered with dust')[115] came to tell the Roman assembly that further defence was useless. He suggested that they carry the war against the French out into the countryside, but this was refused. On the evening of 2 July, he left Rome with his pregnant wife and around 4,000 men and went into the mountains, in an attempt to cross them and reach Venice and fight there against the Austrians. Mazzini stayed on for another few days in the French-occupied city before he too left on 13 July.

Garibaldi's retreat from Rome ended badly. Although the group succeeded in evading capture, falling morale and physical hardship meant that Garibaldi gradually lost men until finally, at San Marino, he disbanded his forces. A remaining few – including Garibaldi and Anita – went on towards the coast in the hope of reaching Venice. Of these, most were caught by Austrian troops and later executed. Garibaldi himself escaped and doubled back across the Apennines towards the Tuscan coast, but Anita died (of malaria or complications with her pregnancy, or both) and he had to leave her in a shallow grave in the marshes near Ravenna. In all, between 3,000 and 4,000 Italians were killed or severely wounded in the defence of Rome, including the volunteer leaders Mameli and Manara. Perhaps some 2,000 French soldiers lost their lives also.[116]

The credit for the brave if bloody defence of Rome was not Garibaldi's alone, but was due to the courage of all the volunteers and to the skill of the other leaders too, perhaps most notably Manara, Bixio and Medici. At the time, and later, Garibaldi was criticised for disobeying orders and for a number of tactical mistakes, especially the arguably futile attack on the Villa Corsini on 3 June, which resulted in such heavy casualties. Garibaldi was not the only leader who became a popular hero in 1849, either in Italy or elsewhere in Europe. Yet his ability both to hold off the French attack and to attract public attention was a winning combination, and it helped hugely in creating widespread international support and the identification of the republican defence of Rome with the broader nationalist struggle in Italy. From 30 April onwards Garibaldi was undoubtedly the 'man of the occasion', to borrow a phrase from the British women's weekly, *The Lady's Newspaper*, which published a front-page portrait of him in May.[117] This achievement was the product of a broad strategy which he had pursued since his return to Italy the previous year.

A key aspect of this strategy was to get men to volunteer and to fight bravely in battle, and to persuade women to encourage them to do so. To this end, Garibaldi made a series of speeches as he moved in late 1848 from Genoa to Livorno, and on to Florence, Bologna, Ravenna and Rome. He presented himself as a specifically Italian hero with certain virtuous qualities – honesty, modesty, bravery – and he called on the audience to identify with him and with them: 'In front of you has come a man, who is with you, an Italian, who has never sold out, never lied'.[118] In Livorno, he likened himself to the celebrated sixteenth-century republican, Francesco Ferruccio, also the hero of Guerrazzi's popular novel *L'assedio di Firenze*: 'I have touched with my sword the ashes of Ferruccio, and I will know how to die like Ferruccio.'[119] All his speeches were short and persuasive. In Florence, he flattered the Florentines: they were the first to honour 'what little I did for America', they were 'the most intelligent and kind of the Italian peoples', their city was 'the Paris of Italy' and the Italian language was 'created in Tuscany'; in Bologna, he thanked them for making him feel better and for 'reinvigorating his soul' with their patriotism; while in both Livorno and Ravenna he confined himself to expressions of pleasure at being among 'strong men'.[120]

In almost every speech before and during the siege of Rome, Garibaldi identified the immediate battle against conservative intervention with an age-old struggle to redeem, with death if necessary, the honour of Italy against foreign oppression/enslavement:

> rise up in the name of unrevenged martyrs, of liberty and the looted fatherland, disgraced by the foreigner, strong like men prepared to die . . . Italians after so many years need men who can teach us to dare and to die. And we have learnt. *Viva l'Italia*, war on Austria . . . the whole population is rushing onward under the standard of redemption . . . Italian honour, and you know how important honour is to a fallen nation, Italian honour has been saved by our brave legionaries.[121]

To convince his soldiers to fight on the terrible morning of 3 June, Garibaldi used sex: 'You are the soldiers who yesterday proudly allowed yourselves to be kissed by Roman women, as thanks for your heroic actions! What would they say today if you are not able to retake the *casino dei Quattro Venti*? They would push you from their breasts, and throw scornfully in your faces the name of coward!!'[122] A week later, he invoked masculine pride and the defence of female honour: 'tomorrow every one of us will come forward, with his head held high, in front of the beautiful Roman women who with a sign of admiration and love will say to us: Thanks to you, brave men, we were not defiled by the barbarian.'[123] But he saved his best, and by far his most famous, speech of 1848–9 for the dramatic moment on 2 July 1849, when his defeated army left Rome for the mountains:

> Soldiers who with me have shared until now the toils and dangers of patriotic battles, who obtained rich rewards of glory and honour: all you who now choose exile with me, this is what awaits you: heat and thirst by day, cold and hunger by night. For you there is no pay but toil and danger, no roof, no rest, but absolute poverty, exhausting vigils, extreme marches, and fighting at every step. Who loves Italy follow me![124]

As popular political rhetoric, the value of these speeches can hardly be denied. They were carefully fashioned, and deliberately linked the immediate military struggle to a higher political and moral ideal which was, in turn, identified with Italy and brought back to the speaker – Garibaldi. His speeches aimed at the emotions, at basic feelings of love, hate, pride, shame and sexual desire. Their sheer theatricality, the constant juxtaposition of danger and death with glory and honour, the appeal to history, beauty and 'the looted fatherland' give us some idea of Garibaldi the performer, and a sense of his qualities as a charismatic leader. As in 1848, we can only speculate about the impact of these speeches on his audience. But it is worth remembering that Garibaldi had by all accounts a compelling and musical voice: 'dolce e vibrante', for Bartolomé Mitre, who met him in Uruguay; and a 'masterly' and 'frank' delivery which produced marvellous results, according to one volunteer who heard him speak in 1849.[125]

Like other revolutionaries in this period, Garibaldi's behaviour in 1848–9 tends to suggest that he lacked a coherent plan and reacted to political–military opportunities simply as they arose. His speeches appear spontaneous and his approach to soldiering energetic and enthusiastic rather than organised. Yet seen as acts of political communication, Garibaldi's 'performances' in 1849 seem far from unscripted. Attention was paid to the specific demands of a given audience. Time was taken to write his speeches down, and a remarkable number of them were published more or less contemporaneously, notably in the Turin newspaper La Concordia. In particular, his 2 July speech to the volunteers became an instant classic. It was circulated widely (as a printed ordine del giorno and as a news item in La Concordia),[126] and was republished and translated in various versions and languages over the next decade. One eyewitness reported that, by early July, Mazzini's name was 'generally abhorred' in Rome for his desire to prolong the resistance to the French, but those who joined Garibaldi were applauded.[127] The effectiveness of Garibaldi as a military commander was probably due in no small measure to his oratory: to his short and rousing speeches which inspired and involved his audience emotionally.[128]

Contemporary impressions of Garibaldi's behaviour in Rome in 1849 differed, and not all were positive. However, they all concur that his physical appearance and behaviour played a key role in his political appeal.[129] One Lombard volunteer, Enrico Dandolo, confided to his family: 'Garibaldi sitting in the simplicity of his costumes is an obvious charlatan from 10 miles away', but he admitted that 'his activity is unparalleled and he knows how to maintain a constant enthusiasm and trust among his soldiers'.[130] 'I had no idea of enlisting,' an Italian artist later told an English clergyman:

but oh! I shall never forget that day when I saw him on his beautiful white horse in the market-place, with his noble aspect, his calm, kind face, his high, smooth forehead, his light hair and beard – everyone said the same. He reminded us of nothing so much as of our Saviour's head in the galleries.

I could not resist him. I left my studio. I went after him; thousands did likewise. He only had to show himself. We all worshipped him; we could not help it.[131]

A Dutch artist, Jan Koelman, wrote of Garibaldi's remarkable clothes and firearms, his 'extraordinary' expressive eyes, his exceptionally wide nose, shoulder-length blond hair and ample two-pointed beard which 'gave a warrior look to his open, oval face, covered in freckles and burnt brightly by the sun'. Garibaldi's nickname was 'lion' and – Koelman tells the reader – he really did look like one, especially in battle 'when his eyes flamed and his blond hair waved around his head like a mane'.[132] Another volunteer, Gustav von Hofstetter, described Garibaldi on horseback, sitting still 'as if he had been born there': small and sunburnt, with long hair which flowed out from a narrow pointed hat with a black ostrich feather on top, and a reddish beard which was so full that it hid half his face. With his friend, the volunteer leader Luciano Manara, he 'marvelled not a little at such a strange way of dressing . . . Manara never got rid of his dislike for those clothes'; even after Manara became friends with Garibaldi he never tired of telling him to put on something 'more modern'.[133]

Garibaldi's personal behaviour and that of his followers were no less the subject of comment. Koelman described Garibaldi's soldiers as 'picturesque' and was amazed that none of them stirred when Garibaldi entered his headquarters; even the sentry kept up his position, half sitting, half lying on the ground.[134] Von Hofstetter 'marvels' at Garibaldi's companions: 'a moor [moro] of vast proportions who had followed him from America, in a black cloak with a lance garnished with a red pennant'. This is Aguyar – 'a Hercules of ebony colour', in Koelman's words – a freed slave who accompanied Garibaldi from Brazil, and who astonished everyone in battle by throwing a lasso over enemy soldiers and pulling them off their horses.[135] Anita was another singular presence, dark and delicate but an 'amazon' all the same, a woman for whom Garibaldi openly expressed his love (on the retreat from Rome, he also told the men stories of her courage during their South American adventures).[136] The garibaldini made camp spontaneously and 'without any order'; soldiers occupied what space they could find, 'with the general in the middle'. Horses were left out to graze freely on long lines; the men went off to kill sheep which were shared out equally; and whilst there was no bread, everyone had wine. When Garibaldi relaxed, the 'spectacle' was equally engrossing: '[u]nder a makeshift parasol, the general put together a pallet with his saddle and a tiger skin, he took off his shirt, lay down and went to sleep'.[137] A Lombard volunteer, Emilio Dandolo, described the scene:

Garibaldi and his officers are dressed in red blouses, all kinds of hats, without distinction of grade ... They ride with American saddles, and take care to show great contempt for everything that is observed and followed with such care by regular armies. Followed by their orderlies (all people who have come from America), they break up, group together, they run here and there in a disorganised way, active, reckless, tireless ... of a patriarchal simplicity which is perhaps a bit forced, Garibaldi seems more like the head of an Indian tribe than a General.[138]

The performance in the press

In Rome, Garibaldi's military activities come across to us not simply as bravery in battle but as a series of almost theatrical set pieces: his wild and passionate appearance in battle; rest and recreation thereafter; the glamorous companions; and his public interventions at crucial moments in the fighting. Furthermore, if the press is anything to go by, in 1849 Garibaldi's appeal was no longer confined to political activists or to an immediate or 'live' audience but had begun to reach a broader reading public. During the fighting for Rome, the Roman satirical daily, *Il Don Pirlone* ('Mr Dickhead', a paper 'with often mediocre lithographs ... and a not elevated sense of humour', in the words of one historian, but 'the freshest *artistic* expression of modern Rome' according to a contemporary),[139] published two memorable cartoons of Garibaldi. The first was entitled *The heart of Garibaldi* and was a simple, but graphic, depiction of his gigantic heart posed against a wall ('What a heart! What a huge heart!' cried one of the well-dressed onlookers); in case readers failed to understand the association, the cartoon was accompanied by a poem dedicated to Garibaldi, 'the lover of good and the hater of evil'. The second image – *Suggestive effects* – showed the king of Naples (a ridiculous figure dressed as Punch) being harassed at the dinner table by a portrait of Garibaldi placed directly opposite him as well as by everyday objects – the bread-board and bread, the wine carafe and glass, the tablecloth and table leg, his chair and the floor – all bearing Garibaldi's name (see figure 3 overleaf).[140] *Il Don Pirlone* also underwent a significant change of attitude in its commentary on events, moving from detached cynicism to direct engagement with the defence of Rome, and it came to celebrate Garibaldi: the 'valiant Garibaldi' who 'knows no defeat' and who 'bites those in power'.[141]

Another Italian satirical paper, *Il Fischietto* of Turin, engaged with Garibaldi only during the retreat from Rome, presumably being stimulated by his ability repeatedly to evade arrest by the Austrians. On 11 August, the paper referred to the presence of 'Garibaldi's tribe' near San Marino and to 'General Garibaldi the head of the *garibaldese* nation'. It also published two cartoons about Garibaldi during the retreat and its aftermath. The first was relatively straightforward, and showed him half submerged in the Straits of Messina struggling between his tormentors France and Naples, depicted as the two monsters of classical legend, Scylla and Charybdis ('Garibaldi shows us that Scylla and Charybdis are not mythical monsters', commented the paper). The second one, published in August, was a comment on Garibaldi's escape from

3 'Suggestive effects': the king of Naples ('Punch') has his dinner disturbed by Garibaldi's renown. *Don Pirlone*, the satirical Roman newspaper which published this cartoon, was one of the earliest to comment on the growing fame of Garibaldi.

the Austrians after the retreat from Rome. In the cartoon, Garibaldi – a 'knavish red devil' – thumbs his nose at a group of stupid and ineffectual soldiers who try vainly to bring him to justice (see figure 4 opposite).[142] Both papers, in other words, reflect the immediate context in which they were published: *Il Don Pirlone* reflects a sense of Roman identity and pride, and *Il Fischietto*, the anti-interventionist and especially anti-Austrian feeling which was prevalent in liberal Turin. Although we know little or nothing about the sales and circulation of these papers, they can tell us that by 1849 Garibaldi had become a widely recognisable public figure, immediately available as a subject of satire to criticise contemporary politics and political leaders.

In terms of public recognition, *Il Fischietto* is especially interesting in that Garibaldi is identified by his clothes and by his physical appearance. In the *Fischietto* cartoons he has long hair and a beard, a large, sloping beret and a loosely tied blouse with rope and tassel. These visual characteristics are taken directly from the portrait which was first reproduced in Turin's illustrated magazine, *Il Mondo Illustrato*, in February 1848 (it borrowed from the portrait by Gallino in South America, which had been copied, subjected to minor changes and lithographed in Turin). In the *Mondo Illustrato* portrait, Garibaldi wears a sloping beret and a loose, long-collared blouse tied with a rope and tassel; his hair is long, wavy and uncontrolled, he has a thick and flowing beard and large, almond-shaped sensuous eyes: his expression is not

—Anche questa volta pirpante diavolo rosso poter scappar per inferna!

4 'Once again the knavish red devil has escaped through hell!' commented *Il Fischietto* on Garibaldi's ability to evade arrest. The paper also made much of Garibaldi's clothes and rebellious behaviour.

overtly threatening but it is fierce, exotic and not entirely pleasant (see figure 2 on page 54). During 1849, this image reached London and Paris. In fact, in May 1849, *The Illustrated London News* and *The Lady's Newspaper* of London, and the Paris magazine *L'Illustration,* all copied and published the same portrait of Garibaldi, this time with the subtitle 'Roman General' and with minor variations in character and quality in each one.[143] So by 1849 there was something of a publisher's market for Garibaldi, with his image circulating in illustrated magazines (one of which was a specifically women's publication) and satirical newspapers across different countries.

The broadening of interest in Garibaldi and the events in Rome seems further confirmed by the fact that in June *The Illustrated London News* went to the expense of sending to Rome its own artist, who drew a series of pictures of Garibaldi and his men together with scenes of the fighting which were subsequently published in the magazine. In a portrait of Garibaldi produced on the spot by *The Illustrated London News* artist ('and', he wrote, 'I have been very particular to get it like him'), Garibaldi has a more dignified and 'European' countenance but – other than his hat, a tall, round ('Puritan') affair with an ostrich feather – his clothes remained more or less the same, and just as unusual. As the artist commented:

> He is a remarkably quiet-looking person, but wonderfully picturesque: he wore a white sort of cloak lined with red, and having a green velvet collar; it had plenty of bullet holes in it. There was no opening visible in the garment, so I imagine he puts it on like a shirt, over his head, like the *poncho* or South American cloak. His trousers were common grey, with a green stripe; and a black slouched hat and feather complete the picture.

The same picture showed Garibaldi's ('now dead') 'negro servant' Aguyar on a prancing horse (see figure 5 opposite). 'He was a fine fellow,' the artist commented, 'his dress a red loose coat and a showy silk handkerchief tied loosely over his shoulders.'[144] Three other illustrations in *The Illustrated London News* offered further information about the appearance and behaviour of Garibaldi's followers. The first, published on 23 June, showed Garibaldi's men outside his headquarters at the San Silvester convent: some stand, some slouch and one sits on horseback; they are all armed and chat and smoke, and form a series of impromptu and relaxed small groups around a central group of three, apparently South American, officers with long hair, blouses and Puritan hats with ostrich feathers (see figure 6 on page 92). The second picture published on 14 July shows a group of 'wonderfully picturesque fellows'. The central figure is very young and again has long hair, a flowing blouse, foulard and a Puritan hat; he smokes a small cigar and is armed with pistol and dagger. Finally, the same issue has a picture of a Garibaldi lancer on horseback: a fierce and determined looking figure dressed in the same flowing clothes and with long hair and beard, galloping at full tilt down a crowded Roman street.[145]

Increasingly, during the course of the siege in 1849, the traditional (or non-illustrated) press outside Italy also took to publishing detailed articles about the

5 'Garibaldi and his negro servant'. This picture from *The Illustrated London News* is perhaps the first image of Garibaldi to be drawn and published directly 'from life'. Many journalists at this time were fascinated by the presence of the ex-slave Aguyar among the soldiers in Rome.

events in Rome. These too emphasised Garibaldi's role in the siege and its aftermath and his striking personal presence. Margaret Fuller wrote a series of important and detailed articles for the *New York Tribune* about the situation in Rome. Much of her enthusiasm was reserved for Mazzini ('a man of genius, an elevated thinker . . . the most powerful and first impression from his presence must always be . . . of his *virtue*'), and for the heroism of the Roman people. However, in July, when the fate of the Republic was entirely sealed, she began to talk mainly of Garibaldi and his followers. If, she told her readers, Garibaldi and his men were really brigands and vagabonds, as 'many "respectable" gentleman' suggested, then they were 'in the same sense as Jesus, Moses, and Eneas were'. When they left Rome at the end of the siege, Fuller was there to see them go. She gave her readers an unforgettable description of Garibaldi, the *garibaldini* and their departure, in which she outlined a romantic political aesthetic based on both the unrestrained physical allure of male youth and a broad, if doomed, vision of political belonging (which included women and the weak: anyone who 'wished to go'):

> the lancers of Garibaldi galloped along in full career. I longed for Walter Scott to be on earth again, and see them; all are light, athletic, resolute figures, many of the forms of the finest manly beauty of the South, all

HEAD-QUARTERS OF GARIBALDI, AT THE CONVENT OF SAN SILVESTRO AT ROME.—(SEE NEXT PAGE.)

6 This illustration of Garibaldi's 'headquarters' is a comment on the exotic, varied and unconventional appearance and behaviour of Garibaldi's volunteers. Note especially the officers in South American dress in the centre of the picture.

sparkling with its genius and ennobled by the resolute spirit, ready to dare, to do, to die . . . Never have I seen a sight so beautiful, so romantic and so sad . . . They had all put on the beautiful dress of the Garibaldi legion, the tunic of bright red cloth, the Greek cap, or else round hat with Puritan plume. Their long hair was blown back from resolute faces; all looked full of courage . . . I saw the wounded, all that could go, laden upon their baggage cars; some were already pale and fainting, still they wished to go. I saw many youths, born to rich inheritance, carrying in a handkerchief all their worldly goods. The women were ready; their eyes too were resolved, if sad. The wife of Garibaldi followed him on horseback. He himself was distinguished by the white tunic; his look was entirely that of a hero of the Middle Ages – his face still young, for the excitements of life, though so many, have all been youthful, and there is no fatigue upon his brow or cheek.

Thus, the symbolic moment at the end of the siege was entirely Garibaldi's. As Fuller commented, '[h]ard was the heart, stony and seared the eye, that had no tear for that moment. Go, fated, gallant band!' [146]

Garibaldi's physical attraction also found its way into the hostile and/or right-wing press. In a series of caricatures published by a conservative Roman paper he appears as a treacherous long-haired brigand, dressed in a huge cloak and large-feathered hat, and shadowed by a large black man.[147] In France, a row broke out in July between, on the one side, the radical paper, *Le National*, which translated and published Garibaldi's 'historic' proclamation at the end of the siege, and praised him for restoring 'prestige to Italian bravery' after 'many centuries of servitude' and, on the other, the conservative paper, *Le Constitutionel*, which accused *Le National* of making a 'hero . . . Napoleon . . . [and a] *petit caporal*' of someone whose real job was 'purely and simply that of a highway robber'.[148] *The Times* of London described Garibaldi variously as a 'chieftain' at the head of 'foreign freebooters', and called Garibaldi, Mazzini and Avezzana 'three strangers of broken fortune, who . . . back up their cause by bands of foreign robbers', and who had planned 'a general sack and plunder . . . when the last hour of defence has arrived'. But, perhaps troubled by its equal antagonism towards the Pope and the French, the paper also allowed some half-ironic admiration of the 'persevering hero', admitting that he had 'shown much talent' in the initial defence of Rome and saying that he had been joined by some 'fine-looking young fellows' from Lombardy, and even that his own men were a mixture of 'wild and truculent-looking savages' and 'heedless young men of a superior class' who had been attracted by the call of a 'free life' but whose conduct was 'as quiet and orderly as any other of the regular military'.[149] Whatever the politics of the reporters, in other words, they all testified to Garibaldi's capacity to attract publicity, and referred to his striking physical presence – his clothes, his gestures, his behaviour – as well as his qualities as a military leader.

Conclusion

The defeat of the 1848–9 revolutions cast a long political shadow across Europe. In some places, for example in France and southern Germany, the democratic movement was subsequently decimated by persecution and exile; elsewhere, including in Italy, it is possible to trace a dwindling of revolutionary militancy during the 1850s and 1860s back to the crushing of radical governments in the spring and summer of 1849. Nevertheless, the revolutions themselves mark a crucial stage in the emergence of mass politics in Europe. For its supporters and detractors, and for those who took part in the events or who reported what they saw or simply read about them, the revolutions represented a transformation of political life and, for many, a novel experience of political 'belonging'. The revolutions introduced a new language, and new rituals, symbols and myths of political mobilisation; and these changes were extended across Europe and to the Americas, being experienced at different times directly, through detailed newspaper reports and/or via the published memoirs and speaking tours of those who had been involved. For all these reasons, the shadow cast by the revolutions was to set the political agenda in the years that followed.

In Italy, Garibaldi played a decisive role both in the broader process of politicisation and in the specific representation and spread of an Italian national identity. He did this first by virtue of his military successes, most notably the spectacular and perhaps truly heroic victory over the French of 30 April 1849. These successes built on his practical experiences in Brazil and Uruguay, and they helped confirm more broadly the Italian revolution's need for military volunteers. Although volunteers were regarded with suspicion by the regular Piedmontese army in 1848 and '49, their youth and enthusiasm was a valuable addition to the nationalist struggle. Moreover, during the fighting for the Roman Republic in 1849, as well as in the defence of other cities during the same year, the volunteers had a second chance, which they took full advantage of. Co-ordinated in part by Garibaldi, their victory over the French in Rome was arguably one of 'the most successful and heroic military engagements of the Risorgimento';[150] it certainly formed a striking contrast to the utter ineffectiveness of the Piedmontese soldiers, crushed twice by the Austrians at the battles of Custoza and Novara. From this point of view, the ultimate defeat of the Roman Republic seemed less important than the proof in many parts of Italy of 'brave resistance and honourable defeat' by an army of young volunteers.[151] Thus, the formation of volunteer militias in 1848–9, and especially the role played in them by Garibaldi, seemed to offer a solution to the twin problems of military weakness and popular apathy which had dogged the Mazzinian party in Italy since the formation of the movement in the early 1830s. Although some military strategists – notably Carlo Pisacane – went on to criticise the tactics used by Garibaldi, a general strategy of forming a national and popular army was henceforth agreed upon by the Italian revolutionary movement.[152]

The defence of Rome by Garibaldi and the volunteer army against French attack has also been described as 'a poet's dream'.[153] Both in Rome and earlier, Garibaldi played a leading part in creating a new – living and contemporary – romantic myth of Italian military heroism. His experiences had all the ingredients of popular Risorgimento narrative: the brave warrior-hero; the community in danger; its defence by a defiant band of 'brothers'; their sacrifice and the death of the heroine (Garibaldi's wife Anita). Indeed, the message of national redemption seems to have been all the more compelling because it was 'true': part of politics and the acts of men rather than something dreamt up by romantic writers. Throughout the events of 1848–9, Garibaldi represented a visible and physical bond between the romantic vision of Italy and Mazzini's ideal of political engagement. In Rome, moreover, he helped to damage (if not entirely dissolve) the symbolic link between the Pope and the nation, an achievement which was reflected in attacks on him in the right-wing and clerical press. Although, as we shall see, it took time – roughly the whole of the 1850s – and a series of writers fully to create this new nationalist formula and establish its close identification with Garibaldi, the main elements were put in place during the events of 1848 and 1849. And both the story itself and its references to the romantic Risorgimento genre were introduced at the time through Mazzinian editorials, in visual images and, perhaps especially, by Garibaldi's own speeches and appearance.

It helped enormously that so many Mazzinians in 1848–9, including Garibaldi, had considerable experience in producing propaganda, in writing good stories and/or in creating better relations with the press, and had long-term friendships with writers and journalists. Indeed, for the historian writing in the twenty-first century, what is most conspicuous, and certainly most familiar, about these events is not so much the street barricades or the acts of military valour as the growing, almost self-sustaining, tide of media interest in them. The 'explosion of journalism' in Europe brought about by the end of censorship in many states in 1847–8 was a clear symptom of political change and participation.[154] The press itself helped to create that change, to publicise and define the revolution and to establish its memory during the ensuing years. Even before 1848, while Garibaldi was still in Uruguay, the press had been a crucial tool in the creation of his fame. In 1848–9, it was the press which launched Garibaldi as a public figure with an appeal beyond the restricted circles of democratic clubs and associations. Throughout 1848, Garibaldi was promoted by the press as an Italian hero, with a clear resonance for the liberal, patriotically inclined elites living in the towns and cities of northern and central Italy. And it was foreign press attention in 1849, thanks to the defence of Rome, which gave him an international reputation both as seductive idol and as dangerous 'freebooter'.

Still, perhaps the most important aspect of Garibaldi's fame in this period is less immediately obvious to us, and lies in the message which he conveys. Of course, most of what we know about Garibaldi's appearances in 1848–9 is mediated through newspaper reports, political commentaries, and scenes imagined by artists or remembered by participants, so its value as historical evidence is far from straightforward. What is clear, however, is the extent to which, as a political symbol, he lies outside any kind of accepted mainstream. For instance, as a soldier, he looks and behaves less like an officer and much more like a bandit. As a national icon, he is neither Jacobin nor Napoleonic; there is little hint of classical beauty or dignity, even less of controlled masculinity, and not much in the way of saintly behaviour. For the readers of *The Illustrated London News* he is 'picturesque', a popular term in the nineteenth century which means natural, exotic and pleasing, and would have reminded the English of seventeenth-century Italian paintings by artists like Salvator Rosa, who peopled their landscapes with soldiers, shepherds and bandits.[155]

Garibaldi seems young, he is sultry, unkempt and hirsute and he dresses unconventionally in flowing, brightly coloured clothes. He is strong and fierce and he makes camp 'like an Indian'; he is sunburnt and he sweats. His look is not self-controlled and classical but that of a hero of the Middle Ages; and while his speeches exalt violence and courage, they also appeal to sex and love. Garibaldi's followers are ill-disciplined, they include strong women and a black ex-slave, and, when they leave Rome, they are beautiful, romantic and sad. A female eyewitness longs for Walter Scott to be alive and see them go. Garibaldi, in other words, is an intensely romantic figure, rebellious, independent and emotive rather than austere, conformist and authoritarian. In political terms, he represents a distinctly democratic and inclusive ideal. He seeks to be a living embodiment of the people's aspirations, and he is part of the community and the nation rather than a 'great man', alone capable of great deeds.

Despite this liberating message, the final legacy of 1848–9 was more negative, and was to cause great damage to the democratic movement in the years to come. The revolutionaries' exceptional talent for self-publicity was not really paralleled by a similar capacity for day-to-day organisation and co-ordination. They were divided in 1848–9, not simply into democrats and moderates (who were not revolutionaries at all), but also into unitarians and federalists; there was a gap between the 'Italian', but also cosmopolitan, Mazzinians and other republican groups with a much more regional or local focus, and/or between all of them and smaller groups with more radical, socialist leanings. It was this tension and lack of co-ordination which partly led to their downfall; it meant that few practical steps were taken to consolidate the revolution, either in preparing for its defence or in seeking to reach out to the provinces and countryside, and to the poorer classes of society.[156] Even on a micro-level, in terms of relations between friends and allies like Mazzini and Garibaldi, the level of discord – especially over the fundamental question of military strategy and tactics – was often striking. If only in this respect, historians are probably right to argue that romanticism provided a flawed and unrealistic basis for political action in 1848–9.

However, such tensions might have been less serious had they not endured and hardened and, in turn, affected democratic thought and practice in the decade after the revolution's end. Paul Ginsborg argues that the republicans learnt the wrong lessons from 1848: 'They became convinced that the most important feature of the Risorgimento was the struggle for independence and unity, to which the[ir] democratic and republican beliefs ... were to be sacrificed.'[157] It is also true that after 1848–9 the generation of Mazzini, Manin and Garibaldi lost much of the intense enthusiasm and fearless optimism which had characterised their political activity up till then. For Garibaldi, revolution left a memory of bitterness, frustration and, after the death of his wife, profound personal grief.[158]

One effect of the 1848–9 revolutions was to inspire a 'poet's dream'. The revolutionaries launched an influential and enduring myth of selfless struggle for national freedom, and they also publicised a republican idea of Italy and a compelling model of political engagement. But this dream worked best for those who had time to read and sleep, or those who came of age thereafter; it appealed most of all to foreigners, to those too young to fight or to those excluded by their sex. Not everyone was taken in by the dream, and those who were not (conservatives, clericals) were often the most powerful groups in European society, with the strongest hold on its poorest members. For the protagonists themselves, and perhaps especially for Mazzinian nationalists, the memory of revolution was more divisive, and henceforth they seemed less able to live up to the message of fraternity they had so successfully promoted. Thus, for those already with an idea of Italy, who had embraced Mazzini's vision of combatant national resurgence long before the spring of '48, the reality of revolution was one of failure. The most lasting impact of this failure was the reintroduction of the more traditional themes of death, decadence and betrayal to the centre of Italy's national story.

CHAPTER 4

EXILE

After the fall of Rome

At the beginning of August 1849, having come within fifty miles of Venice, Garibaldi disappeared for an entire month. The Austrian authorities in Bologna issued a proclamation on 5 August which warned of 'Summary Military Justice' for anyone 'who knowingly aids, shelters or shows favour to the fugitive Garibaldi or to any other individuals of the band led and commanded by him'.[1] Several of the Roman Republic's most celebrated radicals – the priest Ugo Bassi and the popular leader Ciceruacchio, along with his two sons – were captured and executed, but Garibaldi himself managed to escape and went into hiding.

What happened was that following the death of his wife at a farm in Mandriole on 4 August, Garibaldi and his companion 'Leggero' (Battista Colliolo) first hid from the Austrians in the thick pine forest to the north of Ravenna. It was there that they abandoned all hope of reaching Venice, and decided simply to try to get home without being arrested. From the forest they were taken by local sympathisers to a hut in the middle of the marshes and, during the night of 7 August, were moved to the outskirts of Ravenna and on across the Romagna plain towards the Apennines and the Tuscan border. With Leggero (who was wounded in the leg so could only travel slowly) and moving carefully to avoid the Austrian troops, Garibaldi spent some two weeks zigzagging through the mountains between Florence and Bologna, after which they cut south towards Prato. From Prato, they travelled by carriage to Poggibonsi and Volterra, and eventually reached the Tuscan Maremma and the Tyrrhenian coast. In the early morning of 2 September, Garibaldi was moved to temporary quarters at an isolated farmhouse called Casa Guelfi. Here he apparently smoked a cigar and slept for a few hours before being taken to the tiny bay of Cala Martina, from where he embarked for the island of Elba on a fishing boat.[2] After Elba he sailed via Porta Venere to La Spezia, and from

La Spezia travelled by land to Chiavari, which was within the territory of the kingdom of Sardinia. He arrived there on 5 September. Garibaldi's reappearance was announced by *La Concordia* and *La Gazzetta di Genova* on 7 September, by *La Gazzetta di Milano* on 10 September and by *The Times* of London on 14 September. But until his arrival in Chiavari, nobody other than his immediate companions had known where he was or what had become of him.[3]

Throughout August, there had been intense speculation as to Garibaldi's whereabouts. The narratives which emerged were mostly false or based on half-truths at best, reflecting both public interest in Garibaldi and the lack of any real news about him. *The Times*, which carried reports from the main European papers, reported on 17 August that he had escaped but that there was 'great uncertainty' about his movements, and '[s]ome say he re-embarked at La Mesola, with his wife and 30 followers, and reached Venice'. The Turin paper *La Concordia* tried to convince its readers that Garibaldi had reached Venice. It announced on 16 August that Garibaldi had arrived in Venice together with his wife and had been elected admiral: 'Manin received him with great affection and exclaimed "Behold a hero, whom God has sent to save Venice!"' On 29 August, the paper reported that Garibaldi had written to his mother from Venice 'in order to tranquillise her fears' and that, on arrival in Venice, 'he was obliged to keep his bed for a week'. In Paris, at the end of August, he was said to have reached the coast of Dalmatia.

The conservative and Austrian papers initially announced Garibaldi's imminent capture. On 11 August *La Gazzetta di Milano* reported that Garibaldi's boats had been intercepted by the Austrian navy. When driven on to the beach by Austrian guns, Garibaldi had leapt into the waves and abandoned his 'trunk of money'; shouting at 'the few who followed him: "everybody save himself as best he can"', he then threw down his sword and ran off into the woods with his pregnant wife. It was said that she then comforted him and dried his tears. Other papers concentrated on the alleged death of his wife. Anita was said to have died at Chioggia, outside Venice, 'of the excessive fatigue she had endured'; later when her corpse was found near the Mandriole farm she was said to have been murdered – strangled by her hosts – for money. In early September, when Garibaldi arrived in Genoa via La Spezia and Chiavari, a more coherent and persuasive narrative emerged. *La Concordia*, which probably received the news from Garibaldi himself, announced the death of his pregnant wife ('the unhappy woman, who loved, oh too much! her passionate husband, and who wanted to go everywhere with him in his turbulent life'), and described his escape from the Austrians, his perilous journey across the Apennines and his arrival in Chiavari disguised as a fisherman.[4] Its story closely follows the first-hand account given by Garibaldi himself and written down by Augusto Nomis di Cossilla, the intendant of Chiavari. When asked the nature of his business in Chiavari by Nomis, Garibaldi was reported to have replied as follows:

> to have an American passport, under a false name, taken after the surrender of Rome, although to have never used it, never having been in Venice, to have embarked . . . on a fishing boat, to have arrived this morning in Portovenere, without having had anything asked of him, to have come to Spezia, to have there taken the mail coach, to have come here, having relatives and friends, to expect to stay a day or two, and then to continue his journey for Genoa and on to Nice, having there his family, to expect to remain there. All this he said with fine and unusual frankness . . . while this listener heard him talk with no small surprise, curious episode in the very curious history of our time.[5]

Garibaldi's arrival in Chiavari caused quite a stir. Nomis admitted that 'all his adherents . . . make a fuss of him and are preparing a serenade for him'.[6] A Captain Ollandini, the *carabinieri* commander of Chiavari, wrote to Genoa that Garibaldi was recognised on arrival and a large crowd gathered spontaneously to applaud him; in the evening, moreover, 'the most excited' of the national guard put a sentry outside Garibaldi's house and told government officials that any attempt to arrest Garibaldi would be met with armed resistance, and 'they would make the church bells peal'.[7] In fact, Garibaldi's arrest was ordered almost immediately by Alfonso La Marmora, the general in command of Genoa, on the obviously trumped-up charge of entering the country illegally (since he had allegedly forfeited his citizenship by fighting in the defence of Rome, a foreign state).[8] Unsurprisingly, this action did little to calm pro-Garibaldi agitation in Chiavari. When he was taken from Chiavari to Genoa, there was first a demonstration outside the place where he was staying and then disturbances around his carriage. As one official put it, after he got into the carriage, 'the attitude of the numerous bystanders changed, and some broke out in applause for Garibaldi, others in shouts of insults against the king, the government and us, they accompanied us in this way for about a quarter of a mile, forcing the horses to stop at every step so that they could take the time to express to Garibaldi the full extent of their sympathy'.[9] And although in Genoa and Nice officials had the situation more under control, they were still deeply worried by Garibaldi's presence and by his 'immense influence on a great part of the population', and were concerned enough about the threat of disorder to make sure he arrived in Genoa quietly at four o'clock in the morning.[10] When Garibaldi left for Nice from Genoa, *La Concordia* stressed the excited crowds which gathered in boats to watch him leave, and that when he arrived in Nice he was carried in triumph by the crowd to embrace his 'old mother', his aunt and his children. According to the paper, Garibaldi was especially moved by the encounter with his daughter: 'the loss of his wife distresses him deeply, and everything that reminds him of her hurts him terribly'.[11]

Garibaldi's own state of mind is perhaps best summed up by a personal letter written while he was under arrest in Genoa: 'I am in this city from today, having wandered as a refugee around the Romagna and Tuscany for 36 days ... I have lost the beloved companion of my life ... I think I can leave tomorrow for Nice to see my babies and my old mother ... Love, your unhappy brother.'[12] Repeatedly, the correspondence between Chiavari, Genoa and Turin stressed the same message from Garibaldi, that 'his intention ... was to go on to Nice with the aim of returning to the heart of his family ... his only desire is to be able to embrace his mother and children at Nice ... he made known the strongest desire to go to Nice to see there his old mother and his children', after which he was quite prepared to go into exile.[13] Initially he refused money ('a grant') from the Piedmontese government, asking only for help for his mother and children.[14] As it happened, this attitude won the sympathy of government officials, who were also impressed by his 'prudence', 'good sense' and 'frankness', and by his reluctance to encourage popular demonstrations in his favour. Indeed, on the journey from Chiavari, Garibaldi even agreed to use what was termed 'his astonishing influence' to control the crowd, 'which he did to a good degree talking to them in a loud voice, and urging them to calm down'.[15] After his visit to Nice, the intendant wrote to General La Marmora that Garibaldi had behaved 'in the most laudable way' and that actually no public demonstrations had taken place.[16]

It is interesting that Garibaldi managed to make a favourable impression on a man like Alfonso La Marmora. Already, during the siege of Rome in May, La Marmora had expressed a confused – and perhaps not untypical – mixture of patriotic pride and conservative alarm at Garibaldi's achievements ('[t]he French have been taught a good lesson ... on the one hand, there is no harm in their being punished for the contempt in which they hold the Italians, but on the other hand what pride and folly will it arouse in the republicans?').[17] After their first meeting, La Marmora was more unreservedly enthusiastic, writing to army headquarters that Garibaldi 'has attractive features ... rough but sincere; I am ever more convinced that in the right hands we could come to an agreement'. A week later he was even more explicit about the positive impression made on him by Garibaldi:

Garibaldi is no ordinary man, his features however rough are very expressive. He speaks little and well: he has much discernment: I am ever more persuaded that he got into the republican party to fight and because his services had been rejected [by us]. Nor do I think he is now republican by principle. It was a great error not to use him. If a new war proves necessary he will be a man to employ. How he managed to save himself this last time is really a miracle.[18]

Garibaldi's decision to be a calming influence was rewarded by the Piedmontese authorities. They allowed him to see his family, were anxious to treat him with respect and gave him a 'grant' on condition he leave the country. Official policy was to play down Garibaldi's arrest, and to try to pack him off overseas as soon as possible: at first the authorities thought of Montevideo (where they even considered founding an Italian colony under Garibaldi's direction), then the United States and finally Tunisia.[19] A series of carefully conciliatory letters and articles were also published in various newspapers. One such letter appeared in Cavour's paper, *Il Risorgimento*; in it Garibaldi thanked the intendant of Chiavari for all his kindness and support;[20] the semi-official paper *La Legge* also stated that Garibaldi's 'language has been constantly that of a man who understands the necessities of the times, and who would not be even an involuntary source of discord';[21] while the conservative *Gazzetta di Genova*, in a report subsequently published in *La Gazzetta di Milano*, said he had shown 'much deference' to the government on arrival in Chiavari.[22]

Both Garibaldi's and the Piedmontese government's efforts at conciliation were, however, countered by the activities of the radical majority in the Piedmontese parliament. Members included the prominent parliamentarians Urbano Rattazzi and Angelo Brofferio, the editor of *La Concordia*, Lorenzo Valerio, and the deputies for Chiavari and Nice. In its report of 10 September, *La Concordia* had responded angrily to Garibaldi's arrest:

> With our hearts full of joy, we got ready to say to Italy: '*Garibaldi is safe!* He has managed to reach this faraway branch of Italy where the law rules, and the symbol of national thought, for which he accomplished and suffered so much, still waves in the wind above the towers of its cities!' [But] today a despicable and utterly unexpected event forces our hand to take up the pen and cry: Oh infamy! *Garibaldi is in prison!*

The radicals alleged that Garibaldi's arrest was designed to appease the Austrian government, with which Piedmont was still negotiating peace terms (although his arrest was more directly linked to concerns about public order in Genoa, where a major revolt in March had been repressed by a Piedmontese bombardment). Also on 10 September, Sanguinetti, the deputy for Chiavari, presented a petition to the Piedmontese parliament protesting about

Garibaldi's arrest, and this was backed up with a lengthy eulogy by Baralis, the deputy for Nice. Juxtaposing Garibaldi's supposed 'guilt' with the evidence of his accomplishments, Baralis insisted that Garibaldi was guilty of nothing 'but his own valour':

> guilty of having left Montevideo with his brave militia . . . guilty of having offered his sword, his life to the magnanimous Carlo Alberto . . . guilty of having maintained unsullied at Rome the honour of Italian arms, honour which had fallen elsewhere; guilty of having fought against the foreigner . . . guilty of having revived in the Latin land a longing for the Camilli, for the Scipiones; of having swollen the ranks of Carmagnola, of Sforza, of Zeno, of Ferruccio, of Sampieri . . . of having linked the force of Giovanni de' Medici of the *Bande Nere* with the bravery of his compatriot General Massena . . . guilty finally of having rejected the dictatorship of Rome which was offered to him by general acclaim, and of having tried to rescue the dying Venice, in whose deserted fields, tormented and pursued, he heartbreakingly lost his wife.[23]

By identifying Garibaldi with a historical tradition of Italian heroism, and juxtaposing this with a present vision of Italian decadence ('dying Venice') to make a political point, Baralis' speech is a striking indication of the spread of Risorgimento discourse as political rhetoric over the previous four years. These themes of death and redemption – and with them the glorification of Garibaldi – were emphasised again, and more succinctly, by Valerio in the same parliamentary debate:

> Garibaldi is a fellow-citizen, he is the first of our fellow-citizens, he saved the honour of Italian arms, he is martyr and hero of a holy cause, he is the love and pride of the nation, he has the right to our respect, honourable ministers. Imitate him if you can; if you don't know how to imitate him, respect him, but don't arrest him. (*General applause*)[24]

The next day a similar idea was repeated by Valerio's *La Concordia*. The paper warned its readers that the French government had sought Garibaldi's arrest so as to avenge his great challenge to the French army; it 'could not bear to see unpunished the man who had so effectively scorned their insult, throwing the famous phrase *Les Italiens ne se battent pas* into the face of the most distinguished General Oudinot'. In the same issue Garibaldi's letter to Valerio was published, in which he bemoaned the present political climate, recommended 'union and concord' and hoped that Piedmont might one day become 'the bulwark of Italian liberty and independence'. [25]

The radicals' immediate purpose was to use Garibaldi to attack the present government and to bring about a change in its policy towards France. As the deputy Baralis had put it to the chamber amid general cheering, 'perhaps a man blessed with extraordinary courage and integrity without parallel inspires fear in the government? The fear of an individual is a fault only of weak, cowardly and tyrannical governments.' It was also part of a crucial and ultimately successful struggle to safeguard constitutional guarantees in Piedmont and assert the independence of parliament. In the end, after quite lengthy discussion, a motion was passed condemning Garibaldi's arrest as 'contrary to the rights consecrated by the constitution and to the sentiments of Italian nationality and glory'.[26]

The parliamentary motion condemning Garibaldi's arrest was widely publicised, thanks largely to Valerio's efforts, and it formed a significant part of a fairly detailed coverage of the whole episode in the London *Times*.[27] However, the radical protest provoked a backlash from both the Catholic and the moderate liberal press. *Il Cattolico di Genova* criticised the defence of Garibaldi, implying that he was a shady character who was complicit in the death of his wife.[28] And in an article also published in the conservative *Gazzetta di Milano*, Cavour's moderate paper, *Il Risorgimento*, condemned the attack on the government. It 'deplored' the rhetoric and tactics used by the parliamentary radicals as merely 'theatrical', mocked Baralis' eulogy as nonsense and accused the radicals of having no serious interest in the law, in government or indeed in Garibaldi himself. Garibaldi, the paper insisted, was merely a symbol used to divert public attention from the pressing questions of the day: 'Garibaldi is not capable of inciting such rage as an individual or citizen. Garibaldi is an accident in the majority's power. He is a name, he is a system, he is a protest, he is a hope, he is one of many things that destiny prepares and sends out to unlucky peoples, when it is written up there that they should not benefit from free institutions.'[29]

Garibaldi sailed from Genoa bound for exile in Tunisia on 16 September 1849. Although the ten days spent on the Ligurian coast represent a relatively minor incident in his long political career, they are revealing in many ways. The behaviour and reactions of all the political groups and government officials involved are a testimony to Garibaldi's growing fame. If private letters, newspaper reports and parliamentary debates are anything to go by, Garibaldi's name was firmly associated with the currently prevailing, if still partisan, sense of national resurgence, and in particular with deeds of military valour which were seen as belonging to a specifically Italian tradition and which could be used as a rhetorical device to hide and/or belittle more prosaic political realities and interests. It is interesting that Garibaldi himself did little or nothing in these days to encourage such reactions. Presumably exhausted and clearly stricken with grief for the loss of his beloved wife, he played no part in the political furore over his arrest. Indeed he toed the government line to a conspicuous extent. Yet his reluctance to do anything but go home meant that he provided a blank space on which an explicit sense of historical identity and national pride could be inscribed, as well as being a more immediate focus for the hopes, fears and rivalries of Piedmontese politicians at a time of political crisis. Indeed, his disappearance in August, with only brief appearances thereafter, served to increase political fascination with him. The reported death of his wife, and his clear desire to see his 'old mother' and children, also introduced for the first time an element of private intimacy and sentimentality into his heroic reputation.

It became clear in these weeks how difficult it could be to direct or control Garibaldi's fame. Its effects were unpredictable. Garibaldi himself suffered as a result of them – being arrested on home territory as an unlawful immigrant. Subsequently, when he arrived in Tunisia on 19 September, he was refused entry by the Bey, who was frightened of Garibaldi's 'great renown' and feared 'that the mere fact of Garibaldi's disembarking could cause the eruption of a disorderly movement and demonstration in Tunisia'.[30]

In the weeks and months that followed Garibaldi's arrest at Chiavari, La Concordia sought to publicise his sad plight, and published letters and reports on his peregrinations from Tunisia to Sardinia, to Gibraltar (where he met with a frosty reception from the British governor), and on to Tangier, where he spent the winter.[31] La Concordia announced that, in Tangier, Garibaldi had found:

a land which welcomed him hospitably, and which gave him a peaceful refuge. There, neither government officials [intendenti], nor special commissioners, nor carabinieri ask for passports or are concerned for his security . . . in the land of the Bedouins, who eat men; and there he found a friendly and polite welcome, and the kind of peace which Europe and his ungrateful land have so rudely denied him!

Garibaldi wrote to the paper saying: 'Here among the Turks I can live in peace!'[32] In reality, Tangier marks Garibaldi's withdrawal from active politics. In a letter published in La Gazzetta del Popolo on 25 April 1850, he acknowledged receipt (in Nice) of a sword 'dedicated to me by the Italians', and a letter addressed by him to Valerio at La Concordia in June 1850 was published in that paper. Otherwise he spent his time writing his memoirs, and hunting and fishing: seeking to calm his soul 'so traumatised', as he put it, 'by the vicissitudes of a tempestuous life' and 'trying to shake off a kind of dreaded melancholy which for a time has possessed me'.[33]

New York

Garibaldi's letters reveal that money – or more precisely the lack of it – rather than politics was his main concern at this time. He was especially worried by the need to help maintain his mother and children. Out of his financial problems a plan developed to travel to New York, procure a boat and make a living as a merchant seaman.[34] Thus, in June 1850, Garibaldi left Tangier and stopped first at Gibraltar and then at Liverpool, where he spent a week. He then embarked on the *Waterloo* for New York, where he arrived on 30 July.

Garibaldi's brief visit to England received little press attention. *The Times* noticed his arrival in New York ('Garibaldi the celebrated partisan chief in the late wars of Italy and of Montevideo arrived a few days since')[35] but not his stay in Liverpool. *The Liverpool Mail* mentioned his visit to the city, but only after he left. However, the paper did display a fascination with the minute, if often inaccurate, narrative of Garibaldi's life and appearance, which was already becoming a commonplace in public perceptions of him. In a short passage the paper managed to reveal the following details to its readers: that Garibaldi's wife had died 'from fatigue' in the Apennines; that he had then reached the island of La Maddalena to be 'kindly treated and protected by the Sardinian government'; that 'his pecuniary affairs are said to be the reverse of flourishing'; that his mother was looking after his children in Nice; that he was well educated and spoke many languages fluently; that he had fought 'in the war of the Greek revolution, and served . . . under Lord Cochrane, at that time admiral of the Greek fleet'; that he was 'rather below the middle size, stoutly made, with an erect and soldier-like air; and that his manner was 'pleasing and lively, but . . . his demeanour . . . staid and grave'.[36]

Almost a week after Garibaldi's departure for New York, *The Red Republican*, a Chartist paper owned by the 'Jacobin in an English setting', George Harney, and an important vehicle for the views of foreign exiles in Britain after 1848–9, sought to give publicity to Garibaldi's stay in England. Introducing Garibaldi to its readers, the paper used the now familiar trope of denunciation and defence:

'The insufferable domination of Garibaldi and his band' formed the chosen theme, for weeks, of the newspapers subsidized by the great political parties. Reading their lucubrations, you would have imagined that the Roman General was a barbarian of the first order, and that his followers were little better than half-civilized savages. Other, and more impartial testimony, succeeds in proving diametrically the reverse of this. The combined spirit of high chivalrous honour and self-denying patriotism never exhibited itself more strikingly than in the case of the calumniated Garibaldi.

It also published a nine-verse poem ('Lines') by the Reverend John Jeffrey about 'one of the most brilliant episodes of Garibaldi's career, when he ... scattered in "rabble rout" the forces of the King of Naples'. In its way, the poem was very typical of a growing trend in British radical attitudes to Italy – a mixture of Protestant anti-Catholicism ('Popery'), simple juxtaposition of good and evil in the representation of Italian politics, and sheer fantasy in perceptions of Garibaldi:

> Garibaldi! Garibaldi!
>   Thrills the shout through street and square,
> While the legion of the hero
>   Gathers to its thunder there!
> But a handful seems the band,
> As with flushing cheeks they stand,
> Ardent at their chiefs command,
>   To rush forward on the foe, –
> And to crush the slaves of Naples
> By a first and final blow
> . . .
> Garibaldi! Garibaldi!
>   Towering foremost there of all,
> Moves he like destruction's Angel, –
>   Till in circle round him fall,
> Moved by his unresting blade,
> Those who hoped in gore to wade
> One day hence beneath the shade
>   Of St Peter's giant dome:
> 'Romans!' rings his watchword – 'hurl them
>   To the tyrant's hell, – their home!'[37]

Unlike his passage through Liverpool, Garibaldi's arrival in New York was anticipated some time in advance. Hearing of Garibaldi's decision to come to the United States, a welcoming committee of Italian republican exiles was formed. The committee consisted of Mazzini's correspondent from the early 1840s, Felice Foresti (also professor of Italian literature at Columbia University and the Roman Republic's official representative in New York), as well as General Avezzana (the ex-Minister of War in the Roman Republic), Quirico Filopanti (ex-secretary to the Roman triumvirs), and Antonio Meucci (the scientist and entrepreneur). On 26 July, the New York Daily Tribune, a left-leaning paper edited by the prominent labour reformer Horace Greeley, published a statement from '[t]he Italians in New York' that they accepted 'with feelings of gratitude the offers from American, French and other Friends of Liberty, to unite with them in honoring with a public procession the arrival of Gen. Garibaldi, the heroic defender of Liberty in the Old and in the New World'. Those who wanted to take part in the demonstration were asked to inscribe their name and corporation in a register at the Café de la République on Broadway. After his quarantine on Staten Island, it was planned that Garibaldi would be greeted on arrival at the Battery by Mayor Woodhall and that he would be taken to Astor House, where a 'splendid banquet' was to be held a few days later, with speeches in Italian and English. A committee of German and French socialists announced its intention to participate in the Garibaldi demonstrations; 'socialist citizens' were asked to gather at the Shakespere [sic] hotel to collect their red badges, 'as no other color than the red will be admitted'.[38]

There was nothing at all unusual about this kind of welcome. The failure of the revolutions in Europe had produced a stream of political refugees during 1850 and 1851, and various fund-raising exercises and publicity drives were held in New York to help them and their political cause. General Avezzana had arrived some six months before Garibaldi to a great reception. The *Tribune* had published a profile of Avezzana's life, he was presented with a sword, and an enthusiastic ceremony was held in his honour at the chapel of New York University, after which he was received in the City Hall by the mayor and his council.[39] Only a day before Garibaldi's arrival, the Venezuelan leader General Paez arrived as an exile in the city to another organised public greeting. The *Tribune* told its readers that he had 'come to seek, on our shores, the liberty he so vainly sought and suffered for in his own country', while the *New York Herald* dedicated its entire front page to a 'Brief memoir' of his life.[40] Moreover, these kinds of receptions continued to be organised throughout the early 1850s. The most sensational of its kind was for the Hungarian exile, Lajos Kossuth, whose arrival in Manhattan in December 1851 was greeted with 'such a scene as the world seldom beholds', according to the *New York Times*.[41] His speech was interrupted by crowds rushing the podium; there was a huge military parade on Broadway which echoed the exuberant welcome given in 1824 to the French 'hero of two worlds', Lafayette; street vendors did a brisk trade in Kossuth souvenirs ('"Kossuth" everything, from the most delicate lace to the grossest human food', according to the *Tribune*) and detailed descriptions of Kossuth's life and physical appearance appeared in all the papers. Kossuth and those with him were put up in a luxury hotel and enjoyed champagne, madeira and sherry at the expense of the New York government. He later embarked on a 'barnstorming' tour of the West.[42] Hugh Forbes, a British radical who had fought with Garibaldi in 1849, gave lectures on Italy and his experiences, at New York University.[43] Finally, the arrival in early 1853 of the 'hero-priest' Father Gavazzi, Garibaldi's former comrade-in-arms, was hailed as an important public event. There was great enthusiasm about his impressive personal appearance: 'Tall, well made and well-developed ... graceful yet impetuous ... [he] seemed the very symbol of sincerity and power ... his eyes flashing the fire of genuine eloquence'. His lectures in favour of religious liberty and against the Catholic priesthood also received considerable publicity.[44]

In other words, the reception planned for Garibaldi in New York was part of an American political tradition, as was the more general public and popular adoption of foreign exiles as political heroes. More specifically, American politicians and publicists were happy to use the 1848–9 revolutions in Europe for domestic purposes. Reactions to the revolutions, and the greeting given to the exiles, had become a means by which the USA 'took stock of itself'; public opinion in the USA used events in Europe 'to salute US revolutionary origins' and to consider America's political future at a time of growing tension over the issue of slavery.[45] In Garibaldi's case, public opinion was already well disposed, thanks to the publicity given to the Roman Republic by American writers such as Margaret Fuller. All of this suggested that there was great political capital to be made out of Garibaldi's stay in New York.

Yet Garibaldi refused to play any part in the celebrations planned for him. He arrived in Staten Island on 30 July and, after the quarantine, left quietly for Manhattan, from where he moved to the village of Hastings, some twenty miles north of the city on the Hudson river. In Hastings he wrote a letter, published in English in all the New York papers and in Italian in *La Concordia* and *Il Repubblicano della Svizzera Italiana*, in which he declined the honour of 'a public reception'. Pleading ill health and a slow recovery, he insisted that:

> No such public exhibition is necessary to assure me of the sympathy of my countrymen, of the American people, and of all true Republicans in the misfortunes which I have suffered, or of the cause out of which they have flowed. Though a public manifestation of this feeling might yield much gratification to me, an exile from my native land, severed from my children, and mourning the overthrow of my country's freedom by means of foreign interference, yet believe me that I would rather avoid it, and be permitted, quietly and humbly, to become a citizen of this great Republic of Freemen, to sail under its flag, to engage in business to earn my livelihood, and await a more favourable opportunity for the redemption of my country from foreign and domestic oppression.[46]

He spent much of September in Manhattan, staying with his fellow exile Felice Foresti in a friend's apartment on Irving Place, and in the autumn moved back to Staten Island and into the house of Antonio Meucci. During the winter on the island, he spent his time hunting and fishing, and trying to help Meucci by working in his new candle factory (which he said at least kept him warm).[47] He became involved with the affairs of the Italian committee and in helping Italian immigrants, and tried to mediate in the rivalries between the Mazzinian and non-Mazzinian exiles in New York; he also attended the funeral of Avezzana's wife and a concert in aid of Italian exiles. But in none of these activities did he assume a leading role.[48] Garibaldi's letters reveal that his greatest problem was boredom and a sense of idleness, and his major concern was to procure a boat and make a living as a merchant seaman.[49]

American politicians and journalists made various attempts to bring Garibaldi out of his self-imposed obscurity. The veteran politician General Lewis Cass, Democratic Senator for Michigan, ex-presidential candidate and father of the man who had apparently given Garibaldi an American passport in Rome, wrote Garibaldi a public letter of welcome to 'the land of freedom'. He praised Garibaldi for raising 'the standard of liberty upon the Capitoline Hill' and for reviving 'the sprit of ancient Rome amid the monuments of her power and glory'. He told him that his 'glorious exertions, followed by misfortunes born with equanimity, are a passport to the hearts and homes of my countrymen', and invited him to pay a visit to Washington.[50] There were also occasional mentions of Garibaldi in the newspapers. The *Tribune* expressed hope in his re-emergence, praising the 'modest and manly dignity' of his letter of 7 August and anticipating that 'a suitable opportunity may be afforded the public to testify their sympathy with the Italian cause and their regard for its chivalric soldier'.[51] *The Evening Post* published an article on 10 March 1851 which mentioned a projected expedition by the Italian exiles to Italy, and took the opportunity to produce an extended tribute to Garibaldi, whose 'name is a terror, not only to his treacherous countrymen, but to the forces of despotic Austria and disgraced France; [whose] little band of patriots, on every occasion, performed prodigies of valor, and [whose] brilliant defence of Rome, for bravery and skill, has seldom, if ever, been surpassed in the military annals'. According to his friend Foresti, Garibaldi also received 'frequent visits from prominent Americans and foreigners, love letters and expressions of admiration from all parts of the Union, as well as gallant offerings'.[52] Most notably perhaps, he met and impressed the poet Henry Tuckerman and the editor and writer Theodore Dwight.[53]

Dwight seems to have been entirely captivated by Garibaldi, and was keen to publicise his presence in the United States. He persuaded Garibaldi to give him a copy of his memoirs and to sit for a daguerreotype. With the help of Garibaldi and other exiles, Dwight produced the first book-length account of the Roman Republic, which was published in New York in 1851 as *The Roman*

Republic of 1849; with accounts of the Inquisition and the siege of Rome.[54] Although Dwight's main aim was to convince the American reader of a (somewhat unlikely but increasingly popular) theory that Italians were espousing Protestantism and were held back only by papal oppression,[55] the real hero of his account is Garibaldi. Garibaldi's exploits in defence of the Roman Republic take up about half of the book's pages, and it is Garibaldi who most symbolises all that is worthy of American help in Italy.[56] While Dwight damns Mazzini with faint praise (he 'has a great heart and is a pure and enthusiastic patriot: but he seems wanting in experience of men and things'), Garibaldi was '[w]ell fitted by nature to command, he is loved and respected by all who know him'.[57] Thus, in Dwight's hands, Garibaldi becomes a kind of all-American Protestant hero.[58]

The daguerreotype of Garibaldi (by the well-known photographer Marcus Root), reproduced as an engraving for the frontispiece to Dwight's *Roman Republic*, is strikingly different to previous representations of Garibaldi (see figure 7 below). No trace is left of the red blouse, flowing hair and passionate expression. In the portrait, Garibaldi strikes a quiet, gentlemanly pose, with a tree and rising sun in the background. He is still good-looking, but now well groomed in a dark double-breasted coat and neatly tied cravat, with tidy and well-trimmed hair and beard; and he gazes past the viewer with a calm, almost

7   Garibaldi in New York *c.*1851. This portrait shows a drastic change of image from the unconventional figure depicted in figures 2 and 5 above.

melancholy look in his eyes. Dwight presses this point home to his readers: Garibaldi is humble, honourable and physically attractive, with 'penetrating eyes, but . . . mild, gentle and amiable in address and manners, and frank, animated and winning in conversation'. He had an energetic and devoted wife and still has a loving family. He is both brave and steadfast. Garibaldi's 'bravery, perseverance and success in the service of his country, especially at Rome' are, for Dwight, 'equalled only by his decision, equanimity and fortitude during his astonishing retreat after the fall of the city, and the unbroken spirit he still displays after all his sufferings and afflictions.'[59]

None of these attempts at publicity came to anything. In April 1851 Garibaldi left New York for the Pacific Ocean. His friend Carpaneto had finally found a way to buy a ship for Garibaldi, and they sailed together on 28 April for Central America, arriving first in Nicaragua, after which they crossed the Panama isthmus and arrived in Peru in October. From December 1851 to January 1853, nothing more was heard from Garibaldi.[60] In late 1851, Mazzini wrote from London asking Garibaldi to lead an expedition to Sicily, but the letters failed to reach him.[61] During this time Garibaldi crossed the Pacific with a cargo of guano for Canton, and after a side trip to Manila he returned via Australia and New Zealand to Peru.[62] Noting his departure from New York, the *Tribune* wished him 'success in the new path he has chosen', and repeated its admiration for his 'modesty, simplicity and thorough integrity of character . . . pure patriotism and . . . unflinching bravery' as well as for his capacity for 'humble' work. Otherwise there was little public interest in his departure. There was not much more interest in his temporary return to the USA in the autumn of 1853, when he arrived in Boston with a cargo of copper from Chile.[63]

Garibaldi finally left New York for good in November 1853 and returned to Europe. Perhaps because the Piedmontese government had suggested he would be welcome once more on home territory if he agreed not to take part in politics, he travelled again as a merchant seaman, this time as master of a ship with a cargo bound for London and Genoa.[64] From Boston, shortly before leaving the United States, Garibaldi had written a bitter and emotional letter to his friend, Augusto Vecchi:

What can I say to you about my wandering life, my dear Vecchi? I thought that distance might lessen the bitterness in my soul, but sadly [*fatalmente*] this is not true, and I have dragged out a tempestuous existence without happiness, and embittered by memories. Yes, I still yearn for the emancipation of our land . . . although [I am] now worn out and dedicated, so people think, more to the stomach than to the soul, and I shudder at the probable idea that I will never again take up a sword or a gun for Italy.[65]

He told Cuneo that his physical powers were declining, although he hoped more than ever to die for his country. 'At one time', he wrote, 'I sought the affection of men, today I don't care any more, and if I could remove myself entirely from their company, I would believe myself happy.'[66] His main political concern during his last weeks in America was to restore good relations among the quarrelling Italian exiles in New York.[67]

Garibaldi's stay in New York seems a curiously downbeat episode in a career otherwise dedicated to the pursuit and exploitation of publicity for political ends. Why did he not make more use of the undoubted opportunities which New York had to offer? Some of the reasons were personal. On arrival in New York Garibaldi was crippled with rheumatism, 'obliged', in his own words, 'to disembark . . . like a package, by means of a swing hoist'.[68] He was devastated by the loss of his wife; his main aim, repeated often in his letters, was to keep busy and make money to support his mother and children; and he spoke little or no English. But there were political reasons for his inaction too. He was by his own account disillusioned politically, and his presence in New York, and especially the proposed reception for him, caused controversy. Many of his American supporters feared the involvement of socialists (or 'Red Republicans') while the Catholic Church in New York and the powerful Irishman, Bishop Hughes, in particular, were openly hostile to Garibaldi.[69] Thus, as had happened in Liguria at the end of the previous year, pressure may well have been put on Garibaldi to decline all public ceremonies in order to avoid public disorder.

It is also worth considering whether Garibaldi's decision to withdraw from public life was not itself part of a strategy, a 'performance' – however sincere – designed to attract sympathy and increase support for the Italian cause. His letters at this time, including his public letter to the New York papers, express a clear sense of mourning for his 'native land', for his 'beautiful and oppressed country', a mourning which is explicitly identified with his own lonely existence as an exile, bereaved and 'severed' from his children.[70] His 1851 daguerreotype shows a poignant figure in sombre clothes against a dark background, and he made many efforts to identify his personal loss with the greater political loss for Italy. The impression he made on Henry Tuckerman was of a man accompanied by '[s]ad memories . . . a widowed husband, a baffled patriot, an exile from the land for which he had so long toiled and suffered, his limbs racked with chronic pains incident to prolonged exposure; his dearest comrades banished or executed'.[71] In terms of 'staging' this sorrow for public purposes, it was surely more persuasive to refuse rather than entreat publicity and personal honours.

In order to gauge how effective Garibaldi's performance was, it is useful to compare his experiences in the USA with those of other contemporary

political heroes, like Kossuth and Gavazzi, who received such great receptions.
Both Kossuth and Gavazzi were fêted at first. However, Kossuth's speeches
alienated abolitionists and his barnstorming meetings frightened conservatives. Kossuth was quickly abandoned by his supporters – including Senator
Lewis Cass – during a presidential election year and he left the USA, only seven
months after his arrival, amid general indifference and ridicule.[72] Gavazzi's
speeches against the Catholic Church caused great offence; his lecture tour in
French Canada led to riots; and even in New York he was eventually
condemned for stiring up hatred among different American classes and
religions.[73] Garibaldi, by contrast, won widespread praise for his 'modesty',
'good sense', 'high character', disinclination for 'pomp and display' and
willingness to engage – like any other immigrant – in a 'humble occupation' as
a candle-maker.[74] Both Cass and Dwight publicly admired the contrast
between Garibaldi's glorious exploits in Rome and the 'equanimity' with
which he had borne his more recent 'misfortunes' and 'afflictions'. Moreover,
all these qualities – modesty, courtesy, steadfastness – were those exalted by
contemporaries as necessary virtues in American public life.[75] Garibaldi's
decision neither to take part in any reception nor to enter the American
political arena may well have been deliberate and was certainly fortuitous. In
this respect, Garibaldi's real achievement during his stay in the USA was to
have left American shores with his reputation intact.

Garibaldi's American exile also marks the moment when he leaves his
bandit persona behind him. Arriving in London in 1854, he described America
to the Russian exile, Alexander Herzen, as the country of 'forgetting the
fatherland', and he radically changed his image while in New York.[76] The 1851
daguerreotype/engraving of Garibaldi is remarkable for the respectability of
his personal appearance. The Garibaldi who returned to Europe in 1854 after
his 'second exile' was a different figure – older, perhaps sadder and certainly
more 'respectable' than the youthful romantic, the exotic and picturesque
rebel who had fought on the hills above Rome in 1849. A portrait of him in *The
Northern Tribune* shortly after his arrival in England confirms the change in
image. An engraving taken from another photograph, it shows Garibaldi in a
more aggressive pose than in 1851, gazing more firmly beyond the horizon,
but the dark coat remains, as does the tidier hair, as proof of his new, more
respectable social status and his gentlemanly qualities.[77]

As a political move, the change of image turned out not to be a bad one.
During his years away a great deal had altered on the European political scene,
and the Italian question had itself changed dramatically. A series of political
compromises in the aftermath of the 1848–9 revolutions, together with an
ongoing 'revolution' in literacy, publishing and the process of politicisation,
opened up new and different prospects for Garibaldi. Refusing public honours

in New York in 1850, he had said that he preferred to wait for 'a more favourable opportunity for the redemption of my country from foreign and domestic oppression'. The nature and effect of this opportunity, and the use which Garibaldi would make of it, became clear after he returned to Europe.

The 'decade of preparation'

Garibaldi's second exile, and the first real low point in his political career, coincided with the start of major changes both in Italian politics and in public opinion. These changes will be examined in detail in this and the following chapter since they are crucial to understanding all of Garibaldi's subsequent career, both as a military leader and as a national hero. First, although the defeat of the revolutions had demonstrated the international resilience of conservatism, by the mid-1850s the coalition which had sustained conservatives during 1848–9 was in crisis. Austria, the guarantor of conservative stability in Italy, suffered a serious blow to its international standing with the Crimean War of 1854–6; its refusal to stand by its ally, Russia, during the war broke up the conservative coalition, leading to Austria's diplomatic isolation and to particular tensions with Prussia and other members of the German Confederation.[78]

Austrian weakness might have been less serious had Italian conservatism managed to stabilise itself and gain consensus but, in the aftermath of revolution, Italy's conservative rulers made the (arguably understandable) mistake of shifting to the right. During the 1850s, Ferdinando II of Naples ignored the clear need for reform, including in the crucial areas of finance and administration, reimposed press censorship and rejected all compromise with even the most moderate of liberals, preferring to imprison them or send them into exile, while the Austrian authorities in Lombardy–Venetia also brought in censorship and pursued political repression, including executions, with apparent enthusiasm. In Rome, the restored Pius IX set himself firmly against liberalism. During the 1850s, he dedicated himself to matters of Catholic dogma, and left political matters in the hands of his capable but uncompromising Secretary of State, Cardinal Giacomo Antonelli, whose personal dictatorship attracted much political criticism and whose nepotistic tendencies and taste for wealth and luxury encouraged a series of attacks on papal 'corruption'. Once again, censorship, in the notorious form of the Papal Inquisition, was reintroduced. Such high-profile policies of reaction caused a storm of opprobrium and encouraged opposition to the conservative regimes both in Italy and from outside the peninsula. For perhaps the first time, Italian rulers became genuinely, if not universally, unpopular.[79] After the end of the Crimean War, and the shift in international relations away from Austria, they

were also faced with growing international condemnation of their governments. Most notably, at the Congress of Paris in February 1856, the British
minister, Lord Clarendon, raised the 'Italian question', criticising the Pope
and the Bourbons and expressing sympathy for Italian national aspirations.[80]

The problems facing conservatism in Italy opened up new opportunities for
the opposition, but the opposition itself experienced some surprising changes
in fortune. Reaction in 1849 had left only one Italian state – Piedmont – with
a liberal constitution, which limited the power of the monarchy, established an
elected parliament based on limited suffrage and guaranteed important civil
liberties, such as equality before the law and the right of association. There was
also a free press. Moreover, in 1849 the radicals formed a majority in the lower
chamber of parliament. But some two months after the debate on Garibaldi's
arrest had caused such a furore, the king, Vittorio Emanuele II, dissolved
parliament and called new elections, and threaten to revoke constitutional
concessions if the radicals' hostility to the crown was allowed to continue (the
proclama di Moncalieri). In these elections, the radicals suffered a serious
defeat. The moderate liberals, who had fought the election equally as royalists
and as defenders of the constitution, returned with a strong majority and
formed a government. Despite these rather shaky beginnings, the moderates
managed to bring about an extraordinary transformation in Piedmont over
the next ten years. Under, first, Massimo d'Azeglio and, after 1852, Camillo
Benso di Cavour, constitutional government was consolidated, the power of
the Church and the crown was contained, and the Piedmontese economy was
revolutionised through a series of measures which introduced free trade and
improved the country's financial infrastructure and transport system. These
transformations meant that, again for the first time, there existed a real and
successful alternative (a 'middle way' or juste milieu) to both conservatism and
revolution in the Italian peninsula.[81]

Still more worthy of note was the boost which moderate liberal government
gave to Piedmont and to the personal reputations of its ministers. Cavour used
his exceptional political talents to control parliament throughout the 1850s
and, although the scale and stability of his achievement can certainly be
questioned, the great skill with which he outmanoeuvred his opponents and
promoted his policies is undeniable. During this period, Cavour and his party
seized the political and ideological initiative from both the radicals and the
reactionaries in Piedmont. In particular, by creating what was termed an
'unlawful union' (connubio) between the centre right and centre left in the
Piedmontese parliament on the basis of opposition to left and right
extremism, and by establishing an alliance with the radical leader Rattazzi,
Cavour isolated the clerical right and gave the parliamentary radicals a choice
of being either with him and in power, or opposed to him and powerless. He

thereby threw the parliamentary radical movement in Piedmont into a confusion from which it never really recovered.[82] At the same time, the political and economic achievements of the moderate government in Piedmont, and Cavour's capacity to secure a role for Piedmont in European diplomacy especially after the Congress of Paris in 1856, lent a growing attraction to the Piedmontese 'solution' for liberals and radicals all over Italy. This allowed Cavour, in turn, to assume *de facto* leadership of the liberal movement in the Italian peninsula.

Of course, most moderate liberals, Cavour included, were not Italian nationalists. They were anti-Austrian and usually sought the expansion of Piedmontese power and influence; they all despised what Cavour called the 'deplorable influence' of Mazzini's unitarian ideals; and they saw Italian unification as mere 'foolishness'.[83] Yet here, too, a shift took place in the mid-1850s. Cavour became aware of the political advantages of encouraging nationalist feeling, while disillusioned Mazzinians formed the National Society to press for Italian unification under the leadership of the Piedmontese monarchy. These shifts reflected a great surge of political immigration, with an estimated 50,000 refugees arriving in Piedmont in 1849 and some 20–30,000 remaining thereafter. Especially in Turin and Genoa, the impact of these exiles on cultural life was striking and they helped hugely in making Piedmont the nucleus of a reinvented Italian nationalism.[84] In this respect also, Cavour showed a striking ability to adapt to changed circumstances, and to create and hold the centre ground. So by the end of the Crimean War in 1856, Cavour had not only extended his hold over Piedmontese politics, he had come to influence many aspects of the nationalist agenda in Italy as well.

The full significance of Cavour's achievement was to become clear during the climactic years of national unification in 1859–60. Yet already by the mid-1850s, the effect on the Mazzinians was all too evident. Despite enjoying enormous prestige among revolutionary exiles and in the Anglo-Saxon world as the leader of Italian nationalism (perhaps 'the great Italian of this century', according to one Englishman)[85] and a triumvir of the Roman Republic, Mazzini thereafter steadily lost support in Italy and amongst his own followers. In London, he established the National Italian Committee to promote nationalist activity in Italy, saying this represented a 'National Party' (later, 'Party of Action'). He continued trying to organise revolutionary conspiracies, first in Sicily in 1850–1 (which came to nothing) and more notably in Milan in 1853. But the Milan insurrection was a catastrophe for Mazzini. It was misconceived, badly led and poorly supplied, and it severely damaged his image as a revolutionary leader. One conspirator stole most of the money sent by Mazzini to fund the insurrection, and in the Austrian crackdown that followed, sixteen insurgents were executed. When the property of Lombards living in Piedmont was seized by the government, Cavour, not Mazzini, successfully posed as their defender against Austrian bullying. Mazzini even fell out with his fellow revolutionary, Lajos Kossuth, about the use of the Hungarian's name to encourage the uprising.[86]

Not all the Mazzinian conspiracies which followed – Lunigiana in 1853; Massa in 1854; the Bentivegna revolt in Palermo in 1856; Pisacane's expedition in 1857 – were directly organised by Mazzini, but he was widely blamed when they ended in disaster. Pisacane's expedition finished tragically at Sapri on the Calabrian coast with Pisacane's suicide amid the total indifference of the rural population, and the other conspirators were killed or imprisoned. Although Mazzini had not been closely involved in the planning of the expedition but had merely tried to assist Pisacane, the events at Sapri led to a wave of accusations of cowardice and fanaticism against him. Even when Felice Orsini became a hero in 1858 after his attempt to assassinate Napoleon III in Paris, Mazzini, who had deplored Orsini's action, was publicly condemned for it and sentenced to death *in absentia* by the high court in Genoa.[87]

Throughout the 1850s, there was also growing criticism of Mazzini from among his own supporters. A series of rival, and increasingly dissident, organisations were established which challenged his leadership and its base in London: the Latin Committee in Paris (1851) which argued in favour of a federal republic; the Military Committee in Genoa (1852) which sought the military direction of the revolution for itself and which, led by Giacomo Medici, became increasingly opposed to Mazzini; and most notably the afore-mentioned National Society, founded in 1857 by the hero of Venice, Daniele Manin, in Paris and by two exiles in Turin, Giorgio Pallavicino Trivulzio and Giuseppe La Farina. In a famous statement published in 1855, Manin had announced his conditional support of Piedmont ('Make Italy and I am with you. If not, not'). The following year, in a series of letters to 'Caro [Lorenzo] Valerio' and published in the important new paper, *Il Diritto*, Manin openly endorsed the Piedmontese monarchy and advocated political restraint;[88] and in a letter to *The Times* he seemed to criticise Mazzinian conspiratorial methods by declaring that the 'great enemy' of Italy in the present time was 'the doctrine of political assassination or . . . the *theory of the poniard*'.[89]

Although at the time Manin's attack was disapproved of by many on the left, his views increasingly became mainstream during the years which followed. The National Society quickly gained adherents and established local organisations in Piedmont, as well as important – if inevitably more clandestine – contacts in Lombardy, the central Italian duchies, Tuscany and the Romagna. According to its historian Raymond Grew, the formation of the National Society was 'the most dramatic sign that republicans were turning to Cavour, that nationalists would accept unification under Piedmontese monarchy, that the era of Mazzini was really over'.[90] Its methods of peaceful agitation and propaganda now looked more convincing, and won more middle-class and widespread support, than conspiracy and insurrection. In southern Italy, moreover, many began to look to Lucien Murat, the son of Napoleon's king of Naples, Joachim Murat, as a possible alternative to the Bourbon kings. Other revolutionaries continued to follow Mazzini's old rival, Nicola Fabrizi, who was based in Malta, and still others moved towards a more explicitly anarchist and/or socialist position. Their increasing emphasis on the South and Sicily as the new theatre for revolutionary action exasperated Mazzini.[91]

While Mazzini did retain a loyal core of supporters in Italy and among exiles abroad (Saffi, De Boni, Francesco Crispi), many more of them were irritated by his refusal to consult or take criticism, and they distanced themselves from him even where they did not openly endorse Piedmont. His old friend Jacobo Ruffini joked that 'Mazzini thinks he is infallible like the Pope'; the extremist Felice Orsini called him 'the new Mahommed'; and the more moderate Antonio Mordini defined him as 'the tyrant of our party'. Others tended to agree with the satirical poet Cesare Giusti that Mazzini's political clock had stopped in 1848.[92] At the beginning of the 1850s, Italian revolutionaries had suffered the demoralising effects of exile, persecution and financial hardship as a result of their activities. After the disaster of Pisacane's expedition to Sapri in 1857, they were 'deserted' by what Mordini called 'wealth and intelligence', and it became increasingly difficult to agree on a concrete programme with which to reach out and win popular support.[93]

Nor, ironically, did the creation of a myth of revolutionary action do much to help Mazzini. After 1849, a large number of revolutionaries and volunteers published their versions of events as memoirs or pamphlets. These did a great deal to make known what had happened in Rome and made heroes out of those involved.[94] But few were firm followers of Mazzini and they tended either openly to criticise him or to diminish his role. Mazzini also received a great deal of unfavourable publicity from ex-fellow travellers and conspirators. In 1856, the former London exile now living in Piedmont, Antonio Gallenga, published a two-volume history of Piedmont in which he revealed the story of a plot hatched by Mazzini in 1833 to assassinate the king, while during 1857 and 1858 La Farina's paper *Il Piccolo Corriere d'Italia* published a series of attacks on Mazzini, notably the letters of Orsini, which recounted details of Mazzini's treachery and cruelty to his followers.[95]

The break with Mazzini

Garibaldi's political disillusionment and tendency to seek a compromise with the Piedmontese government, evident as early as 1849, was thus part of a broader trend in nationalist circles which developed during the early to mid-1850s. Before leaving the United States for the second time, in 1854, Garibaldi had also seemed to support the idea of an alliance of nationalists under Piedmontese leadership and he expressed equal concern about the utility of Mazzini's methods and tactics ('he is full of hope and fire. I would like him not to act rashly. I am ready to give my life to my country, in any case. [But] I would like to do this to some profit').[96] After his return to Europe, Garibaldi increasingly distanced himself from Mazzini. The two men met in London after Garibaldi arrived there in February 1854, first at a meal on board Garibaldi's ship, and later with a number of prominent European exiles – Herzen, Kossuth and Ledru-Rollin, among others – at a dinner given by American diplomats to celebrate Washington's birthday. Although Mazzini and Garibaldi were by all accounts friendly to each other, henceforth they were in serious disagreement. Garibaldi refused once more to lead an expedition to Sicily.[97] In a somewhat garbled draft of a letter to Mazzini, dated 26 February 1854 (that is, after their first meeting), Garibaldi made his own position very clear:

> . . . or we can do things on our own, overthrowing foreign and domestic obstacles, or we can ally ourselves with a government in which we can place our hopes for Italian unity alone. I don't believe in the first concept, and there are many reasons for my conviction: scarce resources, the masses who can make a revolution are of no use to an army which can support it, not having the peasants fully with us; so I am sure that whatever our maxim, it will serve no other purpose than to make victims, discrediting and weakening the task of redemption. Allying ourselves to the Piedmontese government is a bit tough, I understand that, but I think it to be the best solution, and to combine in that centre all the different colours, which divide us; whatever happens, at whatever cost.[98]

Also in London in 1854, Garibaldi spoke to Alexander Herzen of his differences with Mazzini, and stressed that he was totally opposed to insurrection at that time.[99] Three years later, to his and Mazzini's English supporter, Jessie White, he reiterated that at the present time insurrections had 'no probability of success', that he refused to support 'laughable insurrections' which would make Italians a laughing-stock, and that in his view an alliance with Piedmont had great practical advantages.[100] More seriously for all concerned, he repeated the same anti-insurrectionary, pro-Piedmontese message in public. In London in March 1854 he wrote a (somewhat) restrained address to his 'Lombard friends' which simply stressed the importance of 'union . . . [and] combination of every element . . . at any cost, with the sacrifice, if necessary, of any system, however likeable'.[101] However, five months later, in Genoa, he wrote a letter to the prominent Mazzinian paper, *Italia e Popolo*, in which he told its readers that he had no intention of taking part in the current 'movements of insurrection', and that he felt it his duty to warn young people, eager to fight for 'the redemption of the fatherland', 'not to let themselves be so easily led astray by the easy insinuations of deceived or deceiving men [*uomini inganni o ingannatori*], who push them into untimely attempts which ruin, or at the least discredit, our cause'.[102] In 1855, he wrote an 'Italian programme', presumably intended for publication, which started with the words: 'First of all we must make Italy', and which went on to deplore the factionalism of Italian political life. The choice, according to Garibaldi, was a 'combination' under Piedmontese leadership or being 'destroyed' ('there is no middle way'), and he further recommended that this leadership be 'strictly dictatorial'.[103]

For Mazzini, Garibaldi's attitude was a source of enormous frustration. Mazzini had been unable to understand Garibaldi's departure for the Pacific Ocean in 1851 and his disappearance from politics for nearly two years. 'I don't know where the devil he is, nor how long he will take to come back', he wrote in November 1851, while in June 1853 he complained to Cuneo that there was still no news of Garibaldi, 'who is roving on the high seas far away, and whom I have uselessly tried to contact'.[104] He was briefly cheered by Garibaldi's arrival in London in February 1854, but was soon disillusioned by what he termed Garibaldi's 'vacillation'.[105] Although Mazzini hoped that he could control Garibaldi, as we have seen, Garibaldi refused to co-operate and in private correspondence at least Mazzini became much more hostile. The turning-point for Mazzini was Garibaldi's declaration against republicanism and insurrection published in *Italia e Popolo* in August 1854. 'What is this declaration of Garibaldi's?' he asked Nicolao Ferrari; to Emilie Hawkes he wrote, 'Garibaldi . . . has published a declaration against our Party. I begin to be like Nimrod, all hands against me, and I against all'; while to Nicola Fabrizi he described the declaration as 'cowardly'.[106] Just as 'shameful' and 'sickening' for Mazzini was the evidence that his old friend, Giacomo Medici, had encouraged Garibaldi to make the declaration: 'It is bad to allow Garibaldi to call us, who taught him patriotism, "ingannati o ingannatori": it is bad not to stand up resolutely for our own creed, for our own old friends'.[107]

The quarrel between Mazzini and Garibaldi would probably have been less significant had it not been carried out in public. As it was, the distance between them was intensified and publicised as part of a strategy of attack on Mazzinian loyalists in Genoa by the increasingly broad and pro-Cavourian liberal movement. For example, Antonio Gallenga writing in the pro-Cavourian paper, *Il Parlamento* (edited by Sicilian exiles hostile to Mazzini and with links to Giacomo Medici), immediately picked up on and wrote about Garibaldi's disagreement with the Mazzinian line on his arrival back in Italy.[108] Garibaldi's declaration against Mazzinian methods in *Italia e Popolo* was praised by the moderate papers. However, it met with a barrage of critical letters in the radical press, notably in the pages of *Italia e Popolo* and in the Turin paper, *Il Goffredo Mameli*. Most damaging of all was the dispute which erupted in print between Garibaldi and his old commander from the Roman Republic, Pietro Roselli. Already, in 1853, Roselli had published a pamphlet about the battle of Velletri (19 May 1849), in which he had attacked Garibaldi's conduct, accusing him of insubordination and of responsibility for the failure of this part of the campaign.[109] After Garibaldi's declaration, Roselli reiterated his accusations of the previous year in *Italia e Popolo*. Garibaldi, once again suffering from rheumatism which he acknowledged had put him in a terrible mood, was so angered by the attack that he challenged both the director of *Italia e Popolo*, Francesco Savi, and Roselli to duels.[110] In the end, a 'jury' had to be formed to resolve the dispute, with Medici and Enrico Cosenz acting for Garibaldi. Although it concluded that no offence had been caused to Garibaldi's honour, clear damage was done to personal relations.[111]

Garibaldi's behaviour after his return to Italy in 1854 diminished his standing in Mazzinian circles. As Mazzini put it, commenting on Garibaldi's declaration in *Italia e Popolo*: 'what is he doing? how is he alive to the state and wants of his country? To his own duties? Why does he not feel that the hour has come? and that one word from him and the military nucleus [of Medici] strengthening mine, their names coupled with mine, would be more than sufficient to rouse the people?' On the fallout thereafter, he was even less understanding, writing dismissively to Emilie Hawkes that 'Garibaldi has been walking up and down from place to place in search of duels with – the Italians who protested against his declaration'.[112]

None of this made good publicity and, even before Garibaldi's return, Mazzini had sought to promote another hero. The man was Silvino Olivieri, who had fought in the wars of 1848–9, and who spent the early 1850s leading an Italian legion in Buenos Aires against the dictator Rosas. Mazzini had published an article on Olivieri – 'La legione Italiana in Buenos Aires' – in *Italia e Popolo* of 2 January 1854, which was very similar in content and structure to the early publicity given to Garibaldi. It included a long letter comparing 'the valiant colonel' to Garibaldi and to the Bandiera brothers, and a series of 'official documents' testifying to Olivieri's bravery and selflessness, and to his fame and popularity in Argentina.[113] After the events of the summer of 1854, Mazzini wrote to Nicolao Ferrari in Genoa telling him explicitly to promote Olivieri, as 'he will one day perhaps be our *remplaçant* for Garibaldi'.[114] And although Olivieri was murdered, trying to organise a colony

('New Rome') in Bahia Blanca in Argentina, Mazzini's opinion of Garibaldi did not improve. He persisted in his hope that Garibaldi could be won back for republicanism, but was now consistently disparaging about his political abilities: 'Garibaldi will never start anything', he told Cuneo in November 1855; 'he will follow us if we make it, the monarchists if they make it.' To his English friend Jessie White he was even more forthright:

Garibaldi is good: he loves his country and hates the Austrians; but Garibaldi is *weak*. Therefore, changeful. I believe that he has been really ensnared by the Piedmontese Ministry; I believe that he feels himself now deceived by them . . . Moreover, he believes that I distrust him; therefore, he distrusts me. I do not believe that a cordial understanding can ever take place between us; still I believe . . . call me jesuitical for that . . . even the appearance of such [an understanding] would do good to Italy.[115]

Unfortunately for Mazzini, it was the 'appearance' of quarrelling and disagreement which was the most visible aspect of the democratic movement in Italy in the mid-1850s. Along with Manin's denunciation of Mazzinian methods, Garibaldi's disagreement with Mazzini and the Mazzinians was one of the most public manifestations of what had gone wrong, in terms both of dealing personally with the bitter legacy of 1848–9 and of developing a strategy for responding to moderate liberalism in Piedmont and to political reaction in the rest of Italy. The first beneficiary of this disarray, and of Garibaldi's disaffection as a result of it, was the National Society. Between 1856 and 1859, the National Society largely filled the political vacuum left in nationalist politics, and in Garibaldi's life, by the apparent failure of Mazzinianism. Garibaldi was among the first officially to join the Society by signing its programme, writing to its president, Pallavicino, that '[t]he ideas expressed by you are mine, and . . . I am proud to accompany you in any political demonstration'.[116] His presence was to prove 'in the next two years . . . one of the Party's greatest strengths'; for Pallavicino, they had won the name that would 'add prestige'.[117] Garibaldi also accepted a post as the Society's vice-president, and he even went so far as to write to one supporter that '[t]he National Society is Italy, it is the whole nation!'[118]

Garibaldi's relations with the National Society, and especially with its secretary, Giuseppe La Farina, came to benefit Cavour as well. Cavour was initially very wary of Garibaldi (as he wrote in 1854, 'if he is only coming back to see his family and children, we won't bother him at all; but if he intends to come here to carry out Mazzini's business, we won't tolerate his presence here for one minute'),[119] but gradually, faced with the more 'gentlemanly' Garibaldi and influenced by La Farina, he came to appreciate the advantages of an alliance with him.[120] The two men were introduced by La Farina for the first time in August 1856, and Cavour was said to have been friendly and courteous. They met again in December 1858, at which point Cavour let Garibaldi into some aspects of his plan for provoking a war with Austria. Cavour and Garibaldi apparently met on more than one occasion in the months that followed. In March 1859, Cavour also introduced Garibaldi to the king of Piedmont, Vittorio Emanuele II, and some kind of trust and sympathy seems to have developed between the two men.[121]

Yet despite his friendship with the Piedmontese government, Garibaldi's own political beliefs were much more ambiguous. He never gave up on the idea of revolutionary expeditions. In 1854, at the same time as he told Herzen that he was opposed to insurrections, he extolled the virtues of a seafaring life where, in his words, he and his followers might sail 'over the ocean, hardening ourselves in the rough life of sailors, in conflict with the elements and with danger . . . A floating revolution, ready to put in at any shore, independent and unassailable!'[122] Although he refused to take part in Pisacane's 1857 expedition, throughout 1855 and 1856 he had been quite prepared to help and even to head another expedition to liberate prominent political prisoners being held on the island of Santo Stefano off the coast of Naples.[123] He tried to enlist the National Society's support in persuading Piedmont to pay for three ships in a major campaign which he planned for the spring of 1857.[124] Nor had he abandoned the quintessentially Mazzinian idea of political sacrifice and martyrdom. Refusing to take any part in Pisacane's disastrous expedition, he made his own position very clear to Jessie White:

> if Garibaldi was sure of being followed by a distinct majority . . . and even with a small chance of success, oh my Jessie! do you doubt that I would throw myself, with a feverish joy, into the fulfilment of this idea which has been my whole life, even if the only compensation was the most terrible martyrdom . . . My life is there, for Italy, and my idea of paradise is to take up arms for her. Happiness, a wife, children would not be enough to hold me back and nothing will hold me back when it is a question of the holy cause.[125]

'The years have rather worn me out,' Garibaldi told Cuneo two months later, 'but I am proud to tell you that I have kept my soul together.'[126]

Towards unification

In the 1850s Garibaldi abandoned Mazzini and republicanism for practical reasons but he remained dedicated to Mazzini's nationalist ideals. As he never tired of repeating, Garibaldi believed in the alliance with the Piedmontese monarchy and army but he was equally convinced by Mazzini's religious vision of the nation and by the idea of revolution leading to national redemption.

As an ideological choice, this position was extremely ambiguous. Raymond Grew tells us that, like Garibaldi, the whole of the National Society felt that 'the love of the fatherland [was] . . . a religion', and that the men of the Society were convinced they pursued a 'holy goal'. Pallavicino wrote that the virtues most valued by this 'religion' were a 'disinterested, fervent, holy love of public life', a 'religion of sacrifice' of men with the 'strongest convictions' and 'immaculate lives', and 'civil heroism . . . that faces long martyrdom'.[127] Yet by allying themselves to the Piedmontese monarchy, to an essentially pragmatic, and in many ways conservative, political tradition, and to Cavour, the most opportunistic of politicians, the National Society not only relegated revolution to a secondary phase, they also deprived it of its moral 'vitality'. As Grew comments: 'The concept of the Risorgimento was being changed from a revolution that would remake society to a merely political change brought about by the force of arms'.[128] At the same time, neither Garibaldi nor anybody else ever fully acknowledged this ideological shift. Instead, national unification became a vague and generic imperative, postponing all other decisions, and this catch-all aim obscured all kinds of other political divisions and unresolved issues. The alliance between religion and pragmatism, however productive in political terms, was never entirely clear in either its methods or objectives. Hence, it is not to be wondered at that Garibaldi's involvement with the National Society, and above all with Cavour and the Piedmontese state, came to cause a whole series of equivocations, misunderstandings and betrayals.

Even in practical terms, Garibaldi's attitude could cause difficulties. After the retreat from Rome and the death of his wife in 1849, Garibaldi had been very reluctant to commit himself to political action, and this reluctance persisted following his return to Europe in 1854. In fact, despite his previous reputation as a man of action, there was a curious passivity and lack of real initiative in much of Garibaldi's political activity during the 1850s, and this had a long-term impact on perceptions of him in democratic circles. His attitude was very clear in England in 1854, especially during a visit to Newcastle which he made to buy coal for transport to Genoa. Although the British radicals in Newcastle, led by Joseph Cowen, were keen to hold a demonstration in his honour, Garibaldi refused, and they had to be content with giving him 'an address of welcome and sympathy' and a sword and telescope. In his introduction to the address, Cowen even acknowledged Garibaldi's 'personal dislike' of publicity and added: 'We beg to assure you . . . that we are not here as vulgar *lionizers*'.[129] Over the next couple of years, Garibaldi spent a great deal of time travelling privately as a merchant seaman and away from the political arena. The death of his brother, Felice, in late 1855 partly resolved the financial problems which had obliged him to work for a living, and in early 1856 he used the money inherited from his brother to purchase half of the remote island of Caprera off the north-west corner of Sardinia, where he would then retreat for long periods each year. His life at Caprera removed him from a great deal of the mundane but crucial political activity in nationalist circles in Turin, Genoa and elsewhere in 1857 and 1858.[130]

While Garibaldi gradually came out of his self-imposed political retirement through his involvement with the National Society, he did so on a sporadic and fitful basis. Indeed, after his purchase of Caprera, he developed a lifelong habit of suddenly appearing on the political scene and then disappearing back to Caprera, sometimes disrupting other political action and processes. In a strange way, therefore, he continued to live in exile even after his return to Italy. Although the leaders of the National Society in the 1850s were interested as much in the prestige of his name as in his physical presence, Garibaldi's distance from the daily grind of nationalist activities was still unhelpful. It did little to alleviate the ordinary problems of organisation, assistance and finance which beset many parts of the broader movement. It also constrained his own ability to manoeuvre politically, reducing his knowledge of political develop-ments as well as his capacity to engage in, and influence, political debate or manage events. Already in 1854, over the dispute with Roselli, Garibaldi's lack of political expertise had damaged his personal reputation, and he failed fully to regain the respect of many nationalists thereafter. In 1857, he was only the third man to join the National Society, and although by so doing he saved the whole project – since everyone else in Genoa had refused to sign up – he seemed unaware of this vital fact. Unlike Manin, who managed to maintain a certain distance from the Piedmontese government, Garibaldi gave his open and unconditional support to the same. He subsequently allowed himself to be controlled by La Farina in gaining access to Cavour and, as we shall see in Chapter 6, by Cavour as well in the lead-up to the war of 1859.[131]

Garibaldi found personal happiness at Caprera. He began to build a South-American-style bungalow and went hunting and fishing almost daily. He started to reclaim and cultivate the land, and he planted trees and raised livestock. His diaries from Caprera have survived and are proof of his enthusiasm for, and commitment to, farming the land.[132] Various political friends, like Nino Bixio, came to stay and Garibaldi brought his children there so they could grow up 'strong and active like children of the fields'. His letters speak of the curative powers of gardening, the mild climate and the crystal-clear water.[133] Until it was wrecked in a storm, he also had his own sailing boat which allowed him to move around the Mediterranean as he liked. We can speculate that, for Garibaldi, Caprera represented a kind of ideal romantic socialist community, its inhabitants living in harmony with nature and bound to each other by the ties of hard work and love. When the anarchist Michael Bakunin visited Garibaldi in 1863, he pronounced the little community working in the fields at Caprera to be the prototype of 'a democratic social republic'.[134]

Moreover, Caprera could be said to have served a quite notable political purpose. At Caprera, Garibaldi could hide from his public, and his manifest desire to do so is perhaps an indication of the growing personal burden of his fame. The political importance of privacy, and of the beneficial effects of the island for his health, should not be underestimated, given how serious and incapacitating Garibaldi's attacks of rheumatism had already become. In addition, the near-total seclusion allowed him to pursue various intimate relationships with a series of rich, educated women more or less simultaneously and in complete privacy: first an engagement with the wealthy British widow, Emma Roberts, then a close friendship with her travelling companion, Jessie White, and a relationship with an Italian countess, Maria della Torre (who wrote to him of her pride at being chosen 'as your companion'). He subsequently had a long love affair with the German baroness and writer, Esperanza (or 'Speranza') von Schwartz, to whom he proposed marriage; although she rejected him, she continued to write him passionate letters and to assure him of the 'unbounded affection which I feel for you and will *always* feel for you'. Throughout this time, Garibaldi also enjoyed a sexual relationship with his housekeeper at Caprera, Battistina Ravello, with whom he had a daughter, Anita, in the spring of 1859.[135] In terms of an overall strategy of political display, Caprera was where Garibaldi could go 'backstage', where he could relax and step out of character for a while.[136]

Arguably just as crucial from a political point of view, at Caprera Garibaldi could discuss strategy and plan another 'performance' without being observed by outsiders. By living in Caprera, Garibaldi could control access both to himself personally and to his public appearances and the part he had to play. As Garibaldi's island home, Caprera soon acquired a mythical status of its own, and was to become a kind of second, more privileged, stage in itself.

CHAPTER 5

THE GARIBALDI FORMULA

Print culture and the performance of politics

It is ironic that the Mazzinian movement suffered its greatest setbacks and schisms at a time when the propaganda methods which it had pioneered were being vindicated. Perhaps especially, the changes of the 1850s showed that Mazzini's faith in writing and the printed word as a vehicle for the production and dissemination of nationalist ideas had not been misplaced. In fact, the repression of the 1850s and the restrictions it imposed on press and other cultural and social activity did not really manage to close the new space for political action opened up by the 1848–9 revolutions, and one reason for this was the 'revolution' in reading and publishing sweeping Europe. It was also during the 1840s and 1850s that the market for literature expanded at an extraordinary rate, and it becomes possible to speak of the emergence of modern mass-media print. This phenomenon is worth exploring in some detail as it explains much about public support for national unification in Italy and about the popularity of Garibaldi in particular.[1]

Modern mass-media print developed as the result of a transformation in both supply and demand. Since the eighteenth century, the industrialisation of the printing process had, by the 1840s, made 'the printed word both cheaper and more readily accessibile than it had ever been before'.[2] Supply was also helped by a general increase in mass communications, and specifically by a wide-ranging improvement in transport and distribution networks. Equally, the expansion of the market was the result of a rapid extension of the reading public. During the 1840s and 1850s, first in Britain and the USA, then in France, Germany, and – to a much lesser but still significant extent – Italy, the market for the printed word grew very quickly. This growth was due to a series of factors such as popular education, which led to rising literary rates (for instance, in Britain around 60 per cent of people could read in 1850, and more than 90 per cent in 1900) among populations which were also increasing; the concentration of the same populations in urban areas; the gradual prominence of an educated middle class and, in many places, the reduction of censorship and/or of government duties, which helped to reduce prices further on printed works and boost circulation. The growth in a taste for, and pleasure in, reading is also suggested by the increasing number of books available; for example, in France there were 6,739 titles published in 1830; this had risen to 11,905 in 1860 and 14,195 in 1875.[3] The number of libraries grew in this period, especially in the USA and Britain (where some free libraries were established after 1850), and so did bookshops, which spread throughout provincial towns and became a feature of railway stations.[4] Periodicals could be sold on the street or by colportage, that is, by travelling salesmen going from house to house selling subscriptions and making deliveries; by the same means periodicals, almanacs, pamphlets and flyers (often satirical or sensational *canards*) were also sold in rural areas at fairs or in public spaces in country villages.[5]

For the first time in the 1850s, all kinds of newspapers and magazines achieved a true mass circulation. For example, in Britain, the radical *Reynolds's Weekly Newspaper* achieved a circulation of around 50,000 in 1855 (and reached 150,000 by 1865); the satirical magazine *Punch* had a circulation of 40,000 in the same period. Among daily newspapers, *The Times*' circulation figures were consistently between 50,000 and 60,000, but reached between 90,000 and 108,000 on several occasions, while the mainstream weekly *The Illustrated London News* had a circulation of 123,000 in the mid 1850s (up from 67,000 in 1850).[6] In Germany, Ernst Keil's illustrated family magazine, *Die Gartenlaube*, reached a circulation of 60,000 within four years of its foundation in 1853, and 180,000 by 1863; while in France, the anti-clerical, left-wing paper, *Le Siècle*, achieved a print run of over 52,000, despite the difficult conditions and censorship prevailing under the Second Empire.[7] All these papers went on to publicise the 'Italian Question' during the 1850s and to give a high profile to Garibaldi in the years of unification. Circulation figures in Italy itself were, as we shall see below, much lower but it is worth remembering that throughout Europe the increase in the reading public was far greater than these figures suggest. Magazines and newspapers appeared, along with books, in lending libraries and reading rooms, and they were also to be found in cafés and other public meeting places and, especially in rural areas, they were often read aloud. So it is very likely that several people may have read or otherwise been exposed to a single copy of a magazine or paper.

An equally significant trend was the diversification in print production. Of particular importance to understanding the broad appeal of Italian nationalism for public opinion was the emergence of illustrated news, popular periodicals, family and/or women's magazines alongside the expansion of more traditional printed materials like books, newspapers, pamphlets and learned periodicals. These new magazines offered news items alongside articles of historical interest, essays on self-improvement, general interest stories, serialised novels and advice on fashion, taste, cooking and gardening. A real innovation came from the rapid engraving techniques pioneered by *The Illustrated London News*, established in 1842, which meant that henceforth not only were historical anecdotes or general features accompanied by images but the latest news items could quickly be illustrated as well. It was for this reason, as we saw in Chapter 3, that *The Illustrated London News* sent an artist to Rome in 1849, and that his pictures of the fighting and of the *garibaldini* were rapidly available and used to supplement contemporary accounts of the siege. Since this format was accessible to a very wide public, it quickly became popular and spread rapidly. To give just a few examples: after *The Illustrated London News* in 1842, *L'Illustration* of Paris and *Die illustrierte Zeitung* of Leipzig commenced publication in 1843, followed by *A Illustraçao* in Lisbon in 1845, *Il Mondo Illustrato* in Turin and *The Lady's Newspaper and Pictorial Times* in London in 1847, *Die Gartenlaube* in Leipzig in 1853, and *Frank Leslie's Illustrated Newspaper* and *Harper's Weekly* in New York in 1855 and 1857 respectively.[8]

At the same time, and for similar technological and cultural reasons, there was a general expansion in the market for graphic culture. Books were suddenly full of illustrations, and these could serve a serious scientific or technical purpose; they could also, along with magazines, inform and entertain those with enough time and money to read but not quite enough education to do so easily. Illustrations also led to the diversification of books, from large-format albums to de-luxe editions and travel guides; small illustrated books – 'keepsakes' in Britain; *Taschenbücher* in Germany; *physiologies* in France – were very collectable and made popular gifts, especially for women. The vogue for satirical papers, pamphlets and flyers, such a feature of mid-century political life in Europe, was due in no small measure to the ease with which drawings and caricatures could be reproduced. By the 1840s, short story boards or cartoon strips were also being prepared and printed for mass consumption.[9]

Another manifestation of this same technological trend, of great relevance in understanding the fame of Garibaldi, was the mass production of cheap engravings of saints, historical figures and contemporary personalities. Portraits of famous people became a common feature of illustrated magazines and books, and printed portraits were also popular and indeed became fashionable as individual items: produced and sold in large numbers, and then altered and re-copied several times over to an apparently insatiable public. The fashion for portraits of the famous was intensified by, first, the invention of the daguerreotype (used as the basis of numerous engravings) and then the commercialisation of photographic portraits as *cartes de visite* in the late 1850s. The latter became 'collectable', and were used especially by women in the exchange of gifts and as the basis of sometimes elaborate, hand-painted albums.[10] Some historians talk of the creation by photography of a 'cult of celebrity' from mid-century onwards. Actors, artists and political leaders came to use photographic portraits of themselves as a means of self-promotion through the mass circulation of their image: photography was able to create a sense of immediacy, realism and familiarity.[11] Paradoxically, this kind of fame reflected not just the ubiquity of the printed image but also the emergence of the actor, artist and political leader as exceptional or charismatic figures in their own right.

The 'revolution' in print culture meant that mass communication was now possible in practical terms, via a range of print media which offered different kinds of information in a variety of forms to cater to the diverse tastes of the reading (and, in the case of visual prints, non-reading) public. The writing of fiction was especially affected by this change. Although the price of books seems to have lagged behind the transformation of production, during the 1850s cheap editions and reprints of popular novels began to be produced. Moreover, in a format which proved commercially successful everywhere from the 1830s, much popular fiction was also issued in 'parts' – as 'story papers' in the USA, *feuilletons* in France or *romanzi d'appendice* in Italy – appearing in regular weekly or monthly instalments to be purchased over the course of a year or two. This fiction was sometimes abridged and/or serialised in the new magazines or popular newspapers, and a great deal of the more successful fiction was translated into foreign languages. Not only did part-issues and serialisation greatly increase the availability and circulation of fiction, they also helped to change the genre itself. Since the market was constructed around maintaining a regular supply and demand for fiction, such fiction was based on conventional narrative formulas which guaranteed sales: thus adventure stories, historical novels, adventure romances, crime and sensation novels became extremely successful serial forms in both Britain and France and, from the 1850s, in Italy as well. Stories which proved commercially successful were then republished in cheap editions, perhaps most famously in the 'dime novels' which became so popular in the United States from the 1840s onwards.[12]

Hugely popular too were books on any number of historical subjects. The memoirs and letters, biographies and autobiographies of famous men like Nelson, Napoleon and, as we shall see, Garibaldi, proved strong sellers. Perhaps most noteworthy was Napoleon, who took on a new – more liberal and more romantic – image after his death, thanks to a series of published memoirs. These contributed significantly not only to the creation of a Napoleon myth but also to its constant refashioning during the course of the nineteenth century.[13] More generally, biographical works of various kinds took their place alongside, and overlapped with, an equally popular and widespread religious and morality literature, as well as self-help manuals and books on cooking, medicine, gardening and so on.

By the middle of the nineteenth century, in other words, publishing in Britain had become what has been described as 'a major, multi-million pound industry that both benefited from and contributed to the more general economic and technological developments of the Victorian period'.[14] In France, this was 'the age of the publisher', when book and newspaper publishers built empires and came to be among the most powerful and wealthy figures of middle-class society.[15] Best-selling authors of serialised novels – perhaps most obviously Scott, Dickens, Thackeray and Trollope in Britain; Hugo, Dumas, Sue and Sand in France; D'Azeglio in Italy – could also make money and they certainly became well known, often in more than one language and country. For example, Sue's *Les mystères de Paris* and *Le juif errant* each sold between 50,000 and 70,000 copies between 1841 and 1850, and sales of both were helped by translations into English, German and Italian. In the four years between 1846 and 1850, global sales of Dumas' *Le comte de Monte Cristo*, *Les trois mousquetaires* and *La reine Margot* together may have reached 90,000 copies.[16]

Although the audience for much of this literature was predominantly middle class, a crucial sign of the industry's modernity was its increasing differentiation according to the reading market, and the emergence of a number of important new groups with their own dedicated publications and/or publishers. Especially worthy of note in this period are the growing number of women readers and the diversification of styles and genres within the production of specifically women's fiction and women's magazines. Equally significant in the long term was the gradual development of fiction and non-fiction books, and school textbooks, for children and young people.[17] Already in 1840s Britain, the working-class reading public had its own fiction 'comprising "penny bloods", plagiarisms of mainstream fiction ... and translations of racy continental fiction', along with a number of sensational Sunday newspapers, so much so that by the 1850s there was both intense competition within the popular press, and official concern being expressed about its corrupting influence on the reader.[18] As noted, printed matter could and did reach the countryside via travelling salesmen who relied on the sale of ephemeral material and visual images. The latter in particular can be seen as, in Eugen Weber's words, 'the great bibles of the little people', with a huge impact in isolated rural areas where people had little other visual material to distract and entertain them.[19]

All these trends in publishing and reading should not be overestimated, especially in the case of Italy. The equally revolutionary effect of the printed word and image on eighteenth-century popular culture and politics is widely recognised. It is also worth noting that many of the features described here took full shape only after the 1870s, and that the spread of the reading public was by no means uniform across any national territory. There was also a huge practical gap between the ability to sign one's name (the accepted test for literacy) and reading for pleasure. Nevertheless, the emergence of a more popular literature is of real significance in understanding the political changes of the mid-nineteenth century; specifically, it can help to explain various reactions to the events which occurred in Italy in 1859–60 and the public resonance of Garibaldi's actions. First, it was in this kind of literature that the symbols and tropes of romanticism became part of popular culture. Popular romanticism produced 'patriotic songs, stormy melodramas, gothic romances, and national histories', and it was through this literary and dramatic medium that Garibaldi reached a broader public.[20] Second, as Benedict Anderson points out and as Mazzini had already understood in the early 1830s, the rapid expansion of 'print-capitalism' played a central role in the fashioning of national identity, in that reading books, periodicals and printed images could create a sense of community (however imaginary) by allowing people who had no knowledge of each other, and who lived in different places, to share the same experiences and have the same responses to stories and events in which they had no part.[21] As Mazzini also realised after arrival in England in 1837, the technologies of mass communication could be used to encourage and spread such feelings of empathy far beyond any 'natural' boundaries of national community. By the middle of the nineteenth century, the effects of this nationalising and internationalising print-capitalism had become more widespread. It also became evident that the polite and/or liberal public sphere could no longer be sure of its monopoly of public debate now that it faced increasing competition from, and overlap with, radical and popular culture.[22]

The press – especially newspapers and pamphlets – had always played a direct role in helping to create public opinion and in mobilising it behind political issues but, with the change in scale and scope of press activity in the mid-nineteenth century, relations between press and politics became closer and more immediate. In many mid-nineteenth-century papers and maga-zines, articles with a political content were interspersed with popular stories or advice on household matters, and in this way politics became more ubiquitous and part of daily life. At the same time, the language of popular fiction overlapped with the language of politics. Perhaps most notably, the narrative structures of fiction lent themselves to – and were used explicitly in – the

construction and sale of a political message. Marilyn Butler has observed that
the French Revolution was 'told like a story': it was represented by its
protagonists and adversaries, and received and understood by the public, as a
series of narrative plots through the medium of reading. In this way, narrative
made certain political futures 'thinkable', and excluded or devalued others.[23]
As a result, the language and representation of politics changed definitively.

The effect on politics was intensified by a parallel expansion in popular
entertainment. Especially in the major centres like London and Paris, the
number of new theatres and plays grew rapidly (an estimated 260 new plays
were put on every year in Paris during this period), and new popular genres
developed, such as melodrama, vaudeville and historical drama, in which
songs and dance were a prominent feature.[24] Popular theatre altered the
nature of the 'public' and the performance of politics by making them both
more spectacular and more accessible. It created a new awareness of the
national past by reproducing it as a spectacle for popular consumption and
entertainment: theatre, in other words, acted as a site for the staging of
national (as opposed to classical) history and political ideology. In so doing,
however, it could also become a means of challenging political orthodoxies
and celebrating alternative values.[25] The subversive potential of popular
theatre as political expression was demonstrated clearly by the explosion of
protest around the play *Roma* in 1849, as we saw in Chapter 3 (see pages 80–1),
and by the growing popularity of 'Napoleon plays' in Paris during the
1820s and '30s.[26] Equally interesting was the development of new methods of
staging and acting, and especially important for our purposes was the
emergence of the author and, in particular, the actor ('celebrities' like
Frédérick Lemaître and Jenny Lind) as artistic personalities with a recognised
public role and admired for their emotive and realistic performances. The use
of new optical technologies (the wax display, the Panorama, the phantasmagoria), both inside theatres and as separate shows, attracted large audiences
and 'spectacularised' public entertainement.[27] All these new techniques altered
the relationship between performance and audience and came, in turn, to
affect the structure and presentation of relations in the public sphere more
broadly.

In the course of the nineteenth century, the alliance between politics and
entertainment was democratised. Political radicals in Britain were at the
forefront of commercial publishing, and made the popular press, and
periodicals in particular, a portal through which 'non-respectable' Victorians
could enter the public sphere. Radicals like Ernest Jones turned to publishing,
while writers like George Reynolds embraced mass culture and linked serial
fiction to radical politics; '[i]n the process . . . [they] showed the tremendous
potential of popular fiction for shaping and transmitting a popular political

consciousness'.[28] New political leaders tried to seize control of this process, actively offering themselves as the physical embodiment of a collective identity, and they constructed and publicised their own life stories as the narrativisation of popular demands.[29] They 'began to be judged as believable by whether or not they aroused the same belief in their personalities which actors did when on stage'.[30] Political meetings and demonstrations came to resemble popular theatre, with songs, banners, portraits and the use of elaborate illuminations and other forms of visual entertainment.[31]

In Britain, historians have noted the emergence of leader cults, of 'democratic leading men' like Ernest Jones, Feargus O'Connor, John Bright and William Gladstone, who sought to become 'romantic heroes in a political melodrama of their own scripting'.[32] The process was reciprocal. That is, in this period, the whole spectacle of politics – elections, revolutions, mass demonstrations and political leaders – along with the police, the law, crime and trials, was tapped by writers and dramatists as a colourful and popular source for fiction and poetry.[33] At the same time, the wide spread of political information, and especially the use of photography and biography to promote a cult of political celebrity, could induce feelings of intimacy and indeed 'voyeurism' in the public in relation to its leaders.[34] Thus publishing and theatre, and especially the new methods and genres of mass-circulation literature and drama, helped create a new 'community' of political leaders and their public. It is not surprising that, as part of this transformation of political culture, political events like Italian unification became occasions for mass entertainment. Conflict in the Italian peninsula was re-narrativised as popular melodrama, and the main protagonists were recast to resemble the heroes and villains of historical and adventure novels.

An Italian reading public?

Unfortunately for our purposes, much less is known about reading in Italy during this period. One probable reason for this lacuna is that Italy lagged behind northern Europe in terms of both literacy and public education, so that at the time of unification rates of illiteracy were still high (around 75 per cent of the total population), and there was a considerable and apparently increasing regional variation (53 per cent in Lombardy–Venetia and more than 86 per cent in the Kingdom of the Two Sicilies in 1861; 22 per cent in Lombardy and 79 per cent in Calabria forty years later). Women, moreover, had much higher rates of illiteracy than men (76 per cent compared to 62 per cent in 1871, with over 90 per cent illiteracy in the rural South).[35] Although efforts had been made by the pre-unification states to educate the population, with some positive results especially in Austrian Italy, it was only in 1859 that the principle of general public education was established in law, with the Piedmontese *legge Casati*, which became an Italian law after unification. Even then there was political disagreement about the value of mass education, there was a lack of trained teachers and there were no clear provisions for making education compulsory.[36]

Still, perhaps the most obvious and serious obstacle of all to the creation of an Italian reading public was that most people spoke a series of regional dialects which could (for instance, in parts of southern Italy) be very different from literary Italian. French or the local dialect were more widely spoken than Italian in Piedmont (both Cavour and the Piedmontese king spoke much better French than Italian). According to one estimate, there were around 600,000 Italian speakers at the time of unification, that is, about 2.5 per cent of the total population.[37] Nevertheless, these figures should be treated with some scepticism. Dialects spoken in central Italy, and in Tuscany and parts of the Papal States in particular, were very similar to literary Italian, so that the actual figure for 'Italian' speakers may be closer to three million people, or between 10 and 12 per cent of the population. In much of Italy, moreover, Italian was the official administrative language; the 1861 edition of a Baedeker guide to northern Italy also advised tourists that in order to profit from their stay, it was 'essential to familiarise yourself at least a bit with the Italian language'.[38] Hence the presence of Italian as a language, especially in urban areas, means that a larger percentage of people would have understood Italian when spoken and read aloud to them.[39]

It is evident that many of the conditions that produced mass-media print elsewhere were relatively lacking in much of Italy.[40] High internal and external barriers to trade impeded the arrival and development of new print technology, publishers were slow to embrace techniques of mass production, modern transport networks (notably railways) developed only bit by bit, and the traditionally rigid division – and thus lack of contact – between city and countryside persisted right through the nineteenth century. For all these reasons, reading and the formation of public opinion in Italy was a more regionally based and elitist affair than in many parts of northern Europe. These restrictions had a clear impact on the spread of a sense of imagined community within the peninsula.

Nonetheless, the publishing industry in Italy was at the forefront of political change. Despite the closed markets maintained during the Restoration era, publishers (print-capitalists) challenged press censorship, pressed for the dismantling of internal barriers to trade, and sought government measures which would create a national market in Italy as a means of increasing demand for their goods and boosting their profits. For the same reasons, and even if their distribution networks were circumscribed, publishers were also probably one of the first groups in Italy to establish a more or less national network of contacts.[41] Furthermore, writers, journalists and editors – along with some artists and scientists – effectively constituted a good part of the 'public sphere' in Restoration Italy. From the eighteenth century onwards, it was they who had negotiated new public spaces and established a degree of autonomy for themselves from the centres of political power. After 1815, and despite the harsh constraints of press censorship, it was through the associations and publications of such autonomous intellectuals, scientists and artists that ideas of liberalism and national identity were first circulated and debated. Many of them (Vieusseux, Gioberti, Cattaneo) were publishers as well as writers. Publishing companies in Florence and especially Milan produced a large number of newspapers and periodicals;[42] and in Milan there was also a fairly substantial sector devoted to women's magazines.[43] Radicals were not idle either. As we know, Mazzini was a writer and journalist in Genoa before he became involved in politics, and a constant part of his and his followers' activity consisted in establishing publishing offices and printing presses, and engaging with the practical business of publishing, editing, selling and distributing newspapers, periodicals and books.

Thus, while there may have been no national, liberal public sphere in pre-unification Italy comparable to that in parts of northern Europe, this problem was recognised by nationalists and liberals and resolving it became a political objective which united all sections of progressive opinion.[44] Equally, there was a growing, if still restricted, middle-class market for books in nineteenth-century Italy, and there were publishing 'crazes' in Italy as there were elsewhere. For instance, some political books – Gioberti's *Primato*, Balbo's *Speranze* – became instant sellers, with large numbers of editions being produced in a short period of time. Banned books – Mameli's poems, General Pepe's memoirs – could become cult classics; while other works – the novels of Guerrazzi, D'Azeglio and Manzoni, the poetry of Foscolo – were constant sellers throughout the whole period. Young educated Italians, men and women, read just as voraciously as their counterparts in northern Europe. As Alberto Banti has sought to show, much of their preferred literature was of a 'national–patriotic' inspiration, and the reading of it united this generation and created among them a sense of imaginary community.[45] Publishing and reading, in other words, helped to create and define the Risorgimento.

If the creation of an Italian reading public was difficult before unification, there was a vibrant associational culture. From the end of the 1830s gentlemen's clubs began to open their doors to a wider public and were joined by a plethora of other associations, such as reading clubs, scientific and statistical societies, agrarian associations, arts and craft organisations and traditional coffee houses. Such clubs were concentrated in the cities of northern and central Italy and they were still quite exclusive institutions: unlike the salons of the eighteenth century, they did not admit women; and often they were not interested in philanthropic activities and did little to reach out to the poor and uneducated. Nevertheless, they constituted a public sphere of sorts. They provided a space where male members of the new elite and the traditional nobility could meet, socialise, read and talk, and they helped to form the basis of a new political class.[46]

Equally, the importance and popularity of cultural activities which were less restrictive than reading or joining clubs should not be underestimated. Theatre, and in particular opera, played precisely the kind of 'nationalising' role otherwise largely lacking in Risorgimento Italy. The popularity of opera and melodrama led to a wave of theatre construction in major cities and small towns, and these theatres created a recognisable and uniform public architecture across Italy. Theatres could become alternative civic spaces where a diverse and otherwise segregated public could mingle, or at least could come closer to doing so. The music itself was a powerful vehicle for the popularisation of romantic themes such as oppression, betrayal, struggle and redemption and – most obviously in the Verdi operas – these could be linked to episodes or moments in Italian history. And, whatever the composer's original intentions, during the 1840s and thereafter a section of the liberal public seized on and publicised such music as an example of the growing patriotic spirit in Italy. In this way, both the theatres themselves and the performances in them helped construct an imagined Italian community. Theatrical performances provided a space where people could share responses to the same experience, and not just in one theatre but in repeat performances in theatres throughout the Italian peninsula.[47]

A great deal also changed in Italy during, and as a result of, the 1848–9 revolutions, and subsequently during the 1850s. Partly through the publication of newspapers, the revolutions had given a great boost to the formation of national and nationalist public opinion in Italy. In the aftermath, the nationalist publishing boom continued through the proliferation of memoirs and the appearance of pamphlets and other polemics in print. The centre of public opinion also shifted. As the only Italian state not to reimpose press censorship, and with the only government committed both to dismantling barriers to trade and to improving the transport infrastructure, Piedmont – especially the cities of Turin and Genoa – began to assume the cultural hegemony in Italy previously enjoyed by Milan and Florence. The expansion of cultural life in Turin manifested itself in an unprecedented proliferation of art, literature, clubs, music and theatre, which gave the royal capital an openness and vitality it had hitherto largely lacked. But this expansion was most obvious, and most clearly political, in the publication of numerous newspapers and periodicals. In the fluid and rapidly changing political circumstances of 1850s Piedmont, it was through newspapers, as much as – if not more than – in parliament, that political affiliations were created, altered and maintained. The offices and printing works of daily papers and other periodical and ephemeral publications provided political meeting places and a space to make political contacts, and it was in the pages of these publications that political debate was carried out, and public opinion was formed and kept informed. An added stimulus, and a new national character, to the publishing industry in Piedmont was provided by the influx of political exiles from elsewhere in Italy, many of whom were writers, journalists and/or publishers seeking contacts and gainful employment in their new home; and these people were partly responsible for invigorating cultural life there during the 1850s.

No paper in Piedmont had a large circulation. The daily with the biggest sales, *La Gazzetta del Popolo*, had a maximum of 10,000 subscribers in the early to mid-1850s; *La Concordia* closed due to financial problems in early 1850 with only 1,500 subscribers; and the explicitly Mazzinian *Italia e Popolo* had under 1,000 subscribers. But the sheer number of titles produced suggests that the sector was dynamic in cultural terms. An estimated 117 periodicals were published in Piedmont in 1853, of which fifty-three were in Turin and eighteen in Genoa; in 1854, some thirteen daily papers were published in Turin alone. These figures are all the more worthy of note if compared to those in the other states in the Italian peninsula: in 1857–8, Lombardy–Venetia produced sixty-eight periodicals, Tuscany produced twenty-seven, Rome only sixteen and the whole of the South around fifty.[48] The expansion of the reading public and the publishing industry in Piedmont provided a very vivid contrast to the situation prevailing in the rest of Italy. The openness of Piedmont could be compared to the closed conditions in the Papal States and the South, where the Bourbon government's determination to control and isolate its subjects from the effects of liberalism was equated to enclosing them within a 'Great Wall of Naples', and press censorship was likened to a form of collective imprisonment.[49]

Italy in public opinion

Despite the elitist character of the reading public in Piedmont, the press affirmed and strengthened Piedmontese leadership in the nationalist struggle. Just as nationalists looked increasingly to the Piedmontese government and army for practical help in the 1850s, so nationalist discourse permeated political debate by identifying itself with the moderate liberal or Piedmontese leadership. Nationalists sought ever greater contact with a broader reading public and in the 1850s the political impact of Italian nationalism grew ever greater, thanks largely to a series of carefully orchestrated press campaigns in Piedmont and elsewhere. Yet, although the public sphere became more nationalist, nationalism itself became more moderate. The political meaning of nationalism was transformed, even as its metaphors, symbols and rituals remained apparently the same; at least part of the discourse became less revolutionary, more respectable and more associated with material progress and the Piedmontese monarchy. Here the Italian experience provides a striking contrast to that of Britain (and the USA), where the broadening of the public sphere led to diversification and radicalisation.

At the centre of this nationalist transformation were the press campaigns organised by the National Society, which was itself born out of writing, publishing and other associational activities. Its two leaders, Daniele Manin and Giorgio Pallavicino, had been brought together by press activity aimed at raising the profile of the nationalist question. Campaigns included the 'one hundred cannons' subscription to raise money for the fortifications of Alessandria (on the Lombard–Piedmont border); an attack on the presence of Swiss mercenaries in Naples; and a protest against anti-Italian stereotypes in George Sand's *La Daniella*.[50] During 1856, from his base in Paris, Manin developed contacts with some thirty Italian newspapers and saw to it that articles with a nationalist slant or which discussed national issues were published; these were then cross-published and/or commented on in other papers. With Pallavicino, and especially with Pallavicino's money, he began to publish flyers and pamphlets containing their letters and essays in print runs of between 300 and 3,000 copies. From Turin, these publications were posted to friends, sold in shops or simply left at café tables, clubs and theatres; they found their way in large numbers to Tuscany and the Papal States, and they were also circulated in Lombardy–Venetia, among exiles in Switzerland, Belgium and England; they even reached readers in the USA, Algiers and Malta. In 1857, Pallavicino and Manin acquired direct control of a newspaper – Giuseppe La Farina's *Il Piccolo Corriere d'Italia* – whose news items became dedicated entirely to promoting the issue of national unification and to persuading nationalists outside Piedmont of the necessity of endorsing Piedmontese leadership.[51]

It was this co-ordination of press activity and journalistic production which led directly to the formation of the National Society in August 1857. Thereafter, *Il Piccolo Corriere* assumed a vital role as the crux of the party's operations; as Grew puts it, 'the life of the National Society was centred in the written word'.[52] The Society's secretary Guiseppe La Farina published instructions for the formation of local committees in the paper, as well as more sensational articles attacking the Austrians and papal misrule. He also gave considerable space to Orsini's anti-Mazzinian letters and statements. A significant portion of each issue was devoted to stories from outside Piedmont which emphasised how bad life was in the rest of Italy. Complaints about the repression in Modena, rumours of the wealth of Cardinal Antonelli in Rome, revelations of the abuse of Jewish children by clerics (notably the notorious Mortara affair)[53] and, most common of all, details of the atrocities in the Kingdom of the Two Sicilies were all regular items in *Il Piccolo Corriere* and became part of the accepted narrative of moderate Italian nationalism. The Society also continued to publish pamphlets, which stressed more than ever the benefits of unification for Italy and the need for every Italian to be a nationalist.

Although the evidence is relatively scarce, the Society's message seems to have been widely advertised. *Il Piccolo Corriere* reached a circulation of 4,000 and about 12,000 copies of La Farina's *Credo Politico* were circulated; the latter was incorporated into student songs in Pavia. More broadly, the Society's activities – the circulation of pamphlets, posters and printed images; the promotion and reporting of patriotic slogans and public demonstrations – seem to have contributed significantly to the wave of nationalist (and anti-Austrian) enthusiasm which swept the towns and cities of the Italian peninsula in early 1859. Through its publishing activities, in other words, the National Society played a crucial part in creating and maintaining a common nationalist outlook among its members and adherents, and in presenting 'a simple picture of Italy on the threshold of unity, preparing to fight beside Piedmont'.[54] It was to have a central organisational and propaganda role in the events of 1859–60.

The general acceptance of the National Society's assumption that Italy was a nation, which had simply lost her independence and 'genius' to internal divisions and foreign oppression, shows how far nationalist ideas – dismissed as foolish a decade earlier – had achieved a wide circulation and penetrated political debate, even as Mazzinianism declined as a political movement. Just as striking was the status of this nationalist vision among the reading public outside Italy. As we saw in the previous chapter, there had been great, if not unanimous, enthusiasm for the exiles of 1848–9 in the United States, and American enthusiasm was transformed into broad support for nationalist demands in Italy during the 1850s.[55] In France too, Italian questions were given greater prominence in the press. Edgar Quinet's *Les Révolutions d'Italie*, based on lectures given in the Collège de France, was published in three volumes between 1848 and 1852. In Paris, Manin also made great efforts to promote and control discussion of the Italian question in France. He saw the proofs of all the articles on Italy which appeared in the progressive paper, *La Presse*, while the equally progressive *Le Siècle* published his essays on Italy. Even after Manin's death in 1857, his influence continued. There was a well-supported press campaign in France for a monument to him, and leading French liberals began to use praise of Manin as a means of expressing public sympathy for Italy and of seeking contact with the National Society.[56]

Yet it was in Britain, with its large radical reading public, that Italian nationalism seems to have had most resonance and had the clearest impact on political debate. As in France and the USA, sympathy for Italy in Britain was generated partly by the writings of artists, poets and academics who travelled to Italy and studied its past. Some of these – Arthur Clough, Elizabeth Barrett Browning – had witnessed the 1848–9 revolutions at first hand and published poems about the events. In her famous poem, 'Casa Guidi windows', Barrett Browning praised Italian efforts at 'redemption'; Clough, although more openly cynical, still testified to the fascination of Garibaldi and his followers.[57] In the early 1850s, the negative campaign against Bourbon 'misrule' was given a tremendous political boost by the then High Tory, William Ewart Gladstone, who after a visit to Italy published a famous denunciation of conditions in Neapolitan prisons and of the Neapolitan state as 'the negation of God erected into a system of government' (the 'Two letters to the Earl of Aberdeen').[58] He also helped publish and partly translated Luigi Carlo Farini's history of Rome in the nineteenth century.[59]

Still the single most important reason for the high profile of the Italian question in Britain was the presence of Mazzini. Following his return to London as a hero after the events of Rome in 1849, Mazzini enjoyed even greater fame and influence in Britain than before. His personality 'was appropriated by the supporters of radical politics and likened to that of national radical heroes like Milton or Cromwell'.[60] His philosophy of 'moral regeneration' helped to revive British radicalism in the aftermath of the Chartist defeats; he helped William Linton temporarily revive the republican movement; and his activity in radical circles contributed to the development of a broad liberal consensus which provided a basis for Gladstonian liberalism throughout the 1860s and after.[61] Mazzini also used his position to mobilise and organise public opinion in favour of Italy. In 1851, he established the Society of the Friends of Italy, which spanned a wide section of the progressive middle class and included prominent liberal reformers, religious Dissenters and leading figures of Victorian literary bohemia. Although the Friends of Italy disbanded in 1853, during the fallout from the Milan insurrection, prominent Mazzinians in England – James Stansfeld, William Ashurst, Joseph Cowen – founded a new organisation, the Emancipation of Italy Fund Committee, aimed at the working class, and in 1856 members of the same group set up the Garibaldi Fund Committee. All of these committees had offices and affiliations in provincial centres as well as in London.[62] The committees raised significant amounts of money, indicating a considerable level of support. Initial subscriptions to the Friends of Italy were often as high as £5 and the Friends eventually contributed over £12,800 to the Italian cause.[63]

So Mazzini's declining fortunes in Italy were not reflected in the British public's perception of him. In his first address to the Friends of Italy, Mazzini urged them to win support for Italian freedom through letters, articles in the press, pamphlets and petitions. Mazzini himself continued to write copiously in the new British radical papers of the 1850s. In this activity, he was assisted by a talented group of collaborators and fellow exiles whose publications and lecture tours contributed greatly to publicising the Italian question, and especially the issue of papal and Austrian opression. As well as touring North America, Father Alessandro Gavazzi went on a tour of the British Isles to give a series of anti-Catholic public lectures or 'orations' in the early 1850s which were well attended, while the ex-Roman triumvir Aurelio Saffi in an article in *The Westminster Review* argued that Italy should no longer be considered a Catholic country. Saffi taught Italian literature at Oxford from 1853, and he went on to give public lectures on Dante and Machiavelli in Manchester, and on the Risorgimento in conferences in London, Edinburgh and Glasgow. It was reported that 1,600 people attended his speech in Glasgow. In the same years Garibaldi's friend Jessie White, who had recently returned from Italy enthused by Mazzinian ideals, produced a series of articles on Italy for the *Daily News* said to have been ghost-written by Mazzini, and she too went on a lecture tour of the British provinces. Even those less sympathetic to Mazzini managed to stir up public enthusiasm over the sufferings of Italy. Felice Orsini's lecture tour, which took place shortly after he escaped from an Austrian prison in Mantua, was a sellout. His racy memoirs, published as *The Austrian Dungeons of Italy* in 1856, sold 35,000 copies, and a second edition was published in 1859.[64]

We must not read too much into British enthusiasm for Italian causes. In part, sympathy for Italy in Britain, as well as in France and the USA, masked a distinct sense of cultural and political condescension towards what was seen as a once-great nation, seemingly compromised by misgovernment and unable to liberate itself without assistance. Thus, for many Americans in Rome, papal corruption was fascinating precisely because it seemed so decadent and thus tended to confirm the superiority of their own political system.[65] Having celebrated in print the 1848 revolutions in Florence, Elizabeth Barrett Browning confessed in private to 'a gentle and affectionate approach to contempt' at the fickleness of Italians: 'Poor Rome! Poor Italy! Here there are men only fit for the Goldoni theatre, the coffee houses and the sunny side of the Arno . . .'[66] Even the historian Edgar Quinet was primarily interested in the 1848–9 revolutions in Italy as an example for France of the violence and factionalism which could be caused by Catholic culture and ideals.[67]

Likewise, for British political activists the Italian cause was essentially a 'safe' and workable way for middle- and working-class liberals to assert their own identities and beliefs.[68] For the vocal and popular anti-Catholic lobby in Victorian England, incensed by the Pope's appointment of a Catholic hierarchy in England in 1851, the radical anti-Catholicism of many Italian exiles in England, with their stories of the Inquisition and papal corruption, made them extremely convenient allies.[69] Gladstone's interest in Italy was rooted in his study of Dante, and he found in the issue of Italian reform a means of smoothing his transition from High Tory to Liberal in British politics. His 'Two letters to the Earl of Aberdeen' were in fact 'eminently conservative documents', intended not to support Mazzini (whom Gladstone abhorred) but as a warning that repression was doing the work of Mazzini, by, in his words, 'desolating entire classes upon which the life and growth of the nation depend, undermining the foundation of all civil rule and preparing the way for violent revolution . . .'. Gladstone's 'Letters' were thus not only a plea for reform in Italy, they were also an argument against Mazzini and revolution.[70]

Finally, it is worth remembering that not everyone supported the Italian nationalist cause, either in Britain or elsewhere. Mazzini is said to have 'ruffled the sensibilities of many sympathisers' with his attacks on socialism in Britain. Marx and Engels, as is well known, were especially disparaging about 'the rotten Italians' and their 'revolution', and sought to combat Mazzini's influence in the press with a series of anonymous attacks in the *New York Daily Tribune*.[71] But during the 1850s it was the right, and especially the Catholic Church, which did most to contest support for Italian nationalism. In Rome, the Catholic hierarchy began to mobilise its own anti-nationalist propaganda machine with the foundation of a paper, *La Civiltà Cattolica*. *La Civiltà Cattolica* had been established by the papal authorities in Naples in 1850, and after it was moved to Rome it became a crucial – and all too modern – weapon in the struggle against nationalism in Italy. It had a much greater circulation than any of its nationalist counterparts, with 7,000 subscriptions in the year of its launch (1850), reaching 11,000 in 1853 (with a print run of 13,000 copies). It closely followed and commented on political events in the peninsula, and it attacked without distinction Cavour, the National Society and Mazzini. It also published to great popular success the serialised novels of one of its founders, the Jesuit priest Antonio Bresciani. Bresciani's writings sought to combine the appeal of the historical novel with the duties of strict religious morality: or to entertain readers while teaching them 'the dogmas and moral truths of our holy Religion'. His villains were often revolutionaries and many of the novels had a specifically anti-nationalist theme.[72]

The Catholic press had an international reach, and the Church itself had a call on people's loyalties which could cut across and cancel out the appeal of Italian nationalism and other liberal causes. Under Napoleon III in France, the power of Catholicism was unquestionable, and clerical papers like *L'Univers*, *L'Union* and *Le Correspondant* enjoyed a large circulation.[73] Even in Britain, where the situation was completely different, support for Italian nationalism and for its attacks on the Catholic religion was publicly contested by Catholics. The new archbishop of Westminster, Cardinal Wiseman (whose appointment had caused such a furore of anti-Catholic feeling in Britain), published a counter-attack on Gavazzi,[74] and he went on to make a triumphant tour of Ireland in 1858 to celebrate and honour the man he called the real victim in Italy – the besieged Pope in Rome. In Ireland itself, Paul Cullen, archbishop of Dublin throughout this whole period (1852 to 1878), was a more than able opponent of Mazzini. He had been a student in Rome in the 1830s and a supporter of the arch-reactionary, Pope Gregory XVI, and he had stayed on in Rome at the Irish College and so witnessed all the events and fighting during the 1849 revolution. From the 1850s onwards, Cullen did everything in his power to fight what he saw as the alliance between Protestantism, Freemasonry, revolution in Ireland (led by 'Orange Catholics') and Italian nationalism.[75] An Irish MP, John Francis Maguire, published a defence of the Pope's temporal power – *Rome, its rulers and its insitutions* – to great acclaim in 1856, and this volume was reissued in 1859. Indeed, pro-papal enthusiasm can be said to have fuelled Irish nationalism in the 1850s; it also led to feuds and near-violence in Clerkenwell in 1853 between Italian refugees who insulted local Irish priests and Irish Catholics determined to defend their 'spiritual father'.[76] In the USA too, where the Catholic hierarchy was dominated by the Irish, Italian nationalists did not have everything their own way and Catholics were vocal in their defence of the Pope.[77] Finally, from the 1848–9 revolutions onwards, the Catholic press in the southern German – and traditionally more liberal – states painted an apocalyptic picture of the threat of Mazzini and revolution, and presented the political struggles in Italy as the decisive battle between the 'kingdom of God' and the 'kingdom of darkness'.[78]

Nevertheless, the fact that so many men and women were, by the late 1850s, 'passionately concerned with the fate of the [Italian] peninsula',[79] and that the issue of Italian independence had come to eclipse most other great liberal causes in the international press at this time, is extremely significant. In this respect, the battle with the Catholic Church was deliberately sought by the nationalists: it served to sharpen the rhetorical defences of the nationalists and ensured them wide publicity. Clerical counter-attacks provided them with an occasion to relaunch and restate their core ideas.[80] As the events of 1859–60 were to make abundantly clear, the pressure of international liberal public opinion also helped to give Italian nationalists – including Cavour and the moderates – an ultimately unassailable head start over the Austrians and their allies in the Italian peninsula.

Yet even before these dramatic conflicts took place, the dialogue between Italian exiles, on the one hand, and their readership and audiences, on the other, helped to define the coming struggle and determined perceptions of it. First, the technological and cultural developments of the 1850s opened up new possibilities for Italian nationalists. In this decade, both radical propagandists and the more moderate National Society were able to reach beyond the secret groups of nationalist conspirators and the elite circles of their enthusiasts and connect with a much broader – if educated and still largely middle-class – international reading public. Second, the public debates among nationalists, their language and slogans, even the disagreements between them and the attacks upon them, which were carried out in meetings, lectures, pamphlets, newspapers and books throughout this period, served to promote the new political idea of Italy. The press and public debate publicised the Piedmontese 'solution' and helped give nationalists the appearance (if not the reality) of unity and unanimity. Most of all, the press helped to distil the message of Italian nationalism into a simple but potent narrative, which presented the liberal public with an ostensibly unquestionable moral choice: on the one side, Neapolitan prisons, papal corruption and Austrian repression and, on the other, political freedom, national independence, and the heroism of a few selfless and exceptional individuals.

Stories of love, liberty and adventure

The rapid extension of the reading public in Europe, the consequent broadening of the public sphere and the changes in the language of political debate, as well as the increasing prominence within this debate of the problem of Italy's future, help us to understand the presence and impact of Garibaldi in mid-nineteenth-century European politics. Seen from the perspective of this new political culture, rather than from the more traditional and narrow standpoint of high politics, Garibaldi's extended exile from politics and his political setbacks seem arguably less significant than the continuing spread of public interest in him, expressed through the medium of publishing and reading.

As we know, both the radical and the conservative press had made much of Garibaldi's retreat from Rome. Radical British and American journalists followed his progress from Europe to North America, and only finally lost interest in him when he disappeared into the Pacific. In America Dwight had recast Garibaldi as the 'retiring' and 'noble-hearted' commander and epitome of Protestant virtue, involved in a ceaseless struggle against what Dwight calls 'chronicles' of papal 'despotism'.[81] In France, during the same period, the celebrated novelist Alexandre Dumas fashioned Garibaldi as the passionate, blue-eyed defender of Montevideo – physically beautiful, gracious in his movements, softly spoken – as part of his creation and celebration of the siege of Montevideo as 'a new Troy'.[82] These foreign writers were clearly well aware of the pliability and resonance of Garibaldi's public image. In the aftermath of the revolution, a series of pamphlets were published in Piedmont which commemorated Garibaldi's role in the 1848–9 revolutions, and especially the story of the retreat from Rome.[83] Throughout the 1850s, he remained before the Italian public by means of a series of printed images, as a protagonist in political memoirs, as the subject of a biography, and via appearances in adventure romances. These publications produced a narrative formula apparently so compelling that it structured Garibaldi's political appeal in 1859–60 and thereafter.

In the early 1850s, some of the protagonists in the Roman Republic and in its defence – the political activists Carlo Pisacane, Augusto Vecchi and Luigi Farini; the Lombard volunteer Emilio Dandolo and the Swiss volunteer Gustav von Hofstetter – published their histories and memoirs of recent events. Dandolo and von Hofstetter had fought together in the defence of Rome in Luciano Manara's Lombard legion. Their memoirs aimed and helped to create a romantic memory of the Roman Republic as one of the most tragic and glorious episodes in the whole Risorgimento; in their accounts, young men – 'united by a common sentiment, filled with fervour and enthusiasm' – die stoically as martyrs on the walls of the 'eternal city', and their deaths reunite the Italian family and establish Italy's destiny as a warrior nation.[84] Interestingly, none of these writers was entirely on Garibaldi's side, and Pisacane in particular was critical of Garibaldi's military skills. Yet they were unanimous in praising his bravery in battle and all acknowledged his personal charisma. Dandolo and von Hofstetter wrote at length about Garibaldi's captivating physical presence and radical behaviour, stressing his energy, virility and exotic clothes and gestures (see pages 85–7). Thus, they helped to create and publicise a myth of Garibaldi and to link this myth to an heroic ideal of *italianità*, even while Garibaldi himself had withdrawn from active politics.

It was a sign of the changing times that these writers were able to take advantage of the lack of press censorship and publish their work in Piedmont, and that their work was published abroad as well. Dandolo, Farini and Vecchi were translated into English from Italian; both Dandolo and Vecchi's accounts were published in more than one Italian edition; and von Hoffstetter's was translated from German into Italian. There is evidence, moreover, that these works were widely read and were influential. Dandolo, along with his brother

Enrico and other volunteers who died in the defence of Rome, became heroes
in their own right as a result of the memoir (when Dandolo died in 1859 he was
given a huge funeral in Milan, which provided the occasion for anti-Austrian
demonstrations). Von Hofstetter was with Garibaldi on the retreat from Rome,
and his memoir remains an important source on that episode. At the time, it
helped inspire at least one enthusiast, Garibaldi's future lover and biographer
Esperanza von Schwartz, to seek out Garibaldi at his home in Caprera.[85]

Far closer to Garibaldi than the Lombard volunteers was the journalist
Giovanni Battista Cuneo, a friend and promoter since his South American
days. In 1850, Cuneo published the first real biography of Garibaldi. It was only
a sixty-two-page, cheaply produced book, but it had Garibaldi's co-operation
and full approval.[86] Like the memoirs of Dandolo *et al.*, the biography was to
some extent political intervention: part of the process of creating, promoting
and controlling the memory of 1848–9. Yet Cuneo went a step further and used
narrative elements borrowed directly from fiction to structure the biography,
telling the story of Garibaldi's life as a series of decisively heroic episodes from
his early childhood in Nice until his present-day exile. He adopted a three-stage
sequential narrative (what Northrop Frye has called 'a sequential and
processional form'):[87] the series of minor adventures as a young man (when
Garibaldi's heroism was already evident since he saved no fewer than three men
from drowning); the perilous and character-forming journeys across South
America; and the major 'quest' – the epic battle for Rome where the hero fights
the enemy, finds his destiny and redeems Italian pride against French
accusations of cowardice. In effect, Cuneo employs a standardised literary
formula (the adventure romance), developed to entertain the reader and
encourage his/her identification with the story's protagonist, and applies it to
the construction of a biography as 'exemplary life'.[88]

Cuneo's biography is a striking example of the fusion of politics with
popular fiction. He ties a political (radical, nationalist) message to a popular
narrative formula, he identifies Garibaldi's personal qualities with an ideal of
public virtue, and he constructs his biography so that the life imagined
enhances the appeal of the real. Garibaldi himself is part bold political leader,
part fascinating romantic hero. He is energetic, brave and adventurous, and
his whole life is 'a continual and not unfruitful sacrifice for liberty and the
fatherland'.[89] As a man, he is good-looking and attractive (on the book's
original cover he gazes seductively at the reader in an almost languid pose in
front of Castel Sant'Angelo in Rome):

Of medium height, wide in the chest and shoulders, sturdy and relaxed at
the same time, he gives you an idea of strength and agility. At first glance,
his face seems severe; and the tawny, uncut beard, the long blond hair, the

large forehead which descends from it and which forms with his nose a straight line which falls in perpendicular, and his shrewd and piercing look all give him an imposing aspect; but looking at him more closely, a sweet harmony of line and form jumps out at you and confirms your expectations, and a feeling of trust and sympathy spontaneously rises up within your heart, and mixes with the respect which he had previously inspired in you.

He has a 'chivalrous heart' which is open to 'all displays of beauty'; in particular, 'music and poetry have a magic authority over him'. But he is also strong and steadfast: 'constancy in the face of adversity, a courage which grows in relation to obstacles and dangers, a steadiness of purpose, a flash of the eye which rarely fails to strike in the most dire emergencies, and a serenity in every moment of life' are also features of his personality.[90]

Although it was not until 1859 that publications about Garibaldi achieved a wide circulation, Cuneo's biography created the political–literary formula which structured all future approaches to Garibaldi. Elements of this formula had already arrived in England by the early 1850s, as the short biography of him published in the radical *Northern Tribune* in 1854 shows.[91] The specific information on his early life – unknown in Britain before this time – was lifted from Cuneo's biography (and perhaps from Dwight's *Roman Republic*), with various elements added from British newspapers and periodicals, while others are embellishments invented by *The Northern Tribune*. Crucially, the biography is structured like an adventure story, with many of the familiar episodes included. Thus, we are told that Garibaldi was born in Nice in 1808[92] of 'good family' and that 'his love of adventure led him to the sea'. The paper follows Cuneo in highlighting Garibaldi's dramatic escape after the discovery of the 1833 conspiracy; it has him crossing the River Var in February, and also asserts that this heroic act provides the inspiration for a similar incident in Giovanni Ruffini's novel, *Lorenzo Benoni*, published in Britain the previous year.[93] Like Cuneo, the paper points to Garibaldi's nickname of 'lion' – a medieval symbol of resurrection and a modern euphemism for celebrity – by reproducing the figure of a lion in the accompanying illustration of Garibaldi, and by quoting from Joseph Cowen's address of welcome that his supporters are 'not vulgar *lionizers*'.[94] The article is proof both of Garibaldi's personal capacity to inspire flights of literary imagination, and of the circulation of standardised biographical elements relating to him.

One of the most striking images of Garibaldi during this time is not taken from a photograph: it is an idealised representation of him, printed in Turin, as Christ Pantocrator (probably intended for clandestine circulation in the rest of Italy; see figure 8 overleaf).[95] This image provides us with a clue to one of the great battles of the Risorgimento after 1848–9, which was the struggle between

8   Garibaldi as Christ
Pantocrator, printed in
Piedmont in the 1850s and
circulated clandestinely
elsewhere.

the nationalists and the Catholic Church. Among the first, and in some ways
most revealing, of all contributions to the cult of Garibaldi was produced by the
stridently anti-nationalist Jesuit priest, Padre Antonio Bresciani. His 'historical
novel', *Lionello*, first published in the pages of *La Civiltà Cattolica* in 1852, was
partly set in Rome in the days of the Republic of 1849. During the revolutionary
events, the eponymous hero takes up with Garibaldi, to the surprise of his
friends, who knew Garibaldi as 'a highwayman on land and a pirate on the seas,
who lays waste to every place he lands at, throwing out fire and flame under his
feet, and making blood gush from everything he touches with a deadly hand'.
But, in a parody of Cuneo's *Biografia*, Lionello defends Garibaldi:

> he is of medium stature and with a sturdy and compressed figure but . . . as
> quick as a lion, which combines force with agility, solidity with slenderness,
> the ardent eye with the constant gaze, a proud and merciful heart; the lion
> can most easily be said to resemble him, with his great blond mane which
> descends to the shoulders, the tawny beard, the high forehead, and the grave
> and serious look at first glance, but he who looks at him well sees a generous,
> open and serene face, which inspires reverence, trust and sympathy in you.

Garibaldi, according to Lionello, has a soul which is:

noble, frank, sincere, lofty and entirely harmonious, on which music has a sweet authority, and poetry carries him off on flights which are as sublime as they are strong . . . with his sword he subdued the barbarian, with his pen he sung the triumphs and bravery of Greece, with his mind he made philosophy, and with his heart he burns for the love of freedom.[96]

This satire of Cuneo's biography is continued in the pages that follow. Every episode of Garibaldi's life – his love of Rome, his heroism in South America, his wife Anita – is recounted by Bresciani in a deliberately exaggerated and poor imitation of Cuneo's style and episodic structure. In this way, the real character of the 'hero' Garibaldi – the destroyer of Rome, the insidious conspirator, the perfidious husband – is clearly revealed.

What makes Bresciani's work so interesting for us is his attempt to fuse the traditional reactionary attack on Garibaldi as a bloodthirsty and destructive bandit[97] with a parody of the nationalist 'style' pioneered by Cuneo and others. That Bresciani should have attempted to do so at all is a sign of the wider influence and circulation of this style. The literary impact of Italian nationalism, and of Garibaldi in particular, is also suggested by his appearance in a number of British novels of the period, part of a minor 'pulp' genre which swapped the Italian castles of Gothic romances for the events and places of Risorgimento Italy.[98] The first of these, *Angelo*, was published in 1854 and is the story of a love affair between an ex-Jesuit priest, Angelo Maturin, and the heroine, Leoline, set against the backdrop of the 1848–9 revolutions in Rome.[99] Amid a whole host of exotic and violent characters we find the defender of Rome, 'the notorious Gariboni', the head of a band of mercenaries: 'a character singularly adapted for the execution of the bloody work he had undertaken' and with 'qualities which strongly excited the enthusiasm of his followers'.

'Gariboni' is not just cruel, he is also self-possessed: 'Insensible to the suggestions either of pity or remorse, he could talk calmly, or even jocosely with his victim, and motion at the same instant to his attendants to prepare for his immediate destruction'; but he is a man of principle and honour, if without feeling or mercy. He is, above all, a sexually attractive outsider; he is heavily armed and flamboyantly dressed in a green blouse with red slashed sleeves, red trousers and 'an embroidered pelisse' over his shoulders. His transgressive appearance causes particular excitement among Rome's nuns:

many a female glance, long turned from carnal vanities, rested with satisfaction on his clear blue eye, high forehead, small mouth, luxuriant hair falling in rich curls about his neck, and graceful moustache; and many a heart that ought to have been lost in dreams of Divine love and universal charity, hushed its momentary fears at the appearance of so noble and imposing an invader.[100]

Two years later, Garibaldi appeared in another novel set in Rome during the revolutions, this time a more light-hearted adventure following the journey of an English Catholic family in Italy. In the novel, *Modern Society in Rome*, whose British author was a pro-Piedmontese, liberal Catholic, Garibaldi appears once more as an exotic 'banditto' character, a 'dreaded condottiere', part of 'as wild looking a party . . . as ever went a gypsying on a summer morning'. His dress is described as 'picturesque', and includes: 'Large pointed boots, falling loose round the calves of his legs', short breeches, a green silk scarf around his waist, a scarlet tunic, a large cloak 'with a great capote like that of the Capuchin monks', a broad South American hat and the inevitable pistols and daggers stuck into his belt. Yet despite this alarming appearance, his physical presence is extremely seductive. He is impressive, athletic ('a racehorse or a lion'), beautiful, proud, frank and generous, and his voice is so deep and measured that all 'felt kindly confidence towards him at once'.[101] Anita features in the narrative too, pretty and sweet but 'no less striking than . . . the wild leader himself', as do the thousand athletic men brought by Garibaldi to Rome, '[t]all, dark-visaged, strong men, all nerve and muscle, with hollow eyes and long curling clotted hair, that fell down on their shoulders', who frightened the Romans with their South American dress and manners.[102]

In the novel's climax, the fortunes of the English family become intertwined with those of Garibaldi and Anita, and thus with Italy more generally. This occurs most notably in an absurd plot twist during the retreat from Rome. As Anita lies dying in Garibaldi's arms, which in the novel occurs on 'perhaps the most beautiful of Italian roads' near Ravenna, the two surviving English protagonists – Horace Enderby and Mary Aglethorpe – pass by in a carriage on their way to the Tyrol:

> 'Good heavens, Mary!' exclaimed Horace Enderby . . . 'good heavens, my beloved, it is Garibaldi and Anita!' . . . 'Oh, for a drop of wine!' exclaimed Garibaldi, wildly. Horace sprang back to the carriage and brought forth a flask. 'It is all we have. It is cold tea: but it may refresh her.'

But giving 'an unmistakable look of love' to Garibaldi, Anita dies. Mary bursts into tears. Garibaldi gets up 'with the dignity of unutterable woe', and 'turning from them to hide the tears that streamed down his sunburnt cheeks [and] . . . gently taking the body of his Anita in his arms, he disposed his cloak over it, and strode off into the broken country'. He mourns over her until dark, and then buries her in a mound of sand with his own hands, leaving her in 'that dear land of Italy, from which he himself must go forth a wanderer and an exile'.[103]

One other British novel of the 1850s in which Garibaldi features deserves our attention. *The Exiles of Italy, or Garibaldi's miraculous escapes*, published in 1857, is more openly nationalist than the previous two and is explicitly anti-Catholic, and it calls itself 'a novel' with 'a strictly authentic History of the period embraced'. The female author, C. G. Hamilton, acknowledges the influence of Saffi's lectures on Italy in the formation of her views; and the preface – which calls attention to the 'sufferings and oppression endured by the Italians' – is essentially a virulent attack on papal despotism and the conditions in Neapolitan prisons.[104] The novel's plot turns on the adventures of two exiled Neapolitan noblemen but, once again, significant passages in the novel are given over to Garibaldi. He appears about a third of the way through the story, during the siege of Rome:

> turning an angle of the street ... a noble-looking man on horseback appeared. He was advancing slowly, for the crowd that surrounded him stayed his progress, and as he from time to time returned their acclamations with courteous acknowledgement, the smile with which he regarded them was like that of a father blessing his children. He appeared about fifty years old, of middle stature; his forehead was high, his eyes bright and piercing; the hair of his head and beard was light; and his whole bearing bespoke the dauntless courage that inspired the beholders, and the genial kindness which made him the idol of his followers. He was dressed in a short scarlet cloak, without any insignia of military rank save his cap and sword.[105]

Apart from his dignified countenance, it is Garibaldi's love for Anita which is dwelt upon at length and, once again, their relationship parallels the love affairs of the novel's two heroes and the tragedy of the 1848–9 revolutions. The retreat from Rome is described in considerable, if largely improbable, detail; Garibaldi calls Anita 'my life' and mourns her 'bright elastic spirit that in all their wanderings had shed its sunshine over her husband's perilous and stormy career'. The death of Anita takes place in the Alps, and not even the arrival of a 'shaggy' Saint-Bernard dog who guides the travellers to a mountain hut can save her. Before she dies, she tells her husband: 'I shall be with you, my friend; whether riding by your side, as in days of yore, or looking down upon you from that bright heaven.' This time, he buries her in 'a green, lonely spot, where the dark fig-trees threw their shadows on the grass, and the girdling rocks shut out all human eyes'. He becomes 'a lonely wanderer on the earth'; excluded even from the comfort of his blue-eyed, fair-skinned mother and his four beautiful children.[106]

Garibaldi's emergence as a character in British novels is interesting for a number of reasons, not least because it parallels the wider enthusiasm for Italian nationalism which gathered pace in Britain during the 1850s. As a result, the novels allow us to explore the spread and reception of the cult of Garibaldi in British public opinion. Although it is impossible to trace with any accuracy the sources on Garibaldi for these novels, it is likely that reports in both *The Times* and *The Illustrated London News* were used in the descriptions of his appearance, and that either Dwight or von Hofstetter could have provided some basis for the otherwise wildly romanticised stories of the retreat from Rome. Equally revealing of contemporary attitudes and future trends is the sheer extent of fantasy involved in representations of Garibaldi and his adventures, a fantasy which is nevertheless grounded in the repetition of a formulaic, and already familiar, narrative.

In the three British novels published between 1854 and 1857, the shift in public perceptions of Garibaldi from cruel bandit to picturesque outlaw and then to older gentleman soldier can be read very clearly. More striking still, however, is the element of continuity provided by the fascination of Garibaldi's physical presence. We saw this preoccupation with his personal appearance and behaviour in contemporary reports throughout 1848–9, and again in the accounts of Dwight, Dumas, Dandolo, von Hofstetter, Cuneo and (in negative terms) Bresciani. In the British novels, the sexual overtones of this fascination are made explicit for the first time. Garibaldi is a man who excites nuns and engages in orgies, and his whole appearance 'sends us again to those times, when, by the capture of the senses, reason could be laid asleep'; he is a husband who likes nothing more than to walk hand in hand with his wife and admire the view from under the shade of a chestnut tree; and he becomes a devastated sunburnt lover weeping over the body of his beautiful dead wife.[107] He is not just violent and physically inspiring, he is also sensitive and loving. Here (and not for the last time), the fashioning of an imaginary Garibaldi tailored specifically to the demands of women readers needs to be noted.

Reading Garibaldi

Despite his partial withdrawal from active politics, Garibaldi was far more committed to publicising himself and his political ideas in these years than he liked to let on. We know, for example, that he read and approved Cuneo's biography, and that his help was acknowledged by Dwight in the account of the Roman Republic. That he, too, was involved in the construction of his own biography as 'exemplary life' is indicated by the fact that during these years of exile he wrote his memoirs. He first mentioned his memoirs in a letter to his cousin Augusto in January 1850 (which also referred to an earlier correspondence about them while he was in La Maddalena in October 1849). Before he left Tangier in the spring of 1850, he had apparently completed large sections of his memoirs and a series of biographical sketches of his 'dead companions-in-arms', including an essay on Anita; and during his voyage from Tangier to New York via Gibraltar and Liverpool he sent parts of the manuscript to his cousin and to his friend Francesco Carpaneto in an unsuccessful attempt to get them published.[108] Although this original manuscript of his memoirs was lost, during the 1850s Garibaldi gave copies and authorised publication to a series of friends. He first gave a copy in 1850 to Dwight, who culled them extensively in preparing the sections on Garibaldi for his *Roman Republic* manuscript; subsequently Garibaldi gave another copy to Esperanza von Schwartz, in 1855; and then in 1860 he made available the text both to the Italian officer Francesco Carrano and to the French novelist Alexandre Dumas. In the event, each published a different version in English, German, Italian and French between 1859 and 1861, and each put in their own additions and embellishments.[109]

Written after the tragic end of the retreat from Rome, accompanying Garibaldi into exile in America and being partially lost along the way, as well as being rewritten by others thereafter, the memoirs' relationship with their author is a complex one. Yet it is revealing that during the period when he was most removed from political life, from late 1849 to 1850, Garibaldi was preoccupied by writing and publishing his memoirs. He referred frequently to their preparation for publication; he specified for instance that the biographical sketches should be published separately from the memoirs, he noted that the whole text required substantial correction, and he accepted his cousin's advice that the sketches needed more detail and suggested that this was also true of his memoirs.[110] The fact that at different times during the 1850s Garibaldi gave four copies of his memoirs to four friends of different nationalities, and was apparently happy to let them translate the memoirs and/or add their own narratives and impressions, also suggests a strong commitment to their promotion and international distribution.

Yet the memoirs in general, and the French version published in 1860 by Dumas in particular, have always been treated with suspicion by historians. They are irritated by the significant gaps in the narrative and they find the mixture of personal memory, partisan polemic and novelistic fantasy an impediment rather than an aid to establishing the truth about Garibaldi's actions in the Risorgimento. G. M. Trevelyan says of the Dumas version that, as there is 'no ostensible means of distinguishing Garibaldi's statements from Dumas' romantic inventions', it is impossible for a historian to use it as evidence.[111] Since Garibaldi went on to revise the memoirs and wrote a 'definitive' and considerably altered edition in 1872, the large number of different editions meant that it became more, not less, difficult to separate 'legend from fact'.[112] For the literary critic too, the memoirs are of little significance as they are undeniably badly written. Garibaldi's long-winded

melodramatic style, which relies heavily on superlative and bathos, does little
to commend his narrative to the reader; and the structure of the narrative,
with its extended battle scenes and political digressions, can be equally off-
putting. Yet most historians do agree that the memoirs have some value in
psychological terms. They can, it is suggested, inform us about Garibaldi's
state of mind and they are said to offer clear insights into his emotions and
ideas; as Trevelyan puts it: 'Without knowing that he is making "confessions"',
Garibaldi 'gives himself away as much as Augustine or Rousseau . . . [and] the
gift is pleasant'.[113]

This perception of Garibaldi's memoirs is interesting because, with the
possible exception of the question of their literary interest, it can be challenged
on every count. Broadly speaking, the dismissal of his memoirs as historical
data and their readmission as psychological evidence is based on a
misunderstanding of the nature and importance of memoirs in nineteenth-
century political life. As Pierre Nora has shown convincingly in relation to
France, the memoir genre was not only an immensely prolific one in the first
half of the nineteenth century, but it was also one aimed specifically at 'the
public'; it was a genre which deliberately evoked and produced a sense of
collective past and national belonging, and it was 'deeply engaged in
politics'.[114] Thus, the authenticity and accuracy of Garibaldi's memoirs should
be, for us, of less interest than what they can tell us about the historical context
in which they were produced and about Garibaldi's own relationship to
contemporary concerns. To follow Nora: memoirs 'do not construct actions;
they create a character. They contribute only secondarily to history, yet they
establish a myth', and they propose a strong link between the individual and
the course of history.[115]

In effect, what Nora suggests to us is that Garibaldi's memoirs were central
to the construction of his public persona and to the myth created around it.
Although it would be a mistake simply to place Garibaldi's memoirs within the
French political and literary tradition,[116] 'patriotic memoirs' had from the
start been a prominent and enduringly popular feature of Risorgimento
literature, building on a strong tradition of biographical writing in Italy which
goes back to the lives of saints and to the Renaissance works of Petrach, Bruni
and Cellini, among others.[117] As in France, memoirs in Risorgimento Italy can
be considered a part of political action, whereby the writer asserted his/her role
in history and made a bid to establish and control the memory of a political
event or series of events. In general terms, Garibaldi's memoirs form one in a
series of similar attempts by Risorgimento writers and activists (or writer–
activists) to create a sense of national identity through the construction of, and
appeal to, collective memory. More immediately, his memoirs were part of the
effort, which gathered increasing momentum after 1848–9, to produce a

narrative which would identify these decades as the 'Risorgimento': in other words, to establish and publicise in narrative form an ideal of national resurgence apparently so compelling that people were prepared to fight and die for it and self-evidently so important that it would come to define an epoch. Finally, Garibaldi's memoirs may well reflect the literary influence on him of Argentine oppositional culture, which was similarly engaged in the construction of biography and history for the purpose of creating national memory.[118] Far from giving him away inadvertently, as Trevelyan supposes, Garibaldi's memoirs were an essential aspect of his self-fashioning as a nationalist hero after the events of 1848–9; they were a move to assert himself within the broader Risorgimento myth, and an attempt to establish himself as the symbol of the Italy which he was dedicated to 'resurrecting'.

That Garibaldi's memoirs were conceived of neither as personal auto-biography nor as 'authentic' history but were, from the outset, intended as a form of public intervention is suggested by a series of factors. They are generally concerned far less with minute political recollection than with the broader question of political reputation. Thus, in August 1850, Garibaldi referred to the growing disagreements between Italian republicans, telling one correspondent that he had learnt in New York 'things about the events of Porta S. Pancrazio [in Rome in 1849] that I was ignorant of; although I was quite devoted to my post there; and it upsets me to see those events described by people who didn't witness them'. Despite this, he stressed that he had decided not to write about the 1848–9 revolutions in his memoirs so as to avoid 'obscuring' the 'fame of certain individuals'.[119] In the event, Garibaldi gives overwhelming prominence in these 1850s versions of his memoirs to his South American experiences; and although both Dumas and von Schwartz include in their editions details of the 1849 Roman Republic and the events of 1859, the official part of the published memoirs ends with Garibaldi's return to Europe in 1848. Moreover, only the first few pages of the memoirs are concerned with Garibaldi's early life and journeys to the Black Sea, and here too he has little to say about his own political background. He is much more interested in constructing an exemplary life. He tells the reader of his childhood mishaps and adventures, of his early dedication to the *risorgimento* of Italy, and of his joy at first seeing Rome ('the Rome of the future . . . of the regenerative idea of the people!'), but he says frustratingly little (one paragraph only) about joining Young Italy – he notoriously omits to tell who recruited him – and still less about the failed Mazzinian conspiracy which led him to emigrate to South America.[120]

In this respect, Garibaldi's memoirs reflect the growing tensions in opposition circles and his own ambivalence towards Mazzinian conspiracy. The memoirs express a general desire for Italian 'liberation' but Mazzini, along with other living Italian activists, is scarcely alluded to and the divisive events of 1848–9 are simply excluded from the narrative. Only those companions of Garibaldi who died in 1848–9 – Daverio, Masina, Mameli, Manara, Risso and Bassi – are mentioned, and then only in the biographical sketches published by Dwight in New York in 1859. Instead, Garibaldi adapts a familiar Risorgimento trope first developed to get past the censors: he presents the reader with his own idealised past, against which the situation in 'our poor Italy'[121] can be implicitly compared.

Thus, Garibaldi's South American years resemble a pastoral golden age. He recalls the 'immense and undulating fields' of Uruguay, and his own reaction, as a '25-year-old corsair', to the first sight of the wild, untamed 'stallion of the pampas'.[122] In an extended passage, he praises the 'real kind of independent man' – the matrero of Uruguay (like the gaucho, he says, but 'more illegal, more independent . . . He rules over that vast extensive countryside, with the same authority as a government, [but] he gives no orders; he raises no taxes'):

> A good horse is the first element of the matrero; his arms normally consist of a carabine, a pistol, a sabre, and the inseparable knife, without which the matrero could not exist . . . from the ox he gets the necessary for his saddle, the *maneador* to tie his companion while he grazes . . . *las bolas* which catches the *bagual* (wild horse) in the fury of a race . . . the lasso . . . finally the meat which is the only food of the matrero . . . the field and the forest are his rooms; the sky, his roof.'[123]

His own life there is remembered in idyllic terms. As a 'buccaneer' on the Rio Grande coast, he writes, he had a life full of danger, adventure and physical pleasure:

> but at the same time beautiful, and very suited to my character . . . We had saddles, we found horses everywhere . . . whenever the situation demanded it – we were transformed into not brilliant but awe-inspiring knights, and we were feared . . . Moreover, in almost every place . . . maize, legumes, sweet potatoes and often oranges were to be found . . . The people who accompanied me, a real cosmopolitan crew, were made up of all colours and of all nations. I treated them with kindness, perhaps too much kindness . . . [but] they were not without courage, and this seemed enough to me.[124]

If Garibaldi excludes most living Italians from his memoirs, this does not mean that his pages are unpeopled. He gives lists of those who fought with him in South America and died there; he praises their heroism, bemoans their sacrifice and laments that he can't remember all their names.[125] He stresses the great value of the people who fought with him in the South American wars: the freed slaves, 'true sons of freedom. Their lances, longer than the normal length, their dark black [*nerissimi*] faces, their robust limbs used to permanent and demanding work, their perfect discipline'; and the Italian volunteers, who made charge after charge at the battle of Salto (showing that 'Italians are no cowards'), and who were 'glorious' at the battle of Dayman, 'as solid as a bulwark and highly agile, they rushed to wherever the need took them, and invariably chased away their companions' adversaries'.[126] He pays tribute to the character of Bento Gonçales, his commander in the Rio Grande Republic, 'noble warrior . . . Tall and slim . . . Highly courageous . . . of a moderate and generous heart . . . [yet] simple . . . I shared his meals in the field, with as much familiarity as if we had been friends from childhood and equals' (although, perhaps to prevent Gonçales from stealing too much of his own glory, he points out that he was always defeated in battle). Garibaldi singles out for special admiration the courage and 'purity' (*l'illibatezza*) of a Uruguayan comrade, Juan de la Cruz Ledesma: 'dark-haired, with an eagle eye, with the noble bearing of a fine man'.[127] Most of all, he eulogises those of his fellow exiles who are now dead. He bemoans the loss of his childhood friend Edoardo Mutru, 'the love of my heart'; he describes meeting Luigi Rossetti: 'our eyes met . . . We smiled at each other and became brothers for life. Inseparable for life!'; he recalls Luigi Carnaglia ('another martyr for freedom!'), without a formal education but with a 'high' soul 'which upheld the honour of the Italian name everywhere' and who looked after Garibaldi 'like his own child'; and he praises Francesco Anzani, who brings discipline to the volunteers and who distinguishes himself by his 'courage' and 'cold blood' under fire.[128] Anzani, Rossetti and Mutru all feature in the 'sketches' published by Dwight in New York, as does Garibaldi's closest companion of all, his dead wife, Anita, 'the Brasilian heroine': 'my treasure, no less fervent than myself for the sacred cause of the people, she looked on battles as entertainment and the discomforts of camp life as a pastime.'[129]

All these passages confirm that Garibaldi's memoirs should be seen as a continuation or extension of his political action in 1848–9. The similarities between descriptions of Garibaldi's arresting appearance, behaviour and companions in Rome in 1849 and his own colourful depictions of the 'adventurous life' of the pampas suggest that he not only consciously modelled himself on the matrero but that he also sought to convey this image to the public by political action and by the written word. There is in his memoirs the same attempt at theatrical bricolage that we observed in his gestures and speeches of the 1840s, and here too it is meant for the purposes of public consumption. Moreover, the linking in his memoirs of the pastoral exoticism of his South American exile to examples of individual heroism has a serious political message, whose eclecticism should not mask its intended use as political rhetoric. Garibaldi uses the story of his life to outline a model of nationalism which is international and voluntary.[130] It may not entirely convince us, but his vision of a utopian community is based loosely on a romantic socialist model of political belonging. Its ideals are those of rustic self-reliance and republican virtue, it has a virile martial ethic, and its inhabitants are free and beautiful people: rebellious young Italians, wise elders, freed slaves and liberated women.

Garibaldi seeks, in short, to offer through his own experiences a vision of the nation-at-arms which is also a democratic community. This political vision is conveyed through the actions and appearance of two different but related groups. Much of the narrative is sustained by his interaction with a series of captivating companions with whom he shares the dangers, privations and excitements of a military (and/or seafaring) life. He is careful to emphasise both the fraternal love which grows between these men of different ages, backgrounds and nationality or race, and the importance and glory of their sacrifice (their martyrdom). Here we see outlined in narrative form his ideal of volunteering as the crucible of a national community (volunteers were the basis of Garibaldi's military action in 1848–9, and they were to remain central to his political programme during the 1850s, and in the wars of 1859 and 1860). Yet in stressing the ties of this new fraternal family, he also gives prominence to his own natural family. His memoirs begin with a description of his 'good parents, whose character and loving care had such an influence on my education and on my physical activities': his father, a sailor, who loved his children, did his best for them despite his poverty, and did all he could to give the rebellious young Garibaldi a decent education; and his mother, a 'model for all Mothers', who suffered so much for his 'adventurous career', whose tenderness to Garibaldi was perhaps 'excessive', whose 'angelic' character is responsible for 'the little of good' there is in his, and who, he feels, still watches over him after her death.[131]

There is in Garibaldi's memoirs an attempt to link the republican principles of voluntary political engagement to the affective ties and responsibilities of the traditional nuclear family. In this respect, the central role given to his wife, Anita ('whom I mourn today, and will mourn all my life!'), is especially interesting. It is she who most clearly embodies the Garibaldian fusion of an ideal of intimate love with the ideal of political virtue, and she is also used to represent the reconciliation of the affective life with the life of fighting and adventure. Before their meeting ('one of the defining moments of my life'), he had been convinced that – despite his love of women – his 'independent' and 'adventurous' spirit must necessarily exclude marriage and children. But one day he sees Anita through a telescope from his ship, rushes ashore, and desperately looks for her. He finally finds her, takes one look at her and announces 'you will be mine!!!' He hints that there is a scandal involved in their union, but she becomes 'the only woman in the world for me!'[132] '[M]y incomparable Anita' is, for Garibaldi, 'the Amazon . . . superior to her sex in the discomforts and dangers of war'. She fought alongside him, loaded and fired cannons in battle with him and encouraged his men 'with admirable serenity . . . with her voice, with her gestures, while she brandished the scimitar in a threatening manner'. She is also a loving wife who escaped from enemy hands and crossed the Brazilian forest alone to rejoin her husband, a companion who rode across the American desert at his side and 'consoled me in hard times', and a concerned mother, 'admirable in domestic life', who, with Menotti, their infant son (and a favourite with all the soldiers), on the front of her saddle, endures a disastrous winter retreat across the Serra mountains.[133]

When they were eventually published between 1859 and 1861, Garibaldi's memoirs met with lasting and significant success. Particularly in the version adapted by Dumas, which added more personal and more sensational detail and which restructured the narrative as a set of canonical episodes, the memoirs were an international hit and gave rise to numerous copies and pirated versions. But even before his encounter with Dumas in 1860, Garibaldi had done his best to make the memoirs attractive to the reading public. For instance, the episodic *feuilleton* style used to good effect by Dumas is a feature of the other versions too. It may not be fully successful, but the memoirs attempt precisely the episodic structure, the racy and emotive language, the violent struggle between good and evil, and the all-powerful love between brave hero and spirited heroine which can be found in the historical and adventure novels that were commercially popular at this time. Garibaldi's attention to women (described twice as 'the most perfect of all beings'),[134] not just to Anita and his mother but to the whole number of enchanting women who appear in and inspire his narrative, is typical of the adventure story. It can also be seen as a specific move to entice the female reader to take up his text. Thus, like Cuneo and other radicals near him, Garibaldi sought to construct and sell a political message by the use of a conventional narrative formula. His memoirs are interesting, neither as authentic history nor as a psychological mirror, but as proof that Garibaldi used the printed word to fashion himself as the hero of a political adventure, and sought to reach and extend his public through the leisure activity of reading.

Conclusion

The changes which affected the Italian peninsula in the 1850s and thereafter were not merely the result of high politics. The outcome of the Crimean War, the international isolation of Austria, and the conflicts within and between political groups in Italy may help explain the rise to prominence of the Italian Question in European diplomacy. Yet these events explain little about the public response to the wars of Italian unification or how this response shaped the actions of political leaders. One of the most important political developments of the 1850s was the growth of a liberal public opinion, in Italy and internationally, which was not just sympathetic to Italian nationalism but passionately concerned with Italy's future. This development was the result of new trends in publishing and entertainment which were in turn linked to the emergence of a broader, and more radical, public sphere across Europe.

Nationalism, as the anthropologist Benedict Anderson has shown and Mazzini always knew, was dependent on print culture. Without the expansion of the printed word and image, it was impossible for complex modern societies to 'fashion', 'invent' or 'imagine' a sense of national community and belonging. It is no coincidence that the mid-century revolution in publishing coincided with the first great age of nationalism, and with the creation and consolidation of nation states in much of Europe. More specifically, the unprecedented scope and scale of Garibaldi's fame as a popular leader were largely maintained by the publishing and entertainment industry. The publicity surrounding him – his actions, his appearance, his private life – was sustained by the rapid and extensive supply of information about him, and this was made possible by the revolution in print culture. At the same time, this wide-scale publicity created a new relationship between the 'performer' and his audience, in which a sense of familiarity and intimacy combined with one of admiration and awe.

Content and style also mattered. Like the idea of Italian freedom more generally, Garibaldi's popularity in mid-century liberal Europe was the result both of the spread of democratic ideas and of their fit with the genres of romantic popular fiction. Garibaldi's political appeal was part of a radical style which was structured and told like a story. Garibaldi and those who wrote about him sought to reach and capture the public by presenting him as a romantic hero in his own drama of love, liberty and adventure. Just how far Garibaldi could take, use and promote this narrative formula for political ends became clear during the dramatic events of Italian unification. Here it is important simply to note that the formula itself was established at an earlier stage (during the 1840s and – especially – the 1850s), that there was little or nothing unplanned about its construction and dissemination, and that Garibaldi was responsible for at least part of the final script. One of the most striking features of this script was the apparently seamless blend of fact and fiction, of novelistic fantasy and political truth, and this blend (which could vary, and pick up and discard different elements) seems to have been at the heart of Garibaldi's public success. It helped Garibaldi's appeal to become international in reach and eclectic in nature. It combined the emotive appeal of romanticism with an ideal of republican virtue, and it proposed a persona in which bravery and sensitivity mingled in equal measure. Perhaps especially, his image and its popularity offer proof of what Miles Taylor has called 'the persistence of romanticism in the *mentalité* of mid-nineteenth-century popular politics', or of the 'long reach' of romanticism[135] which the Risorgimento contributed significantly to, and was the beneficiary of.

Finally, it would be a mistake to see the creation – or fashioning – of Garibaldi necessarily as an imposition from above. In many respects, Garibaldi was less a sign of the constraining power of political symbols and more an indicator of their potential to subvert and destabilise. Not only did Garibaldi represent and promote a movement of political radicalism but the diffusion of his fame was a symptom of the democratisation of political culture, a sign of the arrival of 'non-polite' society in the public sphere with a new set of rules and responses. His appeal was tailored to the perceived tastes and demands of this nascent political culture and he helped to create it. Those involved in promoting him came partly (if not always entirely) from outside the traditional establishment. His popularity also reflected a struggle for control of the public sphere. It contributed to the increasing hegemony of nationalist discourse but neither Garibaldi nor Italian nationalism was loved by everyone and his fame only partially masked a significant divergence between rival political visions of the new Italy. Hence it is by no means surprising that the bitter conflicts which beset the Italian peninsula from the 1840s onwards, and which erupted in spectacular fashion in 1859 and after, involved not just diplomacy and battles but also meetings, lectures and theatrical performances, and that they focused, with such remarkable energy, on control over the printed word.

CHAPTER 6

INDEPENDENCE

The 1859 Campaign

On 10 January 1859, at the opening of parliament in Turin, King Vittorio Emanuele II made the most important political speech of his life. Much of the speech was made up of political banalities: the king looked to Piedmont's future with confidence and spoke vaguely of his love of liberty and the 'fatherland'. But one short reference to the 'cries of grief' – reaching him, the king said, from the other regions of Italy and which he found impossible to ignore – received enormous publicity, and cemented the king's reputation as a national leader in Italy and abroad.[1]

The speech was part of a deliberate strategy to provoke a war with Austria. The vivid phrase – 'cries of grief' – was suggested by the French Emperor, Napoleon III, with whom the Piedmontese prime minister, Cavour, had concluded a secret agreement the previous year at the spa town of Plombières. France had agreed to join Piedmont in a war to drive Austria out of Lombardy–Venetia; and it had also agreed to the creation of four states in Italy (a powerful kingdom of Upper Italy ruled by the House of Savoy and comprising Piedmont, Lombardy–Venetia, the central duchies, and the papal Romagna; a kingdom of Central Italy dominated by Tuscany but absorbing other provinces of the Papal States; Rome and its immediate province; and the Kingdom of the Two Sicilies). These would form an Italian Confederation with the Pope as president, 'to console him', in Cavour's words, 'for the loss of the best part of his States'. In return, Napoleon asked for the provinces of Nice and Savoy to be ceded to France and for a marriage between his nephew, the middle-aged and dissolute Prince Jérôme Napoléon, with the king's pious fifteen-year-old daughter, Clotilde. Above all, however, the French promise of military assistance was conditional upon Austria declaring war on Piedmont, so that Austria would be diplomatically and militarily isolated and thus easy to defeat.[2] Everything depended, in other words, on making Italy the victim and Austria the aggressor in the upcoming war.

During the months following the Plombières pact, both the French and the Piedmontese leaders did everything they could to precipitate a conflict with Austria. Initially, it had been hoped to provoke Austrian aggression through a revolt in the Duchy of Modena; but recognising the danger of revolution there they concentrated more on encouraging war fever through a series of inflammatory remarks and actions. Just before Vittorio Emanuele's speech, at a public reception in the Tuileries, Napoleon III had told the Austrian ambassador to Paris that he regretted the strained relations between the two countries: this was widely interpreted as a threat of war. War seemed ever more imminent when, later in January, the forthcoming marriage of Jérôme and Clotilde was announced along with a military alliance between France and Piedmont. However, in February, the British government, which was horrified at the prospect of a European war, began successfully to put pressure on both France and Austria to call off the conflict,[3] and in March the Russian government called for a congress to resolve the differences between the two Great Powers, from which Piedmont would be excluded. By early April, Napoleon III had agreed to the congress and to disarm. But Cavour's plan was saved by an ultimatum from Austria threatening war if Piedmont did not disarm immediately. As Mack Smith puts it, Cavour's 'patient work of provocation was dramatically rewarded when Austria, instead of being grateful for this fortunate respite, decided to make Lombardy a test for the viability of her multi-national empire'.[4] On 26 April 1859, Piedmont refused the ultimatum and Austria declared war.[5]

The war of 1859 was short, messy and violent. Austria was slow to mobilise and Piedmont had apparently little in the way of a military plan, relying instead on the French army 'coming to their rescue'.[6] Thus, much of the military strategy was devised by the French high command, and it was the French army which won the first significant battle of the war, at Magenta on 4 June. As a result of Magenta, Vittorio Emanuele and Napoleon III were able to enter Milan in triumph on 8 June. On 24 June, amid scenes of the most terrible bloodshed and chaos, the allies won an impromptu but major battle at Solferino–San Martino. At the same time, disturbances in central Italy (in Parma, Modena, Emilia–Romagna and Tuscany), which were partly orchestrated by the National Society, led to the overthrow of their rulers and to the establishment of liberal governments in these states. These governments then began actively to seek some kind of union with Piedmont.[7] Subsequently, as a result of both the revolutions in central Italy and the violence and cost of the war, Napoleon III suffered a fatal loss of political and military nerve. In early July, and without consulting Piedmont, he and Franz Josef, the Emperor of Austria, concluded an armistice at Villafranca which brought the war to an end.

The 1859 conflict was a crisis of major European significance. While Russia and Britain had sought urgently to keep the peace, the events revived political debate in the German states after a 'long post-revolutionary torpor'.[8] German conservatives were horrified by revived French aggression and the prospect of revolution; neo-conservatives (including Bismarck) saw advantages in the creation of a strong state south of the Alps; Catholics were alarmed by the probable threat to the Papal States; and liberals were enthused by the success of Piedmont and the apparently declining power of the Catholic Church.[9] In the United States too, the potential for the conflict in Italy to destabilise international relations and alter the European balance of power was widely recognised.[10]

Partly as a result of their international significance and of the crucial military role played by Napoleon III's France, the events of 1859 seem to indicate 'the primacy of foreign policy' in Italian unification, or to demonstrate that royal armies, diplomacy and secret alliances played a far more important role than nationalism. Similarly, Cavour's actions – his deal at Plombières and his provocation of war with Austria – are usually studied as prime examples of his 'Machiavellian' methods and of the use of 'almost pure *realpolitik*' in international relations.[11] Especially after the release of government documents which showed how little Cavour cared about the principle of nationality and how far he was prepared to go to aggrandise Piedmont, the events of 1859 have loomed much larger as a problem in European diplomacy and statecraft than as evidence of the strength of nationalist feeling in Italy.[12]

Yet while the role of diplomacy and armies in 1859 is undeniable, it was accompanied by a no less important, and arguably just as visible, wave of patriotic enthusiasm. Much of this was encouraged by the National Society in a major press campaign. From late 1858 onwards, its publications had predicted that a war with Austria was imminent, and its propaganda was picked up by other papers, such as France's *La Presse*. But although this campaign was clearly linked to the willingness of La Farina, the National Society's secretary, to do Cavour's bidding, the closeness of their relationship should not be over-stressed,[13] nor should the ability of the Society entirely to orchestrate or to control nationalist agitation. The broader process of anti-Austrian nationalist agitation included a tobacco boycott in Milan and Parma, the appearance of nationalist slogans and posters in many northern cities, and patriotic demonstrations in theatres throughout the peninsula.[14] In Pavia, the university was closed down by the authorities at the end of 1858 as a result of anti-Austrian and pro-Piedmontese protests by students.[15]

An especially strong indication of the spread of patriotic enthusiasm was the rush by men from outside Piedmont to volunteer for the upcoming war. According to contemporary estimates, around 20,000 volunteers arrived in Turin between mid-January and the end of March 1859;[16] while a more recent calculation puts the number of those actually enlisted as just under 15,000.[17] Subscriptions were opened to which the public gave generously; horses were even sent to provide a mounted guard.[18] The majority of those who volunteered to fight for Piedmont came from Lombardy, with a significant number also from the central duchies, and this is a strong indication of the success of pro-Piedmontese nationalist propaganda in these states during the previous half-decade. Raymond Grew remarks that this demonstration of nationalist fervour was especially significant if 'one remembers the hazards and expense of the journey' to Piedmont, which involved men leaving their families and homes and risking encounters with police in order to join the army of another state; even more so since many of those who volunteered were property-owners, professionals, students, and crafts- and tradesmen who had much to lose and little to gain by leaving home and interrupting their career or occupation.[19] Here too, the government's hand was obvious. It had been part of Cavour's policy to encourage the formation of volunteer corps and desertion from the Austrian army in Lombardy, and he had expected the National Society to oversee their recruitment. However, both Cavour and the National Society were entirely surprised by the flood, or the 'exodus en masse',[20] of volunteers from neighbouring Italian states into Piedmont from January onwards, and they had no clear strategy for dealing with them.[21] To quote Grew again, if the 'movement of volunteers to Turin' established Piedmont as the centre of nationalist aspirations and 'overshadowed the disappointments the SNI [National Society] had known', it also 'left the Society all but swamped by one of the great demonstrations of the Risorgimento'.[22]

Cavour and Garibaldi

In retrospect, therefore, the months leading up to war in 1859 were marked by an evident contradiction between the expansionist ambitions of Piedmont and the general mood of nationalist expectation and enthusiasm. Yet the protagonists sought to deny or to mask this tension, which led to confusion about the means and aims of military struggle. There is no better expression of this uneasy situation than the alliance which was forged in late 1858 between the Piedmontese establishment and Garibaldi. In December 1858, Cavour let Garibaldi in on some aspects of the Plombières deal, asking him to become involved by organising and training volunteers and getting them ready for action in the following spring. Agostino Bertani, a close friend and ally of Garibaldi, reported that after this conversation with Cavour, Garibaldi came to see him and 'with a radiant face and a voice broken with emotion . . . [said] "At last they have agreed to act . . . I have been empowered at the very highest level to tell our friends to get ready.". . . He kept on repeating that we must all be united and all must take arms if we were going to succeed on our own.'[23] Bertani's comments suggest that Garibaldi initially knew nothing of the alliance with France; he was certainly unaware of the plan to cede Nice (his home town) and Savoy to France.

Garibaldi's letters and actions at this time show that his political game was not entirely clear either. He was very happy to help the Piedmontese, but just as keen to impose his own more radical programme on them. He evidently did his best to please the Piedmontese leadership. On more than one occasion in March 1859, Cavour felt able to reassure those concerned that Garibaldi 'made the most explicit declarations, assumed the most precise responsibilities' and that '[h]e has maintained until now the most reserved and prudent attitude'; he had even remarked that Mazzini was *the greatest enemy of Italy*.[24] At the end of June, despite the fact that relations between them had grown tense, Garibaldi assured Cavour of his personal respect and honour, and of his devotion to Cavour, 'whom I have learnt to identify with Italy'.[25] Garibaldi also tried to endear himself to the king by telling La Farina that the king should act at the head of the army ('and don't mind those who call him incapable') and that a military dictatorship should be established to avoid rivalries and 'stormy uprisings' (although it is of course unlikely that this idea would have pleased Cavour).[26]

Before and during the campaign, Garibaldi's speeches to the volunteers repeatedly recommended discipline, obedience, order and 'cold blood'.[27] Perhaps the most startling transformation, for those who remembered Garibaldi from 1848–9, was in his appearance. The changes begun in America in the early 1850s now reached their logical conclusion. The red shirt disappeared, although the poncho remained for a while. He was now in his early fifties and in a photograph taken around this time his figure appears round and more paternal than athletic, a look which was accentuated by the presence of his oldest son, Menotti, among the volunteers.[28] His famous red-blond hair was growing grey and thin, and he wore it more neatly trimmed and with a short beard. After his incorporation into the army, Garibaldi wore the blue Piedmontese general's uniform with silver lace on the collar and cuffs. The volunteers too were neatly dressed in tidy grey clothes, and there was little or nothing 'picturesque' about their appearance.[29]

Yet it was equally evident that Garibaldi had lost none of his nationalist verve and military ambition. In late 1858 he tried (but presumably failed) to reassure La Farina, and indirectly Cavour, by telling him that '[t]he revolutionary elements are all with us'; in the same letter he praised the student demonstrations in Pavia ('an event which you could increase at your will'), and in January 1859 he confidently told La Farina that the organisation of the volunteers would be on a 'fearsome scale'. In the same period, Garibaldi wrote enthusiastically to friends that 'our affairs are moving forward with giant steps', and that 'our affairs are moving marvellously and we will show them our fists'.[30] He also began to reconstruct his Roman high command from 1849, most of whom were former Mazzinians and some of whom had kept in contact with the revolutionary leader. Thus, Garibaldi invited his old comrade from South American days, Giacomo Medici, to join him and got him to overcome his enmity with Nino Bixio, who was also brought into his high command. He persuaded Bertani (who everyone knew had 'certain *mazzinierie*' in his outlook and loyalties) to run the ambulance service, as he had done in Rome in 1849. Many other Roman veterans, such as the Lombard radical, Giovanni Cadolini, came back to fight with Garibaldi, and Garibaldi involved the Pavian student radical, Benedetto Cairoli, as a fund-raiser along with the rest of his family, as volunteers or as support for the volunteers. Finally, with Medici, he planned the organisation of the volunteers into a national guard, and he instructed Bertani to buy Colt revolvers from America for them: 'they are firearms of great precision . . . they have six shots and are lighter than any other firearm'.[31]

'Oh my dear friend!' Garibaldi wrote to one correspondent in April 1859, 'the day we have longed for for so many years has finally arrived.'[32] For Garibaldi, the war was the political and symbolic moment he had been waiting for since the failure of revolution in 1849. He hoped that his volunteer army would, with the help of Piedmont and France, provide the nucleus and leadership for a revitalised Italy. In February, he approved the wording of a 'hymn' for the volunteers to sing when 'marching against the oppressors of our land ', which began 'The tombs are uncovered, the dead come from far,/ The ghosts of our martyrs are rising to war!'[33] On 24 April (two days before Piedmont refused the Austrian ultimatum), he wrote a letter ('my heart is stirring') to Giovanni Battista Cuneo, his friend from the South American days:

I thank Providence which has brought us to the fulfilment of our desires after so many years. Yes, in a few days we will fight the loathed oppressor of our country. Today Italy offers us a magnificent picture, the parties have all disappeared. The sole idea of throwing out the Austrian dominates our spirits. From every province volunteers are rushing forward to ask for a gun. I have the strongest faith that this blessed land will soon redeem itself.[34]

The next day, he issued a similar proclamation to his soldiers:

We have reached the fulfilment of our desires, the object of our hopes; you will fight against the oppressors of the fatherland. Perhaps tomorrow I will meet the Austrians with a gun in my hand to ask for satisfaction for the thefts and outrages which it disgusts me to remember.[35]

Garibaldi's enthusiasm reflected the nationalist excitement in Turin in early 1859; in turn, his presence provided a focus and encouragement for the great demonstration of nationalist feeling offered by the volunteers arriving in the city ready for action.

However, Garibaldi's agenda was not shared by the Piedmontese establishment. By some accounts, the king liked Garibaldi, and Cavour, Napoleon III and the Piedmontese generals all recognised that Garibaldi had his uses, but they disliked his political image, feared his political friends, and were reluctant to cede any freedom of action to him or the volunteers. Despite Garibaldi's expectations, Cavour had originally envisaged no more than an unofficial part for Garibaldi in organising volunteers; for example, in March he told the diplomat Costantino Nigra 'in confidence and for you alone' that they planned to give 'the deserters to Garibaldi who will know what to do with them'.[36] But he never clarified what Garibaldi's role was to be in the royal war with Austria and was most probably far from pleased at Garibaldi's attempts to reconstruct the spirit and organisation of 1848–9. In reality, Cavour simply wanted Garibaldi and the volunteers to bolster up numbers for the forthcoming war, and perhaps by encouraging desertions from the Austrian army to provoke an act of aggression by the Austrian government; he always intended to keep the volunteers away from the royal armies and felt that the regular business of war should be left to them.[37] Hence, to a suggestion that Italians living in America might want to return to Italy and fight for Piedmont, Cavour advised that:

the Government is not in need of the elements whence to form good soldiers and officers ... What is really needed is not so much military assistance as money. While grateful ... for this offer, and fully appreciating the sentiments that inspire it, the Sardinian government does not consider it expedient that it should be accepted, as there is already a superabundance of the military element ... The greater part of our countrymen now in America can as effectually serve the Italian cause by remaining in the United States and using their influence in favor of our efforts as by returning to Italy.[38]

This diffidence was more than shared by the army itself and by Piedmont's French allies. Perhaps unsurprisingly given the experiences of Rome in 1849, Napoleon III had severe misgivings about involving Garibaldi and his volunteers in the upcoming war.[39] The Piedmontese military hierarchy was equally suspicious of Garibaldi, and they made no attempt to hide their *antipatie* towards the volunteers arriving in Turin, treating them in a way which even a loyal supporter of Piedmont described as 'contemptible'.[40]

The army's hostility to the volunteers led it initially to resist the integration of volunteers into its ranks as distinct units, although some were accepted as normal recruits. Nevertheless, by March 1859 the stream of volunteers and their clear enthusiasm for Garibaldi was so significant that the army was forced to bow to the inevitable, and it was agreed not only to incorporate Garibaldi into the army as a major-general, but also to organise three volunteer corps – around 3,000 men as the *Cacciatori delle Alpi* – under his personal command. Interestingly, while this decision was taken with reluctance, the government had in fact pulled off a considerable coup. As Grew remarks, 'they had purchased a large gain in propaganda with a small concession'. They now controlled Garibaldi, who was no longer free to choose his own men, and he was sent most of the older and less able volunteers, while the royal army took most of the younger men and those with more relevant experience.[41]

Garibaldi's campaign

From the beginning of the campaign, the *Cacciatori* suffered from constant problems due to the lack of supplies of food, bedding or basic clothing, and of any provision for the dead and wounded.[42] Garibaldi and his *Cacciatori* also fought a largely separate campaign, being sent away from the main army towards the Alps on Cavour's instructions to disrupt and cut enemy lines as much as possible.[43] 'They gave him three thousand five hundred badly armed and badly dressed young men, without artillery, without cavalry, and they told him: make the best of it', comments Garibaldi's biographer, Giuseppe Guerzoni, who fought with him in the war.[44] In the event, the volunteers performed surprisingly well. They were the first to come into conflict with Austrian forces and defeat them, at Varese in the Lake Maggiore region of Lombardy, on 26 May. The following day, they marched down towards Como and met with the main body of General Urban's army at San Fermo. Although Urban had about twice the number of men as Garibaldi, Garibaldi decided to charge them in a full-frontal attack – sending his men 'down like a torrent' in Bixio's words[45] – and was successful, after which the volunteers entered Como. After an abortive attack on the fort of Laveno on Lake Maggiore, Garibaldi was forced to turn back to Como on hearing that Varese had been re-occupied by the Austrian army but, following the news of the French victory at Magenta, he re-took Varese and marched eastwards towards Bergamo and Brescia.

At Brescia, his growing band of volunteers finally joined up with the main army, and went on towards Salò on Lake Garda. In return for their successes, Garibaldi and his volunteers received military decorations from the king. However, in mid-June they were sent off again into the mountains, this time to the Valtellina to flush out a derisory Austrian force holding Bormio and the Stelvio Pass.[46] In fact, such was the bad treatment of Garibaldi and his volunteers in 1859 that even G. M. Trevelyan, normally entirely laudatory about the process of Italian unification, admits that the *Cacciatori* were unable to play a decisive part in the war of 1859, and that the decision to send them into the remote Valtellina – 'to the rear' of the army – just when they had become 'formidable in numbers' may have been due to 'professional jealousy'.[47]

Much as in 1848–9, however, Garibaldi was not prepared to let official obstruction hamper his political style. Instead, he used the war and his own progress through the mountains of northern Italy to raise more volunteers for the *Cacciatori* and to promote his nationalist message as widely as possible. His speeches and proclamations at this time all repeated the same point: that Italy needed every able-bodied man to volunteer, that it was their duty to join the 'holy war' to drive out the foreigner, and that they had to fight under both the tricolour flag and King Vittorio Emanuele. Perhaps the most emblematic of all his speeches at this time was the proclamation at the beginning of his campaign, 'to the Lombard people', in which his appeal to a sense of national identity combined history, honour and hatred of the foreigner in a religious call to resurgence:

> You are called to a new life and you must respond to the call, as our fathers did in Pontida and in Legnano. The enemy is still the same, a cruel, murderous despoiler. From every province our brothers have sworn to win or die with us. We must revenge the insults, the outrages, the servitude of twenty past generations, and bequeath to our children an inheritance which is uncontaminated by the stink of a domineering foreign soldier . . . [Anyone] who is capable of taking up arms and does not do so is a traitor.[48]

Garibaldi's appeals were very successful. Giovanni Visconti Venosta, then a local official in the Valtellina, described men volunteering every day: 'people of every circumstance and age, often worn-out and with a tired and sickly air. There were old people and even children.'[49] According to figures given by Trevelyan, the *Cacciatori* numbered around 12,000 men (from an original 3,000) by the end of the campaign; although Garibaldi himself gave the more conservative figure of 9,500 men.[50] Also significant in terms of what they reveal about the spread of Garibaldi's popularity was the number of former exiles and/or foreigners who volunteered to fight with him. Among them were

Quirico Filopanti from New York, the Hungarian Stefano Türr, the English translator of Guerrazzi's *Beatrice Cenci* and, most famously of all, 'the gigantic Peard' – 'Garibaldi's Englishman' – an Oxford-educated 'adventurer' who was immediately useful for his skills as a sharpshooter.[51] One company, observed by a Lombard journalist, included not only young men 'generally belonging to the best classes of Italian society' but Swiss, French and American volunteers as well.[52] London's *Times* reported that the exiled Tuscan writer–activist, Giuseppe Montanelli, had followed his son into 'this perilous adventure', along with many foreigners, including some Spaniards and a man from China.[53]

Garibaldi's movements and those of the *Cacciatori* were also greeted with great scenes of popular enthusiasm. After his entrance into Varese on 26 May, Garibaldi wrote to Cavour that '[a]ll the young people rushed to take up arms and defend the barricades; the population responded with shouts of *viva l'Italia, viva Vittorio Emanuele* to the sound of cannon fire. The church bells rang the tocsin in Varese and neighbouring villages.'[54] Others confirmed his account, and were more forthcoming with details. One officer, Francesco Carrano, described extraordinary scenes in Varese, which the *Cacciatori* entered slowly, in the dark and the pouring rain, to find the town abandoned by the Austrians:

> suddenly a loud shot was heard from not far away, and a large red light was seen to break the darkness of the rainy night. It was the population of Varese who had come out with hundreds of torches to meet Garibaldi and his *Cacciatori delle Alpi*. A thousand cries of joy greeted the famous Italian leader, the man of miracles . . . he was carried in triumph through the city, while men and women came out to shake the hands of the soldiers all dripping with water, and they embraced them like sons and brothers, and quite a few really were[;] Garibaldi saluted with his sword on all sides, and encouraged the people to cheer the King Vittorio Emanuele, and to take up arms against the foreign oppressors, and to come as volunteers to enlarge the ranks of those who were fighting the holy war . . .[55]

On the steps of the town hall, amid a general 'frenzy', Garibaldi and the mayor hugged and kissed each other.[56] In Como too, the population was said to have gone wild. For Giovanni Cadolini, 'the exultation was such that it became almost painful . . . I never saw more impressive scenes of brotherly love.' Carrano saw the people of Como dressed only in their nightclothes and in the rain, unfolding tricolour flags and shouting at the tops of their voices: '"*Viva l'Italia! Viva Garibaldi*" and they vied with each other to see the face and to embrace the legs of the famous Italian warrior'.[57]

These accounts are clearly partisan and some are written much later, so the tendency greatly to exaggerate the extent of enthusiasm and the numbers involved should not be excluded. The weight of evidence suggests nevertheless that there was widespread practical support for Garibaldi and his men, and for the idea of Italy more broadly. One of the doctors who accompanied the *Cacciatori* remarked on what he termed the 'generous support of citizens' for Garibaldi's soldiers. Indeed, he suggested that the soldiers survived the cold rain and hardship of the mountains largely thanks to the general welcome given by ordinary people:

> Throughout Lombardy the care lavished on us by both citizens and town councils was all we could have hoped for. Our soldiers, without packs and with only one shirt and one pair of underpants would certainly not have been able to keep themselves clean and free of lice if the citizens had not come to their help with clean linen, nor would they have been able to put up with the rain for so long were it not for the fact that all the fireplaces in every town and village were made available to them on arrival so that they could dry themselves.[58]

That scenes of patriotic fervour were also quite commonplace is suggested by similar descriptions of the welcome given to the king in cities like Milan and Brescia, and by other patriotic demonstrations such as the making of tricolour flags, the composing and publication of songs and other patriotic pamphlets, and the wearing of tricolour cockades, all of which could involve broad sections of urban society, and which involved the participation of women as well as men. Indeed, it is possible to speak of a wave of nationalist agitation in northern and central Italy during 1859, which had been prepared by the propaganda efforts of the National Society and was spread by the war. Nor did the efforts of the National Society cease during the war; it was its presence in the central Italian duchies during April and May which encouraged the prevailing sense that the Austrian era was over, and that the political future lay with Piedmont and Italian nationalism.[59]

The great welcome given to Garibaldi in places like Varese and Como was the result of his identification with a particular political moment, with his physical affiliation to the nation and to Piedmont; he personally did much to encourage this identification in his speeches and actions. It is equally possible to observe a tendency for Garibaldi's charisma to acquire a life of its own. In 1859, outbreaks of public emotion began to follow his person as much as his politics. Those who heard Garibaldi speak in 1859 agreed that his ability to focus and excite the crowd, and to persuade men to volunteer, was extraordinary. 'One of the characteristic and emotionally moving spectacles of those days [in early July in the Valtellina]', according to Visconti Venosta, 'was the enthusiasm, the irresistible passion, with which people rushed to the sign of Garibaldi, or rose up as if pushed by a turbine if Garibaldi appeared.' He described the 'spell [*fascino*]' which Garibaldi 'cast over the multitude' as something 'marvellous' and 'almost unimaginable' (as well as being worthy of study):

> Garibaldi, when he came through a town, and although at that time he did not wear the red shirt, did not seem to be a general as much as the leader of a new religion, followed by a fanatical rabble. The women were no less enthusiastic than the men, and they even brought along their children so that Garibaldi would bless them, or even baptise them! [60]

Much of this *fascino*, for Visconti Venosta, was due to Garibaldi's speeches and to the way he used his voice, so that his every pronouncement, even the most insignificant, 'had an immeasurable effect' and produced a 'frenzy'. There was, he speculated, a kind of 'magnetic current' between Garibaldi the speaker and the crowd who heard him.[61] The unusual effect of Garibaldi on his listeners was confirmed by an arguably more impartial observer, the British military attaché George Cadogan. He described Garibaldi as a gentle, cautious and rather unrefined man, but with 'an influence on his hearers which a more cultivated intelligence might fail to have. Add to this a voice of singular charm and a manner that brings conviction with it as to the sincerity of speech, and it can be easily imagined that it is no exaggeration to say he could make his followers go anywhere and do anything.' Thus, for Cadogan, Garibaldi had the common touch. He had watched as Garibaldi gave a speech to his soldiers at the outposts. 'It would be impossible', he commented, 'to do justice to the familiar and paternal, though not undignified, character of the few words thus spoken, or to the enthusiasm they produced'.[62]

Villafranca and after

Like so much else in 1859, there was a basic contradiction between these nationalist demonstrations and the prosaic exigencies of international politics. As Garibaldi's campaign of recruitment and mobilisation reached its climax, the tables were turned against him and the entire nationalist movement by the announcement of the armistice between France and Austria at Villafranca. The peace terms agreed by the two emperors recognised the defeat of Austria in Italy, but also tried to save Austria's face. They sought to downplay the victory of Piedmont, and to deny a triumph to the nationalists in the peninsula. So the emperors decided that Lombardy was to be ceded first to France, and only then to be given by France to Piedmont. Furthermore, all the military fortresses of the Quadrilateral (two of which were in Lombardy) were to remain in Austrian hands, as was the entire province of Venetia; and the Habsburg rulers were to be restored to the duchies of Modena, Parma and Tuscany, from where they had fled at the start of the war.

The peace of Villafranca caused consternation among Mazzinian sympathisers and disappointment among the supporters of Italy abroad. Cavour too was frantic to continue the war and furious at the frustration of all his plans; having failed to persuade the king to continue the war without the French, he resigned as prime minister of Piedmont and temporarily retired from politics. But, interestingly, La Farina for the National Society adopted a more conciliatory tone and insisted nothing had been changed by Villafranca. This line seemed to be endorsed by Garibaldi, who issued a proclamation on 23 July which acknowledged the help given by Napoleon and 'the heroic French nation' and insisted that Italy's future still lay with Vittorio Emanuele.[63]

In private, however, it was clear that Garibaldi did not accept the peace. He pleaded personally with the king to be allowed to continue the nationalist struggle; he told the king that he wanted to liberate 'enslaved' Venetia and the other fifteen million Italians in the peninsula, and 'to repeat your cry of national war along the Appennines and the two seas [the Tyrrhenian and the Adriatic]'.[64] He focused his attention on central Italy, where it was obvious that the Habsburg rulers could not be restored without a struggle. On 19 July, he wrote to the Tuscan leader Montanelli that, if offered, he would accept the command of troops in central Italy, and on 27 July he repeated his commitment to (the pro-Piedmontese but also ex-Mazzinian) Antonio Mordini, telling him, 'in any case I think it is indispensable to arm everyone to the death, to bring everyone together whenever we can and to close ranks in the most complete harmony'.[65]

Garibaldi's response to Villafranca – maintaining a public loyalty to the king while in private rejecting and plotting against the political line endorsed by the same – represented the continuation of a policy which he had long pursued, and which had determined his participation in the National Society and his *rapprochement* with Cavour before 1859. Still, there was no doubt that Villafranca revealed cracks in the façade of unity and 'harmony' that he and the National Society had so carefully constructed. Henceforth, some kind of clash between Garibaldi's heroic vision of a 'nation-at-arms' and Cavour's cynical mix of royalist liberalism seems to have been inevitable. Garibaldi's own discomfort and frustration were expressed bluntly in a letter he wrote on 27 July to the founder of the National Society, Giorgio Pallavicino Trivulzio, 'I am with you, with Vittorio and with Italy; I despise all the rest and I hope that before too long we will rise again on the battlefield and finish it off.'[66]

From Villafranca onwards, Garibaldi sought repeatedly to force the government's hand, but he faced difficulties and obstacles at every turn. First, he agreed to resign his commission in the Piedmontese army and to accept the command of troops in central Italy where, despite the armistice agreement, the provisional governments had remained in control. Immediately he began to make plans for the new army; he wanted the volunteers to be transferred to central Italy and he invited his closest officers – Medici, Bixio, Cosenz – to join him.[67] However, to his great irritation, he found himself placed as second in command to General Manfredo Fanti, or 'at the third level', as he put it, also behind Generals Roselli and Mezzacapo.[68]

Garibaldi responded by issuing a series of public appeals to the people of Italy, encouraging them to take arms and calling for military action to drive out the foreigner. He told the people of Tyrol they had not been forgotten; he called on 'our brothers in Naples' to join their brothers in northern and central Italy; and he invited the soldiers in the Papal States to fight with Italy for liberty and unification. These appeals appeared in newspapers and were published as flyers; according to one report, 'thousands' of copies of his appeal to the Neapolitans were circulated in the capital and its provinces.[69] Most importantly, he opened a subscription for a 'Million Rifles'. Its aim was to raise money for a new volunteer national guard, 'made up of every man able to carry a firearm, divided into three categories', or a mass army organised according to physical capacity; the older and more infirm were to be included but confined to policing the cities, while the more active were to be organised into mobile columns.[70] The fund was an implicit rebuke to Piedmont for its material reliance on the French military. The Garibaldian programme, Benedetto Cairoli wrote on 25 September, was 'not local defence but national war'.[71]

Strengthened by his appointment as president of the revived National Society, Garibaldi's 'Million Rifles' campaign gathered pace. Accepting the presidency from La Farina (who maintained practical control of the National Society), he announced that he looked forward to the 'redemption' of Italy: 'we will not lay down our arms while a palm of our land remains unredeemed!'[72] Mazzini arrived in secret in Florence, with money from his English friends. Although it is not clear that Garibaldi was in touch with Mazzini, he did not entirely exclude conspiracy, if the recruitment of his lover, Esperanza von Schwartz, in a highly secret mission to Messina is any indication.[73] Garibaldi also organised an office for the Rifles Fund, with Enrico Besana as director, and he ordered clothes for the soldiers.[74] Committees were formed in Bologna, Milan and New York; money came in from Tuscany, the Romagna and Lombardy; and Pallavicino of the National Society 'supported it vigorously'.[75]

That Garibaldi's fame continued to grow is indicated by the increasing number of public demonstrations in his honour in central Italy. 'Garibaldi is at last in Florence', Thomas Trollope wrote to the *Athenaeum* magazine, '[y]esterday he tried hard, but in vain, to preserve his *incognito*, for brave *"Gallibardi"*, as the Tuscan lower classes . . . invariably call him, is no lover of noisy demonstration.' But he was caught by them in the Piazza della Signoria 'in a tempest of enthusiastic welcome, and could only extricate himself at the cost of a short address to his welcomers'.[76] Even an apparently private visit to his wife's grave in Ravenna became the occasion for nationalist demonstrations, and for a speech in which Garibaldi called for contributions to the Million Rifles Fund.[77] 'This man [Garibaldi] enjoys an immense, universal and almost limitless popularity', the Tuscan leader, Bettino Ricasoli, wrote in October; '[w]e are all aware of the prestige which the name of General Garibaldi brings with it', admitted General Farini at the end of the same month.[78]

However, in mid-November Garibaldi took a step too far. Stationed on the frontier with the Papal States, he responded to the false news of an insurrection in the Marche, and prepared his army to help the rebels. But his order to invade the Marche was cancelled by the Piedmontese army (Generals Farini and Fanti), and Garibaldi, summoned to Turin by the king, was removed from his command in the Romagna. Even this setback failed entirely to stop him, however. He issued a proclamation 'to the Italians' in which he announced his retirement from the army and referred to 'underhand tricks and continual constraints' on his freedom of action; he announced that the subscription for a Million Rifles remained open, and told his colleagues in the fund to carry on their activities because '[w]hen the day of battle returns, I will take one of those guns offered to the fatherland by its loving children and I will rush into battle with my old companions'. He declined the king's offer to re-appoint him general in the Piedmontese army because it would deprive him of that freedom of action 'with which I could still be useful in central Italy and elsewhere', although he did accept the gift of a shotgun and he seems to have carried on wearing a general's uniform.[79] As Trevelyan comments, this quarrel in the autumn of 1859 marked the re-emergence of a 'more dangerous and intractable Garibaldi': 'the long honeymoon of Garibaldi and the cabinet of Turin was at an end'.[80]

Relations did not improve thereafter. More than ever before, according to Raymond Grew, Garibaldi became 'the symbol of a program which competed with Cavour's'. In December, he resigned from the presidency of the National Society. He drew closer to the left deputy Angelo Brofferio, who had begun to organise an increasingly vituperative campaign against Cavour, and he endorsed the programme of Brofferio's *Liberi Comizii*, set up as a rival to the National Society. When the *Liberi Comizii* ran into difficulties at the end of

December, Garibaldi set up his own political organisation, the nation-at-arms (*Nazione Armata*), with openly military aims.[81] His contempt for Cavour and parliamentary government became more unequivocal. He confided his view to Pallavicino that 'our good Vittorio Emanuele' should 'put one of his boots into the head of the Minister and keep for himself alone the army and the Italian nation, with which he could accomplish miracles'.[82] His public speeches and published proclamations were equally inflammatory. In a speech published in *L'Unione* on 14 December, he recalled past examples of 'female patriotism' and asked Italian women to give their 'surplus' to Italy; on the 18th, he challenged the idea of the regular army and called for the national guard to increase its numbers; and on 24 December he addressed the students of Pavia University in a barely coherent tirade against 'a few wicked men', priests and 'the cancer called the Papacy'. Announcing the formation of the nation-at-arms on 31 December, he looked forward to the day when, '[b]ound together in a single phalanx, we will have from that moment but one enemy, the foreign oppressor, and we will live with one hope, Italian freedom'.[83]

Garibaldi's activities seem to have been connected to a plot between the king and Urbano Rattazzi, Cavour's great rival in parliament, to prevent Cavour forming a new government. If so, they failed in this objective, as Cavour was recalled to power in late January 1860. Already, only four days after its foundation, Garibaldi had been told by the king to dissolve the nation-at-arms. He announced its dissolution in a 'Proclamation to the Italians' on 4 January, pointing to the fear it aroused among 'corrupters and bullies, as much within as outside Italy, [where] the crowd of modern Jesuits took fright and cried anathema'.[84] Even for those on Garibaldi's side, the whole episode seemed proof of his political clumsiness. The British ambassador to Turin, Sir James Hudson, described him as a 'well-meaning goose', [85] and Pallavicino observed, 'he is not an *eagle* but a lion. The lion is distinguished by his *strength*, and not by his intelligence.'[86] His close friend Medici lamented that: 'Our poor friend Garibaldi . . . allows himself to be persuaded by discredited men . . . he ruins himself in times of inaction; he talks too much, writes too much, and listens too much to those who know nothing';[87] while the Sicilian revolutionary Francesco Crispi condemned him for being 'as weak as a woman . . . [he] allows himself to be . . . taken in by the very first person who comes along'.[88] Instead of being a means of relaunching the military struggle against Austria, as Garibaldi had hoped, the nation-at-arms had added to his reputation as someone who, in G. M. Trevelyan's words, 'did not understand European politics'.[89]

However, it is worth remembering what Garibaldi had achieved through this frenetic activity. He had sought, and partly managed, to maintain the nationalist organisation and promote international publicity for Italy after the end of the war with Austria. He had established himself as an unassailable force in Italian politics ('one of the greatest forces', admitted Cavour), and his personal popularity grew after Villafranca. Garibaldi had 'in his hands the people of Italy', according to Bertani.[90] As one enthusiast wrote to him from Modena after his resignation from the army: 'We are faithfully awaiting Your return, because we hope that our cause will make its ultimate appeal to the Tribunal of Arms!'[91] At the same time, his reputation for political ineptness could work in his favour, since it added to his standing as a man of affection and integrity. Garibaldi had a warm and tender heart, the poet Walter Savage Landor wrote to *The Times*: he was brave in battle and careful of his men.[92] Most importantly of all perhaps, and thanks to his tireless publicity efforts, his Rifles Fund amassed significant amounts of money and significant amounts of goodwill. One English manufacturer of breech-loading rifles wrote to Garibaldi in December that to honour the 'illustrious son Freedom!' he would 'cheerfully' waive all the patent and service charges relating to their supply.[93] These achievements were to prove vital to the success of his spring expedition to Sicily; the expedition itself was paid for by the Rifles Fund and other related subscriptions organised during these months.[94]

From Nice to Sicily

After the failure of the nation-at-arms, Garibaldi withdrew once more from public life. His political troubles seem to be reflected in his personal life: during the summer of 1859, at the age of fifty-two, he had fallen violently in love with Giuseppina Raimondi, an eighteen-year-old girl from a noble family, and proposed marriage to her.[95] However, his passion for Giuseppina did not stop him from falling in love with another woman, the Marchesa Paulina Zucchini, in October, to whom he also proposed marriage; nor did it prevent him from writing fervent letters to Teresa Araldi Trecchi, the sister of a fellow soldier, or from declaring infatuation to a Sofia Bettini, whom he had met in Staten Island and who had written asking for his autograph. Earlier in the year, his housekeeper in Caprera, Battistina Ravello, had given birth to his child, Anita, and throughout this time his close relationships with Esperanza von Schwartz and Maria della Torre continued (although Esperanza was apparently unhappy about his relationship with Battistina).[96] All this sexual activity reached crisis point in January when he married Giuseppina, only to reject her on the day of their marriage after he discovered her involvement with another man, and that she was pregnant. He wrote furiously to Lorenzo Valerio that he wanted nothing to do with her or her 'foul and loathsome' family, and that she should be prevented from using his name. In February, he wrote again to Valerio that he and Giuseppina could be divorced, as their

marriage was not consummated: he had had sex ('copulations') with her in
December, but not after 20 January, 'so that since the marriage took place on
the 24th and not having copulated again, I think that the marriage can be
considered *unconsummated*'.[97]

It is difficult to know what to make of Garibaldi's behaviour towards
Giuseppina. His treatment of her (he never forgave or acknowledged her
again) is certainly interesting as it reveals to us less attractive aspects of his
private life and personality, otherwise closely guarded 'off-stage' at Caprera.
His passionate letters to her, and his violent over-reaction to her conduct
when he was doing the same as she was, suggest either personal confusion or
considerable hypocrisy, or both. Equally, and most rarely of all, his letters to
her give us an insight into his own view of his fame and its purpose:

> Adorable Giuseppina! I am divided by two sentiments which trouble me to
> an unimaginable extent: love and duty! I love you with all my heart . . . Here
> is the voice of duty: I have in the island a common woman [*una donna
> plebea*], and with this woman I have a child; this would be a minor obstacle,
> because I can't love her any more . . . . [but] uniting with you, most
> beautiful maiden! I would deny that aspect of self-denial which is part of the
> popularity which I enjoy and which I can use for the good of the fatherland,
> when Italian matters call me once more to lead soldiers they will say of
> Garibaldi: he has intrigued fortune! . . . Answer me quickly! I am in such a
> state that I can't wait! . . . For God's sake don't get angry! With someone
> who worships you![98]

Despite his fears, the newspapers mostly kept quiet about his affair and the
fiasco of his marriage, reflecting a general, if somewhat surprising, reluctance
to comment on the more 'scandalous' aspects of his private life. The *New York
Times* published a letter defending Garibaldi and Raimondi's characters
against 'a most infamous aspersion' in 'one or two of the City papers';[99] but
publicly little more than vague rumours circulated. Yet that people knew
about his disastrous marriage is suggested by the private diary of Horace de
Viel-Castel, a Bonapartist writer:

> Garibaldi . . . married a young girl, the heroine of a romance . . . as beautiful
> as anything etc. etc. . . . . Garibaldi, although a republican hero, allowed
> himself to be swayed by every vanity: the old partisan found it quite normal
> that a young girl of seventeen should be madly in love with him, so he
> married her. But, oh bitter disappointment, this enchanting young girl '*was
> four months pregnant!*'[100]

His comments suggest that Garibaldi was not wrong to worry about his romance damaging his 'noble' reputation.

Following these personal and political problems, Garibaldi withdrew to Caprera. 'You have been forced to renounce the Presidency of the nation-at-arms as well?!' one correspondent wrote to him; 'once again I have preached in the desert', Garibaldi wrote to Medici.[101] He spent the whole of February and March at Caprera, refusing all attempts to get him involved with the nascent rebellion in southern Italy. Although he did what he could materially to assist the Sicilian revolutionary, Rosolino Pilo, who was planning a revolt in Sicily, he also felt it necessary to tell him that 'in the present time I don't think that a revolutionary movement is appropriate in any part of Italy, unless it has a really significant chance of success'.[102] That he had chosen once more to take up a life of semi-exile and was planning to pursue politics by another means is indicated by the decision to work on, and try to publish, his memoirs. After his resignation from the army, he wrote to Esperanza von Schwartz asking her for the manuscript back. In January, Alexandre Dumas sought him out in Genoa, and shortly afterwards Garibaldi sent his memoirs to the French novelist.[103] It was clear that there was considerable public interest in anything written by Garibaldi. As William Thackeray wrote to him from London in February: 'We have 500,000 readers. How many more should we have for an article by you? Biography, Italy, America, military tactics . . . how grateful our public would be for any contribution from your pers[on].'[104]

Everything changed, however, with the news at the end of March that Cavour had 'signed away' the provinces of Nice and Savoy to France.[105] The cession of these provinces was the price asked by Napoleon III for French agreement to Piedmont annexing Parma, Modena, Tuscany and the Romagna, and was immensely unpopular, severely damaging Cavour's reputation at home and abroad. Garibaldi's reaction was expressed succinctly in a letter of 26 March: 'My native city is in danger of falling into the claws of the lord protector . . . Thirty years of service for the cause of popular freedom: I will only have won the servitude of my poor land!'[106] In the general election held shortly afterwards, he was returned as a member of parliament, and went to Turin determined to speak against the annexation (which was due to be sanctioned by plebiscite on 15 and 16 April). His speech was applauded but changed nothing ('I knew it would be all a waste of time and breath', he told an Englishman who had accompanied him);[107] and he hatched a plan to travel by ship to Nice, seize the ballot papers and burn them, thus postponing the plebiscite and giving himself more time to stir up enough publicity to prevent the annexation from ever taking place. He decided against this, however, and agreed instead to lead an expedition to Sicily. Encouraged by Rosolino Pilo, an insurrection in Palermo in early April had apparently spread to the countryside, and the Bourbon government faced a serious crisis.[108]

But Garibaldi remained far from convinced by the revolution in Sicily. He lost his nerve more than once before the final departure with his volunteers from Quarto near Genoa in the early morning of 6 May. The news coming in from Sicily was confused, and increasingly suggested that the revolution had failed. In mid-April, 12,000 firearms bought by the Million Rifles Fund for the expedition were seized in Turin, on the orders of the Piedmontese government. Cavour's general attitude, typically equivocal, was largely unhelpful.[109] More moderate colleagues, such as Giacomo Medici, also tried to stop Garibaldi from going.

So it is not clear why exactly Garibaldi did decide to leave for Sicily to help the revolution, although endless efforts at persuasion by Francesco Crispi played a key role.[110] Crispi was helped by the presence of Nino Bixio and the Sicilian baron, Giuseppe La Masa, both of whom were keen to go. Garibaldi's decision may also reflect a highly charged emotional state. The fragment of a letter to 'a relative', written on 25 April, gives us some insight into his feelings:

Everything crushes and humiliates me, my heart is full of mourning. What should I do? Abandon this place, which suffocates me and disgusts me so much that I feel sick. I will do so soon, quite soon ... But honest patriots will always be able to count on me. I will never ask if an expedition is possible or not, so as to buy my fame ... with success on the cheap. For me it is enough that it should be an Italian expedition ... In any case I have only one remaining desire: *To Die for Italy*; and this destiny, these dangers I will risk earlier than I expected ...[111]

The expedition, in other words, followed an established Mazzinian tradition of commiting acts of martyrdom for symbolic purposes. Once again, it reminds us of how much Garibaldi's political outlook and practice continued to be determined by romantic tropes and Mazzinian assumptions.[112]

Considerable momentum had been created by the continual arrival at Garibaldi's headquarters in Quarto of volunteers who had heard about the expedition and wanted to be part of it. There was a striking continuity between the social and geographical background of these volunteers, who eventually numbered just over a thousand, and those of 1859; and many, it seems, had fought with Garibaldi the year before. They came mostly from the cities of Lombardy (434 out of a total of 1,089), with significant numbers from the Veneto and Liguria, and a roughly equal number from Sicily and Tuscany. There were a few foreigners (notably some Hungarian officers), and they were mostly, but by no means all, young (i.e. born in the 1820s and '30s). Many were professionals (lawyers, doctors), others were from the lower middle class (artisans and shopkeepers), and a significant number were also writers, journalists and artists.[113] When it seemed as if the expedition would be abandoned, some of these volunteers wept, others swore, and a few sent a deputation to Garibaldi in an attempt to persuade him otherwise, or at least to give them the money and firearms so that they could go without him. The Tuscan writer, Giuseppe Bandi, then a young man at the beginning of his friendship with Garibaldi, later recalled their disappointment: 'those poor fellows, who had spent the night singing happy songs, who were convinced of going on a glorious voyage to the island of the Vespers, adorned with all the poetry that can dance in the head of young people'.[114] Their presence at Quarto is evidence of what the *New York Times* called at this time 'the magic of [Garibaldi's] name', around which had begun 'to cluster the most passionate hopes and the loftiest aspirations of the patriots of Italy'. Their enthusiasm for the expedition was a clear response to Garibaldi's call to the political generation of 1848 and '59, and proof of their political and emotional engagement with the Risorgimento ideals represented and pursued by him.[115]

Finally, during the night of 5 May, a small group led by Nino Bixio seized two steamships in Genoa from the Rubattino shipping company in order to transport the volunteers to Sicily (they had already managed to get hold of some old rifles from La Farina). They took the two ships, which they had renamed *Piemonte* and *Lombardo*, to the nearby rocks at Quarto, where the volunteers (including Crispi's wife, Rosalie) who had gathered there during the previous days embarked for Sicily. One of Garibaldi's last acts before leaving his bedroom at the Villa Spinola to go down to join his volunteers was to change his clothes. Gone was not just the Piedmontese uniform but also the dark gentleman's clothes in which his other public appearances had been made during the previous decade. In their place, he put on grey trousers and a red shirt and tied a silk handkerchief around his neck; he came out of his room wearing this outfit, with a poncho over his shoulders and on his head a black felt hat.[116] His reportedly radiant appearance left no one in doubt that Garibaldi the revolutionary had returned.

CHAPTER 7

FASHIONING GARIBALDI

Events were to prove Garibaldi right in one sense. The peace of Villafranca was by no means the end of the affair; rather, it was just the beginning of a rapid series of events which culminated in Garibaldi's expedition to Sicily in the spring of 1860, and which were drastically to alter the political map of Italy and European diplomatic relations. Just as remarkable was the public response to Garibaldi and the wars of Italian independence. Enthusiasm for Garibaldi spread across Europe and to the United States, and publications about him found a wide readership in France, Britain and Germany, as well as in Italy itself. A particular feature of these non-Italian publications was the free mixing of history and invention, and the effect of these developments was to produce a new image of Garibaldi with a general European-wide appeal, in which his radicalism tended to be toned down or at least depoliticised. Yet, as we shall see, this new image produced its own tensions and political contradictions, and did not go unchallenged.

A media war

The war of 1859 was the most newsworthy event of the year. Following on from the Crimean War in the mid-1850s, and coming before the American Civil War of the 1860s, the reporting of the 1859 war in Italy was, like them, affected by a new public and 'media' engagement with warfare. This 'enormous demand for information and newspapers' was made possible and encouraged by the new advances in communication and publishing.[1] The significance of photography in raising public awareness of these wars is well known,[2] but perhaps of more immediate importance in explaining the wide coverage of the 1859 war in France, Germany, Britain and the United States, as well as in Italy, was the development of the telegraph. The telegraph allowed correspondents to send their reports, and officials their dispatches, to the newspapers on a daily (if not more than daily) basis; here, the Reuter telegram company (set up by Baron Julius Reuter in 1851), which sent news of the battles and Napoleon III's dispatches to the European press, played a crucial role in publicising the war and providing newspaper editors with regular copy.[3] Equally relevant in accounting for the prominence of the war was the extent to which, in the absence of functioning copyright laws, papers and pamphlets could use information and directly reproduce articles from other newspapers, so that any one episode could be discussed several times in different reports in a single issue of a newspaper.

From the outset of the war, all foreign eyes were fixed on Italy and each battle in the war, especially Solferino, was front-page news.[4] The *New York Times* correspondent sent back detailed letters about the battle, and the paper also published a large map of the battlefield;[5] the London *Times* coverage of Solferino ('one of the greatest battles of modern days . . . a gigantic duel', according to a correspondent) included Reuter's telegrams, extracts from French newspapers, official bulletins and reports from all three armies, and eyewitness accounts sent in from correspondents stationed on both sides of the conflict.[6] Early in the following year, *The Illustrated London News* published a special colour supplement on the battle of Solferino.[7] There was also a broad public interest in the war in Britain and the USA, where it seems to have become something of a spectator sport. One Italian journalist, Charles Arrivabene, noted the presence of British tourists visiting the battlefields near Brescia, and states that this was 'by no means rare at that time'. Sometimes the men 'were loaded with all sorts of projectiles and arms', souvenirs bought from peasants at the Solferino battlefield, although the ladies were content to collect 'stones, flowers, and even branches of slender trees, in commemoration of the places they had visited'.[8] Public engagement with the war is also suggested by the production of souvenirs to commemorate battles and the main protagonists; these included plates, scarves, fans and medals.[9]

Of course, not all the press was in favour of the war, and some journalists focused attention on the suffering it caused. For instance, accounts of the terrible bloodshed ('carnage', according to a *Times* reporter)[10] at Solferino, and of the absence of an adequate medical service to treat the wounded (most notably in Henri Dunant's *Un souvenir de Solférino*) were instrumental in the setting up of the International Red Cross in Geneva five years later.[11] Elsewhere, the war caused considerable political controversy. Even in France, where Napoleon III was only too well aware of the potential of new technology to influence public opinion and there were strict government controls over the press,[12] a debate emerged about Napoleon III's involvement in the Italian war. Alongside the war itself, there took place what one historian has called a 'pamphlet battle' between left and right in France over the correct line to pursue in Italy: 'journalists and polemicists, famous writers, important statesmen and clerical personalities' became actively engaged in a battle for public opinion which manifested itself in print, and which extended and intensified in the following years.[13] The campaign in Italy led to a deterioration in relations between Napoleon III's regime and the Church in France, and it probably helped radical papers like *Le Siècle* to survive government censorship, since Napoleon III needed their support for the campaign.[14]

Le Siècle responded to this opportunity with a blanket reporting of the war, which included reports from special correspondents, daily bulletins, articles from other papers and profiles of the personalities involved. In general and more than in Britain or the USA, in France the immediate requirements of domestic politics intruded into representations and perceptions of the war. Not surprisingly, the war was frequently presented as a positive, patriotic experience, and here political commentaries on the war were both subordinated to, and indirectly expressed as, public entertainment. In this respect, the war also provided an occasion for newspapers and magazines to make money.[15]

A prominent feature of the reporting of the war in France was the production of regular supplements to newspapers and other serial publications, and especially the use of illustrations and other visual material. As early as April, the Paris magazine *L'Illustration* told its readers that it was preparing an atlas of the war and had sent correspondents and established contacts throughout the likely theatre of war. The following month, the magazine increased its circulation and gave its readers a coloured map of Italy and four engravings of the soldiers' departure along with many other illustrations. The magazine, which emphasised that the French progress in Italy 'had been simply one long triumphal march', continued to cover the war throughout the summer; the edition of 28 May dedicated a whole section to a description of the physical landscape of northern Italy with illustrations of lakes and mountains. In effect, *L'Illustration* sought to present the war as a great patriotic adventure and relied heavily on the travel guide formula.[16]

L'Illustration's recasting of the war as public entertainment seems to have been popular, and was adopted elsewhere. Thus, the more modest *Journal pour tous*, with poorer reproduction values than *L'Illustration*, published a regular illustrated supplement to the war – *La guerre d'Italie. Récit hebdomadaire illustré* – which appeared in twenty-six numbers during 1859.[17] Perhaps most revealing of how politics and war could be reworked and presented was the publication of a series of 'war songs', *Souvenirs de la guerre d'Italie*, by a group of radical poets and song-writers led by Pierre Dupont. These songs – 'The departure','The Alpine song', 'To women during the Italian war', 'The cry of the Zouaves', 'The Piedmontese girl', 'Garibaldi' and so on – were published in serial form as part of the weekly illustrated magazine, *Chants et chansons populaires de la France*, complete with sheet music for piano. The accompanying illustrations again included idealised patriotic representations and detailed depictions of soldiers and battle scenes in Alpine environments.[18] Nor was this type of reporting a purely French phenomenon; elsewhere, public interest in the war blended seamlessly with more traditional, 'picturesque' perceptions of the Italian landscape to produce an essentially escapist narrative of events. Much of the coverage offered by *The Illustrated London News* resembled a travel guide to northern Italy. It described the beautiful nature of the local scenery, and maps, landscapes and cityscapes dominated its reporting, along with illustrations of French troops departing, French troops arriving, and even the public receptions held for Napoleon III.[19]

In Italy too, this pattern of reporting was largely followed in the liberal press. Cheap maps, lithographs of battle scenes and portraits of the protagonists were soon produced in large numbers and appeared for sale in the main cities. Sales of such prints were probably responsible for one of the most vivid examples of public engagement with the war, which was the production of higher-quality, illustrated 'Albums'. These were published in series form, each instalment featuring an episode or personality from the war along with an illustration, usually a good-quality portrait or a battle scene. One *Album storico–artistico*, published contemporaneously in Turin and Paris in forty instalments, used reports from the London *Times* to produce what the editors called an 'elegant volume' with '40 beautiful watercolour drawings of the main battles, drawn from life by the distinguished Piedmontese artist Bossoli', along with 'twenty wonderful portraits'. We know very little about the commercial success of these ventures, but a 'sequel' was produced the following year, in which the author referred to the 'extraordinary approval' of the 1859 album, which indicates that, at the least, the format had proven popular.[20] That these albums were indeed popular is also suggested by the publication of another album on the 1859 war – *L'Italia e i suoi difensori. Album storico–biografico* – which used a similar format, this time with a short history of 'Italian resurgence [*risorgimento*] in the nineteenth century', and more emphasis on the biographies of the main protagonists.[21]

The General

Given his proven ability to be picturesque and to capture the attention of the press and the public, it was perhaps to be expected that Garibaldi would loom large in accounts of the 1859 war. The problem facing journalists and editors in France, however, was his reputation as a revolutionary and an enemy of France in 1849. The general response, by the non-clerical press at least, was to de-politicise Garibaldi, and to present him as a kind of broad, all-purpose hero, whose bravery was unparalleled but whose loyalty and discipline were never in doubt. *L'Illustration* made no mention at all of his politics and wrote only of his popularity and prestige. Garibaldi was the 'illustrious leader', 'the intrepid general . . . the indefatigable Garibaldi', an 'intrepid soldier of Italian liberty', and a useful ally of France who, 'always driven by his strong love for Italy, and powerfully attached to the cause of independence', had also been one of the first to ally himself with the king, Vittorio Emanuele.[22] *Le Siècle* was notable for its adulation:

> Garibaldi! what a man! what prestige! He has the ability to excite everyone who sees him, who follows him, everyone who comes near him. His name is on everybody's lips, in everybody's heart . . . The rich man like the peasant has his portrait, his engraving or his lithograph . . . Both men are happy to see the hero of the day up close, and whose lively, piercing eyes are fixed on one single point . . . Italy is his mother and his fatherland, he loves her, he defends her and he wants her to be free. Danger does not exist for him: he is a soldier of liberty.[23]

In stressing Garibaldi's wide appeal ('The rich man like the peasant has his portrait') and his overwhelming love for Italy, the publication was able to dodge his republican past. Interestingly, the British and American liberal press were also often as keen as the French press to stress Garibaldi's decency and respectability; and this approach reflects a quite widespread tendency to present the war, once it started, as a simple struggle for Italian 'liberation' and to emphasise the prevalence of political restraint and moderatism.[24]

9   Garibaldi by Gustave Doré. The artist seeks a compromise between Garibaldi's romantic past and more conventional present by placing a cloak over his uniform and placing him in a rocky landscape.

The iconography of 1859 departed radically from that of 1849 and followed the lead given by Garibaldi himself and the Piedmontese in stressing his 'gentlemanly' qualities and officer appearance. Echoes of his unconventional past lived on. *The Illustrated London News*, for example, showed Garibaldi on horseback in poncho and large hat, with a uniform barely visible underneath, while the French artist Gustave Doré placed a cloak over his uniform and showed him in romantic pose amid a rocky landscape (see figure 9).[25] His romantic side was particularly marked in battle scenes, perhaps especially in representations of the battle for Varese: here Doré produced a spectacular print of Garibaldi standing high on a rocky peak with a jumble of men and horses rushing past him.[26] Still by far the most widely circulated representation of Garibaldi at this time was of him in the Piedmontese general's uniform, with neat, well-trimmed hair and beard: a sterner, stiffer and rather more banal figure than hitherto. *L'Illustration*, for example, published a picture taken from a daguerreotype of Garibaldi in Piedmontese uniform.[27] Considerable effort was also made to place Garibaldi among a figurative pantheon of generals and legitimate national leaders. He appears in the Italian *Album storico–artistico* as a general alongside the other generals of 1859, far down in a hierarchy which includes the king, Cavour and Napoleon III. On the cover of the slightly later album, *L'Italia e i suoi difensori*, he has moved to the head of the group but is still surrounded by respectable figures (this time he is joined by the Tuscan moderate leader, Bettino Ricasoli), and he appears inside as a Piedmontese general identical to the others, using the standard military iconography of the time (see figures 10 and 11). In a French colour print of 1859, *Défenseurs de l'Italie*, he stands, '*Le Général Garibaldi*', with stern expression and about as unattractive as he ever appears in print. He is below Vittorio Emanuele in a stiff little group with Cavour and Generals Cialdini and La Marmora.[28] Henceforth, usually the only mention of Garibaldi the bandit in the press was to remind readers that the Austrians treated him as one, and this was taken as further proof of Austrian superstition and ill intent.[29]

Similar prominence was given to the respectability of Garibaldi's volunteers. They were presented as the best that Italy could offer, and no mention was made of the tensions with the regular army. They were 'the elite of provincial youth', in the words of *L'Illustration*, 'young people, robust, brave, enthusiastic, and within a short time, well disciplined'.[30] An illustration in Claude Paya's *Histoire de la guerre d'Italie* shows a group of them enrolling; one man wears a beard and rough, rural clothes but the majority are well dressed in frock coats.[31] Among the ranks there were 'a large number of gentlemen', according to a *Times* correspondent who saw them in Como:

> sons or themselves small proprietors, farmers, and tradesmen . . . operatives and working men from town and country; all men who had worked honestly

10 'Italy and its defenders': Garibaldi joins a pantheon of royal, military and moderate
liberal heroes. This image was evidently produced after Garibaldi's expedition to Sicily –
note the references to Sicily's broken chains and the volcano (often used to represent the
Risorgimento, especially in southern Italy).

for their living, or did not require to do so, decently and comfortably dressed, and all wonderfully tidy after sleeping so long in their clothes . . . quiet and orderly . . . respectable citizens fighting for their country, carrying into war the same respect for life and property which they showed in peace.

They sat at cafés to write letters home and, according to the correspondent, 'some I saw in the handsome Cathedral, admiring it like ourselves'. Such was '[t]he charm thrown by the hero of Montevideo over the whole Italian population' that, according to another *Times* correspondent, he had managed to enlist 'young men of the highest classes, artists, literary men, professors, and scholars, in his ranks as mere privates'.[32]

Without necessarily denying Garibaldi's physical and personal attraction, it is tempting to see in this emphasis on his personality a consensus to gloss over his political beliefs and so minimise the divisions within the anti-Austrian military coalition. Whatever the reasons, there developed a clear and mounting press obsession with Garibaldi's looks and background in 1859. So, while both *L'Illustration* and *The Times* went 'behind the lines' to Como to obtain interviews with Garibaldi, they sought the personality, not his politics. The two French journalists – a writer and an illustrator – sent back to their readers detailed descriptions of the man and his manner: 'we were well compensated for our trouble [in reaching Garibaldi],' the illustrator wrote, 'by the friendly welcome of the General. His kindness is immense; and while resolve is clearly written on his face, benevolence also reigns there and makes his language and manners most pleasing.' They dined with Garibaldi, and drew his portrait, but apparently did not discuss politics or the war.[33]

Two long reports from *Times* correspondents offer striking evidence of the growing tendency to venerate every detail of Garibaldi's personal appearance and manner. The first, in the form of a diary sent by an Australian on a tour of Switzerland, admitted surprise at Garibaldi's looks: 'From his portraits and warlike exploits I had pictured to myself a very tall large man, of sallow complexion, with long black hair and beard, with something of the romantic air of those Spanish guerrilla chiefs, who sung their songs to the guitar or killed people with equal gusto', so he could 'scarcely believe' that this 'quiet, unaffected, gentlemanly man who entered and sat down with us was Garibaldi'.

He is of middle height . . . a square-shouldered, deep chested, powerful man, without being at all heavy . . . a healthy English complexion, with brown hair and beard, rather light, both slightly touched with gray, and cut very short. His head showed a very fine development, mental as well as moral, and his face is good, though not remarkable to a casual observer . . . but when he spoke of the oppression and sufferings of his country, the lip

11   Garibaldi as a Piedmontese general,
in a typical portrait from 1859.

and eye told the deep feeling long suppressed, and the steadfast daring
character of the man . . . He has the calm manner and appearance of the
English gentleman and officer . . . it was palpable that, strong as may be his
impulses, they are thoroughly under control. Bold and enterprising even to
apparent rashness he is no doubt, but he is also cool and calculating . . . what
impressed me most was the mental calibre of the man.[34]

Strong, intelligent and good-looking but never overbearing; passionate and
driven but controlled, Garibaldi is idealised here as a typical, if unusually
attractive, English gentleman.

A month later, a *Times* 'special correspondent' started his report with the
following lines: 'I am not greatly inclined to hero-worship . . . but I have just
now travelled 150 miles to press the hand of Garibaldi.' He found him ill in
bed, 'with rather a young and good looking' lady sitting next to him:

He has a bright, cheerful look; the colour of his skin and hair betoken a
sanguine temperament. There is not one of the bust, lithographs,
photographs etc that are sold by thousands throughout Italy and Europe as
Garibaldi's portraits, that gives the slightest idea of the expression of that

noble countenance. There is not the least approach to fierceness or wildness about the hero's countenance. He looks intelligent, earnest, benevolent, and affable in the extreme . . . He has a fine head but not very massive; a large, but by no means broad face . . . The hair is brown-red, and has been rich and glossy. The eye struck me as light gray, but with a tint of the lion-red in it. His voice is clear, ringing, silver-toned. Nothing can equal the gentleness, freedom and ease of his address.

Although the correspondent complained loudly of the prevailing tendency to mythologise Garibaldi ('it was neither fair justice nor good taste to represent him as a truculent bandit or as a theatrical hero'), he allowed his own imagination to run wild, associating Garibaldi with a scene from Walter Scott's *Redgauntlet* and attributing to him an innate majesty: 'I fancied I saw the lion-hearted King lying on his lion's hides, and his lovely Queen a suppliant at his feet for the life of the Scotch knight. Truly Garibaldi is one of nature's own kings and leaders to men.'[35]

An imaginary life

The fascination with, and fantasy about, Garibaldi's personal appearance extended to his life story. During and after the war of 1859, journalists and writers rushed to produce biographies of Garibaldi, indeed, no coverage of the war was complete without an account of Garibaldi's life. For example, the supplement to *Journal pour tous* included a serialised biography of Garibaldi; the illustrated work by Claude Paya, *Histoire de la guerre d'Italie,* was little more than a biography of 'this famous man'; the *New York Times* published a 'Sketch of the life, character, and political opinions of General Garibaldi'; and *Harper's Weekly*'s account of 'Garibaldi and his legion' was really a short account of his life, with particular emphasis on his defence of the Roman Republic. The war 'Albums' published in Turin and Florence in early 1860 also contained short biographies.[36] By the summer of 1859, biographies also started to appear in Milan and Florence. These were mostly short, cheap and clearly rushed-out pamphlets; the only expensive production (a 160-page *Biografia* with some fine illustrations) was little more than a pirated version of Cuneo's 1850 biography with details of the 1859 war attached, and in the copy which survives in the Biblioteca di Storia Moderna e Contemporanea in Rome the pages are all in the wrong order, which suggests more haste than care in its preparation.[37] In Britain, a 'Colonel Exalbion' produced a substantial biography, *Garibaldi: his life, exploits and the Italian campaigns;* while publishing houses in Berlin, Weimar, Munich, Zurich and Haarlem all produced biographies of Garibaldi.[38] Above all, in Paris a huge number of biographies appeared, with prominent writers such as George Sand, Alfred Delvau, Pierre Dupont and Hippolyte Castille, among many lesser-known figures, giving their versions of Garibaldi's life.[39]

There was nothing at all unusual about the production of, and public enthusiasm for, biographies of Great Men in mid-nineteenth-century Europe. In the case of Garibaldi, the main narrative of his life had been established some time before, by Cuneo in 1850, and in 1859 English-speaking readers had the additional benefit of Garibaldi's memoirs which were published in New York by Theodore Dwight (and in London later in the year).[40] Almost all Garibaldi's biographers followed Cuneo's format. They stressed his early life and appetite for adventure, his acts of heroism in South America, the events in Italy in 1848–9 and so on, and some, as we saw above, directly copied or abridged Cuneo's text with minor alterations. Most also included a portrait of Garibaldi (always in military uniform), sometimes associated with an image of Italy such as the tricolour; and almost all made a great deal of the close relationship between the seafaring life and his specially passionate nature. Only the references to Garibaldi's life in Caprera and its symbolism were entirely new. 'Don't laugh', Delvau told his readers, 'at the sight of a lion turned into a shepherd, this adventurer become an agricultural expert. Did not Cincinnatus, the Roman dictator, return to his plough after he had nobly taken up arms to defend the honour of his country?'[41]

Even more than Cuneo's study, these biographies shared a tendency to hyperbole, and even a kind of catch-all hagiography in their approach to their subject. Colonel Exalbion wrote that from an early age Garibaldi had 'a spirit bold as that of any of the adventurers recorded in Tasso's pages';[42] while an anonymous French biographer described him as 'dedicated since childhood to this noble idea of Italian independence . . . caring not for danger nor fatigue, always ready to go into battle, to risk his life at the head of his plucky companions . . . how could you not love him?'[43] For Hippolyte Castille, Garibaldi was:

a man of extraordinary bravery . . . with a handsome countenance, well-built, full of strength and agility, imposing, proud and theatrical . . . of a few words and many actions, generous, *tender* . . . [a] blond head, calm, even languid, eyes . . . His life is but a series of adventures, travels, love-affairs, and of great sword-fights, just like the novels of Ariosto.[44]

To his enemies, he was invincible and indeed, according to Castille, perhaps he really was: hit by a bullet in combat in Rome, '[h]e pulled it out with a smile and, holding it out in his hand, he showed it to his soldiers and shouted: "They still can't hurt us!"'[45] Nor were more serious writers like Alfred Delvau and George Sand immune to his charms. Delvau wrote that Garibaldi belonged to that category of 'tiger-men' and 'lion-men': 'he is the knight of adventure, the valiant figure of legend, the Don Quixote of patriotism'.[46] Sand saw him as 'a kind of personification of Italy reborn, with her painful past, her poignant tragedies, her quiet patience, her vital genius, and above all her hatred of the foreign yoke which silences in her all vain pretence and all baneful discord when the hour has come to be or not to be'.[47]

Despite the availability and widespread use of Cuneo's biography, a great deal of what was published as 'biography' of Garibaldi in 1859 and early 1860 was pure invention. Many authors used the basic episodic structure established by Cuneo, and went on to add embellishments, characters and episodes of their own, additions which were then borrrowed by other biographers to produce a narrative of Garibaldi's life which was heavily fictionalised although based on a standard factual chronology. His early life in Nice and his adventures in South America provided the largest scope for narrative fantasy. The novelist Louise Goëthe describes Garibaldi's dramatic birth in a boat in a storm, and this episode was borrowed by the author of the nicely named *Garibaldi et ses hommes rouges* ('Garibaldi and his red men') and by a German biographer, Ludwig von Alvensleben. Dupont and d'Aunay (and later Alexandre Dumas) say Garibaldi was born on dry land, but 'in the room where Masséna was born' (Masséna, a native of Nice, was a Napoleonic general noted for his victories in Italy).[48]

Goëthe seems to have been the original source for an entirely new and substantial episode in Garibaldi's life, after he fled Nice following the failed conspiracy in the early 1830s. She reminds her readers that, 'in the time of which we speak', Garibaldi 'was a very handsome young man, of fine and daring profile, with a look both soft and firm, hair like an eagle, and blessed with prodigious strength and agility', and that his life's story should be read 'at night, in the moonlight, like an Ann Radcliffe novel'.[49] Emboldened by her comparison with this pioneer of the Gothic novel, Goëthe concocts a Gothic episode for her bandit–hero. She says that Garibaldi, 'like Rob Roy' took refuge in the highlands of 'the Black Mountain' (presumably an imaginary version of Montenegro) and became a tutor to Margarita, the beautiful daughter of the Count of Ransbergue at his château. They read books together and fell passionately in love, but when the nobleman discovered them together, he was so infuriated that he struck Garibaldi across the face with a whip. Garibaldi – 'like a wounded lion' – wanted to stab the count, and was only prevented by Margarita's intervention. Instead, he left the château and became a patriot–bandit. He returned, burnt the château to the ground and carried Margarita off into the mountains to marry her. Although Garibaldi was 'hunted like a wild beast' by the Austrians, he and Margarita were happy and their love grew. Margarita made him a father and he wrote her poetry: 'I am King; my kingdom is the deep forest . . . My voice, is a hurricane which wakes up nature . . . I am King, but outlawed, worn down by the tempest, And I have no shelter to put over your head'. But Margarita grew ill and died, and Garibaldi buried her in a rocky place now known as 'Margarita'. Since then, Goëthe tells her readers, Garibaldi is a changed man, and seeks adventure and comfort where he can.[50]

Goëthe's episode appears in various German biographies of Garibaldi[51] and even in a French biography by Juliette la Messine, which cites Garibaldi's own memoirs as its source.[52] The episode itself is entirely emblematic of the mythologising of Garibaldi. There was nothing new about his casting as a heroic character using tropes and techniques borrowed from popular fiction; what was new in 1859 was the almost unrestrained element of fantasy and the subordination of political discussion when it came to selling his life to the reading public. At the same time, the appearance of history – in the sense of biographical truth – was always strictly maintained. For instance, Claude Paya's publisher claimed that his biography was authentic thanks to the author's close 'relations . . . with the most important personalities in Italy', although this was rather unlikely since he had been in prison for ten years (between 1849 and August 1859).[53]

Historical authenticity was maintained in other ways too. All the biographies discussed here are careful to give the date and place of Garibaldi's birth (in Nice in July 1807), and to quote from his speeches and use newspaper reports. Thus, Colonel Exalbion feels able to condemn the 'inflated narratives and official falsehoods' surrounding Garibaldi's part in the war of 1859, and relies instead on 'leading journals' for his account. But he also gives Garibaldi some extra exotic, and entirely imaginary, adventures in South America: 'On one occasion he rolled down a precipice, and found himself in the embraces of a jaguar at the bottom. On another, he with difficulty avoided the embraces of a huge serpent, thirty feet long.' His wife, Anita, had to confront 'a body of mutineers' repeatedly and once nearly fell with her child 'into a frightful mountain abyss' because the rope bridge she was on became entangled in the middle, leaving her suspended halfway across.[54]

In Britain, Garibaldi enthusiasm took on a new guise with the performance of two plays. The first, a one-act play called *Garibaldi's Englishman*, was a satire on political celebrity. The protagonist, John Smith ('Garibaldi's Englishman') is a crook and an impostor: he gives out locks of hair and calls himself a lion, but his suitcase (with MAGENTA pasted on to it) is full of pickles and dried sausages and he leaves a trail of dishonoured cheques in his wake.[55] *Garibaldi*, the other play performed in 1859, was a more elaborate (four-act) piece which took Garibaldi from South America to the Austrian war via the Roman Republic. It mixed 'real' people – Anita, Manara, Bertani, John 'Beard' (Peard) – with more imaginary stock characters like Garibaldi's 'negro attendant',

Procopio, and a villain, Mancini, who is in love with Anita and betrays Garibaldi. Garibaldi himself is a bandit who first appears on stage (in Uruguay) carrying a gun and dead jaguar over his shoulders: 'Holloa! Procopio! Anita! Dinner for as hungry a hunter as ever chawed beef! Holloa – Anita – mia! Dinner!' Anita is unaware that Mancini has stolen her daughter, also called Anita, and brought her up as his own. In the play's climax, all the characters (except Anita, dead at Rome) are reunited on the Stelvio pass in 1859. Procopio discovers that Mancini's daughter is really the daughter of Garibaldi and Anita ('Oh Goramighty, bless you for sure you dat pickaninny. You dat little Anita'); the daughter, Anita, understands why she has always loved Garibaldi 'even when hate of him was inculcated as a duty'; Garibaldi is reunited with his daughter ('Oh! Good God! Is this a dream or a delusion! Anita's self the very face . . . My child! My child! Long lost – here to this lonely heart'); and he fights and kills Mancini, whose dying words are: 'My curse upon you both through life and death, for ever'.[56]

The 1859 war helped commodify Garibaldi as public entertainment, and brought him to the attention of a more popular audience. The main characteristic of Garibaldi's transformation into popular spectacle was the free mix of fact and fiction, especially when it comes to describing Garibaldi's sentimental attachments. Apart from the invented 'Margarita' episode and the invention of a long-lost daughter, the treatment of his real-life wife, the 'Creole' Anita, is also worth noting. Garibaldi's French biographers are clear enough about her death (pregnant, on the retreat from Rome), albeit with embellishments and inaccuracies: Delvau, for example, has her dying for three days under a blazing sun ('[t]he Calvary of Christ – the sublime crucifixion – only lasted one day. And Christ was well weary at the last station of his Calvary!').[57] Another describes her death in the mountains before reaching San Marino; while still another says she is killed 'by the Austrians next to her husband'.[58] There is also a general consensus that she too was something special, 'a heroine worthy of this hero! . . . a great and proud Brasilian creole . . . who had followed her husband everywhere, and who followed him to the end'; 'a virile soul: dressed in soldiers clothes'; 'a great and proud creole . . . with flaming eyes, magnificent black hair . . . Throughout the siege of Rome, our bullets whistled past her ears without disturbing her.'[59] Despite this, only a small minority of them (Delvau, La Messine) get her name right. For the rest, she is Léonta or Florita, an error whose origin is impossible to trace but which is repeated in German and Italian biographies as well as in French editions.[60]

A particularly fine example of novelist's licence dressed up as historical fact is Ludwig von Alvensleben's biography of Garibaldi. In the introduction, he states his aims very clearly. He wants to provide a 'comprehensive and unbiased . . . description' of Garibaldi's life; this is vital, he tells his readers, because the man provokes such strong feelings and responses. Thus, he has tried to find 'as many sources as possible about the hero of the day', and took from the sources (which 'contradicted each other often in stark contrast') everything that seemed to allow him to portray 'the human being Garibaldi' (*den Menschen Garibaldi*), 'as he is, his weaknesses, his sins, where he did really commit them, not in a beautifying sense, but also his better characteristics, amongst which his heroic braveness'.[61] Yet in spite of this admirable statement of commitment to the German historical method, a great deal of von Alvensleben's *Garibaldi* is made up.

For instance, the first meeting betweeen Garibaldi and Anita, a crucial moment in the reader's emotional engagement with the hero, is pure make-believe. Their meeting takes place in a camp, where Garibaldi is being held prisoner. She is called Florita, and is the daughter of a high-ranking officer in Rosas' army. Florita, in love with Garibaldi from afar, bribes the guards to get into his hut. When she enters, he jumps up, steps towards her and grabs her hand, pulls it to his lips and covers it with 'fiery kisses'. Before they can say anything, they fall into each other's arms. She tells Garibaldi that she cannot tolerate the way he is being treated: he can be free, the guards won't follow him, she has bribed them. He replies, embracing her, that he won't leave without her, 'my saviour angel'. She says she is prepared to follow him, but only as his 'lawful wife': will he marry her when he is free and as soon as a priest can be found? 'I am not free,' says Garibaldi, smiling, 'since I am captivated by you, but to put these shackles around me, that is my deepest wish.' Florita 'sank against his chest and willingly moved her lips towards his glowing kisses, which she gave back with the same fire'. They then escape, to the fury of Rosas.[62]

One other work on Garibaldi, produced somewhat later than the others (in the spring of 1860) but belonging to the same fictionalised biography format, is worthy of mention. The book is narrated in the first person and claims to be Garibaldi's memoirs, written 'from day to day, in the midst of a life now as tranquil and serene as a pure and peaceful lake, sometimes as violent and rough as a vast sea raised by unleashed winds'.[63] It is also listed as a copy of Garibaldi's memoirs in the catalogue of the Bibliothèque Nationale de France, with the editors given as Pierre Dupont and Alfred d'Aunay. In reality, it is another invented narrative, presumably the work of Dupont and D'Aunay. The first fifteen or so pages, describing Garibaldi's early life in Nice, is lifted from Cuneo. But the bulk of the 156-page narrative consists of a made-up and complex story, involving Garibaldi's love affair with the beautiful Lucia ('thin, frail, elegant, with the proud and contemptuous look of a duchess'), a famous actress with an extraordinary background.[64]

It is Lucia who dominates the narrative of these 'memoirs'. Garibaldi meets Mazzini and learns to love Italy in a duel to defend Lucia's honour; later, in a crucial episode, he sees off four bandits who are threatening her. After the plot shifts to Venice, Garibaldi and Lucia meet a mysterious Spaniard called Don Fanello. Upset by his presence, she confesses her past to Garibaldi at great length. Fanello seduced her when she was fifteen, and drowned her mother in the Venetian lagoon. Although she escaped, she ended up in a castle with an old man, Don Fabiani, who (she tells Garibaldi) 'abused my excessive trust in him . . . [and] made advances to me', so she was obliged to escape from him as well.[65] Garibaldi kills Fanello in a duel, and learns from Mazzini that Fanello was also an Austrian spy. He marries Lucia and they join forces to fight for Italy.[66] This entire, substantial (over-100-page) account takes place before Garibaldi's departure for South America in 1834. His adventures there and the events of 1848–9 and thereafter are then described cursorily.

These 'memoirs' are a vibrant illustration of the creation of an imaginary Garibaldi, along with a new set of adventures and companions, and its narrative of murder, seduction and mystery is a nice example of the use of a sensationalist style to reconstruct his life story. The memoirs are typical of the format as a whole. Especially interesting is the continuing insistence on the need to tell the truth about Garibaldi, so that even these false and largely ludicrous 'memoirs' make a claim to realism by being narrated in the first person, and they pretend to disparage the mystification of Garibaldi's reputation and life:

> Some present me as an extraordinary man, a hero, a man of providence; others make me, my past, my present, my purpose out to be something quite hideous. The truth is that I am neither that great person nor that bandit. . . . What I am is this: a patriot who loves his nation, ready to go where the common good may call me, and not interested in private gain.[67]

Invented is Garibaldi's return to Caprera to see both his mother and father die (his father's last words are 'God, Italy, the sea . . .'); but the death of Lucia borrows something from the story of Anita. Garibaldi's speech to his soldiers before the war against Austria is imaginary but also uses elements of his 1849 speech at the end of the siege of Rome. He tells them to expect 'thirst and heat by day, cold and hunger by night . . . You are free to be shot like dogs by a Croatian platoon, or to die with the sabre in your chest on the corpses of your enemies shouting: *Vive l'Italie!*' The memoirs conclude on an open-ended but factual note. Garibaldi tells the reader that he has '*rien*' to say about 'the expedition which I am planning for Sicily . . . I will soon be in Palermo.'[68]

Given such a widely advertised dedication to the 'facts', and given that at least some precise details of Garibaldi's life were generally available, it is worth asking why these writers chose to invent so much of his biography. The most obvious answer is that this kind of invention was not unusual. Indeed, a rejection of conventional distinctions between fact and fiction was a feature of French romanticism in the mid-nineteenth century; and the mix of history and melodrama to produce 'realism' was especially prominent in popular historical dramas and in the historical novel, the genre which had such a strong influence on the construction of Garibaldi's biography as exemplary life and which had already been used to great effect by Cuneo.[69] In various portrayals of Garibaldi it is also possible to see a free use of the Gothic style (Goëthe) and the sensationalist (Dupont and D'Aunay); here historical events and the 'real' Garibaldi serve as a background to an imaginary hero's adventures and struggles, much as they do in the contemporary novels of Dumas and Hugo. The manifest taste for the more picturesque and sexual aspects of Garibaldi's story (all the fantasy episodes and characters serve to emphasise that side of his personality and image) should suggest to us that many of these authors were simply following and adapting an already popular romantic style. At the same time, some biographers, such as Hippolyte Castille (whose biography of Garibaldi was part of his second series of 'Historical portraits of the nineteenth century') and the anonymous author of 'Men of today' (whose other subjects included Emperor Franz-Josef, Lord Palmerston, General Filangieri and the prince and princess of Prussia) had to make Garibaldi fit into an established format, with a standard message, structure and page numbers. Here historical reliability probably mattered less than the simple observance of a biographical fashion.

One effect of these biographies is that Garibaldi's personal qualities – his exotic lifestyle, unrestrained sexual appeal, prodigious strength – become more immediately important than his politics. In fact, his politics are seemingly reduced to a dutiful 'decency' and a vague commitment to 'justice' and 'liberty' for an Italy oppressed by Austria. So it may be that, like the newspaper reporting of 1859, these imaginary biographies deliberately attempted either to de-politicise Garibaldi or to diminish his republican past. Perhaps most noticeably in the *Garibaldi* of Hippolyte Castille, a liberal who had decided to co-operate with the regime, there is a move to exalt Garibaldi's personal allure and political actions in order to dismiss both as rhetorical flourish or as nothing more serious than a political fashion ('a man of extraordinary bravery, who seems to combine, in his perhaps excessive and hyperbolic actions, all the heroic and epic vigour of the Italian temperament').[70] Castille's political intention is equally evident in the conclusion to the biography, where he reassuringly compares the wild hero of Rome to the present-day Garibaldi, now an older, wiser and much less radical soldier: 'The Garibaldi of 1859 is not the same man as 1849. His hair has become grey, his spirit has hardened. He has fewer illusions, and perhaps more ardour ... today Garibaldi wears the uniform of a Sardinian general ... This life of devoted heroism has finally been blessed with victory.'[71]

However, the exaggeration of the picturesque can give us a very different hero from the compliant general in Piedmontese uniform, and in some of these biographies a more subversive intent can be discerned. A few of the Garibaldi biographers – Paya, Sand, Delvau and Dupont – were radicals, bohemian 'outsiders' and/or socialists, opposed to Napoleon III's regime. Sand had socialist sympathies, she had been a friend and supporter of Mazzini in 1849, while in 1859 she described herself as a 'young enthusiast' for the events unfolding in Italy.[72] Her *Garibaldi* (a sixteen-page pamphlet) cast him as a popular hero; she claims that the 'devout peasants of Velay and the Cévennes' hang Garibaldi's portrait 'among the images of saints'. What makes Garibaldi special, for Sand, is not his appearance but his 'personal thought . . . his moral work', and here she is careful to define the moral qualities necessary for political freedom:

> he is of a rather delicate nature . . . he is softly-spoken, of modest air and refined manners, with a great generosity and immense kindness tied to an inflexible resolve and a sovereign calm. He is clearly a leader of men, *but he leads by persuasion; he can only command free men* . . . There is a quality of enthusiasm and religion which has no counterpart in regular troops . . . *a small army of partisans, marching to its own tune with the sole concern to conquer or die.*[73]

By likening Garibaldi's popularity to the appeal of a radical secular religion, Sand comes close to recommending the original Mazzinian conception of the democratic hero. Her praise of morality, 'persuasion' and voluntary action can also be seen as a reminder of radical ideals.

Equally, Delvau and Dupont (the former best known for a Parisian slang dictionary and for a series of bohemian and erotic novels; the latter a socialist poet forbidden by the regime to talk about politics) seek out the radical in Garibaldi. Both use fictionalised accounts to emphasise his transgressive appearance and rebellious actions. There is a striking similarity between the illustration for Delvau's *Garibaldi* and the illustration for the song 'Garibaldi', published in Dupont's series *Souvenirs de la guerre d'Italie*. Although the song itself was fairly conventional and non-political, the accompanying illustration was more risky: Garibaldi is dressed in Piedmontese uniform, but his jacket is loose, even untidy, and his trousers are baggy. He wears a scarf and braid around his neck, and a sash tied around his waist; with his hat – a large 'puritan' affair with feather – he waves on his men; and his firearm, complete with long, sharp bayonet, is almost as large as he is. His beard is long, and in the background there is a soldier, and a castle which look suspiciously medieval (see figure 12).[74] Like Dupont's 'Garibaldi', Delvau's hero wears a uniform, but here too the military iconography is persistently denied: Garibaldi's hair is long and wavy, his eyes sloping and seductive, his stance more sensual than martial. Behind him, three volunteers wear the 'medieval' outfits of 1849.

There is a great deal in both these pictures which seeks to remind the viewer of Garibaldi's association with a bandit aesthetic and a medieval past, and so with the republican and revolutionary ideals of 1848–9. Even Paya, whose biography closely follows the regime's established text, and whose illustrations show Garibaldi as a slim and elegant figure in Piedmontese uniform, dwells at length on his defiant actions in Rome in 1849. There is an especially vivid picture of Garibaldi and his men in 1849, on horseback and '[a]rmed with their lassos', out catching cattle for their food.[75] In both Delvau's and Dupont's texts, moreover, there is a celebration of all that is wild, unconstrained and excessive (and medieval) in Garibaldi. He is Don Quixote, 'Fra Moreale', 'Fra Diavolo' and Roland/Orlando;[76] he is 'ardent', he fights duels and kills villains. It thus seems likely that, operating within the constraints of press censorship, these writers deliberately chose to create a transgressive Garibaldi, and that by stressing the picturesque and romantic they sought to recall more radical forms of political belonging.

Conclusion

In the London play, *Garibaldi's Englishman*, 'John Smith' has this to say about his fame:

> everybody takes me for Garibaldi's Englishman and stares at me admiringly – I think I could make a decent thing of it were I to show myself at a shilling a head. It's very agreeable to be so popular. It's astonishing the attention I get by it. Railway porters actually fight for possession of me. Landlords, landladys and chambermaids give me the best rooms and the best beds – waiters do come when they say 'coming' and cabmen are actually civil and content with only twice their legal fare.

The war of 1859 played a central role in fashioning a Europe-wide cult of Garibaldi. It was a leading part of, and contributed significantly to, a myth of Italian resurgence, an entire narrative complete with minor characters, and as much make-believe as historical fact. Garibaldi seemed to symbolise all that was compelling (fair, heroic, poetic) about the Italian nationalist struggle, and he developed an appeal sufficient to mobilise sections of (mostly) urban society behind the idea of an Italian nation.

There seems to be little doubt about the popularity of Garibaldi. We can perhaps raise questions about the numerous reports of patriotic demonstrations and enthusiasm in 1859, which were described in the previous

12   Garibaldi as the hero of a
popular war song: 'Garibaldi'.
This illustration clearly rejects the
traditional military iconography
used in most representations of
Garibaldi in 1859.

chapter, since many of them were written later and with an obvious political
intent. The large number of articles, books and other visual representations of
Garibaldi is, however, clear proof of the spread of the cult and of its
commercial success; it is estimated that Paya's *Histoire* alone had a circulation
of 50,000 copies.[77] Just as noteworthy is the international reach of Garibaldi.
Biographies and other texts were produced in the USA, Britain, Holland,
Germany, Switzerland and, above all, France, as well as in Italy itself, and
details about Garibaldi were copied and reproduced by writers across national
frontiers and languages. This Garibaldi literature is a strong sign of the
existence in the mid-nineteenth century of a liberal and cosmopolitan reading
community, international in character but engaged with nationalism and
nationalist struggle as an idealised representation of itself.

It should be stressed that this cult of Garibaldi was not gender specific.
Although we know almost nothing about who read these biographies, a
significant number of those who wrote them were women. A woman,
Garibaldi's lover Esperanza von Schwartz, took much of the responsiblity for
the production of his memoirs. It is arguable that at least some of these
biographies were aimed also at women readers; the equal emphasis given in

many to Garibaldi's sensitive and sensual side, to his many romances and to his love for Anita suggests authorial attention to a readership which, if not exclusively female, was interested in something else, or more, than battles and brave deeds. In this respect, the cult of Garibaldi both reflects and addresses the existence of a female reading public, with its own tastes and literary genres.

In this chapter, I have outlined the emergence and coexistence of two Garibaldis: the real and the imaginary. As I have sought to explain, Garibaldi was politically quite distinctive – someone who knew how to use his physical charisma to shape and inspire the collectivity – and in 1859–60 he combined this with a great run of military success. These material successes were helped, celebrated and reinterpreted by his imaginary counterpart, the product of articles and biographies which followed separate sets of political priorities and/or literary rules. This kind of coexistence of the real and the imaginary is, of course, quite typical of myth, and it was also a feature of mid-nineteenth-century literature, as writers experimented with first establishing and then dissolving boundaries between fact and fiction. In 1859 no obvious distinction was drawn between the political leader and the literary hero. In the descriptions and 'lives' of Garibaldi, documentary sources were alternately used, ignored and embellished to produce an imagined narrative which was all the more potent by apparently being true.

By the time Garibaldi sailed to Sicily in the spring of 1860, the original Mazzinian purpose of creating a hero who would symbolise and publicise the existence of an Italian people had been fully realised. Yet its extensive success was not without problems. Politically, what Garibaldi stood for could never be that clear; Garibaldi's purpose, for Cavour at least, was to mask the *realpolitik* of 1859, and it is worth remembering that much of the moderate leadership in this period rather despised his capacity to attract so much public attention. Indeed, a deliberate obfuscation of the cult took place, amply demonstrated in the iconography of 1859 with its endless versions of Garibaldi looking awkward in a general's uniform. At the same time, this blander version of Garibaldi never succeeded entirely in obscuring the picturesque bandit, who reappeared in various guises in contemporary illustrations and semi-fictionalised biographies, and whose political message was much more subversive. We can conclude, therefore, that just as the cult of Garibaldi became more widespread and successful, so did it become more eclectic and ambiguous.

It is possible to observe a tendency for the imaginary Garibaldi to 'float free' of the politicians, or to take on a logic and life of its own. The biographies of Garibaldi produced in 1859 and early 1860 were, after all, also vehicles of entertainment, dependent on the skills of the individual writer and the demands of his/her readers. In other words, the cult of Garibaldi was fashioned and elaborated in 1859 in such a way as to make it, if anything, more difficult to control from above by Italy's nation builders. The popular/fantasy dimension to Garibaldi's political appeal was troubling to Italian moderates and to the Piedmontese establishment, already wary of him as a military leader. It may also lie behind the emergence of a substitute element in the Garibaldi cult: that Garibaldi was no good at politics. This view was to gain force in the years that followed, and involved both a recognition of the power of Garibaldi and an attempt to belittle, and so contrast, his significance.

I stress the political purpose of this view – that Garibaldi was politically inept – because it is not entirely accurate. Garibaldi made political mistakes in 1859 (he was plainly too trusting of Cavour), and his impatience with political details and conventions let him down in central Italy during the autumn and winter. But he was not incapable politically, and undeniably possessed what we might call natural political skills which enabled him to connect with individuals and with crowds, and which he used to pursue his political ideals and place them permanently on the political agenda. His speeches and behaviour in 1859 were at times overblown, but they could be very effective, and were the expression of a political leader conscious of his power and aware of how to use it. After Villafranca, as both contemporaries and historians acknowledge, it was Garibaldi who provided the real nationalist counterweight to the stabilisation of Piedmont's deal with European diplomacy. It was he who helped keep the organisation and momentum of the 1859 volunteer movement alive.

What Garibaldi made of the imaginary personality being created alongside him is, unfortunately, not known, but he was certainly attentive to its political possibilities, careful to foster it in his speeches and anxious to protect its appearance. Ironically, however, for a reader with twenty-first-century sensibilities, much of the dramatic tension of the Garibaldi story is derived from the contradictions within it. We find revealing the clash between cynical diplomacy and nationalist enthusiasm; we are intrigued by the contrasts between a military leader and his heroic *alter ego*; and we are amused by the gulf which separates the imagined tendernesses of a young romantic lover from the jealous antics of a lascivious older man. In the last case, the decision by journalists to suppress, apparently voluntarily, the salacious details of Garibaldi's private life may now seem the most interesting aspect of the story. By contrast, what seems to us absurd, and interests us hardly at all, is the glorification of the 1859 war and of Garibaldi's role in it. Yet by dismissing the cult, we fail to understand its impact, and – as I have sought to show in this and the previous chapters – the cult of Garibaldi was crucial politically. His 'heroic' example provided focus and inspiration for nationalist organisations; his public actions placed Great Power diplomacy, and the Piedmontese leadership, under significant pressure; and his imaginary counterpart helped convince a broader European public that Italy existed politically, and that it must be free and independent.

CHAPTER 8

THE THOUSAND

Miracle at Marsala

The expedition which sailed from Quarto for Sicily was ill supplied and under-manned. This problem reflected the hurried circumstances of its departure and Garibaldi's equivocal attitude, as well as the confiscation of its guns by the Piedmontese government. After they left Quarto on 5 May, Garibaldi's thousand volunteers put in at Talamone on the Tuscan coast. There, Garibaldi put on the Piedmontese general's uniform which he had brought along ('[t]oday these clothes should be useful', he is said to have remarked),[1] and talked the military commander into giving them some – but not nearly enough – Enfield rifles and assorted ammunition. They also took a couple of cannons and some other pieces of artillery of antiquarian value which Garibaldi found in the old tower at Talamone. At Talamone, Garibaldi gave a more formal organisation to the expedition – its motto was proclaimed as 'Italy and Vittorio Emanuele' – and he sorted the men into seven companies and appointed a General Staff which included Bixio, Crispi and the Hungarian Colonel Türr. In the same days, in a controversial decision, he sent off a small group of volunteers in an abortive attempt to invade the Papal States.[2]

After Talamone, the volunteers set out for Sicily. The larger boat, the *Lombardo*, was commanded by Nino Bixio, who seems to have spent much of the voyage terrifying his men. He hit one of them across the face with a plate and, according to one memorable description, summoned his men on deck where he stood 'stripped to the waist, bare-headed, irascible', and announced: 'I'm young, I'm thirty-seven years old, I've been around the world. I've been shipwrecked; I've been a prisoner; but here I am and here I command! Here I'm everything, Czar, Sultan, Pope. I'm Nino Bixio!'[3] Those on Garibaldi's *Piemonte* evidently had an easier time, chatting, smoking cigars and trying to sing a hymn composed by Garibaldi.[4] There was some doubt about where exactly they should land in Sicily; indeed, during the night of 10 May the two ships nearly lost each other before they had decided on a landing place. But the following morning, as they were sailing past the port of Marsala (a wine-trading area with a significant British colony) in the direction of Sciacca on the south coast, they saw two British warships in the harbour and decided to land there.

At Marsala, the expedition met with a real stroke of good luck. The Bourbon garrison at Marsala had left for Trapani (the provincial capital), and the Bourbon warships which had been in the harbour had sailed southwards the previous night. This temporary absence of military defence enabled the volunteers to make a very hurried landing on the long harbour wall, even though Bixio had run the *Lombardo* aground at the entrance to the port. One Bourbon ship did return in time to prevent part of the disembarkation. However, its commander was worried by the presence of British ships in the port and perhaps was also reluctant to fire on the town, so he fired low, missing all the men who were running ashore with their supplies. Anecdotal evidence suggests that the only casualties were one man who was hit in the shoulder and a dog, although a Bourbon missile did narrowly miss killing the English manager's wife in one of the wine warehouses.

The first act of the *garibaldini* who got ashore at Marsala was to cut the telegraph link with Trapani. The second – organised by Crispi – was to persuade the town councillors to declare Bourbon rule at an end, and Garibaldi, as the representative of Vittorio Emanuele, to be the dictator of Sicily. Some of the councillors obeyed Crispi, but with considerable reluctance. Generally, the volunteers – the vast majority of whom were from northern Italy – met with very little welcome and a great deal of suspicion in Marsala. One of them, Emilio Zasio from Brescia, remembered their reception eight years later: 'The people were bewildered, ignorant, surprised by the news. We tried to encourage all of them, to raise their enthusiasm with *evvivas* of every type, but with no sign, no response.'[5] Only the Sicilians among them could communicate in (more or less) the same language as the inhabitants of Marsala – a serious problem when the expedition lacked even the most rudimentary maps of the territory they had come to 'liberate'. There were no great scenes of enthusiasm on either side. According to the memoirs of another volunteer, the strong wine they were given by a local man made them all feel ill (Crispi alone could handle it), and they weren't even able to understand the time from the local clock.[6] As the writer Ippolito Nievo (one of the Thousand) wrote to his cousin, '[in] Marsalla [*sic*] squalor and fear; the revolution had been put down everywhere or more accurately had never existed'.[7] Six weeks later, he wrote to the same:

We, the first to land in Marsala, actually brought with us the news of the revolution which had put us all at risk of drowning – In Lombardy it was said and it was written: *Garibaldi has touched dry land: the expedition is assured, Sicily is free.* Instead we all said to each other – *We didn't die at sea, but ridding ourselves of that uncertainty, we have gained the certainty of dying on dry land.*[8]

This strange mix of political daring, military inadequacy, good fortune and personal confusion lent – at least in retrospect – a miraculous quality to the Marsala landing and the ensuing events. The truth is that the volunteers were extraordinarily lucky not to be shot to pieces as they came ashore. This luck stayed with them after Marsala. From there, they marched across the plain towards the hill town of Salemi, where they arrived on 13 May. Although the Sicilian leader, Giuseppe La Masa, had gone ahead of them to warn the town of their arrival, it still caused a stir; one observer, Simone Corleo, described his astonishment at seeing a number of 'small groups' of forty to fifty men who walked up into town from across the plain, 'without firearms, a few with sabres, Garibaldi alone in a red shirt, the rest in military uniforms or civilian dress . . . Tuckory [a Hungarian officer] in a Hungarian uniform'.[9]

At Salemi, Garibaldi once again declared himself dictator of Sicily. He also began to put together a heterogeneous military force. First, he declared the military conscription of all-able bodied Sicilian males between the ages of seventeen and fifty (this decree followed the plans made for the nation-at-arms at the end of the previous year, and divided the men into three categories, with the youngest going into active army service, and the older men being involved with internal policing).[10] He received reinforcements of around a thousand extra men from the surrounding area, organised as peasant irregulars, or into so-called *squadre* by La Masa. In addition, he was joined by a radical Franciscan priest, Fra' Pantaleo, and called on the 'good priests' to lead the revolution against the Bourbons.[11] At Salemi, finally, he received the news that the Bourbon army had caught up with him: a force of around 3,000 men under General Landi had blocked the road to Palermo at Calatafimi, a few miles north-east of Salemi.

Garibaldi went out on the morning of 15 May to meet the Bourbon troops, who were waiting for him on the top of a terraced hill outside Calatafimi. Despite this strategical disadvantage, and being greatly outnumbered in men and weapons, Garibaldi and the volunteers fought their way determinedly and in bursts up the hill, using the terraces for cover. As Ippolito Nievo wrote: 'We thousand attacked, with the General in the lead: every last soldier was used without pause, without care, and without reservation because on that day rested the outcome of the whole expedition'.[12] In a final bayonet charge to the summit, the *garibaldini* managed to scare the Bourbon soldiers into a full-blown retreat across the countryside.

Victory at Calatafimi changed everything. Calatafimi, in Christopher Duggan's words:

gave the expedition an enormous fillip, an aura of success, even of invincibility, and many Sicilians who up to this point had been reluctant to commit themselves now threw caution to the wind and declared openly for 'Italy and Victor Emmanuel'. Garibaldi was no longer just the commander of a band of ill-armed insurgents: he was the leader of an alternative government to that of the Bourbons.[13]

After Calatafimi, Garibaldi pressed on towards Palermo via the Alcamo road. When they reached the high plateau of Renda, with its view of the plain of Palermo (the famous *Conca d'Oro*) and the city itself below, they stopped and made camp. From there, Garibaldi and his General Staff began to plan the invasion of Palermo. It was decided not to go straight down into the town via Monreale, which was well defended, but instead to stay up in the mountains and to move through them to Misilmeri, where they could join up with more of La Masa's peasant *squadre* and enter the city through Porta Termini to the south-east. In this way, they evaded capture by the Bourbon army: they even sent their bags and wounded men south on the Corleone road so that the Bourbons would believe they were retreating.

Towards the end of May, the *garibaldini* had, in effect, disappeared and the Bourbon army was congratulating itself on having seen them off into the Sicilian interior. The men were exhausted and debilitated from sleeping out in the mountains, often in the rain, and most still wore the now ragged clothes and boots they had embarked in at Quarto.[14] However, late on 25 May Garibaldi and his men entered Misilmeri and joined up with La Masa's forces, and on 26 May they left for Gibilrossa, from where they planned to descend the narrow path to Palermo. 'It's Palermo or Hell now!' Bixio told his men.[15] During the following night, keeping as quiet as possible, they came down into the city, taking the Bourbon troops guarding Palermo by surprise ('total surprise', Nievo wrote in his diary).[16] After a brief skirmish at the Ponte dell'Ammiraglio, and encouraged by Garibaldi on horseback, they rushed through to Porta Termini, where they dismantled the temporary gate under heavy fire and charged into the city as far as Piazza Fieravecchia, at the time one of the city's main markets and known for its revolutionary sympathies (the 1848 revolution had started there). From the market in Piazza Fieravecchia, where they arrived at about four in the morning and were reportedly greeted with some enthusiasm, Garibaldi's army fanned out in small groups through the narrow streets. Garibaldi himself led a group diagonally across the city to take the strategic points of Piazza Pretorio (the seat of municipal government, from where the Bourbon troops fled) and neighbouring Piazza Bologni, on either side of the *Quattro Canti* ('Four Corners') at the centre of Palermo.

There followed three long days of brutal street fighting inside Palermo. Barricades were erected across the main streets by the *garibaldini* and their supporters; the main prison was opened; and the Bourbon warships in the port fired on the city, causing great damage to property and loss of life. Throughout this battle, Garibaldi maintained a great public calm. He made a particular display of his indifference to the Bourbon bombs, and spent much of these days sitting on the steps of the over-size Renaissance fountain in Piazza Pretorio by the municipal government (which he had made his headquarters), receiving guests and giving orders, while the bombs crashed around him. On 30 May, the Bourbon government requested a truce. Garibaldi put on his Piedmontese uniform once again, and went off to negotiate terms on board the British warship *Hannibal* in Palermo harbour. After much heated discussion, in which Garibaldi threatened to break off negotiations and continue the fighting, an armistice was agreed, to last until the following day; this armistice was subsequently extended until 6 June, when the head of the government in Sicily, General Lanza, signed a capitulation agreeing to withdraw all his troops (some 20,000 of them) from the city.[17]

There was, and remains, something remarkable about the defeat of a well-equipped regular army by a mixed group of ill-armed enthusiasts and untrained peasants: '20,000 men capitulating to a handful of ill-armed adventurers, that's an astonishing thing!' the French dramatist Prosper Mérimée exclaimed on hearing the news.[18] 'Garibaldi has achieved wonderful results', the philanthropist Lord Shaftesbury wrote in his diary: 'It seems to me that God's protecting and accompanying power has repeated for him the miracle of Gideon and his three hundred.'[19] Luck played an obvious role in explaining their success, especially in the landing at Marsala. Just as important was the major crisis in Bourbon government. This crisis was partly financial, as the Bourbon state had a huge public debt by 1860; it was also partly diplomatic, reflecting an increasing international isolation which had been accentuated by the defeat of its only ally, Austria, in 1859 (whereas the nationalists were helped by the recent election of a British government more favourably disposed to Italy).[20] Also in 1859, the death of Ferdinando II and the accession to the throne of the Two Sicilies of his timid twenty-three-year-old son, Francesco, added a more general problem of legitimacy and political authority; while in April 1860 the insurrection in Palermo had expanded into the countryside, causing widespread revolt, the spread of criminal activity and the breakdown of local government.[21] Put simply, by the time Garibaldi arrived in Sicily, and although the original insurrection had been put down, the government was weak, isolated and unpopular: 'On the one hand was the dissolution of government; on the other there was a spreading lack of confidence in the capacity of the Bourbons to keep law and order'.[22]

This already critical situation worsened with Garibaldi's landing at Marsala. Conditions in Palermo itself rapidly became so threatening that the government was obliged to bring its troops into the city to protect itself; and this action left the provinces dangerously unprotected. Where there were no soldiers, revolts erupted. There were peasant uprisings in the provinces of Girgenti (Agrigento), Messina and Catania, as well as in the areas nearer Garibaldi's forces, and the numbers of criminal gangs – always a problem in the Sicilian interior – increased rapidly. As Garibaldi advanced on Palermo, the more liberal cities of Messina and Catania rose in revolt.[23] Everywhere public officials fled their posts, the police forces gave up their jobs, telegraphic and mail communications were cut, and there was a run on the banks.[24] In effect, the state collapsed in Sicily in the spring of 1860, and Garibaldi and his volunteers were able to step into this vacuum of power.

The role of good luck and good timing does not mean, however, that no merit should go to Garibaldi and his colleagues for the conquest of Sicily. Although I have emphasised the unpreparedness of Garibaldi's expedition as it left Quarto, some aspects of a military strategy were in place before they arrived. The most important of these, or the one that played the most significant role in the immediate success of the Thousand, was the alliance formed by Sicilian revolutionaries, and notably by Giuseppe La Masa, Rosolino Pilo and Giovanni Corrao, with the rural *squadre*. The *squadre* acted as a kind of guerrilla force, disrupting and cutting Bourbon supplies and causing diversions, and they were undoubtedly of crucial help in the taking of Palermo. Equally, the leadership showed real expertise in evading capture in the mountains above Palermo. Here too, the local knowledge of Sicilian revolutionaries, especially Crispi, who persuaded Garibaldi not to go further into the interior but to stay hidden in the mountains and join up with La Masa's *squadre*, was vital.[25]

The kind of warfare which Garibaldi had learnt in South America and had always excelled in – travelling light and fast, using surprise to frighten the enemy, relying on the skill and reckless courage of his officers – was particularly suited to conditions in the empty Sicilian countryside, and to conflict with an enemy which, however well armed, had already been discouraged and dispersed by peasant resistance. Moreover, as Garibaldi had long realised, motivated volunteers had a huge advantage over more self-interested mercenaries and conscripts in close-combat situations where the main weapon was the bayonet. Before the descent into Palermo, Garibaldi was overheard telling the *squadre* chiefs 'for the hundredth time', after they expressed concern about their lack of artillery, 'that it was not long shots which imposed on the well-armed Neapolitans, but a determined rush in advance'.[26] The taking of Palermo was, in its way, an equal triumph of military strategy and local knowledge. Apart from the crucial element of surprise, the leadership was careful to choose one of the city's least defended points, leading into a market area known for its revolutionary sympathies, from where the volunteers could lose themselves in the city, if necessary, or arrive very quickly at the seat of municipal government in Piazza Pretorio, if they were more lucky. Finally, great use was made of Garibaldi's leadership and reputation (and even his Piedmontese uniform) further to demoralise the enemy. When the situation demanded it, Garibaldi showed great skill in producing displays of prodigious courage (exposing himself and his officers to enemy fire at Calatafimi), indifference to danger (sitting in the open during the bombardment of Palermo), and grim determination (threatening to break off negotiations for the truce). These tactics were successful not just in purely military terms but also in helping to intimidate the Bourbon leadership and its soldiers into surrender.

Problems of government

There was evidence of strategy and forward planning in the organisation of the new government and its policies. Here the presence of Francesco Crispi was central. Immediately after the victory at Calatafimi, Garibaldi appointed Crispi as Secretary of State. Crispi went on to introduce a series of measures designed both to re-establish administrative authority in the island and to gain popular support for the regime. First, on 17 May, he announced the appointment of governors in the twenty-four districts of Sicily and he abolished the tax on milling grain (the grist tax or *macinato*); the next day, he set up military courts to try civilian and military crimes, and this was followed ten days later by a decree which established the death penalty for theft, looting and murder. Finally, on 2 June, after the armistice with the Bourbons, he declared that common land should be divided among the peasants, with special privileges given to those who volunteered to fight with Garibaldi. These measures were followed up by other popular reforms, such as the abolition of the title of *Eccellenza* and of the *baciamano* ('hand-kissing' as a sign of social respect). Also on 2 June, the setting up of a civilian government was announced. It was to consist of six ministries: War and Navy; Interior and Finance; Justice; Education and Culture; Foreign Affairs and Commerce; and Public Works.[27] There were also decrees aimed more specifically at the liberal middle class. These included a programme of public works (especially railway construction); the abolition of restrictions on the labour market; investment in education (notably in the universities); and the expulsion of the Jesuits from Sicily along with the confiscation of their wealth and property.[28]

Crispi's aim, as he later explained, was 'to disrupt the enemy's economic resources and win over the masses in any way we could . . . all the decrees of [this] period bear this stamp'.[29] He and the other Sicilians in government remembered only too well the political fallout caused by social disorder during the 1848–9 revolutions.[30] Accordingly, they sought to organise and control the peasantry, to liberate the government from its dependence on the armed irregulars or *squadre* (this by the decree of mass conscription announced before Calatafimi), and to reassure the propertied class on the question of law and order and the protection of its economic interests. There was a widespread recognition of the social hardship and economic problems caused by the prevailing system of land tenure in Sicily and of the pressing need for land reform.[31]

Yet how successful Crispi was in attaining his objectives remains an open question. The decree of land reform – the partition of common land among the peasantry – remained unenacted in many areas, and the disappointment this provoked produced a wave of land occupations and peasant unrest across much of Sicily. Peasant protest was paralleled by a sharp increase in urban crime and rural violence: Alcamo in the province of Trapani was said to be experiencing 'kidnapping, destruction, arson, looting, robbery and homicide' on a daily basis,[32] while in Corleone in the Palermo uplands a bandit named Santo Meli conducted a reign of terror from June onwards. Conscription – through the creation of a national guard as well as an army – was meant to combat the problem of banditry, but even where national guards were set up they were often infiltrated by the bandits themselves. Just as serious were the difficulties in organising provincial and local government. Efforts to set up functioning administrations were persistently undermined by local officials; they were motivated either by old loyalties to the Bourbon regime or more simply by the pursuit of private interests, rivalries and material gain. Increasingly the government was obliged to rely on military force and simple repression to maintain control in the countryside.[33]

The political situation became extremely complex and beset by bitter internal wranglings, particularly when it came to the question of union between Sicily and Piedmont. There were huge issues about Cavour's attitude to the new situation in Sicily. He had done little to help the expedition of the Thousand; indeed his chief contribution may have been 'in not absolutely vetoing the expedition'.[34] Thereafter, Cavour became concerned about the influence of Mazzinians like Crispi in the Sicilian government and by the threat of Garibaldi uniting Italy from the South, which would jeopardise both Piedmont's alliance with France and the moderate liberals' overall direction of

Italian politics. Increasingly, therefore, he concentrated on annexing Sicily so as better to control Garibaldi's and the Mazzinian activities there. Cavour's main agent in Sicily was another Sicilian, Giuseppe La Farina of the National Society. However, La Farina rapidly fell out of favour in Palermo's political circles by pursuing an openly pro-Cavourian, pro-annexation programme, and he quarrelled especially badly with Crispi. But Crispi, in turn, made himself equally unpopular in Palermo by his contempt for Sicilian separatism and by his generally abrasive attitude. At the end of June he was forced to resign from the government and, in early July, Garibaldi, who was furious at the treatment of Crispi, expelled La Farina from the island.[35]

This political disarray – which both La Farina and Crispi contributed to, and to which they both fell victim – reflected, and was accentuated by, the political divisions within Sicily itself. The three main Sicilian political groupings – democrats, moderate liberals and autonomists – had long disagreed amongst themselves. In 1860, they could not agree on a clear policy on the question of annexation by or autonomy from Piedmont, or about precisely how, under what conditions and when Sicily should unite with Piedmont. Even within these three groups there was great disagreement on the question of annexation (as well as other issues: for instance, the democrats were divided between Mazzinians and a smaller socialist party). Moreover, regional splits (most obviously, democrats in Catania; autonomists in Palermo) and rivalry (general resentment of Palermo's dominance within Sicily) added significantly to the factionalism of Sicilian politics.[36]

From Palermo to Naples

What was never in any doubt was Garibaldi and Crispi's intention to continue the struggle against the Bourbons in Sicily, and to use Sicily as a springboard for the war on the mainland. After the departure of Garibaldi and his volunteers for Sicily in early May, a series of organisations in northern Italy – the National Society, the Million Rifles Fund and Bertani's Central Committee in Aid of Garibaldi – continued the work of organising volunteers and raising money for the campaign (and at first for the parallel campaign in the Papal States). It seems that Cavour also sent significant aid, either directly through the National Society or by covering its and/or the Rifles Fund's deficits, presumably in an attempt to influence the conduct of the war in Piedmont's favour.[37] The first small ship carrying guns, ammunition and a few men left Genoa in late May; this was followed some two weeks later by a much larger expedition led by Giacomo Medici consisting of two ships and some 2,500 men and 800 firearms, and in early July by another large expedition under Enrico Cosenz of 2,000 men. An expedition of 800 men was also sent from

Livorno, and throughout July smaller expeditions continued to leave Genoa for the campaign in Sicily; in all, an estimated 21,000 men joined Garibaldi between late May and early September.[38]

After Palermo, Garibaldi's attention was fixed on capturing the Bourbon bridgehead at Messina. Accordingly, the new arrivals were sent out of Palermo into the country in three groups (under Medici, Bixio and Türr) with orders to repress Bourbon resistance and then to converge on Messina. Türr's men went across the interior, and had by all accounts the most 'picturesque' experience,[39] while Bixio and his men proceeded along the south coast and then east towards Catania. At Catania, Bixio's forces became embroiled in peasant land occupations and violence (what the Englishman, Forbes, called 'a small dash of communism')[40] in the area around Bronte, on Mount Etna. Apparently to reassure Sicilian landowners that Garibaldi's revolution did not represent a threat to their property and that he knew how to impose law and order, Bixio brutally crushed the revolt in Bronte and executed the leaders, in a wave of repressive violence.[41] Finally, Medici's column of 2,000 men – which was moving along the north coast between Palermo and Messina – met with a much larger Bourbon force under General Bosco at Milazzo. Although Medici managed to trap the Bourbons temporarily into and around the fortress on the promontory of Milazzo, he called for reinforcements from Palermo in order to prevent Bosco from breaking out and defeating his smaller army. Helped by the arrival not just of fresh troops but also of Garibaldi himself, the next great battle of the 1860 campaign began: the battle of Milazzo of 20 July. Once again, it was an unplanned battle and, once again, Garibaldi's forces won the day against all the odds.

At Milazzo, Garibaldi was as enthusiastic a leader of his men as he had been at Calatafimi. By all accounts, he led and encouraged them from within the thick of the fighting, and sought to inspire them with examples of fearless courage. In one celebrated incident, he found himself standing alone on a road with his aide, Missori, facing a cavalry charge; and, instead of retreating, he stood his ground facing the galloping horses. As they came close, Missori shot the horse from under one officer,while Garibaldi leapt up to cut the same man's throat with his sabre. Missori then continued to shoot at the horses, and Garibaldi went on attacking their riders with his sabre, so terrifying the soldiers that those who were still unharmed fled back to the safety of the fortress. In the afternoon, with his forces established on the bridge to the town, Garibaldi took to a ship and bombarded Milazzo from the sea. By the end of the day, after eight hours of bitter fighting under the Sicilian sun, he had taken possession of the town.[42]

Five days later, General Bosco surrendered the last of the Bourbon forces at Milazzo fortress and, on 28 July, Medici led the volunteers into Messina, riding

Bosco's horse. Although Clary, the Bourbon general in charge of Messina, had 15,000 men and an 'impregnable fortress' at his disposal, he had preferred to sign a treaty whereby Messina would be held by the *garibaldini* and the fortress by the Bourbons, and all hostilities between them were declared at an end. This meant that Garibaldi's ships could cross the straits of Messina 'under the muzzles of the king's cannon to invade his Calabrian provinces' without the Bourbons firing a single shot. Shortly afterwards, most of the soldiers in the Messina fortress were withdrawn to the mainland.[43]

After the defeat at Milazzo, the Bourbons seem to have decided to abandon Sicily in order more effectively to stop Garibaldi on arrival on the mainland. Perhaps aware of this, Garibaldi hesitated for some three weeks before crossing the Straits of Messina into Calabria. On 8 August, he sent a small exploratory force under the Calabrian revolutionary, Musolino, and a trusted officer, Alberto Mario, across to capture the fort at Scilla on the Calabrian side. They failed, and were forced to flee into the Aspromonte mountains. As a result, Garibaldi tried a different tactic, and on 18 August, along with Bixio and a force of some 3,500 men, he crossed the sea to Melito in southern Calabria from a secret embarkation point on the beach below Taormina. They immediately marched inland, away from danger. On 22 August, after some fierce fighting, the combined forces of Garibaldi's and Cosenz's men took Reggio Calabria, and on 26 August met up with Medici's men at Nicotera. Also on the 26th, the town of Catanzaro declared itself for Garibaldi. As Trevelyan comments, '[t]he race to Naples had now fairly begun'.[44] From Nicotera, Garibaldi's army marched north to Monteleone, which the Bourbon garrison of 10,000 men under General Ghio had already abandoned.

By now Garibaldi and his General Staff were on horseback and moving so fast that they 'were acting militarily as their own scouts, politically as their own heralds'.[45] Much of Garibaldi's army was left behind, and the journalists following him were unable to keep up: Charles Arrivabene of the London *Daily News* and Frank Vizitelly, the artist for *The Illustrated London News*, were obliged to cross much of Calabria on foot because Garibaldi and his men had taken all the donkeys and carriages in the area.[46] On 29 August Garibaldi caught General Ghio's men in the high mountains, where they had been blocked by armed bands holding the pass at Agrifoglio, and captured all their weapons and cannons. Garibaldi kept on moving, by carriage and on horseback; he entered the provincial capital of Cosenza on 31 August, and from there descended to the coast and took a boat to Sapri. From Sapri he crossed the mountains of the Cilento, and in Casalnuovo he and his staff got into open carriages and drove into Salerno, just a short train ride away from Naples, on 6 September.

They were met in Salerno by cheering crowds and prolonged celebrations. Garibaldi's arrival had been announced in advance by the English volunteer Colonel Peard, whom many mistook for Garibaldi, and Garibaldi preceded his nearest troops, some 1,500 men under Colonel Türr, by two days' march.[47] The British envoy in Naples, Sir Henry Elliot, was told that 'the whole of the southern part of the kingdom . . . has been conquered by Garibaldi single-handed and without an army at all, for he seems all along to have been from thirty to sixty miles in advance of it, the people rising and the troops falling back or capitulating as he advanced'.[48] 'The royalists dispersed like the dust which followed their flight', commented Marc Monnier, a French resident in Naples, who witnessed these same events.[49]

When the Bourbon garrison left Palermo at the beginning of June, Garibaldi had been there to see them go. '*Au revoir, à Naples!*' he was said to have told the soldiers, and apparently they all believed them.[50] During the events which followed, the Bourbon army had become utterly demoralised. 'Bewilderment and terror was written on every face' according to Alberto Mario, who saw the soldiers in one town: 'to their overstrained imaginations, Garibaldi had gradually assumed the nature and the form of Fate'.[51] Their king too seemed paralysed by fear and anxiety. As early as 4 August, Monnier in Naples wrote of 'reaction on one side, revolution on the other: the king in the middle, helpless and abandoned, the government industriously idle, the population restless . . . a sickening spectacle, inspiring shame and pity'.[52] By the end of August, aware that the city of Naples was almost indefensible militarily, King Francesco II's advisers persuaded him to withdraw from the capital, and to retreat with his army to the fortress of Capua north of Naples. From there they planned to concentrate their forces and launch a counter-attack against Garibaldi.

Thus it came about that Garibaldi was able to enter Naples unopposed on 7 September. He took a train from Salerno in the morning. W. G. Clark, the public orator of Cambridge University, out from England on his annual vacation, went with him from Salerno, and wrote that Garibaldi was sent off to 'the roar of *vivas*'. One member of the crowd collapsed in a convulsive fit, Garibaldi was accompanied by vocal enthusiasts singing 'interminable' songs ('We are Italians/ Fresh young men/ Against the Germans,/ We will fight'), and at every station there was 'a mob of curious people . . . who exchanged cheers with the occupants of the train'.[53] The Anglo-Italian journalist, Charles Arrivabene, who had also 'squeezed' on to the train, wrote that '[f]rom Torre del Annunziata to Naples, we saw nothing but a succession of triumphal arches, festoons of flowers, hangings and flags . . . An interminable scene of movement and gaiety was everywhere visible along the line; a continual shouting of "Viva Garibardo!" [*sic*] "Viva l'Italia!" filled the air.'[54] Garibaldi arrived in Naples itself at lunchtime, and immediately got into a carriage with some of his men. He was driven through an impromptu but reportedly vast crowd, as the streets rapidly filled with 'waving hats and handkerchiefs, hands raised in salute, and a deafening frenzy of shouts and cries'.[55] Garibaldi sat through all this, according to one spectator, 'apparently unmoved, but from time to time he lifted his hat, and smiled, as it were, with the eyes rather than the lips'.[56] Later, on the waterfront, he stood up in the carriage, removed his cap and gazed at the crowd, before retiring to his lodgings at Palazzo Angri.

For two days thereafter, the festivities in Naples continued. In the words of the English follower of Garibaldi, Charles Forbes, an active if not very sympathetic eyewitness: 'the entire population roused themselves into a state of frenzy bordering on madness, which ofttimes became ridiculous, and at others unfortunately dangerous . . . Night and day the entire population were in the streets . . . Bands of ruffians in red shirts invaded hotels and cafes, and forced, arms in hand, every one to join in their orgies.'[57] A correspondent for the Italian radical paper, Il Movimento, offered a more positive, if less coherent, description:

> the whole city in lights, like nothing ever seen before; the long via Toledo just wonderful, with more than 4 thousand carriages going up and down full of beautiful ladies wearing tricolour flags and scarves, the enthusiasm impossible to describe, the shouts in favour of Vittorio Emanuele, of Italia una, to Garibaldi, to Venezia . . . Thousands of radiant faces, every window covered with flags and flowers in the same way; I never saw a more enchanting party.[58]

Unification

After Naples, Garibaldi's attention turned to Rome, and at first he planned immediately to continue the campaign so as to arrive in the papal capital before the winter rains came in November. It was at this point that he learnt about the invasion of the Papal States by the Piedmontese army. Although at first he seems to have believed that Piedmont was on his side, he soon realised that the invasion was part of a Cavourian design to frustrate his plans and prevent him taking Rome. This design also entailed Cavour's plotting to take over the government in Naples and his pressing for immediate annexation by Piedmont of Naples and Palermo. In the middle of September, the differences betweeen Garibaldi and Cavour became publicly irreconcilable, when Garibaldi openly condemned Cavour and asked the king to replace Cavour and Farini in the government. Cavour was under attack from the radicals in Turin, and had become increasingly alarmed by the continuing presence of Mazzinians like Crispi and Bertani close to Garibaldi. He was especially horrified to learn that Mazzini himself had arrived in Naples on 17 September.[59] He spoke of marching on Naples, 'to bring Garibaldi to his senses and hurl that nest of red republicans and socialist demagogues that has grown up around him, into the sea'.[60]

Also during September, the Bourbon army dug in along the River Volturno with some 50,000 men, led by Marshal Ritucci (Garibaldi's army was by now some 20,000 men strong), and prepared to counter-attack for Naples. On 1 October, following a minor victory against Garibaldi's army at Caiazzo, Ritucci attacked Garibaldi's lines between Sant'Angelo and Santa Maria and forced Garibaldi to fight, for the first time in the campaign, a defensive batttle. The battle of the Volturno lasted two days, and although initially the Bourbons had all the advantages, in the end Garibaldi's army were victorious, and saved Naples. According to Trevelyan, the victory at Volturno was due to Garibaldi's great talent as a military leader, and specifically to three factors: 'the personal inspiration of his presence at so many of the important points, the combined caution and vigour of his offensive–defensive tactics and . . . a sound strategy governing the disposition of his men over the whole region of conflict'.[61] Although subsequently played down for political reasons, in reality Volturno was, in Mack Smith's words:

> one of Garibaldi's finest military ventures, in which he defied the pundits by showing himself a master of defensive strategy, and in which he proved fully able to control a larger force of men than the Piedmontese regulars had numbered at Castelfidardo [against the papal army in the Papal States] or indeed in the whole of the Crimean War.[62]

The presence of mind which Garibaldi showed at Volturno is worth stressing because of the fatal political mistake which he also made at this time, and which to an extent overshadowed the rest of his career. Faced with the Piedmontese advance through the Papal States and towards Garibaldi at Naples (rather than towards Rome, as he had hoped), and burdened with the conflicting pressures of radicals and moderates in Naples and Palermo, Garibaldi simply vacillated and did nothing. He seems to have become bored and demoralised by the endless discussions in Naples. As Bertani wrote from Naples to Mordini (the pro-dictator in Palermo) on 28 September:

> On the political side, matters go from bad to worse. The dictator has been struck down by moral paralysis. We can't get anywhere with him, he won't sign anything, he won't be completely on our side and it disgusts him to be with the other side . . . We can't form a government, but no decision is taken to dissolve it. And our enemies profit from this paralysis . . . We are assailed

by hate on all sides. Garibaldi is not fully aware of his strength in Italy – discouraged and irritated at the same time.[63]

'[N]othing can be done without him – very little, I fear, with him', Mazzini commented to his friend Caroline Stansfeld on 2 October.[64]

Garibaldi may have become discouraged about the practicalities of continuing the war without Piedmontese help; in any event, he gradually became convinced that there was no longer any alternative to falling in with Turin, and began instead to place his hopes in a new military campaign for the following summer. During the second week of October, amid scenes of political agitation in Naples and the spread of peasant resistance to the new government in the Abruzzo and Molise mountains, Garibaldi went against the advice of the radicals. Instead of setting up an elected assembly to negotiate the terms of union with Piedmont, he agreed to hold an immediate plebiscite to decide on the question of annexation by Piedmont. Shortly afterwards, pro-Dictator Mordini in Sicily was forced to follow suit.[65]

The decision to hold plebiscites was a decisive victory for Cavour and his supporters in the South. It meant that annexation by Piedmont would be unconditional and immediate. Garibaldi, with this decision, handed over his dictatorial powers to Vittorio Emanuele. 'Cavour has won', complained *L'Unità Italiana* on 17 October: 'the first act of the drama ended at Villafranca, the second is now ending at Naples. God help Italy!'[66] The plebiscites took place on 21 October, and the entire adult male population was asked to vote 'yes' or 'no' to whether they wanted 'to form an integral part of Italy one and indivisible under Victor Emanuel as their constitutional King'. The result was an overwhelming (over 99 per cent), and unsurprising, vote in favour of unification. The vote was in public, and in most places there was tremendous pressure for a 'yes' vote; moreover, as Mack Smith points out, '[t]o vote no . . . had no meaning at all, for the only alternative to Victor Emanuel was Francesco, and the clock could not have been put back short of a bloody counter-revolution'. There was also little or no sense among the population that Garibaldi represented a different political ideal from the Piedmontese king.[67]

Garibaldi stayed on at Naples for three weeks after the vote. On 25 October, he rode north to Teano to meet the king. Although later glorified as a happy and dignified occasion, many contemporary accounts suggest the meeting was a tense and melancholy affair full of bad omens, and that the king became upset when peasant onlookers shouted *Viva Galibardo* [sic]! and ignored the king.[68] On 6 November, the king failed to show up for a review of Garibaldi's troops at Caserta. The next day, after some bitter discussion, the two men rode together in a carriage into Naples during a thunderstorm, both looking sullen and gloomy. 'Garibaldi smiled amidst the storm', a British onlooker remarked, although he seemed 'pale and anxious', while the king 'rolled his eyes and stared in a vacant way quite peculiar to Kings of Italy'.[69] Garibaldi asked to be made viceroy of southern Italy and was refused; the king offered once more to make Garibaldi a general in the Piedmontese army, but his offer was rejected.[70] Although the two men had once liked each other, the king at least was cross with Garibaldi, writing to Cavour some two weeks later that Garibaldi was 'neither as docile nor as honest as people say and as you yourself think'.[71]

Finally, in the early morning of 9 November, Garibaldi left Naples quietly, taking with him only some beans and seedlings for his farm at Caprera. Before departure, he stopped at the British warship *Hannibal* to say a private (but again subsequently celebrated) farewell to Admiral Mundy, the man who had helped negotiate the truce in Palermo. While he told Mundy of his plans to take Rome and Venice, and to put 'a million of men under arms' the following year, Mundy noticed that Garibaldi was gloomy and dejected 'and his whole manner was that of a man who was suffering under a poignant grief'.[72] He was then escorted to the steamer Washington, which would take him to Caprera, by what Marc Monnier called 'a simple entourage of intimate friends' who were all in tears ('it was really simple and sad').[73]

Garibaldi also left behind a number of broken-hearted women. A British resident in Naples, Carlotta Roskilly, expressed her 'profound grief' at his refusal to live 'for a few days in *your room* prepared by me', and blamed herself personally for his decision to leave; while another British woman, signing herself simply 'Your Sauvage', wrote him letter after passionate letter complaining of the 'endless' wait for him, and of her desire to sleep until the moment she awoke and, 'with my hand in yours, I can squeeze it and say "Never apart again"'.[74] The king stayed on for a while longer in Naples. In December he visited Sicily and met with an elaborate reception at Palermo, which included a huge monument to Garibaldi in the Piazza Marina.[75] He then returned home to Piedmont. Italy was officially united the following February, with Vittorio Emanuele II as king, its capital in Turin, and Venice and Rome still under the control of 'foreign oppressors' (Austrian and papal rulers). So ended the story of the Thousand (see map 2 on page 225).

Conclusion

The year 1860 was, as Denis Mack Smith has observed, the '*annus mirabilis*' of the Risorgimento. Garibaldi's actions brought about the collapse of the Kingdom of the Two Sicilies, and led to the political unification of the Italian peninsula. These changes seemed all the more momentous because they were so unexpected and so rapid. For a short time in the summer of 1860, the small army led by Garibaldi – and with him Italian nationalism itself – seemed unstoppable. Yet, as Mack Smith has also shown, 1860 was also a 'complicated and controversial passage of history', involving civil war, diplomatic struggle and peasant unrest. Moreover, in the end, '[f]ew people were more surprised' by Italian unification than Cavour, 'its chief architect', and 'few more disappointed than Mazzini and Garibaldi, the two men who had looked forward to this moment most keenly and who had sacrificed most for its attainment'.[76]

Garibaldi was helped greatly in his campaign by the severe political crisis in southern Italy. He was also able to take advantage of a diplomatic situation, and especially a sympathetic British government, which worked in his favour. Equally, Garibaldi showed considerable military talent in 1860, both in his ability to surprise and improvise – he continually wrong-footed the enemy – and as a leader of his men. As an administrator, with the able assistance of Crispi, he was not unimpressive, especially when the government's lack of resources, the extent of rural unrest, and the scale of the previous government's collapse are taken into consideration. As I will explain in the next chapter, he also proved particularly good at giving his revolution a positive appearance, at making it seem a dramatic and inspiring turning-point in history.

He was much less successful at sustained political negotiation. He provided little leadership during the political crises in Palermo over the summer, and, while he supported Crispi, he seemed unable to stop La Farina. Anecdotal evidence also suggests that Garibaldi became impatient and bored during the prolonged discussions over the question of annexation. If only in this respect, it is clear that he was 'no good at politics'. While his attitude may be understandable, it was also deeply problematic in a revolutionary leader and it caused problems for the democratic movement, as it had done on various occasions during the late 1850s. In 1860, Garibaldi's reluctance fully to resist the Piedmontese solution of immediate annexation led to his defeat by Cavour. This meant that all the political advantages gained in the spring and early summer were thrown away by the autumn. 'Never tire of repeating to the General [Garibaldi]', the Lombard federalist Carlo Cattaneo wrote to Crispi in July, 'that it is not sufficient to know *how to take*, one must also *know how to hold*.'[77] In the end, Garibaldi quietly handed over power to the king and Cavour, and slipped off 'backstage' to Caprera.

It is of course clear that the defeat of Garibaldi's revolution had, to an extent, been determined in advance by the subservient position long taken by many democrats in the alliance made with Cavour's Piedmont. This subservience is clear in 1860, both in the slogan – *Italia e Vittorio Emanuele* – adopted by the Thousand and in succession of decrees which adopted the Piedmontese constitution, legislation and administration in the newly 'liberated' provinces of southern Italy. We might also agree that Garibaldi was unlucky to have been faced with an opponent as endlessly resourceful as Cavour. It is also possible to argue that Garibaldi's real achievement in 1860 was to have forced Cavour's hand, to have obliged him to unite Italy under Piedmont and Vittorio Emanuele, an act which Cavour had never considered seriously before July 1860. Certainly, Cavour's reaction to the expedition reflected the now unstoppable appeal of Italian nationalism and of Garibaldi, its main symbol. Garibaldi's withdrawal to Caprera may also have made good sense militarily and personally, and it definitely worked on a symbolic level. There was no campaigning to be done in the winter, Caprera was good for Garibaldi's rheumatism, and the retirement to his farm added to his mystique as the Cincinnatus or Washington of Italy (both of whom had done the same at the end of their campaigns). For those opposed to the government, Garibaldi's lonely retreat also pointed to a form of internal exile and thus highlighted his shoddy treatment by the Piedmontese.

In the longer term, however, Garibaldi's actions made much less political sense. On the one hand, they left his army without a general, and the democrats without one of their most powerful, and certainly their most popular and famous, representatives during the crucial period between the plebiscite and the consolidation of unity in the spring of 1861. Southern Italy lost the leader of its revolution. Garibaldi's departure for Caprera was essentially an abdication of power. On the other hand, his behaviour offered a political basis for endless recriminations between moderates and democrats, gave rise to a personal bitterness which was to become a destabilising feature of the new Italian politics, and struck a symbolic pose which laid the foundation for a fractured and divisive national memory. In this way, an expedition conceived of in the name of liberty and unity and carried out in the most dramatic form imaginable, ended – in much the same way as the war of 1859 – in a political compromise which satisfied nobody.

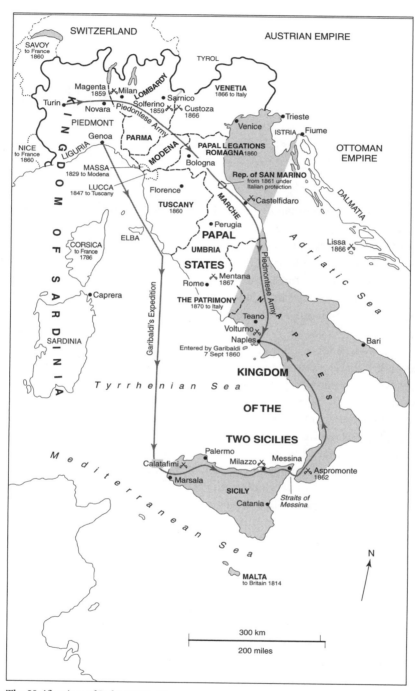

The Unification of Italy, 1859–70

CHAPTER 9

MAKING ITALIAN HEROES

Much has always been made of the unexpected nature of Garibaldi's triumph in Sicily in 1860. Yet his successes were surprising only in terms of the initial disorganisation and the sheer scale of the task which the men had set themselves. In other respects, he and his leadership did have a military strategy which was well suited to the unstable situation in the rural South. They also had a political and social strategy which reflected a clear awareness of the need to get ordinary Sicilians – and, subsequently, Neapolitans – materially on their side.

As is well known, the economic and social measures introduced by Garibaldi's dictatorship ran into problems.[1] Still, these reforms were only one aspect of a general strategy to encourage popular support. In fact, attention to the material aspects of the Sicilian revolution was paralleled by a powerful appeal to people's emotions, and by a series of attempts to put the revolution on display through festivals and other ceremonies of national 'belonging', in order to encourage popular identification with the new regime, and with the idea of Italy more generally. Here what is most striking is the attempt to be inclusive – to appeal to as many sectors of the population as possible – and the use of religious iconography. In particular, Garibaldi and his administration made repeated efforts not to offend the Church and clergy in Sicily, and many of their actions show an explicit recognition that they could accomplish little in the South without the support of the Church.

The religion of revolution

As in 1848–9 and 1859, Garibaldi's progress through Sicily and in Naples was marked by a series of stirring speeches and proclamations. Just as he had done at the start of the campaign in Lombardy in 1859, he issued a call to the population to join him. This time, however, Garibaldi referred not to the northern Italian myths of Pontida and Legnano (see pages 74, 172) but to the central episode in Sicily's 'national' history, the Sicilian Vespers (a thirteenth-century revolt against French rule).[2] 'Everyone to arms! and Sicily will teach us once more the way to free a country from its oppressors.'[3] Throughout the rest of the campaign in Sicily, he alluded to the Vespers and to Sicilian pride. At the end of the fighting for Palermo, he told the crowd assembled at the Palazzo Pretorio that 'my companions and I rejoice that we can fight alongside the children of the Vespers, in a battle that will smash the last link in the chain which has bound this land of genius and heroism' (this speech was published in the *Giornale di Sicilia* on 2 June).[4] Some time later he told the 'citizens of Palermo' that during the fighting for the city 'I understood that I had in my presence the descendants of the Vespers'.[5] Sicilians were 'a great and generous people . . . in this classical land, the citizen rose up in disgust against tyranny, broke his chains, and with his shattered prison irons turned into daggers, fought the hired assassins'.[6] More than once he thanked them for their enthusiasm, the 'brothers of the city' who had fought alongside the 'strong and courageous sons of the countryside', for the support of the priests ('what a change from the dissolute priest of Rome') and for the defiance of women, 'beautiful in their rage and their sublime patriotism'.[7] 'Sicily is a country', Garibaldi wrote in a 'Proclamation to Sicilian Women':

which has no need to look to foreign history for examples of civic virtue by both sexes. In this island blessed by God, the fair sex of all ages has offered proof of such courage to amaze the world . . . The Vespers, a unique moment in the history of nations, also saw the charming women of this island take their place alongside those fighting for the independence of the fatherland.

'Dear and charming women of Sicily,' Garibaldi continued, 'hear the voice of the man who genuinely loves your beautiful country and to whose love he is tied for the rest of life', a man who had never asked anything for himself, only for 'the common Fatherland'. Holding up the example of Adelaide Cairoli of Pavia ('the richest, dearest, kindest woman [*matrona*]'), who had sent her four sons to fight and die for Italy, he urged them: 'Women, send us your sons, your lovers!'[8]

Garibaldi's speeches and proclamations to the Sicilian people are interesting because they follow an established Risorgimento formula – with their references to innate heroism, a glorious history and national 'resurgence' – while also being tailored to flatter and to excite a specific audience, whether Sicilians in general, women, peasants or priests. As in 1859, moreover, these speeches had two related purposes. They aimed to represent and popularise an ideal of virile, popular and inclusive *italianità* and, in so doing, they sought to make the thought of volunteering to fight for this ideal attractive and

emotionally appealing; equally, others (women) were encouraged to participate by giving their material and moral support to Garibaldi's campaign. In
this way, political consent was transformed into active political engagement.
Especially worthy of note, because very unusual, was the attention paid to
priests and the encouragement given to them to join Garibaldi. Indeed, one of
Garibaldi's earliest proclamations, issued at the beginning of the campaign at
Salemi (or possibly even Marsala), had been an appeal to the 'good priests' to
follow 'the true religion of Christ'. He gave specifically to priests the leadership
in the war 'to fight the oppressors' and the task of liberating Sicily ('our land
. . . our children . . . our women . . . our inheritance and . . . us!') from the
domination of foreigners.[9]

Garibaldi's Marsala proclamation re-used one of the most vivid phrases
from his May 1859 call to the 'people of Lombardy': 'Anyone who does not
take up arms is a coward and a traitor to the fatherland.'[10] In Palermo, he
repeated the message: 'So, all to arms, and armed, smash your prison irons and
prepare every means of defence and offence . . . All to arms and armed, I repeat
. . . Who does not take up arms in these three days is a traitor or a coward.'[11]
As Garibaldi moved towards the Straits of Messina and then Naples, his
proclamations began to address the 'Neapolitans': 'I would like . . . to avoid the
spilling of blood between Italians, and so I turn to you, sons of the Neapolitan
continent. I have seen that you are brave, but I don't want to see this again.
Our blood, we will spill together over the corpses of Italy's enemies, but
between us . . . truce!'[12] 'We will win without you; but I would be proud to win
with You', he wrote to the 'Neapolitan Soldiers' in a printed flyer with a
political manifesto attached. The manifesto called on them to revolt against
the king ('destiny is in your hands, oh soldiers of Naples!') and appealed to
their sense of pride and religion. 'Tomorrow you could be respected as soldiers
of the world's first nation, as Italian soldiers', the programme stated; but if they
resisted, they would be fighting against Italy, France and England, and against
a Providence which had protected Italy, put Napoleon on the throne of
France, and 'saved Garibaldi from a thousand deaths'.[13] The (uncommonly)
positive references to France and Napoleon are worth noting here: they are
presumably an acknowledgement of Neapolitan nostalgia for Bonapartism,
and especially for Napoleon's brother-in-law, the king of Naples, Joachim
Murat.

Garibaldi's dictatorship also appealed to the people through the figure of
Garibaldi himself. In 1860, Garibaldi was not just the political dictator of Sicily
(and later Naples), he also became the symbol of revolution in the South and,
with the Piedmontese king, of Italian Risorgimento. As a letter to the radical
Movimento paper put it: 'the Sicilian revolution triumphed with him and in
him'.[14] Following on from the practice established in towns like Varese and

Como during 1859, Garibaldi's public appearances and other commemorative occasions associated with him became the occasion for great public festivities. As in 1859, of course, we know about these festivities and the other scenes of enthusiasm for Garibaldi largely through the descriptions of partial observers, who had an interest in exaggerating the extent of popular involvement and the size of the crowds. Nevertheless, they can tell us something about the frenetic atmosphere in 1860 and the ways in which a cult of Garibaldi was publicly encouraged and staged.

The first great Garibaldi celebration came in Palermo after the armistice with the Bourbons at the end of May. Here Garibaldi made a speech to the crowd telling them of the terms, and of his determination to fight on. 'I can find no words to describe the crowd's reaction', Giuseppe Abba, a volunteer from Bergamo, writes:

> At the terrifying yell that broke out from the Piazza my hair stood on end and my skin went all goose-flesh. People kissed each other, embraced, almost suffocated in their passion. Women, even more than men, demonstrated their desperate readiness to face all dangers. 'Thank you, thank you!' they cried, stretching out their hands towards the General. From the end of the Piazza I, too, blew him a kiss. Such a radiant face had never, I believe, been seen before as on that balcony at that moment. The very soul of the people seemed transfused in him.[15]

The next day, Garibaldi made a tour of the city. Ferdinand Eber, a correspondent of the London *Times* and a huge Garibaldi enthusiast, told his readers:

> I was there, but find it really impossible to give you even a faint idea of the manner in which he was received everywhere. It was one of those triumphs which seem to be almost too much for a man . . . the popular idol, Garibaldi, in his red flannel shirt, with a loose coloured handkerchief around his neck, and his worn wideawake [hat], was walking on foot among those cheering, laughing, crying, mad thousands . . . The people threw themselves forward to kiss his hands, or at least to touch the hem of his garment, as if it contained the panacea for all their past and perhaps coming sufferings. Children were brought up, and mothers asked on their knees for his blessing; and all this while the object of this idolatry was as calm and as smiling as when in the deadliest fire, taking up the children and kissing them, trying to quiet the crowd, stopping at every moment to hear a long complaint of houses burnt and property sacked . . . giving good advice, comforting, and promising that all damages should be paid for.

'Anyone in search of violent emotions', Eber advised, 'cannot do better than set off at once for Palermo.'[16]

An interesting feature of these descriptions is the reference to religion and to religious feeling. In his speeches and appearances in 1860, Garibaldi seemed to develop an ability to adopt a dignified pose ('calm and . . . smiling') while provoking (or recreating) impromptu scenes of popular religious fervour. His use of a religious vernacular to communicate with the people was alluded to by Charles Forbes, the English volunteer, who saw Garibaldi arrive in Messina: 'There is a sort of intimate communion of mind between Garibaldi and the masses which is perfectly electrifying. They look up to him as a sort of link between themselves and the Deity – as a sort of father who would pardon their most venial crimes.' 'I have been many times told,' he wrote later, 'in all sincerity by the peasants, that he is the brother of the Redeemer.'[17] Marc Monnier, observing Garibaldi in Naples, made very similar comments: 'Garibaldi is a saint for the common people [les lazzarones] . . . It is God who has sent him to save the country; several call him Jesus Christ; his officers are the apostles. Alms are asked for in Garibaldi's name.'[18] Moreover, Garibaldi's religious appeal was not confined to the Neapolitan lazzaroni. An English Protestant woman, Harriet Meuricoffre, wrote to her father from Naples in August of his extraordinary, and for her inexplicable, charisma ('You have only to look into his face, and you feel that there is, perhaps, the one man in the world in whose service you would, taking your heart in your hand, follow blindfold to death'), and of his 'devotion to and faith in a holy cause' which were 'written in letters of light' on his face.[19]

That the identification of the cult of Garibaldi with religious cults was deliberate, and created from above, is suggested not just by his speeches praising priests and the use of religious language, but also by his direct participation in religious services and celebrations. As we will see, he also managed to get a significant proportion of the southern clergy on his side. One of his first acts after the battle of Calatafimi was to receive a blessing in the cathedral of nearby Alcamo. On 15 July, for the festa di Santa Rosalia (the patron saint of Palermo), he sat on the high throne of Palermo cathedral, in the role of royal defender of the faith and of the Church, and followed the traditional religious ceremony which affirmed the power of the Pope's representative in Sicily.[20] The day after he arrived in Naples, 8 September, was the popular religious festival of Piedigrotta, traditionally attended by the Bourbon monarchs, and Garibaldi made a point of participating in the religious service and celebrations. According to the journalist Charles Arrivabene, Garibaldi was accompanied by a great procession along the seafront to Piedigrotta: 'lofty green, white and red poles were fixed in a double row in the ground, with flags waving from the summit. Hundreds and hundreds of *carrozelle*, gaily dressed with hangings and banners, and crowded with more people than the half-starved horses could well pull along, followed our carriages.' He was cheered by the fishermen and *lazzaroni*, and women shouted 'May the blessed virgin be with you, *Eccellenza!*'[21] In the tiny church of Piedigrotta, Garibaldi was trapped by the crowds: one of his entourage described 'the frenzy of the people to reach Garibaldi, who passed by, speaking brief words of love'.[22]

On 19 September, Garibaldi went to the cathedral and presided over the liquefaction of the blood of San Gennaro, the patron saint of Naples. This ceremony was a central date in the city's religious and political calendar, and the fact that the saint's blood liquefied in the presence of Garibaldi was celebrated as a good portent for the new regime. As the British envoy, Henry Elliot, commented: Garibaldi treated 'St. Januarius' with 'the greatest respect', so that 'the liquefaction came off last week with the usual *éclat*'.[23] During all these celebrations, Garibaldi took great care to observe and pay his respects to local cults and sensibilities. In so doing he accepted the power of the Church, and identified himself with it in the role of a traditional monarch.[24]

Yet if Garibaldi in his public appearances was careful to follow or borrow elements from traditional religious and royal rituals, he also achieved a familiarity, freedom, and even ordinariness which was entirely democratic (in Forbes' words, he was both 'one of themselves' and 'immeasurably above them all').[25] On the throne in Palermo, he wore his red shirt and scarf: he epitomised, according to one supporter, the 'son of the people' and the 'alliance . . . between altar and law, between religion and reason, between the gospel and progress'.[26] He also took to walking on foot among the people. When in Naples huge crowds greeted Garibaldi, he responded with a great show of friendliness and intimacy. Before his arrival in the capital, in the town of Rogliano, he had allowed himself to be 'almost devoured by kisses', and he had been 'ubiquitous': 'seated on a sofa amidst a bevy of young ladies and children, evidently charmed with the variety of their stupid questions, as he fondled a baby one minute, wrote a few words in an album the next, and from time to time gave orders to the civil and military authorities'.[27] After he arrived, according to the French writer Louise Colet who was in Naples, Garibaldi was 'accessible to everybody, and appreciative of applause and public demonstrations'. He excited the people with his public speeches 'just like in a kind of Greek democracy' and 'was their ideal of a sovereign'. He showed himself frequently on the balcony of his hotel, he came out for walks through the streets and along the seafront, and he greeted, and was greeted by, everyone. 'He conquered this town,' Colet comments, 'not so much by force as by sentiment and real human warmth.'[28] Both Marc Monnier and Harriet Meuricoffre, who had noted his exceptional charisma, stressed equally his ease, openness and 'simplicity'. Meuricoffre wrote of his face 'in which the whole character is written, simple, grand, and loving';[29] while Monnier noted that '[h]e greets all intruders with the patience of a martyr; he does not keep them at a distance; he does not speak to them sententiously. He is simple and kind . . . He is a child of the people, and adored by the people.'[30]

This eclectic mix of the sacred and the everyday – the union of ritualised authority with the casual intimacy of the democratic leader – may explain the popular success of the cult, and in particular help to account for the spontaneous emotional response to Garibaldi's presence. Such spontaneity should not obscure the extent to which popular enthusiasm had been prepared beforehand by nationalist propaganda, and further stirred up by Garibaldi on arrival, through his speeches and behaviour. Even if to a limited extent, Garibaldi's public appearances were planned and choreographed in advance. By 1860, moreover, Garibaldi had the advantage of being very famous. Already he embodied an heroic story of national pride constructed over the preceding two decades and which needed only to be adapted for the conditions of 1860; various tried and trusted mechanisms – such as the press and public appearances and speeches – were already in place to promote a popular cult. To this image was simply added a religious and especially a miraculous vocabulary which seemed particularly suited to the popular culture of Sicily and southern Italy, where there were local traditions of popular festivities for saints from which Garibaldi could benefit. What really distinguished the cult of Garibaldi in 1860 was that, for the first time, he was in power. This major difference meant that the cult could be elaborated in new ways and circulated on a scale which had never been possible before. In short, the cult of Garibaldi in 1860 became official.

An indication of the government's determination to encourage an official cult of Garibaldi can be found in one of the first meetings of the new town council of Palermo on 17 June 1860. To applause, the members agreed on an address to the 'Supreme Italian, General Garibaldi': 'a man from the heroic age, your name hardly had to be uttered and the Sicilians were freed, and became citizens of the great fatherland. The city of Palermo raises a unanimous cry of gratitude to the liberator of Sicily, and from its smoking ruins . . . salutes the Italian hero.' They proclaimed him 'the first among Palermo citizens'; and they decided that Porta Termini should be renamed Porta Garibaldi (and that the via Toledo – one of the two main streets of Palermo – should be renamed via Vittorio Emanuele).[31] More important perhaps than names and speeches was their decision to pay for a birthday celebration in Palermo in honour of Garibaldi.[32] This expenditure was especially significant since the government's lack of money was a serious problem; so serious that, by early August, the town council risked bankruptcy and considered reinstating the unpopular grist tax.[33]

The celebrations for Garibaldi's birthday took place in Palermo on the evening of 19 July (unfortunately without him, as he had been forced to leave Palermo at the last moment for the battle of Milazzo). They were extremely elaborate. According to one report, the church bells started to peal early in the morning;[34] and this was followed by a popular demonstration. *L'Unità Italiana* reported that a children's choir moved around the city singing hymns, and that a group of lively young men carried around an effigy in black (representing perhaps a Jesuit) which they periodically hit with a stick.[35] Thereafter, the official celebrations took over. All the shops were closed and public and private buildings – including the archbishop's palace, the university and the municipal government – were covered entirely in decorations: 'All the balconies crammed full of Chinese lanterns and party decorations, with busts, portraits and flags', commented one newspaper. The decorations on Palazzo Riso attracted particular praise (it was one of the main noble residences in the city, facing Piazza Bologni): 'decorated with magnificent tapestries, of gold and silver braid, along with prestigious military trophies of ancient date ... brocade cloth with gold and sliver braid and numerous candelabra on the balconies. In the middle, an ancient military trophy with a painting of Garibaldi.' Another imposing residence, the Palazzo Sant-Elia, was decorated in lights, flowers and flags, with an image of Garibaldi in the centre and an inscription reading: 'To Giuseppe Garibaldi – Angel of divine justice – Powerful expression – Of eternal Italy.' The various gentlemen's clubs were 'transformed into rooms of *A thousand and one nights*', according to a newspaper.[36] The 'caffè di Sicilia' on the corner of Piazza Bologni and via Toledo displayed the following inscription: 'For Giuseppe Garibaldi – Example of rare modesty – The Italians of Sicily – Celebrate his 53rd year'.[37]

A striking feature of the celebrations was the hanging of large illuminated 'transparent canvases' featuring episodes from Garibaldi's expedition to Sicily and other nationalist allegories. Four of these were hung at the four sides of the *Quattro Canti* at the centre of the city: representing the arrival at Marsala (with '800 Italians'; see figure 13 overleaf), the battle of Calatafimi, and two moments in the battle for Palermo. There were two other canvases, one on the via Toledo and another on the via Maqueda.[38] The via Maqueda canvas showed Sicily 'in the form of Ceres [the goddess of grain and harvests, and a symbol of the cycle of death and rebirth] with a white dress, green scarf and red shawl', standing hand in hand with Garibaldi who, as in all the canvases and the portraits, was 'painted with the classic red shirt and scarf around his shoulders' (see figure 14). Underneath was written a short verse: 'Come child of the sun, you know you must come – Since you are engaged to the King Vittorio.'[39]

Disbarco in Marsala del Generale Garibaldi con 800 Italiani

13 'Landing in Marsala of General Garibaldi with 800 Italians': this version of one of the most emblematic episodes of the Thousand is a copy of a large transparent canvas hung in the centre of Palermo.

There were parades and processions all over Palermo. Troops paraded in Piazza dell'Olivella, and in other squares too, complete with transparent canvases and statues of Garibaldi. The climax of all the celebrations was a general procession, led by a choir and orchestra, and followed by huge crowds, down the via Toledo towards the sea. The procession stopped at various strategic points to sing hymns to Garibaldi. The message of all the hymns was the same and was simple: they presented Garibaldi as the saviour of Sicily, and encouraged Sicilians to fight with him:

> Oh child of the Alps, terrible warrior . . . you unite in joy an entire people/
> How sacred is the day you were born . . . Brave boys the cry of war/
> Encourages us to renewed virtue/ It reminds us that this is the land/ Of
> Guinarde and Procida [a reference to the Vespers] . . . You are the father,
> the friend, the husband,/ The Redeemer of your Sicilian children,/ You are
> that great man, who . . . stole us from cruel servitude.[40]

On the same day, there was a huge festival in Marsala (which lasted five days, according to one paper),[41] with a gun salute, military parade, and Te Deum in

Garibaldi consegna la Sicilia al Re galantuomo

14 'Garibaldi hands Sicily over to the gentleman King': another copy of a transparent canvas hung in Palermo shows Sicily as the goddess Ceres; both figures were dressed in the colours of the Italian tricolour.

the cathedral. In the evening there were illuminations, and a transparent canvas of Garibaldi's landing was hung over the gate by which he had entered the town (although an English observer commented that the painter 'had given rather a stretch to the imagination when he portrayed the people of Marsala receiving them with open arms amid a perfect shower of shot and shell from the Neapolitan ships').[42] The following day, 20 July, there was another – seemingly impromptu – demonstration in Palermo to celebrate Garibaldi's victory at Milazzo, with more illuminations, singing and flag-waving: 'The bells rang out in celebration from every street and district, the crowd vomited into via Toledo with frenzied *evvivas* to Garibaldi, to Italy, to Vittorio Emanuele'.[43]

There seems little doubt about the political intention of these celebrations. Indeed, they appear to be an archetypal example of nation-building from above, of an official attempt to elaborate and utilise a political aesthetic through festivals and visual representations to encourage a sense of national belonging, to foster an emotional attachment to the regime, and to Italianise the public spaces of Palermo.[44] Specifically in this case, we can observe an effort to establish Sicily as part of Italy, identified with the Piedmontese monarchy, through the celebration of the figure of Garibaldi. Yet there was nothing very new about the production itself: the Bourbons had pioneered the use of transparent canvases and elaborate temporary stages and displays for popular festivals (although their origins lie in revolutionary and post-revolutionary France);[45] and although the technology was modern, the spectacle itself was heavy with traditional, and especially religious, symbolism. Garibaldi himself was represented as a saint, responsible for the miraculous liberation of Sicily. In fact, the celebration itself – its timing in the middle of July, the organisation and placing of the procession in the via Toledo and around the *Quattro Canti*, the iconography of Garibaldi as saint – bears an overwhelming resemblance to the popular procession traditionally held in mid-July to commemorate the festival of Santa Rosalia in Palermo. This festival was not celebrated in 1860, allegedly because the Bourbons had stolen the saint's effects and part of her statue from the cathedral.[46]

There were still other official attempts at 'making Italians'. Throughout the summer of 1860, public commemorations sought to establish an official narrative of the events of 1860, or to create and control a nationalist memory of what had occurred. The departure of the Bourbon garrison from Palermo was turned (unsurprisingly) into a general festival of *italianità*, as was the defection of a Bourbon warship, *Veloce*, to the nationalist side: 'you now belong to our family', Garibaldi told the crew.[47] One of the boats which had brought the Thousand to Marsala was refloated and taken to lie in the harbour at Palermo for all to see: '[it's] a wreck,' commented one volunteer, 'but the intention is to remind people of the great event'.[48] Towards the end of June, the final symbol of Bourbon power in Palermo, the fort of Castellamare, was taken by Garibaldi's army. The fort was then demolished (or – more accurately – an attempt was made to demolish it) as part of a great public celebration, involving all the non-combatant groups of Palermo society: priests, women, children, young and old, rich and poor. They reportedly marched together down to the fort shouting '*Evviva all'Italia, evviva al nostro Re e al Dittatore*', carrying flowers, refreshments and the tools of the job to destroy it; and the fort became an open-air site for the staging of *italianità*, visited by prominent political figures, including Garibaldi himself and the archbishop of Monreale, Benedetto d'Acquisto.[49]

The public demolition of the fort at Castellamare was indicative of a more general policy to stage and to encourage public performances of nationalist zeal. Public funerals and other commemorative events were organised to celebrate those 'martyrs' who had died in the Sicilian campaign. Foreigners who had come to fight in Sicily were commemorated, and the biggest funeral of all was ordered personally by Crispi, for his friend, Rosolino Pilo (who had arrived before Garibaldi and was killed in the mountains above Palermo), along with the erection of a monument to him. Pilo's funeral service lasted three hours and took place in the Church of San Domenico, the 'pantheon' of Palermo, on 24 August.[50] Crispi also used the press to make Italians. The two government papers in Palermo, *Il Giornale di Sicilia* and *Il Precursore*, were masterminded by Crispi, and both emphasised the exceptional stature of Garibaldi and sought to glorify specific moments in the revolution. The *Giornale di Sicilia*'s main purpose was to publish the decrees of the dictatorship, but much of its first number was taken up with establishing a detailed, if largely tendentious, narrative of the revolution from the departure at Quarto to the arrival in the mountains above Palermo. Garibaldi, according to the paper, the 'noble Leader [*Duce*]', was a 'genius' with a 'radiant look', whose light shone 'like the brilliant halo of the Italian flag' among the devastation of the Bourbon bombardment and the horrors of a civil war.[51]

This lead was taken up by *Il Precursore* (whose name referred to Pilo). The celebrations for Garibaldi's birthday, the battle of Milazzo, his arrival in Calabria, and other nationalist events: all these gave *Il Precursore* the opportunity to rewrite the idea of the nation in a popular religious vernacular and to hold up Garibaldi as its main interpreter. Reporting on the victory at Milazzo, the paper asked: 'Who can resist the sword of the Hero of Varese and Calatafimi, if his sword is that of the avenging Angel?'[52] 'Where did he go?' it asked after Garibaldi left for Calabria, 'nobody knew, and our answer to those who ask is his: *when you come with me you don't ask where we are going*'.[53] After Garibaldi returned briefly to Sicily in September, *Il Precursore* indulged in an extended hagiography which ran over two issues ('Oh how beautiful it was to see the liberator of Italy, the greatest hero of our day . . . !'). As Garibaldi departed from Porta Felice, the paper reported that 'a thousand kisses' were exchanged, while those who could not kiss him 'began to kiss his red shirt, his arms, his legs, his feet, with the same ardour as they would have kissed a saint'. He was carried to the boat by the people, crying: 'long live the great liberator of Italy, long live our father, long live the Saviour – why are you leaving, why are you abandoning us?'[54]

At a time of political uncertainty and war (for instance, during the battle of Milazzo for Garibaldi's birthday; during Garibaldi's march on Naples for the funeral for Pilo), the amount of attention and resources given to displays of national belonging by Garibaldi's dictatorship is surprising. Indeed, it has never been taken seriously by historians. Yet these kinds of patriotic display in Palermo in 1860 – the role of funerals and the exaltation of death in battle; the promotion of heroes (Garibaldi, the king, Pilo); and the establishment of patriotic rituals and symbols associated with religious practices and vocabularies – represent a significant attempt to sacralise the nation, and to make political action the subject of a religious cult.[55] The patriotic displays of 1860 also tell us that Mazzini's concept of a political religion found official and practical expression before national unification, and well before Francesco

Crispi, as Italian prime minister, introduced a programme of 'making' and educating Italians two decades later.[56]

Many of these celebrations were also politically astute. Not only was a great effort made to be as inclusive as possible (only unrepentant Bourbons and Jesuits were excluded from Garibaldi's revolution), but enormous care was taken not to offend the Church. Moreover, since most of these festivities required a significant amount of expenditure and practical organisation, they presumably served to provide employment for artisans, and so to revitalise the city's economy after the fighting and bombardment and appease this crucial section of Palermo society.[57] The creation of employment opportunities could serve other purposes too. The painters responsible for the large-scale canvases at Garibaldi's birthday celebrations and Pilo's funeral were highly experienced in producing religious and theatrical art, and could therefore be relied upon to produce something spectacular. But they – Giuseppe Bagnasco, Luigi Lo Jacono, Giovan Battista Basile – were also prominent figures known for their liberal sympathies, and it seems very likely that the government sought to reward them for their loyalty and to show other artists and artisans the material advantages which official patronage could bring.[58]

The myth of the 'Mille'

From the outset, Garibaldi's dictatorship had a very keen eye for self-publicity. These publicity efforts were not, however, confined to Sicily; the expedition, and later the government, were extremely attentive to public opinion both in northern and central Italy and internationally. Positive publicity was vital to the success of the expedition, in part because it could translate into the supply of money and men. Widespread and positive publicity was also crucial because, at the outset at least, the expedition to Sicily was part of a broader military strategy which included an attack on the Papal States.

The day before leaving for Sicily, Garibaldi wrote a series of letters, destined for publication in the main democratic newspapers such as Valerio's *Il Diritto*, *L'Unità Italiana* and *Il Movimento*.[59] These letters represent a manifesto for the expedition, in which he justified his action and announced his aims. One of the most important and widely circulated was his 5 May letter to Bertani (who had stayed at Genoa), which asked for practical support in the name of Italian independence:

Try to make Italians understand that if we are duly helped, Italy will be made quickly and at a small cost ... That for an Italy freed today, five hundred thousand soldiers must take up arms, and not a hundred thousand ... With such an army, Italy will no longer need foreign masters who will eat her up bit by bit on the pretext of freeing her. That wherever there are Italians who are fighting the oppressor, there we must incite all the brave men to go and provide them with the necessary for the journey.[60]

That this letter was intended not so much for Bertani as for the rest of the world is suggested by its publication in *Il Diritto* on 9 May, and its translation and circulation to many foreign newspapers, including the London *Times* and the *New York Times* (the latter commented that it was 'in better taste than many of the guerillero's late effusions').[61] A proclamation addressed to *Italiani!*, and which began: 'Sicilians are fighting against the enemies of Italy, and for Italy! It is the duty of every Italian to help them, with word, with money, with firearms and above all with their hands', was also printed and distributed as a flyer.[62]

Arguably the most important sign of Garibaldi's concern with public opinion was the public letter he wrote to the king just before sailing to Sicily. In it, Garibaldi both reiterated the link between nation, monarchy and democracy that he had tried so hard to promote during the previous year, and recast his initially reluctant decision to go to Sicily in a much more conclusive light:

> The cry of torment which arrived at my ears from Sicily has moved my heart, and the heart of a few hundred of my old fellow-soldiers. I did not encourage the insurrection by my brothers in Sicily; but from the moment that they rose up in the name of Italian Union, of which Your Majesty is the personification, against the most vile tyranny of our times, I did not hesitate in placing myself at the head of the expedition. I am well aware that I am embarking on a hazardous enterprise, but I have faith in God, and in the courage and devotion of my companions. Our war cry will always be: *Viva l'unità d'Italia! Viva Vittorio Emanuele*, her first and bravest soldier![63]

In other words, Garibaldi was not responsible for the insurrection, but it was justifiable against such an evil regime; and the expedition itself was a heroic and generous endeavour carried out for Italy and in the name of the king. In this way, Garibaldi sought to establish and control the symbolic representation of the expedition, and to legitimise it by appealing both to revolutionary nationalism and to monarchical devotion.

Garibaldi was also careful to write a letter to the director of the Rubattino Steamship Company in which he justified the theft of his two ships by reference to the 'service to a holy cause', and this letter was published not only in *Il Diritto* and *L'Unità Italiana*, but also in foreign papers like the London *Times*, the *New York Times* and *Le Siècle*.[64] Further evidence of Garibaldi's commitment to getting material and moral support for the expedition is provided by a private letter to Giacomo Medici, asking him to stay behind and organise men and arms: 'Tell the Italians that they should follow you in complete faith, that the hour has finally come to make this Italy that we all yearn for and that by God! they should understand that if we are many we will finish them off quickly and that our enemies draw strength from our fears and our indifference'.[65] This effort did not let up after departure. On 13 May, the *Movimento* published Garibaldi's orders to his troops:

> the mission of this corps will be, as it was heretofore, based upon the most complete abnegation with the object of regenerating our country. The brave Chasseurs have served and will serve their country with the devotion and discipline of the best troops in the world without hoping for any other reward than that of an unspotted conscience. They are attracted to the service by no offer of rank, honors or rewards. When the danger is over they will retire to their simple private life; but now that the hour of combat has come, Italy beholds them in the front rank, joyous and determined, ready to shed their blood.

Everything in these orders was intended for wider dissemination (and, indeed, they were published as far away as New York's illustrated *Harper's Weekly*).[66] Garibaldi's troops were already on board the ships bound for Sicily and committed, for better for worse, to the expedition. It was the young men at home reading about the Thousand in the newspapers that Garibaldi sought to reach, and to encourage to join his volunteers in Sicily. For these readers, the expedition was constructed in heroic terms, mixing religious and military metaphors. The expedition was a matter of individual conscience, a decisive moment to choose bravery and express devotion to a greater cause. Moreover, the expedition's attention to the world outside Sicily did not stop on arrival at Marsala. Indeed, as they sailed into the port, Nino Bixio – perhaps knowing they would have to cut the telegraph wire at Marsala – tried to throw dispatches wrapped in bread to a passing English sailing boat and, when he failed, shouted at them to give out the news that Garibaldi had landed at Marsala.[67]

Immediately after Calatafimi, Garibaldi wrote two other letters, to Bertani and to Rosolino Pilo, which were published in *Il Diritto*. Both began with the same simple but powerful words, 'Yesterday we fought and won', and both emphasised the demoralisation of the enemy, the enthusiasm of the population and the pressing need for volunteers.[68] From Palermo, Garibaldi sent other letters for publication which asked for arms and ammunition,[69] and a series of his letters addressed to British public figures and other groups was published: these thanked the British for their support and asked 'quick' for 'arms, ships, guns and material'.[70] His first proclamations to the Sicilians and Neapolitans reached the *New York Times* on 30 May, and his address to 'Sicilian women', encouraging them to send their sons and lovers, was also intended for a wider audience of women; it was made as Garibaldi prepared to relaunch the expedition by crossing the straits to Calabria, and it was published in *L'Unità Italiana* on 13 August.[71]

The published letters of Garibaldi aimed at maximum publicity, and at gaining material and moral support for the expedition. The letters constructed the expedition to Sicily as a narrative of selfless courage and military daring, where the odds against the expedition – a thousand men against a royal army – added to the miraculous and heroic quality of the final outcome. They were accompanied by a propaganda effort in northern Italy which continued throughout the summer: by speeches, poems and other celebrations. A Sicilian professor, Giacomo Oddo, made a speech in early July to the Institute of Popular Education in Milan which was subsequently published as a pamphlet. In it, he spoke of the joy of being Italian ('allow me to become inebriated on the single idea of being born Italian, and I say to you, oh gentlemen, rejoice, because your fatherland is Italy, and however great were the misfortunes of this unhappy nation, so were its glories, and they are and will always be infinite') and of the greatness of Garibaldi ('the shining star of Italy . . . the man of Providence, the angel of our Italy'). The real purpose of this florid speech was to raise arms and money.[72] The novelist and political activist Francesco Domenico Guerrazzi joined the effort, penning a speech to celebrate the volunteers on the second expedition to Garibaldi and publishing an article in *L'Unità Italiana* and *Il Precursore* in which he praised Garibaldi ('Garibaldi is *the people*, who go forward sword in hand') and criticised Cavour.[73] Bertani was active in this area too; he helped to circulate a poem, 'The guns', which called for volunteers and arms, and in August he organised an elaborate commemoration in Milan – 'Funerals for the martyrs of Milazzo' – which was, above all, a publicity drive and fund-raising activity.[74]

Perhaps most of all, the campaign relied on newspapers to publicise its activity.[75] Around a hundred of the volunteers with the Thousand were writers and/or painters, some of whom (Nievo, dell'Ongaro) had already published poems about their experiences in 1859.[76] A deliberate choice seems to have been made to use their personal accounts, particularly their letters and diaries, to give immediacy and intimacy to the political events being described. In this way, the appeal of first-hand experience was tied to the more abstract, and political, ideal of Italy. That this epistolary formula was perceived as attractive to the reader is indicated by its frequent use in the months that followed, and by many participants and by journalists in 1860 (often the line dividing these two groups was not clear, as many of the journalists were huge Garibaldi enthusiasts). Above all, these letters and diaries stressed the emotional intensity of the events their writers were living through.

A fine example of the use of the epistolary formula to encourage personal identification with Garibaldi's expedition is found in *L'Unità Italiana* of 12 May. The paper published a letter from one volunteer to his mother, in which he asked forgiveness for abandoning her 'to go and help heroic Sicily, but I hope you have forgiven me and will also be a mother to Italy'. He then explicitly identified the love of his own mother with the love of, and need to defend, the Italian family: 'how close it is to my heart . . . dear mother . . . to think you will bless my departure, it gives me greater courage to go and defend other unhappy mothers deprived of their sons, wives deprived of their husbands, and children orphaned by fathers in exile, imprisoned or extinguished by tyranny, because they felt they were Italian'.[77] On 11 May, *Il Movimento* published a similarly intimate letter from another volunteer, but this time an '[o]ld soldier of the fatherland'. He also made a definite link between the personal and the political. He had, he told his readers, seen many 'marvellous events' in his career:

> but the sensations I feel today have something new, so sweetly inexplicable that I have no idea how to define it in words. Alone, in the middle of the wide sea, led by the brave and among the brave, with a great principle as our guide, a glorious flag to defend, we feel ourselves to be great men . . . My sentiments, my impressions I hear repeated around me in all the dialects of Italy. Old conspirators with penetrating eyes and hollow faces mix with the blond and beautiful youngsters sent to us by strong Lombard mothers.[78]

The expedition here is represented as something dramatically important, perhaps the culmination or realisation of Italy's Risorgimento. To belong to the Thousand is seen as a moment of personal fulfilment, and of being part of a microcosm of heroic and beautiful *italianità* ('Alone, in the middle of the wide sea, led by the brave and among the brave . . . we feel ourselves to be great men').

That this glorification of the Thousand was part of a deliberate strategy is further suggested by attempts to do the same for subsequent expeditions to Sicily led by Medici and Cosenz. Long letters from two volunteers with Medici, published in *L'Unità Italiana* and the Florentine paper, *La Nazione*, described their experiences on board and on arrival, along with intimate details of the various personalities: Medici who was seasick; the Englishman Peard, 'a handsome man with long grey hair and beard . . . he adores Garibaldi'; and the welcome given to them by Garibaldi and their 'brothers' in Palermo.[79] A volunteer on the Cosenz expedition, which left Genoa in early July, remarked on the 'solemn silence' of the departure, and the unity and national inclusiveness of the occasion: 'Here and there a sister, a mother, a wife, a lover, tied in close embrace with their dear ones, the tears flowing at such a love scene. All the dialects of Italy could be heard, almost like a prelude to the unity which the nation has longed for through so many years.' The journey itself was 'felicissimo, tranquillissimo', and the men on board were:

> Animated by a flame which even death would extinguish with difficulty, the flame of Italy . . . There were doctors, surgeons and chaplains. Everyone . . . well-behaved . . . the son of the people with hands rough from daily work, and the son of the rich aristocrat, on whose finger precious rings still shone . . . lively and varied groups, with different attitudes, and united together by a single sentiment: Italy.[80]

Both for ideological reasons and because of practical considerations and, as we have seen already, in attempts to 'make' Italians in Palermo, Garibaldi's expedition is represented in the democratic press as an idealised Italian family and a model of democratic inclusiveness.

As the expedition progressed through Sicily, took Palermo and became an army, an increasing amount of emphasis came to be placed on the heroism of those involved, and on the listing of those individuals who had suffered in the struggle. L'Unità Italiana set the tone in late June with a letter from Pietro Ripari, a surgeon and veteran from Garibaldi's 1848–9 and 1859 campaigns, which created a pantheon of heroes – those brave and still untouched, and those wounded but determined to fight on:

> our men are real heroes – I won't talk to you of Garibaldi – the first in any danger, uncaring, disdainful, fully convinced that he cannot die . . . of Sirtori, I tell you that there is no one who exceeds him in fearlessness and cold-bloodedness . . . Bixio, the real live wire of war, he too wounded in the chest . . . he will not take off his uniform until victory is assured. Cairoli, another generous man who accomplished prodigious tasks with his chosen company. Mosto, whose brother was killed . . . is also a hero . . .[81]

Readers were encouraged to follow the convalescence of their wounded heroes: 'Canzio is better, but he has suffered greatly. Damele is much better. Evangelisti is better. The two Cairoli brothers are better, but for the older one it is going to take a long time . . . the younger one is much better.'[82] L'Unità Italiana published on 15 July, 'to satisfy . . . the demands' of its readers, a list of all the dead and wounded garibaldini, complete with their name, origin, age and type of wound sustained.[83] On 28 July, *Il Diritto* published a letter from one of Garibaldi's medical corps (probably the English Mazzinian, Jessie White Mario), stating that none of the wounded volunteers ever complained: '"We have come here to die for Garibaldi", they say, "and we still hope to do so".'[84]

The nationalist press also followed a style of reporting established during the Crimean War, and took a great interest in the heroic doctors and nurses who cared for the wounded and dying. The above letter was followed by another, from a volunteer, which shifted the focus directly on to the medical services. The volunteer praised the doctors and especially the 'signora Mario White' for 'that care which could be called maternal, which is rarely found away from one's own family'. Jessie White was 'the consoling angel of the sick', according to yet another volunteer, with a 'maternal care' for her patients. She was matched only by the 'fatherliness' of the doctor, and the kindness of another nurse who soothed their brows, helped them in their 'most vulgar needs', talked to them 'about our mothers and our countryside', and read them the victory bulletins.[85]

If these letters sought to stress all the suffering, gentleness and consolation of the good Italian family, other letters written from the front line publicised the triumphant progress of Garibaldi's army through Sicily and beyond. On 4 June, *Il Diritto* published Garibaldi's letter to Bertani saying they had arrived in Marsala and were 'welcomed with enthusiasm' by the crowd, who 'joined up with us in large groups'.[86] Letters in *L'Unità Italiana*, *Il Diritto* and *L'Opinione* stressed (equally inaccurately) the enormous welcome given to Garibaldi at Marsala, 'with cheers for the liberator, for Italy and King Vittorio'; 'The enthusiasm of the people is immense . . . the cry of everybody is "*Viva Vittorio Emanuele* our King"'.[87] With somewhat more justification, newspapers stressed the audacity and courage of Calatafimi: 'to describe the marvellous enthusiasm and the miracles of bravery of our young men would be impossible,' *Il Diritto* told its readers on 3 June.[88]

All the epistolary evidence suggests a general consensus to construct and promote a story of the Thousand as an exemplary Risorgimento narrative. After Palermo was taken, all practical and political press restrictions on reporting were lifted, and an information explosion occurred around Garibaldi's expedition. The struggle for Palermo was described in great detail in lengthy letters, as were the city and its inhabitants,[89] and the volume of letters grew still further once Garibaldi had left Palermo for Milazzo, in mid-July, and his intention to cross to Calabria and take Naples became clear. More than ever, the letters glorified the campaign and reflected on its miraculous impact and outcome. 'Dear *Papa!*', one letter began, which described the bravery of the soldiers at Milazzo but added:

we must also admit that there is something heaven-sent which protects them in their holy enterprise. Not just enthusiasm for the national cause which makes them capable of those miracles which have amazed Europe, but its influence extends also over the population which throngs around us and produces a kind of dizziness amongst our enemies.[90]

The welcome Messina gave the *garibaldini* was said to have been 'something from another world!'[91] After Garibaldi reached Naples, letters to the papers spoke of nothing but the festivities surrounding his arrival ('for three days we had an ovation which no other story or people has ever received'), and marvelled at what had been achieved, and how quickly: 'they [Garibaldi and his soldiers] did not come but they were, if you like, pulled to Naples by a rapid, all-powerful, marvellous current . . . It is really something to make your head spin: it exceeds the wildest imagination, spoils the tactical calculations, and makes all diplomatic ventures redundant.'[92]

Of course, the real centre of attention was Garibaldi: his leadership of the expedition guaranteed publicity, and his soldiers' letters from the campaign of 1860 glorified him above all else. This was clear from the beginning. From their stop in Talamone, a volunteer wrote to *Il Diritto* on 7 May that they were all seasick but 'the General is in great form, he does not suffer at all and inspires courage and confidence in everyone'.[93] From the front, other letters repeated the same message, broadly reflecting the official cult of Garibaldi being constructed in Palermo. He was their adored and trusted leader, with powers far greater than their own, but he was also gentle and kind with his followers. From Calatafimi, a volunteer wrote that Garibaldi 'was present at every position; the fear of seeing him hit by enemy fire made us double our efforts';[94] from Messina, another confessed that '[w]ith him command is sweet, and we would go with him to the end of the world'.[95] There was an especially joyous letter sent by a volunteer who had shared a boat trip with Garibaldi from Palermo to Messina at the end of August: 'the brave Italian, affectionate with everyone, he never puts on an heroic act or pretends to be a *great man*'. Garibaldi, the volunteer told his readers, had eaten his meals with the men, he had joined them in singing patriotic songs on board, and he had even taught them a song they didn't know already:

You cannot imagine what ran through my mind . . . my heart beat at a furious rate. That man responsible for miraculous acts, whose name is enough to rout whole enemy legions, that man whose name is spoken with respect throughout the entire world, was there sitting on a barrel of fresh water . . . singing along with us, while the boat steamed along the coast, where an entire population worships him ... oh! it really was something quite incredible.[96]

Once again, the epistolary formula is used to great effect here. Contrasting the intimate experience with the public pose, the humility of the man with his political fame, the letter serves only to intensify the reader's response to Garibaldi's personal greatness.

As if all this was not enough, Garibaldi was joined in June by Alexandre Dumas. Dumas was in the process of editing and embellishing Garibaldi's memoirs for publication, and had been enjoying a lengthy tour and cruise of southern Europe and the Mediterranean. He apparently decided to join Garibaldi in order to get more material.[97] He had an agreement to publish his letters and reports in the French liberal papers, *Le Constitutionel, La Presse* and *Le Siècle*, and later, in Naples, he told Garibaldi that he had a 'great ambition ... to lend my activity to the profit of your popularity'.[98] In effect, Dumas became the first, and self-appointed, historian of the Thousand, and he brought to the task the right blend of journalistic realism, poetic licence and narrative skill. As a clearly envious correspondent of *The Illustrated London News* put it:

> [Dumas] is engaged in writing the history of the revolution, which will in reality be a Sicilian romance, with all the information gleaned right and left, and from opposite sources, crammed into it. No offence to our neighbours across the Channel, but they have a most extraordinary fashion of relating actual occurrences.[99]

Although Dumas was indeed to write a book about his experiences,[100] of more immediate importance in 1860 was a series of published letters from, about, and after the battle of Milazzo. These letters were addressed to the wounded volunteer, Giacinto Carini, but were clearly intended for a much wider national and international readership.

Remarkable both for their intense immediacy (he pulled up anchor at Messina, Dumas tells his readers, and arrived in the Gulf of Milazzo when 'the battle had begun') and intimacy ('the General has opened his eyes, he has recognised me and is looking at me'), it was Dumas' letters which instantly established the battle of Milazzo as a canonic moment in Risorgimento history. The letters were published as a supplement to the Italian paper, *Il Movimento*, in the National Society's *Piccolo Corriere d'Italia*, in the Sicilian *La Forbice*, and in the French *La Presse*. The London *Times* published two official bulletins about 'the battle of Melazzo [*sic*]' on 1 August, together with a lengthy excerpt from Dumas' first letter. In this first and most important letter,

Dumas highlighted the drama of the occasion. Milazzo was a 'battle of the giants'; a '[g]reat battle, a great victory; 7000 Neapolitans have fled in front of 2500 Italians'. The *garibaldini* fought like heroes: Medici was at the head of his men, and his horse was killed under him; Cosenz fell to the ground with a bullet in his neck, 'we thought he was mortally wounded, but then he leapt up shouting: *Viva l'Italia!*'' Of course, the greatest hero of the day was Garibaldi, 'at the head of his men, directing the fire; while twenty paces away the cannon fire rattled'; he was persuaded to pull back only when he had his shoes and stirrups blown off and his wounded horse became uncontrollable.

It was Dumas who made famous the incident of Garibaldi and Missori's reaction to the cavalry charge. Blocked on the road by the Bourbon cavalry:

> The General leapt at the bridle of the officer, shouting: surrender. By way of reply, the officer swiped at him with a downward blow: General Garibaldi parried the blow, and with a backhand strike cut his throat . . . Three or four sabres were drawn on the General, who wounded one of his aggressors with the point of his sword. Missori killed another two and the horse of a third with three pistol shots.

Finally, it was Dumas who gave the reader a memorable – and again intensely personal – description of Garibaldi sleeping on the steps of a church after the battle, in which the private and intimate became a sign of immeasurable historical greatness:

> surrounded by his staff . . . lying on the vestibule, with his head leaning on his saddle, worn out with tiredness: he slept. Next to him was his supper, a piece of bread and a jug of water. My dear Carini, I was taken back to 2500 years ago, and I found myself in the presence of Cincinnatus. May God protect him for you my dear Italians, because if some misadventure were to take him from you, the whole world could not give you another like him.[101]

Journalists and their public

The involvement of Alexandre Dumas best symbolises the remarkable fusion of politics and theatre, news journalism and popular fiction, and the public and the personal which characterised the way the story of the Thousand was accomplished, narrated and remembered. It can hardly be over-stressed how important winning the sympathy of journalists was to Garibaldi. Most obviously, press sympathy was crucial to combat any criticism of what Garibaldi had done. We should remember that at the outset of the expedition Garibaldi's volunteer army had no legal basis whatever, that they had stolen two ships, and that they had attacked without provocation the Kingdom of the Two Sicilies, a recognised and legitimate state, from a base in Piedmont, a non-enemy state. All these actions gave ample opportunity to his right-wing and clerical enemies to attack Garibaldi for being a pirate and a bandit.

In fact, the Bourbon government immediately denounced Garibaldi on this basis, and was quickly followed by the rest of legitimist and reactionary Europe, and especially by the French press. The Neapolitan minister Carafa published a diplomatic note which accused Garibaldi of leading 'a fact of the most savage piracy' with a 'horde of brigands' (as well as saying the British had helped him disembark at Marsala).[102] *La Gazzetta di Napoli* called Garibaldi 'a monster in human shape' and *La Gazzetta di Roma* an 'Antichrist'.[103] On 10 May, *Le Pays*, a Bonapartist paper in France, wrote that '[the] expedition of Garibaldi carried out without a tie to any nationality, without a flag, without a right of any kind, should simply be treated as an act of piracy'; and it was followed on 22 May by the legitimist *Le Correspondant*, which said that Garibaldi had attacked a state he was not at war with, 'at the whim of his fancy and his ambitions'. Also in France, *L'Union* on 2 June called Garibaldi 'an adventurer . . . a bandit, a pirate acting for his own ends . . . a buccaneer', and on 10 June described his volunteers as 'barbarians of the modern age . . . Saracens of the revolutionary idea'.[104] The author of a pamphlet *Halte-là Garibaldi!* described him as a 'bandit-chief subsidised by the foreigner', and repeated the accusation against the British.[105]

Some inkling of how the expedition could be interpreted even by the friends of Garibaldi was provided by *The Illustrated London News*, normally very well disposed towards him. However, on hearing the news of his arrival in Sicily the paper found it impossible to deny that 'the famous partisan General in his present expedition is acting the part of nothing more or less than a buccaneer; that he is guilty of simple piracy', and criticised his 'characteristic impetuosity'.[106] And even though a writer for the *New York Times* hoped 'fervently' for the success of Garibaldi's expedition, he feared 'that the end of the heroic Garibaldi is nigh. Disappointed and heart-sore [a reference to Giuseppina Raimondi], he has, it is said, a desire to meet a glorious death, and it is likely that his fancy will be indulged.'[107] Garibaldi, according to a leader in London's *Times* on 22 May (reprinted in the *New York Times* on 4 June), 'is either a hero or a brigand, all men of his stamp divide the world in admiration or execration'.

As the campaign wore on, however, and Garibaldi went from victory to victory, there was a marked shift in his favour in the attitude of the press. This shift was especially noticeable in France, and probably reflected Napoleon III's view that Garibaldi's conquest of Sicily was a *fait accompli*. The liberal *Journal des Débats* wrote on 23 May that it now seemed impossible 'to prevent the unanimous explosion produced in favour of Garibaldi', and described his progress as 'a serious victory'. 'All eyes are fixed on Garibaldi', the paper proclaimed at the end of May.[108] On 7 June, the radical *Le Siècle* felt able to publish an extended tribute by Louis Jourdain to the 'miracle' brought about by Garibaldi: 'Condottiere, adventurer, officer of fortune, even a brigand . . . what does it matter! Garibaldi is above all a hero, even better, an apostle of liberty and independence . . . he has just won his place – and what a place! – among the greatest and most heroic figures of this century, of all centuries. All honour to this brave captain!' Reflecting and adding to the publicity surrounding Garibaldi, the exiled novelist Victor Hugo made a speech from Jersey in June which was reported, translated and reprinted across the European press:

> Garibaldi! What is Garibaldi? He is a man, nothing more. But a man in the most sublime meaning of the word. A man of liberty; a man of humanity . . . Does he have an army? No. A handful of volunteers. Does he have weapons of war? Not at all . . . So where does his force come from? . . . What does he have with him? The people's soul.

Hugo's speech was also reprinted and published in a Brussels edition of Dumas' *Mémoires de Garibaldi*, with an introduction by George Sand, and the flurry of press activity around his speech can be seen as a furtive political discussion of French policy in Italy.[109] In fact, throughout the summer the *Revue des Deux Mondes* dedicated significant amounts of space to in-depth discussion of the Italian revolution. By the end of the campaign, one of the French artist–writers who had followed Garibaldi in 1860 described the attitude of the French press as follows:

> For some, the famous native of Nice is an adventurer, a seawolf . . . his companions a heap of bandits and buccaneers . . . For others, the erstwhile defender of Rome is a hero, a character from the book of Plutarch, almost a new Messiah surrounded by a phalanx of martyrs and liberators. But there is one point on which the whole world is in agreement, and that is the integrity and unselfishness of the hermit of Caprera.[110]

In Germany too, the press began to express admiration of Garibaldi's courage and ability as a soldier, even while it disagreed with his politics.[111] Karl Marx, never a fan of the Italian nationalists, wrote in the *New York Tribune* on 14 June that Garibaldi was 'the prevailing topic of discussion' in Germany.[112]

In the end, there was no doubt in the international press that 1860 was Garibaldi's year. *The Illustrated London News* wrote about the prince of Wales'

15 'Garibaldi to the rescue'
comments *Punch*. This cartoon
was produced shortly after the
details of Garibaldi's conquest
of Palermo had become known.

GARIBALDI THE LIBERATOR;

visit to Canada and the growth of a volunteer movement in Britain, and
L'Illustration faithfully followed the tours of Napoleon III and his family to his
new provinces in Savoy and the south of France, but there was little really to rival
Garibaldi. On 9 June, New York's *Harper's Weekly* proclaimed that: 'There are
conjunctures in every age when the triumph or defeat of great principles hinges
on the fortunes of individuals'. Thus, 'the course of civilization and human
freedom depends . . . upon the success of Garibaldi'. For the London *Times* on
15 June, Garibaldi was the 'Washington of Italy' who 'descended among a
people whose spirit was broken by long oppression, and whose trust was broken
by frequent treacheries . . . [he] has made war like a Christian gentleman. He has
spoken and he has fought in the old spirit of chivalry.' The British satirical paper,
Punch, published a cartoon the next day, *Garibaldi the liberator: or the modern
Perseus*, showing Garibaldi (Perseus/'Garibaldi to the rescue') chasing off
Francesco II (the serpent/'Bomba junior') while Sicily (the beautiful maiden
Andromeda) lay chained on the rock behind him (see figure 15). Women's
illustrated magazines like *The Lady's Newspaper and Pictorial Times* also
published pictures of Garibaldi. This fascination continued throughout the
summer. 'No such feat', commented the *New York Herald* in September, 'is
recorded in history, nor even amongst the deeds of mythological heroes.' 'It was

truly a most daring and extraordinary enterprise', wrote the *New York World*: 'an enterprise unparalleled in modern times, whether it is viewed in relation to the paucity of the force by which it was achieved, the formidable strength of the potentate against whom it was directed, or the tact, audacity, and military skill of the hero who projected and executed it.'[113] In France, the satirical paper *Le Chiarivari* poked fun at the prevailing obsession with Garibaldi: a middle-class husband criticised by his wife for not caring for the garden replies that it is true, he had forgotten that they had their house to see to and their garden to cultivate, but '*la campagne de Garibaldi me fait oublier la mienne*'.[114]

In this way, the long-term assault on national and international public opinion, prepared by Mazzini since the 1830s, produced a press-led 'Garibaldi-mania' characterised by massive press attention, most of which was entirely positive. In Italy itself, press reporting in 1860 represents an apogee for Risorgimento rhetoric. Nationalists of all political persuasions came to echo each other in praising what had been accomplished, and concurred in emphasising the glorious example set by Garibaldi. Raymond Grew points out that, while the attitude of the National Society and La Farina to Garibaldi's expedition had been 'uncertain' and hesitant, its newspaper – *Il Piccolo Corriere* – 'played happily to the hero-worship of Garibaldi', comparing him to El Cid, a medieval knight, and Napoleon, and complimenting him for the enthusiasm he had engendered in a 'skeptical and materialistic' age.[115] A left-moderate deputy in the Piedmontese parliament, Pier Carlo Boggio ('the *enfant terrible*' of the Rattazzi party, according to *The Times*), who had opposed Garibaldi in the parliamentary debate over Nice in April 1860, and after the campaign was over was to attack Garibaldi again,[116] had nothing but praise for him during the summer. He wrote a short biography of Garibaldi (*Da Montevideo a Palermo*) which was decidedly conventional both in its narrative structure and in the praise which it heaped on him. Boggio differed only in the portrait which he used of Garibaldi (showing him in his dark civilian garb of the 1850s), and in the suggestion – couched in very positive terms – that the hero was an enigma:

> the most extraordinary man! An unresolved and perhaps irresolvable Enigma! . . . he brings alive the fiction of Homeric songs, and of the Round Table . . . the contrast between his physical form, which is quite delicate, and the unyielding energy of his moral gifts – between the sweetness of his gaze and the toughness of his will – everything contributes to endow this man with a prestige which is easier to sustain, than to understand or explain.

Otherwise, he followed entirely the nationalist formula in praising 'Garibaldi, the most powerful, the most marvellous personality that Italy, and perhaps the world, boasts in the field of action.'[117]

More broadly, the moderate press followed the democrats in exalting Garibaldi as a new nationalist saint. He was a 'heroic son of Italy', 'the redeemer of Italy', the 'Genius of Italy' and the 'Archangel Gabriel ... appeared in human shape on earth'.[118] The Turin illustrated paper, *Il Mondo Illustrato*, which was relaunched on 7 July probably in response to the events in southern Italy, fully embraced Garibaldi and the story of the Thousand. In its first number, it began a two-part history of 'Garibaldi in Sicilia' by F. Botto. Botto's history, along with similar accounts in the foreign illustrated press, helped to create a narrative of the campaign as a series of emblematic and picturesque moments. The departure from Quarto, 'They arrive in Sicilia', 'Calatafimi', were followed by 'They win', 'Within sight of Palermo', 'Entrance', and so on until Garibaldi's entry into Naples and the defence at Volturno. All these episodes and characters were constructed as a pictorial history of the events of 1860, with a beginning (Quarto), climax (Naples), and happy ending (the king and Garibaldi at Teano).[119]

There was nothing casual about the involvement of the press with Garibaldi in 1860. Indeed, Garibaldi and those around him consistently did their utmost to endear themselves to journalists. Garibaldi, in particular, used his personal charm to win over journalists, and he encouraged them along with other writers and artists to join his campaign and report on it from the inside. Other than his friendship with Dumas (which predated the departure from Quarto), perhaps the most striking example of Garibaldi's closeness to journalists, and the blurred line between journalism, camp following and soldiering, is his relationship with the *Times* correspondent Eber, a Hungarian officer who had come out to Sicily to fight with, as well as write about, Garibaldi. Eber's articles for *The Times* are among the most vivid contemporary accounts of the experience of being with Garibaldi, but what is most interesting for us is how Garibaldi treated him. Unlike the Bourbon army, Eber had no problem in finding Garibaldi in the mountains above Palermo; he joined up with some American and British sightseers and was taken quickly to Garibaldi's camp at Gibilrossa, on the day before the volunteers were due to go down to Palermo. Garibaldi received the visitors 'with that charming, quiet simplicity which characterizes him, lending himself with great complaisance to the invariably recurring demands of autographs, and answering the numerous questions which were naturally put to him'. Only after the other visitors had gone did Garibaldi resume the pressing business of organising the descent to Palermo and, if the report is to be believed, he immediately let Eber in on all his plans and included him in the invasion party.[120]

Garibaldi's courtesy towards Eber was not at all unusual, and reflects his awareness that the press had become an integral part of modern warfare. As *The Times* pointed out on 8 June 1860:

Battles are now fought in an amphitheatre with the eager public of a hundred nations, in a figurative sense, looking on . . . The duel between Garibaldi and the Neapolitan Viceroy is being fought out under eyes of newspaper correspondents, tourists, artists, and English or American sympathizers, as well as . . . more official spectators.

According to Henry Adams, an American journalist who met Garibaldi shortly after the taking of Palermo, Garibaldi was careful to greet, and shake hands with, every member of his party: 'He talked with each of us, and talked perfectly naturally; no stump oratory and no sham'. When Garibaldi learnt that Adams had come all the way from Naples to see him, 'he turned around thanking me as if I had done him a favor. This is the way he draws people.'[121] Vizitelly of *The Illustrated London News* agreed. He wrote: 'I shall never forget as long as I live the courteous reception given me by the General. He advanced to meet me from his group of officers, and, shaking me by the hand, welcomed me to his roof, which at any time might be splintered into fragments above our heads.'[122] Later on, after the crowds grew too insistent and Garibaldi retreated from the Palazzo Pretorio to the more protected Palazzo Reale, he was still careful to keep his door open to journalists; and he made a great display of the simplicity of his apartments and the beauty of their setting on top of the Porta Nuova, with a splendid view of the city below.[123]

By the time he left Palermo in July, Garibaldi was accompanied by a substantial, increasing, and loyal press entourage. Apart from Dumas and Eber, two Italian journalists based in London – Gallenga and Arrivabene – came to Sicily, as did Texier and Paya from France, and the artists Vizitelly, Nast (a German–American who joined Medici's expedition and worked for *Harper's Weekly* and *The Illustrated London News*),[124] and Devaux and De Fonvielle (for the Paris *Illustration*). Two photographers – Sevaistre and Le Gray – also travelled to Palermo to photograph the war and its protagonists.[125] Later, they were joined by the writers Maxime du Camp and Marc Monnier (who wrote for the *Revue des Deux Mondes*), and by the poet Louise Colet ('Flaubert's muse').[126] All of these people published articles and books about their experiences.[127] Some stayed with Garibaldi, others moved around more: a significant number in Sicily, for instance, seem to have followed General Türr into the wild interior, and sent reports back from there on their activities. These writers were joined by a broader group of political sympathisers or simple admirers: Englishmen like Forbes, Clark and Bucknell, who followed Garibaldi's campaign, sometimes at the front of the army (Forbes was with Garibaldi at Milazzo; Clark on the train with him into Naples). They too sent letters to the papers and published reminiscences – often written as travel books but with their political adventures included – describing, glorifying and promoting their experiences.[128] One of the Italian volunteers, Giulio Adamoli, described the atmosphere in Türr's headquarters as a 'Babel' full of foreign journalists and volunteers, whose only common language was German: 'A caravanserai of the Orient, with all his guests of different races, fashions, colours, can only give some idea of our headquarters and of the respectable or vulgar, pleasant or grotesque, renowned or unknown people who sat at our table during those fantastic months'.[129]

There was never any question about the support of these writers, artists and fellow travellers for Garibaldi. They were also very good at creating a sense of excitement and adventure. Forbes, the British volunteer, thought the members of the press who crowded around the first boat to leave Messina for Calabria as eager as the troops themselves 'for business', and commented that they were 'a plucky lot and going in for the fun of the thing; amongst their number is a French lady, who writes for the *Débats*. All . . . will no doubt fight as well as any one if circumstances require; for they are all out-and-out Garibaldians.'[130] Many of them did get directly involved in the fighting. Ulric de Fonvielle, like Eber, went to Sicily primarily to fight with Garibaldi, and probably saw his painting as a means of paying his passage. A fervent republican and bitterly opposed to Napoleon III ('I hear that liberty is awakening in a corner of the world, I run there . . . come what may!'), he arrived in Sicily in time to fight at Milazzo.[131] Even the politically moderate Charles Arrivabene, less engaged with Garibaldi than most of the others, managed to get caught up in the fighting at Cajazzo (north of Naples), and was wounded and briefly taken prisoner.[132]

The foreign illustrated press, in particular, tended to depict Garibaldi's campaign as an adventure, in which the correspondent himself figured as something of a star. This motif was established by Frank Vizitelly, the writer–artist for *The Illustrated London News* ('a big, florid red-bearded Bohemian' who later covered the American civil war, and was killed during the war for Sudan).[133] Before Vizitelly's arrival in Palermo, when little was known about events in Sicily, *The Illustrated London News* – like the other papers, *Harper's Weekly* and *Illustration* – published general articles and descriptive illustrations featuring the geography of Palermo and its principal monuments, along with accounts of Bourbon torture (*Application of the Tourniquet to a political prisoner* was reproduced in *The Illustrated London News* and *Harper's Weekly*).[134] Vizitelly's arrival shifted the emphasis to war as escapist entertainment, where the difficulties of getting accurate reports became part of the overall excitement. His first article consisted of a lengthy account of his adventures getting to Sicily, while the next began: 'Garibaldi is fighting in the town. I am going to chance the shots. Lots of sketches and a long letter by the next ship. One is now leaving the harbour. Whiz! all the dust dashed up near me. In great haste.'[135]

While the war in 1859 had been reported as a conventional military struggle, with picturesque illustrations and descriptions attached, the events of 1860 were described as a revolution, and could be much more spectacular and fantastical for that. Vizitelly's reports and illustrations gave sensational details of the fighting and disorder in Palermo: pictures included *Defence of the barricade at Porta Felice*; *Catching a goverment spy in the streets of Palermo*; and the most violent of all, with smoke billowing, troops shooting and lots of dead people: *Massacre of people by the royal troops at the convent of the white Benedictines, Palermo* (this picture was also published in *Frank Leslie's Illustrated Newspaper* in New York).[136] As Türr's troops moved out of Palermo and into the wild Sicilian interior, Vizitelly went with them, sending back to London pictures of *Our first bivouac at sunset, near Villafrati*; *A march through Sicily with the centre column of the national army*; and, most vividly, and almost obligatorily, the *Narrow escape of our special artist* from bandits: the picture showed Vizitelly and his driver escaping in a carriage through a mountainous Sicilian landscape under gunfire (see figure 16 below).[137] Other scenes of local colour included *Breakfast-hunting at Roccapalumba*, *A Sicilian village*, an 'amusing' scene of volunteers stealing poultry in the village while the locals screamed in horror, and *Street scene in Naples after the arrival of Garibaldi*: this

16   This illustration by Vizitelly in *The Illustrated London News* is part of a series on the Sicilian landscape, and indicative of the artist–journalist's self-promotion as the hero of an adventure story.

illustration by the American artist, Nast, showed an urchin with an olive branch; an old, fat matron in a tricolour sash with flag; a younger, amazonian female with a dagger; and a man in a uniform, all cheering amid a larger, also cheering crowd.[138]

Through the publication of portraits, the foreign illustrated papers also helped to define the revolution's protagonists as political celebrities. There was a standard image of Garibaldi, more mature than in his previous incarnations, but still instantly recognisable, an attractive figure in (red) shirt and trousers, with beard, hat and sword. Only the German *Die Gartenlaube* persisted in showing Garibaldi in Piedmontese uniform, recycling an *Illustrated London News* portrait from 1859.[139] Equal care was taken to produce portraits of the other combatants (a 'cacciatore of the Alps'; a 'Tuscan volunteer'; 'one of the squadri' [*sic*]).[140] *The Illustrated London News* was especially interested in British involvement with the events in Sicily. It published a portrait by Vizitelly of Mr Edwin James QC, 'the honourable and learned member for Marylebone': a portly middle-aged man in flat cap and with two pistols stuck in his belt, who had taken advantage 'of the leisure afforded to him by the close of the Parliamentary Session and by the long vacation' to go to southern Italy

17   British 'excursionists' in Sicily in 1860, from *The Illustrated London News*. These volunteers posed problems for Garibaldi's army, and the 'Major Styles' depicted here was a very shady character. On his activities as 'Captain Styles', see pages 301–2 below.

and join Garibaldi; and it also published an illustration (from a photograph) of four British volunteers (one dressed entirely in tartan), just arrived from Harwich.[141] The French *Illustration*, by contrast, specialised in vivid illustrations of the general volunteer experience: one picture showed all the volunteers barefoot, another showed a large, vigorous group cheering Garibaldi on a crescent beach with Palermo's Monte Pellegrino in the background, while still another showed a disorderly but enthusiastic bunch of men, riding oxen and mules (see figure 17 opposite).[142]

Towards the end of the campaign, as the fighting and spectacular street scenes wound down, some papers began to lose interest in the campaign. Others, however, responded by producing various forms of commemorative literature. *Harper's Weekly* began to produce poems and cartoons. It celebrated Garibaldi's arrival in Naples in a rousing poem which was the opposite of serious: '*Viva, viva Garibaldi! –* Saver of his native land – *vogliamo, l'Italia, Una – una – una – viva!*'; and it praised him (entirely erroneously) for

THE HERO AND THE SAINT.

18 This cartoon of Garibaldi driving St Januarius out of Naples was published in Britain and the USA. The representation of the saint as a stupid and repellent figure is characteristic of the anti-Catholic rhetoric which circulated among Garibaldi enthusiasts in both countries. Note also the saint's bare feet, a common shorthand for Neapolitan poverty and ignorance at this time.

ridding Naples of religious 'rubbish', by publishing another poem and a satirical cartoon which was first published in *Punch*: *The saint and the hero – Garibaldi driving St. Januarius* [complete with his bottle of blood] *and the winking picture out of Naples* (see figure 18 on page 257).[143] Later on, and although the paper did venture some criticism of the treatment of Garibaldi by the Piedmontese government, it did this again through popular verse: 'The two Kings at Teano' (which said Garibaldi's throne was 'far higher' and 'nobler' than King Vittorio Emanuele's), and 'Two entrances and two exits':

> King Garibaldi to never a crown
> Or royal robe was born.
> He marched to his throne in an old red shirt,
> And a pair of trousers torn.
> No priest at his coronation stood,
> Twixt him and the Power above . . .
> And simple and shabby as he came,
> So shabby and simple goes;
> Back to Caprera's cabbage-beds,
> And early potato-rows.[144]

As part of its Christmas edition, *The Illustrated London News* offered its readers a two-page spread of the meeting at Teano: the king and Garibaldi loom large in the foreground shaking hands on prancing horses, and they entirely fill the page (the paper generally preferred enthusiastic crowd scenes with the protagonists as small figures).[145] Readers were told that a colour portrait of Garibaldi would be presented ('GRATIS') to all subscribers for the following year.[146]

On the whole, therefore, attempts to persuade journalists that the revolution in southern Italy was a heroic act of justice and a marvellous piece of political drama, and not a violent episode of illegal piracy, were entirely successful. As a right-wing pamphleteer in France complained, Garibaldi's 'principal military talent . . . consists of knowing how to open, without shame, the great publicity cash-till'.[147] The coverage of Garibaldi's campaign in the press was remarkable for the sheer amount of visual and textual detail which the reader could choose from. Yet the illustrated press in particular preferred to steer clear of politics and instead offered its readers a fairly light-hearted view of events in southern Italy, one in which they could follow vicariously the adventures of their fearless reporters, marvel at the exploits of the soldier heroes, and be alternately shocked and amused by scenes from the war and its surroundings. In this way, the illustrated press ensured that a section of the reading public would engage with Garibaldi's revolution as a form of entertainment.

This approach loosened the political link between the campaign and its reporting which Garibaldi had sought so hard to establish. Moreover, although spectacular, the illustrated coverage was uneven, and relied on a mixture of styles and authenticity. Some illustrations (notably of the barricades at Palermo and many portraits) were lithographed from photographs; some (the scenes of fighting in Palermo, the battle at the Volturno) were drawn 'from life'; and others (the departure from Quarto, Calatafimi) were entirely imaginary. Thus, careful readers of *The Illustrated London News* must have been surprised by Garibaldi's transformation from the dark, romantic (and imaginary) figure, dressed in flowing robes, leaving Quarto in the paper's 2 June edition, to the blond, more rotund 'gentlemanly' character, wearing tucked-in shirt and trousers, drawn 'from life' on the paper's front page on 23 June. Just as often, it is impossible to tell the imaginary from the authentic. *L'Illustration* and *The Illustrated London News* included detailed illustrations of the battle of Milazzo, and both reproduced a picture of the hand-to-hand combat between Garibaldi and the Neapolitan cavalry – 'Garibaldi cutting down the Captain of the Neapolitan cavalry in the charge made by the latter near the bridge of Melazzo', read the caption in *The Illustrated London News* – but whether this was really drawn 'from life' or simply a visual rendering of Dumas' account is hard to tell.[148]

The recasting of war and revolution as semi-fictionalised popular entertainment was most manifest in the commemorative *Album storico–artistico*, which was issued in parts from September 1860, and was modelled on the war *Album* from the previous year. The album, whose full title was *Historical–artistic Album. Garibaldi in the Two Sicilies or the Italian war of 1860. Written by B.G. with drawings from life, the Palermo barricades, portraits and battles, lithographed by the best artists*, came out every two weeks, and was made up of sixty illustrations along with a historical and geographical account of Garibaldi's adventures.[149] The narrative took second place to the illustrations: these were large and detailed (each occupying a whole folio page), and of higher quality than anything else in 1860. The artists also seemed more experienced and more talented (and, one assumes, more expensive). Everything about the album, including its publication which spread over two years, was intended for the collector, and seems to have been designed to make it an object of status and consumption.

The album followed the established illustrated formula. It focused on the protagonists, with twenty-four portraits clearly reflecting the cult of political celebrity which developed around the events of 1860. Most of these were taken from photographs; and especially worthy of note is the portrait of a virile Garibaldi on the frontispiece (a copy of a photograph taken in Palermo by the French photographer, Gustave Le Gray), and the portrait of 'Frate Pantaleo'.

L'imbarco a Genova del general Garibaldi per la Sicilia

19 'Garibaldi's departure from Genoa for Sicily': the standard representation of this event drawn 'from life' by Girolamo Induno. The romantic farewell scene involving women and children on the right of the picture would seem to be wholly invented.

Pantaleo is a masterly mix of religious and revolutionary iconography, a hirsute, romantic figure in crusading monk's clothes, his right hand raised in exhortation, his left hand grasping a sword.[150] The war scenes were an eclectic mix of fact and fiction which transformed the recent events into a popular spectacle. There were the usual street scenes taken from photographs, and other images lithographed 'from life'. However, 'from life' could mean many things. The departure of the volunteers from Quarto was a version of the painting by the participant Induno, and was a remarkable combination of the realistic (full of historical detail) and the romanticised (replete with melodramatic gestures: it also became the historical source for all subsequent representations of this episode; see figure 19 above).[151] Yet most of the key battle scenes (Calatafimi, Milazzo, Volturno) and the entrances of Garibaldi into cities (Palermo, Messina, Naples) have very little historical or geographical detail and seem entirely theatrical. Milazzo, for example, is represented by a palm tree and a huge, broken, fortified gate. In all of them too, Garibaldi is an exemplary figure: sword always held high, always surrounded by fierce-looking fighting men with fixed bayonets (see figure 20 opposite).

La presa di Milazzo

20 'The taking of Milazzo': Milazzo was a key moment in the story of the Thousand in which Garibaldi's heroism was rarely more spectacular – elements which are clearly reflected in this illustration of the episode.

Arguably, the most vivid picture of all is drawn entirely from imagination: the *Arrival of Garibaldi at Marsala* (*Sbarco di Garibaldi a Marsala*). This episode, one of the most dangerous of the whole campaign and marked by more or less open hostility towards the volunteers, is recast (as it is in almost all the other illustrated accounts of the Thousand) as a festive occasion for a popular hero. Garibaldi, wrapped in a dark cloak, steps calmly off a small rowing boat on to a rocky, mountainous shore (Marsala is flat and has a large jetty), and the crowd hold out their hands towards him in exultation and acclamation. Garibaldi claims Sicily for Italy, and the crowd – a mixed and exotic group of men, women, children, rich and poor – immediately recognise him as their leader. Indeed, one of them has already unfurled a tricolour flag.[152] The whole scene bears a remarkable resemblance to contemporary representations of Christopher Columbus arriving in America (see figure 21 overleaf).[153]

The lives of Garibaldi

The huge, and largely favourable, press coverage of Garibaldi and his campaign in 1860 was accompanied by a fresh wave of histories and

21 'Garibaldi's landing at Marsala'. This almost entirely fictious representation of the expedition's arrival contains a number of typical elements, notably the cheering crowds and the depiction of Marsala as a wild and rocky shore.

biographies dedicated to him and his exploits. These publications are interesting not so much for what they add to our knowledge of events and the man, but for what they can tell us about public interest in him.

A series of histories of the Thousand came out in 1860 and immediately thereafter. They differed in size, quality, and the amount of narrative detail offered; in the number, quality and/or inclusion of illustrations; and in the end-point of the narrative (that is, the early histories came out in June, and ended with the taking of Palermo). Some, such as the *Storia della insurrezione siciliana* by the ex-*carbonaro* and Mazzinian journalist, Giovanni La Cecilia, were extremely ambitious and aimed at a kind of 'total history'. Published in different editions in Milan and Palermo, La Cecilia's history ran into two substantial volumes. It offered its readers an effusive description of the Sicilian landscape; a lengthy account of Sicilian history complete with a detailed account of the Bourbon oppression; a detailed narrative of the events from the outbreak of revolution in April 1860 until the arrival of the king in Palermo in December; a large number of Garibaldi's proclamations and personal letters;

22 Garibaldi as a cover hero. The cover itself is a cheap blue affair and the illustrator relies on a standard – but now out-of-date – representation of Garibaldi as a Piedmontese general.

a series of illustrations and portraits, and a map of Sicily.[154] By contrast, the *Storia popolare della rivoluzione di Sicilia*, by the prolific Milanese writer, Franco Mistrali, was a shorter (160-page), cheaper and less industrious enterprise. But he still managed to cram an enormous amount of material into its pages: a history of Sicily, a number of proclamations, a map and some rather basic illustrations (including a front cover showing Garibaldi in uniform holding sword and flag high above Palermo (see figure 22 above), and the arrival of the volunteers at Marsala to the joyous greetings of its men, women and children).[155]

On the surface, therefore, these two books seemed quite different. La Cecilia was a political writer, who from the 1820s had dedicated his journalistic activity to the Mazzinian cause and had been agitating for an expedition to Sicily since the mid-1850s.[156] Mistrali, while clearly also from the left, produced ephemeral pamphlets and was eclectic in his choice of subject matter. For example, as well as repeatedly recycling and creating new versions of his history of 1860,[157] he produced a vast range of writings, ranging from *The inhabitants of the moon* to *The life of Jesus* and *The death and testament of Urbano Rattazzi*.[158] La Cecilia was more critical of Cavour and Piedmontese policy, and less overblown in his exaltation of Garibaldi (Garibaldi's life, according to Mistrali, was 'a poem of triumph and virtue').[159] Yet the narrative structure of the two books was remarkably similar. The choice of detail and the propensity to praise every aspect of the expedition's history and protagonists was a feature of both. It is hard to avoid the conclusion that both writers were adapting the same narrative formula, combining historical accuracy with romantic invention, and were seeking to make their history as compelling and entertaining as possible to readers.

Apart from the spectacular story of the Thousand itself, writers now also had Garibaldi's memoirs to work with. Dumas had a version ready by June, and they were immediately serialised in Le Siècle as part of its coverage of Garibaldi's campaign.[160] The memoirs met with instant success, going into numerous French editions and versions in the early 1860s, and (unlike Dwight's English version of 1859) were widely translated. By 1861, the memoirs had appeared in Italian (published in Palermo and Livorno), English, Norwegian, Dutch, German (in Zurich, Berlin and Stuttgart), Spanish (in Barcelona and Montevideo), Portuguese, Romanian and Russian.[161] They were serialised in the German illustrated magazine, Die Gartenlaube, and in Italy in the Neapolitan paper, Il Nomade, and the Palermo paper, Il Garibaldi. Also in Italy in 1860, a cheap abridged (and presumably illicit) version was produced – Vita del prode vincitore di Varese – as well as a different version by Francesco Carrano, a Garibaldian officer, this time on the basis of a manuscript given to Carrano by Garibaldi and published as part of his own memoirs of the Cacciatori delle Alpi.[162]

The versions by Carrano and Dumas were only partly the memoirs of Garibaldi. Both men had decided to take the narrative beyond 1848 (where Garibaldi's memoirs had stopped), and to use other published sources and their own recollections and conversations to bring them up to date. Dumas, in particular, embellished the South American episodes and the personality of Anita to great dramatic effect. Again, the interest of these memoirs lies not so much in any new autobiographical details which they reveal about Garibaldi, as in the timing of their publication and fact of their immediate diffusion and multiple translation. The memoirs are a further indication of the continuing and growing appeal of Garibaldi's life to a national and international reading public.

That the expedition of the Thousand had sparked further interest in Garibaldi's life is confirmed by the proliferation of new biographies, alongside the publication of his memoirs. Some of these, like the Vita di G. Garibaldi narrata al popolo by Giuseppe Ricciardi,[163] Louis de la Varenne's Vita del General Garibaldi (an Italian abridgement of the same author's Chasseurs des Alpes, with four pages added about the Sicilian expedition),[164] and Balbiani's Storia illustrata della vita di Garibaldi,[165] were written by those close to

Garibaldi and/or to the sources. Ricciardi's volume aimed explicitly at historical accuracy (he filled his work with published speeches, letters and decrees), although he too was keen to exaggerate Garibaldi's charms (Garibaldi's life was 'the most marvellous life that has ever been lived on this earth . . . more of an epoch than history'). He also added embellishments of his own and glossed over political disagreements.[166] If Ricciardi's biography suggests the problems of maintaining biographical objectivity, Balbiani's *Storia* shows how commercially viable Garibaldi's life could be. Aimed broadly at the same market as the *Album storico–artistico* (every copy was signed by the author), there was again nothing special about Balbiani's narrative, which was little more than a lengthy (817-page) hagiography (indeed, Balbiani specifically compared Garibaldi to Jesus Christ in his looks, background and actions).[167] Much more compelling were the book's high-quality colour prints, which made great use of green, white and red (the colours of the tricolour flag) and which illustrated every key episode in Garibaldi life, with a particular emphasis on the battle scenes of 1859 and 1860. That this illustrated formula worked is suggested by the book's numerous editions (at least five between 1860 and 1866), and the fact that the colour illustrations seem to have been produced, or at least have survived, as historical documents entirely separately from the book.[168] At the same time, alongside these more significant works appeared a huge amount of cheaper, more emphemeral material.[169] These too suggest the circulation of a Garibaldi narrative in a broader mass market, and the growth of a Garibaldi cult in a more popular culture.

There was an equally ready market for Garibaldi biographies and other material outside Italy. In the United States, O. J. Victor published a biography as the first number in the series 'Beadles Dime Biographical Library'. Victor made great claims for his book: no 'complete and authentic biography' existed, and 'the disjointed "autobiographies" of Dwight and Dumas' were full of shortcomings. He, on the other hand, had used records in the Astor Library in New York, and the publisher's blurb claimed his book to be 'The only correct and reliable life of Garibaldi; the Washington of Italy' (the volume was also praised by the *New York Herald* on 22 December as 'a well written and carefully compiled biography of the modern Washington'). In reality, however, Victor relied heavily on Garibaldi's memoirs for his narrative, and was just as happy as everyone else to invent new details. For example, he felt able confidently to assure his readers that Garibaldi had royal blood: 'Garibaldi was Duke of Bavaria, AD 584 – his ancestors having discarded the title of King. Garibaldus . . . was King of Lombardy, AD 673 . . . The blood of *l'ancinne* [*sic*] *noblesse*, then, courses in his veins, and he may consort with kings by "divine right" as well as by right of his own greatness.' Victor also revealed that, while in the United States, the hero had opened a cigar store in Cincinnati.[170] In

Britain, Paya's biography written in 1859/60 was translated into English, without acknowledgement, complete with illustrations;[171] and in France, O. Féré and R. Hyenne published a new illustrated life (*Aventures, expéditions, voyages*), where once more the illustrations were as significant as the largely recycled, if very detailed, narrative.[172] New biographies were published in Germany[173] and in the Netherlands,[174] and a biography based largely on Cuneo was also published in Spain.[175]

'I like Garibaldi's expedition because I love novels and adventure stories!' the dramatist Prosper Mérimée wrote to his friend Antonio Panizzi, the director of the British Museum Library, in May 1860.[176] Alongside biographies and histories, Garibaldi inspired a plethora of poems, plays and novels. In Milan, Vittorio Ottolini published a melodramatic novel, *Cacciatori delle Alpi*, centred around the adventures of a group of Lombard liberals and volunteers in 1859. The novel opens with them drinking a toast to the liberty of Italy, and one of them recites at length the biography of Garibaldi from birth to the present day.[177] Innumerable poems, hymns to Garibaldi, and musical marches for piano were also written and published as fly-sheets or as pamphlets in northern Italy. These included P. Giorzia's *Garibaldi a Palermo: marcia trionfale* (Milan, 1860); G. Predazzi's *L'entrata di Garibaldi a Napoli: marcia per pianoforte* (Genoa, 1860); or more simply E. La Croix, *Garibaldi: marcia: invito all'Italia* (Milan, 1860). In June, G. Azzi published in Ferrara *Garibaldi in Sicilia. Canto nazionale*:

> He arrrived – waving in the wind
> Is the sign of the cross;
> '*Viva Italia!*' he cries, and ten million
> Rise up to the sound of his voice.
> 'Victory or the tomb
> Is my proclamation to you' . . .
> A hundred fires are lit
> On the Sicilian hills;
> A hundred brave men load
> Their terrible rifles.
> 'The Italians don't fight'
> A foreigner said one day:
> While the protector of our despots,
> Pours his last glass away.[178]

This poem, with its emphasis on heroic example, sacrifice and the rejection of foreign accusations of cowardice, confirms the almost instant establishment of the Thousand as a standard story within Risorgimento discourse.

Nor, again, was this literary production confined to Italy. In Madrid, Manuel Gil de Salcedo published a 'historical novel' – *Garibaldi y Procida, ó las Pasquas Sangrientas de Sicilia* – set in Palermo during the 1848 revolutions, with a biography of Garibaldi attached, and the meeting of Garibaldi and the king was marked by two poems, published cheaply in Barcelona as broadsides with an accompanying illustration.[179] In Paris, a satirical play, *L'Ane et les trois voleurs*, set in Naples and with Garibaldi, Mazzini and Cavour as its main protagonists, was performed. In it Garibaldi complains about the attention of foreign correspondents: 'responsible for letting Europe know every time I blow my nose'.[180] The indefatigable Pierre Dupont published a *chant rustique*: 'Sicilienne à Garibaldi'; an 'E. Atgier' published a robust defence of his hero ('O dear Garibaldi! whoever hates you/ Belongs body and soul to the deadly caste');[181] while after Garibaldi's return to Caprera, M. Barthélemy published a seven-page poem, 'Garibaldi or the waking of the lion':

> Such is Garibaldi! . . . His hand holds the oriflamme;
> He is the God of battle, throwing everywhere his flame!
> Tremble, tyrants, tremble! Don't irritate the God . . .
> He takes but one step, and Europe is on fire![182]

In Britain too, the expedition of the Thousand was celebrated in novels and poems.[183] Two plays were performed – *Garibaldi the Italian liberator* and *Garibaldi's excursionists* – in the course of 1860.[184]

The narratives of Garibaldi's expedition in 1860 and the new biographies published in the same year follow a trend established in 1859, and concentrate on selling Garibaldi to as broad a readership as possible. This trend was immensely popular, in that the material was relatively cheap and readily accessible, even to those with a limited reading ability.[185] Moreover, this kind of cultural production gave the public in Italy and elsewhere a choice of reading material. Readers could follow Garibaldi's progress through volunteers' letters and detailed commentaries in the daily press; and they were able to enjoy them again, with accompanying pictures, in the illustrated weekly and satirical magazines. If this was not enough, they might follow up their interest in an illustrated biography or in the great man's memoirs. They could read (or indeed write) a poem dedicated to him, play a tune to him on a piano or even go to the theatre to watch a Garibaldi play. What was significant about the story of Garibaldi in 1860 was the vast extent, pace and variety of its circulation.

Conclusion

There are different memories of the Thousand and its aftermath. The first is a Risorgimento tale of triumph and tragedy: a small group of heroic men overthrow oppression and liberate their enslaved 'brothers', only to be betrayed and defeated by a number on their own side. The second sees the events of 1859–60 as a single, happy continuum: the story of Garibaldi being 'the right man in the right place at the right time', and of opposing political views compromising and coalescing at the right point and with the right objective – Italian unification.[186] Finally, there is the more recent interpretation of the events of 1860 by historians. For them, 1860 was a form of civil war, a moment of intense political conflict and social instability, the results of which were actually damaging to national unity. The first view is represented by the democrats and told in Garibaldi's memoirs;[187] the second was officially sanctioned after unification; and the third was outlined by Marxist historians, and by Denis Mack Smith in Britain, during the 1950s and after.[188] All are useful in explaining and understanding the myth of Garibaldi which developed in and from 1860.

Recent historians are correct to argue that behind the scenes the events of 1860 were driven by a bitter three-way struggle for political control of southern Italy, between conservatives, moderate liberals and democrats/republicans, in which the moderate liberals eventually emerged victorious. The key to understanding what drove this struggle forward lies in the immense ambitions of those democrats who left for Sicily in May. The volunteers – a tiny group of ill-armed men – aimed to overthrow an entire kingdom with a powerful army, and to impose their democratic vision of a future Italy on Piedmont. The leaders then tried to create, in the space of a few months, a new kind of mass volunteer army (the nation-at-arms) based on a revolutionary ideal of active political engagement. They also sought to create a model of national belonging which would exclude as few as possible, and to persuade diverse groups (including priests), classes and regions that their identity was Italian. Garibaldi's government spent considerable time and effort in publicising itself and putting Garibaldi on display. In turn, in his published letters, speeches and personal appearances in southern Italy, Garibaldi himself did a great deal directly to popularise and endorse the idea of Italy. In effect, an official cult of Garibaldi was encouraged in the South, using a potent mix of religious rituals and democratic discourse, of traditional symbols and modern methods, in an effort to persuade its inhabitants to become 'national'. These ambitions predated the expedition to Sicily, and all were traceable – in one way or another – to the political ideas and propaganda methods of Mazzini.

It is not surprising that Garibaldi's actions provoked Cavour's hostility. In the light of its ambitions, Cavour's dislike of the revolution in southern Italy was not at all unexpected. Brilliant politician that he was, he tried consistently to hide his horror at the threat it posed to his domination of Italian politics. Yet it is evident in retrospect that he had little, if any, enthusiasm for Italian nationalism, no interest whatever in southern Italy, and a deep antipathy to the idea of the nation-at-arms. Nor was he much reassured by the use of the king's name to justify the expedition. Cavour was a politician whose strength came from parliament and from resisting the power of the crown, so Garibaldi's royal dictatorship was equally a threat to him.[189] Cavour also had a long-standing antipathy to the Church, and practical experience of bitter Church–state conflict during the parliamentary struggles in Piedmont during the 1850s, so he would hardly have been pleased by Garibaldi's friendliness towards priests.[190]

As we have seen, Cavour was able to trap the democrats and push them politically out of southern Italy. However, he was far less successful in challenging Garibaldi's appeal and the religion of the Italian nation which the southern dictatorship in Sicily had promoted with such skill and dedication. In the end, Cavour managed only temporarily to control Garibaldi and neutralise the threat of Italian nationalism, and he did this by acting as the defender of Italy. In order to control the apparent inevitability of national unification, Cavour was forced to become its main architect. It is in this way that Italian unity was the product both of political conflict and of nationalist feeling. It is also in this light that Garibaldi's achievements – militarily victorious, politically defeated and publicly celebrated – can best be assessed.

In the next chapter, I will assess the evidence of popular support for Garibaldi's expedition and of enthusiasm for him as a heroic figure. The point to note here is how widespread it was imagined to be. Publicity was part of the expedition from its outset, and part of its political ambition. Garibaldi and others with him went to Sicily with a narrative strategy, and they sought to promote the expedition as a popular and morally justified venture, destined for a glorious outcome if only Italians would join them. This aspect of the story of the Thousand was in place even before the volunteers arrived in Marsala, and it follows established Risorgimento discourse. Thereafter, life began to imitate art. Put simply, the lived experiences of the Thousand and the representation of these experiences seemed for a time to converge, a fusion perhaps best illustrated by the heavy use of the epistolary formula in news-paper coverage of the events. The publication of volunteers' letters from the front added a touch of intimacy to these otherwise public affairs. As the expedition faltered with the arrival in Naples of the Piedmontese army, writers

– particularly Garibaldi – fell back on an initially oblique rhetoric of disappointment and betrayal. The use of fictional techniques to describe and justify 'real' political activity was immensely effective: it gained Garibaldi and his expedition unprecedented fame and had a powerful impact on public opinion.

Palermo and Naples may never have become the democratic power base that Cavour so feared, but they did become the centre of ('global') press attention in the summer of 1860. What happened in these cities provided the basis for spreading the nationalist message to the rest of Italy and beyond. In fact, more surprising than the reliance on democratic publishers and writers, and as notable as the process of official nation-building within southern Italy, was Garibaldi's capacity to get substantial sections of the European and American press on his side. Such support had been prepared well in advance, and it reflected a prevailing sympathy with the Italian Question felt by much of liberal Europe. Garibaldi succeeded remarkably well in charming journalists. Press support was reflected in the exceptional amount of printed material produced about him in 1860 and, along with the tendency of journalists to chase copy and copy each other, it produced an elaborate mythology of the man and his actions which drowned out any conservative/clerical criticism. It also became, for a while, self-sustaining. Most of all, the rapport which developed between Garibaldi and his press followers helped construct an image of the expedition with a very broad appeal, in which politics became a form of public entertainment. Thus, however equivocal and divisive the political outcome of Garibaldi's expedition to Sicily, its representation was no less than a propaganda triumph.

By 1860, Garibaldi's story had acquired a powerful fictional element and became a kind of collaborative effort with a structure and logic of its own. Dumas, who has always been taken to task for inventing and embellishing episodes in Garibaldi's life, was anything but unusual, and is really the best example of a much wider fashion. Popular biographies and fictionalised histories were not simply a significant – if inaccurate – way in which news of Garibaldi's expedition reached a broader reading public in 1860. They also became a means through which the public could engage with Garibaldi on an imaginary level. Writers used a novelistic style, or they embellished events and invented episodes and, helped by the spectacular nature of the events they were describing, produced a narrative of revolution which read like an adventure romance. Artists too produced a heavily romanticised visual narrative of the Thousand. In short, the appeal of Garibaldi relied on a strong call on the imagination and emotions. Political principles were not absent, but they were treated as only one aspect of a life which was at once exemplary and entertaining.

To many contemporaries, the events of 1860 seemed miraculous, and even to us they still seem surprising. For Trevelyan, who wrote about them some fifty years later, the 'Garibaldian legend' was true. In his view, Garibaldi's claim 'on the memory of men' lay both in his abilities as a revolutionary soldier and in 'his appeal to the imagination': He is perhaps the only case . . . of the poet as the man of action'.[191] This judgement is not entirely misplaced. In 1860, Garibaldi was both sign and lived existence: he was both a practical instigator of political change and an imaginary symbol of the excitement it could provoke. However, the 'legend' cannot usefully be called 'true'. It appeared spontaneous because it provoked a broad and passionate response. It seemed unrehearsed because its production threw up such a dramatic smoke-screen, and because the motivations, purpose and methods of its creation and diffusion were cloaked in established nationalist rhetoric. Yet the cult of Garibaldi was quite carefully conceived, constructed and publicised; and its purpose was to assist, push through and justify a process of violent and rapid regime change. In short, the cult of Garibaldi was part of the political conflict in 1860, and it contributed to, and reflected, the broader struggle for power.

CHAPTER 10

THE GARIBALDI MOMENT

The year 1860 was Garibaldi's 'moment'. Despite a disastrous personal and political start to the year, he went on to overthrow a kingdom and help construct another. He also achieved a remarkable level of fame: he was cheered by crowds, pursued by journalists and made front-page news throughout the summer, and across the world. The purpose of this celebrity, as we have seen, was political communication. Garibaldi embodied and promoted a political ideal, and he symbolised – and aimed to construct – a sense of national identity which could be transformed into active political consent. The popularity of Garibaldi was meant to convert into support for the Italian nationalist cause. How successful was this process of communication? This is an important issue because by now we know a great deal about the cultural sources and political reasons for Garibaldi's fame, and the various means through which it was produced and expanded. However, there are aspects of the impact and reception of his fame which can still be further investigated.

My purpose in this chapter is to explore possible answers to the difficult question of what the public thought of Garibaldi. I look at the responses of three separate (and loosely defined) groups who were the main audiences for political communication during the events of 1860: the Sicilian public,[1] Italian volunteers, and foreign enthusiasts. We have already noted the tendency, during the events of 1859 and 1860, for an imaginary narrative to emerge and float free of the politics that produced it. In what follows, I assess how the broader public engaged with the cult of Garibaldi. Concentrating on (re)elaborations of the Garibaldi story, and on reactions to the Garibaldi story expressed by associations, in letters and orally, I consider whether the public understood his message, or what specifically they understood from it. In particular, I analyse how far Garibaldi's presence and popularity helped to create or increase a sense of national belonging in Sicily, and to what extent appeals to, or from, Garibaldi boosted practical and political support for the nationalist cause both within and outside Italy. In so doing, I hope to shed some light not just on the process of making Italians, but also on what Italians and others made of this process.

'In the Italian way'

Towards the end of the campaign in southern Italy, a committee in Naples organised a public subscription to honour Garibaldi. The plan was to offer him a ceremonial sword, which was to be made of gold and set with jewels, along with a sabre and a revolver, and to give him any money that was left over to support his future campaigns in Rome and Venice. A design was commissioned, replete with nationalist symbols and epigraphs, and Garibaldi accepted the offer, replying in characteristic terms that 'although superior to my merits I accept the gift with pleasure'. But this subscription met with very little success in Palermo. The substantial volume (with space for 1,440 names) created to record the subscribers in Palermo remained empty: only eleven people signed their names, and four of those came from outside Sicily.[2]

The flop of the Garibaldi subscription in Palermo seems symptomatic of a broader material indifference to the revolution in Sicily. As the naval minister in Palermo in 1860 grumbled to Agostino Bertani: 'I try to do my best for this country, but what can you do when the country does not respond to the pressing needs which present themselves? How can we go forward with this feeble country, without resources and without the will to obtain them?'[3] This problem was put even more bluntly by the British consul in Palermo, John Goodwin, who wrote that 'the reception of Garibaldi in Palermo has been everything the heart could wish, in so far as cheers go, but at "cheers" it stops short. Very little money has been given . . . Manifestos and addresses make a grand show in the papers but the money and materials are wanting.'[4] In many areas of Sicily, people refused to pay taxes, adding to the financial problems of a government already burdened by tax cuts, the cost of the war and the promise of public works ('[t]he truth', according to the democrat Angelo Bargoni, was 'an incredible lack of funds').[5] Equally serious, and seemingly indicative of a lack of patriotic feeling, was the failure of military conscription. As early as the beginning of June, the new governor of Girgenti warned Crispi that conscription had caused 'discontent' in his province,[6] while in Catania the British vice-consul reported that the copies of the published decree had 'been torn from the walls'.[7] In fact, faced with widespread public hostility, the government was forced to modify the decree: it introduced the principle of substitution, allowed a whole series of exemptions (for only sons, married men and priests), and granted a delay to rural communities until after the harvest was brought in.[8] These modifications involved an acceptance that the immediate campaign in southern Italy would have to be fought largely by men from the North, thus dealing a serious blow to Garibaldi's project for the nation-at-arms.

This fragile situation suggests that Sicilian enthusiasm for Garibaldi was indeed entirely superficial, based on 'cheers' and 'addresses' but signifying nothing. Faced with this, many of the *garibaldini* became disillusioned with Sicily, where the welcome was not what they had expected and the culture and geography were so very different from their own. For example, Ippolito Nievo contributed to the myth of the Thousand in public, but was privately very critical of the country and its experiences, identifying the lack of military enthusiasm with feminine weakness: 'Sicilians are all women,' he told his mother in July, 'they have a passion for appearance and uproar', but they had done little, materially, to liberate themselves from the Bourbons.[9] Sometimes, this disappointment was expressed openly in the papers, and again it used a gendered discourse to depict the lack of enthusiasm among Sicilians for the revolution. Women too were included in these criticisms: 'not one of them has a healthy, blooming look', one volunteer letter complained about Sicilian women; '[at] Calatafimi I saw the faces of begging women which had no human form'.[10] This disillusionment with Sicily is of great interest in that it both reflects and anticipates a broader discourse about the problems of the southern 'character'. For our purposes, it is also important in suggesting a process of distancing between the *garibaldini* and the Sicilian people, involving a recognition of their failure to get Sicilians on their side.[11]

The dictatorship's inability to persuade Sicilians materially to support their own liberation was a considerable failure. It points to the essentially elitist, urban and middle-class nature of the Risorgimento as a whole, based as it was on an appeal to those who had the time and ability to read Italian, and perhaps also reflects the waning of democratic revolution by the late 1850s, as Mazzinians and others on the left looked increasingly to Cavour and the Piedmontese monarchy for a partial solution to their political demands. It reminds us that the dictatorship had little understanding of conditions in the countryside and among the poor, that it had largely failed to bring in an effective measure of land reform, and that, when faced with peasant revolt, it sided with the property-owning classes, and harshly restored order. At the same time, by undermining the dictatorship's practical capacity to bring about change in the region, the lack of mass support contributed to the weakness of Garibaldi's revolution and so to his ultimate defeat by Cavour.[12]

It would nevertheless be a mistake to focus exclusively on this failure and its outcome. First, the lack of soldiers and subscriptions from Sicily is not that surprising. Militarism and war was not a major founding myth in Sicilian elite identity (for instance, the Vespers was an act of rebellion rather than war), and exemption from military service was a long-standing, and sometimes jealously guarded, privilege of the Sicilian people: 'better to live as an animal than as a soldier' was one popular saying.[13] Moreover, there was little political tradition of voluntary subscription or association in an island whose modern political identity had been forged both in opposition to, and in material dependence on, the state.[14] Time and a carefully structured policy were needed to transform these deep-rooted attitudes and practices, so their persistence in 1860 does not necessarily mean that there was no real support for Garibaldi in the towns, or even in the countryside. Indeed, where local knowledge and influence was used, as was done by Governor Perroni Paladini in the south-eastern district of Castroreale, men did come forward to volunteer, national guards were formed, and conscription was supported by local communities.[15]

We should recall that, at the start of the campaign, volunteer forces had been successfully formed by sympathetic landowners, into rural *squadre* of so-called *picciotti* ('kids'). These were quite numerous (around 700–1,000 men at Calatafimi, at least 3,000 before the descent to Palermo, and perhaps 7–8,000 by the time they crossed the Straits), and they were extremely helpful to Garibaldi's forces. The problem was that most *garibaldini* – including the Sicilian, Crispi – viewed these volunteers with suspicion, and feared they would prove as violent and uncontrollable as similar peasant bands during the disastrous expeditions of the Bandiera brothers and Pisacane in Calabria, and in the 1848 revolutions. Thus, they abolished the *squadre* as soon as they could decently do so.[16] In other words, political considerations and organisational problems on the part of the government may have played just as important a role in the failure of men to come forward as any popular or elite indifference to the revolution had.

It is also possible that historians have been looking in the wrong place for evidence of support for Garibaldi. As I explained in the previous chapter, the regime's social and administrative policies were part of an ambitious programme of Mazzinian origin, which aimed to 'regenerate' Italy, and which, by encouraging popular identification with the idea of the nation, proposed to unite government and people in a new political religion. The cultural policy of Garibaldi's government was especially interesting because it sought a democratic basis: it differed from some other kinds of nationalism, and especially from the forms of nationalism which developed later in the century, in its inclusive appeal. The vision of national belonging proposed by Garibaldi was aimed not just at intellectuals, or just at the literate, middle-class male, but also at those (women, peasants) who were often given a secondary role in the nationalist hierarchy, or at priests, who were often excluded entirely. The question that we need to address here is whether this policy actually worked. Did Garibaldi gain the support of Palermo intellectuals, and how far did the sphere of culture endorse the project of 'making Italians'? Did priests approve his campaign? Did the new political religion have any impact on popular consciousness? In short, did the cheers of Sicilians mean anything?

Although problems of evidence mean that it is hard to give an accurate, or even certain, answer to any of these questions, a number of developments in Sicily during 1860 and afterwards are significant. In terms of understanding the elite response to Garibaldi, the most important of these was the rapid growth of (often ephemeral) newspapers and the flurry of press activity in Palermo and elsewhere after the lifting of Bourbon censorship: 'Actually more than twenty little papers fill every street corner', wrote one Palermo observer on 19 June.[17] This development was not always seen in a positive light, even by the papers themselves. 'Oof! I can't take any more!!' complained one paper, *Il Vessillo Italiano*, on 15 June: 'Papers here, papers there, high papers, low papers ... oof! I can't take any more ... all of them assume the stance of a periodical without any idea of actual politics, and the benefit of Italian freedom.' 'Mercy! a new paper!' announced *La Frusta* as its opening line of the first issue, 'the *Frusta* too! and so what? Are all those others not enough, which drown the country every day without pity, scrounging our pennies, without the shadow of an idea of useful education?'[18] Despite such (self-)accusations of disloyalty and irrelevance, all the new papers endorsed the lead given by the main government papers: *Il Giornale di Sicilia* and *Il Precursore*. A glance at some of the titles – *The Constancy and Supremacy of Italy; Redeemed Italy; Italian Unity; The War; The New World; The Italian Preacher; Liberty*; and *Garibaldi*[19]– reveals much about the press's desire to proclaim its adherence to the new political order and its principles. Moreover, their articles, letters and editorials consistently followed an established discursive line in glorifying both Garibaldi and the idea of a new, national religion.

Il Garibaldi, as its name suggests, was dedicated to the subject of Garibaldi. It published a version of Garibaldi's memoirs, and along with two other papers (*Il Gazzettino della Sera* and the *L'Unità Italiana*) reprinted Louis Jourdain's fervent tribute to him in the French paper, *Le Siècle*.[20] *Il Corriere di Sicilia* offered its readers a physical portrait of Garibaldi from a 'correspondent': this was really a modified extract from Cuneo's biography.[21] Although *La Forbice* ('The Scissors') promised to be more lively and interesting than *Il Giornale di Sicilia*, it went on to describe Garibaldi in well-worn terms as the 'brave Garibaldi', 'the new Washington', and repeated Cuneo's assertion that '[h]is life is a continual sacrifice in favour of the Italian nation; [he has] a generous and chivalrous soul'; although it did show some originality in mid-June when it referred to him as the 'new Hannibal of war'.[22] Perhaps the best example of the broader diffusion and acceptance of Risorgimento discourse, and of Garibaldi's role within it, by the Palermo papers is the extended tribute to Garibaldi paid by *L'Italia Redenta* in its first number, of 20 June. Proclaiming its programme as the redemption of Italy, 'the beautiful country, source of all knowledge, perpetual theatre of war and civil discord', its main article, entitled

'The sword of Garibaldi compared to the great men of antiquity', concluded that Garibaldi was better than any of them. Charlemagne was a possible comparison, and the paper cited a pantheon of famous Italians:

> Here is the heroic sword of Garibaldi which never fails, and which at the head of the movement routs, beats and conquers the enemy, and hoists the standard of Italian freedom . . . What Dante did for the leadership of Italian thought; what Macchiavelli practised, by seizing the sceptre of politics in Italy; and finally what Galileo discovered, by establishing the movement of the heavens in yearly cycles around the sun, the valiant victor of Varese and Como could properly compete with, as part of the current Italian movement.

'Our admiration is reserved for one man alone, Giuseppe Garibaldi', proclaimed *La Mola* in its first number, and in a rough echo of Mazzini's instructions to Young Italy: 'for the leadership of armed democracy, which liberated us, for the greatest lover of the peninsula, which he believes in and which will be; one Italy, one fatherland for all the people from the mountains to the sea who speak and feel in the Italian way'.[23]

The Palermo press was also very quick to pick up and pursue the regime's proposal of Garibaldi as the leader of a new religion. In various issues of *La Forbice*, Garibaldi was 'our heroic Liberator . . . our immortal Dictator', 'this genius created by God in a moment of divine enthusiasm for the longed-for regeneration of Italy', and the 'destroying angel of tyranny';[24] for *Il Garibaldi*, he was 'the armed missionary of Italian liberation' at the head of a 'holy cause';[25] while for *La Cicala Italiana* he was 'the Holy Man': 'He is life, he is liberty with a lightening glance, with a pure and undefiled soul, with a lofty and extensive mind, and an invincible arm'.[26] Finally, in *L'Unità Italiana*, the new editor, Ignazio Lombardi, told his readers in his first editorial that Garibaldi was the symbol and saviour of Italy, 'the Redeemer of the Ausonian provinces [i.e. Sicily], the Nazarene of Italy . . . the Archangel of wrath . . . the Angel of health and comfort . . . the Man of providence on whom rests the guardian eye of God'.[27]

The papers were equally keen to encourage acts of patriotism, and especially exalted the idea of war and volunteering, making little reference to the problems of conscription. Only *Il Garibaldi* noted that the arrival of volunteers from the continent 'was a tacit and bitter rebuke to those few who still don't understand the inestimable advantage of *conscription*', while *La Forbice* criticised the 'feebleness' of 'idle young men'.[28] However, *La Frusta* expressed confidence in conscription and praised the idea of the free soldier: 'the symbol of civic virtue and military heroism . . . he lives only for the fatherland and

knows how to die with honour for it; but his name will live on in all our hearts
. . . because there is nothing more fitting and more glorious for a man than to
die for the fatherland and for its free institutions'.[29] Almost every issue of *Il
Garibaldi* included a call to arms. '[C]ome, come . . . . come to Palermo,' it
told its readers, 'and be inspired by the scene, truly worthy of Italy, and see
how the rich, the poor and the aristocrats compete with each other to crown
their sons, laying them down on the altar of the fatherland.'[30] *La Guerra*,
perhaps unsurprisingly given its name, also encouraged volunteering, and in a
short article entitled 'The soldier of Garibaldi' summarised the aesthetic,
military and political ideal on which it was based.

> The soldier of Garibaldi is dressed in a red shirt and wide trousers – he has
> an easy gait . . . he is used to hardship, he can withstand the sun, ice, and
> fatigue – he sleeps little, and mostly on straw or the bare earth . . . in battle
> his law is to go ever onward; a *garibaldino* dies, he does not flee – he never
> hides from fire, but faces the bullets with his chest exposed, he fires one or
> two shots and then uses the bayonet – he adores his general, and is
> enchanted by him, he would lay down for him not one but twenty lives.[31]

The press also promoted the virtues of martyrdom, and was particularly keen
to encourage the cult of local martyrs like Francesco Riso and Rosolino Pilo,
as well as those – Tuckory, the Bandiera brothers ('the first heroes of Italian
freedom')[32] – who had come from afar to die for freedom in southern Italy.[33]

Such fidelity to the government line is not altogether surprising, since we
already know that the regime cultivated the press, but it is worth noting as a
cultural contrast to the relative lack of material support. Praise of Garibaldi
and of his government was almost unanimous. Moreover, the language in
which it was expressed, and the symbols referred to, are proof of the full
acceptance of the national–patriotic discourse in Palermo, a city which was
traditionally the centre of Sicilian autonomy rather than of Italian
nationalism. The Palermo press made ample use of existing Risorgimento
tropes like degeneration, regeneration, heroism and martyrdom, and
emphasised almost daily both the virtues of a military life and volunteering
and the idea of Garibaldi as the saviour of Sicily. So, if nothing else, the
government succeeded in getting its patriotic message across to the press.
Indeed, there is little difference in attitude between the Palermo press and
the liberal press elsewhere in Italy during the events of 1860: both
unquestioningly accepted Garibaldi and his dictatorship as representative of
the Italian nation, and opposition was almost entirely silent. Only in October
was some cynicism expressed in Palermo, and then by two nationalist papers,
about the elaborate absurdity of the commemorations of the 'martyrs for

liberty' in the Church of San Domenico.[34] However, this was an isolated moment of dissent; otherwise the papers concurred in praising government-sponsored celebrations such as the demolition of Castellamare fort and Garibaldi's birthday.[35]

Furthermore, journalists and intellectuals were not content merely to echo government propaganda, but also came up with their own associative activities and their own ways of celebrating the revolution. Many of the plays and other performances put on in Palermo at this time had a nationalist theme and/or enacted a nationalist narrative. Thus, the play *Salvatore Maniscalco* (the hated Bourbon chief of police) was immediately followed by *Vittorio Emanuele's entrance in Palermo* at the Teatro Nazionale. The same theatre staged a reading of a new poem 'Garibaldi in Sicily' by the editor of *L'Unità Italiana*, Ignazio Lombardi. The paper was (understandably) keen to stress the success of the event and reported that the author was called back on stage and encouraged to read another poem, 'Il Cacciatore delle Alpi': 'And now to the Vespers – on its fiery earth – We will fight with you – the same war'. At this, the paper wrote, the audience erupted in applause, waved their handkerchiefs and, tying them together in a long chain, sang a nationalist song, 'then shouts, cheers, hands raised and everything else you can imagine from a people enthused for its freedom'.[36] The Teatro San Cecilia organised a huge patriotic celebration. The performance included musical staples of the Risorgimento canon – the overture to *William Tell*, the duet from *I Puritani*, and an aria from *Norma* – as well as specially composed hymns to Garibaldi and Vittorio Emanuele and some ballet. The theatre was decorated with elaborate sets: one was simply a mass of flags, swords and soldiers; another was a recreation of the recent battle scene around the royal palace and Porta Nuova, complete with fortifications and tricolour flags.[37]

On a less spectacular level, literally hundreds of ephemeral publications were produced. These included patriotic flyers, such as a Garibaldi version of the 'Pater Noster' and 'Ave Maria':

Our father who art in Sicily, glorious and content from the liberation of the Italian land, hallowed be thy name, because your love for Italy is as great as your glory, because you came down to earth from heaven for love and to deliver your children with your precious blood . . . Virgin Italy, mother of Garibaldi, pray for your children, now, and until the hour of death of the last tyrant . . .[38]

Poems and songs proliferated, published mostly in newspapers but also separately as pamphlets, and these too followed a standard patriotic formula. One of the most productive writers was Ignazio Lombardi, editor of *L'Unità*

Italiana. He responded to the political crisis of early July with the triumphant national–religious hymn, 'Garibaldi and Italy', which imagined Garibaldi as the 'new Archangel' resurrecting the glories of Italy's past ('now the new heroes embrace the ancient heroes').[39]

This nationalist poetry used an eclectic, arguably even blasphemous, mix of religious, mythological and patriotic vocabularies. It proposed Garibaldi as the saviour of Sicily by referring to him almost simultaneously as a saintly or even Christ-like figure, a classical hero and a mythological creature. 'The Angel of Italy has touched our shores', wrote Pietro Chiara; while, in the words of the liberal priest Carmelo Pardi, Garibaldi was 'sent by heaven': he was the 'lion of Caprera', with 'the soul of Cincinnatus and the heart of Brutus'.[40] One liberal writer, the author of 'Il Torquato Tasso', 'Procida' and the previously banned 'Jacopo Ortis', wrote a tribute to Garibaldi in five *canti*, and told his readers that they could expect thirty-five more:

> Hail immortal Genius, warrior spirit . . .
> you will have at your side
> The sword of Archangel Michael.
> He seemed a brave knight from olden times
> An enchanted being, a God who reigned
> Over nature, and much more besides.[41]

Perhaps the most complete expression of the reception of the Garibaldi cult in Sicilian culture was an extended dramatisation of a Sicilian legend, in which Garibaldi is imagined as the offspring of an angel (Elim) and a young girl. In the final *canto* of the play, Elim gives Garibaldi his mission on earth, which is to follow the model of Christ and save Sicily ('in the midst of so much exhaustion and agitation, of so much life and decay, You will shine, Alone, like the guiding star . . .').[42]

It is extremely significant that the Church in Sicily, for the most part, tolerated the blasphemous use of its own vocabulary to promote an alternative religion of 'humanity' with strong Saint-Simonian overtones. Its attitude is all the more surprising when we remember the considerable, and growing, rejection by Rome of everything that Italian liberalism and nationalism represented in these years. 'Here in Palermo, as in the rest of Sicily, the clergy is truly national', Nino Bixio wrote to his wife in early June: 'what a difference from our lot.'[43] In many cases, moreover, the clergy openly endorsed the nationalist message. 'What is most striking', according to another commentator:

> is the zealous support given by the Sicilian clergy for the insurrectionary cause: priests and monks go through the streets preaching a new crusade

against the Bourbon government, and encouraging the enthusiasm of the islanders for the fight; they fight alongside them in the most awful and bloody frays, raising their spirits with word and deed.[44]

This unusually sympathetic standpoint can be explained both by the careful policies of Garibaldi's regime and by the Sicilian clergy's own ambivalence towards the ecclesiastical hierarchy. Especially in the isolated rural communities of the Sicilian interior, priests lived very close to the people; they were thus well aware of the severe social problems caused by the exploitation of the workforce and by land hunger, and of the pressing need for social reform. They too had often suffered the effects of economic dislocation and poverty, and might feel deep resentment of the bishops and religious bodies like the Jesuits, who had enjoyed enormous wealth and privileges under the Bourbon regime. It was these radicalised priests who responded to Garibaldi's call to 'good priests'. They fought with him, helped organise the peasants into *squadre* on his arrival, encouraged Palermo to revolt, and seized key points in the city during the fighting for the city at the end of May. One of them, Paolo Sardo, even tried to organise a separate 'Ecclesiastical legion' in Garibaldi's army (this was something quite 'extraordinary' according to a northern volunteer, who noted that its stated aim was to 'encourage the fighting men' for the 'great needs of the Italian cause').[45]

In the weeks that followed the seizure of Palermo, some priests publicly rejected their archbishop's official instructions to protect the Pope and his temporal power. A few of them openly condemned the Pope's policy on nationalism and accepted that the abolition of his temporal power was necessary, as it had no spiritual basis. Many lent their symbolic support to the regime. Dominican monks hoisted and blessed the tricolour flag during the fighting for Palermo; and others decorated a main barricade with the figure of Christ surrounded by candles and numerous images of the Madonna.[46] Fra' Pantaleo, the most famous of these radical priests, organised Garibaldi's blessing in the cathedral in Alcamo and adopted aspects of the Crusader's dress, and he went with Garibaldi both to fight and to encourage support for his campaign. The eyewitness, Forbes, observed him in Messina in 'cowl and crucifix', preaching to the people 'in their own *patois*', and finishing the sermon with 'three *vivas* for Garibaldi, three for Victor Emmanuel, and three for the Madonna Sanctissima, who is supposed to have taken the Messinese under her especial protection'.[47]

There is evidence that nuns were equally enthusiastic for the revolution. In volunteer memoirs, nuns become a compelling symbol both of female purity and of the seductive power of the nationalist cause. Alberto Mario commented that 'the romantic figure of Garibaldi had turned the heads of the saintly sisterhood, who were one and all piously enamoured of him'. Fruits, preserves and sweets arrived every day at Garibaldi's residence, wrapped in 'curiously-wrought baskets' with flowers, banners and inscriptions: "'To thee, Giuseppe! Saint and hero! Mighty as St George! Beautiful as the seraphim! Forget not the nuns of ———, who love thee tenderly; who pray hourly to Santa Rosalia that she may watch over thee . . .!'" On one visit to a convent, 'the tables spread for breakfast resembled a fancy fair – sugar castles, cupolas, temples, palaces and domes; and in the centre a statue of Garibaldi, in sugar'. The nuns (young and of noble birth) became so excited by Garibaldi's resemblance to 'our Lord' that they queued up to kiss him on the lips, including the abbess, 'who at first seemed scandalized'.[48] At another convent, Sette Angeli, they got down on their knees to pray before him.[49] One volunteer, Giovanni Nuvolari, even admits to an affair with 'a *simpatica* young nun, an angel of beauty', while another, Abba, sees the nuns as both sexual and unobtainable: 'their lily hands' reach out to him, and he is so aroused by their 'odour of chastity' that he kisses the grille separating the convent from the outside world.[50]

Above all, of course, this evidence reveals much about the sexual attitudes and expectations of the volunteers, but it does also suggest that some Sicilian women were passionate admirers of Garibaldi. We know very little about the general attitude of women to Garibaldi's dictatorship, although there is some limited evidence of support and enthusiasm. There were women's committees which collected money for the dead and wounded,[51] and letters from at least two young educated women express active engagement with the nationalist cause. Felicità Benso di Verdura seems to have known Garibaldi personally: she signed herself *La Garibaldina* and sent best wishes from her mother, father ('*Babbo*') and sister.[52] A young intellectual, Eloisa Abramo, aligned herself explicitly with the Palermo liberals, and expressed happiness at the liberation of 'my country'. 'Sicily . . . has shown herself worthy of that liberty which she was made immense sacrifices to acquire, and the Sicilians of '60 are braver than those of the Vespers . . . the hour of redemption has already rung, and this great task, dreamed of by the divine poet, is about to be achieved after 6 centuries'. She responded with enthusiasm to the news of the victory at Milazzo ('Garibaldi constantly in the line of fire for 12 long hours . . . It is the hand of God which guides this man in the line of fire').[53]

The help given by the Sicilian clergy to Garibaldi was not without controversy. There were, for example, dire warnings of the spread of Protestantism to Sicily, and attempts were made to denigrate Pantaleo and others.[54] On the whole, however, the support of radical priests and nuns can be considered one of the dictatorship's great achievements. It meant that, whatever went on behind the scenes, in public the government could proclaim its message with one voice. At the same time, the clergy helped to publicise the government's attempts to sacralise the nation; and there is plenty of anecdotal evidence, as we saw in the previous chapter, that these attempts produced a wave of quasi-religious celebration in Sicily, which saw the revolution as the people's 'saviour'. Perhaps the most well-known and documented example of a popular cult of Garibaldi is his identification in Palermo with the city's patron saint, Santa Rosalia. He was said to be related to her and to come under her special protection. The anthropologist, Salvatore Salomone-Marino, who researched these and other legends about Garibaldi ('from the mouths of Palermo women, Bourbon soldiers, the *lazzaroni* of Naples'), summarised the Santa Rosalia legend as follows:

> under her personal protection, he received a gift from her, during the journey from Quarto to Marsala, of that rough belt in white leather which he always wears and with which, by waving in the air, he chases away all the bullets and bombs which are aimed at him in the awful moments of battle. And he withdrew every evening to a secluded place, indeed he disappeared completely, because every evening he conferred with the Saint, who taught him the right movements and actions to take and gave them those vivid words with which he provoked fanaticism in his followers and terrified his enemies.[55]

This legend was still in circulation when the historian G. M. Trevelyan visited the city in the early 1900s; according to Jessie White Mario, it was originally created by the nuns of Santa Caterina convent, who observed Garibaldi's fearless behaviour during the bombardment at Piazza Pretorio.[56]

It is possible that Garibaldi was famous among the peasants and urban poor even before he arrived in Sicily. Trying to stir the population to revolt in April 1860, Pilo and Corrao found that their 'only hope' was Garibaldi – 'the man who does not lose battles' – and that his promised arrival spurred the *squadre* leaders into renewed activity.[57] That the arrival of Garibaldi in Sicily had a considerable impact on popular culture and popular memory is suggested by a number of studies undertaken by Salomone-Marino and Giuseppe Pitrè, in the decades after 1860. Pitrè's and Salomone-Marino's interest in folklore and the new discipline of anthropology led them to collect and record Sicilian popular songs: long narrative poems (*cantastorie*) which were passed orally from one generation to the next, and one place or region to the next, often with substantial variations.[58] They found that nationalism and national unification left a strong trace in popular songs and legends, in rural communities as well as in the main cities, and that most of them were still actively in circulation over twenty years later. A large number of these *cantastorie* praised the revolution of 1860 and its aims, and narrated its various episodes and details in ways that were remarkably similar to the official version of events produced by the regime.[59] One song, the work of an illiterate peasant from Etna, was said by him to have been composed after hearing read aloud the letter of Dumas to Carini about the battle of Milazzo; and it repeats its key episode of Garibaldi killing the cavalry captain, with a violent embellishment of its own (Garibaldi kills not one but five soldiers).[60]

Song after song celebrated Garibaldi: 'the Liberator – In his heart there is no place for fear';[61] 'Garibaldi seemed like a God to us – He shouted: Oh my people! Onwards!'[62] 'How handsome Garibaldi is', another song began, repeating the idea of Garibaldi as an eclectic hero bringing together the qualities of the archangel Saint Michael, Jesus Christ and Charlemagne:

> . . . who seems to me
> Saint Michael [*San Micheluzzo*] the archangel in person,
> He has come to liberate Sicily
> and avenge those who died,
> his look is that of Jesus Christ
> his command is like Charlemagne.[63]

Songs depicted Garibaldi as brave and invincible: 'his thunderous voice is frightening . . . he disappears, flies off, and reappears';[64] 'with that horse he rides ever onward and laughs in the midst of gunfire'.[65] His arrival and conquest of Sicily were miraculous: the Bourbon troops had only to see his red shirt to run away, according to one song, while others proclaimed that 'he took control of Palermo in a flash', and that 'when Garibaldi went into battle even the trees and leaves trembled'.[66]

Palpably, these songs share a taste for warfare and violence. One long *cantastoria* recorded by Salomone-Marino delights in the fighting for Palermo and the bravery of all those on Garibaldi's side:

> Old men and young men, and everyone
> Gave a hand against those bad guys . . .
> And huge bombs, from the air they came
> And fell on the ground in their hundreds;
> Our *Squadri*, they were all in their place,
> Stern under fire, no one was scared . . .
> From the barricades we fired
> With a terrible fire like no other,
> And – *Viva Garibardi!* – we cried,
> With a shout which terrified our enemy.[67]

Other songs glorified the volunteer experience: '*Bella*, I'm off with Garibaldi, under his flag to make war – off to make war against the Bourbons';[68] 'We are young men – We have no cares – And if Garibaldi comes – We'll go off with him';[69] or 'Vittorio Emanuele, do me a favour, – Make us a force of Sicilians – Since we must fight the Germans' (this last song, which refers to the Austrians, was an adaptation of a Tuscan volunteer song).[70] And in many songs there were references to liberty, Italy and the fight against 'tyranny': '*Viva la libertà!* Which scares them away – *Viva l'Italia [la Talia]!* Which does not let them escape';[71] '*Viva la Talia e Garibaldi amicu!*';[72] or more directly: 'Sicily mourned, now she laughs – she broke the chains of tyranny – and Garibaldi brave and true – has told us – Now you are free.'[73]

Commenting on the return of Garibaldi to Palermo in September, and on the scenes of popular enthusiasm which greeted his arrival, *Il Precursore* proclaimed, 'Oh how sweet it is to rule not with the bayonet and cannon, but with the love of the people!'[74] The evidence available suggests that the population was not as unmoved by the call of Garibaldi as the new political elite in Palermo privately believed. Now, while 'the love of the people' could not resolve all the problems of men and money, it does point to a degree of political authority and consensus which is relatively unusual in nineteenth-century Italy, and which has been overlooked by historians more interested in explaining the ultimate disappointment of Garibaldi's campaign. From the limited evidence available, the current picture of relations between government and people under Garibaldi's dictatorship, often said to be characterised by political indifference, needs revision. Indeed, it seems likely that the vision of national belonging proposed and promoted by Garibaldi in Sicily did have a broad appeal and impact. In certain circumstances, Sicilians fought with Garibaldi. Garibaldi's patriotic message was endorsed and elaborated both by the press and by the priests, so it reached different, and significant, sections of the population. If popular songs are anything to go by, the story of Garibaldi's expedition, the military and political ideals which it sought to represent, and the images and symbols through which these ideals were expressed, were incorporated into popular culture and reproduced in a local vernacular. Moreover, this story evoked a popular response: at the very least, the songs remained in wide circulation and helped to construct a popular memory of the events of 1860. So, Garibaldi may not have persuaded Sicilians to join up with him *en masse*, but he does seem to have laid some foundations for a state-sponsored religion of the nation.

The nation-at-arms

One of the most remarkable aspects of the war of 1859 was the rush of young men from Lombardy and central Italy to volunteer to fight against Austria.

They did so amid broader scenes of nationalist enthusiasm, such as patriotic demonstrations, the formation of associations and the organisation of public subscriptions. Garibaldi's war against the Bourbons in 1860 provoked a very similar reaction. In fact, his calls for volunteers and material assistance in 1859 had carried on, as we saw in Chapter 7, throughout the winter of 1859–60 and had culminated in his plans for the nation-at-arms in early 1860. These military plans were halted by the Piedmontese government, but the popular appeal of volunteering and otherwise offering aid to the nationalist cause did not cease. The phenomenon of volunteering in 1860 is worth looking at in some detail as it can tell us much about the nature of support for Garibaldi and the national idea which he represented.

One strong indication of public support for Garibaldi was the money given to his Million Rifles Fund during 1860. The Thousand sailed to Sicily, and financed itself until arrival in Palermo, with 90,000 Piedmontese lire from the Rifles Fund (roughly $400,000 in present-day figures).[75] Figures given by Agostino Bertani (who stayed behind in Genoa after Garibaldi's departure for Sicily and was responsible for organising new expeditions)[76] indicate that money continued to be donated thereafter, the fund '[p]rofiting', as Raymond Grew puts it, 'by its association with the General'.[77] In all, the Rifles Fund was able to give a total of 2 million lire (c. $9 million) to the expedition, along with thousands of rifles and muskets. Some of this money came from the Piedmontese government, and some from patriotic municipalities (the city of Pavia donated 37,000 lire and Cremona 130,000 lire to the Thousand); in the latter case money was raised both from municipal funds and via new loans and public subscriptions. Similarly, the National Society received around 450,000 lire (c. $2 million) for the campaign from a combination of official and private sources. Outside these channels, the Sicilian exile, Count Amari, collected around 200,000 lire (c. $900,000); a separate central fund (cassa centrale) set up by Bertani collected over half a million lire (c. $2.25 million); and Garibaldi himself donated approximately 36,000 lire (c. $160,00), apparently from money sent directly to him by his admirers.[78]

The issue of which political groups funded Garibaldi's expedition and campaign is a tricky one, and is connected to the bitter rivalries between moderates and democrats which rumbled on throughout the summer of 1860. For the purposes of assessing both the nationalist response and the popular reaction to Garibaldi, however, these rivalries matter less than the fact that money was given, and from these different sources. The list of sponsors in Bertani's central fund shows a mix of public subscriptions, private donations and municipal funds. One letter to Bertani also suggested opening a bazaar in Genoa to collect money for Garibaldi's expedition. It refers to the frenetic fund-raising activity during May: 'balls are organised . . . flower shows are opened, and the price of the ticket is donated to Garibaldi'. Newspapers had opened subscriptions; and the committee in Bologna had already set up a shop, the letter revealed.[79]

As impressive as the fund-raising was the constant stream of men wanting to volunteer to fight with Garibaldi, or to return to battle with him. In March 1860, a man who had shaken Garibaldi's hand in Rimini wrote him a letter of commendable nationalist orthodoxy:

> Yes, my General, send me wherever you think my few military studies and my limited knowledge can be put to use for the Italian cause: I have no unrestrained ambitions; My profession of faith is this: my life, and that of my two dear sons . . . must end in honour defending the regeneration of our Italy: I, and they, desire nothing else.[80]

Risorgimento rhetoric, and enthusiasm for Garibaldi, reached many during 1859 and early 1860. An English observer, Laurence Oliphant, who was on a train with Garibaldi shortly before the departure for Sicily (but while the expedition had been shelved in favour of defending Nice), was struck by his capacity to provoke a popular response. On the train, Garibaldi read his morning's mail, an 'enormous correspondence' which after reading he tore into small pieces; and the letters were so many that, in Oliphant's words, 'by the time we reached Genoa, the floor of the carriage was thickly strewn with the litter, and looked like a gigantic waste-paper basket'. Oliphant later learnt that these letters were responses to Garibaldi's call for volunteers to Sicily.[81]

Even if it had achieved nothing else, the expedition of the Thousand would have been proof of enthusiasm for the idea of Italy. Indeed, the expedition must be seen as the continuation of a much longer Mazzinian tradition, which began with the Bandiera brothers in the early 1840s and continued through the 1850s, and which has been identified by Paul Ginsborg as a central element in the romantic conception and realisation of Italy as a nation.[82] But it is equally significant that the departure of that expedition from Quarto was part of a much broader movement. Bertani's central committee, and a number of local committees in the Lombard cities of Milan, Bergamo, Cremona and Brescia, and other cities like Modena, Bologna, Florence and Livorno, had the task of encouraging and organising volunteers; and it was to these committees that letters were addressed, from those 'imploring', in G. M. Trevelyan's words, 'to be allowed to serve under Garibaldi'. Cremona, a city of 30,000 inhabitants, alone sent nearly a thousand volunteers.[83] Moreover, from the very day (9 May) when Garibaldi's call for volunteers was published in the papers, but long before the outcome of the expedition was known, offers started to pour into Bertani's central office.

One of the earliest letters in Bertani's files, written on 9 May by an N. Palazzini of Milan, protested bitterly that the expedition had left without him: why, he asked Bertani, was he considered 'unworthy' to serve his country? He accordingly demanded to be reassured that 'on the very next occasion, I will be called on to be part of the elect and given the honour to claim freedom for our Italy'.[84] Another, an officer from Piacenza, begged to be included in the 'other expedition being prepared', adding that he was ready to keep his involvement a secret, to leave immediately, to be accepted in any grade, and to bring other soldiers with him, if only he was allowed to go to Sicily to fight with Garibaldi.[85] Others expressed themselves as 'very anxious to take part quickly in that noble expedition';[86] 'fervent' to offer their lives 'for the patriotic love of Italy';[87] 'fervent . . . to join Garibaldi in any place and to share their destiny with him whatever that may be'.[88] As one man wrote:

> desiring fervently to follow the brave General Garibaldi in any event and in any danger for Italy my fatherland, and to put at your disposal my feeble hand, I turn to you sir . . . begging you to do me the favour of telling me, if or if it is not true that the volunteers are being sent back, and if it is not true, I can tell my companions so that they are convinced and we can leave.[89]

Girolamo Guglielmetti, already in Genoa from Domodossola, expressed an equally 'fervent desire' to go with a new expedition. If Bertani would only let him go, he wrote, he would be 'grateful for ever', adding: 'if in these days you have any need of my person for any purpose whatsoever, I am at your disposal, and I will do what little I can with great pleasure'.[90]

The statements made and questions asked by these volunteers suggest the extent to which bits of information and other rumours rapidly circulated about Garibaldi's expedition in early May, as well as the enthusiasm with which many responded to the news and letters which formally announced his departure. 'Desiring to join up with General Garibaldi as soon as possible', a volunteer wrote in a pompous style on 22 May:

> and not having had from your committee any precise indication, I have taken the liberty of asking you [i.e. Bertani] directly that if I come to Genoa will I be able to leave quickly for Sicily, and how should I regulate myself? I will not seek to hide from you how fervent is my request: but I hope that you will forgive such fervour and the cursive style of my letter, as I care for nothing but the idea which has inspired my resolution.[91]

Some people simply dropped everything and came directly to Bertani's headquarters at Genoa, 'hoping', as two volunteers put it, 'that with your means you can realise our golden dream by taking us to Sicily'.[92] One group of Italians left their homes in 'the centre of Africa' and wrote to Bertani from Algeria asking for advice on how to get to Sicily.[93] Many relied on references from friends or elders with more experience or influence, in an attempt to be accepted by Bertani.[94] Others joined together, and proposed to come as groups of students, artists, enlisted soldiers or from a particular locality. One typical letter of 11 May spoke for a 'few young students from Saluzzo, equally ardent in their patriotic love for Italy', who 'with no other means of dedicating themselves to the same, offer her their lives'; and this group persisted with their offer, writing again on 15 May, and as 'a force of fearless and determined young men' on 6 June.[95]

Often, it is the individual offers that tell us most about the depth of the emotional reaction to the news of Garibaldi's expedition and subsequent campaign. One man wrote a breathless letter – entirely without punctuation – to Bertani asking to be taken on as a volunteer: 'in short how can I be useful to my Fatherland which is my whole life all I have is willing'. Although he was poor, he insisted that if he was accepted as a volunteer he could bring his horse and two saddles.[96] A young Genoese girl wrote to Bertani, stating that: 'Genoa and the world weary me, so far from the heroes of Italy . . . My parents may perhaps be averse to my decision to go to Sicily, but you who are, like Garibaldi, the incarnation of the Italian mind and heart, can find means to persuade them.'[97] That she is not an isolated case, and that some women were desperate to fight with Garibaldi, is suggested by various anecdotes of women dressing as men in order to join his army.[98] A father, a veteran of 1848, offered his son – 'my only son not yet twenty' – to Garibaldi;[99] and a sixteen-year-old told Bertani, 'I want to devote myself because I love Italy, one free independent under the sceptre of King Vittorio Emanuele, and because I adore Garibaldi. And for Italy, for Vittorio Emanuele and for Garibaldi I would be torn to pieces.'[100] Several boys defied their parents and ran away to join Garibaldi. One letter wrote of a sixteen-year-old 'runaway' who had left home 'with the intention of joining the glorious standard of the intrepid Garibaldi';[101] a father asked for the whereabouts of his seventeen-year-old son, 'my only hope', who had managed to leave 'without my knowledge' with Garibaldi and from whom nothing had been heard since Marsala;[102] an uncle asked for news of his nephew, a fifteen-year-old student from Varese, who had run off 'with other young lads . . . full of youthful fire to join up in the ranks destined for Sicily';[103] while still another letter decried the foolhardy actions of two boys from good families but of a lazy disposition ('idle, very idle'), who '[i]n the land of sun will quickly end up as food for misfortune, lost in idleness or pleasure, or they will be shot, at the best . . .'.[104] Towards the end of June, a woman, Giulia Tonelli, wrote to Bertani asking for help. Her husband had abandoned her to go to Sicily, leaving her alone with a child; without financial assistance from Bertani's committee, she wrote, she would be 'obliged to beg for a living'.[105]

Thus, Garibaldi's call for volunteers provoked a great rush to join him. Enthusiasm for his expedition was not confined to the young, reckless or feckless: doctors, pharmacists and government officials all wrote to Bertani asking to be enrolled. Two brothers, both customs officers, wrote before Garibaldi's departure was made public, asking for confirmation of the news so that they could resign their posts to follow him (they wrote again later in the month repeating their offer).[106] A pharmacist who had worked for five years in 'one of the main pharmacies in Turin' was willing to abandon his job 'just to be as useful as I can to the holy cause';[107] and a postal clerk offered his services to the postal office in Sicily but added that he was also prepared to fight as a soldier: 'I too would rush to take up arms to fight for the independence and union of Italy.'[108] A lawyer from Alessandria, an employee in the local government, proposed himself (twice) for a post in the Sicilian administration, but said he was equally prepared to go there as a 'simple soldier';[109] and a professor of chemistry at the University of Pavia wrote that while it was difficult for a man in his position to join the volunteers in the normal way, 'nonetheless I have a strong desire to get myself down there'. 'Don't be discouraged and stay in Pavia', was Bertani's kindly reply to this last request for a place.[110]

A large number of offers came from officers, ex-officers and soldiers. One man, an ex-officer in the Ottoman army (or, as he put it, an officer 'for the Tyrant I hope that the above will soon disappear like mist in the sun') wrote directly to Garibaldi from Constantinople offering his services, and asking him to 'love me as much as I love you'.[111] Another ex-officer, from the Austrian army, wrote that volunteering for Garibaldi would 'cancel out' his past actions.[112] Although Bertani had been instructed by Garibaldi to reject men from the regular Piedmontese army, many refused to be put off and were convinced they could go. A sergeant asked Bertani for advice about being released from the army 'in order to give a helping hand to the Fatherland . . . Viva Garibaldi Viva il Re Viva l'Indipendenza Italiana'.[113] A lieutenant requested three days' notice so that he could ask for his release along with his three brothers ('a fourth one is already with the General').[114] 'Having read about the glorious battles of our brave general in Sicily,' another lieutenant wrote, 'and feeling that it is really there that the Battles of the Fatherland are being fought, and seeing that here we are kept in shameful idleness – while other Brothers are dying in battle, unless you tell me otherwise I will go to Turin and resign my commission.'[115] From Modena, a veteran with twenty years' service wrote furiously, first to La Farina and then to Bertani, about his various efforts to be released from military service and accepted as a volunteer:

> I would have happily given half of my blood in order to be with him and the other half I would happily have shed on to Sicilian soil for the Holy Cause. I am resigned to the fact that I cannot be among the first, but I hope ... I will not be among the last ... to offer his arm and his mind to the brave Sicilians, for my fervent desire to do my duty, the duty of every Italian, to give my all, and to all, and with all my moral and physical faculties for the maximum benefit and the progressive tendency of the common Fatherland, within the limits of honest Justice.

All this passion did not convince Bertani, who rejected his offer of service.[116]

Just as significant was the number of offers coming from men who had previously served as volunteers in other wars. There were one or two sad stories of returning veterans: a Neapolitan, Vincenzo Masi, had fought in 1848 and '49, and after ten years of exile – 'a whole odyssey, an entire Dante's inferno' – he had returned to be rejected as a volunteer in 1859 and imprisoned for 'sedition' in Tuscany; beset by debt and with his wife dying, he asked Bertani for money so that he could come to Italy and take part in the 'heroic expedition' to Sicily, and find 'at least an honourable death on the field of battle'.[117] Another veteran from Napoleon's Russian campaign and the 1821 revolution in Piedmont wrote pathetically to Bertani, twice offering his services 'with all my heart', and asking for 'the day, the time, and the place where I can join myself up with you' (but without success).[118] However, these stories are unusual: the majority of those who wrote to Bertani had had their combat experience during the wars of 1848–9, and/or had been enrolled as *Cacciatori* with Garibaldi or regular soldiers in the war of 1859, and seemed to see these events in an entirely positive light. Their enthusiasm for the fight in Sicily suggests that, for many, participation in the wars of 1859 and 1860 was part of a single struggle for the liberation of Italy.

Overall, these letters offer vivid confirmation of a huge popular response to Garibaldi, at least among the literate urban population of northern and central Italy, and they prove that the Thousand were a fraction of a much more substantial group. We know that at least 21,000 men eventually made it to fight with Garibaldi;[119] Bertani's correspondence reveals that many more sought to go and were turned down. Offers continued to come in to his committees throughout July and August, and were still arriving as late as November and December.[120] The first major expedition to follow Garibaldi to Sicily, which was led by Medici and took around 2,500 men to Sicily on 9 June, was already full by the end of May.[121] On 23 May, after Garibaldi's calls for volunteers had been published in the northern papers but before the news of the victory at Calatafimi was known, a sympathiser in Milan wrote to Bertani asking him what to do with the 'numerous young men' wanting to join Garibaldi: 'around two hundred of them and they besiege me every day . . . Until now I have been trying to calm them down by telling them to wait and that the moment will come and they will be told . . . [but] these brave boys are very impatient and . . . their only aim is: to join Garibaldi'.[122] On 6 June, Giovanni Cadolini, who was helping in Cremona to organise the Medici expedition, told Bertani: 'I am now tired of holding on to these young men, who are impatient with the uncertainty of leaving from one hour to the next'; indeed, if he had not treated with caution the official instructions to encourage volunteers, 'I would have here several hundred men from the provinces without knowing where to send them'.[123] In Tuscany too, the pressure of volunteers was so great that a Florentine activist telegraphed Garibaldi asking him to send 'two or three steamships' to Livorno in order to move them south.[124] Later in June, doctors, pharmacists and other employees had to be told that all further expeditions were full: 'that we already have lots of doctors'; 'we don't need pharmacists'; or 'you can be of use to the Fatherland where you are'.[125] But many volunteers did not take no, or no reply, for an answer, and repeated their offers, sometimes more than once; and they wrote to Bertani of their disappointment – 'We had everything ready'[126] – or insisted on their patriotic zeal: 'we are ready to leave at any moment . . . if I had to walk day and night . . . I am ready for that sacrifice'.[127] Others blamed their local committee for their failure to be accepted.[128] The strain on Bertani, who was already suffering from nervous exhaustion, was seemingly immense: he was ill with a cough for most of June, and unable to eat or speak properly. So, when a complaint came in from Mantua about the failure to take volunteers from this Austrian-held town, it is no surprise that he scribbled crossly on the back of the letter: 'not everyone can go to Sicily: they should adapt themselves to the sacrifice which the fatherland requires'.[129]

The number and enthusiasm of volunteers in 1860 suggests that Garibaldi had succeeded in at least one of his political objectives in 1859–60. His speeches, appearances and actions from 1848 onwards had established a volunteer tradition in northern and central Italy; that is, he had created and publicised a national–military ethos and ideal to which (some) people now felt a passionate and practical commitment. That participation in the war in Sicily was perceived by many as an act of national belonging and political identification is confirmed by the language which they use. Writers don't just beg to join Garibaldi, they seek to put their familiarity with nationalist discourse on display. Thus, Sicilians are 'unhappy' and 'our brothers', whose cry for liberation must be answered (and by late June, Sicily is the 'land of Heroes');

the Bourbons are 'cowards', the 'tyrant oppressors, enemies of our nationality, and independence'; and Garibaldi is 'our General', 'our Leonida', 'the brave' and 'illustrious' 'Hero of Varese' and 'of Italian freedom'. The writers, as we have seen, are 'fervent', seeking nothing less than to offer their lives for the 'sacred' or 'holy' cause of Italian freedom.[130]

One of the earliest letters, addressed to Garibaldi and written by someone who had already tried twice to join him (in Tuscany in 1859), spoke of the need to 'help rise again to freedom' the 'sister . . . provinces' (i.e. Sicily), and of his desire to fight, 'even as a simple soldier to be worthy of the esteem of the greatest General, an esteem which I would jealously guard, and to be able to distinguish myself with great acts or to die'. All he wanted, he added, was to serve his country 'and to have from you, illustrious General, a word which I seek above all others, a *bravo!*'[131] The use here of Risorgimento tropes and symbols – the fight to recover liberty; the nation as family; the virtues of martyrdom; heroism as its own reward – may be crude, but it is also exemplary. 'It is better to die than to see our brothers oppressed by the Bourbon yoke', one volunteer told Bertani at the end of May;[132] 'if I was rich I would offer you gold, to amass firearms, and with that my life, but I am poor and for the fatherland I can offer only my arm and my blood', another one wrote two weeks later.[133] A philosophy student from Alessandria even quoted Garibaldi at Bertani: 'every time that the saying of the Valiant Man of Como and Varese comes to mind, that is: that he who is capable of carrying arms, and does not do so, is a coward and a traitor, I feel myself going red, so for this reason I have a great desire to serve my Fatherland'.[134] The language of these letters tells us that those writing had read the letters and propaganda put out by Bertani *et al.* The letters offer us clear proof of the circulation and use of nationalist discourse in northern and central Italy, and demonstrate a broad engagement with its symbols and ideals.

As ever, however, we must be careful about what we read into the evidence offered by the volunteers' letters. A degree of self-interest or just a simple desire to fight on the part of the volunteers in 1860 can never be entirely excluded. It is clear from the letters that many saw the war in Sicily as part selfless act of national heroism, part adventure with some violence thrown in, and part economic prospect. Some, indeed, openly requested a job in the administration, or in the work of fortification and reconstruction; most of the officers wanted to keep their grades; and as many asked for financial help in getting to Genoa as actually paid for their passage. And it may well be that this combination of emotional resonance and material opportunity best explains the appeal of the whole experience in Sicily. In this respect, the volunteers seemed able to embrace and repeat the propaganda put out by Garibaldi, who presented the war as an inclusive adventure which would glorify all those who participated in it, while ignoring his insistence that they should expect no reward for their actions.

Furthermore, while the volunteers' letters show passionate commitment to the nationalist cause, and a clear identification of the enemies of Italy, there are few hints in them that the volunteers saw Garibaldi as in any way a distinct symbol, different from the Italy represented by Vittorio Emanuele.[135] Indeed, it is hard to see how they could have done, given that the expedition made persistent appeals to the idea of national integration, and had *Italia e Vittorio Emanuele* as its slogan. Moreover, these letters wrote repeatedly of 'liberty' and 'independence'; but there are far fewer references to the need for political unification, even less mention of Rome and Venice, and none at all of the Republic. We can conclude then that the soldiers of 1860 heard the call, identified the enemy and even learnt the language of nationalism, but that they were plainly unable to grasp the details of the democratic message, as these were never made clear, or were never clearly distinguished from the ideals embodied by the king and Piedmont. With the benefit of hindsight, it is hard not to see in these letters also a significant slip in political communication. On a discursive level, and especially if we look at the reception of the nationalist discourse in 1860, we can still observe the reliance of Garibaldi on Piedmont, and foresee his eventual defeat at the hands of Cavour.

The enthusiasm of foreigners

After the expedition to southern Italy was over, the owner of *The Illustrated London News* wrote personally to Garibaldi. She sent him 'two volumes containing pictorial representations of your wonderful progress from Melazzo to Naples', and remarked that her late husband, the previous owner, had 'never omitted an opportunity of despatching Artists to follow you and record in pictures your bold and patriotic deeds'. These pictures had been sent all over the world, she added, and she assured Garibaldi that 'the Artists and Correspondents of this paper will be found wherever your sense of patriotism leads you in future'.[136] Garibald's success with the press was discussed in the previous chapter, and we have also seen the extent to which press reports and illustrations were picked up and elaborated in poems, plays, histories and memoirs in the course of 1860 and afterwards. But the enthusiasm of foreigners for Garibaldi did not stop at plays and publications. Many also expressed their support for him through practical means – namely, the sending of men and money – and by writing directly to Garibaldi to state their admiration for his person and approval of his actions.

Figures suggest that the amount of money sent by the British to Garibaldi was substantial: between them, the Emancipation of Italy Fund and the

Garibaldi Fund raised some £30,000 (just under £2 million in present-day figures) between 1856 and the end of 1860.[137] That Garibaldi became a public cause for British liberals in 1860 is also suggested by various displays of gift-giving. Both Florence Nightingale and Charles Dickens gave money (along with the duke of Wellington's son; however, his donation was anonymous), and the Athenaeum, a gentleman's club in London, raised £300 (c. £19,000) in one night. In Darlington, a Garibaldi Fund Soirée was organised, with the profits from ticket sales going to the Garibaldi Fund; and in Glasgow, a special Working Men's Fund for Garibaldi was set up by John McAdam to consider 'how we can best support the Middle Class Friends of the Cause, who have already remitted to Italy and are preparing for another still larger remittance'.[138]

In fact, Garibaldi's campaign provided the occasion for a host of associative activities. Meetings were held, money was collected and addresses composed in support of Garibaldi. In Staffordshire, some inhabitants of the potteries town of Burslem got together to open a shilling subscription for Garibaldi, and they raised £500 by the end of the year (which suggests that a possible 10,000 people contributed); they also wrote him a letter in which they expressed both their pleasure that the Italians were rejecting Roman Catholicism and 'despotism' and their 'profound admiration' of 'the heroic and statesmanlike qualities displayed by the generous and gallant Garibaldi'.[139] A group in Blackburn sent him £5, and a carefully composed address which described Garibaldi as:

> the noblest of nature's Sons, and the greatest Prince among her Peoples . . . whose heart is set on 'Liberty' whose sympathies are even with the oppressed, whose sacred hand is never raised save in vindication of rights . . . ever ready to face danger and death for the overthrow of despotism, and the defence of the just liberation of the People.[140]

'[T]he men of Sheffield assembled in the Town Hall' on 11 June simply sent a letter to Garibaldi in which they told him of their 'great interest' in events in Italy, expressed their suspicion of 'grasping ambition' and diplomacy, and expressed their sympathy 'with the oppressed people of Italy, who have shown themselves so patient, and so faithful, so prudent and so brave in this great crisis':

> we hail, with all humane and free-minded men, the success of the brave attempt that has, so far, made Sicily free: and we are anxious to tell you that hundreds of thousands of Englishmen think that the course that you have taken was as *wise* as it was brave, and that it will be as really useful as it was most truly great . . . and we pray that you may outlive the storm, and sit

down at last, in the cool of the day, with a free and united Italy to teach the people the arts of a lasting peace as faithfully and as well as you have taught the arts of a just and manly war.[141]

William Johnson, the secretary of the Southampton Athenaeum, wrote on behalf of its members – 'the loving and loyal subjects of our devoted and beloved Queen Victoria (under whose beneficient reign we enjoy perfect freedom)' – to offer Garibaldi 'their most hearty congratulations' for his liberation of the people of Italy 'from a cruel and oppressive tyranny' (this latter phrase was underlined in red pen).[142]

There was similar activity in New York, from where an estimated $100,000 (c. $2.3 million in present-day figures) was sent to Italy between 1859 and 1860.[143] Two Italian committees (one under Garibaldi's old colleague, General Avezzana) were set up there in late 1859 and successfully organised sub-scriptions and other fund-raising activities for the Million Rifles Fund; these were joined by a third committee of prominent Americans which convened with great publicity in the City Assembly Rooms in February 1860. During the summer, publicity for Garibaldi was widespread. There was a concert in aid of Garibaldi in New York in July, to which artists and musicians donated their services free, and mass meetings of support for 'the immortal Garibaldi' were held in Cincinnati, Ohio and Newport, Rhode Island. From Philadelphia, Henry Roney wrote directly to Garibaldi to tell him that he and his friends were members of a secret society and they wished to make a donation to his campaign, while Thomas Schaffer wrote to inform Garibaldi that he had been elected an 'Honarary [sic] member of the Franklin Library Institute of Centenary College of Louisiana'.[144] Money was sent from San Francisco, and from Italian groups in Montevideo and Valparaiso, Chile.[145] A letter also reached Garibaldi from 'The Committee of the Fraternity of all Nations', signed by various exiles whose current location was not stated:

From the land of exile, we send to you, Dear General, our sentiment of respect and admiration, for your glorious achievements, and of those who have nobly shed their blood for the cause of humanity. We all look at you as the noble initiator of the emancipation of all the different peoples of Europe, and we fervently hope that you will fulfill to the last your heroic undertaking.[146]

Volunteers and other kinds of practical assistance also arrived from Britain and America. The Americans lent their particular support by providing ships to transport volunteers: the *Charles and Jane*, the *Franklin*, the *Washington* and the *Oregon* were American, or bought with American money, while the British supplied the *Amazon*.[147] In July, the *New York Herald* led a public outcry after the *Charles and Jane* was briefly seized by the Bourbon navy; when the ship's first mate, Watson, refused to allow her to be boarded he became something of a hero, and was offered (and acccepted) a post in Garibaldi's navy. Other American volunteers, most of whom were attached to General Avezzana's staff and arrived with him in time to fight at the Volturno, included two surgeons studying in Paris, two generals who had fought in the Mexican war during the 1830s, and the nephew of Senator Jefferson Davis.[148] John Litchfield offered himself and his men in the Volunteer Rifles – 'strong hands with willing hearts' – from Kingstown, Canada.[149] Britain sent more than its share of colourful characters. Apart from 'the gigantic Peard', who had already fought with Garibaldi in 1859, and went with a small group of other British volunteers to Sicily with Medici's expedition in July, there was Colonel John Dunne, who arrived in late May on a secret mission from Cavour, formed a peasant *squadre* of his own with which he entered Palermo during the fighting, and stayed on to form an English 'regiment', which was made up mostly of adolescent street boys from the 'Garibaldi foundling hospital'.[150] In mid-October, a second group of British volunteers arrived in Naples: these so-called 'excursionists' were around 600 strong and they fought with the army at Capua.[151] Finally, there is also evidence that British sympathisers, and notably the Glaswegian John McAdam, helped encourage and materially assist Hungarian volunteers for Garibaldi.[152]

In France, government restrictions prevented such open expressions of support. However, liberal newspapers like *Le Siècle* and *L'Opinion Nationale* did manage to receive and distribute funds for Garibaldi throughout the summer. A group in Marseille also sent a small sum to Garibaldi via Alexandre Dumas, and an attempt was made in September to circumvent political restraints by setting up a fund for a monument to Paul de Flotte, a Breton socialist and volunteer for Garibaldi killed in Calabria at the end of August. A list of seventeen subscribers (who had each donated between two and ten francs) was published in *Le Siècle* and *L'Opinion*, but the fund was quickly suppressed by the police.[153] Similar restrictions probably affected the formal organisation of a French volunteer legion for Garibaldi. Nevertheless, between 300 and 500 men made it to southern Italy via Genoa to fight with Garibaldi, and in July the French consul in Sicily was sent several complaints from parents whose young sons had run away to join Garibaldi (there was particular concern about boys from Nice, now under French control). The same Paul de Flotte organised a group of around fifty men who stayed with him from Genoa onwards, and after his death, towards the end of the campaign, Garibaldi ordered the formation of a French legion: the *légion de Flotte*.[154] Also towards the end of the campaign in October, Johann Becker, a former member of

Young Germany, arrived in Naples to form a corps of German volunteers to fight with Garibaldi.[155]

Alongside these more organised efforts, many individuals wrote privately to Garibaldi offering material support, their services, or simply their fervent admiration. At the beginning of August, Alexander Andrews wrote to Garibaldi from East Bengal of his longing 'to join the banner of liberty under the heaven Conferred destroyer of Tyrants', and offering his services as a subaltern. An American surgeon, William Holcome, wrote offering his and his wife's services ('we will *both* come to any *place* you may mention and work heartily for your cause which is an immortal one'); while William Forster wrote from Newcastle that he had been training 'for a soldier's life' in the hope that 'I might aid in the great work of Redemption'.[156] Some writers sent Garibaldi their own music and poems. A woman signing herself 'Violet' wrote from High Wycombe to express her 'deep and earnest admiration'; and she sent Garibaldi a bookmark: 'although it is a very humble offering yet it comes from one who has a warm and patriotic heart'.[157] 'Although I am a stranger to you, I will not be happy unless I express in a letter the feelings of admiration which I feel for you, for the real nobility, and the pure generosity of your character', another English woman, Fanny Blews from Birmingham, wrote to Garibaldi (in Italian). This sentiment, she claimed, was shared by all 'English women': 'The eyes of women were full of tears on reading about the glorious and intrepid actions of Garibaldi and his devoted band; and many prayers were offered to almighty God to look after the head of the general on the field of battle and glory'. She had followed his progress since 1848: 'your name was a guiding star for me . . . in this time it has become the symbol of a man who is more honourable and more loved than all the heroes of antiquity'.[158] Others wrote with requests. Thomas Watson asked Garibaldi for his autobiography ('it would gladden . . . [my] heart to look on the lines traced by the gallant hand that has so often led to victory. Don't refuse me General');[159] a Swiss baroness sent Garibaldi a copy of his own portrait and asked him to sign it and return it to her;[160] while George Barker ('a plain Englishman') asked Garibaldi for an autograph to add to his collection (which included those of Wellington and Nelson), as did a writer from Melbourne, Australia, on behalf of his seventy-five-year-old mother who had told him to 'ask the General not to delay in sending it'.[161]

Many of these letters are especially interesting for the sense of a personal relationship and of intimacy, as well as political involvement, which their authors convey to their hero. Some had met Garibaldi, and wrote to renew their acquaintance. Sarah Barfield, who had met Garibaldi in Messina and published an account of their meeting in the *Daily News*, wrote: 'May God long preserve your valuable life and when you visit England I hope you will come and see me'.[162] The wife of the British consul in Tangier in 1850 wrote to remind Garibaldi of 'the quiet and happy times' they had spent together: 'no one has followed your career with more interest and pride than I have done'; and an American who had met him in 1853 wrote with a message of political support, a lengthy account of his own life, and an invitation to visit in Boston.[163] More usually, however, such confidence was entirely imagined. As one passionate supporter of Garibaldi wrote angrily to Joseph Cowen, Mazzini's great supporter in Newcastle: 'Garibaldi, remember, is THE *man of action* at *the present* moment, and he deserves all the support we can collect. I have nothing to do with the Italian Committee here . . . I work for and with *Garibaldi & no one else* at PRESENT. The money that I receive shall be sent to HIM direct *if possible*.'[164] A fifteen-year-old, 'F. Keel' from Birmingham, sent two letters to Garibaldi asking to be allowed to join him:

> I hope that you will allow me to come to you now for I love you as I did my parents . . . [I] can stand or go through any danger or hardships for those I love, as I do you, I will do every thing in my power to please or enjoy you I will be unto you as a son should be to a father. do not think that this step is without due consideration . . . I hope you will send a letter as soon as possible for I am impatient to come to you. Please do not say no. for I shall be obliged to disobey this one request for my determination is fixed to come & serve you [*sic*].

'Hoping you are quite well and happy . . . Goodbye till we meet', the boy ended the letter.[165] By way of contrast, but still displaying this sense of personal closeness, William Cobbit sent Garibaldi a nine-page diatribe about taxes and government spending in September, along with a similar letter to a newspaper, from a debtors' prison.[166]

Many letter-writers saw in Garibaldi an expression of their own religious beliefs, especially their faith in Protestantism and their horror of Roman Catholicism.[167] Margaret Davis from Aberdare in Wales, a 'profound admirer of Garibaldi', wrote to him both of her desire to go as a nurse 'to his wounded soldiers' and of her 'involuntary' ability to do so, and of her conviction that Garibaldi would help in 'opening the door of that blessed gospel of Jesus Christ which alone makes nations as well as individuals'.[168] Religious fervour also inspired another Welsh writer, William Rayner from Swansea, to write a long letter in which he compared Garibaldi to Cromwell, and assured him that:

> prayers from my heart and thousands of Christian hearts and pulpits in this country are constantly ascending on your behalf and for your preservation in every danger until your work is done. Oh! may it be done in your own

humane and loving way and not by blood ... My dear friend your little island [Caprera] is your throne and your work the Crown set not in polished jewels or diamonds but with great and worthy deeds that shall sparkle through the distant mists of time and nothing but the great conflagration shall obliterate its light.[169]

John Spear, 'a staunch friend of Italian freedom', wrote from Dublin of his disgust at the formation of the Irish brigade to defend the Pope. They were, he assured Garibaldi, only '400 misguided fanatics' and should not be allowed to colour his attitude to Ireland. 'Now your Excellency, is a great nation to be answerable for such a *paltry piece of papal intrigue*? I almost hear a *determined* negative, thundering from your lips, and grasp the auspicious moment, to implore of you, not to listen to the voice of those, that say "*my country is your foe*".' He accordingly asked permission of Garibaldi to organise a band of excursionists, 'a noble *Irish* Legion'.[170]

That so many of these letters come from British or Anglo-Saxon sources suggests that British support for Garibaldi was especially strong. However, this may not necessarily be the case, since it may be that only the British letters to Garibaldi have survived, or were kept, while others were lost. In general, the most striking aspect of foreign support for Garibaldi was its international or cosmopolitan character, and it is possible to speak of a wave of international enthusiasm for Italy and for Garibaldi: along with Britain, the USA and France, Hungary, Poland and Germany sent volunteers to Sicily and the South. Moreover, throughout 1860, expressions of foreign support for Garibaldi, and the presence of foreign volunteers in his army, received huge attention and publicity. Foreign backing added force to the prevailing feeling that Garibaldi's campaign was both just and unstoppable, and it formed part of his government's self-image and propaganda.

Such enthusiasm is further evidence of the success of Mazzini's international publicity campaign for Italy, which had begun some twenty-five years previously. It also shows us the effect of the press and publishing in creating a community of readers with shared interests and common sentiments. Subscriptions, letters and the act of volunteering suggest the extent to which readers in Paris, London and New York had become personally and emotionally involved with Garibaldi and his fate, and they tell us that some were inspired to become more than mere spectators to political events and had decided to invest materially in their result.

As before, however, we must be careful lest we too are drawn into, and convinced by, the powerful nationalist rhetoric of 1860. The appeal of events in Italy for the British public lay in the apparently simple triumph of good over evil, and their enthusiasm reflected a sense of national satisfaction at being on the right side (and 'subjects of our devoted and beloved Queen Victoria', as the secretary of the Southampton Athenaeum wrote). It is evident from their letters and statements that many people were as transfixed by Bourbon 'tyranny' as they were fascinated by the heroism of Garibaldi. For example, a visit to, and description of, the Bourbon prisons in Naples (condemned by Gladstone in the mid-1850s) became a seemingly obligatory ritual for all the British writers who made it out to join Garibaldi in 1860.[171] So all this enthusiasm should be treated with some scepticism: a taste for morality tales and the spectacular did not always translate into lasting political engagement. Internal politics and preferences had always played a significant role in defining foreign support for Garibaldi: resistance to Napoleon III in the case of France; and a strident Protestantism (characterised by 'extraordinary wildness and nastiness', according to one of its historians)[172] in the case of Britain and the USA.

Most important of all, we must note that – with the exception of one or two officers with previous military experience – the foreign volunteers for Garibaldi were never a huge help to him and were, on occasion, a positive hindrance. There was jealousy between the French and Italian volunteers and the French men were allegedly difficult to control.[173] The British 'excursionists' caused very serious problems. These started before they even left Britain, and were created by a fake *garibaldino*, 'Captain Styles', who convinced the committee in London he was an agent of Garibaldi (see his picture in *The Illustrated London News*, figure 17 on page 256). He went about selling commissions but kept the money for himself, so that when the men arrived in Italy to find that their commissions were not recognised by Peard, their new commander, they were understandably furious. Further difficulties were caused by the Foreign Enlistment Acts, which forbade the recruitment for foreign armies on British soil. Although this problem was avoided by calling the volunteers 'excursionists', the published announcement read like a tourist advertisement, and many who went to join Garibaldi were ready for adventure and little else.[174] One journalist, who published a highly fictionalised account of his experiences as an 'excursionist', wrote of his decision to go to Sicily with friends: 'we all loved adventure, were sick of the dull routine of idle bachelor's life in town, and thought "it would not be such bad fun after all" . . . And thus it was we three friends became Garibaldini'.[175] Some were what Trevelyan calls 'roughs' from Glasgow and London, 'who considered that they were out on a holiday at other people's expense' and, although they were happy to fight, 'expected a maximum of food and good quarters and a minimum of discipline'.[176] They got drunk on the cheap wine, a group of them robbed a peasant on the Volturno, and there were real problems involved in getting them home when the campaign was over.[177] Even medical volunteers were not immune to criticism. One of them, a Dr Wolfe who went out in July with drugs and medical instruments, fell out so badly with Garibaldi's doctors (and with Jessie White Mario in particular) that he was arrested and placed in Caserta prison.[178]

Finally, while much of the material looked at in this chapter would suggest that the whole world loved Garibaldi, this was actually not the case. As we saw earlier, the right-wing press in France attacked Garibaldi in newspapers and pamphlets: they argued that Britain was the true instigator and economic beneficiary of the collapse of the Two Sicilies, and that the real victim was Francesco II.[179] One of the most passionate of all the letters to Garibaldi came from 'a patriotic Frenchman, a friend of truth, [and] enemy of falsehood', who wrote to condemn his actions ('What have you done, brigand!') and who was entirely unconvinced by the attempts to justify his attack on the Two Sicilies:

> what is the good of adding hypocrisy to all the horrors of your life? . . . no! Everyone will understand what they already know: and what your apologists also know: that your aim is to bring disorder to humanity . . . and that were your desires to be fulfilled, Europe and perhaps the universe, would be nothing more than a vast sewer of mud and blood in which you and those like you would crawl until Judgment Day.[180]

Even in Britain, the Garibaldi committee was sued more than once by an anti-Garibaldi group which objected to its recruitment for the nationalist cause.[181]

Most importantly, the combination of Piedmontese expansion into the Papal States and Garibaldi's expedition to the Two Sicilies put Catholics everywhere on the defensive against Italian nationalism. In 1859, Pius IX had adopted a visible public stance of no compromise with the Piedmontese state and this had produced 'a wave of emotion' which 'drew the hearts of Catholics towards Rome' across Europe and America.[182] Huge amounts of money were sent, in the form of a revived 'Peter's Pence', to help the Pope defend Rome and the Papal States against attack, and a wave of addresses were sent to the Pope, totalling over five and half million signatures.[183] In 1860, the French General, Lamoricière, issued a proclamation: 'The revolution now menaces Europe as once Islam used to menace it. Today as in old days the cause of the Pope is the cause of the civilization and liberty of the world'; he then went to Rome to raise an army of volunteers for the Pope.[184] French bishops responded to his call and encouraged young men to join what would be called 'the ninth crusade'. In Catholic Ireland, Archbishop Cullen launched a massive pro-papal agitation, and between February and July 1860 he organised a collection which raised a 'prodigious' £80,000 (or c. £5 million in present-day figures) for the Pope.[185] A brigade of over 1,000 Irish volunteers formed and went out to join the 500 French zouaves and 600 Belgians, and they fought at the battles of Spoleto, Castelfidardo and Ancona against the Piedmontese army.[186]

In Catholic Ireland, in other words, Garibaldi's campaign was not seen in a positive light at all, but as a threat to the Pope's temporal power. Moreover, the defence of the Pope contributed to the formation of an Irish–Catholic consciousness which could distinguish itself neatly from pro-Italian, Protestant, British identity.[187] In general, 1860 saw the mobilisation of the Catholic Church against Italian nationalism, broadly associated with the revolution and perceived as a threat to European civilisation. As one French zouave wrote: 'Nowadays the forces of Hell are known by a name that incorporates them all: the Revolution. Italy is the battleground where the great armies of Christian civilization and barbarism meet.' This campaign was extremely successful, producing a popular response on a scale which in many ways surpassed support for Italian unification. Appeals to the Catholic community were made via pamphlets and newspapers, the organisation of subscriptions, and networks of voluntary associations; and some of the French zouaves attached the Sacred Heart insignia to their uniforms, using a symbol of Catholic identity developed during the French Revolution as protection against the sign of 'Marianne'.[188] Hence the Catholic war on 'Italy' relied on propaganda methods which were all too clearly 'artefacts of political modernity'.[189]

Conclusion

Although support for Garibaldi in 1860 was not unanimous, he was definitely hard to ignore. In Sicily, he had the support of an intellectual elite and of sections of the Church, and his government was celebrated in newspapers, plays and poetry. He enjoyed considerable mass popularity, even if this popularity was tough to define and control. In the rest of Italy, his expedition to Sicily resulted in subscriptions and associations, and he quickly amassed a large and enthusiastic volunteer army. Throughout the summer, he was inundated with offers of foreign support and expressions of admiration. He posed as the 'saviour' of Sicily, and was seen as the 'Redeemer' (Saint Michael, Jesus Christ and/or Charlemagne). His calls to the nation-at-arms were reflected in volunteers' letters to their 'father' at the head of a 'holy cause'. His careful cultivation of foreign support was amply repaid by the declarations of support for the gallant (Protestant) General, fighting for the benefit of humanity (and against Rome and the Papacy).

The response of volunteers to Garibaldi's call can also be seen as a triumph for Mazzini's ideas and methods. Mazzini's propaganda strategy finally came good in 1860 and produced practical results on a significant scale.

'Garibaldianism', according to his British follower, Charles Forbes, was for Garibaldi's troops in 1860 'as completely a religion as was Mohammedanism with the fanatical followers of the prophet in the earlier days of the Koran'.[190] His statement reflects the steps taken in 1860 towards establishing nationalism as a political religion. Just as striking is the variety of understandings of Garibaldi's message. Above all, it is clear that the radical and republican aspects of the revolution were submerged beneath a more generic discourse of national revival, whose broad appeal masked a variety of sometimes self-interested and contradictory motives. Equally, we should not suppose, as many of his supporters seemed to in 1860, that Garibaldi carried all before him, or that his conquest of southern Italy represented the inevitable defeat of political conservatism and the Roman Catholic religion.

In August 1860, as Garibaldi prepared to relaunch his war against the Bourbons on the Italian mainland, he made the following speech to his officers and soldiers:

> Among those qualities which must prevail among the Officers of the Italian Army, apart from bravery, there must also be kindness, which will attract and keep the affection of the soldier . . . A strict discipline can be obtained with severity; but it is preferable to obtain it with affection and leadership . . . It would be impossible . . . for a soldier in the field of battle to abandon his dear officer, who has treated him kindly, who has smiled at him in times of need, and with whom he has shared the trials and glories of a campaign. For this reason an officer must take special care to stay with his soldiers, and to look after them, as if they were his own family.[191]

In this passage, Garibaldi recognises the importance of affective ties to the functioning of his army and, more broadly, of appeals to emotion as the basis of his popularity. It was a sense of belonging (to a 'family') and affection for the national 'community' which lay at the root of the decision of so many men to leave their homes and fight with him for 'Italy' in 1860. These emotions offer powerful evidence for the formation of a national community in Italy, however complex, contingent or constructed.[192]

Although I have stressed caution in approaching much of the evidence presented in this chapter, it still suggests that the achievement of Garibaldi's dictatorship in creating a passionate sense of political identity in 1860 was quite considerable. These elements of a nationalist religion created by Garibaldi were neither especially authoritarian nor entirely one-way. The reactions to Garibaldi which I have looked at here point to his appeal being based on a fusion of authoritarian and democratic symbols. It was his capacity to be both magnificent and humble to which people responded; and it was the juxtaposition, beloved of democratic iconography and used so frequently in the letters and stories of 1860, of political achievement and private simplicity which seemingly made the most impression on the public imagination. Although, by 1860, he had left his more dangerous bandit persona far behind, Garibaldi still appealed to radicals, or to those who sought political, religious and social change, and to those who sought, more simply, an alternative form of political identity or a means of social escape.

Equally, Garibaldi fashioned himself, but he was not the only source of the cult which surrounded him. In the vast theatre which characterised the production of the Garibaldi cult in 1860 – the symbols and associations, speeches and newspapers, the memoirs, novels, plays and letters – it is not always clear who is controlling whom, or who is the 'transmitter' and who the 'receiver' in this process of communication. The creation of the cult of Garibaldi can perhaps be more accurately defined as, in Marjan Schwegman's words, 'a dynamic, highly international, interactive work of art created by many different men and women', a product which was political because it publicised and inspired adherence to a political project 'that the public was supposed to act out in their own life'.[193] This 'interactive' nature of Garibaldi's appeal can explain why such a wide range of groups found in him something to react to. It may also help to account for the intensely emotional response to Garibaldi (the feelings of personal involvement with his programme, or of intimacy with and confidence in him) which is typical of the correspondence of those, like volunteers or foreign women, who had never actually met him or known the places he fought for. So, while Garibaldi's message in 1860 may seem somewhat equivocal and his charisma artificially constructed and promoted, its reception was in many ways spontaneous and creative, and the responses to him were genuinely felt.

CHAPTER 11

UNIFICATION

Caprera

Garibaldi threw away a huge political advantage when he agreed to hand over power to Piedmont and retired 'backstage' to Caprera in November 1860. At least initially, however, he was not aware of the scale of his defeat. On 18 October, he wrote simply to Mazzini that 'if one must concede it is better to do so with good grace'.[1] He was careful to thank everybody who had helped in the expedition, which may suggest he was planning to call on their support another time. He wrote a public letter to the Garibaldi committee in New York, in which he thanked them and the 'generous American people', and told them that 'the enterprise is not completed. There is a part of our family still oppressed by atrocious despotism . . . you must not abandon your work for us.'[2] He explicitly told the Italian committee, in another public letter, 'don't disband. Do not abandon the enterprise half-way. What you did in the name of Sicily and Naples, you must also do for Rome and Venice.'[3] He wrote to the Polish émigré Ludwik Mieroslawksi that 'my withdrawal to Caprera is not a desertion of the cause of the people to which I have dedicated my whole life.'[4] Finally, he even wrote as much to the king, telling him that he was going to Caprera in order to get himself ready, that 'soon Your Majesty will be called to finish that great task for which Providence has destined you', and that, in this case, 'I would consider myself very fortunate to be numbered among your soldiers.'[5] With his generals, Garibaldi also envisaged the creation of five armed divisions – the *Cacciatori delle Alpi* – made up of his southern army, foreign volunteers, and any other volunteers not subject to the national conscription laws; and these were to be stationed in various regions of Italy in readiness for the next war against Austria.[6] Everything suggested, in other words, that Garibaldi left for Caprera planning another campaign for Venice and/or Rome over the following summer, and did not consider that the struggle for Italy was over.

The winter spent in Caprera did little to alter his expectations and ambitions. Fund-raising activities continued, and in January Bertani relaunched the 1860 'committees of aid' as 'committees of assistance' for Rome and Venice with Garibaldi as president. Accepting the appointment, Garibaldi wrote to the committee that they must have 'as the password for every day, every moment, repeated incessantly to every committee and tried by every other means to be absorbed into the minds of every Italian: – that in the forthcoming spring of this year 1861 Italy must, without mercy, put a million patriots to arms'. To that end, he recommended that they set up a newspaper, *Roma e Venezia*.[7] At this point, he still saw Austria – rather than the Pope – as the main adversary. His letter to Mieroslawksi, in which he also stated his support for 'our brave Poles', was re-dated and published in *Il Diritto*.[8] To Mazzini he wrote that he would prefer to fight for Venice first: 'We have a vast theatre of operations: – that is from the mouth of the Danube to the mouth of the Po'.[9] 'I am sure that Italy can fight its war of redemption again this year', he wrote to the British political leader 'John Russel' [*sic*], in London in early March.[10]

Garibaldi had good reason to be confident. His prestige in early 1861 was immense: 'dominating the picture we have the gigantic figure of Garibaldi growing bigger and bigger on his rock at Caprera and casting his enormous shadow even at this distance', the diplomat Costantino Nigra wrote to Cavour from Naples in March.[11] In the national elections of January 1861, Garibaldi won seats in several constituencies, and chose to represent Naples (although he did not travel to parliament when it met in February). Letters of support and various honours were sent to Garibaldi by many municipal governments, including those of Pavia and Turin, the Workers' Club of Parma and a women's group in Como.[12] The Council in Lodi declared 11 May (the date of arrival in Marsala) a 'citizens' holiday', with money to be given to the families of those who had fought with Garibaldi.[13] At the end of March, the Italian Unitary Association in Milan made him their president (his letter of acceptance was published in the main nationalist papers); and in early April he received a delegation from the workers' clubs (*società operaie*), and the speeches made on that occasion were published in *Il Diritto*.[14] In Palermo, a new version of the paper *Il Garibaldi* was published in January and February; a collection of poetry appeared in Catania to celebrate his name-day (San Giuseppe);[15] and the priest Carmelo Pardi gave a published speech to commemorate the first anniversary of the April revolt which had brought Garibaldi to Sicily.[16]

Caprera itself was the centre of intense activity. Apart from his children, Teresita and Menotti, there was Fruscianti, who looked after the farm, the Deideri couple, who had acted as Teresita's parents when she was a child, and various other semi-permanent residents, including Specchi, Carpeneto and

Basso, who worked as his secretaries. Moreover, Garibaldi's celebrated solitude was, in his own words, 'shattered by visitors'.[17] His close political friends, Bixio and Vecchi, came to stay for extended periods; a number of artists came to paint and sculpt him; and Timoteo Riboli, a phrenologist, came to study his skull. The latter became a friend of, and physician to, Garibaldi, and made a public announcement that his head was 'remarkable ... the craniology of the head ... offers an original phenomenality of the rarest kind, one might even say unprecedented: the harmony of all the organs is perfect ... a marvellous, organic, faultless head'.[18] Johann Becker, the 'German Garibaldi', came to Caprera to discuss his plans for an Italian–German alliance against Austrian and French 'despotism'.[19] The Scottish radical, John McAdam, arrived (after a terrible journey in midwinter) with money from the Glasgow Ladies Sick and Wounded Fund, and conceived an elaborate plan to set up a salmon hatchery on Caprera.[20] A stream of uninvited admirers also arrived almost continuously and were seemingly always welcomed. Vecchi remarked that 'the presence of the General in Caprera' was a 'god-send' to the neighbouring village of La Maddalena: a 'sort of inn' even opened to put up the tourists.[21]

Garibaldi's home at Caprera became an integral part of his fame. This process had begun in 1860, when Garibaldi's sometime lover, Esperanza von Schwartz, published an account of her visit a few years earlier, in German, English and French. She described the wild beauty of Caprera, where 'the Cincinnatus of our time has withdrawn himself from the world and its delusive hopes [in 1858]', as well as offering a host of details about his private life: the design of his house; the well-kept garden; his books; his children and the family's lifestyle on Caprera; and his love for his late wife.[22] Thereafter, Garibaldi's simple life on Caprera became a form of public display. However genuine his own commitment may have been to farming the land and making a personal life for himself, the image of a 'modern Cincinnatus' captured the public imagination and made Caprera anything but a private place. Frank Vizitelly of *The Illustrated London News* went specially to Caprera on his way home at the end of the campaign 'to close my correspondence with a few illustrations of the island home of the modern Cincinnatus'. Although he warned his readers not to expect intimate descriptions ('I visited General Garibaldi as a friend ... and doubtlessly, he will expect from me but gentlemanly treatment in whatever I may write respecting him and his home'), he offered them exhaustive details of the house, and of Garibaldi and his family's behaviour, along with seven illustrations of Garibaldi at home.[23] These included *General Garibaldi spearing fish by night off Caprera* ('it is impossible to conceive anything more picturesque', see figure 23 opposite), and *The farmyard*, which showed a

GENERAL GARIBALDI SPEARING FISH BY NIGHT OFF CAPRERA.—FROM A SKETCH BY OUR SPECIAL ARTIST, FRANK VIZETELLY.—SEE PAGE 72.

23   This illustration by Vizitelly of Garibaldi spearing fish both reflects, and contributed to, the mythology of his life at Caprera.

bucolic scene of Garibaldi feeding his dog with his horse 'Marsala' impatiently pawing the ground next to him.

From Caprera, Vizitelly's prose and pictures took up the juxtaposition of the public figure and the private man which had already been a potent feature of journalism in 1860, and turned the glimpses of Garibaldi's intimate life into a form of popular theatre:

here am I, sitting peaceably under the roof and partaking of the hospitality of the man who seven months since . . . raised the standard of freedom on the shores of Sicily, and threw his gauntlet at the feet of Francis II and his legions. As I write this I can see Giuseppe Garibaldi, the undoer and maker of Kings, trundling along a barrowful of roots that he has grubbed from the rocky soil . . . Little dreamt I when, nearly seven months ago, I shook hands with that daring revolutionist, the morning after his entry into Palermo, that seven months later I should congratulate him on his complete success in his cottage at Caprera.

The iconographic fascination of Caprera persisted into the following year, and thereafter. In May 1862, a colour print of *Garibaldi in his island home* was published in Newcastle 'and dedicated to the People of United Italy'. Garibaldi's pose was copied from a famous photograph, but the landscape was pure invention: a mix of classical and romantic references featuring a stormy sea, an overhanging rock, and two goats grazing nearby.[24] The same attraction can be observed in the first numbers of a serialised Italian Album, published by Terzaghi of Milan. This took up the story of Garibaldi's life after his departure from Naples; and illustrations included *The hermit of Caprera* (Garibaldi with spade, surrounded by farm animals, looking tired and downcast, see figure 24 below); the happier and openly patriotic *Garibaldi in the heart of his family* (Garibaldi sits on a sofa in front of a map of Italy and reads *Il Diritto*, surrounded by his personal and political family); and the more sensational *A young Spaniard who prefers to kill himself than leave Garibaldi* (the accompanying text explains that the man 'had made an idol of Garibaldi, and no longer being able to live with him, had decided to die where he lived'; see figure 25 opposite).[25] In 1866, the German illustrated paper, *Die*

Il Romito di Caprera.

24 'The hermit of Caprera': a popular representation of Garibaldi at Caprera. Contemporary prints made much of his solitary existence, his work in the fields (suggested by the spade) and his relationship with the farm animals.

Un giovane Spagnuolo che preferisce d'uccidersi anziacché allontanarsi da Garibaldi.

25 'A young Spaniard who prefers to kill himself than leave Garibaldi'. Note also Garibaldi's white house in the background here and in figure 24: an essential element of the established iconography of Caprera.

Gartenlaube, published an article on 'the Cincinnatus of Caprera', with the usual details of his happy family life.[26] These publications also helped define a new phase in the cult of Garibaldi, in which interest in his private life and character competed with awareness of his political concerns and objectives.

In turn, however, Caprera acquired a political significance as the physical representation of Garibaldi's reputation. Engaging loosely with a symbolism inherited from the American and French revolutions, where public greatness was matched by private virtue, Garibaldi's lifestyle on Caprera seemed proof that he was a 'genuine' hero, whose personal modesty was unaffected by his political fame. Each writer used this juxtaposition in different ways, but the rhetorical point remained the same. 'All eyes are turned at this moment on a little, almost inaccessible and completely barren island, lost in the heart of the Mediterranean', the French volunteer Emile Maison wrote, praising Garibaldi's military talent and his personal diffidence. Riboli published his description of Garibaldi's exceptional head and ordinary life in the French radical paper *Le Siècle*.[27] A British visitor described Garibaldi's friendliness to him at Caprera: 'I was soon impressed with the belief that the General was not only the bravest of warriors and the purest of patriots, but also the prince of gentlemen.'[28] In Modena, an Abate Bazzani dedicated an Ode 'To Garibaldi in Caprera', in which he praised equally his greatness and his selflessness; and in Naples, a priest, Domenico Jonata, wrote a 'political constitutional catechism' designed to teach 'the people' democratic principles, and dedicated it to the 'immortal Giuseppe Garibaldi' on his 'humble . . . home, the happy island of Caprera'.[29]

The person who probably did most for Caprera was Colonel Vecchi, whose book, *Garibaldi a Caprera*, was translated into English, Dutch, French (published in Holland presumably to avoid censorship problems), Swedish and German.[30] Like the others, Vecchi made a great deal of the simplicity of Caprera and the dedication of Garibaldi to his farm; like the others, he described in detail his frugal but happy private life, the feminine talents of his daughter, Teresita, and the names of his animals (notably the fact that one donkey was called Pius IX). He too stressed Garibaldi's greatness ('[t]he days that I passed by the side of my General are like a fugitive but brilliant dream') and his gentleness (there is one passage in which Garibaldi searches all night for a lost lamb).[31] But Vecchi went one step further, and sought to sacralise Caprera and, with it, the man who had made his home there:

> Who can visit Caprera without emotion? . . . He is about to step on a shore made illustrious by the highest human excellence, and he feels his thoughts softened, elevated and enchanted. Even at the distant point where the boat lands, perched amid great lumps of granite rock, that little white house is visible, an object of deep affection to how many human creatures! Within dwells an exceptional, I might say an almost superhuman being. It is the den of the Italian Lion. It is the refuge of the friend of mankind. It is the fountain-head of all that is noble, generous and holy. It is the oasis of peace of Giuseppe Garibaldi![32]

In reality, Garibaldi spent most of the winter engaging in a vast correspondence: 'there were three people employed in answering the heaps of letters that arrived daily for the General', according to Vecchi, who also helped out with answering letters.[33] John McAdam noted that Garibaldi worked incessantly on his correspondence, continuing to write after supper, dictating to his secretaries in bed, and getting up before dawn to work with them again.[34] 'My correspondence quite exceeds my capacity, and the capacity of those who assist me in writing', Garibaldi admitted to Mazzini;[35] and many of his letters of this period are written in another hand and bear just his signature.

As in 1860, it was foreign letters which filled Garibaldi's postbag. For example, Elisanter, the editor of *Die Deutsche Zeitung*, wrote from Berlin of the support of his paper (which showed, he said, that not all Germans thought like the Austrians), and to invite him to the city.[36] Many were content to send Garibaldi gifts or expressions of their admiration. A company in Milan sent him 'the proverbial *Panettone*' for Christmas 1860; a *garibaldino* sent him nougat and mustard from Cremona; Zeffira Levi made him a flag ('what an Italian woman who can't do more must do'); while Margherita de Sanctis, of the Institution Dolet in Naples, composed a verse: 'Napoli calls you, Palermo desires you. Your brave men invoke your name. The whole world admires you! ... Venezia cries sighs and waits for you. Rome quivers, but hopes. Only Caprera is happy. The heavens bless and protect you. The fair sex adores you, and I hold you carved in my heart.'[37] One group wrote from Brussels to tell Garibaldi that they had 'woken his spirit' in a seance: the spirit had told them that he had landed in Catania with two friends disguised as him, and that his soul 'was that of Hannibal'.[38] Manfred Warmund wrote enclosing a song and expressed his great esteem for Garibaldi ('Believe me, 100,000 young Germans think like me'); and an anonymous fan letter arrived from Bremen written in Latin.[39] A French writer sent a letter from Aix-en-Provence to tell Garibaldi: 'You are great! you are noble! ... I admire you, I envy you ... Heaven has elected you to change completely the destiny of *beautiful Italy* ... so *Courage* ... *Courage, Courage!*';[40] while a professional female companion, 'E. Birkardt', wrote to Garibaldi from Nice to ask if she could come and live with him in Caprera.[41]

Perhaps excited by the prospect of a war for Rome, British Protestants were especially frequent correspondents. Few were as colourful as Paul Doig, who from Stirling sent Garibaldi a handwritten extract from the Book of Revelation: 'Fall of Rome by Fire' ('[t]he great whore spoken of (as you will observe) is a city, and that city, terrible Rome'), but all were hugely enthusiastic. Another Scot, Julia Lees, wrote from 'poor, Priest-ridden Ireland': she filled eight dense pages with religious fervour and sent him a copy of the New Testament, 'not too large, I hope, to be easily carried about, so as to be your friend, a companion'.[42] Culling Eardley, the president of the Evangelical Alliance, asked for Garibaldi's help in the battle against Catholic intolerance, and William Ashley, of the same, sent him a copy of the 'Polyglot bible'.[43] Thomas Scott, secretary of the Reformed Romanist Priests Protection Society (whose motto was 'Christ and not the crucifix all over the world'), wrote from Dublin to invite Garibaldi to speak in Ireland, and assured him (rather implausibly) that he would be given a good 'Irish welcome'. A final indication of the strength of these religious associations with Garibaldi comes from a Charles Turner in London, who wrote nine detailed pages to tell him of the error of his ways: 'you have gone forth with the deadly sword against your Brothers in the same faith'. In the letter's climax, the author asked Garibaldi:

Can you obtain Mercy, can you be forgiven, can you repent, can you humble yourself in dust and ashes. Can tears run down like a river before God. Can you lift up your eyes to *Christ* . . . Sir, you have sent many down to death . . . You Sir are grievously sinning against God, against men and against your own *Soul* . . . Sir tremble at his Majesty – *go not forth again with the Sword of war.*[44]

Parliament

Garibaldi's remarkable stature in this period, and the strong public reaction to him, are worth stressing because they masked less happy political developments and, to an extent, prevented serious discussion of them. During 1861, divisions began to open up in the democratic movement, as activists took stock of the new political situation. In particular, they had to respond to the extension of a parliamentary system throughout almost the whole Italian peninsula, and to reconsider their policy on revolutionary action. Alessandro Galante Garrone has identified three main currents which emerged within the democratic left immediately after unification: the first, led by the Tuscan democrat, Antonio Mordini, which concentrated entirely on parliamentary activity; a second led by Francesco Crispi, who insisted that 'we must remain within the law'[45] but also pursued extra-parliamentary agitation and associations; and a third, more 'extreme' left, headed by Bertani, which, while not excluding parliamentary action (and thus disagreeing with Mazzini), remained fully committed to the idea of revolution in Italy. Garibaldi leaned mostly towards Bertani's line, and even grew closer to Mazzini in these months, but part of his leadership in 1860 – Medici, Bixio, Türr and Sirtori – moved towards a compromise with the Piedmontese government, and accepted positions in the Piedmontese army. Garibaldi himself continued to believe that King Vittorio Emanuele could in some way lead the revolution.[46] Effectively, therefore, the democrats lacked a clear policy or an agreed single response to the achievement of national unification; or as Garibaldi wrote to Mazzini: 'In terms of projects – I have none. I limit myself to gathering the means.'[47] Cavour was less charitable, writing (in late September 1860) to one close colleague that 'Garibaldi has not a single clear political idea'. Yet Garibaldi's prestige meant that these problems were rarely discussed openly, and that members of the left felt obliged publicly (if not privately) to unite behind him.[48]

The confusion in the democratic camp gave Cavour a great advantage. In the first elections following the October plebiscites in January 1861, government candidates won a major victory, while leading democrats were defeated. At the same time, Cavour and his allies began to move against the *garibaldini* in southern Italy, determined both to oust them from their positions in government and administration and to prevent Garibaldi's volunteer army from being incorporated into the Piedmontese military.[49] Particularly ruthless was the decision, planned and put through by General Fanti, essentially to liquidate Garibaldi's army. By a decree of 16 November 1860, all his officers and soldiers had to pass before a special commission, and this commission excluded huge numbers of them, notably all foreign volunteers (apart from a few Hungarian officers) and the volunteers from southern Italy.[50] In January 1861, the national guards in southern Italy were also disbanded and replaced with the much more elitist Piedmontese model.[51] By the spring of 1861, it was clear that very few of Garibaldi's officers or soldiers had been transferred into the regular army and, in April, new regulations were introduced putting an absolute limit on the numbers that could be admitted.

However, the action against the democrats in the South was a disastrous mistake. It removed a relatively sound basis of political support and material force for the government, and created in its place a large pool of disaffected, displaced young men, to add to the security problems of crime and brigandage and to create a series of political threats (reaction and republicanism) in southern Italy.[52] The mistake was even recognised by the king who, unlike Cavour, had seen the enthusiasm of the volunteers in Naples and wrote that their dissolution was 'bringing with it a great hatred ... has done grave damage, and may yet do more'.[53] Its more immediate effect was to infuriate Garibaldi. He decided to leave Caprera in early April and travel to the new capital of Italy, Turin, to take his seat in parliament and there protest publicly against the treatment of his volunteers and oppose the measures for the national guards. He wrote a letter to Urbano Rattazzi, the president of the Chamber of Deputies, in which he decried '[t]he deplorable conditions in southern Italy and the unjust abandonment of my brave companions-at-arms' and expressed his distaste 'towards those who are the cause of so much disorder and injustice'. The letter was widely publicised: it was read out by Rattazzi in parliament and published in *Il Diritto*.[54]

Garibaldi followed the letter up by his first public appearance since his departure from Naples in November 1860, this time at the parliament in Turin. His appearance was delayed by a few days due to an attack of rheumatism, during which Garibaldi added to general speculation by refusing to speak to members of the press (although he did find time to seduce two British women, who subsequently wrote him letters filled with passionate personal and political prose).[55] His arrival at parliament on 18 April caused enormous media and public interest: 'such a multitude as I never saw assembled at this place ... an unusual swarming, even in the square before the

Palace and the adjoining streets', the *Times* correspondent commented.[56] Garibaldi entered the chamber to the wild applause of a packed gallery (full of women, according to one account) but to the 'cold silence' of most of the deputies, and he took his seat on the extreme left. His political attitude was expressed clearly in his clothes. Instead of wearing a suit like all the other politicians (as he had done in parliament during the previous session), he had put on what one French diplomat called 'his usual dress, his immortal red shirt with a grey overmantle . . . [which] made him look like a prophet – or, if you prefer, like an old vaudeville actor'.[57] His appearance was obviously theatrical and intended to mark his political distance from parliamentary proceedings. If there had been any doubt about his meaning, it was dispelled by his speech. He began slowly and fumblingly, only to launch swiftly into a tirade against Cavour. First rejecting any hope of reconciliation with a man 'who has made me a stranger in Italy' (both a specific reference to the cession of Nice, and a wider appeal to a standard Risorgimento trope),[58] he then caused uproar in the chamber by accusing Cavour of provoking a 'fratricidal war' in his treatment of the volunteers.[59] He repeated the accusation, at which point, in the words of the *Times* correspondent: 'the din of voices became terrific . . . The *mêlée* in the centre of the hall . . . was truly appalling. In the midst of it all Crispi was seen bawling, gesticulating like a maniac. Chaos reigned for 15 or 20 minutes.'[60]

The political fallout from Garibaldi's speech was considerable. Widely reported in the press, it made public and visible, almost for the first time, the real disagreement about Italy's future which divided Garibaldi and his followers from the moderate liberals. The parliamentary debate which followed was less violent than Garibaldi's opening salvo, but, in the discussions of the treatment of his volunteers in 1859 and his management of the campaign of 1860, the depth of bitterness and contempt on both sides was plainly revealed. At the time, Nino Bixio tried to cover up the cracks by telling the chamber that 'Garibaldi's words should not be taken too literally or be given the same weight as if they were written', but he seems to have convinced no one.[61] Moreover, the dispute continued in the press. Two days after these events, General Cialdini wrote a public letter to Garibaldi – 'You are not the man I thought you were' – criticising his attitude to the king and his 'outlandish costume' and stating that the Piedmontese army had saved his volunteers at the Volturno.[62] Garibaldi, of course, replied in print defending his military and political conduct (and adding, '[a]s for my way of dressing I will continue to wear [those clothes] until I am told that I am no longer in a free country where anyone can dress as they please'), and his letter was published in *Il Diritto*, *L'Unità Italiana*, *La Nuova Europa* and *Il Popolo d'Italia*. The quarrel was halted only by a meeting between the main protagonists, brokered by the king but, at the meeting, 'I did not shake

Cavour's hand or seek a reconciliation', Garibaldi confirmed to his secretary, Guerzoni.[63]

This particular episode was brought to a close by Cavour's sudden death of a fever in early June, but the clash between Cavour and Garibaldi had a long-term significance. First, it offered vivid evidence of a substantive struggle for power between moderates and democrats, which focused on a central issue for the new Italy: control of the armed forces. Second, the public staging of the struggle – Garibaldi's theatrical appearance; the debate in parliament; and the detailed personal and political accusations – points us to the importance the antagonists placed on establishing and controlling the public memory of recent events. Finally, Garibaldi, and the left in general, came off rather the worse in the struggle. Garibaldi succeeded admirably in displaying his contempt for Cavour and the parliamentary hierarchy, but it is difficult to see what else he achieved. By late April, it was really too late to save his southern army; and Garibaldi himself seems to have recognised this fact by leaving the chamber before the crucial vote, and writing to Cavour some weeks later of the need once more for them to work together.[64] Moreover, while Cavour won considerable praise and sympathy for his dignity during the parliamentary debate,[65] nobody sought to defend Garibaldi's behaviour (as we saw, even Bixio told the deputies not to take him seriously; and Sir James Hudson, the British minister in Turin, called him a 'wild amphibious creature').[66] Thus, while unquestionably spectacular, Garibaldi's first foray into Italian politics after national unification cannot be considered a success. It did little to solve the problems of leadership, organisational unity and policy-making which beset the radical movement as it confronted the changed circumstances of national unification.

Aspromonte

After the clash in parliament, Garibaldi returned to Caprera, and seems to have accepted that there would be no military action that summer. For a while, he considered going back to the United States, where civil war had broken out, and taking up a command in the Union army.[67] There were rumours that he would lead an expedition to Montenegro; the Austrian government feared he would organise an uprising in Dalmatia to coincide with one in Hungary; and the French government heard that he was planning to land in Catalonia to provoke a revolution in Spain.[68] However, the real initiative came much closer to home. In the course of 1861, Agostino Bertani worked furiously to bring together the various workers' clubs, democratic committees and patriotic associations into a single, broadly based radical movement. 'This', as Bertani wrote to Crispi, 'will give us freedom of action, put Garibaldi in his place, and allow us to direct him to wherever our fatherland needs him.'[69] In December, these groups met in Genoa and agreed to form a single organisation: the Italian Freedom Association (*Associazione Emancipatrice Italiana*), which held its inaugural meeting in March 1862. Garibaldi attended as president, and he made the opening speech calling on the left to unite their forces (like the 'Roman fasces') and focus on Rome and Venice.[70]

This conference coincided with important shifts in government policy at Turin. King Vittorio Emanuele saw in Cavour's death an opportunity to involve himself more directly in politics and, as a result of his political machinations, a new government was formed in March 1862 by the king's ally, Urbano Rattazzi. The responsibility for what happened next was denied by the king and by Rattazzi. However, it seems likely that they both contacted Garibaldi in the hope of bypassing parliament and gaining a political advantage over their opponents. The king seemingly sought to involve Garibaldi in two different schemes for the Balkans: first, to attack Austria somewhere in Dalmatia as a means of gaining control of Venice; and second, to put pressure on Greece so that the government there would accept the king's second son as the country's new monarch. Rattazzi made a million lire available to Garibaldi for purposes which remained deliberately vague.[71]

Throughout this time, Garibaldi remained as popular as ever. He was inundated with letters from every group and every corner of Italy and abroad: by men and women offering their services, pleading with him to liberate Rome and Venice, sending him poems and gifts, and asking for his autograph or for permission to dedicate a book to him.[72] Altogether, they testify to Garibaldi's continuing capacity to encourage multiple forms of political ambition and attract an intense sense of personal belonging. For example, a Spanish general, a veteran of the Peninsular war, wrote offering his 'feeble services' as a soldier ('old officers are ever young, when the hour comes to do their duty');[73] while Victor Clément, a Parisian cobbler, wrote a poem to him as a fellow artisan ('Leave futile joys to others, Garibaldi only needs truly useful things').[74] 'Some women' from Brandenburg saw in him a way of becoming public. They asked him for a piece of his red shirt so that they could match the colour and make shirts for themselves, and in this way 'pay you homage in the face of the whole world, not just in an intimate way, but also in our external clothing'.[75] A radical priest in Genoa sent Garibaldi his publications on popular education (for 'both sexes to distribute also in the countryside'), and assured him that 'in my small way with my voice and my pen, I will not cease being a priest of God and of the people';[76] and someone wrote from Livorno simply to tell him that Italy and the world were ready for his call: just the smallest sign would be enough to show that 'the Lion of Caprera is returning . . . to the field of action . . .'.[77]

It was in this mood of popular and political expectation that Garibaldi embarked on a government-sponsored tour of Lombardy. The aim of the tour was to promote the new rifle clubs (*Società del tiro a segno*); and, while royal control of these clubs was obvious from the start (Crown Prince Umberto was the president), Garibaldi saw in them the possibility of reviving his military idea of the nation-at-arms and of linking it to the new political initiative made by the democratic Freedom Association. The tour was a publicity triumph. It was the occasion for speeches and commemorations, for a celebrated meeting in Milan with the novelist, Alessandro Manzoni, and for huge public demonstrations in support of 'Rome and Venice'.[78] During all these events, Garibaldi used his personality to recruit men and raise money for Venice, as well as to promote the idea of the nation-at-arms to a very wide cross-section of the population. He personally sought to establish local clubs in every town and small village that he visited.[79] Through his indefatigable correspondence, he tried to reach an even larger audience. In innumerable letters he encouraged the recruitment of peasants ('[j]oin up, my good friends of the fields, most noble class of agricultural workers; come together in fraternal maniples'); accepted the presidency of workers' clubs and local patriotic associations throughout Italy; welcomed priests; and sought to involve women's groups from all over Italy.[80] The results reflect the tangible impact of Garibaldi's presence, and the continuing appeal of his name. Letters of support for the rifle clubs followed his route through the provinces of Bergamo, Brescia, Cremona and Parma. From the South and Sicily, letters of support also arrived from local governments and other groups anxious to identify themselves with this new initiative and the 'already legendary figure of Garibaldi'.[81]

But this spectacle of patriotic unity was brought to an abrupt halt in early May. A group of volunteers, led by the *garibaldino* Francesco Nullo, was arrested by the Italian army at Sarnico on Lago d'Iseo, near the Austrian border. The government claimed that they had been preparing to attack Austria in the south Tyrol. A popular demonstration in favour of the arrested men took place in Brescia, but was broken up by the police, who fired on the crowd killing some of them. Garibaldi published a letter condemning the 'massacre of Brescia' in *Il Diritto*.[82] Crispi and Rattazzi clashed dramatically in parliament. Crispi accused Rattazzi of inventing a plot for his 'personal advantage': Sarnico was 'a fairy tale, a phantasmagoria, one of those dramatic incidents orchestrated by the government' and designed to discredit Garibaldi.[83] For the left, Sarnico raised again the dilemma of choosing between parliamentary action and revolution. All hope for Venice seemed lost, and Garibaldi took himself off to Caprera.

In Caprera, however, events took an entirely new turn. Towards the end of

June, Garibaldi left Caprera, but this time he sailed south to Sicily, apparently once more with the support of the government.[84] His plans at this stage were quite unclear: 'yes . . . we will go to Palermo and there we will see', he is said to have remarked to his companions as they approached the coast of Sicily.[85] He was greeted by the prefect of Palermo, his old friend Giorgio Pallavicino Trivulzio, and was taken to the royal palace, where he was given the same rooms in the 'pavilion' above the Porta Nuova which he had used in 1860. The sense of unfinished business was palpable. To Crispi, Garibaldi wrote on 8 July: 'things are going well, although I don't know what we will do next. In any case, we must get out of this mud, with the same programme and the right men.'[86] A week later he wrote to the British journalist, James Stuart, asking him to raise a loan of £20,000 in England 'for Rome' ('[i]n Italy this can't take place without compromising the secrecy which is necessary for my plans').[87] He wrote a series of letters to Masonic lodges asking for their help in taking Rome ('[s]tupid and wicked are those who do not rush to the defence of their own mother').[88] And on 23 July, he wrote a lengthy address to 'Roman women' (published in *Il Diritto* and *L'Unità Italiana*) in which he told them:

> Women [*Matrone*] of Rome, *Rome or Death* has rung again in the land of the Vespers. Have hope! In this land of volcanoes a flame leaps which will burn the throne of tryants! *Rome or Death!* . . . Rome, the mother of Italian greatness! . . . Rome, oh Rome! He who pronounces your name and is not moved to take up arms and redeem you did not deserve the gentle touch of his mother, or the ardent kiss of his lover . . . I am with you until death, oh women.[89]

So Rome it was to be. In Sicily itself, where Garibaldi was followed closely by the press, he made speech after speech, and created a new style of impromptu dialogues with his audience. From the Hotel Trinacria, the town hall, the Teatro Garibaldi, and the Convento della Gancia in Palermo, he travelled to Cefalù, Termini Imerese, Corleone, Misilmeri and Trapani, making short, emotive statements and establishing dialogues with the crowd ('You know I am a friend of the people, yes, friend, of the people, and above all of the Sicilian people . . . People of Palermo . . . Rome is ours [*the crowd: Ours, ours*] . . . out, out with Napoleon! [*Out, out*]'). Finally at Marsala, he raised the cry which was to set the tone for the expedition, and which he used again and again: 'Rome or Death'.[90] In rhetoric and in practice, Garibaldi's attempt to raise a volunteer army in Sicily in 1862 and seize Rome from the Pope followed a familiar Risorgimento formula. In order to gain momentum, he relied heavily on the force of his own appeal to the people and on publicity in the press; and the absence of any detailed planning suggests that he hoped, once again, to wrong-foot his opponents, rush to Rome with his men and present the government with a seemingly spontaneous *fait accompli*. At the very least, by his actions he hoped to gain publicity, and maintain the questions of Rome and Venice as issues on the political agenda.

For this plan, he had certainly chosen the right place to start. Apart from the evidence of Rattazzi's collusion with the campaign, the security forces in Sicily had very little control over the island. Local officials lacked proper instructions about how to deal with Garibaldi, and even senior members of the administration believed – quite understandably – that he had the full support of the government. Volunteers later questioned about their motives for joining Garibaldi claimed to have been convinced that 'everything would go like it did in 1860'.[91] For all these reasons, Garibaldi was allowed to pass south-eastwards and unimpeded through the interior of Sicily, raising the cry of 'Rome or Death' and encouraging men to join his campaign. In August, he and his volunteers (now some 4,000 men) converged in three columns on Catania, which they entered at 2 a.m. on 19 August and were 'met by an immense crowd'.[92] Although on the following day the government finally responded by declaring martial law in Sicily and the mainland South, on 25 August Garibaldi was allowed openly to cross the Straits of Messina with his men, and to land on the shores of Calabria.[93]

Having done up to then remarkably little to stop Garibaldi, the government now cracked down with considerable force. On 26 August, the arrest of all those 'who were part of the band of Garibaldi or took part in any way in the rebellion' was ordered. On 28 August, three left-wing parliamentarians were arrested in Naples. On the same day, emergency powers were introduced in Catania, which included a general disarmament and a ban on the wearing of red shirts and berets.[94] On 29 August, Garibaldi and his volunteers were halted by Italian troops in the mountains of Aspromonte. In the resulting confusion, firing broke out and Garibaldi was badly wounded in the foot. Another group of *garibaldini*, left in Sicily in the hills above Acireale, was also caught by the army, which shot dead seven of them. General Cialdini, who had arrived in Messina on 27 August, issued a decree stating that 'all those who are caught armed and vagrant in the countryside and villages . . . [should] be considered and treated as brigands'. During the same days, the government took advantage of martial law to suspend the freedom of the press, and to dissolve the Societies for Freedom, set up by the democrats in Genoa during the previous March. There followed a general military crackdown throughout Sicily which lasted until mid-November.[95]

'Aspromonte', as the whole episode came to be known (the name coincidentally means 'sour mountain'), was a disaster for all concerned. In the South, it was just the beginning of a violent campaign of military repression and emergency legislation which lasted throughout 1863, and which then dragged on more or less unsuccessfully until late 1866. Aspromonte hugely discredited the government, and prime minister Rattazzi in particular. Stories of his involvement were heard everywhere, and in December 1862 his government was forced to resign. Many on the left, including Crispi and Bertani, had been against Garibaldi's expedition and advised him against it; so Aspromonte revived the divisions with the democratic movement and halted the steps taken in early 1862 towards the construction of an effective political party. During 1863, efforts were made to reconstruct this alliance around resistance to the government's campaign in the South, but in the end these came to nothing. Bertani tried to orchestrate a mass resignation of deputies from parliament in protest at government policy in Sicily ('I have no faith left in your system', he announced), but this was not a success.[96] The majority, led by Crispi and Mordini, chose to remain in parliament, while only a small minority, which included Garibaldi, resigned their seats in protest.[97] The great divergence in political attitudes on the left was also obvious in the reaction to the split of 1863. Crispi wrote of Garibaldi that 'God did not endow him either with Cromwell's mind or Napoleon's ambition . . . his arena is not parliament but the public piazza and the field of battle', while Mazzini was delighted by Garibaldi's decision, and urged all those who had resigned to turn to the masses, 'who must learn to see in you the future leaders of a revolution, that cannot fail to break out sooner or later'.[98] Thus, Aspromonte and its aftermath deepened the divisions in the democratic movement, and did nothing to resolve the political crisis on the left.

Garibaldi suffered great and lasting pain from the wound to his foot. After the skirmish at Aspromonte, he was arrested and taken with his family and immediate associates to the fortress of Varignano near La Spezia, and for a while it seemed he would be put on trial. However, at the end of October he was allowed to leave Varignano, and moved to La Spezia and then Pisa; he had an operation to remove the bullet from his foot, and finally in late December he was able to return to Caprera. After Aspromonte, he was physically never the same. He spent the winter with his leg strapped in bandages and could move only in a bath chair or on crutches; and he failed to recover full mobility thereafter, walking almost always with a limp and the help of a stick.[99] Despite the outbreak of revolt in Poland, which attracted great public sympathy and to which a group of Garibaldi volunteers rushed to fight, he was unable to move from Caprera during the whole of 1863. In truth, his health was already compromised by chronic rheumatism, but hitherto this had been relatively well hidden; now Aspromonte marked the permanent and public loss of Garibaldi's physical vitality.

Aspromonte seemed at first to deal a major blow to Garibaldi's political reputation as well. The Turin satirical paper, *Il Fischietto*, immediately published

26 Mazzini is an 'insatiable Saturn who devours his children big and small indiscriminately one after the other', according to *Il Fischietto* in the aftermath of Aspromonte.

a large cartoon of Mazzini depicted as death – an 'insatiable Saturn' – eating his children, the last of whom was Garibaldi (see figure 26 above).[100] The episode was also seized on by the right-wing and clerical press in France. *L'Union* described Garibaldi as 'a bandit in a comic opera' caught in a mountain gorge by 'a handful of bersagliers', while Augustin Cochin in *Le Correspondant* announced: 'The redeemer descends again to a scoundrel',[101] and claimed his defeat was the result of divine intervention. For the main government paper, *Le Constitutionnel*, Aspromonte was 'the victory of order over anarchy', while the liberal press remained largely silent on the subject.[102] Even *The Times* in London saw Aspromonte as a major defeat for Garibaldi, writing as soon as the news came in:

> What made Garibaldi an idol to his friends . . . was the prestige of his invulnerability, the conceit of his omnipotence, his certainty of success, his faculty to peform miracles in everything he undertook . . . But now blood has been drawn from the veins of the charmed man . . . the hero sinks to the level of mere mortals . . . He has tempted Providence, and his star pales in heaven; his final defeat may be deferred, but his fall is no less inevitable.

Four days later, the paper had not changed its mind: 'Garibaldi is on the ground, never again to rise. Whatever events the future may have in store for Italy, Garibaldi's game is played out. He is old, prematurely old, broken in health, worn by fits of excessive activity . . . The gout tortures and paralyses his limbs, sorrow will soon gnaw into his very soul.'[103]

Despite all these setbacks, Aspromonte became something of a propaganda success for the left in Italy. However politically divided by this episode, the left responded with a public show of support for Garibaldi, and this was accompanied by a major publicity exercise intent on showing Garibaldi, the hero of Italy, to be the victim of government brutality and duplicity. This effort began as soon as his men got him off the mountain at Aspromonte, and it was instigated by Garibaldi himself. On board the ship taking him to Genoa, he wrote a long letter to *Il Diritto* in which he defended his actions. In a dramatic opening sentence, he pushed the blame on to the government. 'They were thirsty for blood! And I sought to save it.' He had told his men not to fire and, although wounded and unable to see the whole conflict, 'I am . . . assured in all conscience that . . . from the lines under my command and the command of my adjutants, not a single shot was fired.' He even went so far as to praise the conduct of Colonel Pallavicini, the commanding officer at Aspromonte, in order further to express his contempt for Rattazzi's government. He concluded the letter with a brief, but masterly, piece of Risorgimento rhetoric which contrasted his and his men's voluntary martyrdom for Italy with the apathy of its official representatives:

> What pains me most is the fatal mistrust (by the head of State) which contributes in no small way to the non-fulfilment of Unity. But however it may be, this time too I can present myself to Italy with my head held high, sure that I have done my duty. This time too, my indifferent life, and the more precious life of so many generous young men, was offered as a sacrifice to the most holy of causes, untouched by cowardly self-interest.[104]

Garibaldi's letter to *Il Diritto*, cast as a defence of national honour, was widely published and translated. It was followed up by another open letter, this time to the 'English nation' and written from prison in Varignano, in which he denounced the 'immoral monstrosity which is called the Papacy' and acclaimed England as the land of liberty.[105] In Italy itself, press restrictions seem to have muted the immediate response. However, a series of pamphlets was produced semi-clandestinely in order, as they put it, to combat the 'lies' put out by Rattazzi and to defend the selfless heroism of Garibaldi. One anonymous author wrote from prison to back up Garibaldi's account written from 'his bed of pain': they had done everything they could to avoid a conflict with their 'brothers' in the army.[106] An officer, R. Maurigi, also wrote from prison to give more details of the episode. Forced by his wound to sit down, Garibaldi had continued shouting *viva l'Italia,* and in the end the regular soldiers cried *viva Garibaldi* and they had all exchanged 'fraternal embraces'.[107] Alexandre Dumas, who claimed to have obtained an eyewitness account from a Hungarian officer, told his readers that Garibaldi had continued smoking while he was hit, and his face never changed expression;[108] while a volunteer, another eyewitness, observed that Garibaldi was hit in front of all his men, implying that he had been fired at deliberately. The volunteer quoted the Book of Genesis at his readers: 'and it came to pass, when they were in the field, that Cain rose up against Abel his brother, and slew him'.[109]

Thanks to these propaganda efforts, Aspromonte ceased to be seen as the defeat of Garibaldi. Instead, it was recast as one more painful event in Italy's national history, a tragic example of civil strife (another writer quoted Manzoni: 'brothers have killed brothers'),[110] and an emblematic illustration of the nation's betrayal by the perfidy of a few Italians (Rattazzi) and the tyranny of its foreign oppressors (Napoleon III).[111] At the centre of this tragedy was the treatment of Garibaldi, and his suffering acquired conspicuous religious overtones. Two French writers explicitly compared Garibaldi's pain to that of Christ on the cross. One pamphlet, by Felix Pyat (a French political exile, and later member of the Paris Commune), spoke directly to Garibaldi:

> Your sacrifice ... seems a *Transfiguration.* All of you that was earthly has disappeared with your blood. Your wounds render you divine. Aspromonte recalls the peaks of Calvary, your martyrdom recalls the Passion. Your glory becomes a cult. The people loved you, now they adore you. They glorified you, now they deify you. You were great, now you are a saint ... 'Behold the Man!'[112]

A. Mancel called on the whole Christian world in verse:

> World, cover your head in mourning!– Garibaldi,
>   your earthly Redeemer has fallen.
> Cry! – his wounds bleed.
> Pray! – his heart suffers. . .
> By his death, the heavenly Redeemer re-ascended
>   to the throne of his father.
> By his fall, the earthly Redeemer has only increased
>   his glory:
> *It is a station on his Way of the Cross!*[113]

Objects relating to the affair at Aspromonte were collected and conserved as 'relics'. These included the wooden stretcher used to carry him down the mountain; the blanket with which he was covered after he was wounded; and the boot he was wearing with the bullet hole in the ankle.[114] Garibaldi was photographed, in prison at Varignano and subsequently, with his wounded foot displayed like a stigma; these photographs were heavily retouched (some were simply photo-montages) to emphasise his imprisonment, pain and sacrifice, and they were widely circulated as cartes-de-visite and lithographed copies.[115] The final illustrations of the pictorial album, *Giuseppe Garibaldi da Caprera ad Aspromonte*, represented Aspromonte in three key episodes. The first was the conflict itself, defined by the caption, '"Don't fire!" cried Garibaldi'; the second, *The transportation of Garibaldi to Scilla*, showed him being carried down the mountain by his loyal volunteers; and the third was *Garibaldi on his bed of pain*. The album made Rattazzi the villain of the drama, and Garibaldi the sacrificial victim.[116] 'To the greatness of the hero', in Alexander Herzen's words, 'was added the crown of the martyr.'[117]

27 'Cain and Abel', comments the satirist Adolfo Matarelli. Italy, flanked by Rome (the wolf) and Venice (the winged lion), reproaches Rattazzi for wounding Garibaldi. This casting of Rattazzi as the villain of Aspromonte became standard, and was agreed upon by left and right on the Italian political scene.

Images of the martyred Garibaldi were especially popular with caricaturists, and it is in satirical papers and flyers that we find the strongest reaction to Aspromonte. The artist Matarelli, working mostly for the Florentine satirical paper, *Il Lampione*, produced a long series of comments on the events of 1862. An early sketch by him, *The trial of Garibaldi*, was published on 12 September and reflects a legal concern about his arrest and possible trial; but by 10 December the same artist had picked up on the religious theme: in *Cain and Abel*, Abel (Garibaldi) lies wounded in a loincloth, while mother Italy reproaches Cain (Rattazzi) for his violence (see figure 27 opposite). Many of the outstanding caricatures from this period rely on religious references to produce an anti-clerical message. One, *The Calvary of Garibaldi at Aspromonte*, represents Garibaldi as Christ on the cross, surrounded by weeping women (Italy), while his tormentors (the Pope, Napoleon II) dance in the background (see figure 28 below). Garibaldi is also the 'Sacred Heart' and a saint in various guises who kills the serpent; Rattazzi, Napoleon III and/or General Cialdini are Judas and/or Pilate. A particularly effective anti-clerical religious allegory can be found in a colour calendar for 1863, which shows a bust of Garibaldi as the saint on an altar, surrounded by guns and cannons in the place of candles and candlesticks ('These are your candles and this is your saint' reads part of the caption).[118]

28 Garibaldi's 'Calvary' ('Aspromonte 28 August 1860') is the most explicitly religious comment to come out of the events of Aspromonte.

Other caricatures dating from this time pursue the idea of Aspromonte as the final trial of an exemplary life. The popular pictorial *Life of Garibaldi* represents his life in thirty-five patriotic pictures from birth (breast-fed by 'mother' Italy), through exile and adventure to Aspromonte (two dark images of Napoleon's hat and a leg wrapped in bandages); and culminating in his victory in the arms of a winged lion: a personal triumph over physical suffering and the oppression of crown and altar. Rather more sophisticated, but still depicting Garibaldi's life in visual and exemplary terms, is the colour lithograph, *The 12 labours of Hercules*, which represents Garibaldi as the mythical hero Hercules, who overcomes the obstacles of human greed and folly by virtue of his superior (moral and physical) strength.[119] These last two prints, and the colour calendar, are especially significant in that they carry a positive political message. They make explicit an attempt to reconcile Garibaldi the victim with Garibaldi the personification of strength and courage, and to emphasise his role as the redeemer of Italy who will show the people the way to the promised land (Rome and Venice).

It is just as clear that Aspromonte did not lead to the loss of Garibaldi's popular support. From the moment that the news came out, men and women wrote to Garibaldi with money, messages of support and poems, and, as well as from Italy, they wrote from Britain, France, Belgium, Holland, Germany, Switzerland, Spain, Greece, Latvia and Russia (and often received replies).[120] If anything, Aspromonte served to increase religious fervour among Garibaldi's supporters. 'The people of Italy', according to the 1863 journal of a British tourist, 'idolize Garibaldi, they have *tabooed* him, and no one ventures to touch him.'[121] Emilio Ferrari sent him a poem, written for the 'wounded of the Italian Calvary', and added: 'I kiss your holy hand tortured in the new world [a reference to his torture while a prisoner in Brazil], and your holy foot tortured in the old world.'[122] An anonymous poem in French, sent to '*Joseph Garibaldi. Prisonnier*', assured him that he was not defeated because through his rejection of glory '[y]ou have taken on the Man God's fatal inheritance'.[123] A group of men and women wrote passionately if falteringly from Rovigo, in Austrian Venetia, to tell him that 'We cannot describe to You, oh General, our feelings of supreme hope, of unexpressible anxiety, then of profound heartache, which agitated our hearts, during the days in which you carried out your glorious attempt, which from the place, which witnessed your sublime sacrifice, took the name of Aspromonte'. 'Oh!' they went on: 'You are so great, that every expression towards you falls short: so great, as to form the pride, not just of your brothers in the fatherland, but of an entire generation.'[124]

Moreover, for many, Aspromonte added another element – namely, concern about his health and comfort – to their sense of personal intimacy with Garibaldi. Public subscriptions paid for surgeons to come from France,

Germany and Britain to visit Garibaldi in Varignano (although the twelve doctors that attended him could not agree about the correct treatment).[125] George Burney wrote on behalf of a meeting in Tower Hamlets (London) to tell him with 'how much pain [I] have followed the accounts of your serious illness; which pain is shared by every truly English heart'.[126] Thomas Stevens sent Garibaldi a portrait he had painted of him, with wishes for a speedy recovery.[127] On a single day, 10 November, Carl Weidlich wrote from Neu Rappen near Berlin to ask about his health and to tell him that the 11,000 people of Neu Rappen loved him and his son Menotti; a fifteen-year-old girl from Switzerland wrote in great concern about his health; and a set of enthusiasts in Lake Constance, who had built a club house in their village and called it Garibaldiburg, told him they were feeling his pain and a great 'contempt' for his 'persecutors'.[128] As Garibaldi recovered, huge interest was taken in his convalescence. The 'Fratelli Hauser' wrote to invite him for a cure at their Swiss spa: 'You will find our spot to be a calm and alpine village which will certainly not displease you', and one man wrote from Brussels to invite him to a performance of Les Misérables.[129]

One of the most widely distributed and copied images of Garibaldi in this period is of him in bed, writing letters with a studious expression.[130] In fact, Garibaldi's correspondence shows that Aspromonte did little to diminish his political energy. While he was still in prison at Varignano, workers' clubs and other political associations from all over Italy sent money to him for those wounded at Aspromonte, and they continued to do so after he was transferred to La Spezia and Pisa and operated on; they all received signed replies from Garibaldi and sometimes personalised notes of thanks.[131] In Palermo, a new pro-Garibaldi paper was published, called L'Aspromonte, and Garibaldi wrote a letter to the editor, saying that '[t]he cry of Rome or Death which they tried to destroy, has risen like a giant after Aspromonte'.[132] Although poor health did oblige Garibaldi to remain in Caprera for the whole of 1863, he continued to maintain a huge correspondence. He wrote to the group from Rovigo, assuring them that '[i]f the foreigner continues to trample over our fatherland, thousands of brothers will keep their arms at the ready for the complete liberation of Italy . . . And I am confident of being among you before too long' (the letter was published in L'Unità Italiana).[133] He revived his project for a Million Rifles Fund, and sent out a circular letter calling for donations.[134] He sent messages of support to Poland, and attempted to link the Polish revolt to the struggle in Hungary;[135] and he took a particular interest in Sicilian politics, and seemed for a time to see in Sicily a real hope for revolutionary action. Indeed, some of his letters to Sicilian revolutionaries show clear signs of the shift to the left and towards sympathy with socialism which was to mark the latter stages of his political career (it was over Sicily that he resigned his seat in parliament in December 1863).[136]

London

In the spring of 1864 Garibaldi left Caprera. His departure caused consternation among Italian governing circles, or, as one British representative in Turin put it:

> The activity with which the party of action had been labouring in conjunction with the Hungarian refugees to bring about a combined movement in Hungary and Venetia, and Garibaldi's own addresses to the Italians calling upon them to be ready for action, sufficed to render his sudden departure for Caprera the occasion for innumerable conjectures.[137]

To the 'evident relief' of the government, Garibaldi went instead to England. Still, there were concerns about this visit. Emanuele d'Azeglio, the minister in London, argued that Garibaldi's visit could be used to encourage British public opinion in Italy's favour, and that he could be presented as 'the most distinguished Italian who has however spoken and committed the most distinguished nonsense'. The king, however, was less convinced, instructing D'Azeglio 'not to become involved in Garibaldi-type [*Garibaldesche*] banquets and grand demonstrations to make the British government aware that those kinds of great parties don't amuse me nothing myself personally [*sic*]'.[138]

Garibaldi's reasons for travelling were not entirely clear. He may have hoped to put pressure on the British government in the war between Prussia and Denmark, or to establish closer links with the National League for the Independence of Poland, whose members were also supporters of Italian nationalism.[139] We know that since 1860 he had been subjected to a relentless round of invitations from his British admirers.[140] He may even have seen his visit as a mostly private affair, or at least as an opportunity simply to thank his supporters on the various Garibaldi committees, and to visit his many old and new friends in Britain. Indeed, on arrival in England he issued a press release calling for calm: 'Dear Friends, I do not want political demonstrations. PS. – Above all, don't incite riots.'[141]

In fact, the idea for the visit seems not to have come from Garibaldi at all, but from the Mazzinians Aurelio Saffi and Agostino Bertani. They were in no doubt at all about its purpose. 'I am ever more convinced that Garibaldi's visit to England would help to sway English public opinion in our favour and so push the Government to support public opinion', Bertani wrote as they hatched this plan. He had very specific ideas about how Garibaldi should be used, and this purpose realised: 'Garibaldi must not hold meetings – he must not shake money boxes – He must place in the papers a few words which explain the aim of his journey . . . say a couple of words in a public place to the people, get them published in the papers – create a committee and leave having seen no more than 3 or 4 cities.' The precise message of Garibaldi was also to be clear. 'From his mouth the cry of Rome will be a bolt of lightning amongst those Protestants and Francophobes . . . Garibaldi should appear twice at the most – say little and appeal to the English people as the embodiment of a young nation, resolved to take up its place in the world and finish its achievements . . .'[142] Much as Mazzini had done twenty years earlier, Bertani saw in Garibaldi the silent symbol of a political idea which had itself changed little in those twenty years. Garibaldi was to represent, promote and encourage a distinct vision of Italy, but he was not himself to become involved in any separate political activity.

What happened thereafter confounded all their expectations. Far from being either a private visit or an orchestrated propaganda exercise, Garibaldi's stay in England became a political 'moment', an extraordinary demonstration of 'radical chic',[143] trade union pageantry, popular Protestantism and private passion, 'given', in the words of a *Times* correspondent, 'with such an earnestness and goodwill as has seldom been equalled, and probably never excelled'.[144] From the moment his ship arrived in Southampton on 3 April, Garibaldi was mobbed by journalists, fans, politicians and other official representatives, many of them wearing red shirts or jackets, and tricolour ribbons. He was taken off to a civic reception and a huge parade ('such a sight', one reporter wrote, 'has never been witnessed here before').[145] From there, Garibaldi went to the Isle of Wight, where he stayed for eight days at the home of Charles Seely, a radical MP. He paid a visit to the poet laureate, Alfred Tennyson, and planted a tree in his garden (they recited Italian romantic poetry to each other and Tennyson advised Garibaldi not to discuss politics in England). Tennyson's wife and sons were greatly taken by Garibaldi; in her diary Mrs Tennyson described him as 'a most striking figure . . . His face very noble powerful & sweet, his forehead high & square. Altogether he looks one of the great men of our Elizabethan age.'[146]

After the Isle of Wight, Garibaldi and Seely, along with a small entourage, travelled by train to London on 11 April, where a reception had been arranged to welcome him. The organisers were very lucky with the weather: 'The day was magnificent,' D'Azeglio commented, 'as hot as a summer's day'.[147] Huge crowds greeted Garibaldi's arrival at Nine Elms station in Vauxhall. After a series of welcoming addresses, he got into a carriage with the duke of Sutherland, and they tried to drive through the vast crowd filling central London in order to reach the duke's home in St James's. The writer and parliamentarian, John Morley, wrote that London had 'seldom beheld a spectacle more extraordinary or more moving . . . vast continuous multitudes, blocking roadways, filling windows, lining every parapet and roof with eager gazers. For five hours Garibaldi passed on amid tumultuous waves of passionate curiosity, delight, enthusiasm.'[148] 'Call it bad management, or call it the irrepressible excitement of the people,' commented *The Times*, 'the fact is that the General's carriage could hardly make any progress at all ... the multitude ... closed round the General, holding out their hands to be shaken, and testifying with rude cordiality their admiration for the hero of the day.'[149]

An estimated 500,000 people had turned out to greet Garibaldi. They formed an 'impassably dense' crowd mostly from 'the lowest classes', in the words of the government clerk, Arthur Munby, who stood happily among them: 'a very shabby and foul smelling crowd; and the women of it, young and old, were painfully ugly and dirty and tawdry'. Garibaldi's carriage was preceded by a long trade union procession, and when he came in view, the crowd, which had until then 'behaved with the utmost good humour and peacefulness', erupted with excitement:

> when this supreme moment came, it resulted in such a scene as can hardly be witnessed twice in a lifetime. That vast multitude rose as one man from their level attitude of expectation: they leapt into the air, they waved their arms and hats aloft, they surged and struggled round the carriage, they shouted with a mighty shout of enthusiasm that took one's breath away to hear it: and above them on both sides thousands of white kerchiefs were waving from every window and housetop ... And He ... sat aloft ... sitting quiet and gazing around and upwards as if he could scarcely believe that this great greeting was meant only for him.[150]

People climbed on railings, lampposts, signs and trees to get a view of Garibaldi; and at Trafalgar Square they hung from the plinth of Nelson's column and the equestrian statue of Charles I. As *The Times* put it:

> For five hours did the acclamations of the people last and the acknowledgements of Garibaldi answer them. It was half-past 2 when the first cheers greeted his ears on the arrival of the train, and it must have been nearly 8 o'clock when he reached the hospitable shelter of Stafford House [the duke of Sutherland's London residence].[151]

Lord Palmerston wrote that 'Garibaldi met with such a reception as no one ever had before'.[152] 'This', according to Alexander Herzen, 'is Carlyle's hero-worship in real life.'[153]

Garibaldi stayed for twelve more days in London. He attended a reception at St Pancras, and two receptions in his honour at the Crystal Palace. Around 25–30,000 people came to the first Crystal Palace reception, which was organised by the social and political elite and was a celebration of all things Italian (Italian music, flags and speeches in favour of Rome and Venice). The second was equally well attended, and was billed as 'the people's reception', designed, in the words of the *Annual Register*, 'to give the humbler classes in various parts of the country an opportunity of enjoying the presence of the great object of their admiration'. The price of admission to the reception was fixed at one shilling, special trains were laid on from all over Britain, and Garibaldi was presented with ceremonial addresses from organisations like the Temperance Society, the Emancipation Society, the Young Men's Christian Association, and the 'Garibaldi reception Testimonial Fund and Working Men's committees'. The duke and duchess of Sutherland put on an elegant social gathering for him at Stafford House (depicted in *The Illustrated London News*); he went to the opera at Covent Garden (where he heard *Norma* and *Masaniello* and was mobbed by women 'delirious with excitement');[154] he attended a banquet at the Reform Club; he was given the Freedom of the City of London, followed by a banquet and reception; and he visited Ugo Foscolo's tomb in Chiswick. In addition to these public occasions, Garibaldi went to smaller private functions in his honour and received guests who called on him at Stafford House. He met Lord Palmerston, Lord Russell, Lord Derby and Gladstone ('[t]hey have all lost their heads', commented Emanuele d'Azeglio;

" THIS IS THE NOBLEST ROMAN OF THEM ALL ! "

29 This full-page cartoon in *Punch* is a sign of the media excitement surrounding Garibaldi's arrival in England. His casting as a 'noble Roman' is typical of the eclectic response to him, and may reflect concurrent celebrations for Shakespeare's tercentary and/or be an anti-papal comment.

'both Whigs and Tories are disgraced for ever', wrote the Catholic archbishop of Dublin, Paul Cullen).[155] He also met 'stars' like Florence Nightingale, Lord Shaftesbury and the prince of Wales, and old friends, including Colonel and Mrs Chambers, Alexander Herzen and Mazzini.[156]

Garibaldi's visit to England in 1864 is one of the most closely documented and studied episodes in his political career, and it is justifiably famous. Above all perhaps, it is significant as an unusually successful example of 'spectacular politics':[157] hugely well attended, seemingly spontaneous and with a visible impact on elite and popular culture. Coverage of Garibaldi saturated a wide section of the press. *The Times*, *The Illustrated London News*, *The Scotsman*, *Reynolds's Newspaper* and *The Bee-Hive* gave huge amounts of column space to his arrival and welcome. *Punch* proclaimed him the 'noblest Roman of them all' on 9 April (see figure 29 on page 333); and before his arrival *The Operative Bricklayers' Trade Circular* instructed its readers to give 'a working man's welcome' to this 'great, good and honest patriot'.[158] Staffordshire figures, Wedgwood china and decorative biscuit tins were produced to commemorate his visit (although the famous 'Garibaldi biscuit' probably dates from 1860–1); in 1865 a new football club, Nottingham Forest, adopted red as its colour in honour of Garibaldi and, dressing its players in red-tasselled caps, won fame as the 'Garibaldi reds'. Streets and pubs were named after him; and both men

30   This brightly coloured Staffordshire figure of 'Garibaldi at home' in his red shirt was one of a series, and it points to the enduring fascination with his life at Caprera. Note the presence of his spade (see also figure 24 on page 310).

and women went about wearing red shirts, red jackets and Garibaldi 'aprons'. The number of Staffordshire figures of Garibaldi – at least fifteen were produced in the early 1860s – is especially interesting. These brightly coloured earthenware ornaments, which were usually collected and placed on Victorian mantelpieces, represent Garibaldi in various movements and activities: Garibaldi and his horse (in three sizes, a copy of an 1861 *Illustrated London News* engraving); Garibaldi and Vittorio Emanuele at Teano (also from *The Illustrated London News*); Garibaldi paired with his 'Englishman', John Peard, with General Napier and with William Shakespeare (whose tercentenary was in 1864); and Garibaldi at home. The latter showed him sittting bareheaded in shirt and trousers, holding a spade between his legs with his left hand (see figure 30 opposite).[159] Hyam & Co. of Leeds advertised 'The Garibaldi, a new over-coat' as part of its 'leading styles for the present season'.[160]

Garibaldi's visit also prompted the proliferation of Garibaldi sheet music for piano: tunes included 'Garibaldi's hymn arranged as a march', 'Garibaldi's popular march' and 'The Garibaldi polka'. One tune, 'Garibaldi's hymn', had a solo piece ('He fought not for self, all his thought was for others, All earth was his country, Th'oppresst were his brothers, yet dear to his heart was the land of his father, And freely his life for his country he gave') as well as a final chorus ('Come forth sons of freedom Come join in our welcome! The cry's "Garibaldi" who lives but to save'). Popular verse published in 1864 ranged from 'London's latest citizen' to 'Garibaldi: why we welcome him', and a collection of songs entitled 'A wreath for Garibaldi'. These songs contained no surprises. The first line of one 1864 song, 'The red shirt', is 'Garibaldi, Italia's saviour, for ever', and its chorus goes

> The red shirt, the red shirt, the red shirt, for ever,
> The red shirt henceforth will be famous in story,
> The red shirt with Freedom is one now and ever,
> Hurra, for the red shirt! Garibaldi and glory.[161]

Janet Hamilton, 'the radical bard of the Glasgow workers', may have sung her welcome to Garibaldi in 'Auld Scottish' ('The warm bluid's swalling' like the tide – Through my auld heart'), but the sentiment – 'Blest among women was the mither – That bore thee, Garibaldi!' – was entirely standard.[162]

A Garibaldi fashion was created in 1864, and the British public's enthusiasm expressed itself in clothes, china and songs. What makes these ephemera interesting is their sheer repetition and banality: quality or novelty was not nearly as important as conformity to the style. Equally, Garibaldi's visit provided the occasion for a new round of biographies which closely followed the established formulas. Titles from 1864 include the illustrated *Garibaldi: his life and times. Comprising the revolutionary history of Italy from 1789 to the present time. Illustrated with numerous engravings, and a coloured portrait of Garibaldi*; the reformatted *Garibaldi: his career and exploits, reprinted . . . from the 'Morning Star' of April 2, 1864*; E. H. Nolan's *The liberators of Italy* (a serial, which came out in twenty-five parts); and *The life of Garibaldi . . . Interspersed with anecdotes illustrative of his personal character. Compiled from authentic and original sources*, a fairly straightforward cull of existing accounts from *The Times* and from Vecchi. None of these writers took any chances with their approach to the subject. 'There is no man of the present day whose life abounds in more stirring incidents than that of the hero of Italian freedom, Giuseppe Garibaldi', began *The life of Garibaldi*; '[n]ever has the muse of history or song touched a nobler theme than the soldiership and manhood of the patriot hero who lands to-day on English soil', proclaimed the *Morning Star*.[163] The 1860 biography, *Garibaldi*, by O. J. Victor of New York, came out in a London edition in 1864. Perhaps the only 1864 biography with any pretence to originality was *Garibaldi and Italian unity*, written by Garibaldi's close friend, Colonel Chambers ('the writer being convinced that there was much unknown in the history of General Garibaldi'), which claimed to tell the story of Aspromonte 'for the first time . . . to the world'. In reality, Chambers' study was more overtly political but equally tendentious in its approach to Garibaldi, and just as formulaic in its methodology and sources as the other 1864 biographies.[164]

So Garibaldi's visit to London was a broad and spectacular confirmation of the success of the Garibaldi cult. At the time, as we have seen, there was a general consensus that the welcome given to him was unique, or at least unprecedented in the history of London. How can this enthusiasm for Garibaldi be explained? The first point to make is that however novel it may have seemed, the welcome given to Garibaldi was part of a longer tradition. Only a year before, the prince of Wales had passed through London with his bride-to-be in front of a huge cheering crowd (indeed, Queen Victoria complained that Garibaldi had received the kind of honours 'usually reserved for Royalty').[165] In 1851–2, the arrival of the Hungarian revolutionary, Lajos Kossuth, had provoked an 'ecstatic reaction': 'London has never . . . witnessed such a sight as it has seen today', commented one paper; in Birmingham, his reception was said to have 'eclipsed all the great occasions of public note since 1832', and 500,000 people were reported to have turned out to see him.[166] The obvious similarities between Kossuth's and Garibaldi's receptions tell us that a kind of radical choreography had already been created for welcoming democratic heroes to England, and that this choreography was being practised in 1864. Equally, the vast crowds were not amorphous: each had its own banners, speeches and rituals, and their presence reflects a political culture based around an existing associational life.[167]

The British enthusiasm for Italian revolution (and for Kossuth) reflected British concerns and a British sense of identity. British support for Italy was closely connected to evangelical Protestantism and, as in 1860–2, many Garibaldi admirers in Britain saw him as above all an opponent of 'Popery', the 'Lord's battleaxe' against the Roman 'Babylon'.[168] One British man even wrote to Garibaldi at this time to suggest a new tricolour flag for his volunteers: red, orange (signifying anti-papal Protestantism), and blue ('the colour of the Scotch covenanters').[169] Admiration for Garibaldi was often expressed in terms of approval of his 'English' or 'gentlemanly' virtues; or as a sense that, as Gladstone put it, 'there was something English about this blue-eyed Latin!' (his eyes were probably light brown).[170] This identification of 'Englishness' was also literary and romantic. Mrs Tennyson's reaction to Garibaldi as an 'Elizabethan' hero has already been mentioned. Shakespeare and Garibaldi were manufactured as a pair of Staffordshire figures. A biographer likened Garibaldi to a litany of native heroes: to Raleigh, Frobisher, Drake, 'Blake the admiral' and Rob Roy; he also speculated that Garibaldi had Scottish or Irish ancestry ('Baldy Garrow' = 'Garret Baldwin' = 'Garibaldi'), and compared the 'horrors' of the retreat from Rome in 1849 to 'the disasters and miseries which attended the flight of the Young Pretender after Culloden'.[171] The Times was keen to show that the welcome given to Garibaldi was better than any foreign 'pageant':

> in every country of the Continent there may be seen brilliant pageants and well drilled battalions. It is in England only that associations of workmen could conduct a revolutionary hero, through a capital thronged with their own class, and yet not excite a fear in the mind of any politician . . . With not a soldier visible, and with only a few police to clear the way, that wonderful combination of order and disorder, an English crowd, conducted Garibaldi . . . to the mansion of his noble host.[172]

Thus, for The Times, Garibaldi's welcome became a sign of English superiority: of the country's social cohesion, native liberty and freedom from political interference. That this impression was at least partly intentional is suggested by Palmerston's comment to the queen: contained by the aristocracy, he told her, Garibaldi's visit would afford 'great pleasure to the bulk of the nation, as a proof of the community of feeling among all classes of the nation'.[173]

Yet perhaps unsurprisingly, behind the official façade of one nation lay a divided response to Garibaldi. Even before he arrived in England, aristocratic enthusiasts, middle-class radicals and working-class activists had disagreed about what Garibaldi represented and who was to welcome him. The great social diversity in the British and Italian committees who greeted and celebrated Garibaldi in London, and the organisation of separate receptions to honour him, is as suggestive of political competition for control of his name as it is of any class unity in enthusiasm for him. Although his entry into London was a celebration of social belonging, the readings of it varied. Middle-class publications tended to downplay the prominent presence of trade unions in the ceremony, whereas the working-class press stressed the presence of labour associations, as well as highlighting a speech by Garibaldi in which he identified himself as working class. Both groups united when Garibaldi was 'captured' by the aristocrats and kept under the duke of Sutherland's control. They were particularly angry that Garibaldi was allowed only occasional visits to radicals like Cowen and McAdam, and a dinner in Chiswick with the foreign exiles Mazzini, Herzen and Karl Blind.[174]

In Italy and elsewhere, Garibaldi caused controversy by his association with the radicals. His dinner with Herzen, more specifically his widely publicised toast to Mazzini as 'a man who has performed the greatest services both to my native land and to freedom in general . . . the counsellor of my youth . . . my friend, my teacher!', was criticised in the moderate and clerical press.[175] King Vittorio Emanuele was said to be equally offended – 'angry and sore' – because he resented Garibaldi's English reception 'as an ovation to a rival'.[176] In turn, Mazzini and the radicals were angry with Garibaldi for allowing himself to be hijacked by the British elite. As Minghetti, the Italian prime minister, had foreseen: 'Garibaldi is rather unyielding to the designs of others; so he prefers to initiate his own plan: and this plan will probably not be that of Mazzini.'[177]

All these disagreements probably account for the unexpected conclusion to Garibaldi's visit. Pleading ill health, Garibaldi abruptly cancelled his plans to visit Manchester, Newcastle and Glasgow, and paid only brief visits to Cliveden (the duke of Sutherland's country house), Eton College and Cornwall (to see his friend, Colonel Peard, and he was given a huge public welcome). He then left for Caprera on 28 April in the duke of Sutherland's yacht. It was widely felt that illness was not the reason for his sudden departure. Instead it was alleged that the British government, and Gladstone in particular, had put pressure on Garibaldi not to undertake a tour of the provinces for fear of stirring up radical agitation and popular disorder. There were also rumours that the government had been subject to pressure from the French and Italian governments to contain him.[178]

Whatever the real reasons for Garibaldi's departure, the struggle to manage him and his visit suggests that he had a political significance in Britain that went beyond (even as it depended on) a popular taste for his 'style'. Emanuele d'Azeglio and many others noticed the predominance of the poor and working class in the crowds that welcomed him, and of radical symbols and leaders in the ceremonies of welcome.[179] In fact, Garibaldi's presence in 1864 helped to bring about a major shift in British radicalism. As Margot Finn argues, the great resentment felt by radicals at Garibaldi's departure served to mobilise a popular movement for domestic reform and, in particular, an extension of the franchise which was to culminate in the Second Reform Act of 1867. Agitation over his visit brought to prominence new radical leaders 'capable both of expressing class interests and of bridging them', who used their sympathy with continental nationalism 'to gain admittance to the public sphere of politics and economics'.[180] As well as the extension of the franchise in 1867, this political coalition brought about a change in the language of radicalism, introducing new definitions of national belonging and a debate about women's suffrage.[181]

Garibaldi provoked an equally vigorous response among those opposed to him, and they saw him as a real threat to British society. Queen Victoria was in no doubt about what had happened. 'Garibaldi – thank God! – is gone!' she wrote to her daughter: 'It has been a very absurd and humiliating exhibition and was becoming very dangerous by the connection with Mazzini and all the worst refugees.'[182] British conservatives denounced 'the fumes of this intoxication' and wrote that the working-class celebration of Garibaldi represented a coded threat of 'revolution' and 'socialism'.[183] Catholics were infuriated by Garibaldi's visit, as they had been two years previously by the outcry over Aspromonte, which had led to riots in Hyde Park between Irish supporters of the Pope and pro-Garibaldi demonstrators.[184] 'What a degrading and disgraceful exhibition of English feeling in favour of Garibaldi', Archbishop Cullen wrote from Dublin on 14 April (it had 'offended everybody in Rome', Odo Russell confirmed).[185] Only two political figures in Britain professed indifference to Garibaldi. Disraeli refused to meet him for fear of alienating Irish Catholic MPs, while Karl Marx mocked the popular enthusiasm for 'a pitiful . . . donkey'.[186]

So we can explain a great deal about the reaction to Garibaldi's visit by contextualising it in British politics and by reference to prevailing British sensibilities. However, the emotional intensity of people's responses to him should perhaps be reflected on further. Everyone who saw him in London seemed touched by the experience. Arthur Munby did not get close to him but, as he wrote in his diary, 'one would have known that heroic face among a thousand'. A friend of Munby, who was nearer Garibaldi's carriage when it passed, was 'instantly converted', and told Munby that Garibaldi's face was 'by many degrees more beautiful than any face he ever saw'.[187] 'We who then saw Garibaldi for the first time', Gladstone remarked, 'can many of us never forget the marvellous effect produced upon all minds' by his presence.[188] Even the prince of Wales professed himself 'much pleased with him . . . nobody who sees him can fail to be attracted by him'. Lord Granville noticed that both Lord Shaftesbury and the duchess of Sutherland had been driven 'temporarily a little out of their minds' by the company of their hero.[189]

Lord Granville was not wrong: the duke of Sutherland's wife, Anne, seemed to have fallen fervently for Garibaldi. As Garibaldi prepared to leave England, and after his departure, she wrote him a series of despairing letters (in French). 'Have you really not understood, my General?' she wrote on 24 April, 'that I have given you everything I have – a real cult for your beautiful life, your noble actions – a *veritable* and profound affection, made holy by my admiration for your great character.' 'You have filled my thoughts since I left you this morning', she wrote on another occasion: 'I love you with an affection which will last *forever*. I so wanted to kiss you when saying goodbye . . . Let me believe that you are coming now, and for the future, into our life.'[190] Her mother-in-law, the dowager duchess, wrote (also in French) on 27 April to tell Garibaldi of 'all my regrets for your departure, and to tell you of the void you have left. Come back, dear General.'[191] She evidently had a close and intimate sense of identification with him. She was concerned for his happiness ('I think so often about your sad words on life! How I would like to bring it some consolation! Can you give me the friendship of your beautiful spirit?'); and worried incessantly about his health. 'Do you remember the day that you took my finger and placed it on the deep scar of your wound. Dear General, how you have suffered in your noble life, and I worry so, and often, that I did not express all the sympathy [*sympathie*] that I felt and will always feel.' She also told him that she kept his portrait with her always: 'It is next to me and looks at me with great indulgence.'[192]

There was, moreover, nothing unusual about the passion that the two duchesses felt for Garibaldi. Mary Seely, who with her husband Charles had entertained Garibaldi for a week on the Isle of Wight, wrote him letter after letter filled with adoring prose. 'Beloved General', one letter began:

When, alas! you had left me yesterday, and my heart was heavy with grief – I went to your little bed – full of emotion – and sorrow, that your dear and revered head, would not rest there again – for long. I stood – so sad – and from below the quilt *there* was the corner of a handkerchief that you had used. Oh! dearest Garibaldi, it was there to comfort me! I cannot send it away! I may surely keep it, to love, and to delight in – it is the grey one, that used to hang around your neck . . . and I have helped to cover your dear head with it . . . I had longed to possess that handkerchief, but could not frame the expression of my wish – and now it is here – do say it may be mine.[193]

'Your visit has been the great glory of my life', she told him in another: 'Dearest General, *when* will you return to England?' 'Do you know that since your visit I find everything that is not associated with you, has ceased to interest me. If *you* have not used a room, I do not care to enter it, if *your portrait* is not in a collection, I do not care to look at it. If people do not speak of you, I wish them to be silent.'[194] As well as the handkerchief, she kept a half-cigar and a lock of his hair as 'treasured mementoes'. She sent him a Stilton cheese, and she kept on writing to him:

> Dearest dearest General, who can tell how deeply you are beloved? or how justly? . . . The room you occupied is sacred ground, no one shall sleep in it again . . . except those who love, and honour and revere Garibaldi . . . I was telling Charles last night, that if our house was ever on fire – I would save your letters first, of all my possessions.[195]

Everyone shared her passion, she told Garibaldi. 'My husband and I, sit at nights talking of your probable return, and of our true love for you – and we never tire'; and after Garibaldi had kissed her daughter, Fanny, 'she told her husband *never* to touch that little part of her cheek! And then she wept long'. Even her baby grandaughter knew Garibaldi's portrait ('[s]he kisses her darling little hand to it, and dances with pleasure'). Tennyson's sons had sent Garibaldi seeds, and '[m]any people beg of me to send you Odes in your honour and verses without end'. Even the police, apparently, had declared their work for him 'a labour of love'.[196]

Fame itself can help to explain this passion for Garibaldi. He came to London as a cult figure and, as Munby noticed, he enjoyed instant public recognition. This was largely due to the wide circulation of papers, books and printed images of him, so that people felt as if they knew him personally, and identified emotionally with his life story (or, as an American woman who had met him once wrote: 'I forget . . . that it is not an old and intimate friend I address so long have you had a *home in my heart*').[197] What captivated mid-Victorian Britain most of all was the contrast between the greatness of Garibaldi's reputation and his 'simplicity' as a man; enthusiasts saw this kind of charisma as an innate quality or defined it as a form of moral 'character' (something 'English', as we saw above),[198] and never wondered if it might be staged. In Mary Seely's words, he seemed 'the grandest, gentlest, most beloved and admirable of men'.[199] There was, to quote Munby again, 'in his bearing and looks . . . a combination utterly new and most impressive, of dignity and homeliness, of grace and tenderness with the severest majesty'.[200] Gladstone selected 'from every other quality' his 'seductive simplicity of manner': 'the union of the most profound and tender humanity with his fiery valour . . . one of the finest combinations of profound and unalterable simplicity with self-consciousness and self-possession'.[201] Trying to explain Garibaldi's fascination to a hostile Queen Victoria, Lord Granville told her that he had:

> all the qualifications for making him a popular idol in this country. He is of low extraction, he is physically and morally brave, he is a good guerilla soldier, he has achieved great things by 'dash', he has a simple manner with a sort of nautical dignity, and a pleasing smile . . . His mountebank dress, which betrays a desire for effect, has a certain dramatic effect.[202]

In this way, and as Granville partially perceived, Garibaldi actually added to the personal impact of his fame by appearing to deny or distance himself from it.

The passionate reaction of many women to Garibaldi is especially interesting. This passion was surely due in part to his physical allure, or to his apparent skill at using sexual attraction to personalise his political appeal. Garibaldi's capacity to attract women through a powerful mix of the personal and the political was already evident in the 1850s (in his relations with von Schwartz and Jessie White), and continued through the early 1860s. Although sex is never openly discussed in any of these letters, we can perceive sexual desire in the constant allusions to Garibaldi's body, his bedroom and/or his bed. Like Mary Seely, Florence MacKnight (who met Garibaldi in Turin in 1861) also wrote to him of her 'lonely pilgrimages' around his bedroom, and of the 'caresses' given to his bed and pillow; and of her love for '*you – just you* . . . for the real, loyal, and tender man'; while another woman, 'Sauvage', wrote of her insatiable 'hunger' for a letter from him ('I devour any writing of yours in the papers with an avidity which is perfectly frightful, as I feel more hungry and wish for *more* the instant after').[203] Sex, or at least feelings of intimate physical passion, was thus one basis of Garibaldi's personal charisma. As Mary Seely said to him: 'You free the body, and enchain the mind'.[204] Of course, women were by no means alone in responding to Garibaldi's powerful physical magnetism, but since they felt able to express their feelings for him in more openly sentimental ways, it is much easier for us to recognise this aspect of their response.

It is also apparent that Garibaldi's special relationship with women was the result of a conscious and long-term political strategy to get them on his side. He had begun addressing women directly in Rome in 1849 and, as we have seen, a huge number of his speeches and public letters were addressed specifically at the patriotic woman during Italian unification and in the years that followed. Equally, it is more than likely that he encouraged the personal displays and expressions of affection described above. He certainly replied more or less scrupulously and tenderly to all their letters. To Mary Seely he wrote: 'Allow me to kiss your beneficent hand and to express the immense gratitude I owe to you, angelic woman! . . . believe me that my heart will remain with you all my life'; and he later wrote of his joy at receiving her letters: 'recalling the angelic support of your arm in ascending and descending the stairs, the gentle care you took of me . . . and your face which I carry with me in my soul, I forget all my sorrows and I am happy'.[205] He wrote the same, but more delicately, to the duchess of Sutherland ('I kiss your beneficent hand; and . . . I thank you for your generous hospitality . . . Never so well as with you, in any corner of the world');[206] while to another admirer, Julie Salis Schwabe, he confessed: 'I can never repeat enough, how much I owe to your kindness, and will be more than happy every time you demand [anything of] me.'[207] When reading these words, however, we must be careful to remember that Garibaldi's relationships with these women were not purely personal. All of them were well connected politically to different currents of radicalism (Schwabe was a rich German widow, and a friend of Cobden and Bright; MacKnight was the daughter of a British peer favourable to Garibaldi), and all of them were recruited to do his political bidding in one way or another. It is also clear that these women were conscious of their role in his life; indeed, when the emotional demands of Julie Schwabe on him became especially insistent, Garibaldi put her off by referring to the 'terrible responsibility' of his political position, and to his 'anxious concern to complete' his life's mission, and she wrote to him that she entirely understood.[208]

Presumably, the tactics used by Garibaldi worked as well as they did because he had little competition. No one else, except perhaps Mazzini before him, made political use of British women in quite this way at this time. It is also worth noting what participation in the moral and material struggle for Italian liberation offered to middle-class and aristocratic women in Britain. While we should be clear that involvement with Italian patriotism never fully challenged the ideology of separate spheres (women usually worked as nurses or fund-raisers), through this work they could nevertheless acquire a personal autonomy and public authority that they did not enjoy elsewhere.[209] As a result, many of these women became what Julie Schwabe described as Garibaldi's 'sister[s] *for life*!': their enthusiasm for Garibaldi's politics insepar-able from their interest in his private welfare and emotions. MacKnight wrote to Garibaldi of her unhappiness at having to stay in Turin without him but concluded, 'but I'll be brave [*allons courage*]! I'm a soldier too.'[210] Schwabe told Garibaldi that she acted for him out of 'pure, unselfish, loving interest in you and the cause you represent'; and in 1864 she fought hard (if unsuccess-fully) to have him stay in her house in Manchester: 'I have overcome all female dignity and modesty and tell you frankly that for your and your party's personal ease and comfort, as well as for your public interests you can be at *Manchester* not in better hands than mine.'[211] Along with her expressions of undying affection, the duchess of Sutherland sent Garibaldi a bible, and lengthy analyses of religion;[212] her mother-in-law wrote seriously to him about slavery and the American civil war;[213] and another 'sister', Caroline Gifford Philipson, offered him her reflections on Protestantism as well as poetry and a jacket for his rheumatism.[214] They all helped organise subscriptions, meetings and press campaigns in aid of the Italian cause. Thus, for these women, and perhaps especially for Schwabe (a relative outsider), love for Garibaldi and support of Italian liberation were indivisible, and both can be seen as a strategy to assert a public identity of their own.

Conclusion

In the final version of his memoirs, written between 1871 and 1872, Garibaldi dedicates very little space to the years immediately following Italian unifica- tion. Only Aspromonte is mentioned and it is given eight terse pages; and he describes his life in its aftermath as 'idle and useless.'[215] Yet this is not entirely fair. In Italian politics, the period between 1860 and 1865 was one of transi- tion, and Garibaldi played a central role in establishing the direction of political life. Through a prodigious correspondence and relentless publicity in the press, he did an enormous amount to keep the issues of Rome and Venice alive, and constantly in front of the Italian and European public. He continued to attract huge popular support, and reached out to a broad cross-section of society. As well as the literate, male middle classes, he encouraged peasants, priests, workers and women to become involved in political action; he maintained political contacts with groups all over Italy, in the South as well as in the North; and he worked hard, and not unsuccessfully, to establish reciprocal links between the nationalist struggle in Italy and similar political struggles all over Europe and beyond Europe. He helped set the political agenda for liberal Italy in the years after unification, and made sure it would be a radical nationalist one. He also developed a mass political style, unique in Italy at this time, of using open spaces and theatres to make short speeches and hold impromptu dialogues with the crowd.[216] For all these reasons, a study of Garibaldi's activity after unification can add considerably to our under- standing of the ideas and political opportunities of the democratic movement in the period between the defeat of traditional conservatism in the late 1850s and the rise of mass socialist parties some twenty years later.

Garibaldi's career is equally revealing of the problems which faced the democratic movement. In Italy, and like their socialist counterparts later in the century, democratic activists had to choose between the parliamentary route to achieving their political ambitions or reliance on revolution; and, as their socialist counterparts were also to find out, this choice was an extremely divisive one, leading to lasting bitterness which their opponents were quick to take advantage of. Here, Garibaldi was no help at all. In the changed circumstances of a united Italy, his continuing loyalty to the crown and persistent belief in revolutionary action were incompatible; so his political attitude merely mirrored the left's dilemma rather than offering a solution to it. Moreover, some of his activities – his withdrawal to Caprera, his sudden appearance in parliament, Aspromonte – contributed significantly to the disarray on the left, and further stunted its capacity for practical political action. Although he was involved with political discontent in the South, his encouragement helped create a vast and diffuse southern opposition rather than an organised movement of democratic opposition to government policy.[217] Even his behaviour in England – allowing himself to be controlled by liberal aristocrats and then leaving with the tour half done – was typical of a disdainful attitude to practical political activity which was very obstructive. In this respect, Garibaldi's political career prefigures the disconnection of the democratic movement during the early 1870s.

The immediate years following 1860 are equally interesting in terms of the representation of politics. Garibaldi's function as a symbol of Italy probably revealed more than it should have about Italy after 1860. His withdrawal to Caprera, and his behaviour there and elsewhere, indicated a deep dissatisfaction with the outcome of national unification. His image was used satirically to attack the prime minister as well as the Pope; and his reception in London both embarrassed the Italian government and irritated Italian radicals. On the left, there was a growing tendency to sanctify Garibaldi, even as political criticism of him grew, to place him on a rocky island, altar or cross, away from or above the struggles and setbacks of daily politics. After Aspromonte, this strategy was useful for rhetorical purposes; it helped turn a political disaster into a propaganda triumph and it probably helped greatly in the popular dissemination of his image. Yet this heavy use of traditional symbolism did little to clarify what Garibaldi really stood for in political terms. As we saw, during his visit to London Garibaldi could be made to represent a vast range of different characters: a 'noble Roman', a working-class radical, an English gentleman and a romantic Italian lover. So in Britain too he seems to have represented a style or a 'look' as much as a real set of political issues.

In fact, part of Garibaldi's activity in these years should be understood as a struggle by him to direct his own role, to invest it with a political meaning of his choosing, and to use it to further his own programme – namely the nation-at-arms, and union with Rome and Venice – rather than simply to endorse the programmes of political colleagues like Crispi or Bertani. Still, in the end, neither he, nor the left, nor the government entirely controlled the use of his image. Indeed, the need to fashion and manage the political image of Italy, which had occupied Mazzini since the early 1830s, continued to trouble political leaders in the years after national unification; so, as such a potent symbol of Italian identity, Garibaldi started to become a reflection of its problems. Hence, a study of Garibaldi's function as a political symbol in this period can shed light on the broader difficulties of directing the process of political communication in liberal Italy, now that its metaphors and ambitions had become fully visible and its mechanisms freely available.

Equally interesting is the public reception of, and reaction to, Garibaldi. Although it is difficult to calculate accurately the extent of his support, it was undoubtedly considerable. It was not unique. Indeed, as I have sought to show, public enthusiasm for Garibaldi can best be explained by reference to a wider European and American cult of 'hero worship', which was a prevalent feature of support for democratic leaders like him. However, its scale, duration and intensity was unusual. As historians, we should cast a sceptical eye on descriptions of the crowds in London and elsewhere, and we can deconstruct the language and purposes of letters to Garibaldi. Nevertheless, they still offer us glimpses of an intense individual response to Garibaldi, and of a passionate engagement with the ideals which he was held to represent; and this response is all the more interesting as the voices of support for Garibaldi were often marginal to, or excluded from, the political system. Equally, we can perceive the presence of political acting in Garibaldi's humble home on Caprera, and see his simplicity as deliberate or staged. Yet our understanding of his private life as political statement should not obscure the importance of it to him as a model of democratic identity and behaviour, or lead us to ignore his audience, who found it so appealing and convincing. All the evidence, in other words, points not to the loss of support, but rather to the continuing vitality and potency of the popular cult of Garibaldi in the years immediately following the unification of Italy.

CHAPTER 12

CULTURE WARS

Rome and death

Garibaldi lived for twenty more years after his defeat at Aspromonte, and he was involved in three more military campaigns. The first of these was in the summer of 1866 when he fought with his volunteers on the side of the king and the royal army, who had joined Prussia in the war against Austria. Once again in this war, his volunteers were armed at the last minute, and they were sent away from the main action around the Po and Mincio rivers, up into the mountains of the Tyrol. There they engaged in two battles, at Monte Suello and Bezzecca, neither of which was a clear victory; at Bezzecca, Garibaldi was incapacitated by a thigh wound and had to direct the fighting from a carriage, and his army had heavy casualties.[1] The war itself was a dramatic failure. Indeed, the Italian army was so poorly prepared, and so badly co-ordinated and directed, that it stumbled into a major defeat at Custoza against an army which was less than half its size and before most of its divisions were engaged. Shortly thereafter, the Italian navy suffered an equally bad defeat at the island of Lissa by a smaller Austrian naval force. Italy's humiliation was completed by its ally, Prussia, which made a separate armistice with Austria. By the terms of the peace settlement, and in an echo of 1859, Austria ceded the Veneto to France, which only then handed it over to Italy, and the Tyrol remained in Austrian hands.[2]

The war of 1866 was considered a national disaster. Venice was taken without any great scenes of popular enthusiasm, although the population dutifully voted in a plebiscite for union with Italy. Although the numbers of Italian casualties were relatively small (600 dead at Lissa and 750 at Custoza),[3] the poor performance of the military was a terrible embarrassment. 'To be Italian was something we once longed for,' Crispi wrote to Bertani in August, 'now, in the present circumstances, it is shameful.'[4] Pasquale Villari, a respected intellectual and politician of the right, asked 'Whose fault is it?' and pointed to 'our colossal ignorance, our multitudes of illiterates, our machine bureaucrats, childish politicians, ignoramus professors, hopeless diplomats, incapable generals, unskilled workers, primitive farmers, and the rhetoric which gnaws our very bones'. 'Never again', he announced, 'can we look at ourselves quite as we used to do.'[5] If this was not bad enough, in mid-September, a week-long rebellion resulted in the seizure of the city of Palermo. Police and government officials were assaulted and murdered; the prefect and mayor of Palermo barricaded themselves into the royal palace; a political committee was formed to direct the revolution; and the revolt spread to the outlying provinces. The government declared martial law, and took three days of bitter street fighting to restore its authority in the city, and an even longer, equally violent campaign to do so in the countryside. During the official inquiries which followed, the extent of elite disaffection, popular deprivation and government incompetence in this part of Sicily was vividly revealed.[6] 'The result is dispiriting,' the academic and literary critic Francesco de Sanctis announced a few years later in a lecture on Mazzini, 'Italy is as it always was.'[7]

The war of 1866 and its aftermath represent a turning-point of sorts for the new state and the idea of the Italian nation. It marks the public emergence of a mood of national disillusionment, a sense of moral disappointment with Italy as a nation, and the first explicit use of disappointment as a rhetorical device in political debate after the achievement of national unification. At the end of the war, Garibaldi both accepted the peace publicly and expressed his displeasure with it in a celebrated one-word telegram to the king – '*Obbedisco* [I obey]' – and retired to Caprera. The government fell in early 1867 following a vote of no confidence, and a more left-leaning government under Rattazzi was formed. However, this mood of disillusionment was not confined to feelings about the government, but stretched beyond it to encompass the opposition. The old democratic left of Mazzini, Bertani and Crispi found itself under attack for political failure from a younger generation of revolutionaries influenced by socialist and anarchist ideas; some also revived the criticisms which Pisacane had made of Garibaldi's military tactics in the 1850s, and criticised him for accepting the peace terms with Austria rather than continuing the war in the Tyrol. Meanwhile, the divisions within the democratic left remained unresolved. Although Garibaldi and Mazzini grew closer during this period, Crispi had broken very publicly and definitively with Mazzini over the question of the monarchy (when Crispi accepted the monarchy, Mazzini loudly accused him of opportunism). In turn, Crispi and Bertani, despite repeated efforts to work together, grew further apart. They collaborated to produce a new paper of the left, *La Riforma*, and although the paper was an important one (and a mouthpiece for Crispi), it had financial problems and not very many readers, and it proved unable to maintain a single editorial line on the main political issues facing the left, notably its attitude to the monarchy. [8]

It was in the midst of this unstable political situation that the attention of both Garibaldi and the government turned to Rome. Some two years previously, the government had concluded a treaty with France: the so-called 'September convention' of 1864, whereby the Italian government recognised and guaranteed papal Rome and moved its capital from Turin to Florence, and Napoleon III agreed to withdraw his troops guarding the Pope in Rome. This treaty, which seemed to represent a relinquishment of Rome as the capital of Italy, was unpopular and caused a wave of protest, and there were riots in Turin over the loss of its status as capital city. However, the arrival of Rattazzi as prime minister in 1867 seemed to add new life to the idea of winning Rome for Italy. In fact, Rattazzi and the king hatched an essentially nefarious plan secretly to encourage Garibaldi to invade the Papal States. They gave him money and arms, but seemingly intended to use his invasion as 'an excuse for the Italian army to cross the frontier in pursuit, so that the temporal power and the forces of radicalism could be destroyed in one blow'. Suspecting this, and fearing a second Aspromonte, many on the left advised Garibaldi against any such action.[9]

Nonetheless, in the early months of 1867 Garibaldi left Caprera and embarked on a frenetic bout of political activity. He came first to the new Italian capital, Florence, and went on a triumphant tour via Bologna and Rovigo to Venice, where he arrived to a great welcome in late February. He made a series of violently anti-clerical speeches, in which he also put pressure on the government for action on Rome.[10] He then stayed on the mainland throughout the spring and summer. During this time, his son, Ricciotti, raised money in Britain for a new Roman campaign, and the campaign received a large donation from the Tuscan democrat and financier, Adriano Lemmi (a former secretary of Kossuth's, and active in anti-clerical and Masonic circles in Britain and the USA).[11] Garibaldi also established a series of contacts with a committee of Roman exiles in Bologna (an anti-clerical city), and a Centre of Insurrection in Rome; the latter appointed him their 'Commander-in-Chief' in April. During the summer, Garibaldi toured a series of towns – Pistoia, Siena and Orvieto – which brought him ever closer to the frontier with the Papal States. He issued a call to the Masonic lodges of Palermo and Naples to unite, and published a statement supporting radical proposals for compulsory free lay education and the extension of equal civil and political rights to women. In September, he travelled to Geneva to speak at the Congress of the International League of Peace and Liberty, and called not just for peace but also for an end to the Papacy.[12] He then went back to Florence, where he began final plans for the invasion of the Papal States, and travelled south towards the frontier at Orvieto. It is clear from his activities in 1867 that Garibaldi saw the seizure of Rome not just as a nationalist objective but also, and above all, as the destruction of the Papacy and the liberation of 'humanity' from priestly oppression.[13]

At this point, however, the king and Rattazzi, who were under great pressure from Napoleon III over the threat to Rome, lost their nerve and arrested Garibaldi, who was taken back to his home on Caprera.[14] Yet even the arrest of Garibaldi was not the end of the story. Rattazzi, now in contact with Crispi, apparently still had designs on Rome. Instead of a direct invasion of Rome, which would have been an open breach of the September convention with France, they hatched a new plan to encourage a popular insurrection in the Papal States, which they hoped would appeal to Italian (and international liberal) public opinion, and make it seem that the government had no choice but to invade Rome. Accordingly, large sums of money were passed to clandestine volunteer groups and a committee of assistance to encourage insurrection; Crispi mounted an intense nationalist campaign in the press; and in mid-October Garibaldi was allowed to escape from Caprera and come to Florence. However, two days before his arrival the French government announced its decision to send another expeditionary force to Rome to protect the Pope; and on the day of his arrival Rattazzi resigned as prime minister.[15] Nonetheless, in the delay before the formation of another government, he continued to assist Garibaldi, who finally managed to enter papal territory on 24 October and join up with other volunteers (including his son, Menotti) at Monterotondo.

On 3 November, Garibaldi's volunteers met with papal troops at Mentana. Although Garibaldi had experienced problems of morale and discipline with his forces, they gradually gained the upper hand and, by the afternoon, had forced the papal troops into a retreat.[16] The arrival of the French expeditionary force cancelled this advantage. The French were equipped with the new *chassepot* rifle, which enabled them to fire repeatedly from a long distance; and Garibaldi's tactics of enthusiastic charging with a large body of men were simply no match for this weapon. By the evening, his volunteers had fled the battlefield in confusion and Garibaldi was defeated. The next day, he retreated with part of his army across the border to Italy and was immediately arrested and placed once again in the fort at Varignano. During the same days, a Mazzinian-inspired insurrection had started in Rome, but was quickly suppressed by papal troops amid the general indifference of the population.[17]

'Mentana', as this episode now came to be called, was even more disastrous for the government than the war for Venice. 'Ill-designed, badly-conceived, and miserably executed', was the comment of the American consul in Rome.[18] Mentana made the king unpopular at home; it showed how many of Italy's politicians were, at heart, conspirators rather than statesmen; and it not only failed to achieve its objective but also offered, again, the humiliating spectacle of Italy as the territory of foreign (French) invasion. The government's action in failing to protect the integrity of the Papal States was condemned in Berlin, Vienna and Paris; and the British politician, Lord Clarendon, remarked on the 'universal agreement that Victor Emanuel is an imbecile . . . a dishonest man who tells lies to everyone'.[19] Much like the war for Venice, in other words, Mentana pointed to the failure of the new Italy. On the one hand, it represented the public betrayal of the Risorgimento promise while, on the other, it added to Italy's reputation as a weak power and unreliable ally.

Mentana also led to further shifts on the left. Some younger radicals distanced themselves from Mazzinianism and Garibaldi; and the Neapolitan radical paper La Situazione pronounced Garibaldi dead at Mentana: 'and history will say of him that, born of the people, he neither understood nor fought for them; he lived an immensely glorious but fatuous life, and died consumed by the tabes dorsalis of the party system: [a mixture of] incapacity and utopia'.[20] A new anti-clerical paper, Libertà e Giustizia, criticised those who joined Garibaldi for their inability to understand popular religious sentiment.[21] At the same time, Mentana helped to define the left's opposition to the government. Bertani (who had opposed the expedition but had followed Garibaldi into battle) spoke openly against the monarchy in parliament: '[at] Mentana something solemn and serious occurred; at Mentana was ruptured the solidarity . . . between the volunteers and the monarchy';[22] Lo Zenzero, a Florentine radical paper, proclaimed: 'Italy was born from revolution; and the day that Italy deviates from its revolutionary policy will be the last day of its greatness . . . General Garibaldi has always been the personification of revolutionary politics in Italy, from 1848 to this time.'[23] The kind of political and popular fallout Mentana could cause is demonstrated clearly by the case of Bologna, an anti-clerical city where, until this time, there had been very little left-wing opposition to the moderate liberal hegemony over the local administration. However, in the aftermath of Mentana, the refusal of the City Council to give a public funeral to two 'martyrs' of the campaign caused days of street protests and a public row. Indeed, so angry was the crowd that Bologna's leading moderate politician, Marco Minghetti, had to be protected by bodyguards and hurredly left the city. So, for Bologna's ruling elite, Mentana marked the end both of a post-Risorgimento consensus and its division into openly hostile political camps.[24]

Garibaldi's motives for trusting the king and Rattazzi in 1867 are not entirely clear. He never trusted them again and became, henceforth, an outspoken critic of the monarchy and the political system in liberal Italy. After his arrest, he agreed to return to his home on Caprera and, although he was obliged to stay only for six months, in the end he remained there in a kind of internal exile for almost three years. He resigned as a deputy in the national parliament. These decisions reflect his political disillusionment and may also have been made partly for personal reasons: he was now in his sixties, and suffering badly from rheumatism. He also had a new family in Caprera, this time the result of a relationship with his daughter's wet-nurse, Francesca Armosina, with whom he had two daughters, Clelia in 1867 and Rosa in 1869, and a son, Manlio, in 1873. He wanted to marry her but, since he was still married to Giuseppina Raimondi and could not divorce her, he was unable to do so (and, indeed, they only married in 1880, when the Court of Appeal finally accepted Garibaldi's argument that his marriage to Raimondi was unconsummated).[25]

Nevertheless, Garibaldi's decision to remain on the island was also political; it represented an 'abstention' rather than a retirement.[26] As we shall see, he continued to write in abundance, publishing a multitude of comments on national politics, addresses to clubs and meetings, and letters to newspapers; and all of these pronouncements were uncompromisingly radical and anti-clerical. He followed the lead of his Neapolitan colleague Giuseppe Ricciardi and endorsed the formation of an *anticoncilio* in opposition to the convocation of the first Vatican Council in Rome.[27] He did not see Mentana as the end of his military career. At the end of December 1867, he wrote an address to the Mentana veterans: 'A woman has sent me the following motto: Perseverance wins. I hope that the Italians will remind the world of this next spring.'[28] On the anniversary of the departure from Quarto (in 1860), he wrote to the Sicilian veterans of Milan: 'Yes! I know that not all the brave men in Italy are dead and I hope that with your help, the priests, mercenaries and traitors will know this soon. To another 5th of May!'[29] He also wrote two novels while at home in Caprera, *Clelia* and *Cantoni il volontario* (both published in 1870), which represent, among other ambitions, a forceful attempt to publicise his anti-clericalism, and which express his personal and political frustration at the conditions prevailing in Italy.[30]

In 1870, France declared war on Prussia. The war was the final stage in a protracted diplomatic stand-off between Bismarck and Napoleon III and in it France suffered a series of swift losses and a crushing defeat at the battle of Sedan on 1 September. After Sedan, Napoleon III abdicated and left France as a German prisoner. Shortly before, he had withdrawn all his troops from Rome and, on 19 September, the Italian army (led by General Cadorna but without Garibaldi) made a breach in the Roman walls at Porta Pia and seized Rome from the Pope. In France, a republic was declared and a Government of National Defence was formed, which then set about creating a new army to defend the nascent republic. As part of this programme, an auxiliary army was

created, in which all non-regular troops – *mobiles* and *francs-tireurs* operating
as guerrilla forces – could be given commissions and appointed to any rank.
These *francs-tireurs* were a popular success: their numbers quickly reached
over 55,000, and volunteers came from Spain, Poland, America, Britain and
Italy to fight for the new French republic. Garibaldi decided to join them.
Encouraged by Philippe Bourdon or 'Bordone', a French 'disciple' (and a
volunteer from 1860),[31] he wrote to the provisional government: 'What
remains of me is at your service. At your command.'[32] He then left Caprera
and came to Tours, France's temporary capital during the siege of Paris. There
he was appointed commander of the Army of the Vosges, a force of some
15,000 *francs-tireurs* and *mobiles* in eastern France.[33]

The radical press (notably *Le Siècle*)[34] welcomed Garibaldi, and a journalist
in besieged Paris published a paper, 'Garibaldi, the defender of oppressed
peoples', which declared: 'Garibaldi does not belong to Italy; he belongs to the
whole world.'[35] But the French authorities were not pleased to see him. His
reception was not helped by the presence of Bordone, who was widely
considered an unsavoury character and had a criminal record.[36] Garibaldi had
annoyed everyone before arriving by writing two letters to *Il Movimento* in
Genoa: one in which he proclaimed the historic independence of Nice, and
another where he praised his 'brothers in Germany' for having rid the world
of that 'incubus of tyranny' which was Bonapartism (this pro-German stance
was not uncommon at the time).[37] The Catholic right was openly furious, and
the archbishop of Tours lamented: 'I thought that divine Providence had
reached its fill of the humiliations which it had heaped on our country; I was
wrong: one supreme humiliation was kept back for us, that of seeing Garibaldi
arrive here, having given himself the mission of saving France.'[38] According to
an English commentator, French civilians considered Garibaldi to be 'a
presumptious intruder, who felt that, because he had beaten a few miserable
Neapolitans in a little enterprise that had become famous for the mere
romance of it, he could conquer the great armies of Germany, before which so
many French generals had been compelled to retreat in disaster'.[39] All the
commanders of the regular French divisions in eastern France were said to
despise and resent Garibaldi. There was also no denying that Garibaldi was
now old and suffering from ill health; plus he had no experience of fighting in
a northern European winter. So there were real doubts about how much help
he and his 'collection of revolutionaries' could really be.[40] As one hostile
French historian of the war put it a few years later: 'Garibaldi, this so-called
saviour of France, was nothing but an invalid in body and spirit, who
constantly let himself be dominated by his entourage and above all by his
favourite, Bordone. In return, he always refused to submit to government
orders.'[41]

In the event, Garibaldi's campaign in eastern France was not a success. His son, Ricciotti, won a brief victory over a German command in Châtillon-sur-Seine, but Garibaldi himself proved repeatedly unable to recapture Dijon for the French. Only at the end of December, after the Germans had evacuated the city, did he prepare to move; but then he delayed the troops' departure from their base in Autun due to the lack of trains and, after arrival, he was incapacitated by an acute attack of rheumatism. And, although his army was able to fight off a German counter-attack for Dijon on 21 January (commanded from a carriage by Garibaldi), they later abandoned it to the Germans after the armistice. They also did nothing to help General Bourbaki's army at Besançon, which now collapsed or fell into 'a kind of instanteous decomposition' and started to surrender to the Germans; later they were interned in Switzerland.[42]

The French government surrendered Paris to the German army at the end of January, and brought the war to a close. Garibaldi stayed on after the armistice, and was elected as a deputy in the new National Assembly for Dijon, Paris, Nice and Algiers. Although he announced his intention of resigning his seat(s) and returning to Caprera, he first travelled to Bordeaux (where the assembly was temporarily located) to cast his vote in favour of retaining the Republic. Garibaldi's arrival, 'in a red jumper, with his large felt hat, [and] the rough, calm air of a soldier' (according to the eyewitness Emile Zola), caused a terrible uproar in the chamber, which was dominated by conservatives and monarchists who despised him as a republican and had accused him of military insubordination during the war.[43] They argued that, as a foreigner, he could not be elected, and the president of the chamber told him he could not speak as he had just resigned his seat. Garibaldi repeatedly tried to speak but was shouted down. Eventually he left the chamber, and Bordeaux, for Marseille, from where he travelled to Caprera in the middle of February. A popular demonstration took place outside the chamber to protest at his treatment, but it subsided after Garibaldi's departure became known. Three weeks later, Victor Hugo caused another uproar in the French assembly when he sought to defend Garibaldi ('I don't wish to be offensive,' he told the deputies, 'but I must say that, among all the French generals fighting in this war, Garibaldi alone did not suffer a defeat'); he too was shouted down.[44] If nothing else, this bitter episode at the end of a deeply divisive war showed just how intensely French public opinion was divided over Garibaldi.[45]

The years 1870–1 were a major turning-point in nineteenth-century history. The defeat of France by Prussia, following the defeat of Austria four years earlier, and the creation of the German Empire marked the emergence of Germany as the dominant power in continental Europe, and a new phase in international relations. These years also saw an important shift on the democratic left. Two events dominated political life in Italy: the capture of Rome from the Pope in the autumn of 1870, and the revolution in Paris (the Paris Commune) of spring 1871. By removing any further reason for insurrection, the capture of Rome seemed to eliminate the tensions between the 'loyal' parliamentary opposition and the 'extreme' left (*Estrema*). But the Paris Commune separated them again, pushing some towards greater political compromise and the formation of the Historic Left (*Sinistra Storica*), which four years later took power in the parliamentary 'revolution' of 1876, and pushing others (a series of radical organisations, and various socialist and anarchist groups) further to the left. Within this radical left, a crucial division emerged. Mazzini utterly condemned the Paris Commune as a socially divisive mistake, and sought to regroup the workers' clubs to combat the danger of socialism.[46] However, many other radicals in Italy followed the socialist lead and mythologised the Commune as a social revolution ('the glorious harbinger of a new society' in Karl Marx's words).[47]

As a result, the Paris Commune allowed a significant section of the radical left, especially a younger generation of radicals led by the poet and satirist Felice Cavallotti and grouped around the newspaper *Il Gazzettino Rosa*, to break openly and decisively with both Mazzini and the principles and methods of Mazzinian politics. *Il Gazzettino Rosa* praised Mazzini as the 'saviour' and teacher of Italy but insisted:

> We have no more idols, we don't accept abstruse, incomprehensible formulas ... What we object to in Mazzini is not his opinion in itself, as much as his opinion erected into a system and a political dogma. We are materialists, but we don't make a political school out of our materialism. To us it does not matter if one believes or does not believe in God ... instead Mazzini wants to impose a new religion on us.[48]

The emphasis by younger radicals on the 'social question' was paralleled by an increase in what was called 'internationalist' or socialist activity (mostly Bakuninist anarchism) throughout northern and southern Italy, which was given a big boost by the Paris Commune. The rise of socialism represented a genuine challenge to Mazzini and the Mazzinian emphasis on politics and culture; and Mazzini's death early in 1872 only served to underline the prevailing sense that his political era was over.

Garibaldi now broke definitively with Mazzini, and this time he moved to the left of him. He came out entirely in favour of the Paris Commune and internationalism, and his stance brought him much closer to the younger radicals, especially Cavallotti, and gave him a new lease on political life. From his support was born an initiative to relaunch a broad party of the radical left.

'Why', Garibaldi wrote from Caprera, 'don't we pull together in one fasces [organised group] the Freemasonry, democratic societies, workers' clubs, Rationalists, Mutual Aid etc., which have the same tendency towards good?'[49] He became involved in organising a general democratic congress, a Congress of Unity, which was to be held in the Colosseum in Rome in November 1872. As well as having the support of radical organisations, the Congress was endorsed by the anti-clerical free-thinking group, the socialist groups in Emilia–Romagna, the social workers' movement in Tuscany, and the *Plebe* group from Lodi, and was a striking example of the unifying power of Garibaldi's name.[50] Although the Congress was banned by the government, the committee itself went ahead and held a meeting in the Teatro Argentina. There they signed the Pact of Roma on the basis of a package of radical policies which included universal suffrage, compulsory lay education, progressive taxation, administrative reform and the abolition of the death penalty.[51]

Nor was this the end of Garibaldi's political activity. After his return from France, he substantially revised and republished his memoirs, and produced a new novel, *I Mille*, which was both anti-clerical and anti-Mazzinian.[52] In 1873, he issued a public declaration in support of the new republic in Spain and, in the same year, he endorsed the programme of an anti-clerical meeting held in Milan, attended by radical groups, Masonic lodges and various atheistic and free-thinking societies.[53] Amid a deepening economic crisis, he then stood for parliament as a radical candidate and was elected for Rome in the general election of 1874. He had long been interested in public works, and in early 1875 he travelled to Rome to take his seat, and to present a grandiose project to revitalise the city by diverting the course of the Tiber from Rome and reclaiming the surrounding land, so making the river navigable and the city free of disease. He was now sixty-eight and increasingly infirm, but still dressed in red shirt and poncho, and huge crowds greeted him in Civitavecchia, where he disembarked, and in Rome's railway station, where he was taken in triumphal procession to his hotel.[54] Although the Tiber project came to nothing, Garibaldi still refused to retire. Also in 1875, he wrote to parliament protesting at the emergency legislation proposed for Sicily and the South, and the following year he proposed limiting the size of government pensions and salaries (this was part of a broader attack on the privileges of public life, including a critique of the king's very substantial civil list).[55] In 1879, in the midst of widespread dissatisfaction with the political record of the new government of the *Sinistra*, he went to Rome again to help launch a new campaign with his old comrade-in-arms, Alberto Mario. The League of Democracy founded by him, Mario, Bertani and Cavallotti, among others, restated the 1872 programme of electoral, administrative and financial reform; it also called for the legal and political emancipation of women, the replacement of the regular army by the nation-at-arms, and a plan of public works to improve the Roman countryside.[56]

In 1880, Garibaldi issued a series of manifestos and addresses calling for universal suffrage. He also went to Genoa to protest at the arrest of his son-in-law, Stefano Canzio, for political sedition, and travelled to Milan for the inauguration of the monument to those fallen at Mentana. Since he was too ill to speak at the ceremony, Canzio read his speech out for him, which ended with a call for universal suffrage.[57] In March 1882, at the age of seventy-four, Garibaldi left Alassio (on the Italian Riviera, where he had spent the winter for health reasons), and travelled to southern Italy; he arrived first in Naples, and then took the train to Palermo in order to attend the commemoration of the 600th anniversary of the Sicilian Vespers. According to his daughter, Clelia, who was with him, Garibaldi had said that he wanted to see 'the *palermitani*' before he died, and was especially keen to greet those who had fought with him in 1860.[58] But Garibaldi also had immediate political reasons for going to Palermo. These were connected to the French government's recent seizure of Tunis, traditionally seen as an Italian (and specifically Sicilian) sphere of influence. So, the radicals saw the celebrations for the Sicilian Vespers as an opportunity for anti-French, anti-government agitation, and Garibaldi sought to support them, much to the alarm of government repesentatives, who wanted to use the ceremony as an official festival of unity and national belonging. As it turned out, Garibaldi was so ill that he could not attend the main ceremony on 31 March, although he did manage to go to the inauguration of a monument to the Thousand in the mountains at Gibilrossa.[59]

Garibaldi returned to Caprera in mid-April and two months later, in early June, he died in bed after an attack of acute bronchitis. In the end, he died quickly, so only his eldest son, Menotti, and his third wife, Francesca, were with him. He left what have been called 'plans of remarkable precision' for his funeral.[60] He gave strict instructions that he was to be cremated, and told his doctor that he wanted:

> a pile of firewood two metres high, of acacia, mastic, myrtle and other aromatic wood. On the pile a small iron bed should be placed and on this the uncovered coffin, with my remains inside, adorned in a red shirt. A handful of ashes should be placed in an ordinary urn, and this should be placed in the graveyard where the ashes of my children Rosa and Anita lie.

He told his family not to tell the political authorities until the ceremony had been carried out.[61]

Allegedly inspired by the cremation of the poet Shelley (on an open fire at the beach in Viareggio), Garibaldi's funeral instructions reflect his enduringly romantic beliefs and sensibilities; but they are also a curious, if entirely typical, combination of the personal and political. His death was conceived as a 'last battle against the Vatican',[62] and it was defiantly secular. In his 'political testament' (1871–2), he had stated his rejection of 'the odious, despicable and wicked ministry of a priest, whom I consider to be the atrocious enemy of humankind and of Italy in particular' at the moment of his death,[63] and we must remember that cremation was an illegal procedure in Italy until 1888, and condemned by the Church (and that Garibaldi had lent his support to the radical *filocremazionista* League which had agitated for a change in the law during the 1870s).[64] So his instructions are interesting for what they tell us about Garibaldi's enduringly political attitude to his life and fame. Even in death, he fought for control of his body and of the means of its representation, by seeking to leave the public stage in a political manner and moment of his own choosing.

Unfortunately, the Italian authorities found out about his plans, and they insisted on an official commemoration. So instead Garibaldi's body was made to lie in state in his bedroom at Caprera surrounded by funeral wreaths and with a crimson rose fixed to his red shirt. The body was viewed by veterans, admirers and politicians; and the funeral itself was an elaborate ceremony, attended by royalty, officials, and 1,200 different associations, and with 100 flags. Garibaldi was not cremated; instead, to the sound of firing cannons, his coffin was carried by members of the Thousand and placed in a tomb covered with a large granite block. The funeral ended in a violent storm which trapped many of the dignitaries on Caprera for the night.[65]

This ceremony was followed by other elaborate funeral processions in the major Italian cities. In Milan, the procession was attended by some 50,000 people, including military veterans, Masons, workers' organisations, women's groups and mutual aid societies, with a huge bust of Garibaldi at the centre of proceedings. In Rome, the commemorations were even more elaborate. As part of a vast procession which started in Piazza del Popolo and moved towards the Campidoglio, a bust of Garibaldi (which had been crowned with a laurel wreath by a statue of liberty placed alongside the bust) was drawn in a carriage by eight white horses dressed in mourning (see figure 31 opposite). Carved into the sides of the carriage were representations of Garibaldi's triumphal entrances into Rome, Naples and Palermo.[66]

A wave of national mourning swept across Italian public spaces. Black edges framed the front pages of newspapers, and flags were lowered to half-mast on town halls and almost every other public and private meeting place. All public and political events, including Constitution Day and other local festivals, were cancelled, and many politicians and veterans made a public display of their grief; some were said to have wept openly. These demonstrations were

31 The transportation of Garibaldi's bust to the Campidoglio in Rome. This colour lithograph was one of many produced to commemorate the elaborate 'funeral' celebrations held after Garibaldi's death.

accompanied by a succession of speeches by public figures and poems by famous writers like Giosuè Carducci, as well as by minor speeches, songs and patriotic hymns; and parades were held in towns and villages across Italy. Often these were also published as separate pamphlets and/or as items in the local papers.[67] 'His death has pierced the heart of Italy with a universal, deep, and unutterable pain', Enrico Panzacchi announced to the Progressive Constitutional Association in Bologna; 'death's scythe reaped the life of the brave of the braves, Giuseppe Garibaldi, yesterday evening at 6 o'clock', the citizens of Conegliano, near Venice, were told.[68] In Codogno, a small rural community in the Milan hinterland, a service to honour Garibaldi was held in the local theatre, which was decked out in black flags, with a bust of Garibaldi similarly draped in mourning; in Pisa, a huge choreographed procession was organised on 15 June; in Siracusa, a commemoration was held in the Greek theatre; while in Macerata in the Marche, the whole of the following April was given over to a prolonged celebration of Garibaldi, which involved every social club, democratic association, mutual aid society, veterans' group, bank, library and musical band in the district.[69]

Death came to be seen as the apotheosis of Garibaldi's life, and provided an occasion for the unrestrained use of Risorgimento rhetoric. 'I salute you . . . I place on your venerable forehead the laurels of immortality', one of the Thousand, Eugenio Dionese, announced in a speech in Lipari, in the Æolian islands.[70] 'He is dead? That's a lie! . . . Garibaldi is not a man, he is a symbol, an idea, he is Jacob reborn . . . Ideas don't die, Garibaldi lives', the students at the University of Messina were told; while in Trapani, the head of the local school, Gino de' Nobili, made a speech in the Teatro Garibaldi, where a bust of Garibaldi was again crowned with a laurel wreath by a figure representing Italy; in his speech he declared Garibaldi's apotheosis and described him as 'a Greek soul spirtualised by the Christian world'.[71] 'Garibaldi is dead! *Viva Garibaldi!*' Matilde Caselli wrote in Naples.[72] He 'personified the courage and sacrifice of Leonidas, the loyalty and patriotism of Washington. Like a marvellous meteor which leaves a sparkling and dazzling trail in its wake', the speaker at a ceremony in Pachino (in the extreme south-eastern corner of Sicily) informed his audience.[73] Many of the visual images produced at this time show Garibaldi sanctified or deified, received into paradise by a complete pantheon of Italian

32   '2 June 1882': this lithograph imagines Garibaldi's arrival in paradise. Welcoming him in the clouds are Cavour, Vittorio Emanuele and Mazzini, and behind them are other Risorgimento heroes. Ranged around this central group are examples of Garibaldi's heroism and at his feet are Italy, France, America and a volunteer. The picture is a striking example of attempts to create a conciliatory pantheon of nationalist heroes and of the pervasion of nationalist rhetoric by religious discourse.

heroes (see figure 32 opposite); in others, he is already a monument, standing above the Italian people or riding his horse off into the clouds.[74] There was a marked tendency to idealise every aspect of his life, and to establish a hagiographic script which was to endure during the decades which followed. Even the moment of his death was idealised as a peaceful slumber surrounded by his loving family, with Garibaldi's two dead daughters represented as birds outside his bedroom window, ready to take him to paradise.[75]

In New York, *Harper's Weekly* presented Garibaldi's life as a triumph. He 'lived to see the completion of a work that none but himself could have perfected'; he 'waved his magic wand . . . and all was changed'; 'not Gracchus, nor Cicero, nor any Roman patriot who labored for freedom in the classic age, has so well deserved the grateful tears of every Roman'; Garibaldi was 'one of the figures of romance which occasionally appear in history, and are remembered as the personification of heroic qualities'.[76] The London *Times*, as we shall see, was less positive in its assessment (and dwelt at length on the dispute over his funeral), but it still agreed that he was 'the last hero of the heroic age of new Italy'.[77] In Paris, the *Revue des Deux Mondes* printed a sharply critical article entitled 'The last of the *condottieri*', but it too grudgingly paid tribute to Garibaldi's sincerity, bravery and sang-froid, as well as his sense of theatre: 'famous men should always arrange to end their lives on an island, nothing makes them greater than the solitude which it creates around them. The smaller the island, the greater the man appears, and Caprera was just a tiny little island.'[78]

The funeral of Garibaldi, and the political events leading up to his death, offer us a valuable insight into the struggle for control of his image and memory, a struggle which I will examine in the last sections of this chapter. Before I do so, however, I want to stress the importance of his last years in political terms. The late 1870s mark the beginning of *trasformismo* in Italy, or the formation of government majorities based on parliamentary alliances between left and right, and this strategy helped to create a more or less unified party of the ruling elite. This system was unstable and often unpopular, and helped bring the parliamentary system in Italy into considerable disrepute.[79] However, as Axel Körner has pointed out, the rise of *trasformismo* also saw 'a strengthening of the opposition on the Radical Left, despite the ideological differences between *Garibaldini*, Republicans and oppositional democrats'.[80] At least part of the credit for this achievement must go to Garibaldi's tireless political activity in the fifteen years after Mentana.

Garibaldi is unusual in that he became more, not less, radical as he grew older. It is possible to disparage his futile attempts to defend the French Republic, but they represent a striking commitment to the principles of international republicanism.[81] We should also be clear that his internationalism was not socialist in the Marxist sense, but more a mix of early-nineteenth-century cosmopolitanism, Saint-Simonianism, and Masonic associationalism; equally, Garibaldi distanced himself from Bakunin and anarchism in the early 1870s.[82] His stated aim was merely to turn what he called 'such a strong association' to 'a good end rather than a bad'.[83] Nevertheless, his commitment to the First International did a great deal to help the diffusion of socialism in Italy and encourage the adherence of a younger generation to socialist and anarchist groups.

The Italian radical movement in the 1870s was not especially successful. Garibaldi's Tiber project was a failure, the various programmes of political reform remained unenacted, and the broadly constructed, mass-based party that he envisaged was never established. Nevertheless, the policies promoted by Garibaldi publicised a concern with the 'social question': they were an attempt to resolve the problems of Italy's poor and of Italy's landscape, and to prevent the growth of social unrest. Thus, Garibaldi's support of radical policies in public works, education and taxation helped place these issues clearly on the political agenda; furthermore, along with Bertani and Mario, he helped promote the issue of female emancipation, and women activists were consistently involved in his last campaign with the League of Democracy.[84] Although universal suffrage was not attained, the suffrage was widened in 1882, and the campaign for a new suffrage in that year relaunched radicalism as a political movement.[85] Perhaps especially, Garibaldi's relationship with younger radicals (notably Cavallotti but also a large number of lesser-known activists) helped create a heterogeneous but arguably national network of radical associations and clubs. The new methods of political communication pioneered by the radical movement, through speeches and dialogues with the crowd and mass meetings in open spaces and theatres, which tended to challenge and overcome the otherwise narrow, elitist basis of political life in Italy, were at least partly the invention of Garibaldi.[86] His energetic, physical style – *garibaldinismo*, a 'romanticism which translates into political action',[87] based on a fusion of religious and secular symbols – was to prove remarkably influential in Italian politics. In all these ways, Garibaldi's later political career, along with those of other radicals, provides a crucial link between the democratic movement of the Risorgimento and the rise of mass socialist parties towards the end of the nineteenth century.

It is often argued that the last period of Garibaldi's career was unhappy and even futile, that he was worn down by personal illness and political failure. As *The Times* commented in its obituary, 'had he, like Cavour, died at the opportune moment, [he] would have been deemed absolutely without fault', but there was 'a weak side' to his nature which made him commit an 'extraordinary number of blunders' ('happy if he had spoken less and written

33 Garibaldi at the Augustus Mausoleum in 1875. The occasion was a banquet for workers' societies and, despite his gravely ill appearance, was part of a renewed bout of political activity.

nothing!').[88] Photographs of him as an old man show a tired figure stiffened by rheumatism (at a democratic meeting in the Augustus Mausoleum in 1875, he slumps in a chair, visibly ill, covered with a poncho which seems more like a blanket; see figure 33 above); and a late painting of him at Caprera by the avant-garde *macchiaolo* artist Vincenzo Cabianca, holding his wounded foot and with his crutch beside him, anticipates his death by casting him in a shadowy, melancholy light.[89] The view that his last years were 'empty and mundane' was put forward in compelling terms by Garibaldi's biographer, his secretary Giuseppe Guerzoni:

It is sad to tell of these last years: sad, like the spectacle of greatness which declines and lives beyond itself. Garibaldi was now but the ghost of a giant, obliged to drag across the earth the weight of his past greatness . . . fortune, which had bestowed so many favours on our Hero, refused him the greatest one of all: that of resting on the last trace of his victories and dying at the right time.[90]

A crucial aspect of the later legend of Garibaldi is that, as Daniel Pick writes, he 'found . . . little solace and contentment in old age'; he suffered 'political marginalisation', and he was self-destructive, prone to melancholy and inclined to obsessive behaviour.[91]

As I have sought to show here, Garibaldi was not politically marginal, and there is another way of interpreting his obsessive behaviour. Although Garibaldi was severely ill and visibly frustrated in his final years, it seems likely that at least some of his melancholy and neurosis was staged for public consumption and for political purposes, and that this was a tactic ably supported by artists, writers and his first serious biographers, men like Guerzoni, most of whom were also his political colleagues.[92] I would suggest that, since Garibaldi was no longer able or willing to press his good looks and physical energy into the service of the national cause, personal sadness became for him an alternative form of political display. In the context of post-unification political disillusionment, it seems evident that Garibaldi's ill, tired and broken body served as a symbol of national suffering, and was a very effective means of publicly personifying the social injustices of liberal Italy, the 'sickness' of Rome, and the betrayal of the Risorgimento.

The politics of memory

National unification posed many problems for Italy's rulers. In the 1860s, the political divisions and clerical opposition caused by the circumstances of unification combined with economic depression and widespread poverty, social disorder (especially brigandage in southern Italy) and the humiliations of foreign policy to create a clamour of opposition to the right-wing government. After 1876, the disillusionment caused by the meagre political record and *trasformismo* of the new left government produced a climate of political and social instability. The increasingly visible issue of Italy's regional diversity, notably the political, economic, cultural and geographical difference between North and South, added to these problems and seemed to offer clear proof that unification had still not been achieved. National unification was meant to resolve Italy's difficulties, not increase them, and the inability of Italy's new governing class to solve these problems undermined its legitimacy, and provided both the radical movement and the Church with ample opportunity to attack its legislative record and the conduct of political life. Crucially, these practical problems of unification were paralleled by problems with nationalism itself. As we have seen, Italy lacked national symbols such as the monarchy and the army, the Italian language was spoken by a minority of the population, and illiteracy rates were extremely high. Unification, by profoundly alienating the Catholic Church, neutralised (at the very least) the role of traditional religion as a source of Italian national identity. In this way, nationality could not unite Italians; it became another one of liberal Italy's disappointments.

It is now a commonplace that the rulers of Italy were faced after unification with the prodigious task of 'making Italians'. Involved was a process both of nation-building (what Umberto Levra calls a process of 'amalgamating' and 'homogenizing' Italians) and of organising political consent through the invention of Italian national traditions, and the creation of symbols of *italianità*.[93] As part of this process, the Risorgimento was quickly appropriated and recast as the latest episode in Italy's foundation story, or as a recent heroic past which could inspire and consolidate a sense of national community and belonging.[94] There has been an enormous amount of scholarly interest in this political project. Research has focused on a number of related themes and issues, but especially on the moment of nation-building after the broadening of the suffrage in 1882 and thereafter (the construction of monuments to dead heroes like Garibaldi and King Vittorio Emanuele; commemorations, anniversaries and museums of the Risorgimento; educational policies; and the writing of a national history). The prevalence of personality cults (the glorification of Garibaldi and Vittorio Emanuele; and the promotion of historical heroes of *italianità* like Dante, Columbus and the boy insurgent Balilla) was also a characteristic feature of the late-nineteenth-century process of nation-building in Italy.[95]

Francesco Crispi, in particular, used Garibaldi to promote his own nationalising agenda. He assiduously fostered the cults of both Garibaldi and Vittorio Emanuele in the 1880s, and sought specifically to turn Garibaldi into 'a sacred symbol . . . of the unity of the nation, of the people bound in selfless faith and duty to Italy and to its main political incarnation, the monarchy'. In speeches, articles and in his paper, *La Riforma*, Crispi presented Garibaldi as a 'divine' and 'exceptional being'; a man devoted to the king and even an anti-socialist, as well as a nationalist and anti-clerical.[96] At the same time, and as Crispi's language suggests, attempts were made to sanctify Garibaldi and his work in the construction of the Italian nation state. These were part of broader efforts to create a new civic religion in Italy, by simultaneously promoting secular moral values through institutions such as schools and the army, and appropriating and recasting the symbols and rituals of the Catholic Church.

Yet despite the evidence of so much effort, most historians of the period have found that the process of making Italians had little impact either on Italian culture, which remained largely local and regional in character, or on popular ignorance (illiteracy rates remained high). They have also concluded that many of the new symbols and rituals of the nation were unpopular or failed largely to affect popular emotions or otherwise 'impact upon the collective imagination'.[97] Hence, historians tend to stress the difficulties,

34 Garibaldi in a more mature
incarnation, on the occasion of the
war in 1866.

narrowness and ultimate failure of the nationalising project in Italy, especially
compared to similar programmes in France and/or Germany.[98]

In the rest of this chapter, I will look at the role played by Garibaldi and his
radical colleagues in making Italians and in the construction of national
memory *before* his death in 1882, which was also the year that the suffrage was
widened. Although there has been much less interest in the period before
1882, there was little that was qualitatively new about the late nineteenth-
century attempts to make Italians; indeed, remarkably similar policies were
tried out in Sicily in 1860. Many of the problems which frustrated the process
of making Italians in the 1880s and after were either caused by, or prefigured
in, the political stance taken by Garibaldi during the last years before his
death. Furthermore, the clash for control of his image and its symbolic
associations involved more protagonists than has hitherto fully been
recognised. A study of this earlier conflict can tell us much about the obstacles
to nation-building in later nineteenth-century Italy, and the equivocal outcome of this process.

An important, if obvious, point to remember is how famous Garibaldi had
become by the 1860s and '70s. The potent combination of media interest and
popular enthusiasm established in 1859–60 did not desert him in his old age.

Pictorial albums were produced to commemorate the war of 1866 and the Franco-Prussian war of 1870–1, and the coverage of the former war, in particular, continued to propose Garibaldi as an emblem of manly vigour and Italian military success, while admitting that he had grown older (see figure 34 opposite).[99] 'So the star of Garibaldi still shines', was the comment of Le Siècle.[100] His efforts to destroy the Papacy in 1867 attracted huge international attention. Le Siècle continued to support him, and if The Times in London was openly concerned about the diplomatic consequences of his actions, and was a strong advocate of Franco-Italian understanding, even it could not entirely contain its excitement at his escape from Caprera, and at the prospects of the 'Garibaldi movement' thereafter.[101] His actions were widely applauded in the American press as proof of the resolute power of republicanism. The Philadelphia Inquirer used the Roman Question to press home its republican message: the king had no desire for Rome, the paper insisted, but Garibaldi did, and the king 'is not nearly so beloved as Garibaldi'.[102] Harper's Weekly described Garibaldi as a

simple hero . . . [who] inspires a nation with a word and confounds the astutest politics of the most experienced statesmen . . . it is Garibaldi who plays the first part in Italian regeneration . . . No King could grasp by sympathy the popular heart like Garibaldi, and the character and life of the present monarch chill the national ardour . . .[103]

The events around Mentana also inspired popular demonstrations and poetry. John Greenleaf Whittier's 'Garibaldi' instructed him to 'Rejoice', as one day his aims would be realised: 'All men shall be priests and Kings – One royal brotherhood, one church made free – By love, which is the law of liberty!'[104] The Times reported that Mentana had even revitalised Guy Fawkes Day (5 November) in London: 'At the East End a large representation of the Pope was carried on poles, Garibaldi, with uplifted sword, being about to strike him down'.[105]

As the example of Guy Fawkes Day suggests, Garibaldi's ability to appeal to the crowd was equally undiminished by political failure and physical infirmity. Indeed, the political events described in the previous section must be imagined against the backdrop of cheering crowds and mass celebrations:

He came at last, the commander, the most romantic hero of our century, the most famous human being on the planet, the leader most sure of living in the hearts of future generations, a living man whose legend is already as firmly implanted as that of Wallace or William Tell [an Englishman wrote of Garibaldi's arrival in southern France in 1870] . . . this hero came amongst us, and [as he] walked through the station to his one-horse carriage we saw his face very clearly in the gaslight. It was a pale, grave face, much more like that of a student and philosopher than a hero of great exploits. We cried '*Vive Garibaldi*' with some energy, but he answered with a tone of extreme gravity and sadness '*Vive la République Française!*'

'It is finished', wrote the correspondent of the *Daily News*, when Garibaldi left some five months later: 'Garibaldi has quitted the soil of France . . . I think the entire population of Marseilles was on foot at dawn . . . "There", cried a working man, "there goes our last hope!" . . . All is blank and tame, and void of interest. I never felt so forlorn.'[106] An English woman who saw Garibaldi arrive in Rome in 1875 was astonished by his ill appearance ('his face corpse-like . . . carried like an infant in the strong arms of his son Menotti') but also by the 'wild yell of love' which rose from the crowd on his arrival, 'so shrill and piercing in its intensity that it could be heard half over the city'.[107] His arrival in Palermo in 1882 was an even more remarkable spectacle: almost entirely immobilised by rheumatism, Garibaldi had to be carried on a specially designed bath chair through a crowded but hushed city (the crowd had been told to welcome him with a 'religious silence' for the sake of his health).[108] For *Harper's Weekly*, his arrival was 'inexpressibly pathetic': 'As the train rolled into the dépôt, a shout was raised, which was quickly hushed when his illness was announced. He lay like a dead man on the couch, which was placed in an open carriage, and followed by a mourning, silent crowd.'[109]

> I can't begin to understand, even today [Garibaldi's daughter Clelia wrote in 1948], how that enormous flood of people managed to control the enthusiasm in their hearts and succeeded in obeying the orders [to be quiet] . . . The carriages passed between two wings of people gathered together around Garibaldi, in great silence . . . so many shining eyes, so many kisses blown from women's, men's, children's hands, from every social class! Papa was moved too, [and] with a sign of his hand responded to the greeting of that huge crowd gathered around him.[110]

Surrounded by this heady fusion of political radicalism ('*Vive la république française!*') and popular religiosity, Garibaldi expired gradually but publicly in front of his audience; in contrast to these emotional scenes, his funeral at Caprera represents the victory of secular officialdom, and of a much more hierarchical vision of national belonging.

Indeed, we should not be surprised at the scale and persistence of Garibaldi's celebrity, which was the fruit of almost forty years of unrivalled publicity. More interesting is the use which he and the radicals made of this fame to score rhetorical and symbolic points against their political opponents.

One way in which Garibaldi sought to undermine the government's legitimacy was by promoting a specific kind of Risorgimento memory, and he did this through his presence and speeches at commemorative events. Garibaldi's presence at any public event tended to evoke a more splendid past and better leaders, thus serving as an implicit rebuke to the government, or he could directly remind the audience of the government's betrayal of the Risorgimento. His 1880 speech for the monument to Mentana had all of these ingredients; and is a skilful piece of Risorgimento rhetoric in which he explicitly juxtaposed reminiscences of revolutionary glory with evidence of government treachery:

> Legnano and the Five Days show that this people will not suffer tyranny. You have kindly asked me to assist at the erection of a monument to our heroic martyrs of Mentana, fallen under the sword of Bonapartist soldiers [*soldatesche*] who had joined up with the cops of the papal monster, and were assisted and *guaranteed* by an immoral government to the misfortune of Italy.[111]

In the later years of his life, Garibaldi's speeches and public announcements were rarely, if ever, occasions for self-congratulation or satisfaction, but were usually treated as opportunities for political attack, as moments of high emotion directed against Italy's enemies. 'Italy is not made', he told the crowd in Orvieto in August 1867. 'Who prevents us from finishing our task are first the priests, then Bonaparte ... We must go to Rome; without Rome Italy cannot make itself. We must remove that cancer from the middle of our country.'[112] To the president of a workers' club which had made him honorary president, he advised: 'tell the brother workers from me not to believe the priests ... because the priests are the greatest obstacle to Italian redemption';[113] and to the editor of the French paper, *Le Rappel de Provence*, he declared: 'The truth above all, my friend, and let's call everything by its name: the priest is the murderer of the soul'.[114] In 1870, he told the inhabitants of Trieste (still part of the Austrian Empire) that 'a priest, in whatever name or guise he presents himself, is an impostor, and an enemy of God.'[115]

'Who will deny', he wrote in an English magazine in the same year

> that the prime cause of brigandage in Italy is Bonaparte, with the priests for his myrmidons and the Italian government for his accomplices? Does not this son of Hortense, with his crocodile's devotion, bring about the misery of my country by maintaining in the heart of Italy that den of assassins [the Papal States] ... ?[116]

The main focus of Garibaldi's attack in his later years was the Church. His novels, in particular, offer us a fascinating glimpse into the culture of anti-clericalism in the early years of liberal Italy. As he wrote to Edgar Quinet (the French translator of *Cantoni*), 'by writing Novels ... I sought to make my ideas on Papal Theocracy (the plague of the World) more accessible ... because I believe – every honest man must contribute ... with word – and deed – when he can – to overthrowing such disgusting – and corrupting obstacles to human progress'.[117] Each of his novels, moreover, had the same plot: 'in each a priestly villain conceives an illicit passion for the young heroine, and the novel tells of his attempts to satisfy that passion, the eventual foiling of his schemes, and *en passant* reveals a considerable amount of hypocrisy and moral corruption within the Church'.[118] This basic plot allows Garibaldi to press into service one of the favourite tropes of radical anti-clericalism, which is the illegitimate, uncontrollable sexuality of the clergy.[119] In *Clelia*, Cardinal Procopio ('the factotum and favourite of His Holiness') instructs an aide to procure him the eponymous heroine: 'Go Gianni ... go and procure this gem for me at any cost. I can no longer live if Clelia is not mine. Only she can relieve my boredom and bless the stupid existence which I drag out alongside that old imbecile [i.e. the Pope].'[120] In *I Mille*, one of the heroines, Marzia, is the daughter of a priest, Monsignor Corvo, who, having stolen her from her mother and then abandoned her, fails to recognise her when they meet so rapes her, after which he places her in a convent (and kills himself when she reveals her true identity later in the novel). Although *Cantoni* has a slightly less racy plot, the heroine, Ida, does have to fight off the Jesuit priest ('the Jesuit! the Jesuit! another human anomaly'), Fra Gaudenzio, who tries to rape her when she is unconscious and a prisoner: 'he bent his snake's face over Ida's gagged mouth and tried to kiss her'. It also has a lengthy description of the horrors of the papal dungeons ('that filthy bastion of priestly tyranny'), including a diabolic scene where Cantoni's gaolers die in a drunken stupor amid the ruins of the burning prison.[121]

Garibaldi's diatribes against 'priestism' (*pretismo*) are set against the background of real episodes in the Risorgimento – 1849 (*Cantoni*), 1860 (*I Mille*) and 1867 (*Clelia*) – in which he figures personally and in which he intervenes to make explicitly contemporary political comments. The wars described here are all moments of high national drama where the volunteer fights heroically against 'priestism' (the volunteer can say, 'with his head held high ... I have served no one but my country!'),[122] but is let down by the politicians. In both *Cantoni* and *Clelia* the hero dies defending national honour. Thus, Garibaldi takes Italy's recent history – the Risorgimento – and restructures it as a canonic Risorgimento narrative. In the process, he uses the plot to turn the government into something like a Judas figure who betrays the nation for personal gain. 'I consider it absurd to deny that the Monarchy supported national aspirations for unification out of its own interests', Garibaldi comments at the start of *I Mille*. 'Your misdeeds are too many, the hate too great which the population in all justice feels for you: tricked, humiliated, plundered, betrayed by you!'[123] he tells Italy's monarchs later in the novel. In *Cantoni*, even the Bourbons are victims of Piedmontese hypocrisy ('[t]he inexperienced Francesco II, betrayed by the northern fox').[124]

'I will be accused of pessimism [Garibaldi wrote in the preface to the 1872 edition of his memoirs]; but . . . [t]oday I am entering my 65th year, and having believed for the best part of my life in human progress, I am embittered to see so much misfortune and corruption in this self-styled civilised century.'[125] 'The priest!' he exclaimed a few pages later. 'Ah! He is the real Scourge of God. In Italy, he props up a cowardly government in the most degrading humiliation . . . !'[126]

> My first reason for writing a novel [he told the readers of *Cantoni*] is to remind Italy of those brave men who fell on the field of battle for her sake . . . Secondly I want to appeal to the youth of Italy. I want to put before them the deeds which other young Italians have done and remind them of their duty to finish the task. In particular I want to point out the base and deceitful conduct of governments and priests.[127]

Here Garibaldi revives a traditional, and essentially Risorgimento, opposition between young, 'brave' Italians and their 'deceitful' rulers, and he does so on the basis of a radical memory of the Risorgimento.[128] 'Oh Thousand!' he wrote at the beginning of *I Mille*, 'in this time of shameful misfortune – I am happy to remember you – it lightens my soul to think of you.'[129] At the end of the novel, he has a political dream: 'in the snake pit which had poisoned Rome for so many centuries . . . a lightning bolt had fallen'; there was a 'government for all by all'; a temporary dictatorship ('a wise and energetic man elected by a popular majority'); a national guard kept the peace; there was a monument to the heroes of 1849; and 'instead of the desert, beautiful farmsteads with verdant gardens and trees loaded with every kind of fruit, vast plains covered in gold-coloured grain'. But he wakes up, 'pained' by the 'nauseating reality of present-day society', and leaves, 'sorrowful', for 'my isolated and deserted home'.[130]

This self-image as preacher in the desert was one of Garibaldi's favourites,[131] and it is revealing that he uses it here in opposition to the 'nauseating reality' of present-day Italy. Introducing Ida, Cantoni's companion who dresses as a man to fight alongside him in the defence of the Roman Republic, Garibaldi has the following to say about women:

Angel of life! . . . if the Almighty had a human form, it would be that of a woman. If mind was to prevail over matter – intelligence over brute force – the man over the elephant – the woman would lead the human family. If instead of the formless compound of hermaphrodites who govern Italy, we substituted a woman, she certainly would not allow us to be subjected to so many humiliations.[132]

There are two points being made in this passage. One the one hand, there is the proposal to include women in public life; Garibaldi repeatedly pressed for female emancipation, and saw the education of women as the means of their liberation from the tutelage of priests ('these ministers of Satan').[133] On the other, there is the juxtaposition of true 'virility' (which can be male or female, and is associated with maturity, courage and intelligence)[134] and perverse, effeminate sexuality, which is here identified with Italy's governing class. Now, there is nothing unusual about the use of metaphors of sexual and moral degeneracy to denigrate Italy's rulers; indeed, as Silvana Patriarca has shown, the use of these negative stereotypes to indicate Italy's decline was a prominent and lasting feature of Risorgimento discourse.[135] But it is surprising to find these metaphors being used within the Risorgimento discourse to characterise and disparage those who, in theory at least, represented the fulfilment of the Risorgimento in liberal Italy. In his novels, as in his later political life, Garibaldi seeks to set up, or in a sense to revive, the rhetorical discourse where not just the Church but the government too is the enemy of Italian 'resurgence', and both are placed on the same degenerate side.

It follows from Garibaldi's stance and public pronouncements that, in their struggle to make Italians and create a civic religion whose moral code would substitute for Catholicism, Italian nationalists did not speak with a single voice. There was nothing entirely new about this either: moderates and democrats had long disagreed about the future of Italy. However, as we have also seen, this disagreement was not especially evident before the early 1860s: moderates and democrats had 'shared common sentiments and cultural conceptions about that obscure object of desire, the nation',[136] and in 1860 the democrats were unable to distinguish their political language and symbols from those of moderate, monarchical Piedmont. But after unification, and especially after the divisive events of the mid-1860s (the September convention; the 1866 war; Mentana), this common patriotic discourse began to disintegrate, and nowhere was the damage more visible than in the speeches, writings and actions of Garibaldi. Yet he was so famous, and so closely identified with an official image of Italian resurgence, that it was difficult for the government to fight back without seeming to betray itself. Reflecting the symbolic corner it found itself in, the government greeted most of Garibaldi's attacks either with silence or with an attempt to deny him a serious political role: Garibaldi, in the words of the government paper, *L'Opinione*, was a man 'in whom the most essential political qualities were lacking', so that he was unable to 'judge the needs of the country' or assess 'the conduct of government'.[137]

In assessing the political impact of Garibaldi's hostility to the new Italy, we must also situate his memoirs, novels and speeches in a much broader radical tradition of symbolic opposition to political institutions. The radicals may have been relatively ineffective in parliament or as a practical revolutionary party, but they were far more successful in publicising their political antagonism, in challenging and subverting official representations of national belonging, and in promoting a cult of the Republic.[138] One tactic, which we have already seen used by Garibaldi, was to deflate the monarchy and its achievements and to emphasise instead a sense of disappointment and frustration. At the same time, the radicals set about constructing and promoting an alternative, radical myth of the Risorgimento. This myth was opposed to the official memory and was based on revolutionary traditions and memoirs; it involved the exaltation of 'martyrs' like the Bandiera brothers and Carlo Pisacane, and of 'apostles' like Mazzini. Radicals also began to organise public commemorations of revolutionary events such as the Five Days of Milan in 1848 and the Roman Republic of 1849.[139] One of the most successful commemorations was the 1880 monument to the 'martyrs' of Mentana. Constructed in two years by public subscription and opened by Garibaldi, it provided the basis for a lengthy challenge to government attempts, undertaken in the same period, to commemorate the contribution of Napoleon III to the Risorgimento by a monument in Milan.[140]

Garibaldi was a major focus of this alternative radical mythology. From the late 1860s, a growing radical publishing industry concentrated on producing the works of Garibaldi cheaply, and in serial and/or illustrated formats, along with the writings of Mazzini and other anti-clerical and radical novels. Probably its most important single publication was Jessie White Mario's *The life and times of Garibaldi*, which was published in 1882 to tremendous acclaim (new editions came out in 1884, 1887 and 1905). Other important alternative histories included Guerzoni's *Garibaldi* (1882) and Bandi's *I Mille da Genova a Capua* (1886), while the poetry of Giosuè Carducci also largely reinforced a democratic myth of Garibaldi.[141] In this radical symbology, efforts were made to reunite Mazzini and Garibaldi (whose disagreements were the subject of public debate).[142] Their name-day, 19 March, was celebrated as the day of the 'two Josephs [*due Giuseppe*]'; and an 1871 print shows them, each with a halo, working together as carpenters on the construction of the 'European ship', under the eyes of the female figure

'Democracy' (who is tying together a bundle of sheaves [*fasci*] representing political unity).[143] The radical press also made use of Garibaldi in caricature as a means of ridiculing or denigrating the government. Thus, although his 1875 Tiber project was a practical failure, it was a visual gift to caricaturists. One paper, *Il Pappagallo*, represented him as 'the new Italian Gulliver': 'the pygmies think they have tied the giant down, but in the end he will get fed up, will get up and will shake them all off. In the meantime, he has presented to parliament three useful projects for Italy.'[144]

Garibaldi's novels were not especially successful. Only the first, *Clelia*, was published widely in translation; he had difficulty finding an Italian publisher for *I Mille*; and a fourth novel, *Manlio*, remained unpublished until 1982. The critics were often hostile,[145] and his later memoirs did not meet with the popular acclaim of the 1859–60 versions.[146] Yet these semi-autobiographical works should not be seen as an isolated publishing episode, but as just one element in a more substantial production of memoirs and novels by his colleagues and other volunteers in the wars of the Risorgimento. That this literary production, commonly known as 'Garibaldian literature' (*letteratura garibaldina*), added significantly to the Garibaldi cult after unification, and especially after his death, has long been recognised.[147] Rather less well known is the extent to which many of the writers concerned sought to produce a memory of the Risorgimento which would be far from comforting or favourable to the government.

One of the most important works in Garibaldian literature is the 1886 memoir, *I Mille da Genova a Capua*, written by the republican journalist Giuseppe Bandi. Bandi offered his readers a deliberately anti-Piedmontese, anti-annexationist version of the events of unification, and he sought explicitly to 'de-sacralise', though not de-heroicise, Garibaldi through a series of intimate narratives of the man, his habits and his actions. Bandi's work has been somewhat overshadowed by the much more congratulatory memoir, the *Noterelle* by Giuseppe Cesare Abba, also published in the 1880s.[148] But the tone and direction of Bandi's memoir was paralleled in the work of other volunteer-writers – Alberto Mario, Emilio Zasio, Felice Cavallotti, Achille Bizzoni, Eugenio Checchi and Ettore Socci[149] – whose memoirs of the Risorgimento were either overtly republican and anti-government or else adopted a deliberately anti-heroic, even irreverent approach to their Risorgimento past. Thus, both Mario and Zasio attacked the government for its treatment of the *garibaldini*: Mario refers (in 1865) to 'four disenchanting years [which] have swept away belief and hope', and to their shoddy treatment at the hands of the king and his entourage at Teano;[150] Zasio returns time and again to the betrayal of Risorgimento ambitions for Italy.[151] Cavallotti's memoir of Mentana, *L'insurrezione di Roma*, stressed the tragedy of the event. The volunteers who died were 'martyrs' for 'the independence of the fatherland', who were 'mown down like the harvest in the fields' in front of the lethal *chassepot* rifles; and 'Garibaldi seemed transformed; gloomy, hoarse, pallid, only his eye lively and focused; thinking of everyone but himself: no one ever saw him look so old as on that day'.[152]

Bizzoni, Checchi and Socci were, like Cavallotti, younger radicals influenced by the bohemian *scapigliata* ('dishevelled') movement. They adopt a less obviously polemical but still political, *bozzettino* ('sketchy') style, which relied heavily on the evocation of informality, confusion and chaos in order to poke fun at Italy's grandiose sense of itself.[153] He had learnt the following lesson from the war of 1866, Checchi told his readers: 'that you can go off to war with your spirits full of excited, vigorous expectation, with healthy and robust limbs, and return filled with bitter disappointment and minus a few broken ribs'. In his memoirs, first serialised in *La Gazzetta del Popolo* in 1866, the war itself is a 'miserable series of troubles', where they were all hungry, tired and freezing with cold, 'badly dressed in a poor red shirt'. While waiting for the war to begin in the Apulian town of Barletta, the setting for the novel *Ettore Fieramosca* and a central episode in Risorgimento narrative, Checchi is bored and disappointed by what he finds. The volunteeers get drunk every night and they swim every day, and are looked at with suspicion by the local population, 'as if we were brigands from the Sila [forest] or the Gargano [peninsula]'. Their commander, Giovanni Nicotera (a Risorgimento hero and future government minister), is a self-important and rather preposterous figure:

> a handsome man . . . with the fine baritone voice of a democratic Deputy . . . He began with a great eulogy in our honour, he told us that he had baptised us as brave men, that he had only one ambition, to die well: and that at the end of the war we would be proud to have belonged to the sixth regiment . . . that we would always win, that we would astound Europe with our bravery. In short, it seemed as though we and he would astound the world.

Only Garibaldi escapes the sarcasm. He stays above the military chaos 'in an all-white little house', and he takes care to visit and talk personally to the wounded. Leaving the hospital, 'he removed his hat, and shook his poor fellow-soldiers by the hand, saying goodbye! Until we meet again! and left accompanied by the cheers of us all.'[154]

Even in these most deflating accounts, the power of Garibaldi as an authentic symbol of national heroism is still confirmed. Mario remembers Palermo in 1860 as 'a sort of delicious ecstasy', where 'faith in the future was boundless' and 'Garibaldi, in his pavilion, was a magician'.[155] Garibaldi could be (and often was) attacked for his political mistakes, but on a symbolic level he was more or less untouchable. Even the young radical left which had ventured to criticise him in the 1860s had been, as we have seen quite clearly, won over by the '70s. None of this is that surprising, although it does confirm Garibaldi's enduring ability to appeal to a very broad audience; but what is worth dwelling on is the extent to which this iconic status and widespread fame posed problems for the government. After 1867, Garibaldi adopted a very public attitude in opposition to the state. He refused to take part in any official ceremonies of *italianità* (although he paid a private visit to the king in 1874, he refused to make a public announcement in his support, even on the occasion of his funeral in 1878), but he lent his considerable presence to anti-government meetings and ceremonies. Moreover, since he did all this prior to the government's developing, in the 1880s, a thorough programme of 'making Italians', he helped the radical, anti-government myth to promote and consolidate itself some time before the government even got started. George Mosse tells us that the purpose of the secular religions established by nation states in the course of the nineteenth century was to bind government and people together,[156] but the experience of liberal Italy offers us a different lesson entirely. Thanks in part to Garibaldi's actions, a sense of *italianità* was invented in the years after unification, but it was effective and convincing largely as an ideology of opposition to the nation's official leaders.

The death and funeral of Garibaldi form an interesting contrast to the rites celebrated four years previously for the king, Vittorio Emanuele, which represented a partial reconciliation between Church and monarch.[157] The service for Garibaldi established a tradition of 'lay death' from which the Church was entirely excluded; and this secular rite was subsequently adopted for other heroes of the Italian nation. However, although Garibaldi's death appeared to produce a mood of national reconciliation around admiration for the Hero, it also provided a new stage for the articulation and promotion of conflict between rival conceptions of that nation. We have seen that Garibaldi was not given the radical funeral he wanted, but something more official and pro-government instead. This divergence between the radical and official Garibaldi was evident in every other aspect of the commemorations. Many on the government side wanted his body to be brought to Rome: as Crispi's paper, *La Riforma*, put it, Garibaldi should be made to lie '[i]n front of the Vatican, in this Rome, mother of ancient heroes . . . Garibaldi . . . does not belong to a party but to the nation';[158] others proposed a common tomb to house Cavour, Vittorio Emanuele and Garibaldi, 'the mind, the heart, and the arm of the fatherland'. But there is evidence that the new king, Umberto I, was quite unhappy with this notion and resisted any such proposal. It was certainly opposed by the radicals, who insisted on Caprera as the burial place for

Garibaldi. 'In a Pantheon, next to certain false heroes he would feel uncomfortable', was the opinion of one Bologna university student.[159]

The flurry of public and printed eulogies to Garibaldi after his death seems,
on the surface, to offer striking confirmation of his role as a unifying symbol
of the Italian nation. His death halted Italian public life and led to an immense
display of national emotion. Most of the eulogies adopted the same
biographical structure and exalted his death as a secular apotheosis. Beyond
this, however, there were huge differences. In parliament, the prime minister,
Agostino Depretis, described Garibaldi as 'the great citizen' and the most
'disinterested collaborator of the great King who established national unity';
others stressed his sense of duty (the *obbedisco*) and sacrifice to the greater
cause of Italy. But the radicals announced that 'the living legend of the
fatherland' had died with Garibaldi.[160] Anton Barilli warned against making
too much of a cult out of love for the 'fatherland': 'Too many enemies are still
alive: too many friends are lukewarm; too much envy, not enough support for
our chances'; while in a passionate political speech, Giosuè Carducci directly
questioned the identification of Garibaldi with a present-day Italy where 'our
co-nationals are . . . sought out to be killed in the streets of foreign cities',
where Trieste and Trento were still 'unredeemed', where Tunisia was in the
hands of the French and 'we are the friends and second-compass bearers of
Bismarck'.[161] 'Socialists, republicans, all true democrats, let's join hands',
announced the young socialist leader, Andrea Costa, 'and go forward together
in the name of Garibaldi.'[162]

Rival Romes

In assessing the achievements (or otherwise) of the cultural process of nation-
building in early liberal Italy, we should keep in mind that the radicals were
not alone in being one symbolic step ahead of the Italian state. The Church too
was well on its way to challenging all secular conceptions of *italianità* and
offering an extremely successful rival form of identity. With national
unification, all liberal hopes of compromise with the Church had faded
drastically. In 1861, Cavour had tried to reach an agreement with the Church
on the basis of 'a free Church in a free state', but these negotiations had come
to nothing and, thereafter, the Pope rejected all possibility of conciliation.
Loyal Catholics were even urged to follow a policy known as *non expedit*, that
is, they were told to abstain from either standing or voting in any political
elections in Italy. There followed a series of much-publicised battles between
Church and state: over Church property, control of education, and the
appointment of bishops. After the Italian army seized Rome in 1870, Pius IX
withdrew behind the walls of Vatican City and declared himself a 'prisoner'.

Although the government passed a law of guarantees, giving the Pope the effective status of an independent sovereign power, the Pope continued to play the part of the hostage, and never again left the Vatican (and, once elected, none of his successors set foot outside the Vatican walls until 1929).[163]

During the same period, the Pope assumed an ever more aggressive stance towards the wider liberal world, and worked tirelessly to reassert his traditional authority over the Church. In 1861 he issued an allocution refusing to compromise with 'modern civilisation'; and in 1864, an encyclical *Quanto Cura* together with a Syllabus (list) of the eighty errors of modernity (the eightieth stated, 'It is wrong to believe that the Pope can and ought to reconcile himself with progress, liberalism, and modern civilisation'). The Syllabus of Errors was followed by the summoning of a General Vatican Council, attended by some 700 bishops, and in 1870, shortly before the arrival of Italian troops in Rome, it declared the dogma of papal infallibility, which stated that when the Pope spoke *ex cathedra* (in an official capacity and on matters of doctrine) he was 'possessed of that infallibility with which the divine Redeemer willed that his Church should be endowed for defining doctrine concerning faith and morals'.[164] The dogma of papal infallibility confirmed the victory of ultra-montanism, so that the Church which emerged at the end of the political upheavals in Italy, and after the loss of the Pope's temporal power, was 'more uniform, more centralised and more "Roman"' than its predecessor.[165]

Pius IX called on loyal Catholics for their support in his intransigent stance, and met with a great and enthusiastic response. In fact, the cultural conflicts of this period in Italy can be better understood if we remember that the growing authoritarianism of the Pope was justified as a popular defence of Catholic liberty against political interference, and that the clerical activism inspired by Rome converged with a period of popular religious revival, especially with the growth of extra-sacerdotal expressions of popular piety (pilgrimages, miraculous encounters and other acts of devotion).[166] Women, in particular, began to find in the Church a space for themselves which was closed off by the state.[167] From the 1850s onwards, Pius IX embarked on an intense programme of sanctifications and beatifications, of religious commemoration and festivals, in a way which was quite different from that of his predecessors, and which can be seen as an attempt to combat (or, indeed, pre-empt) the creation of secular heroes in Italy and elsewhere.[168] He also made a direct appeal to the faithful. He identified modernity, liberalism and secularisation with the all-encompassing enemy – revolution – and developed a personal cult based on his own suffering and victimhood at the hands of this enemy. As Christopher Clark tells us:

> Catholics were encouraged to see in the suffering, despoliation, 'imprison-ment' and 'martyrdom' of the pontiff the embodiment of the troubles

currently afflicting the church. The Pope's intransigence in negotiations with the Kingdom of Italy was likened to Christ's steadfastness in the face of Satan's blandishments. There was even a widespread tendency to equate the Sacred Heart of Jesus with the person of the 'suffering' pontiff.[169]

Pius IX was a new kind of pontiff. His image was 'more personal' and less regal; 'the office was lent a magic by flesh, and speech, and smile, and greeting, and blessing'; anyone who talked to him 'felt that at that moment he cared about him or her more than about anyone else in the world'.[170] Part of his appeal lay in the contrast with the Piedmontese monarchy. After 1870, there were two courts in Rome: one at the Quirinale, presided over by Vittorio Emanuele, an essentially foreign sovereign who missed his native Piedmont and 'was bad at public functions'; the other in the Vatican, with a pope–king 'who was superb with crowds'. The Quirinale was 'cold and formal'; the Vatican 'warm and emotional'.[171] When both men died, within three weeks of each other in 1878, three times as many people turned out for the funeral of the Pope in St Peter's as had turned out for the king (although, when the Curia tried to move the Pope's body across Rome to its burial place in San Lorenzo in 1881, there were riots and the coffin was nearly thrown into the Tiber by a hostile, anti-clerical crowd).[172]

While the divisions between Church and state were far from monolithic, and there is evidence of *de facto* co-operation and agreement, especially over the threat of socialism,[173] it is undeniable that both sides competed for the rhetorical high ground. Moreover, the Pope's resolute stance against modernity did not include a rejection of its technology. As we saw earlier, Catholic mobilisation against the unification of Italy involved the very successful use of modern methods of mass communication, notably newspapers and prints. Railways also made pilgrimages to Rome much easier. Pius IX's warm personality combined with modern transport to alter the quality of his audiences with the faithful and of their response to him. He was the first pontiff to be photographed, and people's sense of personal intimacy with their Pope was encouraged by photographic portraits, and by reports and other pictures of him in the Catholic press. Thus, the use of the new mass media defined the so-called 'culture wars' between Catholics and anti-clericals, and between Church and state, which broke out all over Catholic Europe in the latter decades of the nineteenth century. These were, above all, 'wars of words and images',[174] or a 'communicative phenomenon' where 'the bugles and drums of the media spectacle' were as crucial to both sides in the conflict 'as the heavy guns of legislative or police action'.[175] There was a striking similarity between the communicative methods of Catholic Europe and those used to promote Garibaldi, which I have described in the course of this book.

Unfortunately, there has been relatively little research on the role of the Catholic media in the struggle for Italy and to 'make Italians' in this period.[176] What is clear, nonetheless, is that its presence made the struggle a three-way process, in which the monarchy's efforts to represent and unite the nation were undermined as much by the clerical right as by the radical left. Ironically perhaps, one of the most popular targets of the Church's counter-attack on the kingdom of Italy was Garibaldi, another of the kingdom's adversaries. Rome had always been hostile to Garibaldi, but in the aftermath of Mentana it felt able to launch a major new assault on his reputation in the press and by publication of numerous pamphlets and histories of the recent events. For *La Civiltà Cattolica*, Garibaldi was a coward, a hypocrite and, increasingly, a clown. The paper mocked his fame:

> Wherever Garibaldi goes he has been accustomed to be met with cheers, drums, trumpets, bells and frantic applause. Fashions of dressing *alla Garibaldi* have given work to tailors, and makers of hats and shoes. Cafés have been called after him. His sulky face was shown in shop windows, and his pictures figured on the walls of taverns and public lavatories.

But at Monterotondo (before Mentana), he was just 'a comic hero' who had 'sneaked off under cover of night':

> Why did you turn tail, O hero? . . . Surely it is better to die bravely than to run away like a coward. You yourself had given the watchword 'Either Rome or death', and no one would have imagined that you had a third alternative up your sleeve – flight! . . . Poor Garibaldi! Until now he has been the hero of Marsala. Henceforward he will be the coward of Monterotondo.

'It is not our fault if mention of his name makes soldiers of any regular army burst out laughing', the paper went on, warming to its subject: 'We too, it must be confessed, have also been tempted to laugh when studying this "legendary epoch from Montevideo to Marsala"':

> This valiant lion, this Achilles, this Hercules, this Mars, this Jove – the more you try to force him into the light of day, the more he retreats into the shadows, the more he melts before your very eyes. Finally he is no bigger than a puppet – gross, bearded, red-shirted, made to dance by other people without him ever perceiving the fact.

'[N]o puppet is more obedient than Garibaldi', the paper wrote, seeking to deflate his heroic reputation by revealing its empty substance. For the Church, in this representation, Garibaldi was ridiculous – a mere performer in a drama directed by the Savoy monarchy.[177]

For the majority of the Catholic press there was no difference between the Italian nationalists: they were all in it together and as dangerous as each other. Garibaldi was 'the armed hand of Mazzini', both had a 'marriage' with Vittorio Emanuele, and Rattazzi was behind all their actions.[178] According to General Kanzler, who led the defence of Rome and published his report to the Pope, the events of 1867 were a political scandal. 'A government, which calls itself legitimate, favoured a treacherous invasion: a General of this government dared, with the cry of *Rome or Death*, to order a war against the most August of Thrones.'[179] In the Catholic version of Mentana, Garibaldi was a coward (leaving Mentana, he changed 'the godless cry: "Rome or death" with the other "get out if you can"') but he was also a dangerous fanatic – 'a modern blasphemer' who promised to 'demolish all the altars of the living God, in order to replace them with the abominable orgies of the she-god *reason*, and convert St Peter's into a grand Masonic lodge'.[180]

In one history of Mentana, Garibaldi is reinvented once more as the brutal bandit of 1849. He rides on horseback into a church:

his head was covered with a round grey cap with a wide brim ... with flowing locks; the blond beard mixed with white hair fell down to his chest: a bright red tie edged in black was tied around his neck: an old overcoat came down to his knees ... With a lit cigar in his mouth, with a fine whip in his hand, he let his gaze fall to this side and that: and since from every side his followers cheered him to the skies; now and then he slowly bent his head, showing them that he enjoyed the applause, or signalling that it was now time to quieten down.[181]

He was accompanied by 'a proud Amazon in a garibaldi skirt', and his followers were violent, undisciplined and sacrilegious: a 'revolutionary horde'; a 'furious revolutionary phalanx'; a 'garibaldish torrent'; 'new Muslims'; and 'children of Satan'.[182] All of the histories of Mentana recounted the actions of the *garibaldini* in gruesome detail: confessionals were destroyed, churches burnt and sacred images defamed. In one convent 'they vandalised and sacrilegiously cut an arm off the image of Saint Anthony; they rolled down the stairs an image of the Baby Jesus; they stole the holy Pyx from the holy ciborium; they irreverently squandered the sacred communion wafers, and gave themselves over entirely to sack and to pillage'.[183] Sermons were preached to the 'God Garibaldi'; a pulpit was used as a latrine; his men stole and drank the communion wine and they used the churches as brothels: 'they committed outrages against women'.[184] The worst insults were said to have been aimed at the Madonna: 'their most usual blasphemies were against the Holy Madonna and against her inviolable Virginity, using such shameful and disgusting words that the pen shakes just to think of them!'[185]

In general, the Catholic representations of Garibaldi and his followers follow a well-defined stereotype of the revolutionary as a dangerous and savage 'other'. The events of Mentana had, in the words of General Kanzler, shocked 'the entire civilised World'.[186]

> It is clear that future generations will be astonished [another writer confirmed], nor will they be able to understand how, in the heart of this Italian land, mother to so many famous heroes, creator of so much noble genius, masters of every science, seat of every virtue, there could emerge men of such savagery and excess as to emulate the terrible bondage of the Goths and Saracens.[187]

Yet this juxtaposition of Catholic 'civilisation' with revolutionary 'barbarism' bore a striking rhetorical similarity to the terms of Garibaldi's opposition between revolutionary 'virility' and corrupt 'priestism'. It used the same demonisation of the enemy and, notably, the same identification of the enemy with degenerate or 'incontinent' sexuality; and each accused the other of offending the native genius of Italy. Both appealed to Italian identity by referring to a remarkably analogous sense of family, place and model of heroism, and both recognised the affirmation of Italian-ness in the heroic defence of a holy cause.

More than one clerical writer described the victory at Mentana using topoi which we tend to associate with Risorgimento discourse. The papal soldiers were an invincible 'handful of heroes' led by courageous leaders; and they defended Catholicism against 'a formidable army . . . that enormous mass of garibaldini'.[188] One writer, Paolo Mencacci, wrote of 'the heroism of Papal soldiers, a heroism which placed them at the front of the most hardened armies in the world'.[189] Those who died were martyrs, whose biographies were published along with letters of tribute from priests and other clerical dignitaries. An obituary for an English zouave, Julian Waits Russell, was published first in the Rome periodical, Il Divin Salvatore, and then translated into English and published as a pamphlet. His father was said to be consoled by the heroism of his son's death, and announced: 'If I had ten sons, I would willingly sacrifice them for God in so holy a cause.' Readers were assured that there were many more like Julian: 'all were chosen victims and glorious heroes, whose memoirs, if collected, would read like a page out of the history of the crusades, or even the Acts of the Martyrs'.[190] In Rome, General Kanzler was given a triumphal welcome, and both the Pope and the king and queen of the

Two Sicilies (in exile in Rome) made a great show of caring for the wounded. The dead were given 'splendid' funerals, and Pio IX ordered a monument to be erected to the 'martyrs' of Mentana in the Church of San Lorenzo (where he was eventually buried).[191] Catholics were told that '[t]he sect will make still more gigantic efforts, but in vain. The Hand of God hangs visibly over it and the defeat of Mentana has brought about its fatal Downfall.' The victory at Mentana revived memories of the historical victories of Catholicism, notably its triumph over the Ottoman Empire at the battle of Lepanto.[192]

Although the absence of research permits us to do little more than guess at the popular reception of papal propaganda, we do know that it had a wide international reach. In London, Father Beste of the London Oratory called Garibaldi a 'cruel blasphemer [who] has dared to call a Pope the vampire of Italy, and Rome its plague spot . . . he, too, has cursed his Father and his Mother – he, too, will die the death!'[193] In Catholic Ireland, the capture of Rome in 1870 as well as Mentana was marked by the publication of songs and pamphlets celebrating the 'Downfall of Garibaldi', 'The Pope's triumph over Garibaldi', 'The sorrowful lamentation of Garibaldi' and 'A new song on the capture of Garibaldi'. Archbishop Cullen of Dublin held what he called 'a grand high mass' in a crowded church for the papal soldiers killed at Mentana. He delivered the funeral oration which lasted for an hour, and did, in his words, 'all I could to extol the Zouaves, but I think I succeeded better in assailing Garibaldi. I told . . . [the] story of . . . how he got into the church of the conventuals, and hid himself in the confessional – the poor Catholics were delighted to hear the scoundrel so well abused.'[194] Above all in France, where there was a vibrant group of Catholic publicists well used to tackling any sign of sympathy with Italian nationalists, the Catholic press attacked Garibaldi. Catholic writers belittled Garibaldi, pointed out his lack of military skill and the slightness of his achievements; while other publications stressed the involvement of the Italian government and of Rattazzi in particular.[195] As for Garibaldi's wicked reputation, there was no doubt that it was true: he was a 'brigand . . . who has spent his life conspiring and fighting in the two worlds'; a '*Wandering-Jew* of the revolution'; and the 'master' of Italy who 'declares war at will; and is stopped every time he runs any kind of risk'.[196] The French volunteers were all selfless heroes, 'beautiful souls' and glorious martyrs.[197]

Furthermore, if the government was embarrassed and silenced by its casting as a national villain at the hands of Garibaldi after 1867, the Church had no such problem. Indeed, after the death of Pius IX in 1878, when there seemed to be a possibility of better Church–state relations in Italy, a renewed clerical assault was mounted on Garibaldi's reputation. In 1878, the Catholic historian Cesare Cantù judged Garibaldi's legacy to be a divisive and destructive one. Garibaldi was an arrogant and vulgar man, Cantù insisted, who '[a]lways . . .

gave himself airs as though he were another Washington . . . He could destroy, but did not know how to build.'[198] *La Civiltà Cattolica* initiated a major attack on Garibaldi in 1879, 'maximum idol of the Italian Revolution', at the time of his organisation of the League of Democracy. Calling him the '*hero of two millions*' (a reference to a government pension he had accepted in the mid-1870s), the paper mocked his physical incapacity, his political ideas and his literary pretensions.[199] It took the side of his estranged wife, Giuseppina Raimondi, and protested against 'the shameful insinuations circulated about her' in Garibaldi's ongoing attempts to divorce her. Giuseppina was the victim of Garibaldi's self-interest, and '*the hero of two millions*' wanted simply to 'get rid of Giuseppina, so that Francesca is able to enjoy the pension rights of a General's widow and of *that* General'. All this was proof, the paper wrote, that 'the rotten source' of the proposed divorce law in Italy was Freemasonry.[200]

Most of all, *La Civiltà Cattolica* issued dire warnings about Garibaldi's republicanism and socialism, all the while glorying in any evidence of bad feeling among the nationalists. In a review of the anonymous pamphlet *Garibaldi politico*, one of the few liberal publications openly hostile to Garibaldi in this period,[201] the paper likened the revolution to Saturn devouring his own offspring (recycling a Piedmontese comment on Aspromonte in 1862).[202] The Italian revolution 'has been until now a great devourer of its children', and while the monarchist party had been eaten by the democrats it was now trying for a 'return match, helping others to devour its devouring party'. This 'spectacle', concluded the paper, was inevitable: 'all that is done against God and his Church is foolish and transient . . . in this world the eternal justice of the Almighty frequently punishes the sect which hates Christ'.[203]

Conclusion

In this chapter, I have sought to show that there is a great deal of political and symbolic interest in the last years of Garibaldi's life. He was a more successful, and much less marginal, figure than is often assumed. His perception of the economic, social and political problems affecting early-liberal Italy was not wholly misplaced, nor were his unstinting efforts to establish a broad-based radical movement with as wide an appeal as possible. For somebody so established and successful, he showed a remarkable ability to reinvent himself, and to adapt to the different political circumstances prevailing after Mentana; and in his willingness to risk his fame and defy infirmity by continuing to campaign for radical change we should recognise an impressive display of physical and intellectual courage. Much of what we perceive as disappointing in Garibaldi's later career is a product of the political conflict in this period: of his convincing attempt (ably reinforced by his colleagues) to pose as the victim of political betrayal and of official efforts to marginalise him or to deny him a serious political role.

A study of Garibaldi in this period can also tell us a great deal about the broader process of nation-building in liberal Italy, and especially about its problems. First, Garibaldi and his radical associates claimed to represent the Risorgimento, and they appropriated its symbolic system. They spoke for the 'real' Italy which had been betrayed and excluded by a dishonest and feeble government, and in so doing they pre-empted and challenged government attempts to symbolise the nation and inspire a more official sense of national belonging. Second, in his attacks on the Church, identified as the true enemy of the nation, Garibaldi also placed part of the blame on the government for failing to combat clericalism, and for collaborating in its policy to mislead and corrupt the Italian people. At the same time, the Church was far from idle. In the person of the Pope and through its control of the Catholic press, the Church entered the modern battle for the hearts and minds of Italians. It set up the Pope as the victim of Italian aggression, it mocked all efforts to construct a secular sense of community, and it identified Garibaldi as the symbol of demonic 'Revolution'. In effect, the task of nation-building in liberal Italy was not just frustrated by the persistence of regional and local loyalties or the prevalence of popular ignorance; nation-building was also undermined by disagreements among the nationalists, and by the Church, which proposed and promoted a very potent, rival version. In the process, both the radicals and the Church adopted extreme rhetorical stances and forced the governing party to occupy a weak and unconvincing middle ground.

The struggle to invent official symbols of Italian national identity was more than just a stand-off between the king, Vittorio Emanuele, and the General, Garibaldi. It was also a three-way fight between these two figures and the Pope. It is unfortunate that we know relatively little about the impact of this struggle on public opinion, although it might help to account for the perception of failure long associated with the Italian experience of nation-building. It is even hard to say who came out in front at the end of the culture wars, although it is very unlikely that it was the new state and its official version of national belonging. Not only had the state suffered a preventative propaganda strike at the hands of Garibaldi and his associates, but it was also faced with the charisma of Pius IX, who had 'the Hand of God' and a significant section of international public opinion on his side.

The extent of the radical victory can also be questioned. One aspect of the Italian national discourse which emerges very clearly from a study of Garibaldi's efforts in these years is the rather narrow range of discursive options open even to the radical nationalists. Until the early 1860s, the radicals proved unable (or unwilling) to distinguish their language and symbols from those of the moderates; and increasingly thereafter, a kind of linguistic convergence occurred around the symbols and metaphors of the Catholic religion. Although we have seen in this book that the means of production and dissemination of the nationalist discourse were modern, linked to the expansion of print culture, popular theatre and associational life, at least part of the content and structure of this discourse was deeply traditional, based on biblical narrative and on the use of religious metaphors and symbols which divided the world into heroes, villains, victims and martyrs. This mixture of the secular and religious can explain both the emotional reach of Italian nationalism and its equivocal political impact. We have seen that Garibaldi was a master of the technique of modern politics – the short speech and the striking look – but there was also much in his presence which was pure *ancien régime*. As Garibaldi grew older, he left his bandit role far behind, and it became increasingly difficult to separate his image from that of a suffering saint. This elaboration worked rather well as an anti-government metaphor, but it was a weak weapon against the rhetoric of the Church, and it laid him particularly open to the kind of scornful attacks and political mockery which became a feature of the Catholic press' approach to him. There are some striking similarities in the representations and descriptions of Garibaldi and Pius IX, but we should not assume that Garibaldi was always the more convincing public personality.

The view of Italy as a weak and failed nation is a persistent one and, in the years after national unification, Italy's foundation story was recast as a tragic romance. Yet, as I have suggested in this chapter, this narrative is in part the product of political embellishment. That is, the 'failure' of Italy reflected the significant economic, social and political challenge of national unification but it was also the result of a polemic, in which the political loser(s) sought to denigrate and diminish the achievements of the victorious side. The effect of this polemic on the national discourse was to maintain at its very centre the persuasive contrast between a poetic vision of national belonging and the prosaic disenchantment of Italy's governments; in this way, the contrast which had been such a powerful weapon in the hands of the political opposition during the Risorgimento was to remain in place after the unification of Italy. On the radical side, few used it with more skill or to greater lasting effect than Garibaldi.

The crucial point to recognise, however, is not so much that Italy was an unsuccessful nation as that it was a politically divided one. In many ways, the emphasis on a failed Italy in this political conflict, the strong focus on national heroes and national martyrs, on national 'resurgence' and national betrayal, points us to the overwhelming victory of the Italian nationalist discourse. Its success is shown by the dominance of patriotic language in political debate and the great capacity of the nationalist imaginary to provoke a passionate sense of political involvement. Perhaps what emerges most clearly from a study of the culture wars of early-liberal Italy is the absolute centrality of ideas of the nation to an increasingly bitter struggle for political power.

CONCLUSION

THE MYTH OF GARIBALDI

We only believe in a romance when we see it in a newspaper.
Wilkie Collins, *The Moonstone*

When Garibaldi died in 1882, *The Times* expressed its shock at the loss of a man who had 'fascinated two hemispheres for thirty years'. He had, according to the paper, accomplished 'a miracle of national regeneration . . . To him . . . Italy is indebted for an ideal of manliness and individual self-reliance.' 'A nation is better for an ingredient of romance in its history', the paper concluded, and Italy had 'that ingredient copiously in the entire career of Garibaldi'.[1] These words sum up neatly the combination of political wonder, literary fantasy and physical excitement which Garibaldi's name evoked for the nineteenth-century reader. In the conclusion, I want to reflect further on the ingredients of his 'fascination'.

In the course of the preceding chapters, I have shown how a political cult of Garibaldi as an Italian hero was conceived of, fashioned and promoted during the crucial transition years of the Risorgimento and Italian unification. The original purpose of the cult was to embody and publicise a political sense of *italianità*, to identify an imaginary narrative of romantic heroism with a living, military leader, and to encourage Italians to 'regenerate' themselves. The cult was prepared and executed with remarkable precision by Mazzini and his followers and, in the long decade of 1848–60, it combined with a broader campaign in the press and accompanied a programme of political–military action. By unification, the cult of Garibaldi had helped make visible and convincing a heroic ('manly') ideal of Italy which had hitherto existed in literature, music and the visual arts, or only in the closed, underground circles of political conspirators. After the unification of Italy, the heroic image of Garibaldi was at once the most prominent and persuasive symbol of the new Italy, and a constant reminder of its varied disappointments.

I have suggested that a study of the Garibaldi cult can show us how nineteenth-century revolutionary and radical leaders, without a hold over

government, administration or public finance, and long before the organisation of mass political parties in the 1880s, made use of the new technologies of
mass communication to reach, constitute and persuade a substantial radical
public. During the events of 1859–60 the cult became a myth in and of itself,
based on a narrative which was at least partly invention and which embodied
key themes and ideas of Risorgimento culture. A striking feature of this myth
was the free, and outwardly flawless, mix of fact and fiction, and the recasting
of political struggle as popular entertainment. There seems little doubt that
Garibaldi's image was something manufactured and 'managed', which
borrowed the tropes of adventure romances, harnessed the techniques of
theatrical performance, and took on the liturgical and ritual aspects of
religious practice.[2] In this way, the creation of the myth of Garibaldi reflects
both the political possibilities of modern communication techniques and the
scavenging tendencies of nationalist rhetoric, which seeks to construct a
popular and persuasive political ideology by appropriating and manipulating
pieces of existing discourse and practice.

Yet the process of political communication did not flow in one direction
only, and the nationalist scavenging was far from random. First, the political
'fascination' of Garibaldi was very carefully staged for particular and/or
different audiences: Garibaldi and those around him strove to establish a fit
between his image and the fashionable tastes for fictional heroes, and much of
his popular success was due to an acute sensitivity to the narrative demands of
his public. So we should not assume that his audience was passive, and must
recognise instead that they played an active role in creating the hero they
desired. Second, Garibaldi's style was not entirely eclectic, but drew on three
main sources. It was based on an established set of republican rituals, it pressed
into service romantic metaphors and narratives of rebellion, and it made great
use of his personal, and physical, attraction. Garibaldi's charisma was
artifically fashioned, but it also fitted the man, his politics, and his audience's
expectations.

Garibaldi represents an alternative, and democratic, tradition of political
heroism often overlooked by historians more interested in the origins of the
authoritarian personality cults of the twentieth century. His popularity also
reflects changes in the public sphere, from an elite-dominated world of letters
to the more democratic world of popular or 'low' literature enjoyed by both
men and women. By looking at press reports, popular biographies, prints and
songs about Garibaldi, and at reactions to them, we can trace the popularisation of romanticism, and its partial fusion with political culture. In attacks on
Garibaldi, we can also follow the struggle for control of the new, popular
(although not yet 'mass') culture produced by this union. Perhaps most
importantly, through the creation of a cult of Garibaldi we can gain an

understanding of how activists tried to connect with cultural change and direct
it to specifically political ends. Garibaldi reminds us that in our attempt to
understand the formation, language and impact of nationalist movements in
modern societies we cannot just focus on cultural production but should also
seek to analyse political action, and that we should also consider the role of
political struggle in creating a language of nationality and the public response
to it.

In my view, the cult of Garibaldi was the product of a vibrant movement of
political radicalism which flourished in the mid-nineteenth century, and it was
part of radicalism's attempt to promote, and insert itself into, an international
mood of popular romanticism. The mix of romanticism and radicalism
anticipated and helped to form a new, more spectacular style of political
communication, characterised by the cult of personality, the borrowing of
techniques developed for literature and the theatre, and the use of the press.
This style, and the political symbolism which it produced, represents an early
and in some respects defining stage in the emergence of mass politics in the
nineteenth century.

Since this 'radical moment' has been relatively neglected in recent research,
we can only speculate about the reasons for its decline or, more accurately, for
its diversion into the more antagonistic and chauvinistic political symbolism
of the later-nineteenth and twentieth centuries. Nevertheless, if we look at
Garibaldi we can observe a tendency for the charismatic construction to float
free from its political moorings. The biography of Garibaldi was something of
a collaborative effort, and while this 'interactive' aspect of Garibaldi's celebrity
helps to explain its success, it also means that its political significance could be
disputed. Garibaldi's image was always vulnerable to manipulation. Although
the reworking of his legend occurred mainly after his death, along with the
gradual defeat of radicalism, it was foreshadowed in Garibaldi's controversial
attempts to maintain control over the use of his image in the years before he
died. Just as radicals had been able to contest and reshape the public sphere by
appropriating new methods of communication, so could conservatives and
clericals wrest control from them using the very same techniques.

Long before his death, control of Garibaldi's image had become a powerful
instrument of political propaganda and political authority, and this was
because popular identification with him could reach fanatical levels. The cult
of Garibaldi was very successful. The creation of his heroic reputation owes a
great deal to existing cults of hero worship, but it had a reach and a resonance
which was almost unprecedented, especially when we remember that he was
excluded from political power. It was international (he really was a 'hero of
two worlds'), visually spectacular, and it worked; Garibaldi was immensely
famous, his presence could provoke mass demonstrations of popular enthu-

siasm, and from the late 1850s his name guaranteed large donations of money and encouraged a rush of volunteers to fight with him. Garibaldi's charisma provoked intensely passionate feelings of political belonging. Men and women felt personally involved with Garibaldi and were emotionally touched by his experiences. They not only supported his political aims but also identified their own romantic sensibilities, radical ambitions and/or religious hatreds with his struggle to 'free' Italy from foreign or 'priestly' oppression.

This unusual achievement comes down largely to timing and to place. Garibaldi's emergence and definition as a popular hero was a symptom of political modernisation. It coincided with a popular revolution in publishing and reading, which helped writers, publishers and readers to challenge elite control of the public sphere, and made it possible to promote him – a revolutionary outsider – on a hitherto unparalleled scale. Garibaldi reached much of his public through the leisure activity of reading and other forms of visual entertainment, and the public's response to him was conditioned by these media. Mazzini and Garibaldi were among the first to seize this development for political purposes, so that lack of competition also helps to explain the unrivalled nature of their publicity triumph. At the same time, the popular resonance of Garibaldi owed much to the persistence of tradition. That is, his appeal as an exceptional leader made sense to a culture where notions of the superhuman and (especially) the sacred still had a real political and social significance, and where people believed in kings, saints and miracles, or were at least nostalgic for them. This is perhaps most obvious in the case of Italy itself, with its strict religious hierarchy built around the charismatic figure of the Pope and popular faith in the miraculous power of saints,[3] but it is also evident, if sometimes expressed more obliquely, in the press reactions to Garibaldi's successes in Britain and the United States. It is perhaps this nineteenth-century mix of tradition and modernity, and of democracy and dictatorship, which best explains the political reach and emotional impact of Garibaldi.

But how special was Garibaldi? To what extent was his charisma also the result of genuine political or personal achievement? In an age when fame is ubiquitous and we no longer believe in Great Men, this is an especially tricky question to answer. Nevertheless, throughout this book I have sought to stress Garibaldi's singular importance as a political actor. He remained in the public eye for nearly forty years, and his life spanned the shift from nationalism as a revolutionary movement to nationalism as the official ideology of an established regime. In particular, I have contended that Garibaldi's military ideas, and especially his vision of volunteering, were both politically innovative and broadly popular, and that his military successes played a key role in the construction of his political appeal. I have also suggested that the period of dictatorship in Sicily in 1860 was a more significant political experiment than is often assumed, and that his later political career contains much that is noteworthy. Primarily, I have argued that his outstanding talent for political communication should be taken seriously. If the reports and letters about Garibaldi are to be believed, he learnt (or he naturally possessed) great dramatic timing: he knew how to strike a pose, he knew how to use his voice, his body and his smile, he knew when to be brave and when to be humble, and he knew (perhaps too well for his colleagues) when to abandon the stage and distance himself from the public furore created by his presence. He applied what was by all accounts a powerful physical and sexual magnetism to the purpose of political persuasion, and he followed this up with an unparalleled display of modesty and openness. He seems instinctively to have understood that, in the extended imaginary communities created by mass print culture and entertainment, nothing succeeded so well as the personal, intimate touch.

Historians have long struggled to distinguish between fact and fiction in the making of Garibaldi, to find the man behind the mask, and to destroy or confirm Garibaldi's heroic reputation by revealing the truth about his military failures, his political mistakes and/or his private obsessions. In a sense, however, this is to miss completely the point about his life. With Garibaldi, image and reality were effectively indistinguishable. Both were part of a prolonged process of political display which took in South America and Caprera, his political battles and his private life, which became part of a public memory that defined an 'epoch' (the Risorgimento), and which seemingly only ended with his death (and even then, as we have seen, not entirely).

In conclusion, the myth of Garibaldi may not be true, but it was uncommonly effective. Garibaldi showed how Italians could be 'made', and his presence helped to create, encourage, and greatly increase support for political radicalism and nationalism. In turn, the popularity of Garibaldi offers us insights into the general role and function of myths in nationalist movements. It tells us that successful nationalist myths are neither genuine nor invented but a compelling blend of both; and that they are neither spontaneous nor imposed, but can far better be characterised as an intricate process of negotiation between actor and audience where the author (or source of authority) is difficult to discover. Most of all, it suggests that, in the complex and contingent processes which go into making a national community and in the political struggle to control and use this sense of belonging, there are few symbols more potent and more plastic than a living, breathing man.

NOTES

Author's Note

All emphases in the text are in the original unless otherwise stated.

List of Abbreviations

ACS	Archivio Centrale dello Stato, Rome
ASM	Archivio di Stato di Milan
ASP	Archivio di Stato, Palermo
ACP	Archivio Comunale, Palermo
BL	British Library, London
Epistolario	*Epistolario di Giuseppe Garibaldi*, 11 vols, Rome, 1973–2002
MCRR	Museo Centrale del Risorgimento, Rome
MRG	Museo del Risorgimento, Genoa
MRM	Museo del Risorgimento, Milan
NA	The National Archives (Public Record Office), London
SSSP	Società Siciliana per la Storia Patria, Palermo
Scritti	*Scritti editi ed inediti di Giuseppe Mazzini*, Imola, 1906–86
Scritti e discorsi	*Edizione nazionale degli scritti di Giuseppe Garibaldi*, vols 4–6. *Scritti e discorsi politici e militari*, 3 vols, Bologna, 1934–7

Introduction

1. J. Butler, *In memoriam Harriet Meuricoffre*, London, 1901, p. 50; also in D. Mack Smith (ed.), *Garibaldi. Great lives observed*, Englewood Cliffs, NJ, 1969, p. 130.
2. *Minuta di proclama agli Italiani*, Genoa, 5 May 1860 (or Talamone, 8 May 1860), in Garibaldi, *Scritti e discorsi*, 1, pp. 239–41.
3 . There is a huge number of popular and academic biographies of Garibaldi. Among the most up to date are, in English, D. Mack Smith, *Garibaldi. A great life in brief*, London, 1957 and J. Ridley, *Garibaldi*, London, 1974; and in Italian, G. Monsagrati, 'Garibaldi Giuseppe', *Dizionario biografico degli italiani*, 52, Rome, 1999, and A. Scirocco, *Garibaldi. Battaglie, amori, ideali di un cittadino del mondo*, Bari and Rome, 2001.
4. M. Amari, *Carteggio di Michele Amari*, ed. A. d'Ancona, 3 vols, Turin, 1896, 2, p. 134.

5. G. C. Abba, *The diary of one of Garibaldi's Thousand*, trans. E. R. Vincent, London, 1962, p. 77.

6. Quoted in D. Beales, 'Garibaldi in England. The politics of Italian enthusiasm', in J. A. Davis and P. Ginsborg (eds), *Society and politics in the age of the Risorgimento. Essays in honour of Denis Mack Smith*, Cambridge, 1991, pp. 188, 190.

7. C. Duggan, *Francesco Crispi. From nation to nationalism*, Oxford, 2002, pp. 426–50; idem, 'Francesco Crispi, "political education" and the problem of Italian national consciousness, 1860–1886', *Journal of Modern Italian Studies*, 2/2, 1997, pp. 141–66.

8. On the burial, see B. Tobia, 'Una forma di pedagogia nazionale tra cultura e politica: i luoghi della memoria e della rimembranza', in *Il mito del Risorgimento nell'Italia unita*, Milan, 1995, pp. 194–207; U. Levra, *Fare gli italiani. Memoria e celebrazione del Risorgimento*, Turin, 1992, pp. 110–13. On the 1884 pilgrimage, see B. Tobia, *Una patria per gli italiani. Spazi, itinerari, monumenti nell'Italia unita*, Rome and Bari, 1991, pp. 100–42.

9. I. Porciani, *La festa della nazione*, Bologna, 1997.

10. Tobia, *Una patria per gli italiani*, pp. 143–8.

11. M. Baioni, *La 'religione della patria'. Musei e istituti del culto risorgimentale (1884–1918)*, Treviso, 1994.

12. The most thorough study of the *Vittoriano* is C. Brice, *Le Vittoriano. Monumentalité publique et politique à Rome*, Rome, 1998. On the official political iconography of nineteenth-century Italy, see S. von Falkenhausen, *Italienische monumental Malerei im Risorgimento, 1830–1890*, Berlin, 1993.

13. See E. Gentile, *The sacralization of politics in fascist Italy*, trans. K. Botsford, Cambridge MA, 1996, pp. 1–18; idem, *Le religioni della politica. Fra democrazia e totalitarismi*, Rome and Bari, 2001; M. Ridolfi, C. Brice and F. de Giorgi, 'Religione civile e identità nazionale nella storia d'Italia: per una discussione', *Memoria e Ricerca*, 13, 2003, pp. 133–52.

14. On the 'national pantheon' of great Italians, see E. Irace, *Italie glorie. La costruzione di un pantheon nazionale*, Bologna, 2003, pp. 121–208. See also Levra, *Fare gli italiani*, pp. 27, 153–4, and M. Isnenghi, *L'Italia in piazza. I luoghi della vita pubblica dal 1848 ai nostri giorni*, Milan, 1994, pp. 24–7.

15. Isnenghi, *L'Italia in piazza*, p. 25. For a comprehensive list of the monuments to Garibaldi in Italy, see G. Massobrio and L. Capellini, *L'Italia per Garibaldi*, Milan, 1982.

16. Levra, *Fare gli italiani*, pp. 153–4.

17. Duggan, *Francesco Crispi*, pp. 693–4; the quote by Crispi is on p. 294.

18. E. Garibaldi (ed.), *Qui sostò Garibaldi. Itinerari garibaldini in Italia*, Fasano, 1982; J. Grévy, *Garibaldi*, Paris, 2001, pp. 160–2.

19. One survey of commemorative pamphlets and patriotic ephemera published in this period has found that those dedicated to Garibaldi almost outnumber those of all other Italian national heroes put together. F. Dolci, 'L'editoria d'occasione del secondo Ottocento nella Biblioteca di storia moderna e contemporanea di Roma', in *Il mito del Risorgimento*, p. 146.

20. Grévy, *Garibaldi*, pp. 146–60.

21. J. Woodhouse, *Gabriele D'Annunzio. Defiant archangel*, Oxford, 1998, p. 196.

22. Grévy, *Garibaldi*, pp. 183–201; M. Isnenghi, 'Usi politici di Garibaldi dall'interventismo al fascismo', in F. Mazzonis (ed.), *Garibaldi condottiero. Storia, teoria, prassi*, Milan, 1984, pp. 533–40; M. Brignoli, 'Bruno, Costanzo e la presenza garibaldina nella grande guerra', in Z. Ciuffoletti *et al.* (eds), *I Garibaldi dopo Garibaldi. La tradizione famigliare e l'eredità politica*, Manduria, 2005, pp. 155–64.

23. C. Fogu, '"To make history": Garibaldianism and the formation of a fascist historic imaginary', in A. Russell Ascoli and K. von Henneberg (eds), *Making and remaking Italy. The cultivation of national identity around the Risorgimento*, Oxford, 2001, pp. 203–40.

24. On the film, see D. Forgacs, '*Nostra patria*: revisions of the Risorgimento in the cinema', ibid., esp. pp. 257–63. For a general discussion of the uses of the Garibaldi myth during Fascism see Grévy, *Garibaldi*, pp. 202–12; Isnenghi, 'Usi politici di Garibaldi', pp. 540–4.
25. M. Isnenghi, 'Garibaldi', in idem (ed.), *I luoghi della memoria. Personaggi e date dell'Italia unita*, Rome and Bari, 1997, pp. 41–3; Grévy, *Garibaldi*, pp. 212–18.
26. On which, see S. Gundle, 'The "civic religion" of the Resistance in post-war Italy', *Modern Italy*, 5/2, 2000, pp. 113–32.
27. Grévy, *Garibaldi*, pp. 223–9, 241–56.
28. On the role and purpose of the 'exemplary life' in modern politics, see G. Cubitt, 'Introduction: heroic reputations and exemplary lives', in idem and A. Warren (eds), *Heroic reputations and exemplary lives*, Manchester, 2000, esp. pp. 7–9.
29. Among the most important of these biographies of Garibaldi are G. Guerzoni, *Garibaldi*, Firenze, 1882; J. White Mario, *Garibaldi e i suoi tempi*, Milan, 1884; G. E. Curàtolo, *Giuseppe Garibaldi*, Rome, 1925; and G. Sacerdote, *La vita di Giuseppe Garibaldi*, Milan, 1933. The *Garibaldi* 'trilogy' published in England by G. M. Trevelyan between 1907 and 1911 takes an equally reverent attitude towards its subject matter, but for less immediate (although no less evident) political reasons.
30. On this trend in the political arena, see M. Marsili, 'De Gasperi and Togliatti: political leadership and personality cults in post-war Italy', *Modern Italy*, 3/2, 1998, pp. 249–61.
31. A. M. Ghisalberti, 'Di una buona bibliografia e di alcuni discutibili giudizi', *Rassegna Storica del Risorgimento*, 58, 1971, pp. 629–30.
32. Idem, 'Ancora sulla partecipazione popolare nel Risorgimento', ibid., pp. 31–3, 1944–6, p. 6, his emphasis.
33. Idem, *Momenti e figure del Risorgimento romano*, Milan, 1965, p. 183.
34. Ibid., p. 189. The titles of the essays included here are themselves revealing: 'Among the minor figures of the Roman Risorgimento' ('*Fra i minori del Risorgimento romano*') and 'Pietro Rosselli, a forgotten figure of '49' ('*Pietro Rosselli, un dimenticato del '49*').
35. Quoted in D. Mack Smith, *Cavour and Garibaldi. A study in political conflict*, Cambridge, 2nd edn, 1985, p. x.
36. L. Riall, 'Rivoluzione, repubblicanesimo e Risorgimento: Roma e i suoi storici, 1798–99 e 1849', *Roma moderna e contemporanea*, 9/1–3, 2001, pp. 291–2.
37. For a discussion, see Grévy, *Garibaldi*, pp. 229–41. A partial exception to this rule, as Grévy argues, is the work of Denis Mack Smith, but this is hardly surprising since he comes from a different (Anglo-Saxon) historiographical tradition with different institutional constraints (and Mack Smith himself stresses his position as an outsider in *Cavour and Garibaldi*, pp. xi–xii).
38. A. Gramsci, *Il Risorgimento*, Turin, 1949.
39. The literature on Gramsci's analysis of the Risorgimento is very substantial. In English, see, in particular, J. A. Davis, 'Introduction: Antonio Gramsci and Italy's passive revolution', and P. Ginsborg, 'Gramsci and the era of the bourgeois revolution in Italy', both in J. A. Davis (ed.), *Gramsci and Italy's passive revolution*, London, 1979. For a brief summary, see L. Riall, *Sicily and the unification of Italy. Liberal policy and local power, 1859–1866*, Oxford, 1998, pp. 8–14.
40. Riall, 'Roma e i suoi storici', p. 290.
41. See Ghisalberti's remarks in the *premessa* to *Momenti e figure del Risorgimento*, pp. x–xii, and the comments of Franco della Peruta about Morelli in 'Il Mazzini di Emilia Morelli', *Rassegna Storica del Risorgimento*, 82/4, 1995, pp. 513–14.
42. A. Gramsci, *Selections from prison notebooks*, ed. and trans. Q. Hoare and G. Nowell Smith, London, 1971, pp. 61, 204.
43. For a summary of the findings of Italian social historians, see L. Riall, *The Italian Risorgimento. State, society and national unification*, London, 1994, esp. pp. 20–49.

44. E. Gellner, *Nations and nationalism*, Oxford, 1983; E. Hobsbawm, *Nations and nationalism since 1780*, London, 1990; B. Anderson, *Imagined communities*, London, 1991 edn.
45. See the comments by Hobsbawm on why in general 'historians should address their attention to such phenomena' in E. Hobsbawm, 'Introduction, inventing traditions', in idem and T. Ranger (eds), *The invention of tradition*, Cambridge, 1983, p. 12.
46. A. M. Banti, *La nazione del Risorgimento. Parentela, santità e onore alle origini dell'Italia unita*, Turin, 2000. He discusses and lists the 'canonical' texts on pp. 44–55.
47. See I. Porciani, 'Stato e nazione: l'immagine debole dell'Italia', in S. Soldani and G. Turi (eds), *Fare gli Italiani. Scuola e cultura nell'Italia contemporanea*, Bologna, 1993, 1, pp. 385–428.
48. See the analyses in Grévy, *Garibaldi*, pp. 139–267 and Isnenghi, 'Garibaldi'.
49. F. della Peruta, 'Il mito del Risorgimento e l'estrema sinistra dall'Unità al 1914', in *Il mito del Risorgimento*, pp. 32–70.
50. Fogu, 'To make history', pp. 206–15.
51. M. Agulhon, 'Le mythe de Garibaldi en France de 1882 à nos jours', in idem, *Histoire vagabonde, vol II. Idéologie et politique dans la France du XIXe siècle*, Paris, 1988, pp. 85–131. For the myth of Garibaldi in England, see Beales, 'The politics of Italian enthusiasm', and M. Finn, *After Chartism. Class and nation in English radical politics*, Cambridge, 1993, pp. 189–223; and in Germany, C. Dipper, 'Helden überkreuz oder das Kreuz mit den Helden', in *Jahrbuch des Historischen Kollegs*, Munich, 1999. For a general discussion, see Grévy, *Garibaldi*, pp. 93–138.
52. Scirocco, *Garibaldi*; D. Pick, *Rome or death. The obsessions of General Garibaldi*, London, 2005; M. Schwegman, 'In love with Garibaldi: romancing the Risorgimento', *European Review of History–Révue européene d'Histoire*, 12/2, 2005, pp. 363–81. Grévy, *Garibaldi*, looks directly at the myth of Garibaldi but focuses largely on the period after his death.
53. C. Crocella, 'La storiografia su Garibaldi militare', in Mazzonis (ed.), *Garibaldi condottiero*, p. 481.
54. R. Villari, 'La prefigurazione politica del giudizio storico su Garibaldi', *Studi Storici*, 23/2, 1982, pp. 261–4.
55. In his 1954 study, *Cavour and Garibaldi*, Denis Mack Smith observed Garibaldi's capacity for political realism, while in 1963 Virgilio Titone made a plea for historians to look more seriously at Garibaldi's political strategy ('Garibaldi', in *Quaderni Storici*, 2, 1963, pp. 52–65, with a translated extract published in Mack Smith (ed.), *Garibaldi*, pp. 168–73). Both Rosario Villari and Franco della Peruta have suggested that Garibaldi was both more representative and more politically astute than traditional Risorgimento historiography would have us believe (Villari, 'La prefigurazione politica'; F. della Peruta, 'Garibaldi fra mito e politica', *Studi Storici*, 23/1, 1982, pp. 5–22). However, none of these useful suggestions has given rise to more in-depth research.
56. For a comparison, see Alan Forrest on Napoleonic strategy: 'Propaganda and the legitimation of power in Napoleonic France', *French History*, 18/4, 2004, pp. 426–45; and, for an earlier period, P. Burke, *The fabrication of Louis XIV*, New Haven, CT, and London, 1992.
57. D. Cannadine, *G.M. Trevelyan. A life in history*, London, 1992, p. 67.
58. A. D. Smith, 'National identity and myths of ethnic descent', in idem, *Myths and memories of the nation*, Oxford, 1999, p. 58.
59. See the comments of R. Girardet, *Mythes et mythologies politiques*, Paris, 1986, pp. 13–14.
60. On the use of symbols in the construction of political authority, see D. Kertzer, *Rituals, politics and power*, New Haven, CT, 1988; and G. Schöpflin, 'The function of myth and a taxonomy of myths', in G. Hosking and G. Schöpflin (eds), *Myths and*

nationhood, London, 1997, pp. 19–35. R. Gewarth, *The Bismarck myth. Weimar Germany and the legacy of the Iron Chancellor*, Oxford, 2005, B. Schwartz, *George Washington. The making of an American symbol*, New York, 1987, and I. Kershaw, *The 'Hitler myth'. Image and reality in the Third Reich*, Oxford, 1987, have been of particular help to me in understanding the political function of hero cults.

61. On this point, see most obviously G. Mosse, *The nationalisation of the masses. Political symbolism and mass movements in Germany from the Napoleonic wars through the Third Reich*, New York, 1975, esp. pp. 6–12.

62. M. Weber, *Economy and society*, 2 vols, Berkeley, CA, 1978, 2, pp. 241–2.

63. E. Shils, 'Charisma, order and status', *American Sociological Review*, April 1965, p. 200; C. Geertz, 'Centers, kings and charisma: reflections on the symbolics of power', in J. Ben-David and T. Nichols Clark (eds), *Culture and its creators. Essays in honor of Edward Shils*, Chicago, 1977, p. 171.

64. Shils, 'Charisma', pp. 200–1.

65. This is a feature of political charisma in Italy more generally. See S. Gundle and L. Riall, 'Introduction' to 'Charisma and the cult of personality in modern Italy', *Modern Italy*, 3/2, 1999, p. 157.

66. For instance, C. Lindholm's interesting study, *Charisma*, Cambridge, MA, 1990, focuses entirely on right-wing dictators and violent cult leaders like Charles Manson. Kertzer, *Rituals*, is one of the few studies which considers revolutionary movements as well as rulers in analysing the uses of political symbolism.

67. Weber, *Economy and society*, pp. 246–54.

68. Kershaw, *The 'Hitler myth'*, pp. 4, 253; R. Tucker, *Stalin in power*, New York, 1992, p. 171; J. Gottlieb, 'The marketing of megalomania: celebrity, consumption and the development of political technology in the British Union of Fascists', *Journal of Contemporary History*, 41/1, 2006, pp. 35–55.

69. See, by way of contrast, the comments of Nell Painter that the nineteenth-century American preacher and feminist, Sojourner Truth, 'remains more sign than lived existence . . . like other invented greats, Truth is consumed as a signifier and beloved for what we need her to have said.' N. W. Painter, 'Representing Truth: Sojourner Truth's knowing and becoming known', *Journal of American History*, 81/2, 1994, p. 480.

70. G. Eley, 'Nations, publics, and political cultures: placing Habermas in the nineteenth century', in C. Calhoun (ed.), *Habermas and the public sphere*, Boston, MA, 1994, pp. 289–339.

71. J. Smith Allen, *Popular French romanticism. Authors, readers and books in the nineteenth century*, Syracuse, NY, 1981, pp. 6–12.

72. This point is also recognised by Schwegman, 'In love with Garibaldi', pp. 370–2.

Chapter 1: Nation and Risorgimento

1. 22 Oct. 1843, in *Scritti*, 24, p. 316. Mazzini was referring specifically to an argument between Cuneo, Garibaldi and another 'Young Italian', Rossetti, which had caused temporarily what Mazzini called 'a kind of separation' between the two friends.

2. On the Italian secret societies, see A. Lehning, 'Buonarotti and his international secret societies', *International Review of Social History*, 1, 1956, pp. 112–40; R. J. Rath, 'The Carbonary: their origins, initiation rites and aims', *American Historical Review*, 69, 1964, pp. 353–70. On Mazzini's involvement with the Carbonari see E. Hales, *Mazzini and the secret societies: the making of a myth*, London, 1956.

3. F. della Peruta, 'Mazzini della letteratura militante all'impegno politico', *Studi Storici*, 14/3, 1973, p. 546.

4. On Saint-Simon, see J. Hayward, *After the French Revolution. Six critics of democracy and nationalism*, London, 1991, pp. 65–100.

5. Quoted in R. Sarti, *Mazzini: a life for the religion of politics*, Westport, CT, 1997, p. 60. For Mazzini and Saint-Simonianism, see ibid., pp. 58–60.

6. 16 Dec. 1846, to Carlo Fenzi, in *Scritti*, 30, p. 308.

7. F. della Peruta, *Mazzini e i rivoluzionari italiani. Il 'partitio d'azione' 1830–1845*, Milan, 1974, p. 70.

8. Sarti, *Mazzini*, p. 60.

9. On Buonarotti and conspiracy, see E. L. Eisenstein, *The first professional revolutionary: Filippo Michele Buonarotti (1761–1837)*, Cambridge, MA, 1959, and more generally J. M. Roberts, *The mythology of the secret societies*, New York, 1972.

10. Quoted in Della Peruta, 'Mazzini', pp. 508, 552; the hero in Italian political culture is discussed in more detail below, pp. 59–67.

11. Mazzini was strongly influenced by the pamphlet published in 1830 by the Piedmontese exile Carlo Bianco di Saint Jorioz, *Della guerra nazionale d'insurrezione per bande, applicata all'Italia*. For a discussion and the text, see F. della Peruta (ed.), *Democratici, premazziniani e dissidenti*, Turin, 1979; on Mazzini, V. Parmentola, 'Carlo Bianco, Giuseppe Mazzini e la teoria dell'insurrezione', *Bollettino della Domus Mazziniana*, 2, 1959, pp. 5–40.

12. Sarti, *Mazzini*, p. 54.

13. Extracts in A. M. Banti, *Il Risorgimento italiano*, Rome and Bari, 2004, pp. 189–92.

14. E. Gentile, *The sacralisation of politics in fascist Italy*, Cambridge, MA, 1996, p. 4.

15. There is a substantial literature on this subject: on the 'ethnic' and historical origins of nations, see A. D. Smith, *Nationalism and modernism*, London, 1998, and A. Hastings, *The construction of nationhood: ethnicity, religion and nationalism*, Cambridge, 1997; on nationalism and modernisation, E. Gellner, *Nations and nationalism*, Oxford, 1983; and on the 'invention' of nations, see J. Breuilly, *Nationalism and the state*, Manchester, 1993 edn; B. Anderson, *Imagined communities. Reflections on the origins and spread of nationalism*, London, 1991 edn; and E. Hobsbawm, *Nations and nationalism since 1780*, Cambridge, 1990.

16. A. M. Banti, *La nazione del Risorgimento. Parentela, santità e onore alle origini dell'Italia unita*, Turin, 2000, p. 150. Similar points are made by A. Lyttelton, 'Creating a national past: history, myth and image in the Risorgimento', in A. R. Ascoli and K. von Henneberg (eds), *Making and remaking Italy: the cultivation of national identity around the Risorgimento*, Oxford, 2001, esp. pp. 27–9.

17. See e.g. F. Venturi, *Settecento riformatore. I. Da Muratori a Beccaria*, Turin, 1969; also D. Carpinetto and G. Ricuperati, *Italy in the age of reason, 1685–1789*, London, 1987, p. 89; and S. J. Woolf, *A history of Italy 1700–1860*, London, 1979, pp. 75–80.

18. R. Grew, 'Culture and society, 1796–1896', in J. A. Davis (ed.), *Italy in the nineteenth century*, Oxford, 2000, p. 206.

19. Perhaps the best short summaries of the impact of the French on Italy are A. Grab, *Napoleon and the transformation of Europe*, London, 2003, pp. 152–75 (which despite its title has useful information on the revolutionary period as well), and idem, 'From the French Revolution to Napoleon', in Davis (ed.), *Italy in the nineteenth century*, pp. 25–50. See equally J. A. Davis, *Naples and Napoleon*, Oxford, 2006.

20. Grew, 'Culture and society', pp. 207–10.

21. Banti, *La nazione*, pp. 3–29.

22. There was remarkable continuity in those aspects of the revolutionary and Napoleonic traditions which modernised government administrations and strengthened the power of the state, as well as a fairly ambivalent attitude towards restoring the *ancien régime* privileges of Church and nobility. For a general discussion, see D. Laven and L. Riall, 'Restoration government and the legacy of Napoleon', in Laven and Riall (eds), *Napoleon's legacy. Problems of government in Restoration Europe*, Oxford, 2000, pp. 1–26; and on the specific policies of Restoration Italy, see D. Laven, 'The age of Restoration', in Davis (ed.), *Italy in the nineteenth century*, pp. 51–73.

23. For the text of De Staël's essay and the debate between 'classicists' and 'romantics' which ensued, see E. Bellorini (ed.), *Discussioni e polemiche sul romanticismo (1816–1826)*, Bari, 1943.
24. E. Raimondi, *Romanticismo italiano e romanticismo europeo*, Milan, 1997; C. Springer, *The marble wilderness: ruins and representation in Italian romanticism*, Cambridge, 1997; see also Grew, 'Culture and society', pp. 211–15.
25. Banti, *La nazione*, p. 29.
26. On the Italian version of the historical novel, see S. Pinto (ed.), *Romanticismo storico*, Florence, 1974; for a more general discussion, see B. Hamnett, 'Fictitious histories: the dilemma of fact and imagination in the nineteenth-century historical novel', *European History Quarterly*, 36/1, 2006, pp. 31–60.
27. Quoted in Banti, *La nazione*, p. 69. Lyttelton notes that *L'assedio di Firenze* was in fact considered too inflammatory to be published in Italy when it first appeared in 1836: 'Creating a national past', p. 59.
28. Ibid., pp. 52–8.
29. M. Praz, *The romantic agony*, London, 1933, esp. pp. 58–69. See also P. Ginsborg, 'Il mito del Risorgimento nel mondo britannico: "la vera poesia della politica"', in *Il mito del Risorgimento nell'Italia unita*, Milan, 1995, pp. 386–7.
30. N. Frye, *The anatomy of criticism*, Princeton, NJ, 1957, pp. 33–4.
31. G. Mosse, *The image of man. The creation of modern masculinity*, New York, 1996, p. 18.
32. G. Dawson, *Soldier heroes. British adventure, empire and the imagining of masculinities*, London, 1994, pp. 69–74.
33. Banti, *La nazione*, p. 123.
34. On both these novels, see ibid., pp. 93–6.
35. For a discussion of images of war in Scott's poetry, see S. Bainbridge, *British poetry and the revolutionary and Napoleonic wars. Visions of conflict*, Oxford, 2003, esp. pp. 120–47, 159–70.
36. I. Porciani, 'Der Krieg als ambivalenter italienischer Gründungsmythos – Siege und Niederlagen', in N. Buschmann and D. Langewiesche (eds), *Der Krieg in den Gründungsmythen europäischer Nationen und der USA*, Frankfurt and New York, 2003, pp. 193–212.
37. D. Laven, 'Machiavelli, *italianità* and the French invasion of 1494', in D. Abulafia (ed.), *The French descent into Renaissance Italy, 1494–95. Antecedents and effects*, Aldershot, 1995, pp. 355–69. I discuss this theme in 'Eroi maschili, virilità e forme della guerra', in A. M. Banti and P. Ginsborg (eds), *Il Risorgimento*, Turin, forthcoming.
38. This issue is discussed in more detail below, Chapter 5, pp. 135–6.
39. Lyttelton, 'Creating a national past', p. 31.
40. D. Laven, 'Italy: The idea of the nation in the Risorgimento and liberal era', in T. Baycroft and M. Hewitson (eds), *What is a nation? Europe 1789–1914*, Oxford, 2006, p. 269.
41. Banti, *La nazione*, p. 150.
42. Lyttelton, 'Creating a national past', p. 42.
43. Della Peruta, 'Mazzini', p. 507.
44. See G. Pirodda, 'Giuseppe Mazzini e il romanticismo democratico', in *La letteratura italiana. Stori e testi*, 7, pt. 1, Bari, 1970–80, esp. pp. 252–9.
45. A. Galante Garrone, 'I giornali della Restaurazione', in idem and F. della Peruta, *La stampa italiana del Risorgimento*, Bari, 1976, p. 141.
46. Sarti, *Mazzini*, p. 54; Della Peruta, 'Mazzini', p. 507.
47. Galante Garrone, 'I giornali della Restaurazione', p. 156.
48. Ibid., pp. 157–64.
49. Ibid., p. 156.
50. *Scritti*, 34, p. 29 (the whole article is at pp. 27–48, and was first published in the London radical weekly, the *People's Journal*, in 1846).

51. S. Hazareesingh, 'Memory and political imagination. The legend of Napoleon revisited', *French History*, 18/4, 2004, p. 476.
52. D. Mack Smith, *Mazzini*, London, 1994, pp. 31, 40, 65.
53. D. Laven, 'Mazzini, Mazzinian conspiracy and British politics in the 1850s', *Bollettino Storico Mantovano*, nuova serie, 2, 2003, pp. 267–82.
54. Sarti, *Mazzini*, p. 3; Mack Smith, *Mazzini*, p. 2.

Chapter 2: In Search of Garibaldi

1. On Mazzini's experiences in England before the revolutions of 1848, see E. Morelli, *L'Inghilterra di Mazzini*, Rome, 1965; R. Sarti, *Mazzini. A life for the religion of politics*, Westport, CT, 1997, pp. 95–126; D. Mack Smith, *Mazzini*, London, 1994, pp. 20–48.
2. For the disagreement between Mazzini and Fabrizi, see F. della Peruta, 'Le teorie militari della democrazia risorgimentale', in F. Mazzonis (ed.), *Garibaldi condottiero. Storia, teoria, prassi*, Milan, 1984, pp. 67–9.
3. See M. Finelli, *'Il prezioso elemento'. Giuseppe Mazzini e gli emigrati italiani nell'esperienza della Scuola Italiana di Londra*, Verucchio, 1999.
4. Cited in Mack Smith, *Mazzini*, p. 41.
5. See below, pp. 139–46.
6. 'Byron et Goethe', *Scritti*, 21, pp. 233–4.
7. Quoted in Sarti, *Mazzini*, p. 112.
8. Mack Smith, *Mazzini*, pp. 42–3.
9. E. Yeo, 'Some practices and problems of Chartist democracy', in J. Epstein and D. Thompson (eds), *The Chartist experience: studies in working-class radicalism and culture, 1830–60*, London, 1982, pp. 345–80.
10. I. Haywood, *The revolution in popular literature. Print, politics and the people, 1790–1860*, Cambridge, 2004, pp. 139–61.
11. J. Vernon, *Politics and the people: a study in English political culture, c.1815–1867*, Cambridge, 1993, p. 258; the whole chapter, pp. 251–91, is a useful analysis of the creation of British radical heroes (including Garibaldi). For a discussion of the British popular radical tradition over a longer time-span, see J. Brewer, *Party ideology and popular politics at the accession of George III*, Cambridge, 1976; J. Belchem, *Orator Hunt. Henry Hunt and English working-class radicalism*, Oxford, 1985, and R. McWilliam, *Popular politics in nineteenth-century England*, London, 1998; and on the influence of British thought on Mazzini, G. Monsagrati, 'Garibaldi e il culto vittoriano dell'eroe', *Studi Storici*, 42/1, 2001, pp. 165–80.
12. J. Plunkett, *Queen Victoria. First media monarch*, Oxford, 2003.
13. On European exiles and their impact, see S. Freitag (ed.), *Exiles from European revolutions. Refugees in mid-Victorian England*, Oxford, 2003; see also M. Isabella, 'Exile and nationalism: the case of the *Risorgimento*', *European History Quarterly*, 36/4, 2006, pp 493–520.
14. See G. Claeys, 'Mazzini, Kossuth and British radicalism, 1848–1854', *Journal of British Studies*, 28/2, 1989, pp. 225–61.
15. Sarti, *Mazzini*, p. 116; idem, 'La democrazia radicale: uno sguardo reciproco tra Stati Uniti e Italia', in M. Ridolfi (ed.), *La democrazia radicale nell'ottocento europeo*, Milan, 2005, pp. 140–4.
16. 24 Dec. 1846, to Enrico Mayer, in Mazzini, *Scritti*, 30, p. 321.
17. On Italian communities in the Americas during this period, see the general discussion in D. Gabaccia, *Italy's many diasporas*, London, 2000, esp. pp. 45–52, and M. Sanfilippo, 'Nationalisme, "italianité" et émigration aux Amériques (1830–1990)', *European Review of History*, 2, 1995, pp. 177–91. Before the arrival of Mazzinian ideas with the emigrations of 1833–4, many Italian political exiles had made their home in

Latin America. A. Scirocco, *Garibaldi. Battaglie, amori, ideali di un cittadino del mondo*, Rome and Bari, 2001, pp. 29–30.

18. M. A. de Marco, *Bartolomé Mitre*, Buenos Aires, 1998; W. H. Katra, *The Argentine generation of 1837: Echeverría, Alberdi, Sarmiento, Mitre*, London, 1996; N. Shumway, *The invention of Argentina*, Berkeley, CA, 1991. More generally on the development of Argentine oppositional culture in this period, see C. A. Román, 'Caricatura y politica en *El Grito Argentino* (1839) y *¡Muera Rosas!* (1841–1842)', and E. J. Palti, 'Rosas como enigma. La génesis de la fórmula "civilización y barbarie",' both in G. Batticuore, K. Gallo, J. Myers (eds), *Resonancias románticas. Ensayos sobre historia de la cultura argentina (1820–1890)*, Buenos Aires, 2005, pp. 49–84.

19. See S. Candido, 'L'azione mazziniana in Brasile ed il giornale "La Giovine Italia" di Rio de Janeiro (1836) attraverso documenti inediti o poco noti', *Bollettino della Domus Mazziniana*, 14/2, 1968, pp. 3–66; idem, 'La "Giovine Italia" a Montevideo (1836–1842). Contributo alla storia mazziniana nelle Americhe', ibid., 21/1, 1975, pp. 53–76; idem, *La rivoluzione riograndese nel carteggio inedito di due giornalisti mazziniani: Luigi Rossetti e G.B. Cuneo (1837–1840). Contributo alla storia del giornalismo politico di ispirazione italiana nei paesi latinoamericani*, Florence, 1973.

20. T. Olivari, 'I libri di Garibaldi', *Storia e Futuro*, 1, 2002, pp. 1–16, see www.storiaefuturo.com.

21. Both Mazzini and the carbonari were also influenced by Saint-Simon and the romantic socialists. For recent reassessments of the Saint-Simonians and romantic socialism, see L. Sharp, 'Metempsychosis and social reform: the individual and the collective in romantic socialism', *French Historical Studies*, 27/2, 2004, pp. 349–79; P. Pilbeam, 'Dream worlds? Religion and the early socialists in France', *Historical Journal*, 43/2, 2000, pp. 499–516; J. Beecher, *Charles Fourier*, Berkeley, CA, 1986, pp. 409–30; E. Berenson, *Populist religion and left-wing politics in France, 1830–52*, Princeton, NJ, 1984.

22. According to two letters which Garibaldi wrote from Rio in January 1836: to Canessa on 25 Jan. and to Mazzini on 27 Jan. In *Epistolario*, 1, pp. 6–10.

23. 27 Dec. 1836, to Cuneo, ibid., p. 12.

24. There is a substantial literature on Garibaldi as a 'corsair'. See in particular S. Candido, *Giuseppe Garibaldi. Corsaro riograndese (1837–1838)*, Rome, 1964. Also important is R. Ugolini, *Garibaldi. Genesi di un mito*, Rome, 1982, pp. 93–124, while Scirocco, *Garibaldi*, pp. 28–74 and J. Ridley, *Garibaldi*, London, 1974, pp. 47–104 have useful accounts both of Garibaldi's activities and of the broader context of the war between Brazil and the fledgling republic of Rio Grande do Sul.

25. Ibid., p. 133.

26. D. McLean, 'Garibaldi in Uruguay: a reputation reconsidered', *English Historical Review*, 113, April 1998, pp. 351–5.

27. J. Lynch, *Argentine caudillo. Juan Manuel de Rosas*, Wilmington, DE, 2001, pp. 83–6.

28. Ridley, *Garibaldi*, pp. 109, 127, 133, 140–1, 181, 201.

29. A. Saldías, *Historia de la confederacíon Argentina*, 9 vols, Buenos Aires, 1929, 7, pp. 20–2.

30. McLean, 'Garibaldi', p. 351.

31. 15 March 1846.

32. On Garibaldi in Uruguay, see McLean, 'Garibaldi'; also Ridley, *Garibaldi*, pp. 94–206; Ugolini, *Garibaldi*, pp. 125–41; Scirocco, *Garibaldi*, pp. 83–124; and S. Candido, *Giuseppe Garibaldi nel Rio della Plata, 1841–1848*, Florence, 1972.

33. A. Dumas, *Montevideo ou une nouvelle Troie*, Paris, 1850; S. E. Pereda, *Garibaldi en el Uruguay*, 3 vols, Montevideo, 1914–16; idem, *Los extranjeros en la guerra grande*, Montevideo, 1904. On the myth of Garibaldi in Brazil, see A. Boldrini, 'Il mito di Garibaldi nella letteratura del Rio Grande do Sul', *Quaderni Storiografici dell'Istituto*

internazionale di studi Giuseppe Garibaldi, 8, 1993, pp. 3–25.

34. Quoted in McLean, 'Garibaldi', pp. 360–6.
35. Ridley, *Garibaldi*, pp. 47–9.
36. On Sarmiento: T. Halperín Donghi *et al.* (eds), *Sarmiento. Author of a nation*, Berkeley, CA, 1994.
37. There is a large hagiographic literature on Anita, about whom comparatively little is known. For a recent biography, see A. Valerio, *Anita Garibaldi. A biography*, Westport, CT, 2001.
38. Ridley, *Garibaldi*, pp. 139, 159.
39. On Zambeccari, see the special issue 'Tra il Reno e la Plata: la vita di Livio Zambeccari studioso e rivoluzionario', M. Gavelli, F. Tarozzi and R. Vecchi (eds), *Bollettino del Museo del Risorgimento*, 46, 2001.
40. D. Mack Smith, *Garibaldi: A great life in brief*, London, 1957, p. 19.
41. 9 March 1851, in *Epistolario*, 3, pp. 38–9; McLean, 'Garibaldi', p. 366.
42. The quotation is from D. F. Sarmiento, *Facundo*, La Plata, 1938, p. 59, quoted in J. Lynch, *Caudillos in Spanish America, 1800–1850*, Oxford, 1992, p. 412. For the typology of the gaucho see ibid., pp. 10–13.
43. G. Guerzoni, *Garibaldi*, Florence, 1882, 1, pp. 211–13. The quotations are translated in D. Mack Smith (ed.) *Garibaldi*, Englewood Cliffs, NJ, 1960, p. 95.
44. It is not known when, or whether or not, Anita's first husband had died, or why the couple decided to get married when they did. Ridley, *Garibaldi*, pp. 106–8.
45. For a discussion, see A. Filippi, 'Simón Bolívar e la nascita delle nuove repubbliche ispanoamericane nel pensiero politico italiano dell'Ottocento', *Pensiero Politico*, 18, 1985, pp. 182–207; see also Lynch, *Caudillos*, pp. 6–9.
46. Gaucho culture has also been used as a social and cultural explanation for the establishment of the ferocious dictatorships established by Rosas and others. See Lynch, *Caudillos*, pp. 412–16.
47. Idem, *Argentine caudillo*, pp. 45, 83. For a discussion of the Rosas 'style' and its purpose, see ibid., pp. 44–52.
48. G. Monsagrati, 'Garibaldi', in *Dizionario biografico degli Italiani*, 52, Rome, 1999, pp. 317–19.
49. 18 Oct. 1842, in *Epistolario*, 1, p. 43.
50. On the concept of the 'soldier hero' in British literature, see G. Dawson, *Soldier heroes. British adventure, empire and the imagining of nationalism*, London, 1994.
51. C. Jean, 'Garibaldi e il volontariato nel Risorgimento', *Rassegna Storica del Risorgimento*, 69/4, 1982, pp. 399–419.
52. According to Lord Howden, who knew Garibaldi in Montevideo. Quoted in Mack Smith (ed.), *Garibaldi*, p. 87. See also the comments of William Gore Ouseley, who knew Garibaldi during the same period, ibid., p. 93.
53. E. Feraboli, 'Il primo esilio di Garibaldi in America, 1833–1848', *Rassegna Storica del Risorgimento*, 19/2, 1932, p. 264.
54. H. F. Winnington-Ingram, *Hearts of oak*, London, 1889, p. 93.
55. Ibid.
56. Feraboli, 'Il primo esilio', pp. 264, 266.
57. In MRG, there are two paintings of Garibaldi from 1841 and 1842, and another, executed by Gaetano Gallino in Genoa in 1848.
58. From *Gaçeta Mercantil* 13 July 1843; *British Packet and Argentine News* 2 Jan. 1846, Ridley, *Garibaldi*, pp. 125, 148, 167, 180, 191, 217; Scirocco, *Garibaldi*, p. 126.
59. Ridley, *Garibaldi*, p. 167.
60. *The Times*, 1 Jan. 1845, 'Seizure of the Argentine squadron'; Ridley, *Garibaldi*, p. 181.
61. The emphasis is Mazzini's, to Cuneo, on 20 Oct. 1846, in *Scritti*, 30, p. 235.
62. Both Cuneo's letter and Mazzini's reply (8 Aug. 1841) are in *Scritti*, 23, pp. 274–82.
63. To his mother, 4 Oct. 1842, ibid., pp. 290–1. Garibaldi is almost always referred to as

coming from Genoa rather than Nice in this early correspondence.

64. On which see Saldías, *Historia*, 6, p. 18.
65. To his mother, 19 Nov. 1842, *Scritti*, 23, pp. 335.
66. 9 May 1845, ibid., 27, pp. 274–9.
67. 7 Oct. 1842, ibid., 23, p. 293.
68. 25 Nov. 1842.
69. 22 June 1845, *Scritti*, 28, p. 36; 23 Dec. 1845, ibid., p. 240.
70. 'The Italian legion in the service of Montevideo', *The Times*, 30 Jan. 1846; on his efforts to circulate the pamphlet in Europe, see Scirocco, *Garibaldi*, p. 130.
71. 2 Oct. 1846, *Scritti*, 30, p. 199.
72. The text of the letter is in *Scritti e discorsi*, 1, pp. 79–81.
73. 6 Oct. 1846, *Scritti*, 30, pp. 208–9.
74. On this period of Pius IX's Papacy, see O. Chadwick, *A history of the Popes, 1830–1914*, Oxford, 1998, pp. 61–77.
75. 20 Oct. 1846, *Scritti*, 30, pp. 238–9.
76. On Turchetti's speech, see the note to Mazzini's letter to Lamberti of 18 Oct. 1846, ibid., p. 231.
77. The book was published in Livorno (a town well known for its liberal leanings), in 1846. On Cesare de Laugier, see N. D. Vasoli, 'Cesare de Laugier e la figura dell'eroe militare italiano tra l'età napoleonica e la prima guerra d'indipendenza', in J. Joly (ed.), *Mythes et figures de l'héroisme militaire dans l'Italie du Risorgimento*, Caen, 1982, pp. 37–49.
78. On the spread of publications and interest in Garibaldi see Scirocco, *Garibaldi*, p. 133.
79. F. de Boni, *Così la penso. Cronaca*, 1, Lugano, 1846, pp. 367, 369, 370 (the whole article was some twenty pages long, and is at pp. 365–84).
80. The text of the circular is in Feraboli, 'Il primo esilio', p. 270.
81. Ibid.
82. See the series of letters from Mazzini in November and December in *Scritti*, 30, pp. 272, 278, 312, 318–20, 279, 300, 308.
83. Scirocco, *Garibaldi*, p. 133.
84. Mack Smith, *Mazzini*, p. 157, describes Harro-Harring as 'slightly unbalanced'. See also the exchange of letters between Cuneo and Mazzini in which Harro-Harring's name is mentioned as the contact, 8 Aug. 1841 and 18 March 1842, in *Scritti*, 23, pp. 277, 286–97.
85. P. Harro-Harring, *Dolores. A historical novel. With an introduction to Mazzini*, New York and London, 3rd edn, 1853, p. 95.
86. Ibid., pp. 100–2.
87. A. Galante Garrone, 'I giornali della restaurazione', in idem and F. della Peruta, *La stampa italiana del Risorgimento*, Bari, 1976, p. 233.
88. 13 April 1847, in *Scritti*, 30, p. 108.
89. Cuneo's account is in nos 9, 11, 12, 13, 14, 15 and 16, and reprinted in G. B. Cuneo, *Biografia di Giuseppe Garibaldi*, Rome, 1932 edn.
90. Ibid., pp. 72, 88.
91. Ibid., pp. 71–3, 81, 83, 85–8.
92. 6 May 1847, 'The River Plate'.
93. L. Mariotti [pseud. of A. Gallenga], *Latest news from Italy*, London, 1847, pp. 13–14. On Gallenga's relations with Mazzini, see T. Cerruti, *Antonio Gallenga. An Italian writer in Victorian England*, Oxford, 1974, pp. 100–8.
94. A. Viarengo, 'Mito e politica. Lorenzo Valerio e Giuseppe Garibaldi', in A. Trova and G. Zichi (eds), *Cattaneo e Garibaldi. Federalismo e Mezzogiorno*, Rome, 2004, pp. 271–300; also Scirocco, *Garibaldi*, pp. 134–5.
95. Garibaldi's letter, dated 8 Aug. 1847, is in *Epistolario*, 1, pp. 239–41, and published in *Concordia*, 5 Jan. 1848.

96. G. Bertoldi, *Alla legione Italiana in Montevideo ed al colonello Giuseppe Garibaldi*, Lugano, 1847; on the pamphlet, see Valerio's letters to Giacomo Ciani, 14 April, 5 May, 12 May 1847, in L. Valerio, *Carteggio (1825–1865), vol II (1842–47)*, ed. A. Viarengo, Turin, 1994, pp. 449, 458, 460.

97. *La Patria*, 28 Oct. 1847.

98. To Cuneo, 13 April 1847, *Scritti*, 32, p. 109; to Medici, 7 Nov. 1847, ibid., 33, p. 52. On the English-based National Fund, see Mack Smith, *Mazzini*, pp. 54–5.

99. Pereda, *Garibaldi en el Uruguay*, p. 15. For a discussion of this early portrait, see *Garibaldi. Arte e storia*, 2 vols, Florence, 1982, 1, p. 58.

100. In MCRR, and published ibid., cat. II, 28, p. 27.

101. 5 Feb. 1848.

102. To Lamberti, 29 Jan. 1847, *Scritti*, 32, pp. 31–2; to Foresti, ibid., 33, pp. 106–7.

103. 12 Oct. 1847, in *Epistolario*, 1, p. 245.

104. For details of Garibaldi's last year in Montevideo, see Ridley, *Garibaldi*, pp. 224–33, and McLean, 'Garibaldi', pp. 363–6.

105. On the concept of *bricolage* applied to the 'opportunistic appropriations' of Napoleonic propaganda, see C. Prendegast, *Napoleon and history painting. Antoine-Jean Gros's La bataille d'Eylau*, Oxford, 1997, pp. 8, 32, 78.

106. See A. Lyttelton, 'Creating a national past: history, myth and image in the Risorgimento', in A. Russell Ascoli and K. von Henneberg (eds), *Making and remaking Italy. The cultivation of national identity around the Risorgimento*, Oxford, 2001, pp. 33, 36.

Chapter 3: Revolution

1. L. Hunt, *The family romance of the French Revolution*, London, 1992, esp. pp. 17–52.

2. F. Furet, *Interpreting the French Revolution*, Cambridge, 1981, pp. 46–7.

3. M. Agulhon, *Marianne into battle. Republican imagery and symbolism in France, 1789–1880*, Cambridge, 1981, pp. 13, 16.

4. L. Hunt, *Politics, culture, and class in the French Revolution*, London, 1986, pp. 54, 72–83.

5. M. Ozouf, *Festivals and the French Revolution*, Cambridge, MA, 1988, esp. pp. 8–11; see also foreword by Lynn Hunt, pp. xi–xii.

6. On Hercules, see Hunt, *Politics*, pp. 94–113; on the lion and on Marianne, see Agulhon, *Marianne*, pp. 14–32.

7. Furet, *Interpreting*, p. 48. See also the discussion in Hunt, *Politics*, esp. pp. 11–15, 24 and for a critical analysis, R. Spang, 'Paradigm and paranoia: how modern is the French Revolution?', *American Historical Review*, 108/1, 2003, pp. 119–47.

8. A. Soboul, 'Religious feeling and popular cults during the French Revolution: "patriot saints" and martyrs for liberty', in S. Wilson (ed.), *Saints and their cults. Studies in religious sociology, folklore and history*, Cambridge, 1983, pp. 217–32; A. Potts, 'Images of ideal manhood in the French revolution', *History Workshop Journal*, 30, 1990, pp. 1–21 (on Bara).

9. Soboul, 'Religious feeling', pp. 221–9, Ozouf, *Festivals*, pp. 262–7.

10. Potts, 'Images', esp. pp. 1–6. For a discussion of the relationship between the classical revival promoted by Johann Joachim Winckelmann and revolutionary art and politics see G. Mosse, *The image of man. The creation of modern masculinity*, Oxford, 1996, pp. 28–39; A. Potts, *Flesh and the ideal. Winckelmann and the origins of art history*, New Haven, CT, 1994; and H. Honour, *Neo-classicism*, London, 1977 edn, pp. 69–80.

11. T. Crow, 'Patriotism and virtue: David to the Young Ingres', in S. F. Eisenmann, *Nineteenth-century art. A critical history*, London, 2002 edn, pp. 18–23, 26–38.

12. D. Outram, *The body and the French Revolution. Sex, class and political culture*, New Haven, CT, and London, 1989, pp. 78–9.

13. Ibid., p. 82, author's emphasis. For a more detailed discussion see J. B. Landes, 'Republican citizenship and heterosocial desire: concepts of masculinity in revolutionary France', in S. Dudink *et al.* (eds), *Masculinities in politics and war. Gendering modern history*, Manchester, 2004.

14. Hunt, *The family romance*, p. 81, see also pp. 28–42, 53–75.

15. On Napoleon and history, see A. Jourdan, *Napoléon. Héros, imperator, mécène*, Paris, 1998. See also the discussion of Napoleon's use of the arts in N. Petiteau, *Napoléon, de la mythologie à l'histoire*, Paris, 1999.

16. P. G. Dwyer, 'Napoleon Bonaparte as hero and saviour', *French History*, 18/4, 2004, p. 385.

17. Mosse, *The image*, p. 7.

18. Ibid., p. 51.

19. Ibid., p. 6.

20. G. Mosse, *Nationalism and sexuality. Middle-class morality and sexual norms in modern Europe*, Madison, WI, 1985, p. 16.

21. K. Hagemann, 'A valorous *Volk* family: The nation, the military, and the gender order in Prussia in the time of the Anti-Napoleonic wars, 1806–15', in I. Blom *et al.* (eds), *Gendered nations. Nationalisms and gender order in the long nineteenth century*, Oxford, 2000, pp. 186–91.

22. Mosse, *Nationalism and sexuality*, pp. 50–3. See also Potts, 'Images', pp. 4, 15, and for the twentieth century, A. Caesar, *Taking it like a man. Suffering, sexuality and the war poets*, Manchester, 1993, pp. 1–3.

23. T. Carlyle, *On heroes, hero-worship and the heroic in history*, Lincoln, NB, and London, 1966 (1841), esp. pp. 12–13, 198–9.

24. On military heroes, see J. MacKenzie, 'Heroic myths of Empire', in idem (ed.), *Popular imperialism and the military, 1850–1950*, Manchester, 1992, pp. 109–38. On Napoleon's image in Britain, see S. Semmel, *Napoleon and the British*, New Haven, CT, and London, 2004, and S. Bainbridge, *Napoleon and English Romanticism*, Cambridge, 1995, and on other celebrity cults, below pp. 130–2, 134–5.

25. L. Mascilli Migliorini, *Il mito dell'eroe*, Naples, 1984, pp. 10–15, 148–9.

26. Both quoted in C. Crossley, *French historians and romanticism. Thierry, Guizot, the Saint-Simonians, Quinet, Michelet*, London, 1993, pp. 55, 230.

27. B. Schwartz, *George Washington. The making of an American symbol*, New York, 1987, pp. 50, 179. Of course this model too was beset by political tensions: I am referring here to an ideal type.

28. *Scritti*, 29, pp. 92–4.

29. See above, pp. 24–6.

30. Adrian Lyttelton, 'Creating a national past: history, myth and image in the Risorgimento', in A. R. Oscoli and K. von Henneberg (eds), *Making and remaking Italy. The cultivation of national identity around the Risorgimento*, Oxford, 2001, pp. 31, 33.

31. Honour, *Neo-classicism*, pp. 184–90; T. Crow, 'Classicism in crisis: Gros to Delacroix', in *Nineteenth-century art*, pp. 55–81.

32. On Byron and the 'anti-heroes' of romanticism, see M. Praz, *The romantic agony*, London, 1933, pp. 58–69.

33. W. Scott, *Rob Roy*, Boston, MA, 1956 (1817), pp. xxxiv, 218, 285, 300. See also the comments of A. Welsh, *The hero of the Waverley novels*, Princeton, NJ, 1992 edn, pp. 40–8.

34. Scott, *Rob Roy*, pp. 296, 305, 308–9, 354.

35. Lyttelton, 'Creating a national past', pp. 33.

36. Ibid., p. 36.

37. Ibid.

38. J. Farr, 'Understanding conceptual change politically', in T. Ball *et al.* (eds), *Political*

innovation and conceptual change, Cambridge, 1989, pp. 24–49.

39. J. Tulard, *Napoleon. The myth of the saviour*, London, 1985; see also R. Gildea, *The past in French history*, New Haven, CT, 1996, pp. 89–111 and S. Hazareesingh, *The legend of Napoleon*, London, 1994.
40. Lyttelton, 'Creating a national past', p. 29; see also pp. 46–61.
41. C. Jean, 'Garibaldi e il volontariato italiano nel Risorgimento', *Rassegna Storica del Risorgimento*, 64/2, 1982, pp. 401–3; C. Cesari, *Corpi volontari italiani dal 1848 al 1870*, Rome, 1921, pp. 1–84.
42. There is a vast literature on the 1848–9 revolutions; the best and most up-to-date general survey in English is J. Sperber, *The European revolutions, 1848–1851*, Cambridge, 1994.
43. See *Scritti*, 35, pp. 140–1.
44. Both reports are reprinted in A. Cavaciocchi, 'Le prime gesta di Garibaldi in Italia', *Rivista Militare Italiana*, 6, 1907, pp. 5–87.
45. *L'Italia del Popolo*, 28 June 1848.
46. *Scritti e discorsi*, 1, pp. 87–8.
47. 11 July and 15 July 1848, in *Scritti*, 35, p. 248.
48. D. Mack Smith, *Mazzini*, London, 1994, pp. 58–9.
49. R. Sarti, *Mazzini. A life for the religion of politics*, Westport, CT, 1997, pp. 132–3.
50. 2 July and 8 July, 1848, in *Scritti*, 35, pp. 239, 246.
51. J. Ridley, *Garibaldi*, London, 1974, pp. 242–3.
52. D. Laven, 'The age of restoration', in J. A. Davis (ed.), *Italy in the nineteenth century*, Oxford, 2000, pp. 67–9.
53. Mack Smith, *Mazzini*, p. 62; on 'the first war of independence' in 1848, see P. Pieri, *Storia militare del Risorgimento. Guerre e insurrezioni*, Turin, 1962, pp. 197–263.
54. *Scritti*, 35, p. 260.
55. 27 July 1848, in *Scritti e discorsi*, 1, pp. 89–90.
56. Its printed programme is reproduced in *Edizione nazionale degli scritti di Garibaldi, vol. 1. Le memorie di Garibaldi in una delle redazioni anteriori alla definitiva del 1872*, Bologna, 1932, pp. 80–1.
57. 31 July 1848.
58. There is a useful chapter in Ridley, *Garibaldi*, pp. 243–54, on the 1848 campaign. See also, P. Pieri, *Storia militare del Risorgimento*, Turin, 1962, pp. 337–43 and *Garibaldi condottiero*, Rome, 1932, pp. 63–85. Both Cavaciocchi, 'Le prime gesta', and L. Giampolo and M. Bertolone, *La prima campagna di Garibaldi in Italia (da Luino a Morazzone) e gli avvenimenti militari e politici nel Varesotto 1848–1849*, Varese, 1950, have an extensive selection of original documents relating to Garibaldi in 1848 (the latter includes correspondence of the Austrian army).
59. 13 Aug. 1848, the communal clerk of Castelletto Ticino to the governor of Novara, in Cavaciocchi, 'Le prime gesta', p. 20.
60. See ibid., esp. pp. 35–8, 48–50; Giampolo and Bertolone, *La prima campagna*, pp. 313–49.
61. Giampolo and Bertolone, *La prima campagna*, p. 348.
62. The *protesta* is in *Scritti*, 38, pp. 207–9. 'Agli Italiani' is also published in F. della Peruta (ed.), *Giuseppe Mazzini, Scritti politici*, 3 vols, Turin, 1976, 2, pp. 314–19.
63. In *Scritti*, 39, pp. 3–70.
64. *Scritti e discorsi*, 1, pp. 92–4.
65. Ridley, *Garibaldi*, p. 246; Giampolo and Bertolone, *La prima campagna*, p. 317 has a copy of the manifesto conserved in the Kriegs Archiv, Vienna.
66. G. Candeloro, *Storia dell'Italia moderna, 3. La rivoluzione nazionale, 1848–49*, Milan, 1960, pp. 271–343.
67. 27 July 1848, in *Scritti e discorsi*, 1, pp. 89–90.
68. 3 Aug. 1848, ibid., pp. 90–2.

69. See P. Brunello, 'Pontida', in M. Isenghi (ed.), *I luoghi della memoria. Simboli e miti dell'Italia unita*, Rome and Bari, 1996, pp. 15–28 and Lyttelton, 'Creating a national past', pp. 46–50.

70. Pieri, *Storia militare*, p. 331.

71. 11 Sept. 1848, republished in *Scritti*, 35, p. 321.

72. 9 Sept. 1848, to the minister of war and navy, Cavaciocchi, 'Le prime gesta', pp. 81–2.

73. *Scritti*, 37, pp. 33–5. Garibaldi's speeches in Nice and Oneglia are in *Scritti e discorsi*, 1, pp. 95–6.

74. 28 Sept. 1848, from the military commander of San Remo to the governor of Nice, in Cavaciocchi, 'Le prime gesta', pp. 82–3.

75. Sperber, *The European revolutions*, p. 1.

76. Ibid., p. 148.

77. Ibid., p. 165. There is a substantial literature on the process of politicisation in the 1848–9 revolutions: see especially M. Agulhon, *The republic in the village: the people of the Var from the French Revolution to the Second Republic*, Cambridge 1982; P. McPhee, *The politics of rural life. Political mobilisation in the French countryside, 1846–1952*, Oxford, 1992; and J. Sperber, *Rhineland radicals: the democratic movement and the revolution of 1848–1849*, Princeton, NJ, 1991.

78. On newspapers in 1848–9, see F. della Peruta, 'Il giornalismo dal 1847 all'Unità', in A. Galante Garrone and F. della Peruta, *La stampa italiana del Risorgimento*, Rome and Bari, 1979, pp. 331–465.

79. S. La Salvia, 'Nuove forme della politica: l'opera dei circoli popolari', *Rassegna Storica del Risorgimento*, 86, 1999, pp. 227–66; R. de Longis, 'Tra sfera pubblica e difesa dell'onore. Donne nella Roma del 1849', *Roma Moderna e Contemporanea*, 9/1–3, 2001, pp. 263–83; R. Balzani, 'Consenso "patriottico" o consenso "repubblicano"? La Repubblica Romana a Forlì', in S. Mattarelli (ed.), *Politica in periferia. La Repubblica Romana del 1848 fra modello francese e municipalità romagnola*, Ravenna, 1999, pp. 11–27; F. Rizzi, *La coccarda e le campane. Comunità rurali e Repubblica Romana nel Lazio (1848–1849)*, Milan, 1989; A. de Clementi, *Vivere nel latifondo. Le comunità della campagna laziale fra '700 e '800*, Milan, 1989, pp. 167–87.

80. Della Peruta, 'Il giornalismo', p. 421.

81. F. Fonzi, 'I giornali romani del 1849', *Archivio della Società Romana di Storia Patria*, 72, 1949, pp. 197–220.

82. Sarti, *Mazzini*, pp. 137–40.

83. H. Hearder, 'The making of the Roman Republic, 1848–49', *History*, 60, 1975, p. 171.

84. L. Naste, *Le feste civili a Roma nell'Ottocento*, Rome, 1994; C. Tacke, 'Feste der Revolution in Deutschland und Italien', in D. Dowe, H.-G. Haupt and D. Langewiesche (eds), *Europa 1848. Revolution und Reform*, Bonn, 1998, pp. 1045–88.

85. A. M. Ghisalberti, 'Il marzo romano di Mazzini', in idem, *Momenti e figure del Risorgimento romano*, Milan, 1965, pp. 149–50. On the broader international and historical significance of Rome, see C. Edwards (ed.), *Roman presences: receptions of Rome in European culture, 1789–1945*, Cambridge, 1999; N. Vance, *The Victorians and ancient Rome*, Oxford, 1997; W. L. Vance, *America's Rome*, 2 vols, New Haven, CT, and London, 1989.

86. Ghisalberti, 'Il marzo romano', pp. 146–7, 156–8, 174–9.

87. Mack Smith, *Mazzini*, pp. 67–9; the description of the festival ('Very queer you will say; but it was really fine') is in a letter of 23 April 1849, in A. H. Clough, *The poems and prose remains of Arthur Clough with a selection from his letters and a memoir*, 2 vols, London, 1869, 1, pp. 143–4.

88. Some historians argue that the years 1848–9 are the real watershed in Church–state relations in Italy, rather than the later date of 1870 (when Rome became the capital of united Italy): G. Battelli, 'Santa Sede e vescovi nello stato unitario. Dal secondo

ottocento ai primi anni della Repubblica', *Storia d'Italia. Annali. La chiesa e il potere politico*, Turin, 1986, pp. 809–10.

89. Rizzi, *La coccarda*; see also D. Demarco, *Una rivoluzione sociale. La repubblica romana del 1849*, Naples, 1944; N. Roncalli, *Cronaca di Roma, 1848–1870*, 2 vols, Rome, 1997, 2, esp. pp. 9–22.

90. Mack Smith, *Mazzini*, pp. 69–70. The origin of the phrase is not entirely clear, and great capital was made of it by the nationalists after they had beaten the French. See G. Belardelli, 'Gli Italiani non si battono', in idem *et al.*, *Miti e storia dell'Italia unita*, Bologna, 1999, pp. 63–9.

91. Clough, *The poems*, 1, pp. 143–4.

92. Vance, *America's Rome*, 2, p. 132; H. James, *William Wetmore Story and his friends*, Boston, MA, 1903, p. 157.

93. In *Scritti*, 40, p. 75.

94. Ibid., p. 73.

95. Sarti, *Mazzini*, pp. 144–5.

96. G. M. Trevelyan, *Garibaldi's defence of the Roman Republic*, London, 1907, p. 2.

97. On the European-wide wave of repression against the radical governments of 1849, see Sperber, *The European revolutions*, pp. 225–36.

98. 9 May 1849, published in M. Castelli, *Il Conte di Cavour. Ricordi*, Turin and Naples, 1886, p. 132.

99. According to *The Times*, 18 June 1849.

100. P. Vermeylen, *Les Idées politiques et sociales de George Sand*, Brussels, 1984, pp. 149–50.

101. 27 May 1849, reprinted in A. B. Fuller (ed.), *At home and abroad. Or things and thoughts in America and Europe*, Boston, MA, 1874, p. 382.

102. Vance, *America's Rome*, 2, pp. 128–9. See also T. Roberts, 'The United States and the European revolutions of 1848', in G. Thomson (ed.), *The European revolutions of 1848 and the Americas*, London, 2002, pp. 88–9.

103. 24 May 1849.

104. On this popular Parisian theatre, famous for its melodramas, see J. McCormick, *Popular theatre in nineteenth-century France*, London, 1993.

105. 30 Sept. 1849, to Lorenzo Valerio, in *Carteggio di Lorenzo Valerio (1825–1865), 4 (1849)*, ed. A. Viarengo, Turin, 1994, p. 348.

106. C. Bouneau, 'Opinion publique parisienne et question romaine, novembre 1848–novembre 1849', Université de Paris, I, Centre de Recherches en Histoire du XIXe Siècle, Mémoire de Maîtrise, 1982, pp. 311–21.

107. Roncalli, *Cronaca*, pp. 232–4.

108. 25 Oct. 1848, *Scritti*, 37, p. 83; see also Mazzini's letters to Emilie Hawkes, 15 Nov. 1848, and to George Sand, 16 Nov. 1848, ibid., pp. 118–25; 127–30.

109. On Sterbini's comment, see Roncalli, *Cronaca*, p. 84; in general, see Ridley, *Garibaldi*, pp. 256–62.

110. 27 March 1849, in *Epistolario*, 2, p. 116.

111. 19 April 1849, in D. Mack Smith (ed.), *Garibaldi*, Englewood Cliffs, NJ, 1969, p. 20; also in *Epistolario*, 2, p. 144.

112. 22 April 1849 and 1 May 1849, ibid., pp. 147, 152.

113. On the agitation in Paris, see J. Beecher, *Victor Considerant and the rise and fall of French socialism*, Berkeley, 2001, pp. 246–9.

114. Trevelyan, *Garibaldi's defence*, p. 187.

115. According to the eyewitness Gabussi, in Mack Smith (ed.), *Garibaldi*, p. 21.

116. Various estimates are given in Trevelyan, *Garibaldi's defence*, pp. 342–3, and Trevelyan's book still remains one of the most complete accounts of the fighting for Rome. See also Ridley, *Garibaldi*, pp. 270–307, and there is a shorter account in D. Mack Smith, *Garibaldi. A great life in brief*, London, 1957, pp. 43–52.

117. *The Lady's Newspaper*, 19 May 1849.
118. 24 Feb. 1849, in *Scritti e discorsi*, 1, p. 111.
119. 30 Oct. 1848, ibid., p. 98.
120. 30 Oct., 3 Nov., 12 Nov., 20 Nov. 1848, ibid., pp. 97–103.
121. 18 Oct., 30 Oct., 12 Nov. 1848, 24 Feb., 20 May 1849, ibid., pp. 97–8, 103, 111, 127.
122. 3 June 1849, ibid., p. 136.
123. 11 June 1849, ibid., p. 139. For an analysis of this and the previous speech, see M. Isnenghi, *Le guerre degli italiani*, Milan, 1989, pp. 55–6.
124. There are two versions in *Scritti e discorsi*, 1, pp. 147–8; see also Trevelyan, *Garibaldi's defence*, pp. 231–2, who gives another version and refers to other variants and their sources.
125. B. Mitre, *Ricordi dell'assedio di Montevideo (1843–1851)*, Florence, 1882, p. 13; G. von Hoffstetter, *Giornale delle cose di Roma nel 1851*, Turin, 1851, p. 29.
126. *La Concordia*, 24 July 1849; the *ordine del giorno* of 4 July is in Roncalli, *Cronaca*, p. 197.
127. Ibid., pp. 190–1.
128. See Isnenghi, *Le guerre*, pp. 12–16; Winston Churchill's words in his famous speech to the House of Commons on 13 May 1940: 'I have nothing to offer but blood, toil, tears and sweat' were seemingly borrowed from Garibaldi.
129. For a discussion of personal appearance as political sign, relating to the French Revolution, see R. Wrigley, *The politics of appearance. The symbolism and representation of dress in revolutionary France*, Oxford, 2002; also Hunt, *Politics*, p. 53 and idem, *The family romance*, pp. 76–82.
130. M. Bonsanti, 'Una generazione democratica: amore familiare, amore romantico e amor di patria', in A. M. Banti and P. Ginsborg (eds), *Il Risorgimento*, Turin, forthcoming.
131. Quoted in Trevelyan, *Garibaldi's defence*, p. 119.
132. J. P. Koelman, *Memorie romane*, 2 vols, Rome, 1963, p. 245.
133. Von Hofstetter, *Giornale*, pp. 28–9.
134. Koelman, *Memorie*, pp. 245–6.
135. Von Hofstetter, *Giornale*, pp. 29; Koelman, *Memorie*, p. 331.
136. Von Hofstetter, *Giornale*, pp. 327, 355.
137. Ibid., pp. 32–3.
138. E. Dandolo, *I volontari ed i bersaglieri lombardi*, Turin, 1849, pp. 176–7.
139. Della Peruta, 'Il giornalismo', p. 426; Vance, *America's Rome*, p. 127.
140. 16 May, 29 May 1849.
141. 18 May, 21 May 1849.
142. 31 July, 21 Aug. 1849.
143. *The Illustrated London News*, 19 May 1849; *The Lady's Newspaper and Pictorial Times*, 19 May 1849; *L'Illustration. Journal universel*, 26 May 1849; *Il Mondo Illustrato*, 5 Feb. 1848.
144. 21 July 1849.
145. 23 June, 7 July, 14 July 1849.
146. Fuller, *At home*; the comment about Mazzini is on 20 March, p. 367, and the letter describing the departure of Garibaldi and his men, on 6 July 1849, pp. 413–14.
147. *Garibaldi. Arte e Storia*, 2 vols, Florence, 1982, 1, cat II, 7. 1–4.
148. Quoted in P. Gut, 'Garibaldi et la France, 1848–1882. Naissance d'un mythe', *Rassegna Storica del Risorgimento*, 74/3, 1987, pp. 299–300. The '*petit caporal*' refers to Napoleon.
149. 12 May, 16 May, 24 May, 29 May, 14 July 1849.
150. Mack Smith, *Mazzini*, p. 69.
151. F. della Peruta, 'Le teorie militari della democrazia risorgimentale', in F. Mazzonis (ed.), *Garibaldi condottiero. Storia, teoria, prassi*, Milan, 1984, p. 73.

152. Ibid., pp. 72–9; Jean, 'Garibaldi e il volontariato', pp. 404–5; L. Riall, 'Eroi maschili, virilità e forme della guerra', in Banti and Ginsborg (eds), *Il Risorgimento*.
153. Trevelyan, *Garibaldi's defence*, p. 3.
154. Sperber, *The European revolutions*, p. 151.
155. See the discussion in N. Moe, *The view from Vesuvius. Italian culture and the Southern Question*, Berkeley, CA, 2002, pp. 2–3, 16–19.
156. For a discussion, see P. Ginsborg, *Daniele Manin and the Venetian revolution of 1848–49*, Cambridge, 1979.
157. Ibid., p. 376.
158. For an attempt to link some of Garibaldi's subsequent political actions to his personal loss, see D. Pick, *Rome or Death. The obsessions of General Garibaldi*, London, 2005.

Chapter 4: Exile

1. Quoted in J. Ridley, *Garibaldi*, London, 1974, p. 336, emphasis in the original.
2. On the legend which grew up around Casa Guelfi, and especially the 'relic' made from the cigar smoked by Garibaldi, see G. Guelfi, *Il sigaro di Garibaldi*, Genoa, 1992.
3. On Garibaldi's escape from the Austrians across the Apennines, the most detailed source is G. M. Trevelyan, *Garibaldi's defence of the Roman Republic*, London, 1907, pp. 288–321.
4. All these reports are also summarised in *The Times*, 17,18, 22, 23, 29 Aug. and 17 Sept. 1849.
5. 5 Sept. 1849, in C. di Biase, *L'arresto di Garibaldi nel settembre 1849*, Florence, 1941, pp. 76–7.
6. Ibid., p. 76.
7. 5 and 6 Sept. 1849, ibid., pp. 75, 82.
8. 6 Sept. 1849, ibid., pp. 79–81.
9. 7 Sept. 1849, from Captain Basso, ibid., p. 88.
10. 7 Sept. 1849, from Major Ceva di Nuceto, ibid., p. 90.
11. 11 and 17 Sept. 1849; also reported in *The Times*, 19 and 24 Sept. 1849.
12. 7 Sept. 1859, in *Epistolario*, 2, p. 197.
13. 5, 6 and 7 Sept. 1849, in Di Biase, *L'arresto*, pp. 75, 84, 91.
14. 8 Sept. 1849, from La Marmora, ibid., pp. 94–6.
15. 6 and 8 Sept. 1849, pp. 82, 87–8.
16. 13 Sept. 1849, in Di Biase, *L'arresto*, p. 116.
17. H. Nelson Gay, 'Il secondo esilio di Garibaldi (1849–1854)', in idem, *Scritti sul Risorgimento*, Rome, 1937, p. 196.
18. 8 and 15 Sept. 1849, in Di Biase, *L'arresto*, pp. 96, 118.
19. See the correspondence of 6, 7, 10 and 15 Sept. 1849, ibid., pp. 79, 100–3, 107, 117.
20. 22 Sept. 1849, ibid., p. 85.
21. As reported in *The Times*, 20 Sept. 1849.
22. 7 and 10 Sept. 1849.
23. *Atti del parlamento subalpino. Camera dei deputati. Discussione*, 10 Sept. 1849, p. 375.
24. Ibid., p. 379.
25. 11 Sept. 1849; this letter was also reported in *The Times* of 17 Sept. and, according to Di Biase, *L'arresto*, p. 121, a whole series of versions of this letter exist, suggesting that it was widely circulated.
26. *Atti del parlamento*, pp. 375, 382–3.
27. See Valerio's letter of 10 Sept. 1849, in Di Biase, *L'arresto*, pp. 105–6, and the coverage in *The Times*, 17 Sept. 1849.
28. Ridley, *Garibaldi*, pp. 346–7.
29. *La Gazzetta di Milano*, 15 Sept. 1849.
30. 21 Sept. 1849, from the Piedmontese consul in Tunis, in Di Biase, *L'arresto*, p. 126.

31. On Garibaldi's movements in 1849–50, see Ridley, *Garibaldi*, pp. 347–57 and Gay, 'Il secondo esilio', pp. 197–205. The main source for his time in Morocco is D. Guerrini, 'Giuseppe Garibaldi da Genova a Tangeri (1849)', *Risorgimento Italiano, Rivista Storica*, 1/4, 1908, pp. 588–607.

32. 27 Dec. 1849.

33. 14 Oct and 10 Nov. 1849, *Epistolario*, 2, pp. 205, 209; ibid., 3, pp. 11, 20. On Garibaldi's memoirs, see below, pp. 154–61.

34. See his letter to his cousin, Augusto, 12 Jan. 1850; to the American consul in Tangier, 22 Feb. 1850; and others to Francesco Carpeneto, 7 May and 22–23 June 1850, ibid., pp. 3–4, 6–7, 15–16, 22–3; see also Gay, 'Il secondo esilio', p. 203.

35. 8 Aug. 1850.

36. 29 June 1850.

37. 6 July 1850.

38. *Tribune*, 26, 27 and 29 July 1850.

39. H. R. Marraro, *American opinion on the unification of Italy, 1846–1861*, New York, 1932, pp. 165–6.

40. *Tribune* and *Herald*, 29 July 1850.

41. D. S. Spencer, *Louis Kossuth and Young America. A study of sectionalism and foreign policy, 1848–1852*, Columbia and London, 1977, pp. vii, 7.

42. Ibid., pp. 7–9, 121–4; T. Roberts, 'The United States and the European revolutions of 1848', in G. Thompson (ed.), *The European revolutions of 1848 and the Americas*, London, 2002, p. 93; Gay, 'Il secondo esilio', p. 206.

43. Marraro, *American opinion*, p. 207.

44. Ibid., pp. 169–71; on Gavazzi, see L. Santini, *Alessandro Gavazzi*, Modena, 1955.

45. Roberts, 'The United States', p. 77.

46. *Tribune, Herald, Evening Post*, 8 Aug. 1850 (the letter is dated 7 Aug.); *La Concordia*, 2 Sept.; *Il Repubblicano della Svizzera Italiana*, 5 Sept. The Italian version of the letter is published in *Epistolario*, 3, pp. 27–8.

47. 'Next to the oven there is an almost Cuban heat', to Eliodoro Specchi, 10 Feb. 1851, ibid., p. 36.

48. Ridley, *Garibaldi*, pp. 360–5; Gay, 'Il secondo esilio', pp. 207–11.

49. See his series of letters to Carpaneto, 12 and 23 Aug. and 7 Sept, and to Carpenetti, 11 Sept. 1850, in *Epistolario*, 3, pp. 28–9, 31–3; and the letter from Foresti in Gay, 'Il secondo esilio', pp. 207–9.

50. *Herald*, 27 Aug. 1850.

51. *Tribune*, 8 Aug. 1850; see also 17 Feb. 1851.

52. Quoted in Gay, 'Il secondo esilio', p. 209.

53. Garibaldi's other American publicist, Margaret Fuller, had died in a shipwreck off Long Island in early 1850, returning to the USA with her husband and child.

54. Tuckerman also published his impressions of Garibaldi: see his anonymous article 'Garibaldi' in *North American Review*, 92, 1861, pp. 15–56.

55. G. Spini, *Risorgimento e Protestanti*, Naples, 1956, pp. 323–5.

56. W. L. Vance, *America's Rome, 2. Catholic and contemporary Rome*, New Haven, CT, 1989, pp. 135–8.

57. T. Dwight, *The Roman Republic of 1849; with accounts of the Inquisition and the siege of Rome*, New York, 1851, pp. 93–4.

58. Vance, *America's Rome*, 2, pp. 137–8.

59. Dwight, *The Roman Republic*, pp. 94, 96, 197.

60. In fact, remarkably little is known about this period of his life. One first-hand account exists: E. Reta, 'Ricordi del viaggio di centro America', which includes a pencil sketch of Garibaldi, in MRG.

61. See *Scritti*, 47, 14 and 25 Nov. 1851, pp. 87–9, 116; see also D. Mack Smith, *Mazzini*, London, 1994, p. 80.

62. Ridley, *Garibaldi*, pp. 365–73; Gay, 'Il secondo esilio', pp. 211–12.
63. *Tribune*, 30 April 1850; Gay, 'Il secondo esilio', p. 212.
64. Ridley, *Garibaldi*, pp. 373–4.
65. 19 Sept. 1853, in *Epistolario*, 3, p. 51.
66. 21 Sept.1853, ibid., p. 53.
67. 19, 21, 22 Sept 1853, ibid., pp. 51, 53, 55–6.
68. To Carpaneto, 12 Aug. 1850, ibid., p. 28.
69. *Evening Post*, 28 June 1859; Marraro, *American opinion*, pp. 166–8.
70. See his letter of 7 Aug. 1850, and his letter to L. J. Cist, 23 Aug. 1850, *Epistolario*, 3, p. 31.
71. Tuckerman, 'Garibaldi', p. 34.
72. Spencer, *Louis Kossuth*, pp. 145–70; Roberts, 'The United States', pp. 94–7.
73. Marraro, *American opinion*, pp. 170–3.
74. *Tribune*, 8 Aug. 1850 and 28 April 1851; *Herald*, 27 Aug. 1850; *Evening Post*, 28 June 1859; Dwight, *The Roman Republic*, p. 94.
75. For a discussion, see M. S. Miller, 'Rivoluzione e liberazione. Garibaldi e la mitologia americana', in *Giuseppe Garibaldi e il suo mito. Atti del LI congresso di storia del Risorgimento italiano*, Rome, 1984, pp. 220, 229; more broadly, C. Smith-Rosenberg, 'The republican gentleman: the race to rhetorical stability in the new United States', in S. Dudink, K. Hagemann and J. Tosh, *Masculinities in politics and war. Gendering modern history*, Manchester, 2004, pp. 61–76; B. Schwartz, *George Washington. The making of an American symbol*, New York, 1981, esp. pp. 127–30, 149–92, and D. Wecter, *The hero in America*, New York, 1941, esp. pp. 11–15.
76. A. Herzen, *My past and thoughts*, 6 vols, London, 1924–7, 3, p. 77.
77. *Northern Tribune*, I, Jan.–July 1854, p. 151; W. Settimelli, *Garibaldi. L'album fotografico*, Florence, 1982, p. 35, fig. 3.
78. On the diplomatic context, see P. Schroeder, *Austria, Great Britain and the Crimean War. The destruction of the European concert*, Ithaca, NY, 1972; W. Baumgart, *The Crimean War, 1853–1856*, London, 1999, pp. 34–42, 211–17.
79. On the Italian states during the 1850s, see A. Scirocco, *L'Italia del Risorgimento*, Bologna, 1990, pp. 320–37; on Antonelli, see F. Coppa, *Cardinal Giacomo Antonelli and papal politics in European affairs*, New York, 1990.
80 . D. Mack Smith, 'Cavour, Clarendon and the Congress of Paris, 1856', in idem, *Victor Emanuel, Cavour and the Risorgimento*, London, 1971, esp. pp. 81–2.
81. There is a vast literature on Cavour, Piedmont and 'the decade of preparation'. The most exhaustive study is R. Romeo, *Cavour e il suo tempo*, 3 vols, Rome and Bari, 1969–84, and see the same author's *Dal Piemonte sabaudo all'Italia liberale*, Turin, 1963. A. Cardoza, 'Cavour and Piedmont', in J. A. Davis (ed.), *Italy in the nineteenth century*, Oxford, 2000, pp. 108–31, is an up-to-date summary in English.
82. The work of Romeo offers a very positive assessment of Cavour's achievement, but there is an important historical debate about its broader implications and problems. For a much more negative judgement see, for example, D. Mack Smith, *Cavour*, London, 1985; and for a critical assessment of the *connubio* see P. G. Camaiani, *La rivoluzione moderata: rivoluzione e conservazione nell'unità d'Italia*, Turin, 1978.
83. Mack Smith, *Mazzini*, p. 78; R. Grew, *A sterner plan for Italian unity. The Italian national society in the Risorgimento*, Princeton, NJ, 1963, p. 45.
84. G. Candeloro, *Storia dell'Italia moderna, 4. Dalla rivoluzione nazionale all'unità*, Milan, 1964, pp. 211–15.
85. Quoted in Mack Smith, *Mazzini*, p. 111.
86. G. E. Curàtulo, *Il dissidio tra Mazzini e Garibaldi. La storia senza veli*, Milan, 1928, pp. 125–8.
87. There is a detailed discussion of Mazzini's activities during this period, ibid., pp. 77–128; see also R. Sarti, *Mazzini. A life for the religion of politics*, Westport, CT,

1997, pp. 147–79.
88. Grew, *A sterner plan*, pp. 28–30, 36–7.
89. 28 May 1856; see also ibid., pp. 37–8.
90. Ibid., p. x; see also pp. 38–41, 89–98.
91. G. Berti, *I democratici e l'iniziativa meridionale nel Risorgimento*, Milan, 1962, pp. 539–740.
92. Curàtulo, *Il dissidio*, p. 154; Ridley, *Garibaldi*, p. 380.
93. Mordini's remark is in A. Scirocco, *I democratici italiani da Sapri a Porta Pia*, Naples, 1969, p. 15; see also A. Scirocco, 'Le correnti dissidenti del Mazzinianesimo dal 1853 al 1859', in *Correnti ideali e politiche della Sinistra Italiana dal 1849 al 1861*, Florence, 1978, pp. 49–69; and C. Lovett, *The democratic movement in Italy*, Cambridge, MA, 1982, pp. 157–86.
94. E. Dandolo, *I volontari ed i bersaglieri lombardi*, Turin, 1849 (London, 1851; Milan, 1860); L. C. Farini, *Lo stato romano dall'anno 1815 all'anno 1850*, Turin 1850–1 (London, 1851–4); C. Pisacane, *Guerra combattuta in Italia negli anni 1848–49*, Genoa, 1851; C. A. Vecchi, *La Italia. Storie di due anni, 1848–9*, Turin, 1851 (2nd edn 1856).
95. Sarti, *Mazzini*, pp. 175–6; Grew, *A sterner plan*, pp. 103–4.
96. 22 Sept. 1853 and 9 Jan. 1854, in *Epistolario*, 3, pp. 56, 59–60.
97. Mack Smith, *Mazzini*, pp. 106–7; 119.
98. *Epistolario*, 3, p. 62.
99. Herzen, *My past and thoughts*, 3, p. 77.
100. 3 Feb. 1857, in *Epistolario*, 3, pp. 150–1.
101. 4 March 1854, ibid., p. 66.
102. Dated 4 Aug. 1854, ibid., p. 80.
103. Ibid., Appendice 4, p. 202.
104. 25 Nov. 1851, in *Scritti*, 47, p. 116; 8 June 1853, ibid., 49, p. 224.
105. 24 Feb. 1854, ibid., 50, p. 282.
106. 9, 10, 13 Aug. 1854, ibid., 53, pp. 51, 59, 64.
107. Ibid., p. 64; 2 Feb. 1855, ibid., 54, p. 36.
108. For a discussion, see ibid., 52, pp. 5–6, and on the *Parlamento*, F. della Peruta, 'Il giornalismo dal 1847 all'unità', in A. Galante Garrone and F. della Peruta, *La stampa italiana nel Risorgimento*, Rome and Bari, 1979, pp. 484–6.
109. P. Roselli, *Memorie relative alla spedizione e combattimento di Velletri avvenuto il 19 maggio 1849*, Turin, 1853.
110. Curàtulo, *Il dissidio*, pp. 131–9; and the documents pp. 345–52. Garibaldi's letters of 28 Aug. and 2 Sept. 1854 are also in *Epistolario*, 3, pp. 82–3.
111. A. Scirocco, *Garibaldi. Batttaglie, amori, ideali di un cittadino del mondo*, Rome and Bari, 2001, pp. 205–6.
112. 1 and 26 Sept., 1854, in *Scritti*, 53, pp. 97, 160.
113. Mazzini's article on Olivieri is in *Scritti*, 51, pp. 175–85. On Olivieri, see G. Bernardi, *Un patriota italiano nella repubblica Argentina. Silvino Olivieri*, Bari, 1946 [1861].
114. 20 Dec. 1854, ibid., p. 297.
115. 8 Nov. 1855, in *Scritti*, 56, p. 44; 12 March 1856, ibid., Appendice, 5, p. 112 (part of the original letter is missing).
116. 20 May 1857, in *Epistolario*, 3, p. 157.
117. Grew, *A sterner plan*, pp. 84, 90.
118. 15 June 1858, *Epistolario*, 3, p. 171; Grew, *A sterner plan*, pp. 83–4, 90; Scirocco, *Garibaldi*, p. 210.
119. 4 April 1854, in *Cavour e l'Inghilterra. Carteggio con V. E. d'Azeglio*, 1, Bologna, 1933, pp. 22–3.
120. Grew, *A sterner plan*, p. 117.
121. See the series of letters from Garibaldi in Dec. 1858 in *Epistolario*, 3, pp. 191–8; on

Garibaldi's relation with the king, see D. Mack Smith, 'Victor Emanuel and the war of 1859', in idem, *Victor Emanuel*, pp. 92–3.

122. Herzen, *My past and thoughts*, 3, p. 77.

123. D. V. Reidy, 'Panizzi, Gladstone, Garibaldi and the Neapolitan prisoners', *Electronic British Library Journal* (eBLJ), 2005, pp. 7–12.

124. Grew, *A sterner plan*, p. 49.

125. 3 Feb. 1857, *Epistolario*, 3, p. 151.

126. 23 March 1857, ibid., p. 155.

127. Grew, *A sterner plan*, pp. 154–5.

128. Ibid., p. 143.

129 . See the report in the *Northern Tribune*, 1854, pp. 173–6.

130. A. Falconi, *Come e quando Garibaldi scelse per sua dimora Caprera*, Cagliari, 1902.

131. Grew, *A sterner plan*, pp. 83–4, 117–18.

132. G. E. Curàtulo, *Garibaldi agricoltore*, Rome, 1930.

133. To Speranza von Schwartz, 17 June 1858, *Epistolario*, 3, p. 173; to Cuneo, 27 Nov. 1858, ibid., p. 188.

134. E. H. Carr, *Michael Bakunin*, London, 1937, p. 301.

135. On Roberts and White, see E. Daniels, *Jessie White Mario. Risorgimento revolutionary*, Athens, 1972, esp. pp. 5–10, 33; Della Torre's letter, 4 Aug. 1856, in MRM, Garibaldi Curàtulo, f. 364; Schwartz's letter, 24 Jan. 1858, ibid., b. 693; on all of them and Ravello, see G. E. Curàtulo, *Garibaldi e le donne*, Rome, 1913.

136. On the concept of 'backstage', see E. Goffman, *The presentation of self in everyday life*, London, 1969, pp. 109–40.

Chapter 5: The Garibaldi Formula

1. What follows is an attempt to contextualise the growing support for Garibaldi as part of the rapid expansion of the reading public in Europe and North America. The literature on this process is very large and increasing, although more restricted for Italy. Useful and up-to-date surveys for Britain and France, which also give an idea of the very different approaches now prevailing in the two countries, are: J. Plunkett and A. King (eds), *Victorian print media. A reader*, Oxford, 2005; I. Haywood, *The revolution in popular literature. Print, politics and the people, 1790–1860*, Cambridge, 2004 (which concentrates on popular readers and radical publishers); P. Brantlinger and W. B. Thesing (eds), *A companion to the Victorian novel*, Oxford, 2002; and the encyclopaedic R. Chartier and H.-J. Martin (eds), *Histoire de l'édition française. Vol 3. Le temps des éditeurs, du romantisme à la belle époque*, Paris, 1990 edn.

2. R. D. Altick, *Victorian people and ideas*, New York, 1973, p. 64.

3. M. Crubellier, L'Elargissement du public', in Chartier and Martin (eds), *Histoire de l'édition française*, p. 31; E. Weber, *Peasants into Frenchmen. The modernisation of rural France, 1875–1914*, London, 1977, p. 453.

4. F. Barbier, 'Libraires et colporteurs', in Chartier and Martin (eds), *Histoire de l'édition française*, pp. 256–302.

5. See the description in Weber, *Peasants into Frenchmen*, pp. 452–63.

6. R. D. Altick, *The English common reader. A social history of the mass reading public, 1800–1900*, Chicago, IL, 1957, appendix C, pp. 394–5.

7. K. Belgum, *Popularizing the nation. Audience, representation and the production of identity in Die Gartenlaube, 1853–1900*, Lincoln, NB, 1998, p. 10; C. Charle, *Le Siècle de la presse (1830–1939)*, Paris, 2004, p. 96.

8. J. Watelet, 'La presse illustrée', in Chartier and Martin (eds), *Histoire de l'édition française*, pp. 369–82; P. Anderson, *The printed image and the transformation of popular culture, 1790–1860*, Oxford, 1991.

9. M. Merlot, 'Le Texte et l'image', ibid., pp. 329–55 (see also 'les keepsakes', pp. 507–8);

Weber, *Peasants into Frenchmen*, pp. 455–9. On caricature, see J. Watelet, 'La Presse illustrée', pp. 369–73; and R. J. Goldstein, *Censorship of political caricature in nineteenth-century France*, Kent, OH, and London, 1989.

10. P. di Bello, 'The female collector: women's photographic albums in the nineteenth century', *Living Pictures*, 1/2, 2001, pp. 3–20.

11. J. Plunkett, *Queen Victoria. First media monarch*, Oxford, 2003, pp. 244–65, 338–63; P. Burke, *Eyewitnessing. The uses of images as historical evidence*, London, 2001, pp. 17–28; H. K. Henisch and B. A. Henisch, *The photographic experience, 1839–1914. Images and attitudes*, Philadelphia, PA, 1993, pp. 244–65, 338–63. On actors, see R. Sennett, *The fall of public man*, London, 1986, pp. 195–205.

12. M. Lyons, 'Les Best-sellers', in Chartier and Martin (eds), *Histoire de l'édition française*, pp. 422–3; A.-M. Thiesse, 'Le Roman populaire', ibid., pp. 509–19; Brantlinger and Thesing (eds), *A companion to the Victorian novel*, chs 13–15; M. Denning, *Mechanic accents. Dime novels and working-class culture in America*, London, 2nd edn, 1998; L. James, *Fiction for the working man, 1830–1850*, London, 1963.

13. S. Hazareesingh, *The legend of Napoleon*, London, 2004, esp. pp. 151–208; N. Petiteau, *Napoléon, de la mythologie à l'histoire*, Paris, 1999; R. Gildea, 'Bonapartism', in idem, *The past in French history*, New Haven, CT, and London, 1994, pp. 89–111. On the 'memoirs tradition' in France see P. Nora, 'Memoirs of men of state: from Commynes to De Gaulle', in idem (ed.), *Rethinking France. Les lieux de mémoire. Vol 1, The State*, Chicago, IL, 2001, esp. pp. 403–14, and below, p. 156.

14. K. J. Mays, 'The publishing world', in Brantlinger and Thesing (eds), *A companion to the Victorian novel*, p. 12.

15. R. Chartier and H.-J. Martin, 'Introduction', in idem (eds), *Histoire de l'édition française*, pp. 5–6.

16. Lyons, 'Les Best-sellers', pp. 422–3; see also the analysis of reading tastes in mid-century Britain in J. Rose, 'Education, literacy and the reader', in Brantlinger and Thesing (eds), *A companion to the Victorian novel*, pp. 39–44.

17. H. M. Schor, 'Gender politics and women's rights', ibid., pp. 172–88; L. C. Roberts, 'Children's fiction', ibid., pp. 353–69; A. Sauvy, 'Une Littérature pour les femmes', in Chartier and Martin (eds), *Histoire de l'édition française*, pp. 496–507; J. Glénisson, 'Le Livre pour la jeunesse', ibid., pp. 461–95.

18. Haywood, *The revolution in popular literature*, pp. 139–40, 237–42; M. Taylor, *Ernest Jones, Chartism and the romance of politics, 1819–1869*, Oxford, 2003, pp. 137–94.

19. Weber, *Peasants into Frenchmen*, p. 458; J. Rose, *The intellectual life of the British working classes*, New Haven, CT, and London, 2001.

20. J. Smith Allen, *Popular French romanticism. Authors, readers, and books in the nineteenth century*, Syracuse, NY, 1981, pp. 5–6.

21. B. Anderson, *Imagined communities*, London, 1991 edn, pp. 37–46; see also the discussion in Belgum, *Popularizing the nation*, pp. xvi–xx.

22. G. Eley, 'Nations, publics and political cultures. Placing Habermas in the public sphere', in C. Calhoun (ed.), *Habermas and the public sphere*, Cambridge MA, 1992, pp. 289–339.

23. M. Butler, 'Telling it like a story', *Studies in Romanticism*, 28, Fall 1989, pp. 345–64.

24. C. Molinari, 'La guerra dei teatri da Napoleone a Victor Hugo', in R. Alonge and G. D. Bonino, *Storia del teatro moderno e contemporaneo*, 2, Turin, 2000, pp. 467–511; J. McCormick, *Popular theatres of nineteenth-century France*, New York, 1993.

25. S. E. Wilmer, *Theatre, society and the nation. Staging American identities*, Cambridge, 2002, pp. 1–3.

26. M. Samuels, *The spectacular past. Popular history and the novel in nineteenth-century France*, Ithaca, NY, 2004, pp. 106–50.

27. Ibid., pp. 26–62; on Lemaître, see Sennett, *The fall of public man*, pp. 204–5.

28. Haywood, *The revolution in popular literature*, pp. 140–1, 172; R. McWilliam, 'The

mysteries of G. W. M. Reynolds', in M. Chase and I. Dyck (eds), *Living and Learning: Essays in honour of J. F. C. Harrison*, Aldershot, 1996, pp. 182–98.

29. Although this too had roots in the eighteenth century. See John Brewer's comment about Wilkes that he 'not only made politics commercial; he made it entertaining and sociable', in *Party ideology and popular politics at the accession of George III*, Cambridge, 1976, p. 191.

30. Sennett, *The fall of public man*, p. 196.

31. S. Gundle, 'Le origini della spettacolarità nella politica di massa', in M. Ridolfi (ed.), *Propaganda e comunicazione politica*, Milan, 2004, esp. pp. 17–22.

32. P. Joyce, *Democratic subjects. The self and the social in nineteenth-century England*, Cambridge, 1994, p. 214, and for a broader discussion see ibid., pp. 147–223; see also J. Belchen and J. Epstein, 'The nineteenth-century gentleman leader revisited', *Social History*, 22/2, 1997, pp. 174–93; E. Biagini, *Liberty, retrenchment and reform. Popular liberalism in the age of Gladstone, 1860–1880*, Cambridge, 1992, pp. 369–425; J. Vernon, *Politics and the people: a study in English popular culture, c.1815–1867*, Cambridge, 1993, pp. 251–91.

33. J. R. Reed, 'Laws, the legal world and politics', in Brantlinger and Thesing (eds), *A companion to the Victorian novel*, pp. 155–71.

34. Plunkett, *Queen Victoria*, pp. 144–98.

35. R. Romanelli, *L'Italia liberale, 1861–1900*, Bologna, 1979, p. 436.

36. B. Tobia, 'Una cultura per la nuova Italia', in G. Sabbatucci and V. Vidotto (eds), *Storia d'Italia, 2. Il nuovo stato e la società civile*, Rome and Bari, 1995, pp. 427–34.

37. T. de Mauro, *Storia linguistica dell'Italia unita*, Rome and Bari, 1979, p. 40.

38. K. Baedeker, *Italie septentrionale*, Coblenz, 1861, p. xv.

39. A. Castellani, 'Quanti erano gli italofoni nel 1861?', *Studi Linguistici Italiani*, new series, 8/1, 1982, pp. 3–26. See also the discussion in D. Beales and E. F. Biagini, *The Risorgimento and the unification of Italy*, London, 2002 edn, pp. 74–80.

40. For the background, see R. Pasta, 'The history of the book and publishing in eighteenth-century Italy', *Journal of Modern Italian Studies*, 2/10, 2005, pp. 200–17.

41. L. Perini, 'Editori e potere in Italia dalla fine del secolo xv all'unità', in C. Vivanti (ed.), *Storia d'Italia. Annali 4. Intellettuali e potere*, Turin, 1981, pp. 838–46; A. Lyttelton, 'The national question in Italy', in M. Teich and R. Porter (eds), *The national question in Europe in historical context*, Cambridge, 1993, pp. 89–90.

42. M. Berengo, *Intellettuali e librai nella Milano della Restaurazione*, Turin, 1980; U. Carpi, *Letteratura e società nella Toscana del Risorgimento. Gli intellettuali dell'Antologia*, Bari, 1974. On journalists, see G. Ricuperati, 'I giornalisti italiani fra poteri e cultura dalle origini all'unità', in *Storia d'Italia. Annali 4*, pp. 1085–132.

43. P. Landi, 'Non solo moda. Le riviste femminili a Milano (1850–1859)', in N. del Corno and A. Porati (eds), *Il giornalismo lombardo nel decennio di preparazione all'Unità*, Milan, 2005, pp. 221–39; S. Franchini, *Editori, lettrici e stampa di moda*, Milan, 2002.

44. Tobia, 'Una cultura', pp. 428–32.

45. A. M. Banti, *La nazione del Risorgimento. Parentela, santità e onore alle origini dell'Italia unita*, Turin, 2000, pp. 37–53.

46. There is a very substantial literature on associational life in Risorgimento Italy. See M. Meriggi, 'Società, istituzione e ceti dirigenti', in G. Sabbatucci and V. Vidotto (eds), *Storia d'Italia, 1. Le premesse dell'unità*, Rome and Bari, 1994, pp. 190–217; and the special issue of *Quaderni Storici*, 77, 1991, 'Elites e associazioni nell'Italia dell'Ottocento'. Two useful case studies – from different ends of Italy – are A. Signorelli, *A teatro, al circolo. Socialità borghese nella Sicilia dell'Ottocento*, Rome, 2000, pp. 105–209; and M. Meriggi, *Milano borghese. Circoli ed élites nell'Ottocento*, Venice, 1992.

47. C. Sorba, *Teatri. L'Italia del melodrama nell'età del Risorgimento*, Bologna, 2001; Signorelli, *A teatro*, pp. 9–104; on music, see S. Pivato, *La storia leggera. L'uso pubblico*

della storia nella canzone italiana, Bologna, 2002, pp. 7–65; and R. Monterosso, *La musica nel Risorgimento*, Milan, 1948.

48. F. della Peruta, 'Il giornalismo dal 1847 all'Unità', in A. Galante Garrone and F. della Peruta, *La stampa italiana del Risorgimento*, Rome and Bari, 1979, pp. 319–20, 468.

49. M. Petrusewicz, *Come il meridione divenne una questione. Rappresentazioni del Sud prima e dopo il Quarantotto*, Catanzaro, 1998, pp. 113–16.

50. R. Grew, *A sterner plan for Italian unity. The Italian national society and the Risorgimento*, Princeton, NJ, 1963, pp. 52–61.

51. Ibid., pp. 67–77.

52. Ibid., p. 104.

53. D. Kertzer, *The kidnapping of Edgardo Mortara*, New York, 1997.

54. Grew, *A sterner plan*, p. 105; for a complete description of the National Society's propaganda activities, ibid., pp. 101–23.

55. H. R. Marraro, *American opinion on the unification of Italy, 1846–1861*, New York, 1932, pp. 206–21.

56. Grew, *A sterner plan*, pp. 68, 100–1.

57. Barrett Browning's poem was written in 1848 (with an additional section on Garibaldi written in 1851); Clough's poem 'Amours de voyage' first appeared in the *Atlantic Monthly* in 1858. For a discussion of the context, see L. Riall, 'Rappresentazioni del Quarantotto italiano nella storiografia inglese', in R. Camurri (ed.), *Memorie, protagonisti e rappresentazioni del 1848 italiano* (forthcoming); on the link between their poetry and nationalism: M. Reynolds, *The realms of verse, 1830–1870. English poetry in a time of nation-building*, Oxford, 2001, pp. 27–48.

58. 'Two letters to the Earl of Aberdeen on the state prosecutions of the Neapolitan government', London, 1851; see also D. M. Schreuder, 'Gladstone and Italian unification, 1848–1870: the making of a liberal?', *English Historical Review*, 85, 1970, pp. 475–501; O. Chadwick, 'Young Gladstone and Italy', *Journal of Ecclesiastical History*, 30, 1979, pp. 243–59.

59. *The Roman state from 1815 to 1850*, 4 vols, London, 1851–4.

60. M. Isabella, 'Italian exiles and British politics before and after 1848', in S. Freitag (ed.), *Exiles from European revolutions. Refugees in mid-Victorian England*, Oxford, 2003, p. 71.

61. Ibid., pp. 71–3. See also M. Finn, *After Chartism. Class and nation in English radical politics, 1848–1871*, Cambridge, 1993, esp. pp. 62–81; Biagini, *Liberty*, pp. 41–50, G. Claeys, 'Mazzini, Kossuth and British radicalism', *Journal of British Studies*, 28/3, 1989, pp. 228–44, 255–61.

62. Isabella, 'Italian exiles', p. 74; Finn, *After Chartism*, pp. 166–72; M. O' Connor, *The romance of Italy and the English political imagination*, London, 1998, pp. 79–91.

63. Finn, *After Chartism*, p. 166; O'Connor, *The romance*, p. 90.

64. Isabella, 'Italian exiles', pp. 74–7; on Jessie White's activity, see E. Daniels, *Jessie White Mario. Risorgimento revolutionary*, Athens, OH, 1972, pp. 41–54.

65. W. L. Vance, *America's Rome, 2. Catholic and contemporary Rome*, New Haven, 1989, pp. 110–22.

66. Quoted in J. Pemble, *The Mediterranean passion. Victorians and Edwardians in the South*, Oxford, 1987, p. 138; for a broader discussion see Riall, 'Rappresentazioni'.

67. C. Crossley, *French historians and romanticism. Thierry, Guizot, the Saint-Simonians, Quinet, Michelet*, London, 1993, pp. 173–4.

68. Isabella, 'Italian exiles', p. 78; Biagini, *Liberty*, p. 372; Finn, *After Chartism*, pp. 203–25.

69. S. Matsumoto-Best, *Britain and the papacy in the age of revolution, 1846–1851*, London, 2003, pp. 137–71.

70. Schreuder, 'Gladstone', p. 480. On Dante, see A. Isba, *Gladstone and Dante: Victorian statesman, medieval poet*, London 2006.

71. Claeys, 'Mazzini', pp. 231–2, 253.

72. A. Coviello Leuzzi, 'Antonio Bresciani Borsa', in *Dizionario Biografico degli Italiani*, 14, Rome, 1972, pp. 182–3.

73. J. Godechot et al., *Histoire générale de la presse française*, 2, Paris, 1972, pp. 259–60.

74. N. P. Wiseman, *Recollections of the last four Popes and of Rome in their times*; first published in London without date (but before or in 1857), then in 1858 and 1859.

75. C. Barr, 'Giuseppe Mazzini and Irish nationalism', in *Proceedings of the British Academy* (forthcoming); D. Bowen, *Paul Cardinal Cullen and the shaping of modern Irish Catholicism*, Dublin, 1983.

76. S. Gilley, 'The Garibaldi riots of 1862', *Historical Journal*, 16/4, 1973, pp. 700–1.

77. Marrao, *American opinion*, pp. 48–63, 166–8; Vance, *America's Rome*, pp. 129–30.

78. J. Petersen, 'Das deutsche politische Italienbild in der Zeit der nationalen Einigung', in idem, *Italien-Bilder–Deutschland-Bilder*, Cologne, 1999, pp. 61–5.

79. D. Laven, 'Mazzini, Mazzinian conspiracy and British politics in the 1850s', *Bollettino Storico Mantovano*, 2, 2003, p. 278.

80. For example, Gavazzi used Wiseman's attack to give a new lecture, and publish it as a reply to Wiseman: *My recollections of the four last Popes and of Rome in their times. An answer to Dr. Wiseman*, London, 1857 and 1858.

81. T. Dwight, *The Roman Republic of 1849; with accounts of the Inquisition and the siege of Rome*, New York, 1851, pp. 94, 209–23.

82. A. Dumas, *Montevideo ou une nouvelle Troie*, Paris, 1850, pp. 84–5.

83. *Ultimi fatti dei Croati in Lombardia con un soneto improvvisato in lode del Gen. Garibaldi*, n.d. but after 1848; G. Scarpari, *L'addio di Garibaldi e morte di sua moglie. Racconto storico*, Turin, 1850; E. Ruggieri, *Della ritirata di Giuseppe Garibaldi da Roma. Narrazione*, Genoa, 1850.

84. E. Dandolo, *I volontari ed i bersaglieri lombardi*, Turin, 1849, p. 32; G. von Hofstetter, *Giornale delle cose di Roma*, Turin, 1851, p. 13.

85. Dandolo, *I volontari*, was also published in London in 1851 and Milan in 1860; von Hofstetter was originally published as *Tagebuch aus Italien 1849*, Stuttgart, 1851. Also: L. C. Farini, *Lo stato romano dall'anno 1815 all'anno 1850*, Turin, 1850–1 (and London, 1851–54); C. Pisacane, *Guerra combattuta in Italia negli anni 1848–49*, Genoa, 1851; C. A. Vecchi, *La Italia. Storie di due anni, 1848–9*, Turin, 1851 (2nd edn 1856). A short account of Dandolo's life is in G. Mariani (ed.), *Antologia di scrittori garibaldini*, Bologna, 1958, pp. 240–1. Von Schwartz mentions von Hofstetter in *Garibaldi at home: a visit to the Mediterranean Islands of La Maddalena and Caprera*, London, 1860, p. 231.

86. G. B. Cuneo, *Biografia di Giuseppe Garibaldi*, Turin, 1850; see Garibaldi's letter to Cuneo which acknowledges the receipt of the biography and praises it, 12 March 1850, in *Epistolario*, 3, pp. 9–10.

87. N. Frye, *Anatomy of criticism. Four essays*. Princeton NJ, 1957, pp. 186–7.

88. J. G. Cawelti, *Adventure, mystery and romance: formula stories and popular culture*, Chicago, 1976, pp. 6–9.

89. Cuneo, *Biografia*, p. 73.

90. Ibid., pp. 19–23.

91. *The Northern Tribune. A periodical for the people*, 1, Jan.–July 1854, pp. 150–7.

92. He was born in 1807.

93. G. Ruffini, *Lorenzo Benoni or passages in the life of an Italian*, Edinburgh and London, 1853 (Genoa, 1834).

94. On the original photograph, see above, p. 114. In the copy, Garibaldi stands leaning on a mantelpiece with a lion pedestal. The Chartist leader Feargus O'Connor was known as the 'lion of freedom': see J. Epstein, *The lion of freedom: Feargus O'Connor and the Chartist movement, 1832–1842*, London, 1982.

95. In *Garibaldi. Arte e storia*, 2 vols, Florence, 1982, 1, cat II/3, 67, p. 220.

96. A. Bresciani, *Lionello*, Rome, 1852, pp. 73–4.

97. This did not let up after 1849, see e.g. the pamphlet *Saggio di stile epistolare e di sapienza politico-civile-militare di parecchi personaggi che furon la gloria della quinimestre Repubblica Romana con opportune annotazioni*, Rome, 1850.

98. See also, for example, H. Geale, *Ernesto di Ripalto. A tale of the Italian Revolution*, London, 1849; M. Roberts, *Mademoiselle Mori: a tale of modern Rome*, 2 vols, London, 1860; and, above all, G. Meredith, *Emilia in England*, London, 1864, and *Vittoria*, London, 1897.

99. Anon., *Angelo. A romance of modern Rome*, London, 1854.

100. Ibid., pp. 232-5.

101. J.R. Beste, *Modern Society in Rome*, 3 vols, Rome, 1856, 2, pp. 78-81.

102. Ibid., pp. 81, 91-2.

103. Ibid., 3, pp. 282-4. The departure from Rome and the retreat is described on pp. 257, 266-7.

104. C.G. Hamilton, *The exiles of Italy, or Garibaldi's miraculous escapes. A novel*, London, 1857, pp. v-viii, xxxi.

105. Ibid., p. 71.

106. Ibid., pp. 100-30, 177-83, 247-8.

107. Anon., *Angelo*, p. 234; *Modern Society in Rome*, 3, pp. 143-5, 283-4; Hamilton, *The exiles of Italy*, pp. 99-100, 120-9. Elizabeth Barrett Browning had also dwelt on the death of Anita and her unborn child in the second part of 'Casa Guidi windows', written in 1851.

108. 12 Jan., 6 April, 21 and 31 May, 15 and 22/23 June, 12 Aug. 1850, in *Epistolario*, 3, pp. 4, 13, 17-19, 21-3, 29.

109. *The life of General Garibaldi written by himself with the sketches of his companions in arms*, New York, 1859; F. Carrano, *I Cacciatori delle Alpi comandati dal generale Garibaldi nella guerra del 1859*, Turin, 1860 (pp. 9-86 are Garibaldi's memoirs); *Mémoires de Garibaldi*, Paris, 1860; *Garibaldi's Denkwürdigkeiten nach handschriftlichen Aufzeichnungen desselben und nach authentischen Quellen bearbeitet und herausgegeben von Elpis Melena*, Hamburg, 1861.

110. 31 May, 15 and 22 June 1850, in *Epistolario*, 3, pp. 19, 21-2, 23.

111. G. M. Trevelyan, *Garibaldi's defence of the Roman Republic*, London, 1907, p. 354.

112. M. Thom, 'How I made Italy' (review of G. Garibaldi, *My life*), *Times Literary Supplement*, 17 June 2005, p. 8.

113. Trevelyan, *Garibaldi's defence*, p. 354.

114. Nora, 'Memoirs', pp. 405-6, see also G. Egerton (ed.), *Political Memoir*, London, 1994.

115. Ibid., p. 434.

116. An obvious referent is Napoleon's *Mémorial de Sainte-Hélène*, on which see D. Le Gall, *Napoléon et le Mémorial de Sainte-Hélène: analyse d'un discours*, Paris, 2003.

117. M. McLaughlin, 'Biography and autobiography in the Italian Renaissance', in P. France and W. St Clair (eds), *Mapping lives. The uses of biography*, Oxford, 2002, pp. 37-65. On Risorgimento memoirs, see G. Trombatore, 'Introduzione', *Memorialisti dell'Ottocento*, I, Milan and Naples, 1953, pp. ix-xxv; Banti, *La nazione del Risorgimento*, pp. 54-5; M. Petrusewicz, 'Giuseppe Ricciardi, ribelle, romantico europeo', *Archivio Storico per le provincie Napoletane*, 117, 1999, esp. pp. 244-6.

118. G. Fitzpatrick and F. Masiello, 'Introduction', and R. Piglia, 'Sarmiento the writer', both in T. Halperín Donghi *et al.* (eds), *Sarmiento. Author of a nation*, Berkeley, CA, 1994, pp. 1-16, 127-44.

119. 12 Aug. 1850, in *Epistolario*, 3, pp. 29-30.

120. *Le memorie di Garibaldi in una delle redazioni anteriori alla definitiva del 1872*, Bologna, 1932, pp. 9-10, 12.

121. Ibid., p. 150.

122. Ibid., pp. 16-17.

123. Ibid., pp. 112-13.

124. Ibid., pp. 29–30.
125. Ibid., pp. 35, 40–2.
126. Ibid., pp. 64–5, 136, 143.
127. Ibid., pp. 28, 113.
128. Ibid., pp. 13, 22, 41, 102, 121.
129. Ibid., p. 53; 'Anita', ibid., Appendice A, p. 365.
130. This point is made by Thom, 'How I made Italy', p. 8.
131. *Memorie*, pp. 5–6.
132. Ibid., pp. 37, 44–6.
133. Ibid., pp. 51, 52–3, 74–5, 365, 367, 370–2, 375.
134. Ibid., pp. 11, 45.
135. Taylor, *Ernest Jones*, pp. 9–10.

Chapter 6: Independence

1. D. Mack Smith, 'Victor Emanuel and the war of 1859', in idem, *Victor Emanuel, Cavour and the Risorgimento*, London, 1971, p. 93.
2. According to Cavour's correspondence with the king, 24 July 1858, in *Il Carteggio Cavour–Nigra dal 1858 al 1861*, 1, Bologna, 1961, pp. 103–14.
3. On British policy in this period, see D. Beales, *England and Italy, 1859–60*, London, 1961, pp. 36–92.
4. D. Mack Smith, 'An outline of Risorgimento history, 1840–1870', in idem, *Victor Emanuel*, p. 29.
5. For detailed descriptions of the origins of the 1859 war, see F. Coppa, *The origins of the Italian wars of independence*, London, 1992, pp. 74–91; A. Blumberg, *A carefully planned accident. The Italian war of 1859*, London, 1990, pp. 27–104; M. Walker (ed.), *Plombières: secret diplomacy and the rebirth of Italy*, New York, 1968.
6. Mack Smith, 'Victor Emanuel', p. 95.
7. See R. Grew, *A sterner plan for Italian unity. The Italian National Society in the Risorgimento*, Princeton, NJ, 1963, pp. 193–217.
8. J. Petersen, 'Il mito del Risorgimento nella cultura tedesca', in *Il mito del Risorgimento nell'Italia unita*, Milan, 1995, p. 454.
9. Ibid., pp. 454–62; idem, 'Das deutsche politische Italienbild in der Zeit der nationalen Einigung', in idem, *Italien-Bilder–Deutschland-Bilder*, Cologne, 1999, pp. 73–80. See also F. Valsecchi, *Italia ed Europa nel 1859*, Florence, 1965, pp. 121–69 (and, for a broader discussion on Great Power politics and the Italian Question in 1859, see pp. 52–84).
10. H. R. Marraro, *American opinion on the unification of Italy, 1846–61*, New York, 1932, pp. 225–35.
11. D. Beales and E. Biagini, *The Risorgimento and the unification of Italy*, London, 2002 edn, pp. 114–20.
12. An example of this kind of approach is in Coppa, *Origins*, who pays hardly any attention at all to the role of nationalism in the Italian wars. But even an organisation as pro-nationalist as the Istituto per la Storia del Risorgimento at Rome sees the war of 1859 purely in terms of international relations: see the essays in *Nel centenario del 1859. Atti del XXXIX congresso di storia del Risorgimento italiano*, Rome, 1960.
13. Grew, *A sterner plan*, pp. 111–22.
14. Ibid., pp. 122–3.
15. A. M. Isastia, *Il volontario militare nel Risorgimento. La partecipazione alla guerra del 1859*, Rome, 1990, p. 103.
16. These figures are given in L. de la Varenne, *Les Chasseurs des Alpes et des Apennins. Histoire complète*, Florence, 1860, p. 307 and are used in the official government publication, *La guerra del 1859 per l'indipendenza d'Italia, vol 1. Narrazione*, Rome, 1910, p. 117.

17. See the breakdown of figures in Isastia, *Il volontario*, pp. 189–242.
18. De la Varenne, *Les Chasseurs*, pp. 302–5. He reports that money also came from overseas and from as far away as the USA.
19. Grew, *A sterner plan*, p. 178. Isastia suggests that the movements of these men can be seen as a kind of political and economic 'migration', but offers little evidence to substantiate this claim. *Il volontario*, p. 14.
20. Ibid., p. 101.
21. Grew, *A sterner plan*, pp. 174–5.
22. Ibid., p. 170.
23. D. Mack Smith (ed.), *Garibaldi*, Englewood Cliffs, NJ, 1969, pp. 31–2.
24. Cavour to Nigra, 6 & 7 March 1859, in *Cavour–Nigra*, 2, pp. 61, 64. See also his comments on 9 March, p. 74.
25. 30 June 1860, in *Epistolario*, 4, p. 85.
26. 22 Dec. 1858, ibid., 3, p. 195.
27. See speeches nn. 113–16, 128, 133–4, in *Scritti e discorsi*, 1, pp. 164–6, 176–7, 181–2.
28. *Epistolario*, 4, facing p. 80.
29. See the report in *The Times*, 20 June 1859. The writer also says that the volunteers still wore no uniform, 'just a small tricolour cockade', although G. M. Trevelyan says they 'dressed after the ugly, conventional patterns of the line regiments'. *Garibaldi and the Thousand*, London, 1908, p. 90.
30. *Epistolario*, 3; see also his letters of 20 Dec. 1858 to Deideri and Specchi, ibid., pp. 191–3, and to La Farina, 30 Jan. 1859, in ibid., 4, p. 7.
31. See esp. 21 Dec. 1858, in *Epistolario*, 3, p. 193, and 8 and 30 Jan, 15 March, 4 and 17 April 1859, in ibid., 4, pp. 3, 6–7, 14, 19–20, 27. For Cairoli's accounts, see ibid., pp. 277, 229–30, 238–9.
32. To Planet de la Faye, 23 April 1859, ibid., p. 31.
33. 26 Feb., 7 March, 10 April 1859, ibid., pp. 11, 13, 22. Translation in G. M. Trevelyan, *Garibaldi and the making of Italy*, London, 1911, pp. 299–300.
34. 24 April 1859, ibid., p. 33.
35. 25 April 1859, in *Scritti e discorsi*, 1, p. 164.
36. 9 March 1859, *Cavour–Nigra*, 2, p. 74.
37. Isastia, *Il volontario*, pp. 97–101.
38. In *L'Eco d'Italia*, 16 Feb. 1859 and New York *Evening Post*, 21 May 1859. Quoted in Marraro, *American opinion*, p. 241.
39. J. Ridley, *Garibaldi*, London, 1974, pp. 402–3.
40. Luigi Carlo Farini to Cavour, 28 March 1859, quoted in Isastia, *Il volontario*, p. 10. For a discussion of the differences between volunteering and the regular army as a military model, see L. Riall, 'Eroi maschili, virilità e forme della guerra', in A. M. Banti and P. Ginsborg (eds), *Il Risorgimento*, Turin, forthcoming.
41. Grew, *A sterner plan*, p. 175; Isastia, *Il volontario*, finds that the vast majority of those enrolled in the royal army were aged between eighteen and twenty-six, while over 40 per cent of those in the *Cacciatori* were twenty-seven years of age or older, pp. 212–13, 239.
42. Isastia, *Il volontario*, pp. 10–12.
43. See Garibaldi's letter to Cavour, 21 May 1859, in *Epistolario*, 4, pp. 52–3.
44. G. Guerzoni, *Garibaldi*, 2 vols, Florence, 1882, 1, p. 471.
45. Quoted in Trevelyan, *The Thousand*, p. 99.
46. There are a number of contemporary sources for Garibaldi's part in the 1859 war. See, in particular, F. Carrano, *I Cacciatori delle Alpi comandati dal Generale Garibaldi nella guerra del 1859 in Italia*, Turin, 1860, and W. Rüstow, *La guerra d'Italia del 1859*, Turin[?], 1859. Other sources are: *La guerra del 1859*, 1, pp. 116–21, 275–96; A. Rocca, 'La campagna del 1859', *Garibaldi condottiero*, Rome, 1932; and there are useful shorter accounts in P. Pieri, *Storia militare del Risorgimento*, Turin, 1962, pp. 621–3;

and Trevelyan, *The Thousand*, pp. 82–109.

47. Ibid., pp. 106, 108.
48. 23 May 1859, *Scritti e discorsi*, 1, p. 168.
49. G. Visconti Venosta, *Ricordi di gioventù: cose vedute o sapute (1847–1860)*, Milan, 1904, p. 453.
50. Trevelyan, *The Thousand*, p. 106; Garibaldi to the king, 3 July 1859, *Epistolario*, 4, p. 89.
51. *Epistolario*, 4, pp. 88–9; on Peard, see also G. M. Trevelyan, 'The war journals of Garibaldi's Englishman', *Cornhill Magazine*, 24, Jan.–June 1908, pp. 96–110. De la Varenne says that volunteers came from France, Baden and Poland as well as Hungary and England, and he is the source of the information about Guerrazzi's translator, Charles Scott: see *Les Chasseurs*, pp. 307, 319–22.
52. C. Arrivabene, *Italy under Victor Emmanuel. A personal narrative*, London, 1862, pp. 299–300.
53. 26 July 1859.
54. *Epistolario*, 4, p. 55.
55. Carrano, *I Cacciatori*, pp. 253–4.
56. This description is by Giovanni Cadolini, *Memorie del Risorgimento dal 1848 al 1862*, Milan, 1911, p. 319, and is confirmed by Carrano, *I Cacciatori*, p. 254, and G. della Valle, *Varese, Garibaldi ed Urban nel 1859 durante la guerra per l'indipendenza italiana*, Varese, 1863, pp. 38–9.
57. Cadolini, *Memorie*, p. 332; Carrano, *I Cacciatori*, p. 310.
58. Luigi Gemelli to Agostino Bertani, MRM, Archivio Bertani, Cartella 9, plico viii, n.120/15; partly quoted in Isastia, *Il volontario*, p. 10.
59. Grew points out that the Society's propaganda efforts were much more successful than their efforts at co-ordination and organisation, but suggests that this mattered little if at all during the confused events of May–June 1859. *A sterner plan*, esp. p. 205.
60. Visconti Venosta, *Ricordi*, pp. 543–4.
61. Ibid., p. 544.
62. 31 Oct. 1859, in Mack Smith (ed.), *Garibaldi*, p. 102.
63. *Scritti e discorsi*, 1, p. 184.
64. 18 July 1859, *Epistolario*, 4, pp. 97–8.
65. Ibid., pp. 99, 102. See also his letter of 21 July to Lorenzo Valerio, ibid., p. 100.
66. 27 July 1859, ibid., p. 102.
67. See his letter to the king, 13 and 15 Aug., and to Ricasoli, 22 Aug. 1859, ibid., pp. 120–1, 123–4.
68. 29 Aug. 1859, ibid., p. 128.
69. *Scritti e discorsi*, 1, pp. 190–1, 201–11.
70. To Valerio, 21 Sept. and 5 Nov. 1859; to Vincenzo Malenchini, 18 Dec. 1859, in *Epistolario*, 4, pp. 142, 182–3, 209–10.
71. Quoted in Trevelyan, *The Thousand*, p. 119.
72. 19 Nov. 1859, in *Epistolario*, 4, p. 166.
73. 2–4 Nov. 1859, ibid., pp. 151–3.
74. 25 Oct. and 8 Nov. 1859, ibid., pp. 175, 183.
75. 11 and 22 Oct., 9 and 14 Nov, ibid., pp. 161, 172, 184, 186–7. Grew, *A sterner plan*, p. 223.
76. T. Trollope, *Social aspects of the Italian revolution in a series of letters from Florence*, London, 1861, p. 95.
77. Ridley, *Garibaldi*, p. 418, who also describes the ceremony transferring her remains. *Scritti e discorsi*, 1, pp. 191–6.
78. A. Scirocco, *Garibaldi*, Rome and Bari, 2001, p. 223.
79. 19 and 23 Nov. 1859, *Scritti e discorsi*, 4, pp. 211, 215–16; 16, 25 and 29 Nov. 1859, *Epistolario*, 4, pp. 187, 191, 195. Pagliano's portrait of Garibaldi from life, in Dec-

ember 1859, shows him still wearing the General's uniform (in MRM).

80. Trevelyan, *The Thousand*, p. 123.
81. Grew, *A sterner plan*, pp. 229–31.
82. 21 Dec. 1860, *Epistolario*, 4, p. 213. In late October, Garibaldi had told the king that he should become the dictator of central Italy, 'just like in Piedmont', ibid., p. 180.
83. His speech to the students of Pavia is ibid., pp. 215–18, the others are in *Scritti e discorsi*, 1, pp. 217–21.
84. *Scritti e discorsi*, 1, pp. 223–4.
85. Ridley, *Garibaldi*, p. 423.
86. Scirocco, *Garibaldi*, p. 225.
87. Trevelyan, *The Thousand*, p. 165.
88. C. Duggan, *Francesco Crispi, 1818–1901. From nation to nationalism*, Oxford, 2002, p. 168.
89. Trevelyan, *The Thousand*, p. 178.
90. Ibid., p. 166.
91. From Giuseppe Cacciari [?], Modena, 24 Nov. 1859, MCRR, b.45 n.26/ 75.
92. *The Times*, 29 Nov. 1859.
93. Joseph Kerr to Mr Vetter, 8 Dec. 1859, MCRR, b.52 3/33.
94. Trevelyan, *The Thousand*, App. K, pp. 340–1.
95. On this episode, see M. Mulinacci, *La bella figlia del lago. Cronaca intima del matrimonio fallito di Giuseppe Garibaldi con la marchesina Raimondi*, Milan, 1978.
96. Ridley, *Garibaldi*, pp. 424–6; see his letters to Teresa Araldi Trecchi, 22 Sept. 1859, and to Sofia Bettini, 24 Oct. 1859, in *Epistolario*, 4, pp. 143, 174.
97. 28 and 29 Jan., 26 Feb. 1860, ibid., 5, pp. 34–5, 43–4.
98. 30 Nov. 1859, ibid., 4, pp. 195–6.
99. 6 March 1860.
100. H. de Viel-Castel, *Mémoires du comte Horace de Viel-Castel sur le règne de Napoleon III (1815–1864)*, 6 vols, Paris, 1883–4, 6, 8 March 1860, p. 45.
101. From Luigi Reali, 6 Jan. 1860, MRM, Garibaldi Curàtolo, f. 603; 5 Jan. 1860, in *Epistolario*, 5, p. 6.
102. 15 March 1860, ibid., p. 48; for more details about the planned insurrection, see Duggan, *Francesco Crispi*, pp. 168–79.
103. 26 Nov. 1859, *Epistolario*, 4, p. 192; 11 Jan. 1860, ibid., 5, p. 14 (this letter also mentions that Carrano, his Italian editor, had a copy of the memoirs), and 28 March 1860, ibid., 5, pp. 25–6. On the encounter with Dumas, see G. Pécout, 'Una crociera nel mediterraneo con Garibaldi', in A. Dumas, *Viva Garibaldi*, Turin, 2004, p. xvi.
104. 2 Feb. 1860, MCRR b.47 2/1. Thackeray was writing as the editor of *Cornhill Magazine*. See also Garibaldi's letter to Dall'Ongaro of 21 Jan. 1860, where he refuses to give him a copy of the ms. and mentions that a 'Signor Troloppa' [Trollope?] was also interested in his memoirs, 28 March 1860, *Epistolario*, 5, p. 55.
105. Trevelyan, *The Thousand*, p. 169.
106. *Epistolario*, 5, p. 53.
107. L. Oliphant, *Episodes in a life of adventure*, Edinburgh and London, 1887, p. 171.
108. On the Palermo insurrection, see L. Riall, *Sicily and the unification of Italy, 1859–66. Liberal policy and local power*, Oxford, 1998, pp. 66–71.
109. D. Mack Smith, 'Cavour and the Thousand, 1860', in idem, *Victor Emanuel*, esp. pp. 184–6.
110. On the complexities surrounding Garibaldi's decision and Crispi's role, see Duggan, *Francesco Crispi*, pp. 180–6.
111. *Epistolario*, 5, pp. 73–4.
112. For a discussion, see P. Ginsborg, 'Risorgimento rivoluzionario: mito e realtà di una guerra di popolo', *Storia e Dossier*, 47, 1991, pp. 61–97.
113. The list of the Thousand was compiled by the Italian Ministry of War in 1864–5, and

formed the basis of a pension given to them by a law passed in 1865: see *Legge colla quale è assegnata una pensione vitalizia a ciascuno dei Mille fregiato della medaglia d'onore a ricordo della spedizione di Marsala, Torino, 22 gennaio 1865*, Milan, 1865. See also A. Pavia, *Album dei Mille*, Genoa, 1862, idem, *Indice completo dei Mille*, Genoa, 1867 (and M. Pizzo, *L'Album dei Mille di Alessandro Pavia*, 2004).

114. G. Bandi, *I Mille da Genova a Capua*, Milan, 1977 (1886), pp. 16–18.
115. R. Balzani, 'I giovani del Quarantotto: profilo di una generazione', *Contemporanea*, 3/3, 2000, pp. 403–16.
116. Trevelyan, *The Thousand*, p. 205.

Chapter 7: Fashioning Garibaldi

1. C. Bellanger, J. Godechot *et al.*, *Histoire générale de la presse française. Tome II, De 1815 à 1871*, Paris, 1972, p. 277.
2. H. K. Henisch and B. A. Henisch, *The photographic experience, 1839–1914. Images and attitudes*, Philadelphia, PA, 1993, pp. 365–95.
3. A. Briggs and P. Burke, *A social history of the media*, Cambridge, 2002, pp. 135–6.
4. See the comments in H. R. Marraro, *American opinion on the unification of Italy, 1846–61*, New York, 1932, pp. 244–9; and G. Lutz, 'La stampa bavarese negli anni dell'unificazione italiana (1858–1862)', *Rassegna Storica del Risorgimento*, 53/1 (1966), esp. pp. 35–47.
5. *New York Times*, 12, 20 and 22 July 1859.
6. *The Times*, 27 June, 2, 3, 4, 6 July 1859; it should be noted that *The Times* changed its stance from an anti-Italian position to a much more favourable view in 1859.
7. 25 Feb. 1860.
8. C. Arrivabene, *Italy under Victor Emmanuel. A personal narrative*, London, 1862, pp. 304–5.
9. *Garibaldi. Arte e Storia*, 2 vols, Florence, 1982, 2, cat. VII, 22 & 25, p. 54; ibid., pp. 115, 120–1.
10. *The Times*, 2 July 1859.
11. J. Ridley, *Garibaldi*, London, 1974, p. 413.
12. Bellanger et al., *Histoire générale*, pp. 8–10; C. Charle, *Le Siècle de la presse (1830–1939)*, Paris, 2004, pp. 91–4.
13. M. Milan, 'Opinione pubblica e antigaribaldinismo in Francia: la querelle sull'unità d'Italia (1860–66)', *Rassegna Storica del Risorgimento*, 70/2 1983, pp. 143–4.
14. M. Bernardi, 'Garibaldi et l'opinion publique française de 1860 à 1882', Université de Paris I, Centre de Recherches d'Histoire XIX–XXe Siècles, Mémoire de Maîtrise, 1982, p. 19.
15. Bellanger *et al.*, *Histoire générale*, p. 277.
16. See especially 23 April, 7, 14 and 21 May 1859, for the outbreak of war; and 28 May and 25 June 1859 on the movement of the military.
17. *Journal pour tous*. Suppl. au.n.218: n.1. 4 June 1859; suppl. au. n.232: n.26, 10 Sept. 1859.
18. *Souvenirs de la guerre d'Italie. Chants guerriers par messieurs Auguste Barbier, Pierre Dupont, Fernand Denoyers, Gustave Mathieu, Charles Vincent. Musique et accompagnement de piano par MM. Darcier, Pierre Dupont, Hector Salmon et Mme Mélanie Dentu*. Paris, n.d. but 1859.
19. 7, 14, 21 and 28 May, 4, 11, 18 and 25 June 1859.
20. *Album storico–artistico. 1859 Guerra d'Italia. Scritta dal corrispondente del Times al campo Franco–Sardo con disegni dal vero di C. Bossoli. Lith. par les Freres Fd & Charles Perrin*. Paris and Turin, 1860; *Album storico–artistico delle guerre per l'indipendenza italiana. Pubblicato in due parti*, Turin, 1860–1.
21. *L'Italia e i suoi difensori. Album storico–biografico dell'avv. Giuseppe Pistelli, ornato da*

ritratti e stampe litografiche, Florence, 1860.
22. *L'Illustration*, 4 June 1859.
23. *Le Siècle*, 2 June 1859. This 'hommage' to Garibaldi, by H. Lamarche was reprinted with Anatole de la Forge's biography of Garibaldi as *Histoire du Général Garibaldi*, Paris, 1859.
24. Marraro, *American opinion*, pp. 246–57; D. Beales, *England and Italy, 1859–60*, London, 1961, pp. 64–8. In both countries, however, there was considerable divergence of opinion, due to the presence of Mazzinians, who criticised the war, and to anti-French feeling in Britain.
25. 14 June 1859, p. 545; the same image was published on the cover of New York's *Harper's Weekly*, 9 June 1860; *Journal pour tous*, suppl., 4 June 1859, n. 1, p. 20.
26. *Garibaldi. Arte e storia*, 1, p. 97.
27. 3 June 1859, p. 392.
28. *Epistolario*, 4, facing p. 176.
29. See e.g. *Le Siècle* and *L'Illustration*, both 4 June 1859.
30. Ibid., 25 June 1859.
31. C. Paya, *Histoire de la guerre d'Italie. Garibaldi*, Paris, 1860, p. 165.
32. *The Times*, 20 June and 26 July 1859.
33. *L'Illustration*, 18 June 1859.
34. *The Times*, 20 June 1859.
35. Ibid., 26 July 1859.
36. *Journal pour tous*, suppl. 4 June 1859; 11 June 1859; 18 June 1859; 10 Sept. 1859; Paya, *Histoire*; *New York Times*, 31 May 1859; *Harper's Weekly*, 18 June 1859; *Album storico–artistico. 1859* and *L'Italia e i suoi difensori*.
37. *Biografia di Giuseppe Garibaldi*, Florence, 1859. See also *Biografia del Generale Giuseppe Garibaldi prode difensore della indipendenza italiana*, Milan, 1859; *Garibaldi ed i Cacciatori delle Alpi. Cenni biografico–storici colla narrazione dei più recenti fatti d'arme*, Milan, 1859; M. Carletti, *Biografia del Generale G. Garibaldi*, Florence, 1859.
38. *Garibaldi. Eine biographische Darstellung nach bisher unbekannten Documenten*, Berlin 1859; L. von Alvensleben, *Garibaldi. Seine Jugend, sein Leben, seine Abenteuer und seine Kriegsthaten*, Weimar, 1859; W. Raible, *Leben und Abenteuer des berühmten Freischaarenführers Joseph Garibaldi, General der sardinischen Armee und der italienischen Liga*, Munich, n.d. but 1859; *Leben und merkwürdige Abenteuer Joseph Garibaldi's, kühnen Aufwieglers und tapferen Bandenchef*, Zurich, 1859; L. C. Cnopius, *Garibaldi. Zijn Leven, Krijgsbedrijven en Avonturen*, Haarlem, 1859. See also T. Moegling, *Ein Besuch bei Garibaldi im Sommer 1859*, Zurich, 1860, and in general on German interest in Garibaldi in this period, W. Altgeld, 'Giuseppe Garibaldi in zeitgenössischer Sicht von der Verteidigung Roms bis zur Niederlage bei Mentana (1848–1867)', *Risorgimento*, 1982–3, pp. 175–8.
39. G. Sand, *Garibaldi*, Paris, 1859; A. Delvau, *G. Garibaldi. Vie et aventures, 1807–1859*, Paris, 1859; P. Dupont and A. d'Aunay, *Mémoires sur J. Garibaldi*, Paris, 1860; H. Castille, *Garibaldi*, Paris, 1859.
40. G. B. Cuneo, *Biografia di Giuseppe Garibaldi*, Turin, 1850; T. Dwight, *The life of Garibaldi written by himself*, New York, 1859. The London edition does not seem to have enjoyed a large circulation in Britain: the BL has no record of a copy, although there is a London edition in the library of the University of Birmingham.
41. Delvau, *Garibaldi*, p. 23.
42. Colonel Exalbion, *Garibaldi: his life, exploits and the Italian campaigns*, London, 1859, p. 6.
43. *Hommes du jour, L'empereur Francois-Joseph, Garibaldi, Lord Palmerston, Le prince Schwarzenberg . . . Le général Filangieri, Le roi Ferdinand II, Le duc de Modène, Le prince régent de Prusse, Madame la princesse de Prusse, Le maréchal Canrobet*, Paris, 1859, p. 31.

44. Castille, *Garibaldi*, pp. 3–4, 7–8. In Ludovico Ariosto's famous narrative poem *Orlando furioso* (1532), the hero is driven mad by love but eventually cured, and his return to the ranks of Charlemagne's army leads to the end of the siege of Paris and the defeat of the pagan armies. The suggested parallel with Garibaldi and the war of 1859 seems obvious.

45. Ibid., pp. 35–6.

46. Delvau, *Garibaldi*, p. 2.

47. Sand, *Garibaldi*, p. 16.

48. L. Goëthe, *Garibaldi, sa vie, son enfance, ses moeurs, ses exploits militaires*, Paris, 1859, p. 10; *Garibaldi et ses hommes rouges*, Paris, 1860, pp. 10–13; von Alvensleben, *Garibaldi*, pp. 7–10; Dupont and d'Aunay, *Mémoires*, p. 11.

49. Goëthe, *Garibaldi*, p. 18.

50. Ibid., pp. 19–52.

51. Von Alvensleben, *Garibaldi*, p. 23; *Garibaldi. Eine biographische Darstellung*, p. 15; Raible, *Leben und Abenteuer*, pp. 10–17.

52. J. la Messine, *Garibaldi*, Paris, 1859, p. 20. Juliette also published under the name 'Lamber' and 'Adam'; and an 1860 edition of the same *Garibaldi* is authored by Alexis la Messine.

53. J. Godechot, 'Un Journaliste français libéral ami de l'Italie: Charles Paya (1813–1865)', in *Il liberalismo moderato nel Risorgimento. Atti del XXXVII congresso di storia del Risorgimento italiano*, Rome, 1961, pp. 111–13.

54. Exalbion, *Garibaldi*, pp. 11–12, 152.

55. *Garibaldi's Englishman*, performed in St James Theatre, Dec. 1859, BL, Lord Chamberlain's plays, ADD 52988 U.

56. *Garibaldi*, by Tom Taylor, performed Oct. 1859, ibid., 1859 ADD 52985 H.

57. Delvau, *Garibaldi*, p. 20.

58. C. Pita, *Biographie du Général Garibaldi*, Paris, 1859, p. 40; De la Forge, *Garibaldi*, p. 6.

59. Delvau, *Garibaldi*, p. 14; Pita, *Biographie*, p. 40; *Hommes du jour*, p. 37.

60. Castille and Pita give her name as Léonta, as do the authors of *Hommes du jour*, *Biografia del Generale Garibaldi* and *Leben und merkwürdige Abenteuer Joseph Garibaldis*.

61. Von Alvensleben, *Garibaldi*, pp. 5–6.

62. Ibid., pp. 79–80.

63. Dupont and D'Aunay, *Mémoires*, p. 8.

64. Ibid., p. 15.

65. Lucia's story is ibid., pp. 33–120.

66. Ibid., p. 122.

67. Ibid., pp. 5–6.

68. Ibid., pp. 152–3, 156.

69. B. Hamnett, 'Fictitious histories: the dilemma of fact and fiction in the nineteenth-century historical novel', *European History Quarterly*, 36/1, 2006, pp. 31–60; M. Samuels, *The spectacular past. Popular history and the novel in nineteenth-century France*, Ithaca, NY, 2004.

70. Castille, *Garibaldi*, p. 3; see also pp. 4–5, 8, 42.

71. Ibid., pp. 59–60, 62.

72. P. Vermeylen, *Les Idées politiques et sociales de George Sand*, Brussels, 1984, pp. 150–1.

73. Sand, *Garibaldi*, pp. 4, 14, my emphasis.

74. 'Garibaldi', in *Souvenirs*.

75. Paya, *Histoire*, p. 14.

76. Delvau, *Garibaldi*, p. 2; for a general discussion, see J. R. Dakyns, *The Middle Ages in French literature, 1851–1900*, Oxford, 1973, esp. pp. 96–109.

77. Godechot, 'Paya', p. 112.

Chapter 8: The Thousand

1. G. Bandi, *I Mille da Genova a Capua*, Milan, 1977 (1886), p. 45.
2. Still the most complete account of the expedition is G. M. Trevelyan, *Garibaldi and the Thousand*, London, 1909, pp. 211–64. There is a very detailed description of the movements of the volunteers between Marsala and Palermo in C. Duggan, *Francesco Crispi*, Oxford, 2002, pp. 187–96. Much of the following description is based on these two works.
3. G. C. Abba, *The Diary of One of Garibaldi's Thousand*, London, 1962 (1880), pp. 11, 19; Trevelyan, *The Thousand*, p. 222.
4. Bandi, *I Mille*, pp. 42, 67–8.
5. E. Zasio, *Da Marsala al Volturno. Ricordi*, Padova, 1868, p. 34.
6. G. Nuvolari, *Come la penso*, Milan, 1881 (1861), p. 250.
7. 28 May 1860, in I. Nievo, *Lettere garibaldine*, Turin, 1961, p. 7.
8. 24 June, ibid., p. 17.
9. S. Corleo, *Garibaldi e i Mille a Salemi*, Rome, 1886, p. 7.
10. F. Brancato, 'L'amministrazione garibaldina e il plebiscito in Sicilia', in *Atti del XXXIX congresso di storia del Risorgimento Italiano*, Rome, 1961, p. 181.
11. On Pantaleo, see B. E. Maineri, *Fra Giovanni Pantaleo, Ricordi e note*, Rome, 1883; Garibaldi's proclamation is in *Scritti e discorsi*, 4, pp. 250–1.
12. 28 May 1860, in Nievo, *Lettere*, p. 8.
13. Duggan, *Francesco Crispi*, p. 191.
14. See Nievo's letter of 24 June, *Lettere*, p. 18.
15. Abba, *Diary*, p. 64.
16. 27 May, first published in *Il Pungolo* in June 1860, reprinted in Nievo, *Lettere*, p. 157.
17. Trevelyan, *The Thousand*, pp. 295–327. The description of the commander of the *Hannibal*, Rear-Admiral Mundy, is probably the best eyewitness account of the taking of Palermo: R. Mundy, *H.M.S. 'Hannibal' at Palermo and Naples during the Italian Revolution, 1859–1861*, London, 1863.
18. In a letter to the Italian exile, Antonio Panizzi, quoted in G. Dethan, 'Réactions françaises à l'enterprise des "Mille" en Sicile (mai–août 1860)', *Revue d'Histoire Diplomatique*, 99/3–4, 1985, p. 199.
19. 12 June 1860, in E. Hodder, *The life and work of the seventh Earl of Shaftesbury, K. G.*, London, 1892, p. 563.
20. D. Beales, *England and Italy, 1859–60*, London, 1961, pp. 131–62.
21. L. Riall, *Sicily and the unification of Italy. Liberal policy and local power, 1859–1866*, Oxford, 1998, pp. 62–71.
22. D. Mack Smith, 'The peasants' revolt in Sicily, 1860', in idem, *Victor Emanuel, Cavour and the Risorgimento*, London, 1971, p. 205.
23. Riall, *Sicily*, pp. 73–4.
24. Ibid.; Mack Smith, 'The peasants' revolt', p. 206.
25. Rosolino Pilo was killed in a skirmish in the mountains, which deprived the revolutionaries of an important leader. Duggan, *Francesco Crispi*, pp. 194–5.
26. *The Times*, 8 June 1860.
27. Duggan, *Francesco Crispi*, pp. 192–3; Riall, *Sicily*, pp. 86–90.
28. Riall, *Sicily*, pp. 87–9.
29. Quoted in Duggan, *Francesco Crispi*, p. 192.
30. G. Fiume, *La crisi sociale del 1848 in Sicilia*, Messina, 1982.
31. L. Riall, '"Ill-contrived, badly executed [and] . . . of no avail?" Reform and its impact in the Sicilian *latifondo* (1770–1910)', in E. dal Lago and R. Halpern (eds), *The American South and the Italian Mezzogiorno. Essays in comparative history*, London, 2002, pp. 132–52.
32. 10 Aug. 1860, in ASP, Ministero e Real Segretaria di Stato presso il Luogotenente

Generale, Polizia. Miscellanea. b.1510, f. personale del distretto di Alcamo.

33. For a general analysis of all these problems, see Riall, *Sicily*, pp. 92–107.
34. D. Mack Smith, 'Cavour and the Thousand', in idem, *Victor Emanuel*, p. 108.
35. The classic analysis of these early conflicts in Sicily is idem, *Cavour and Garibaldi, 1860. A study in political conflict*, Cambridge, 2nd edn 1985, pp. 22–99, and see also Duggan, *Francesco Crispi*, pp. 199–201.
36. Riall, *Sicily*, pp. 80–3.
37. R. Grew, *A sterner plan for Italian unity. The Italian National Society in the Risorgimento*, Princeton, NJ, 1963, pp. 298–301.
38. Ibid., 301–2; see the detailed list in G. M. Trevelyan, *Garibaldi and the making of Italy*, London, 1911, App. B, pp. 316–18.
39. Abba, *Diary*, pp. 95–100; G. Adamoli, *Da San Martino a Mentana. Ricordi di un volontario*, Milan, 1911 (1892), pp. 109–30.
40. C. S. Forbes, *The campaign of Garibaldi in the Two Sicilies. A personal narrative*, Edinburgh and London, 1861, p. 126.
41. There is a substantial literature on the revolt at Bronte: see L. Riall, 'Nelson versus Bronte: land, litigation and local politics in Sicily, 1799–1860', *European History Quarterly*, 29/1, 1999, pp. 39–73; M. S. Messana Virga, *Bronte 1860*, Caltanissetta & Rome, 1989; Mack Smith, 'The peasants' revolt', pp. 212–15.
42. Trevelyan, *The making of Italy*, pp. 80–90.
43. Ibid., pp. 99–100.
44. Ibid., p. 138.
45. Ibid., p. 146.
46. C. Arrivabene, *Italy under Victor Emmanuel. A personal narrative*, London, 1862, p. 148.
47. Trevelyan, *The making of Italy*, pp. 151–65.
48. H. Elliot, *Some revolutions and other diplomatic experiences*, London, 1922, p. 71.
49. M. Monnier, *Garibaldi. Histoire de la conquête des deux Sicilies. Notes prises sur place au jour le jour*, Paris, 1861, p. 296.
50. Ibid., p. 155 (according to the speech in *Scritti e discorsi*, 1, p. 266, Garibaldi said, 'We will see each other again! We will meet again on the continent and this time, by God, we will not be enemies!').
51. A. Mario, *The red shirt. Episodes*, London, 1865, p. 160.
52. Monnier, *Garibaldi*, pp. 215–16.
53. W. G. Clark, 'Naples and Garibaldi', in F. Galton (ed.), *Vacation tourists and notes of travel in 1860*, Cambridge, 1861, p. 24.
54. Arrivabene, *Italy under Victor Emmanuel*, p. 190.
55. Zasio, *Da Marsala*, p. 88 (Zasio was in the carriage with Garibaldi).
56. Clark, 'Naples', p. 25.
57. Forbes, *The campaign*, p. 237 (see also his lengthy description at pp. 232–4).
58. 11 Sept. 1860, in M. Menghini (ed.), *La spedizione garibaldina di Sicilia e di Napoli nei proclami, nelle corrispondenze, nei diarii del tempo*, Turin, 1907, p. 305.
59. Mack Smith, *Cavour and Garibaldi*, pp. 204–21, 243–50.
60. Quoted in Duggan, *Francesco Crispi*, p. 211, from R. Romeo, *Vita di Cavour*, Rome and Bari, 1984, p. 481.
61. Trevelyan, *The making of Italy*, p. 257.
62. *Cavour and Garibaldi*, pp. 310–11.
63. Quoted in M. Rosi, *Il Risorgimento italiano e l'azione d'un patriota cospiratore e soldato*, Rome, 1906, pp. 414–15.
64. Quoted in Mack Smith, *Cavour and Garibaldi*, p. 310.
65. Ibid., pp. 311–19; Duggan, *Francesco Crispi*, pp. 213–16.
66. Quoted in Mack Smith, *Cavour and Garibaldi*, p. 403.
67. Ibid., p. 388, and, in general, pp. 376–91.

68. Mario, *The red shirt*, pp. 276–90.
69. A. S. Bucknell, *In the tracks of the Garibaldians through Italy and Sicily*, London, 1861, p. 122.
70. Mack Smith, *Cavour and Garibaldi*, pp. 408–9.
71. Idem (ed.), *Garibaldi. Great lives observed*, London, 1960, p. 59.
72. Mundy, *H.M.S. 'Hannibal'*, pp. 282, 285.
73. Monnier, *Garibaldi*, p. 383.
74. Carlotta Roskilly, 13 Nov. 1860, in MRM, Garibaldi Curàtulo, f. 612; 'Sauvage', ibid., f. 627; see also the letters from Felicità Benso di Verdura, 21 Dec., ibid., f. 268.
75. M. C. Ruggieri Tricoli, *I giochi di Issione. Segni ed immagini della modernità nelle architetture provvisorie della Palermo borbonica*, Palermo, 1990, pp. 143–8.
76. Mack Smith, *Cavour and Garibaldi*, p. 1.
77. 18 July 1860, in T. Palmenghi-Crispi (ed.), *The memoirs of Francesco Crispi, 1. The Thousand*, London, 1912, p. 300.

Chapter 9: Making Italian Heroes

1. L. Riall, *Sicily and the unification of Italy, 1859–66. Liberal policy and local power*, Oxford, 1998, pp. 91–102.
2. On the centrality of the Vespers to Sicilian revolutionary identity, see G. la Mantia, 'I ricordi di Giovanni di Procida e del Vespro nei proclami rivoluzionari dal 1820 al 1860', *Rassegna Storica del Risorgimento*, 28, 1931, suppl., pp. 217–19; and more generally, see G. Giarrizzo, 'Note su Palmieri, Amari e il Vespro', *Archivio Storico per la Sicilia Orientale*, 69, 1973, pp. 355–9; and F. Brancato, *Storiografia e Politica nella Sicilia dell'Ottocento*, Palermo, 1973, pp. 196–208.
3. 11 May, *Scritti e discorsi*, 1, p. 249 (all dates henceforth are 1860 unless stated).
4. 30 May, ibid., p. 255.
5. June, ibid., pp. 264–5.
6. 2 June, ibid., p. 258.
7. Ibid., p. 259; 13 June, p. 265; 20 June, p. 269.
8. 3 Aug., ibid., p. 283.
9. 11 or 14 May, ibid., pp. 250–1.
10. 11 May, ibid., p. 249.
11. 1 June, ibid., p. 258.
12. 6 Aug., ibid., p. 289.
13. Aug., ibid., pp. 291–3.
14. In M. Menghini (ed.), *La spedizione garibaldina di Sicilia e di Napoli*, Turin, 1907, p. 119.
15. G. C. Abba, *The diary of one of Garibaldi's Thousand*, London, 1962 (1880), p. 74.
16. *The Times*, 15 June; see also similar eyewitness descriptions in E. Zasio, *Da Marsala al Volturno. Ricordi*, Padova, 1868, p. 58, and E. Lockroy, *Au hasard de la vie. Notes et souvenirs*, Paris, 1913, pp. 29–30.
17. C. S. Forbes, *The campaign of Garibaldi in the Two Sicilies. A personal narrative*, Edinburgh and London, 1861, pp. 118, 195.
18. M. Monnier, *Garibaldi. Histoire de la conquête des deux Siciles. Notes prises sur place au jour le jour*, Paris, 1861, p. 302.
19. J. Butler, *In memoriam Harriet Meuricoffre*, London, 1901, p. 50; on Garibaldi's assistance to the Protestants in Naples (including the granting of land to build a church), see M. Pellegrino Sutcliffe, 'Victorian congregations and Anglican chaplains in unified Italy (1861–1891)', MA thesis, Birkbeck College London, 2001, pp. 24–5.
20. G. Tricoli, 'Il mito di Garibaldi in Sicilia', *Archivio Storico Siciliano*, serie 4, 9, 1983, p. 100; F. Brancato, 'La partecipazione del clero alla rivoluzione siciliana del 1860', in *La Sicilia verso l'unità d'Italia*, Palermo, 1960, p. 22.

21. C. Arrivabene, *Italy under Victor Emmanuel. A personal narrative*, London, 1862, p. 230.
22. R. Tosi, *Da Venezia a Mentana (1848–1867)*, Forlì, 1910, p. 90; W. G. Clark, 'Naples and Garibaldi', in F. Galton (ed.), *Vacation tourists and notes of travel in 1860*, Cambridge, 1861, pp. 29, 54.
23. H. Elliot, *Some revolutions and other diplomatic experiences*, London, 1922, p. 85. On the San Gennaro miracle and its meaning, see M. P. Carroll, *Madonnas that maim. Popular Catholicism in Italy since the fifteenth century*, Baltimore, MD, 1992, pp. 115–19.
24. For a useful discussion, see E. Muir, *Ritual in early modern Europe*, Cambridge, 1997, esp. pp. 232–46.
25. Forbes, *The campaign*, p. 118.
26. G. Oddo, *I Mille di Marsala. Scene rivoluzionaria*, Milan, 1863, p. 568.
27. Forbes, *The campaign*, p. 204.
28. In D. Mack Smith (ed.), *Garibaldi*, Englewood Cliffs, NJ, 1969, p. 131, from L. Colet, *L'Italie des Italiens*, 4 vols, Paris, 1862–3, pp. 66–7.
29. Butler, *In memoriam*, p. 51.
30. Monnier, *Garibaldi*, p. 302.
31. ACP, Atti del Consiglio Comunale di Palermo, Deliberazioni Consiglio Comunale, n. 1.
32. That is, on 27 Sept. the council approved unanimously the expenditure for the celebrations.
33. 1 July, the *pretore* to the president of the *consiglio civico*, ACP, Corrispondenza Finanza, n. 17/4.
34. *La Mola, Gazzetta popolare di Sicilia*, 20 July.
35. 27 July, in Menghini (ed.), *La spedizione*, p. 182.
36. *La Forbice, Gazzetta popolare di Sicilia*, 21 July.
37. From the *Nazione*, 29 July, in Menghini (ed.), *La spedizione*, pp. 443–4.
38. *Il 19 luglio 1860. Festa popolare in Palermo pel giorno natalizio del generale Giuseppe Garibaldi*, Palermo, 1860, pp. 12–14.
39. Menghini (ed.), *La spedizione*, p. 445.
40. *Il 19 luglio*, pp. 6–10.
41. *La Forbice*, 28 July.
42. H. F. Winnington-Ingram, *Hearts of oak*, London, 1889, p. 212.
43. Raffaello Carboni to Agostino Bertani, 21 July, in MRM, Archivio Bertani, Cartella 11, plico xii. See also the description in Crispi's paper, *Il Precursore*, 21 July.
44. There is now a huge literature relating to this aspect of nationalism; for a recent study of the same period, S. Hazareesingh, *The Saint-Napoleon. Celebrations of sovereignty in nineteenth-century France*, Cambridge, MA, 2004.
45. M. C. Ruggieri Tricoli, *I giochi di Issione. Segni ed immagini della modernità nelle architetture provvisorie della Palermo borbonica*, Palermo, 1990; on France: M. Samuels, *The spectacular past. Popular history and the novel in nineteenth-century France*, New York, 2004, pp. 18–62.
46. *La Nazione*, 29 July, in Menghini (ed.), *La spedizione*, p. 442. For a discussion of the cult of Santa Rosalia in Palermo, see S. Cabibbo, *Santa Rosalia tra terra e cielo*, Palermo, 2004; and on Italian popular Catholicism more generally, M. P. Carroll, *Veiled threats. The logic of popular Catholicism in Italy*, Baltimore, MD, 1996.
47. 10 July, *Scritti e discorsi*, 1, p. 273.
48. *La Nazione*, 29 July, in Menghini (ed.), *La spedizione*, p. 443.
49. See the report in *Il Garibaldi. Giornale Politico*, 19 June, pp. 21–2 and *La Nazione*, 8 July (in Menghini (ed.), *La spedizione*, pp. 132–3); Brancato, 'La partecipazione del clero', pp. 23–4.
50. F. Venosta, *Rosolino Pilo e la rivoluzione siciliana. Notizie storiche*, Milan, 1863,

pp. 130–3; *Il Giornale di Sicilia*, 25 Aug. On the creation of the church of San Domenico as a Sicilian 'pantheon' in the nineteenth century, see P. Antonino Barilaro OP, *San Domenico di Palermo. Pantheon degli uomini illustri di Sicilia*, Palermo, 1971, pp. 74–5.

51. *Giornale Officiale del Governo Provvisorio di Sicilia*, 29 May, a.1, n.1.
52. 25 July.
53. 21 Aug.
54. 18 and 19 Sept.
55. E. Gentile, *The sacralization of politics in fascist Italy*, Cambridge, MA, 1996, pp. 2–5; M. Ridolfi, 'Per una storia della religione civile: il "caso italiano" in prospettiva comparata', *Memoria e Ricerca*, 13, 2003, pp. 133–40.
56. On which, see C. Duggan, *Francesco Crispi*, Oxford, 2002, pp. 426–50.
57. Artisans had also been at the centre of popular revolt against the government; for example the 1820 revolt in Palermo was largely caused by the government's attempt to abolish the trade guilds or *maestranze*. See O. Cancila, *Palermo*, Rome and Bari, 1988, pp. 47–52; Riall, *Sicily*, pp. 39–41, 207–11.
58. L. Sarullo (ed.), *Dizionario degli artisti siciliani*, 2, Palermo, 1993, pp. 27–8, 81–2, 300–1; M. Accascina, *Ottocento siciliano. Pittura*, Palermo, 1982 (1939), pp. 59–63, 93–100, 140–1. Bagnasco went on to have a career as an official 'nationalist' artist. He worked on the monument to Pilo and produced a famous curtain for the Teatro Garibaldi which showed Garibaldi sitting at the fountain in Piazza Pretorio (see *Garibaldi alla fontana pretoria in Palermo*, *Sipario*, Palermo, 1895, and the sketch in the Museo del Risorgimento, Palermo). On Lojacono, who took part in the fighting with his still more famous painter son, Francesco, see M. Vitella, 'Una traccia per Luigi Lojacono', in G. Barbera *et al.*, *Francesco Lojacono, 1838–1915*, Palermo, 2005, pp. 369–75. The main designer for the Pilo monument was the architect, Giovan Battista Basile, later responsible for the *giardino Garibaldi* in Piazza Marina and the Teatro Massimo, Palermo's monumental opera house. See more generally N. and M. C. Bullaro, 'L'impresa dei "Mille" nei pittori garibaldini', *Nuovi Quaderni del Meridione*, 80, 1982, esp. pp. 559–62.
59. For a discussion of Italian journalism in this period, see V. Castronovo, 'Stampa e opinione pubblica nell'Italia liberale', in idem, L. G. Fossati and N. Tranfaglia, *La stampa italiana nell'età liberale*, Rome and Bari, 1979, pp. 15–56.
60. 5 May, *Epistolario*, 5, p. 92.
61. *The Times*, 12 May; *New York Times*, 24 May.
62. 5 May, in *Scritti e discorsi*, 1, pp. 239–41; a facsimile of the flyer is in *Garibaldi. Arte e storia*, 2 vols, Florence, 1982, 2, cat. x, 13, pp. 56, 58.
63. 5 May, in *Epistolario*, 5, pp. 90–1.
64. 5 May, ibid., p. 95, and *Scritti e discorsi*, 1, p. 239.
65. 5 May, *Epistolario*, 5, p. 96.
66. 9 June (from which this translation is taken). The original is dated 7 May, in *Scritti e discorsi*, 1, p. 242.
67. G. M. Trevelyan, *Garibaldi and The Thousand*, London, 1909, p. 230.
68. 16 May, *Epistolario*, 5, pp. 104–5. Bertani's letter was published on 4 June, Pilo's on 27 May.
69. To Besana and Finzi, 28 May, *Epistolario*, 5, p. 116 (published in *Il Diritto*, 11 June); see also to Bertani, 3 June, ibid., p. 124.
70. To Thomas Parker, 24 June, ibid., pp. 139–40 (published in the *Morning Herald* and *L'Unità Italiana*, 11 July); see also 'Agli ufficiali della crociera inglese', May, ibid., pp. 120–1 (published in *L'Unità Italiana* of 1 June); 'Alla Regina Vittoria', 22 June, ibid., pp. 137–8 (published in *Il Diritto*, 15 Aug.); 'Al Presidente del comitato londinese per i soccorsi alla Sicilia', 24 June, ibid., pp. 141–2 (published in *L'Unità Italiana*, 10 July).

71. 3 Aug., in *Scritti e discorsi*, 1, pp. 282–4; see also above, p. 227.

72. *Garibaldi. Discorso di Giacomo Oddo. Letto all'Istituto d'istruzione popolare in Milano*, Milan, 1860, pp. 6–7, 11, 14.

73. F. D. Guerrazzi, *Addio ai giovani soldati volontarii della impresa italica capitanata dal Generale Garibaldi*, 1860; *Il Precursore*, 18 Sept.

74. In MRM, Bertani, cartella 12, plico xiii, n. 5; the material on the '*funerali*' is in ibid., cartella 11, plico xii, n. 99.

75. See, e.g., the letter from the editor of the Florentine paper, *La Nazione*, in which he says that he would have liked to have known more about the expedition at the outset, but is still pleased to publish information and letters relating to it. 9 May, to Bertani, ibid., cartella 12, plico xiii, n. 21.

76. F. dell'Ongaro, *É Garibaldi. Canzone*, Florence, 1859; I. Nievo, *Gli amori garibaldini. Con poesie e introduzione*, Como, 1911; S. di Paola, 'Il mito di Garibaldi nella poesia italiana', in F. Mazzonis (ed.), *Garibaldi condottiero. Storia, teoria, prassi*, Milan, 1984, p. 510.

77. Letter from Andra Fasciolo, 5 May, in Menghini (ed.), *La spedizione*, p. 7.

78. Ibid., p. 9.

79. *La Nazione*, 18 June; *L'Unità Italiana*, 22 June, ibid., pp. 105–9.

80. *Il Diritto*, 6 and 16 July, ibid., pp. 146–7, 151.

81. 27 June, ibid., p. 94.

82. *Il Movimento*, suppl. to 18 June, ibid., pp. 97–8.

83. Menghini (ed.), *La spedizione*, pp. 162–7.

84. Ibid., p. 173.

85. *L'Unità Italiana*, 5 Aug. and 9 Sept., ibid., pp. 225, 292.

86. 13 May, *Epistolario*, 5, p. 101.

87. 18, 21 and 29 May, in Menghini (ed.), *La spedizione*, pp. 21–3.

88. Ibid., p. 31.

89. Ibid., esp. pp. 57–80 (in *Il Diritto*, *Il Movimento*, *La Gazzetta di Genova*, *L'Unità Italiana*, and *La Nazione*).

90. *L'Unità Italiana*, 4 Aug., ibid., p. 243.

91. *Il Movimento*, 3 Aug., ibid., p. 249.

92. *L'Opinione*, 15 Sept., ibid., pp. 311–13.

93. 13 May, ibid., pp. 14–15.

94. 3 June, ibid., p. 33.

95. 5 Aug., ibid., p. 214.

96. 28 Aug., ibid., pp. 271–2.

97. G. Pécout, 'Una crociera nel mediterraneo con Garibaldi', in A. Dumas, *Viva Garibaldi. Un'odissea nel 1860*, Turin, 2004, pp. xii–xiii.

98. 16 Oct. in MRM, Garibaldi Curàtulo, f. 378.

99. 4 Aug.

100. *Les garibaldiens. Révolution de Sicile et de Naples*, Paris, 1861, which he then republished with additions in *Le Monte-Cristo* in 1862. An English translation was published in 1861: see the translator's note to another version of the same text, *On board the Emma. Adventures with Garibaldi's 'Thousand' in Sicily*, trans. R. S. Garnet, London, 1929, pp. xi–xii. For a discussion, see F. Boyer, '"Les Garibaldiens" de Alexandre Dumas: roman ou chose vue?', *Studi Francesi*, 4, 1960, pp. 26–34.

101. Suppl. to *Il Movimento*, 18 Aug. in Menghini (ed.), *La spedizione*, pp. 183–204. The phrase 'my dear Italians' was changed to 'my dear Sicilians' in the Sicilian papers.

102. Quoted in Monnier, *Garibaldi*, p. 136.

103. *The Times* 15 June; *L'Unità Italiana*, 10, 18 April, 23 June and 3 July, in G. Rondoni, 'Garibaldi nei vecchi giornali della patria', *Garibaldi, numero unico*, 1907, p. 49.

104. M. Bernardi, 'Garibaldi et l'opinion publique française de 1860 à 1882', Université de Paris I, Centre de Recherches d'Histoire XIX–XXe Siècles, Mémoire de Maîtrise, 1982,

pp. 23–4; for an analysis of anti-Garibaldi opinion in France, see M. Milan, 'Opinione pubblica e antigaribaldinismo in Francia: La *querelle* sull'unità d'Italia (1860–1868)', *Rassegna Storica del Risorgimento*, 60/2, 1983, pp. 147–8.

105. *Halte-là Garibaldi!*, Paris, 1860, p. 3.

106. *ILN*, 19 May, p. 465.

107. 24 May.

108. G. Dethan, 'Réactions françaises à l'enterprise des "Mille" en Sicile (mai–août 1860)', *Revue d'Histoire Diplomatique*, 99/3–4, 1985, p. 203.

109. *Mémoires de Garibaldi par Alexandre Dumas, précédés d'un discours sur Garibaldi par Victor Hugo et d'une introduction par George Sand*, 2 vols, Brussels, 1860, pp. viii–ix.

110. H. Durand-Brager, *Quatre mois de l'expédition de Garibaldi en Sicile et en Italie*, Paris, 1861, pp. i–ii.

111. D. Stübler, 'Guerra e rivoluzione in Italia nella stampa liberale prussiana (1859–1860)', *Contemporanea*, 1/3, 1998, pp. 590–2; W. Altgeld, 'Giuseppe Garibaldi in zeitgenössicher Sicht (1848–1867)', *Risorgimento*, 1982–83, pp. 178–83, 186–9; G. Lutz, 'La stampa bavarese dal 1858 al 1862', *Rassegna Storica del Risorgimento*, 53/2, 1966, pp. 221–2.

112. On Marx and Engels' attitude to Garibaldi and the Thousand, see Altgeld, 'Giuseppe Garibaldi', pp. 183–6.

113. H. Marraro, *American opinion on the unification of Italy, 1846–61*, New York, 1932, p. 280.

114. Bernardi, 'Garibaldi', p. 44. This is a play on words: '*campagne*' means both 'campaign' and 'countryside' in French.

115. R. Grew, *A sterner plan for Italian unity. The Italian national society in the Risorgimento*, Princeton, NJ, 1963, pp. 291, 293.

116. Regno di Sardegna, Camera dei Deputati. Seduta del 12 aprile, in *Garibaldi in parlamento, 1. Dalla Repubblica Romana a Aspromonte*, Rome, 1982, pp. 64–7; P. G. Boggio, *Cavour o Garibaldi?* Turin, 1860, to which see Brofferio's reply, *Garibaldi o Cavour?* Genoa, 1860. The comment from *The Times* is from 25 Nov. 1862, on the occasion of another attack by Boggio on Garibaldi.

117. P. G. Boggio, *Da Montevideo a Palermo. Vita di Giuseppe Garibaldi*, Turin, 1860, pp. 5, 7.

118. *The Times*, 15 June; *L'Unità Italiana*, 10, 18 April, 23 June and 3 July, in Rondoni, 'Garibaldi nei vecchi giornali', p. 49.

119. Rondoni, 'Garibaldi', pp. 48–9.

120. Eber's long article, which takes the reader from the camp above Gibilrossa to Palermo under siege, is in *The Times*, 8 June.

121. *Boston Courier*, 10 July, also in Mack Smith (ed.), *Garibaldi*, p. 128.

122. 16 June.

123. See, for instance, the description of the French journalist Lockroy, *Au hasard de la vie*, p. 31.

124. On Thomas Nast, see the article in *Harper's Weekly*, 11 May 1867, and A. Boime, *The art of the Macchia and the Risorgimento*, Chicago, IL, 1993, pp. 29–32.

125. *Garibaldi. Arte e storia*, 1, p. 314.

126. F. du Plessix Gray, *Rage and Fire. A life of Louise Colet – pioneer feminist, literary star, Flaubert's muse*, London, 1994, esp. pp. 299–307. She and Du Camp also loathed each other, and Du Camp was much more critical of Garibaldi in private.

127. Monnier, *Garibaldi*; M. du Camp, *Expédition des Deux-Siciles: souvenirs personnels*, Paris, 1861; L. Colet, *L'Italie des Italiens*, Paris, 1863, vol. 3. Charles Arrivabene also wrote a book about his experiences (*Italy under Victor Emmanuel*, London, 1862), as did the artist De Fonvielle (*Souvenirs d'une chemise rouge*, Paris, 1861).

128. Forbes, *The campaign*; A. S. Bucknell, *In the tracks of the Garibaldians through Italy and*

Sicily, London, 1861; W. G. Clark, 'Naples and Garibaldi', in F. Galton (ed.), *Vacation tourists and notes of travel in 1860*, Cambridge, 1861.

129. G. Adamoli, *Da San Martino a Mentana. Ricordi di un volontario*, Milan, 1911 (1892), p. 145, and see his more detailed description on pp. 141–6.

130. Forbes, *The campaign*, pp. 130–1.

131. F. Boyer, 'Les Volontaires français avec Garibaldi en 1860', *Revue d'Histoire Moderne et Contemporaine*, 7, 1960, pp. 129–30.

132. Arrivabene, *Italy under Victor Emmanuel*, pp. 263–85.

133. Mrs Burton Harrison, *Recollections Grave and Gay*, New York, 1911, pp. 133–4; another American described Vizitelly as a 'bummer' (a Union guerrilla): J. Johns, 'Wilmington N.C. during the blockade', *Skedaddle*, 12 April 2004, p. 17.

134. 9 June; in *Harper's Weekly*, 7 July.

135. 9 and 16 June.

136. 16 and 23 June, 7 July.

137. 28 July, 4 Aug.

138. 8 and 29 Sept.

139. See Vizitelly's illustration in the *ILN*, 23 June, and another portrait by Orsani ibid., 14 July. *Die Gartenlaube*'s portrait is in n. 9, p. 133.

140. *ILN*, 28 July. This picture had a wide circulation: published in *Harper's Weekly* on 25 Aug. and *Die Gartenlaube*, in n. 36, pp. 564–6.

141. 21 July, 13 and 21 Oct. The paper was careful to state that the British volunteers were middle class and especially prized by Garibaldi, but it also confessed that they were motivated by a 'love of adventure, as much, perhaps, as a love of freedom'. On this problem, see below, pp. 301–2.

142. 14 and 21 July, 18 Aug.

143. 21 Sept., 13 and 20 Oct.

144. 8 Oct., 23 March 1861.

145. See J. Plunkett, *Queen Victoria. First media monarch*, Oxford, 2003, pp. 48–52.

146. 12 and 29 Dec.

147. *Halte-là Garibaldi!*, p. 3.

148. Both magazines' coverage of Milazzo is on 18 Aug.

149. Published by Fratelli Terzaghi in Milan, 1860–2. See the *programma* at the start of the book, which explains the plan and layout of the album.

150. Ibid., p. 78.

151. See the various illustrations ibid., pp. 10, 12, 22, 24, 26, 28, 32, 68; Induno's lithograph is on p. 2, the painting is in the Museo del *Risorgimento* in Milan, and it formed the basis for the departure scene in Alessandro Blasetti's 1934 film, *1860*.

152. *Album storico–artistico*, p. 4.

153. *Garibaldi. Arte e storia*, 1, pp. 94–5.

154. G. La Cecilia, *Storia della insurrezione siciliana, dei successivi avvenimenti per l'indipendenza ed unione d'Italia e delle gloriose gesta di Giuseppe Garibaldi compilata su note e documenti trasmessi dai luoghi ove accadono*, 2 vols Milan, 1860 (there were two different editions in Milan, and in Palermo the book was serialised in six parts, each with illustrations).

155. F. Mistrali, *Storia popolare della rivoluzione di Sicilia e dell'impresa di Giuseppe Garibaldi*, Milan, 2nd edn. 1862.

156. La Cecilia is best known for his *Memorie storico–politiche*, Rome, 1876–8; see also the 'prefazione' by R. Moscati to a 1946 edition of the memoirs.

157. Among other editions, Mistrali produced *Da Palermo a Gaeta. Storia popolare della campagna dell'Italia meridionale*, Milan, 1861; a three-volume *Storia anedottica politico-militare della guerra d'Italia nel 1859 e 1860*, Milan, 1863; and a 442-page *Storia anedottica politico-militare della guerra d'Italia, nel 1860 . . . Da Caprera ad Aspromonte*, Milan, 1875.

158. *Gli abitanti della luna*, Bologna, 1874; *Vita di Gesù*, Milan, 1863; *Morte e testamento di Urbano Rattazzi*, Milan, 1863. For a full list of Mistrali's publications, see *Clio. Catalogo dei libri Italiani dell'800*, Milan, 1991, 4, p. 3060. Pagnoni, the Milan publisher of his Garibaldi volumes, had specialised in historical novels and after 1859 began to publish works of a nationalist nature.

159. *Storia della insurrezione*, 2, pp. 518–19; *Storia popolare*, p. 60.

160. Dumas's first letter to *Le Siècle* was published on 25 May; the memoirs began on 8 June and were serialised throughout the rest of the month.

161. M. Martenengo, 'Garibaldi narratore. Vicende editoriali e stato attuale dei manoscritti', *Il Risorgimento*, 55/1, 1996, pp. 90–1.

162. Turin, 1860: the memoirs are inserted in the volume at pp. 9–86.

163. G. Ricciardi, *Vita di G. Garibaldi narrata al popolo . . . e continuata sino al suo ritiro nell'Isola di Caprera [9 novembre, 1860]*, Florence, 1860.

164. L. de la Varenne, *Vita del General Garibaldi*, Bologna, 1860.

165. A. Balbiani, *Storia illustrata della vita di Garibaldi*, Milan, 1860.

166. Ricciardi, *Vita*, pp. 1, 6, 14–15.

167. Balbiani, *Storia illustrata*, p. 12.

168. These illustrations (printed by Rossetti in Milan) are, for example, preserved separately in the collections of both the Museo del Risorgimento in Turin and the Biblioteca di Storia Moderna e Contemporanea in Rome.

169. *Il Generale Garibaldi. Italia luglio del 1860; Storia di Giuseppe Garibaldi*, Genoa, 1860; G. Marchese, *Giuseppe Garibaldi*, Turin, 1860; F. Santi, *Vita aneddotica politico–militare del Generale Giuseppe Garibaldi*, Milan, 1860 (this volume had the same publisher, Pagnoni, as Franco Mistrali).

170. O. J. Victor, *Life of Joseph Garibaldi. The Liberator of Italy. Complete up to the withdrawal of Garibaldi to his island home after the Neapolitan campaign, 1860*, New York, 1860, pp. 5, 9–10, 81.

171. [Anon], *The illustrated life and career of Garibaldi*, London, 1860.

172. O. Féré and R. Hyenne, *Garibaldi. Aventures, expéditions, voyages. Amérique, Rome, Piémont, Sicile, Naples. 1834–1848–1859–1860*, Paris, 1861.

173. *Garibaldi, der Held und Befreier Italiens, dessen Lebensbeschreibung und Bildniss*, Reutlingen, 1860; *Garibaldi, das Haupt des jungen Italiens; sein Leben, seine Abenteuer und Heldenthaten*, Berlin, 1861.

174. Dr D. Burger, *Een vorlooper van Garibaldi*, Amersfoort, 1860; *Garibaldi, zijn leven, krijgsbedrijven en avonturen, etc. (Met portret.)*, Haarlem, 1859; *Garibaldi en de Profetiën*, Amsterdam, 1860; *Garibaldi en het Duizendjarig Rijk, gevolg van Garibaldi en de Profëtien*, Utrecht, 1860.

175. A. Altadill, *Garibaldi en Sicilia ó la unidad italiana*, Madrid/Barcelona, 1860.

176. Dethan, 'Réactions françaises', pp. 198–9.

177. V. Ottolini, *Cacciatori delle Alpi (1848–59). Scene storico-militari*, Milan, 1860, pp. 119–29.

178. *Garibaldi in Sicilia*, p. 5.

179. D. Manuel Gil de Salcedo, *Garibaldi y Procida, ó las Pasquas Sangrientas de Sicilia. Novela Histórica Contemporánea*, Madrid, 1860; 'Rendicion de Capua y triunfal entrada de S.M. el Rey Victor Manuel y el Garibaldi', Barcelona, 1860.

180. *L'Âne et les trois voleurs. Proverbe garibaldien en un acte et en vile prose*, Paris, 1860, pp. 7–8.

181. E. Atgier, *Garibaldi le Filibustier*, Rochefort-sur-mer, 1860 and 1861, p. 5.

182. M. Barthélemy, *Garibaldi ou le réveil du lion*, Paris, 1861, p. 5.

183. M. Roberts, *Mademoiselle Mori. A tale of modern Rome*, London, 1860; A. B. Edwards, *Half a million of money*, London, 1865; W. Somerville Lach Szyrma, *Heroes of the day: Franklin and Garibaldi. Poems*, Plymouth, 1860; M. Braddon, *Garibaldi and other poems*, London, 1861.

184. BL, Lord Chamberlain's plays, ADD 52994 K and 52997 J (*Garibaldi's excursionists* by H. J. Byron was also published as *The Garibaldi excursionists*, London, 1860).

185. Here I use 'popular' not in the sense of mass culture *per se*: see Samuels, *The spectacular past*, p. 5.

186. G. M. Trevelyan, *Garibaldi and the making of Italy*, London, 1911, pp. 3, 296.

187. F. della Peruta, 'Il mito del *Risorgimento* e l'estrema sinistra dall'Unità al 1914', *Il Risorgimento*, 47/1–2, 1995, pp. 32–70. I refer here to the final version of Garibaldi's memoirs, written in 1872, *Le memorie di Garibaldi nella redazione definitiva del 1872*, Bologna, 1932.

188. See Mack Smith's comments on the effect of his book in the preface to the 1985 edn of *Cavour and Garibaldi. A study in political conflict*, Cambridge, 1985, pp. ix–xvi.

189. Idem, 'Cavour and parliament', in idem, *Victor Emanuel, Cavour and the Risorgimento*, London, 1971, pp. 56–76.

190. O. Chadwick, *A history of the Popes, 1830–1914*, Oxford, 1998, pp. 132–9.

191. Trevelyan, *The making of Italy*, pp. 296–7.

Chapter 10: The Garibaldi Moment

1. In looking at the response to Garibaldi in Sicily, I focus largely on Palermo, where most of the nation-building effort was concentrated, and where there is a large collection of nationalist memorabilia kept in the library of the SSSP.

2. 'Album per la sottoscrizione alla spada di onore che offre l'Italia all'immortale eroe Giuseppe Garibaldi', Naples, 1860. The Palermo record book is in the SSSP. The subscription ran into other problems, see Garibaldi to Federico Bellazzi, 22 April and 3 June 1861, *Epistolario*, 6, pp. 88–9, 113–15.

3. 7 Aug. 1860 [henceforth 1860 unless stated], G. Piola to Bertani, in MRM, Bertani, cartella 11, plico xii, n. 62/8.

4. 8 and 21 July, in NA, FO 165/134.

5. 27 Aug., in *Memorie di Angelo Bargoni, 1829–1901*, Milan, 1911, p. 142.

6. 12 and 13 June, Giacinto Scelsi to Crispi, in F. Crispi, *Memoirs of Francesco Crispi. The Thousand*, vol. 1, 3 vols, London, 1912–14, pp. 226–7.

7. 15 June 1860, NA, FO 70/317.

8. 17 June, in Crispi, *Memoirs*, 1, pp. 228–9.

9. 1 July, I. Nievo, *Lettere garibaldine*, Turin, 1961, p. 27.

10. M. Menghini (ed.), *La spedizione garibaldina di Sicilia e di Napoli*, Turin, 1907, pp. 76, 104, 117–19.

11. See the analysis in N. Moe, *The view from Vesuvius. Italian culture and the Southern Question*, Berkeley and Los Angeles, 2002, pp. 156–83.

12. For a discussion of some of these issues, see F. Renda, 'Garibaldi e la questione contadina in Sicilia', in G. Cingari (ed.), *Garibaldi e il socialismo*, Rome and Bari, 1984; and for a broader analysis of the historiographical approach to which it relates, L. Riall, *Sicily and the unification of Italy. Liberal policy and local power, 1859–1866*, Oxford, 1998, pp. 1–29.

13. G. Falzone, 'Volontarismo siciliano', in *Atti del XXXIX congresso di storia del Risorgimento italiano*, Rome, 1961, p. 147.

14. L. Riall, 'Elites in search of authority: political power and social order in nineteenth-century Sicily', *History Workshop Journal*, 55, 2003, pp. 25–46.

15. F. Brancato, *Francesco Perroni Paladini, garibaldino e uomo politico*, Palermo, 1962, pp. 31–5.

16. Falzone, 'Volontarismo siciliano', pp. 166–70.

17. Rosario Lentini to the Marchese di Torralta, in C. E. di Torralta, 'La spedizione garibaldina del 1860 in alcune lettere di contemporanei', in *La Sicilia verso l'unità d'Italia*, Palermo, 1960, p. 63.

18. *La Frusta. Gazzetta semiquotidiana*, 10 July.
19. *La Costanza e la Supremazia d'Italia; L'Italia Redenta; L'Unità Italiana; La Guerra; Il Mondo Nuovo; Il Predicatore Italiano; La Libertà;* and *Il Garibaldi*.
20. *Il Garibaldi*, 6 and 23 June; *Gazzettino della Sera*, 27 June; *L'Unità Italiana*, 19 June (this paper should not be confused with the democratic paper published in Genoa). For Jourdain's article, see above, p. 249.
21. 6 June.
22. 4, 5 and 15 June.
23. 19 July.
24. 15 and 26 June, 21 July.
25. 6 June.
26. 13 Aug., 21 Sept.
27. 9 June.
28. 23 June; 13 Aug.
29. N.d., 1, n.3.
30. 21 June, and 6, 11, 14, 16 June.
31. 12 June.
32. *Il Vessillo Italiano*, 5 June.
33. *Il Garibaldi*, 6 June; *La Forbice*, 5 and 6 June; *L'Unità Italiana*, 9 June; *La Cicala Italiana*, 13 Aug.
34. See *La Forbice* ('*Quanto pasticci*'), 2 Oct., and especially *Tom Pouce* ('Signor Basile, if Garibaldi only knew!!!'), 3 Oct.
35. See e.g. *Il Garibaldi*, 19 June; *La Mola*, 20 July; *La Forbice*, 21 July.
36. 15 June.
37. ASP, Ministero e Segreteria di Stato presso il Luogotenente Generale, Ripartimento dell'Interno (1818–1864), b.1608, f.pubblica spettacoli dal n. 1 al n. 3 da giugno a dicembre (which includes the programme and illustrations of the show).
38. These flyers are in the Biblioteca di Storia Moderna e Contemporanea in Rome, and published in D. Bertoni Jovine (ed.), *I periodici popolari del Risorgimento*, 2 vols, Milan, 1959, 2, pp. 139–40.
39. 9 June and 4 July.
40. P. Chiara, *Garibaldi dall'Italia alla gran giornata della Sicilia già mossa*, Palermo, 1860; C. Pardi, *A Giuseppe Garibaldi. Ode*, Palermo, 1860.
41. V. Navarro di Ribera, *Il Garibaldi*, Palermo, 1860.
42. L. Capuana, *Garibaldi, leggenda drammatica in tre canti*, Catania, 1861.
43. 12 June, quoted in F. Brancato, 'La partecipazione del clero alla rivoluzione siciliana del 1860', in *La Sicilia verso l'unità d'Italia*, p. 17.
44. 5 June, ibid.
45. From *La Nazione* of 29 July, in M. Menghini (ed.), *La spedizione garibaldina*, p. 446.
46. Brancato, 'La partecipazione', pp. 18–26.
47. C. S. Forbes, *The campaign of Garibaldi in the Two Sicilies. A personal narrative*, Edinburgh and London, 1861, p. 128.
48. A. Mario, *The red shirt. Episodes*, London, 1865, pp. 3–4.
49. G. Tricoli, 'Il mito di Garibaldi in Sicilia', *Archivio Storico Siciliano*, series 4, 9, 1983, pp. 90–1.
50. Mario, *The red shirt*, pp. 3–4; G. Nuvolari, *Come la penso*, Milan, 1881 [1861], p. 299; G. C. Abba, *The diary of one of Garibaldi's Thousand*, Oxford, 1962, pp. 67, 71, 79, 84–5.
51. Francesco Lanza, 5 Nov. MRM, Garibaldi Curàtulo, f. 470.
52. 21 Dec., 23 March 1861, ibid., f. 268.
53. C. E. di Torralta, 'La spedizione garibaldina del 1860 in alcune lettere di contemporanei', in *La Sicilia verso L'Unità*', pp. 55, 69, 73.
54. Brancato, 'La partecipazione', pp. 24–5, 27–8.

55. S. Salomone-Marino, 'Garibaldi e le tradizioni popolari', *Archivio per lo studio delle tradizioni popolari*, 1, 1882, pp. 459–60.

56. G. M. Trevelyan, *Garibaldi and the Thousand*, London, 1909, pp. 306–7 (Trevelyan was told the legend by Giuseppe Pitrè); Tricoli, 'Il mito di Garibaldi', pp. 91–3.

57. C. Duggan, *Francesco Crispi, 1818–1901. From nation to nationalism*, Oxford, 2002, pp. 179–80.

58. S. Salomone-Marino, *Leggende popolari siciliane in poesia*, Palermo, 1880, pp. vii–xxii.

59. E.g.'La rivuluzioni di lu 1860'; 'Lu cummattimentu di Calatafimi'; 'Lu sbàrchitu di Canibardi a Marsala'; 'La trasuta di Canibardi a Palermu'; 'Lu bummardamentu di Palermu', in Salomone-Marino, *Leggende popolari*, pp. 343–53.

60. Ibid., pp. 361–2.

61. Idem, *Canti popolari siciliani in aggiunta a quelli di Vico*, Palermo, 1867, n. 741, p. 287.

62. Idem, *La trasuta di Garibaldi a Palermu. Storia popolare siciliana in poesia*, Palermo, 1885, p. 10.

63. C. di Mino, 'Il Risorgimento italiano nei canti del popolo siciliano', *Rassegna Storica del Risorgimento*, 18, 1931, suppl. p. 226: see also in S. di Paola, 'Il mito di Garibaldi nella poesia italiana', in F. Mazzonis (ed.), *Garibaldi condottiero. Storia, teoria, prassi*, Milan, 1984, pp. 512–13.

64. B. Messana, 'Dialogu tra lu Generali Lamoriciere e lu Cardinal Antonelli doppu l'entrata di Garibaldi in Napuli', in *Poesie liberali siciliani*, Palermo, 1860, pp. 93–4.

65. Salomone-Marino, 'Garibaldi e le tradizioni popolari', p. 461.

66. Ibid., pp. 460–1.

67. Salomone-Marino, *La trasuta di Garibaldi*, pp. 11–12.

68. Idem, 'Garibaldi e le tradizioni popolari', p. 59.

69. T. Cannizzaro, 'Frammenti di canti popolari politici', *Archivio per lo studio delle tradizioni popolari*, 7, 1888, p. 140.

70. Salomone-Marino, *Canti popolari*, p. 288.

71. Ibid., p. 287.

72. Idem, *La trasuta di Garibaldi*, p. 9.

73. Di Paola, 'Il mito di Garibaldi', p. 514.

74. 18 Sept.

75. These (very approximate) figures and those below are obtained from C. Cipolla, *Le avventure della lira*, Bologna, 1975, table. A6, p. 145, and http://eh.net/hmit.

76. On Bertani's role in 1860, see A. Galante Garrone, *I radicali in Italia, 1849–1925*, Milan, 1973, pp. 42–6.

77. R. Grew, *A sterner plan for Italian unity. The Italian national society in the Risorgimento*, Princeton, NJ, 1963, p. 296.

78. See the breakdown of figures, ibid., pp. 396–404; Trevelyan, *The Thousand*, App. K, pp. 340–1; G. M. Trevelyan, *Garibaldi and the making of Italy*, London, 1911, App. C, pp. 321–2. Bertani gives the subscription list for his fund in *Resoconto della cassa centrale soccorso a Garibaldi, 1860*, Genoa, 1860, and for the other funds in *Le spedizioni per i volontari per Garibaldi*, Genoa, 1861. On his work, see C. Maraldi, *La spedizione dei Mille e l'opera di Agostino Bertani*, Palermo, 1940.

79. 29 May, Carlo Strada, in MRM, Bertani, cartella 12, plico xiii, n.121.

80. 22 March, Filippo Collo Cavanna in Molazzano, MCRR, b.45, n. 26/76.

81. L. Oliphant, *Episodes in a life of adventure*, Edinburgh and London, 1887, p. 174.

82. P. Ginsborg, 'Risorgimento rivoluzionario: mito e realtà di una guerra di popolo', *Storia e Dossier*, 47, 1991, pp. 61–97.

83. Trevelyan, *The making of Italy*, pp. 36–7, 321.

84. MRM, Bertani, cartella 12, plico xiii, n. 6.

85. 11 May, Cesare Pescetto, ibid., n. 26.

86. 12 May, Giovanni Guarlotti in Galliate, ibid., n. 28.

87. 11 May, Giacomo Abelli in Saluzzo, ibid., n. 31.

88. 18 May, Filippo Torricelli in Turin, ibid., n. 33.
89. 19 May, Romano Campagnola in Casale, ibid., n. 73.
90. 25 May, ibid., n. 110.
91. Demetrio Cialdini in Modena, ibid., n. 99.
92. 10 May, C. Moreto and T. Brocchieri from Milan, ibid., n. 17.
93. 22 Aug., Giovanni Camponovo in Coleah, ibid., cartella 13, plico xvi, n. 42.
94. E.g. 14 May, Pontoli in Parma, ibid., cartella 12, plico xiii n. 104; 25 May, Marchetti, ibid., n. 109; 15 June, Santo Polli in Gallarate, ibid., plico xiv, n. 6; 16 June, Gaspare Finali in Turin (Camera dei Deputati), ibid., n. 14; 4 June, Giuseppe Levi in Milan, ibid., n. 133; 29 June, Antonio Sergent in Milan, ibid., n. 192.
95. 11 and 15 May, from Giacomo Abelli, ibid., plico xiii, n. 31; plico xiv, n. 144; see also e.g. 10 May, Pietro Massa, ibid., plico xiii, n. 20; 11 May, P. Cacciò in Piacenza, ibid., n. 25; 18 May, Filippo Torricelli in Turin, ibid., n. 33; 19 May, the *comitato di soccorso per la Sicilia* in Brescia, ibid., n. 69.
96. 10 June, Volpino Volpini in Tredozio, ibid., plico xiv, n. 218.
97. 4 July, Teresa Penco, ibid., plico xv, n. 180; quoted in Trevelyan, *The Thousand*, p. 38.
98. Most of these relate to Garibaldi's companion, Maria della Torre, but see the mentions in W. B. Brooke, *Out with Garibaldi: or from Milazzo to Capua*, London, 1860, pp. 238–9; and E. Maison, *Journal d'un volontaire de Garibaldi*, Paris, 1861, pp. 96–7; and the discussion in L. Guidi, 'Patriottismo femminile e travestimenti sulla scena risorgimentale', *Studi Storici*, 41/2, 2000, pp. 571–87.
99. 14 May, Defendente Mapelli in Monza, MRM, Bertani, cartella 12, plico xiii, n. 62.
100. 30 May, Luigi Bergeno in Saluzzo, ibid., n. 127. See also the letter of 23 May, Francesco Allegro in Oneglia, ibid., n. 98.
101. 17 May, G. Giucciardi in Milan, ibid., n. 38.
102. 15 June, Giuseppe Briasco in Genoa, ibid., plico xiv, n. 24.
103. 18 June, Stefano Castiglioni in Angera, ibid., n. 33.
104. 17 June, Salvolini in Novi, ibid., n. 15.
105. 28 June, in Sarzana, ibid., n. 250.
106. 7 May, Cesare Crugati in Montespluga, ibid., plico xiii, n. 13.
107. 13 June, Pietro Gillio in Turin, ibid., plico xiv, n. 213.
108. 13 June, Giacomo Talassano in Savona, ibid., n. 208.
109. 21 June, Giovanni Moro, ibid., n. 67.
110. 29 May, Angelo Pavesi, ibid., plico xiii, n. 123.
111. 26 Sept., Stefano Canessa, ibid., Garibaldi Curàtulo, f. 471.
112. 23 May, Vincenzo Ghirardini in Cremona, ibid., Bertani, cartella 12, plico xiii, n. 100.
113. 14 May, in Brescello, ibid., n. 66.
114. 22 May, Enrico Ruspini in Cuneo, ibid., n. 91.
115. 11 June, Carlo Romagnani in Lugo, ibid., plico xiv, n. 99.
116. 1, 4, 5 and 14 June, Marco Fasolis de Salineri, ibid., n. 85, 151, 188, 190.
117. 12 June, ibid., n. 320.
118. 20 June, Domenico Casanova in Pinerolo, ibid., n. 49. His second letter (25 June) is published in Maraldi, *La spedizione dei Mille*, pp. 157–8, along with a selection of other letters begging to be allowed to volunteer.
119. Trevelyan, *The making of Italy*, App. B, pp. 316–19.
120. MRM, Bertani, cartella n.13, plichi xv–xvi; cartella 15, plico xxii.
121. Trevelyan, *The making of Italy*, App. B, pp. 316–19. See the comment added to the letter of 30 May 1860, MRM, Bertani, cartella 12, plico xiii, n. 126.
122. 23 May, Giorgio Gilette, ibid., n. 97.
123. Ibid., plico xiv, n. 89.
124. F. Conti, *L'Italia dei democratici*, Milan, 2000, p. 78.
125. 21 June, MRM, Bertani, cartella 12, plico xiv, n. 64; 11 June, ibid., n. 99; 23 June 1860, ibid., ns. 116 and 121. These comments are instructions apparently written by Bertani

to his secretaries on the back of each letter: the actual letters of rejection are missing.

126. 13 June, Antonio Scotti in Lodi, ibid., n. 228.

127. 31 May, Paolo Francesco Ramella in Turin, ibid., plico xiii, n. 131 (and see 12 May, ibid., n. 34).

128. E.g. 24 May, Pietro Venchi in Robbio Lomellina, ibid., n. 106; 10 June 1860, Luigi Monari in Novara, ibid., plico xiv, n. 187.

129. 13 June, ibid., n. 226; on Bertani's state of health, see Trevelyan, *The making of Italy*, p. 38.

130. E.g. 6 May, MRM, Bertani, cartella 12, plico xiii, n. 10; 7 May, ibid., n. 12; 10 May, ibid., nn.18 and 20; 11 May, ibid., n. 25; 16 May, ibid., n. 49, 15 May, ibid., n. 59; 14 May, ibid., nn. 65 and 66; 19 May, ibid., nn. 69 and 72; 20 May, ibid., n. 79; 21 May 1860, ibid., n. 96; 20 June, ibid., plico xiv, nn. 51 and 53.

131. 6 May, Giuseppe Redaelli in Lande St Maurizio, ibid., plico xiii, n. 10.

132. 30 May, Achille Regard in Casale, ibid., n. 125.

133. 12 June, Giacomo Taricchi in Chesrasco, ibid., plico xiv, n. 234.

134. 27 June, Ottavo Ferrero, ibid., n. 246.

135. One or two correspondents complain about the 'lack of energy' of the Piedmontese government: e.g. 21 May, Nob. Gio. Batt. Contarini in Milan, ibid., plico xiii, n. 96; and another, Angelo Pavesi, complains about 'hardships of every kind' in Pavia, 29 May, ibid., n. 123.

136. 1 Feb. 1861, Anna Ingram in London, ibid., Garibaldi Curàtulo, f. 449.

137. M. O'Connor, *The romance of Italy and the English political imagination*, London, 1998, p. 90; M. C. Finn, *After Chartism. Class and nation in English radical politics, 1848–74*, Cambridge, 1993, pp. 206–7. The currency figures are based on calculations given by http://eh.net/hmit.

138. J. Ridley, *Garibaldi*, London, 1974, p. 459.

139. According to a flyer dated 20 June, and a letter from the 'Honorary Secretary' dated 29 Dec. in MCRR, b.53 11/4.

140. 19 Dec., in MRM, Garibaldi Curàtulo, f. 449.

141. MCRR, b.52, 3/96.

142. 30 Nov., in MRM, Garibaldi Curàtulo, f. 449.

143. H. Marraro, *American opinion on the unification of Italy, 1846–61*, New York, 1932, p. 304; http://eh.net/hmit.

144. 18 Sept., and n.d., both in MRM, Garibaldi Curàtulo, f. 449.

145. These details are in Marraro, *American opinion*, pp. 287–95, and Ridley, *Garibaldi*, p. 462.

146. N.d., in MRM, Garibaldi Curàtulo, f. 449.

147. Trevelyan, *The making of Italy*, pp. 48–9; App. B, pp. 316–20.

148. Marraro, *American opinion*, pp. 285–7.

149. 19 Nov., in MRM, Garibaldi Curàtulo, f. 449.

150. Trevelyan, *The making of Italy*, pp. 64–5; see also Dunne's obituary in *The Times*, 3 Dec. 1906.

151. Trevelyan, *The making of Italy*, pp. 259–61.

152. J. Fyfe (ed.), *Autobiography of John McAdam (1806–1883)*, Edinburgh, 1980, pp. 44–5; McAdam's letter to Holyoake, 28 May, ibid., pp. 130–1.

153. F. Boyer, 'Souscriptions pour Garibaldi en France (1860)', *Rassegna Storica del Risorgimento*, 47/1, 1960, pp. 69–74.

154. Idem, 'Les Volontaires français avec Garibaldi en 1860', *Revue d'Histoire Moderne et Contemporaine*, 7, 1960, pp. 126–7, 142–3; see also the same author's 'Journalistes, volontaires et armateurs français à Gênes en 1860', in *Genova e l'impresa dei Mille*, 2 vols, Rome, 1961, 2, pp. 539–50.

155. M. Paolino, 'Johann Philipp Becker ed il Risorgimento Italiano', *Rassegna Storica del Risorgimento*, 85/2, 1998, p. 219.

156. 2 Aug., 16 Sept. and 14 Dec., in MRM, Garibaldi Curàtulo, f. 449.
157. 18 Sept., ibid.; see also John Connor's letter of 5 Oct. and Elisabeth Hodges' letter of 8 Dec., also ibid.
158. 19 Nov., ibid.
159. 27 Nov., in MCRR, b.53, 11/3.
160. 27 Aug., signed 'La Barone de Walniew', in MRM, Garibaldi Curàtulo, f. 470.
161. 10 Nov. and 25 Nov., ibid., f. 449 (the latter writer had also fought with Garibaldi in Brazil).
162. 18 Aug., ibid.
163. N.d., from Elisabeth Murray; 5 Nov., from John Sullivan, ibid.
164. Quoted in Ridley, *Garibaldi*, p. 460.
165. 10 Nov., in MRM, Garibaldi Curàtulo, f. 449.
166. 24 Sept., ibid.
167. On the importance of Protestantism in Britain and the USA, see G. Spini, *Risorgimento e Protestanti*, Naples, 1956, esp. pp. 274–365, and more generally G. Best, 'Popular Protestantism in Victorian Britain', in R. Robson (ed.), *Ideas and institutions of Victorian Britain. Essays in honour of George Kitson Clark*, London, 1967, pp. 115–42.
168. 6 Aug., in MRM, Garibaldi, Curàtulo, f. 449.
169. 23 Nov., ibid.
170. 1 Nov., ibid.
171. W.G. Clark, 'Naples and Garibaldi', in F. Galton (ed.), *Vacation tourists and notes of travel in 1860*, Cambridge, 1861, pp. 35–6 (he suggests that they were taken to visit the prisons on government orders); Forbes, *The campaign*, pp. 252–6; R. Mundy, *HMS 'Hannibal' at Palermo and Naples during the Italian revolution, 1859–61*, London, 1863, p. 255; A. S. Bucknell, *In the tracks of the Garibaldians through Italy and Sicily*, London, 1861, pp. 132–8.
172. Best, 'Popular Protestantism', p. 117.
173. Boyer, 'Les Volontaires français', pp. 133–5.
174. G. J. Holyoake, *Bygones worth remembering*, London, 1905, pp. 244–54.
175. Brooke, *Out with Garibaldi*, p. 6.
176. Trevelyan, *The making of Italy*, p. 260.
177. John McAdam had to go to considerable trouble to get them home, going out to Naples with money and borrowing more, and he was left personally 'out of pocket' from the whole experience. Fyfe (ed.), *Autobiography*, pp. 47–8, and his letters, pp. 140–9.
178. See the correspondence in MCRR, b.53, n.11/1, 2, and 5a and b.
179. M. Milan, 'Opinione pubblica e antigaribaldinismo in Francia: la *querelle* sull'unità d'Italia (1860–1868)', *Rassegna Storica del Risorgimento*, 70/2, 1983, pp. 150–4.
180. N.d. MCRR, b.53, f. 11/52.
181. Ridley, *Garibaldi*, pp. 460–1.
182. O. Chadwick, *A history of the Popes, 1830–1914*, Oxford, 1998, p. 145.
183. C. Clark, 'The new Catholicism and the European culture wars', in idem and W. Kaiser (eds), *Culture wars. Secular–Catholic conflict in nineteenth-century Europe*, Cambridge, 2003, p. 21.
184. Ibid., pp. 148–51.
185. E. Larkin, *The consolidation of the Roman Catholic Church in Ireland, 1860–70*, Dublin, 1987, p. 13.
186. G. F. H. Berkeley, *The Irish battalion in the papal army of 1860*, Dublin, 1929, pp. 32–9, 240–1.
187. Larkin, *The consolidation*, p. 50; this is an important point, as in other respects the Irish brigade suffered great problems of morale and discipline, leading to what Larkin calls a 'perceptible cooling' in Irish–Roman relations: Cullen himself anticipated this, writing on 21 June that '[p]robably the whole affair will end up a fiasco – like some of

the Crusades'. Ibid., p. 19.
188. R. Jonas, *France and the cult of the sacred heart. An epic tale for modern times*, Berkeley, CA, 2000, pp. 3–5, 158–60.
189. Clark, 'The new Catholicism', p. 13.
190. Forbes, *The campaign*, pp. 340–1.
191. 6 Aug., in *Scritti e discorsi*, 1, pp. 285–8.
192. See L. Cole, 'Introduction: re-examining national identity in nineteenth-century Central Europe and Italy', in idem (ed.), *Different paths to the nation: regional and national identities in Central Europe and Italy, 1830–1870*, Basingstoke, 2006, pp. 1–15.
193. M. Schwegman, 'In love with Garibaldi: romancing the Italian Risorgimento', *European Review of History*, 12/2, 2005, pp. 371–2.

Chapter 11: Unification

1. 18 Oct. 1860, *Epistolario*, 5, p. 266.
2. End Nov. 1860, ibid., p. 285, first published in the *New York Herald*, 14 Dec. 1860.
3. 6 Nov. 1860, *Epistolario*, 5, p. 278, first published in *Il Diritto*, 17 Nov. 1860, p. 278.
4. 30 Dec. 1860, in *Epistolario*, 5, p. 293.
5. 7 Nov. 1860, ibid., p. 281.
6. P. Pieri, *Storia militare del Risorgimento*, Turin, 1962, p. 733.
7. 13 Jan. 1861, *Epistolario*, 6, pp. 8–9. On the *comitati*, see A. Galante Garrone, *I radicali in Italia, 1849–1925*, Milan, 1973, pp. 57–9.
8. 30 Jan. 1861, *Epistolario*, 6, p. 27.
9. 4 Feb. 1861, ibid., p. 30.
10. 4 March 1861, ibid., p. 54.
11. 17 March 1861, from Costantino Nigra, in D. Mack Smith (ed.), *The making of Italy, 1796–1866*, London, 2nd edn, 1988, pp. 366–7.
12. See his letters in *Epistolario*, 6, pp. 13, 15, 29, 37.
13. 13 March 1861, ibid., pp. 56–7.
14. 30 March 1861, ibid., pp. 63–4. On the *società operaie*, see Galante Garrone, *I radicali*, pp. 59–61.
15. *La libera parola. Foglio estraordinario pel giorno onomastico del Generale Garibaldi*, Catania, 19 March 1861.
16. C. Pardi, *Pel primo anniversario del 4 aprile. Orazione*, Palermo, 1861.
17. 25 Feb. 1861, to Flora Dorant, *Epistolario*, 6, p. 48.
18. Riboli's letter is in E. Maison, *Caprera. Les loisirs de Garibaldi*, Paris, 1861, App., pp. 25–31. On the popularity of phrenology among radicals (in Britain), see T. M. Parssinen, 'Popular science and society: the phrenology movement in early Victorian Britain', *Journal of Social History*, 8/1, 1974, pp. 1–20.
19. M. Paolino, 'Johann Philipp Becker ed il Risorgimento Italiano', *Rassegna Storica del Risorgimento*, 85/2, 1998, pp. 216–37; the title 'German Garibaldi' is Jenny Marx's. See also the correspondence between Garibaldi, Becker and Mieroslawski in MRM, Garibaldi Curàtulo, f. 266.
20. J. Fyfe (ed.), *Autobiography of John McAdam (1806–1883)*, Edinburgh, 1980, p. 63. See McAdam's letter to Garibaldi, 13 Jan. 1861, in MCRR, b.54 f. 1/8.
21. Col. Vecchi, *Garibaldi at Caprera* (trans. Mrs Gaskell), London, 1862, pp. vii–xi, 22–3, 58, 94. See also the descriptions of various visitors in Riboli's letter in Maison, *Caprera*, App., pp. 25–6.
22. Writing as Elpis Melena, *Hundert und ein Tag auf meinem Pferde und ein Ausflug nach der Insel Maddalena*, Hamburg, 1860; *Garibaldi at home: a visit to the Mediterranean islands of La Maddalena and Caprera*, London, 1860; *Recollections of General Garibaldi; or travels from Rome to Lucerne: comprising a visit to the Mediterranean islands of La Maddalena and Caprera*, London, 1861; *Excursion à l'île de Caprera*,

Geneva, 1862. She also published a version of Garibaldi's memoirs (*Garibaldi's Denkwürdigkeiten*) in Hamburg in 1861.

23. The illustrations are in *ILN*, 26 Jan. 1861, pp. 71 (the front page), 74–5, 79 (this edition also had a colour portrait); Vizitelly's description is in the 2 Feb. edition, pp. 105–6.

24. *Garibaldi, Arte e storia*, 2 vols, Florence, 1982, 1, cat. 3.3.11, pp. 105–6.

25. *Giuseppe Garibaldi da Caprera ad Aspromonte, 1860–61–62. Memorie storiche raccolta da Felice Venosta*, Milan, n.d., pp. 4, 5, 11.

26. *Die Gartenlaube*, 1866, n.2. p. 32.

27. Maison, *Caprera*, p. 6, App., p. 25.

28. C. MacGrigor, *Garibaldi at home. Notes of a visit to Caprera*, London, 1866, p. 39.

29. *Il tributo all'immortale Giuseppe Garibaldi o sia catechismo politico costituzionale italiano per la necessaria istruzione del popolo*, Naples, 2nd edn, 1861, p. 5.

30. *Garibaldi a Caprera*, Turin, 1861; *Garibaldi e Caprera*, Naples, 1862; *Garibaldi en Caprera*, Utrecht, 1861; *Garibaldi et Caprera*, Utrecht, 1862; *Garibaldi på Caprera*, Stockholm, 1862; *Garibaldi auf Caprera*, Leipzig, 1862. I have used the English version, see above, note 21.

31. Vecchi, *Garibaldi*, pp. 7–8, 38, 43–5.

32. Ibid., p. 2.

33. Ibid., pp. 55, 75.

34. Letter of 3 Jan. 1861, in Fyfe (ed.), *John McAdam*, p. 51.

35. 4 Feb. 1861, *Epistolario*, 6, p. 29.

36. 2 Feb. 1861, MCRR, b.47 f. 2/2; 9 April 1861, MRM, Garibaldi Curàtulo, f. 383 (and see Garibaldi's reply in *Epistolario*, 6, pp. 62–3).

37. 28 Oct., 14 Nov., 22 and 24 Dec. 1860, MRM, Garibaldi Curàtulo, f. 470.

38. 25 Dec. 1860, ibid., f. 453

39. 6 May 1861, MCRR, b.54 f. 1/4; 2 March 1861, ibid., b.53, f. 11/9.

40. 26 Feb. 1861, ibid., b.53, f. 57.

41. 3 Dec. 1860, MRM, Garibaldi Curàtulo, f. 566.

42. 30 Jan. and 8 Feb. 1861, ibid., f. 449.

43. 31 Jan. 1861, in MCRR, b.53 f. 11/7 (Garibaldi's reply in *Epistolario*, 6, p. 65, and published in *Il Diritto* and *L'Unità Italiana* on 6 April). Ashley's letter of 9 April is in MRM, Garibaldi Curàtulo, f. 449.

44. Both letters 30 Jan. 1861, ibid.

45. C. Duggan, *Francesco Crispi, 1818–1901. From nation to nationalism*, Oxford, 2002, p. 245.

46. Galante Garrone, *I radicali*, pp. 49–50, 56.

47. 4 Feb. 1861, in *Epistolario*, 6, p. 30.

48. Galante Garrone, *I radicali*, pp. 53–4, 72.

49. L. Riall, *Sicily and the unification of Italy. Liberal policy and local power, 1859–66*, Oxford, 1998, pp. 123–30; A. Scirocco, *Il Mezzogiorno nella crisi dell'unificazione, 1860–1*, Naples, 1981.

50. Pieri, *Storia militare*, pp. 734–5; F. Molfese, 'Lo scioglimento dell'esercito meridionale garibaldino 1860–1', *Nuova Rivista Storica*, 44, 1960, pp. 1–53.

51. E. Francia, *Le baionette intelligenti. La guardia nazionale nell'Italia liberale (1848–1876)*, Bologna, 1999, pp. 57–86; P. Pieri, *Le forze armate nella età della Destra*, Milan, 1962, pp. 66–7.

52. Riall, *Sicily*, pp. 138–55; F. Molfese, *Storia del brigantaggio dopo l'unità*, Milan, 1964; J. A. Davis, *Conflict and control. Law and order in nineteenth-century Italy*, London, 1988, pp. 168–86.

53. 22 Nov. 1860, to Cavour, in D. Mack Smith (ed.), *Garibaldi*, Englewood Cliffs, NJ, 1969, p. 60.

54. 11 April 1861, in *Epistolario*, 6, pp. 78–9.

55. Florence MacKnight, MRM, Garibaldi Curàtulo, f. 566; Caroline Gifford Philippson, ibid., f. 580.
56. *The Times,* 23 April 1861.
57. H. d'Ideville, *Journal d'un diplomate en Italie,* Paris, 1871, 1, pp. 179–80, and in Mack Smith (ed.), *Garibaldi,* p. 60; see also the description in Madame C. de Bunsen, *In three legations. Turin, Florence, The Hague,* London, 1909, pp. 136–9.
58. M. Isabella, 'Exile and nationalism: the case of the Risorgimento', *European History Quarterly,* 36/4, 2006, p. 496.
59. The speech is in Mack Smith (ed.), *The making of Italy,* pp. 348–52.
60. 23 April 1861.
61. Mack Smith (ed.), *The making of Italy,* p. 352; the full text of the debate is in *Garibaldi in parlamento, 1. Dalla repubblica romana a Aspromonte,* Rome, 1982, pp. 89–237.
62. J. Ridley, *Garibaldi,* London, 1974, pp. 519–20.
63. 29 April 1861, *Epistolario,* 6, pp. 94–6. See also 22 April 1861, ibid., pp. 89–90.
64 . 18 May 1861, ibid., pp. 104–6.
65. At least from the foreign audience in parliament, see *The Times,* 23 April; D'Ideville, *Journal,* and De Bunsen, *In three legations.*
66. 12 April 1861, NA, 30/22/68.
67. On this episode, about which there was considerable debate, see Ridley, *Garibaldi,* pp. 520–4; and a recent discussion in *The Times,* 9 Feb. 2000.
68. Ridley, *Garibaldi,* pp. 525–6.
69. Duggan, *Francesco Crispi,* p. 248.
70. Galante Garrone, *I radicali,* pp. 64–71.
71. D. Mack Smith, 'Constitutional monarchy, 1861–1865', in idem, *Victor Emanuel, Cavour and the Risorgimento,* London, 1971, pp. 283–8; Duggan, *Francesco Crispi,* p. 249.
72. Most of these letters can be found in MCRR, b.50, f. 1–2; b.45, f. 26–7.
73. 23 Jan. 1862, from Leopold Comte Ribarola, ibid., b.50 f. 2/19.
74. Dec. 1861, ibid., b.47 f. 2/5.
75. N.d. (but in 1861–6 file), ibid., b.316 f. 32/5.
76. Jan. 1862, ibid., b.45 f. 26/53.
77. 17 Oct. 1861, ibid., b.52, f. 3/54 (the letter is partly destroyed).
78. G. Guerzoni, *Garibaldi,* 2 vols, Florence, 1882, 2, pp. 284–7.
79 . G. Pécout, 'Les Sociétés de tir dans l'Italie unifiée de la seconde moitié du XIXe siècle', *Mélanges de l'Ecole Française de Rome,* pp. 544–50. Garibaldi's letters to the Rifle Clubs (March and April 1862) are in in *Epistolario,* 7, pp. 12–13, 18, 51, 61, 63–4, 68, 77–81.
80. Ibid., pp. 19–20, 28–9, 32–7, 39–40, 44–8, 53–60, 65, 69–70, 76–8, 83–7, 89, 91–5.
81. Pécout, 'Les Sociétés de tir', pp. 550–1.
82. 19 May 1862, *Scritti e discorsi,* 2, pp. 80–1 (see also his follow-up letter, pp. 81–2).
83. Duggan, *Francesco Crispi,* p. 250.
84. Mack Smith, 'Constitutional monarchy', p. 288.
85. Guerzoni, *Garibaldi,* 2, p. 300.
86. *Epistolario,* 7, p. 158.
87. 16 July 1862, ibid., p. 164.
88. July 1862, ibid., pp. 289, 292–5.
89. Ibid., pp. 165–7.
90. Almost all these speeches were published in *Il Diritto* and are republished in *Scritti e discorsi,* 2, pp. 96–123.
91. These were soldiers being tried for desertion, in ACS, Tribunali militari di guerra di Palermo, Messina, Catania e Catanzaro, 1860–6, b.1.
92. 19 Aug. 1862, telegram from the prefect of Catania to the prefect of Palermo, in G. Scichilone (ed.), *Documenti sulle condizioni della Sicilia dal 1860 al 1870,* Rome, 1952, p. 141.

93. Riall, *Sicily*, pp. 162–3; Mack Smith, 'Constitutional monarchy', pp. 289–91.
94. The decree is in MCRR, b.668, f. 34/5.
95. Riall, *Sicily*, pp. 163–7.
96. A. Bertani, *Scritti e discorsi*, 2 vols, Florence, 1890, 2, pt 1, p. 42.
97. Galante Garrone, *I radicali*, pp. 72–3, 78–9.
98. Quoted in Duggan, *Francesco Crispi*, pp. 259–60; on Sicily in 1863, see Riall, *Sicily*, pp. 167–78.
99. Guerzoni, *Garibaldi*, 2, p. 332; on his wounds, see E. Albanese, *La ferita di Garibaldi ad Aspromonte. Diario inedito della cura*, Milan, 1907.
100. '*Io e il popolo*', 4 Sept. 1862.
101. August 1862, vol. 56, p. 833.
102. P. Gut, 'Garibaldi et la France, 1848–1882. Naissance d'un mythe', *Rassegna Storica del Risorgimento*, 74/3, 1987, pp. 309–10.
103. 1 and 5 Sept. 1862.
104. *Epistolario*, 7, pp. 300–2; *Scritti e discorsi*, 2, pp. 146–9. *Il Diritto* was already involved with a polemic over Garibaldi's support of those arrested at Sarnico (see 'Garibaldi e la legge. Risposta all'opuscolo dell'Avvocato P. C. Boggio', published as a supplement to the paper, and as a separate pamphlet), so led the controversy over Aspromonte in Italy. Garibaldi's letter was also published in *The Times* on 10 Sept. 1862.
105. *Scritti e discorsi*, 2, pp. 150–3; quoted in M. Finn, *After Chartism. Class and nation in English radical politics, 1848–1874*, Cambridge, 1993, p. 208. This letter was also published in *Il Diritto*.
106. *Una voce dalle prigioni. Il fatto d'Aspromonte*, Lugano, 1862, p. 7.
107. *Aspromonte. Ricordi storico–militare*, Turin, 1862, p. 59.
108. *La verità sul fatto di Aspromonte, per un testimonio oculare*, Milan, 1862, p. 55.
109. *Cinque giorni in Calabria o la catastrofe d'Aspromonte per un volontario garibaldino*, Palermo (?), 1862, pp. 33–4.
110. C. Bianchi, *I martiri d'Aspromonte, cenni storici*, Milan, 2nd edn, 1863, title page.
111. Napoleon III was widely presumed to be behind the government's action at Aspromonte.
112. F. Pyat, *Lettera al Generale Garibaldi*, n.d. but 1862, p. 8.
113. *Garibaldi et la civilisation. La rédemption – les puissants – le Pape – mensonges de la civilisation – l'avenir*, Turin, 1862, pp. 7–8.
114. *Garibaldi, Arte e Storia*, 2, cat. 12, nn. 12–14, pp. 67–70.
115. W. Settimelli, *Garibaldi. L'album fotografico*, Florence, 1982, pp. 59–63.
116. *Giuseppe Garibaldi da Caprera ad Aspromonte*, p. 73.
117. A. Herzen, *My past and thoughts*, 6 vols, London, 1924–7, 5, p. 36.
118. Civica Raccolta delle Stampe A. Bertarelli, Milan, ASM, 36–65; *Arte e storia*, 2, pp. 219, 229–33 (which has other examples of the same theme).
119. Both are in *Epistolario*, 8, pp. 66, 130 (from MCRR).
120. See e.g. MCRR, b.52, f. 3, b.47, f. 2 & b.53, f. 11. For typical examples of Garibaldi's replies see his letter to Teodorina Muller, 7 Nov. 1862, *Epistolario*, 7, p. 220; to the students of Utrecht, 6 Dec., ibid., p. 244; and to the surgeon Nikolai Pirogov, 6 Aug. 1863, *Epistolario*, 8, p. 127.
121. Christopher Wordsworth's travel journal (1863), quoted in H. W. Rudman, *Italian nationalism and English letters*, London, 1940, p. 318.
122. 2 Nov. 1862, in MCRR, b.52, f. 3/52.
123. 3 Sept. 1862, ibid., f. 3/55.
124. Jan. 1863, ibid., b.51, f. 1/16.
125. Ridley, *Garibaldi*, p. 544.
126. 25 Oct. 1862, MCRR, b.54, f. 1/22.
127. 17 Oct. 1862, ibid., f. 1/19.

128. Ibid., b.53, f. 11/30–2.
129. 4 Dec. 1862 and 15 April 1863, ibid., f. 11/39 and 52.
130. Settimelli, *Garibaldi*, pp. 60–1.
131. Various '*indirizzi*' and subscriptions are in MCRR, b.51, f. 1/1–19; b.316, f. 32. Many of his replies are published in *Epistolario*, 7, pp. 199–200, 213–14, 245–7.
132. 19 Jan. 1863, ibid., 8, pp. 18–19.
133. 24 Feb. 1863, ibid., pp. 37–8.
134. Aug. 1863, ibid., pp. 128–30.
135. 1 and 2 March 1863, ibid., pp. 44–7.
136. See his letters to various priests, 11 and 15 Jan. 1863, ibid., p. 16; to Perroni Paladino [*sic*] and the editor of *L'Aspromonte* about the election of a candidate, 19 Jan., ibid., pp. 17–19; to the republican Giovanni Corrao, 1 March, ibid., p. 45; to '*alcuni amici palermitani*', 3 Nov., ibid., p. 166; and to the socialist Saverio Friscia, 25 Dec. ibid., p. 187.
137. Quoted in N. Blakiston, 'Garibaldi's visit to London in 1864', unpublished paper, BL, p. 3.
138. Quoted in L. Elda Funaro, 'Il viaggio di Garibaldi in Inghilterra e la crisi della democrazia italiana dopo l'unità', *Studi Storici*, 7/1, 1966, pp. 134–5, and more generally on the attitude of the Italian government, pp. 137–40.
139. Finn, *After Chartism*, pp. 214–17.
140. Fyfe (ed.), *John McAdam*, p. 67; D. Beales, 'Garibaldi in England: the politics of Italian enthusiasm', in J. A. Davis and P. Ginsborg (eds), *Society and politics in the age of the Risorgimento. Essays in honour of Denis Mack Smith*, Cambridge, 1991, p. 194.
141. 3 April 1864, in *Epistolario*, 8, p. 212: it was published in *The Times*, 4 April, and *Il Diritto* & *Unità Italiana*, 7 April.
142. Quoted in Elda Funaro, 'Il viaggio', pp. 147–8.
143. According to R. McWilliam, *The Tichbourne claimant: a Victorian sensation*, London, forthcoming.
144 . 12 April 1864.
145. Quoted in M. O'Connor, *The romance of Italy and the English political imagination*, London, 1998, p. 168. Her volume, along with Ridley, *Garibaldi*, pp. 546–64, Beales, 'Garibaldi in England', pp. 184–216, and J. A. Davis, 'Garibaldi in England,' *History Today* 32, 1982, pp. 21–6, are the most detailed accounts of Garibaldi's visit to England.
146. M. Reynolds, *The realms of verse. English poetry in a time of nation-building*, Oxford, 2001, pp. 3–8.
147. 12 April 1864, in Elda Funaro, 'Il viaggio', App. p. 155.
148. Mack Smith (ed.), *Garibaldi*, p. 132.
149. 12 April 1864.
150. Munby's diary, 11 April 1864, in D. Hudson (ed.), *Munby. Man of two worlds*, London, 1972, pp. 186–7.
151. 12 April 1864.
152. Diary entry for 11 April 1864, quoted in Beales, 'Garibaldi in England', p. 191.
153. Herzen, *My past and thoughts*, 5, p. 32.
154. Quoted in Beales, 'Garibaldi in England', p. 137.
155. Elda Funaro, 'Il viaggio', p. 139; Paul Cullen to Patrick Moran, 12 April 1864, Cullen papers, Dublin diocesan archives, f. 40/4 (also in C. Barr (ed.), *The correspondence of Paul Cullen*, Dublin, forthcoming).
156. Ridley, *Garibaldi*, pp. 549–51, 555–61; O'Connor, *The romance of Italy*, pp. 172–4.
157. The phrase is Matthew Truesdell's, *Spectacular politics. Louis-Napoleon Bonaparte and the 'Fête Impériale', 1849–1870*, Oxford, 1997.
158. E. Biagini, *Liberty, retrenchment and reform. Popular liberalism in the age of Gladstone, 1860–80*, Cambridge, 1992, p. 374; Beales, 'Garibaldi in England', p. 189.

159. Beales, 'Garibaldi in England', pp. 188–9; O' Connor, *The romance of Italy*, pp. 153–5, P. D. Gordon Pugh, *Staffordshire portrait figures and allied subjects of the Victorian era*, Woodbridge, 1970; R. McWilliam, 'The theatricality of the Staffordshire figurine; *Journal of Victorian Culture*, 10/1, 2005, pp. 107–14. On the Garibaldi biscuit, see http://en.wikipedia.org/wiki/Garibaldi_biscuit'. This British biscuit (two crackers with a currant filling) also bears a resemblance to a fruit bread, *pane dei pescatori*, still sold today on the Ligurian coast.

160. 'Hyam & Co.'s leading styles for the present season', advertising sheet, BL.

161. In M. Smith, *A wreath for Garibaldi*, London, 1864.

162. Quoted in Biagini, *Liberty*, p. 373.

163. Both on p. 3.

164. Colonel Chambers, *Garibaldi and Italian Unity*, London, 1864, p. 3.

165. Quoted in Finn, *After Chartism*, p. 221; on Princess Alexandra's arrival, see J. Plunkett, *Queen Victoria. First media monarch*, Oxford, 2003, pp. 51–2.

166. G. Claeys, 'Mazzini, Kossuth and British radicalism', *Journal of British Studies*, 28/3, 1989, pp. 227, 245–7.

167. J. Davis, 'Radical clubs and London politics, 1870–1900', in D. Feldman and G. Stedman Jones (eds), *Metropolis London. Histories and representations since 1800*, London, 1989, pp. 103–28; S. Shipley, *Club life and socialism in mid-Victorian London*, London, 1971.

168. Beales, 'Garibaldi in England', p. 186.

169. 18 April 1864, MRM, Garibaldi Curàtulo, b.449.

170. O'Connor, *The romance of Italy*, pp. 152–60, 177–8; see also the comments of J. Vernon, *Politics and the people*, Cambridge, 1993, pp. 265–6.

171. Anon. *The life of Garibaldi . . . Interspersed with anecdotes illustrative of his personal character. Compiled from original and authentic sources*, London, 1864, pp. 4, 17, 60.

172. 12 April 1864.

173. Quoted in Finn, *After Chartism*, p. 218.

174. Ibid., pp. 217–24.

175. Mack Smith (ed.), *Garibaldi*, p. 75.

176. Blakiston, 'Garibaldi's visit to London', p. 5.

177. Elda Funaro, 'Il viaggio', pp. 145, 152.

178. Beales, 'Garibaldi in England', pp. 199–216.

179. Elda Funaro, 'Il viaggio', p. 155.

180. Finn, *After Chartism*, pp. 223–5.

181. See Catherine Hall *et al.*, *Defining the Victorian Nation: Class, Race, Gender and the Reform Act of 1867*, Cambridge, 2000.

182. Quoted in O'Connor, *The romance of Italy*, p. 182.

183. H. E. Manning, *The visit of Garibaldi to England. A letter to the Right Hon. Edward Cardwell, M.P.*, London, 1864, p. 6; see also R. J. Cooper, *Three letters to the conservatives of England ... on the subject of Garibaldi and Revolution*, London, 1864.

184. S. Gilley, 'The Garibaldi riots of 1862', *Historical Journal*, 16/4, 1973, pp. 697–732.

185. To Myles O'Reilly, National Library of Ireland, MS 17,886; in Barr (ed.), *The correspondence of Paul Cullen*, forthcoming; N. Blakiston (ed.), *The Roman Question*, London, 1962, p. 285.

186. Quoted in Beales, 'Garibaldi in England', p. 193.

187. Hudson, (ed.), *Munby*, p. 187.

188. Mack Smith (ed.), *Garibaldi*, pp. 132–3.

189. Quoted in Ridley, *Garibaldi,*, pp. 558, 560.

190. MRM, Garibaldi Curàtulo, f. 657.

191. Ibid., f. 656. It was also considered surprising that at Stafford House she took him to her boudoir and allowed him to smoke there: Earl of Malmesbury, *Memoirs of an ex-minister*, London, 1885, pp. 593–4.

192. 29 April, 15 and 29 June 1864, MRM, Garibaldi Curàtulo, f. 656; see also her letters of 31 May, 11 July, 13, 26 and 31 Aug. 1864.
193. 23 April 1864, ibid., f. 632.
194. 24 April, 2 May and 1 June 1864, ibid.
195. 'May', 2 May, 20 June, 4 Aug., 5 Sept. 1864, ibid.
196. 2 and 24 May 1864, ibid.; MCRR, b.54, f. 1/42 (quoted in G. Monsagrati, 'Garibaldi e il culto vittoriano dell'eroe', *Studi Storici*, 42/1, 2001, p. 176).
197. Nanette Malleim, 14 Dec. 1866, MRM, Garibaldi Curàtulo, b.449.
198. O'Connor, *The romance of Italy*, pp. 154–6.
199. 24 May 1864, MRM, Garibaldi Curàtulo, f. 632.
200. Hudson (ed.), *Munby*, p. 187.
201. Mack Smith (ed.), *Garibaldi*, p. 133.
202. Quoted in Beales, 'Garibaldi in England', pp. 187–8.
203. 12 April ('Sauvage') and 15 May (MacKnight) 1861, both in MRM, Garibaldi Curàtulo, f. 566.
204. 20 Oct. 1864, ibid., f. 632.
205. 24 April and 13 June 1864, *Epistolario*, 8, pp. 57, 92–3.
206. 24 April and 7 June, ibid., p. 58.
207. 3 May 1864, ibid., p. 63.
208. According to a letter she wrote to him, 9 Oct. 1864, ibid., f. 629; and see also her frantic letter to him of 12 May, ibid.
209. This point is also made by O'Connor, *The romance of Italy*, pp. 112–15.
210. 15 April 1861, MRM, Garibaldi Curàtulo, f. 566.
211. 10 April and 9 Oct. 1864, ibid., f. 629.
212. 1 and 17 June 1864, ibid., f. 657.
213. 28 April and 22 Oct. 1864, ibid., f. 656.
214. G. Curàtulo, *Garibaldi e le donne*, Rome, 1913, pp. 59–65; see also her letter of 14 Oct. 1862, MCRR, b.54 f. 1/17.
215. *Le memorie di Garibaldi nella redazione definitiva del 1872*, Bologna, 1932, p. 499.
216. E. Mana, 'La "democrazia" italiana. Forme e linguaggi della propaganda politica tra Ottocento e Novocento', in M. Ridolfi (ed.), *Propaganda e communicazione politica*, Milan, 2004, p. 149.
217. Galante Garrone, *I radicali*, p. 157.

Chapter 12: Culture Wars

1. J. Ridley, *Garibaldi*, London, 1974, pp. 566–70.
2. D. Mack Smith, 'The king and the war of 1866', in idem, *Victor Emanuel, Cavour and the Risorgimento*, London, 1971, pp. 306–32.
3. Idem (ed.), *The making of Italy, 1796–1866*, London, 1988 edn, p. 392.
4. Quoted in C. Duggan, *Francesco Crispi, 1818–1901. From nation to nationalism*, Oxford, 2002, p. 283.
5. *Il Politecnico*, Sept. 1866, in Mack Smith (ed.), *The making of Italy*, pp. 392, 395.
6. L. Riall, *Sicily and the unification of Italy. Liberal policy and local power, 1859–1866*, Oxford, 1998, pp. 198–221.
7. Quoted in E. Gentile, *The sacralization of politics in fascist Italy*, Cambridge, MA, 1996, p. 6.
8. A. Galante Garrone, *I radicali in Italia, 1849–1925*, Milan, 1973, pp. 82–95; Duggan, *Francesco Crispi*, pp. 263–96.
9. D. Mack Smith, 'Victor Emanuel and the occupation of Rome', in idem, *Victor Emanuel*, pp. 344–5.
10. G. Verucci, *L'Italia laica prima e dopo l'unità, 1848–1876*, Rome and Bari, 1996 edn, p. 285.

11. D. Mack Smith, *Garibaldi*, London, 1957, pp. 159–60; on Lemmi, see C. Lovett, *The democratic movement in Italy, 1830–1876*, Cambridge, MA, 1982, pp. 177, 220.

12. *Scritti e discorsi*, 2, pp. 394–5, 399–401, 411. See also S. Morelli, *I tre disegni di legge sulla emancipazione della donna, riforma della pubblica istruzione e circoscrizione legale del culto cattolico nella chiesa. Preceduti da un manifesto di Giuseppe Garibaldi*, Florence, 1867.

13. For a discussion of anti-clerical culture and the left in Italy during this period, see Verucci, *L'Italia laica*, pp. 266–311.

14. Ridley, *Garibaldi*, pp. 573–82.

15. Duggan, *Francesco Crispi*, pp. 296–302; Mack Smith, 'Victor Emanuel', pp. 346–9.

16. Although some observers insist the Papal troops were winning, see the letter of Edwin Cushman, 14 Nov. 1867, in H. R. Marraro, 'Unpublished American documents on Garibaldi's march on Rome in 1867', *Journal of Modern History*, 16/2, 1944, pp. 119–21.

17. Mack Smith, 'Victor Emanuel', pp. 346–9; Ridley, *Garibaldi*, pp. 586–90.

18. In Marraro, 'Unpublished documents', p. 121.

19. Quoted in Mack Smith, 'Victor Emanuel', p. 352.

20. Quoted in Galante Garrone, *I radicali*, p. 96; on *Situazione*, see Verucci, *L'Italia laica*, pp. 314–15.

21. Verucci, *L'Italia laica*, p. 317.

22. Quoted in Galante Garrrone, *I radicali*, p. 98.

23. 7 Nov. 1867, quoted in C. Ceccuti, 'Garibaldi e la stampa democratica fiorentina fra 1860 al 1870', *Garibaldi e la Toscana. Atti del convegno di studi, 1982*, Florence, 1984, p. 94.

24. A. Körner, 'Local government and the meaning of political representation: a case study of Bologna between 1860 and 1915', *Modern Italy*, 10/2, 2005, pp. 139–42.

25. Raimondi had miscarried the child that she was pregnant with when she married Garibaldi.

26. On 'abstentionism', see Galante Garrone, *I radicali*, p. 98, 101–4.

27. Verucci, *L'Italia laica*, p. 201 (on the Vatican Council, see below, p. 378).

28. 22 Dec. 1867, in E. Ximenes (ed.), *Epistolario di Giuseppe Garibaldi*, Milan, 1885, p. 320.

29. 11 May 1868, ibid., p. 326; *Scritti e discorsi*, 3, pp. 8–9.

30. *Clelia, ovvero il governo del monaco (Roma nel secolo XIX)*, Milan, 1870 (it was preceded by an English translation); *Cantoni il volontario*, Milan, 1870. On the editorial history of these novels, see M. Martinengo, 'Garibaldi narratore', *Il Risorgimento*, 55/1, 1996, pp. 95–100; on their importance as political intervention, see below, pp. 370–2.

31. F. Boyer, 'Les Volontaires français avec Garibaldi en 1860', *Revue d'Histoire Moderne et Contemporaine*, 7, 1960, pp. 127–9.

32. *Scritti e discorsi*, 3, p. 47.

33. M. Howard, *The Franco-Prussian war. The German invasion of France, 1870–1*, London, 1961, pp. 205–56; for the numbers of men (said to be 16,645 at the end of the campaign), see R. Molis, *Les Francs-tireurs et les Garibaldi*, Paris, 1995, p. 260.

34. P. Gut, 'Garibaldi et la France, 1848–1882. Naissance d'un mythe', *Rassegna Storica del Risorgimento*, 74/1, 1987, p. 317.

35. Quoted in R. Paris, 'L'Italia fuori d'Italia', in *Storia d'Italia, 4. Dall'unità a oggi*, pt. 1, Turin, 1975, p. 510.

36. Ridley, *Garibaldi*, pp. 602–3.

37. 7 and 12 Sept. 1870, Ximenes, *Epistolario*, pp. 356–7; *Scritti e discorsi*, 3, pp. 46–7; for a discussion, see J. Petersen, 'Garibaldi und Deutschland 1870–71', in idem, *Italien-Bilder–Deutschland-Bilder*, Cologne, 1999, pp. 120–40. Thomas Carlyle proclaimed Germany's defeat of France as 'the hopefullest public fact that has occurred in my time',

quoted in J. Joll, *Europe since 1870. An international history*, London, 1990 edn, p. 1.

38. Quoted in Howard, *The Franco-Prussian war*, p. 253.
39. In D. Mack Smith (ed.), *Garibaldi*, Englewood Cliffs, NJ, 1969, p. 121.
40. Howard, *The Franco-Prussian war*, pp. 254, 407.
41. A. Vuilletet, *Garibaldi en France*, Paris, 1876, p. 99.
42. Quoted in Howard, *The Franco-Prussian war*, p. 429, and for a description of all these events, pp. 407–31.
43. Paris, 'L'Italia fuori d'Italia', p. 512.
44. Mack Smith (ed.), *Garibaldi*, p. 122; Gut, 'Garibaldi et la France', pp. 321–2; Ridley, *Garibaldi*, pp. 614–16.
45. K. Varley, 'Contesting concepts of the nation in arms: French memories of the war of 1870–1871 in Dijon', *European History Quarterly*, 36/4, 2006, pp. 548–83.
46. F. Cammarano, 'La costruzione dello Stato e la classe dirigente', in G. Sabatucci and V. Vidotto (eds), *Storia d'Italia, 2. Il nuovo stato e la società civile*, Rome and Bari, 1995, pp. 73–5.
47. Joll, *Europe since 1870*, p. 50.
48. Quoted in Galante Garrone, *I radicali*, p. 113.
49. *Scritti e discorsi*, 3, pp. 93–4.
50. Verucci, *L'Italia laica*, pp. 223–30.
51. Galante Garrone, *I radicali*, pp. 127–9.
52. On these works, see Martinengo, 'Garibaldi narratore', pp. 91–4, 100–8.
53. Verucci, *L'Italia laica*, pp. 300–1.
54. D. Pick, *Rome or death. The obsessions of General Garibaldi*, London, 2005 pp. 1–9.
55. 15 June 1875 and 13 May 1876, *Scritti e discorsi*, 3, pp. 155, 239.
56. F. Conti, *L'Italia dei democratici. Sinistra risorgimentale, massoneria e associazionismo fra '800 e '900*, Milan, 2000, pp. 88–113; A. Scirocco, 'Garibaldi e la lega della democrazia', in G. Cingari (ed.), *Garibaldi e il socialismo*, Rome and Bari, 1984, pp. 121–43; Galante Garrone, *I radicali*, pp. 193–5.
57. *Scritti e discorsi*, 3, pp. 308–9.
58. C. Garibaldi, *Mio padre*, Florence, 1948, pp. 136–7.
59. F. Brancato, 'Il vi centenario del vespro e l'ultimo viaggio di Garibaldi in Sicilia', *Nuovi Quaderni del Meridione*, 20, 1982, pp. 573–4, 586–90.
60. Pick, *Rome or death*, pp. 219–20.
61. Quoted in A. Scirocco, *Garibaldi. Battaglie, amori, ideali di un cittadino del mondo*, Rome and Bari, 2001, p. 391; and see the similar set of instructions in his 'Testamento politico', pp. 316–18, and its 'Appendice' 2 July 1881, *Scritti e discorsi*, 3, p. 318.
62. D. Mengozzi, *La morte e l'immortale. La morte laica da Garibaldi a Costa*, Manduria, 2000, p. 187.
63. Ibid., p. 316.
64. Verucci, *L'Italia laica*, pp. 235–6.
65. *The Times*, 10 June 1882; Scirocco, *Garibaldi*, pp. 391–3.
66. Mengozzi, *La morte e l'immortale*, pp. 213–14, 221–4. There is a photograph of the Roman 'funeral' in *Garibaldi. Arte e storia*, 2 vols, Florence, 1982, 2, fig.18.3, p. 91.
67. For a description, see Mengozzi, *La morte e l'immortale*, pp. 188–95.
68. *A Giuseppe Garibaldi. Parole di Enrico Panzacchi dette alla Associazione Progressista Costituzionale delle Romagne nell'adunanza dell'11 Giugno 1882*, Bologna, and Conegliano, 1882. F. Dolci, 'L'editoria d'occasione del secondo Ottocento', in *Il mito del Risorgimento nell' Italia unita*, Milan, 1995, pp. 124–48, counts 220 commemorative pamphlets published in 1882 alone; see also the list in idem (ed.), *Effemeridi patriotiche*, Rome, 1984.
69. *In morte di Giuseppe Garibaldi. Commemorazione. Codogno 8 giugno 1882*, Codogno, 1882; *Funebri onoranze a Giuseppe Garibaldi in Pisa, 15 giugno 1882*, Pisa, 1882; E. Befardeci, *Cenno necrologico di Giuseppe Garibaldi letto nel teatro greco di Siracusa il*

25 giugno 1882, Siracusa, 1882; *Commemorazione della morte del Generale Giuseppe Garibaldi, 30 aprile 1883*, Macerata, 1883.

70 . *Alla venerata memoria del prode dei prodi Giuseppe Garibaldi*, Messina, 1882, p. 12.

71. Avv. L. Fulci, *Garibaldi. Conferenza tenuta nella grande aula della Università di Messina*, Messina, 1882; G. De' Nobili, *Apoteosi di Garibaldi. Discorso*, Trapani, 1882.

72. M. Caselli, 'Garibaldi è morto!', Naples, 1882.

73. *A Giuseppe Garibaldi. Parole di cordoglio pronunziate il 17 giugno 1882 nella ricorrenza delle civile onoranze resegli in Pachino*, Noto, 1882.

74. *Arte e storia*, 1, cat. II, 9, 158–67, pp. 256–8; S. Abita and M. A. Fusco, *Garibaldi nell'iconografia dei suoi tempi*, Milan, 1982, pp. 184–6.

75. 'Morte di Giuseppe Garibaldi a Caprera', Civica Raccolta delle Stampe A. Bertarelli, Milan, ASM, 42–6.

76. 17 June 1882.

77. 3 June 1882.

78. Vol. 52, juillet–âout 1882, p. 204.

79. G. Sabbatucci, *Il trasformismo come sistema. Saggio sulla storia politica dell'Italia unitaria*, Rome and Bari, 2003; L. Musella, *Il trasformismo*, Bologna, 2003.

80. Körner, 'Local government in Bologna', p. 138.

81. Although Garibaldi did not fight in the Paris Commune, many *garibaldini* did, including his son, Menotti, and he sent a message of support to its leaders. Paris, 'L'Italia fuori d'Italia', pp. 513–19.

82. F. della Peruta, 'La concezione del socialismo in Garibaldi'; L. Briguglio, 'Garibaldi e l'Internazionale'; A. A. Mola, 'L'internazionalismo massonico di Garibaldi'; all in Cingari (ed.), *Garibaldi e il socialismo*, pp. 81–95, 97–118, 147–64.

83. 14 Nov. 1871, to Giorgio Pallavicino, in Mack Smith (ed.), *Garibaldi*, p. 83.

84. E. Mana, 'La "democrazia" italiana. Forme e linguaggi della propaganda politica tra Ottocento e Novocento', in M. Ridolfi (ed.), *Propaganda e communicazione politica*, Milan, 2004, pp. 152–4.

85. E. Mana, 'La democrazia radicale italiana e le forme della politica', in M. Ridolfi (ed.), *La democrazia radicale nell'Ottocento europeo*, Milan, 2005, pp. 197–202.

86. Mana, 'La "democrazia" italiana', pp. 147–155.

87. Conti, *L'Italia dei democratici*, pp. 75–87.

88. 3 and 5 June 1882.

89. W. Settimeli, *Garibaldi. L'album fotografico*, Florence, 1982, figs 81–3, pp. 78–9; *Arte e storia*, 1, cat. 1, 3.1.8., p. 87. On the 'Macchiaioli' and their relationship to nationalism, see A. Boime, *The art of the Macchia and the Risorgimento*, Chicago, 1993.

90. G. Guerzoni, *Garibaldi*, 2 vols, Florence, 1882, v. 2, pp. 585–6.

91. Pick, *Rome or death*, pp. 145–6, 185, 204–10.

92. I discuss this in greater detail below; see also M. Isnenghi, 'I due volti dell'eroe. Garibaldi vincitore–vinto e vinto–vincitore', in S. Bertelli and G. Clemente (eds), *Tracce dei vinti*, Florence, 1994, pp. 265–300.

93. U. Levra, 'Vittorio Emanuele II', in M. Isnenghi (ed.), *I luoghi della memoria: personaggi e date dell'Italia unita*, Rome and Bari, 1997, pp. 49–52.

94. See I. Porciani, 'Italien. "Fare gli Italiani"', in *Mythen der Nationen. Ein europäisches Panorama*, Berlin, 1998, pp. 199–222.

95. For a discussion and bibliography of this substantial literature, see above, pp. 3–5.

96. Duggan, *Francesco Crispi*, pp. 436–40.

97. I. Porciani, 'Lo statuto e il Corpus Domini. La festa nazionale dell'Italia liberale', in *Il mito del Risorgimento*, p. 171.

98. Recently, the work of Catherine Brice on the monarchy has suggested that this negative view needs to be modified: 'La Monarchie et la construction de l'identité nationale italienne, 1861–1911', Doctorat d'Etat, Institut d'Etudes Politiques de Paris, 2004.

  99. *Album della guerra del 1866*, Milan, 1866–7, illustrations on pp. 9, 12, 68, 76–7.
 100. 25 Sept. 1866.
 101. 26–31 Oct. 1867.
 102. 31 Oct. 1867.
 103. 9 Nov. 1867.
 104. *Atlantic Monthly*, 1869, in Mack Smith (ed.), *Garibaldi*, p. 146.
 105. 7 Nov. 1867.
 106. Both in Mack Smith (ed.), *Garibaldi*, pp. 120–3.
 107. F. M. Elliot, *Roman gossip*, London, 1894, p. 142.
 108. C. Garibaldi, *Mio padre*, p. 136; the Museum of the Risorgimento in Palermo displays the chair as one of its Garibaldi 'relics'.
 109. 26 June 1882.
 110. C. Garibaldi, *Mio padre*, p. 137.
 111. *Scritti e discorsi*, 3, p. 308. The word 'guaranteed' refers to the law of guarantees, with which the Italian government tried to regulate its relationship with the Vatican by guaranteeing its sovereign status.
 112. 26 Aug. 1867, *Scritti e discorsi*, 3, pp. 407–8.
 113. 5 May 1869, Ximenes, *Epistolario*, pp. 334–5.
 114. 7 Sept. 1869, ibid., pp. 344–5.
 115. Letter to the *Gazzettino Rosso*, 21 June 1870, *Scritti e discorsi*, 3, p. 43.
 116. *Cassell's Magazine*, 1870, in Mack Smith (ed.), *Garibaldi*, p. 82.
 117. Quoted in C. E. J. Griffiths, 'The novels of Garibaldi', *Italian Studies*, 30, 1975, p. 90.
 118. Ibid., pp. 95–6.
 119. M. Borutta, 'La "natura del nemico": rappresentazioni del cattolicesimo nell'anticlericalismo dell'Italia liberale', *Rassegna Storica del Risorgimento*, 88, 2001, pp. 124–8.
 120. *Clelia*, p. 2.
 121. *Cantoni*, pp. 26, 96, 111, 147–9.
 122. Ibid., p. 11.
 123. *I Mille*, Bologna, 1874 edn, pp. v, 57.
 124. *Cantoni*, p. 79.
 125. *Le memorie di Garibaldi nella redazione definitiva del 1872*, Bologna, 1932, pp. 12–13.
 126. Ibid., p. 14.
 127. *Cantoni*, pp. i–ii, in Mack Smith (ed.), *Garibaldi*, pp. 80–1.
 128. For further discussion, see L. Riall, 'Eroi maschili, virilità e forme della guerra', in A. M. Banti and P. Ginsborg (eds), *Il Risorgimento*, Turin, forthcoming.
 129. *I Mille*, p. 1.
 130. Ibid., pp. 399–408, 410.
 131. See above, p. 182.
 132. *I Mille*, p. 31.
 133. *Cantoni*, p. 33.
 134. L. Guidi, 'Patriottismo femminile e travestimenti sulla scena risorgimentale', *Studi Storici*, 41/2, 2000, pp. 574–5.
 135. S. Patriarca, 'Indolence and regeneration: tropes and tensions of Risorgimento patriotism', *American Historical Review*, 110/2, 2005, pp. 380–408.
 136. Ibid., p. 380.
 137. Quoted in R. Villari, 'La prefigurazione politica del giudizio storico su Garibaldi', *Studi Storici*, 23/2, 1982, p. 266.
 138. Conti, *L'Italia dei democratici*, p. 15.
 139. F. della Peruta, 'Il mito del Risorgimento e l'estrema sinistra dall'Unità al 1914', in *Il mito del Risorgimento*, pp. 38–50.
 140. B. Tobia, *Una patria per gli italiani*, Rome and Bari, 1991, pp. 168–80.
 141. C. Ceccuti, 'Le grandi biografie popolari nell'editoria italiana del secondo Ottocento',

in *Il mito del Risorgimento*, pp. 111–16, 122–3; I. Biagianti, 'Jesse White Mario e la "cultura garibaldina"', in Cingari (ed.), *Garibaldi e il socialismo*, pp. 238–40; on the more compromised attitude of Carducci, see G. Spadolini, *Fra Carducci e Garibaldi*, Florence, 1982.

142. Della Peruta, 'Il mito', pp. 61–2.

143. *Arte e storia*, 1, p. 245.

144. Ibid., 2, pp. 103–5 (see also the illustrations in *Don Pirloncino* and *Omnibus*).

145. A reviewer in the *Athenaeum* called it 'an impetuous, angry, unwise book, which can have no good result to Italy' and which risked damaging Garibaldi's reputation. Griffiths, 'The novels of Garibaldi', p. 87.

146. See above, pp. 154–6, 161, 264.

147. See G. Stiavelli, *Garibaldi nella letteratura italiana*, Rome, 1901; B. Croce, 'Letteratura garibaldina', in *La letteratura della nuova Italia. Saggi critici*, vol. 6, Bari, 1940; G. Trombatore, 'Introduzione', *Memorialisti dell'Ottocento*, Milan and Naples, 1953, 1, pp. xxvi–xxvii, 721, 751–2, 897–9, 1007–8, 1052–3, 1085–8, M. Tedeschi, 'Memorialisti garibaldini', in *La letteratura italiana. Storia e testi: il primo ottocento. L'età napoleonica e il Risorgimento*, Rome and Bari, 1975, 8, pt. 2, pp. 433–83.

148. For the publication history of Abba's *Noterelle*, see G. Mariani (ed.), *Antologia di scrittori garibaldini*, Bologna, 1958, pp. 73–5. Bandi's memoir was rediscovered in the post-'45 period: see esp. Croce's comparison of Bandi and Abba, and his criticisms of Abba's work for its '*sforzi letterari, di necessità artificiosi*', 'Letteratura garibaldina', p. 13.

149. A. Mario, *The red shirt. Episodes*, London, 1865 (the first Italian version, 'La camicia rossa', was published in *Rivista Contemporanea* in 1869, and in a series of editions thereafter: see A. P. Campanella (ed.), *Giuseppe Garibaldi e la tradizione garibaldina*, 2 vols, Geneva, 1971, 1, pp. 378–9); E. Zasio, *Da Marsala al Volturno. Ricordi*, Padua, 1868; F. Cavallotti, *L'insurrezione di Roma dai sui primordi fino alla esecuzione di Monti e Tognetti*, Milan, 1869–70; A. Bizzoni, *Impressioni di un volontario all'esercito dei Vosgi*, Milan, 1871 and 1874; E. Checchi, *Memorie di un Garibaldino/ Memorie alla casalinga di un garibaldino*, Livorno, 1866; E. Socci, *Da Firenze a Digione. Impressioni di un reduce garibaldino*, Prato, 1871.

150. Mario, *The red shirt*, p. 9.

151. Zasio, *Da Marsala al Volturno*, pp. 1–22, 69–70, 130–5.

152. Cavallotti, *L'insurrezione di Roma*, pp. 629–30. The volume was illustrated, and came out in parts, in the publishers' series, 'Collana dei martiri italiani'.

153. G. Mariani, *Storia della Scapigliatura*, Milan, 1967.

154. *Memorie*, pp. 1, 14, 20–3, 26, 73, 187.

155. Mario, *The red shirt*, p. 9.

156. G. Mosse, *The nationalization of the masses. Political symbolism and mass movements in Germany from the Napoleonic wars through the Third Reich*, New York, 1975, p. 6.

157. B. Tobia, 'Una forma di pedagogia nazionale tra cultura e politica: i luoghi della memoria e della rimembranza', in *Il mito del Risorgimento*, pp. 194–207.

158. Quoted in Duggan, *Francesco Crispi*, p. 437.

159. Mengozzi, *La morte e l'immortale*, pp. 199–200.

160. Ibid., pp. 203–5.

161. 'Le tre Italie per Giuseppe Garibaldi. Le orazioni funebri', *Il Pensiero Mazziniano*, 11–12, 1982, pp. 14, 27–8.

162. Quoted in Mengozzi, *La morte e l'immortale*, p. 208.

163. D. Kertzer, 'Religion and society, 1789–1892', in J. A. Davis (ed.), *Italy in the nineteenth century*, Oxford, 2000, pp. 190–6.

164. O. Chadwick, *A history of the Popes, 1830–1914*, Oxford, 1998, pp. 161–228.

165. C. Clark, 'The new Catholicism and the European culture wars', in idem and W. Kaiser (eds), *Culture wars. Secular–Catholic conflict in nineteenth-century Europe*,

Cambridge, 2003, pp. 11, 19.

166. Ibid., pp. 13–23; Chadwick, *A history of the Popes*, pp. 38–9.
167. Borutta, 'La "natura del nemico"', pp. 122–4.
168. A. Scattigno, 'Caterina da Siena: modello civile e religioso nell'Italia del Risorgimento', in A. M. Banti and R. Bizzocchi (eds), *Immagini della nazione nell'Italia del Risorgimento*, Rome, 2002, pp. 177–8.
169. Clark, 'The new Catholicism', p. 22.
170. Chadwick, *A history of the Popes*, pp. 244, 284.
171. Ibid., p. 238.
172. Ibid., pp. 268–72.
173. M. Pappenheim, '*Roma o morte*: culture wars in Italy', in Clark and Kaiser (eds), *Culture wars*, pp. 207–8, 225–6.
174. Clark, 'The new Catholicism', p. 36.
175. Pappenheim, '*Roma o morte*', p. 214.
176. Research tends to focus more on the anti-clerical media, see ibid.; Borutta, 'La "natura del nemico"'; Verucci, *L'Italia laica*.
177. *La Civiltà Cattolica*, Rome, 1867, vol. 12, pp. 396–407; 1868, vol. 2, pp. 408–11, in Mack Smith (ed.), *Garibaldi*, pp. 114–18.
178. T. Salzillo, *I fatti d'arme delle prodi legioni pontificie nella invasione garibaldesca di ottobre e novembre 1867 del patrimonio di S. Pietro*, Rome, 1868, pp. 6, 13; P. Mencacci, *La mano di Dio nell'ultima invasione contro Roma. Memorie storiche*, 3 vols, Rome, 1868, vol. 3, p. 149.
179. Generale Kanzler, *Rapporto alla santità di nostro signor Papa Pio IX. Felicemente regnante . . . sulla invasione dello Stato Pontificio nell'autunno 1867*, Rome, 1867, p. 3.
180. Mencacci, *La mano di Dio*, 3, pp. 147–8, 215; see also C. Brezzi, 'La "mano di Dio" a Mentana', in F. Mazzonis (ed.), *Garibaldi condottiero. Storia, teoria, prassi*, Milan, 1984, pp. 425–39.
181. A. Vitali, *Le dieci giornate di Monterotondo. Racconto Storico*, Rome, 1868, pp. 85–6.
182. Mencacci, *La mano di Dio*, 2, p. 301; Vitali, *Le dieci giornate*, pp. 57, 64, 66; Salzillo, *I fatti d'arme*, p. 48.
183. Salzillo, *I fatti d'arme*, p. 29; see the almost identical description in Mencacci, *La mano di Dio*, 2, p. 251.
184. Vitali, *Le dieci giornate*, pp. 44–5, 57, 120; Mencacci, *La mano di Dio*, 2, pp. 301–6.
185. Mencacci, *La mano di Dio*, 2, p. 304.
186. Kanzler, *Rapporto*, p. 3.
187. Vitali, *Le dieci giornate*, p. 2.
188. Ibid., pp. 26–7, 38, 49; Salzillo, *I fatti d'arme*, pp. 11, 14, 30–1, 47.
189. Mencacci, *La mano di Dio*, 1, p. vii.
190. Father V. Cardella, *Julian Watts Russell, pontifical zouave*, London, 1868; Mencacci, *La mano di Dio*, also has a long biographical section devoted to the martyrs of Mentana, 3, pp. 465–518.
191. *L'Osservatore Romano*, 7 Nov. 1867; Chadwick, *A history of the Popes*, p. 271.
192. Mencacci, *La mano da Dio*, 3, pp. 303–4.
193. K. Beste, *The victories of Rome*, London, 1868, p. 43.
194. 20 Dec. 1867, to Thomas Kirby, Kirby papers, Irish College Rome Archive, K-67–466 (in C. Barr, *The correspondence of Paul Cullen*, Dublin, forthcoming).
195. See, in particular, F. Dupanloup, *Lettre a M. Ratazzi [sic] ... sur les entreprises de Garibaldi*, Paris, 1867; J. C. P., *Les Pontificaux et les Garibaldiens ou histoire anecdotique d'après les documents officiels et les correspondances*, Paris, 1868; F. Ribeyre, *Histoire de la seconde expédition française à Rome*, Paris, 1868; M. Roget, *Les Diplomates italiens et Garibaldi devant l'Europe*, Paris, 1868. In general, see M. Milan, 'Opinione pubblica e antigaribaldinismo in Francia: La *querelle* sull'unità d'Italia (1860–1868)', *Rassegna Storica del Risorgimento*, 70, 1983, pp. 141–66.

196. R. Huguet, *Les Victoires de Pie IX sur les garibaldiens en 1867 et les soldats du pape devant l'histoire,* Paris and Brussels, 1868, p. 38; Ribeyre, *Histoire,* p. 18; J. C. P., *Les Pontificaux,* p. 107.

197. See the volunteer memoirs, *Glorieuse victoire de Mentana ... par les troupes du Saint-Père,* Paris, 1868; and Comte Eugène de Walincourt, *Les Héros de Mentana,* Paris and Lille, 1868.

198. C. Cantù, *Della indipendenza italiana, cronistoria,* Turin, 1878, 3, pt 2, pp. 580–13, trans. in Mack Smith (ed.), *Garibaldi,* p. 154.

199. 1879, vol. 9, pp. 360–1; vol. 10, pp. 487–9, vol. 13, p. 79.

200. Vol. 12, p. 336; vol. 13, p. 363.

201. 'Fe...Gio...Gi' [anonymous author], *Garibaldi politico,* Rome and Florence, 1879, and the same author's *Garibaldi l'ingrato. Compilazione funebre,* Rome and Florence, 1879.

202. See above, p. 323.

203. Vol. 13, pp. 78–82.

Conclusion: The Myth of Garibaldi

1. 5 June 1882.

2. For a discussion, see S. Gundle, 'The death (and re-birth) of the hero: charisma and manufactured charisma in modern Italy', *Modern Italy,* 3/2, 1998, pp. 173–89.

3. See the discussion in L. Cavalli, 'Considerations on charisma and the cult of charismatic leadership', ibid., pp. 164–6.

SELECT BIBLIOGRAPHY

Sources

There is a vast amount and huge variety of sources for the study of Garibaldi's life, career and myth. A very detailed bibliography (to 1971) is provided in A. P. Campanella (ed.), *Giuseppe Garibaldi e la tradizione garibaldina*, 2 vols, Geneva, 1971; however, its uses are somewhat limited by the author's decision to follow a chronological and hagiographical approach, and not to distinguish between the various types of publications on Garibaldi. Readers seeking a straightforward biography of Garibaldi in English can choose between D. Mack Smith, *Garibaldi. A great life in brief*, London, 1957, and J. Ridley, *Garibaldi*, London, 1974, while D. Pick, *Rome or death. The obsessions of General Garibaldi*, London, 2005, is an interesting experiment with psycho-biography. In Italian, A. Scirocco, *Garibaldi. Battaglie, amori, ideali di un cittadino del mondo*, Rome and Bari, 2001, is a useful recent study. Still fundamental in many ways is G. M. Trevelyan's *Garibaldi*, published in London between 1907 and 1911.

Among the published primary sources, indispensable are the two versions of Garibaldi's memoirs published by the Edizione Nazionale degli scritti di Garibaldi in the 1930s, along with the various editions produced by Alexandre Dumas in 1860–1, the *Denkwürdigkeiten* by Esperanza von Schwartz/Elpis Melena published in Hamburg in 1861, and the rarer English version edited by Theodore Dwight, *The life of General Garibaldi written by himself*, New York, 1859. The *Edizione Nazionale* also published three volumes of Garibaldi's *Scritti e discorsi politici e militari*, Bologna, 1934–7, which complement the more recent publication of his letters, *Epistolario di Giuseppe Garibaldi*, in eleven volumes (Rome, 1973–2002), which has now reached the year 1866. For the years 1867–82, the reader must still rely on E. E. Ximenes, *Epistolario*, Milan, 1885. Also useful is the huge correspondence of Mazzini, *Scritti editi ed inediti di Giuseppe Mazzini*, Imola, 1906–86, which amounts to over one hundred volumes.

The two main Garibaldi archives are in the Museo Centrale del Risorgimento, Rome (on which, see E. Morelli, *I fondi archivistici del Museo Centrale del Risorgimento*, Rome, 1993), and the Museo del Risorgimento, Milan. Although the catalogues of both archives make them difficult to use, they have an extraordinary wealth of material relating to Garibaldi, and indeed to all the protagonists of the Risorgimento. Particularly worthy of note in the Museo del Risorgimento, Milan are the Carte Garibaldi 'Raccolte Storiche del Comune di Milano', the Archivio Bertani (for the events of 1860, including the letters of volunteers) and the Archivio Garibaldi Curàtulo. The latter, along with the collection donated by Clelia Garibaldi to the Museo Centrale del Risorgimento, contains a large numbers of letters to Garibaldi from his admirers, which were of particular use to the present study. The Archivio di Stato and the Archivio Comunale in Palermo have a limited amount of material on the cult of Garibaldi in 1860, and Foreign Office records in the National Archives in London are helpful on official British reactions to Garibaldi. The Biblioteca Labronica in Livorno and the Garibaldi museum on Caprera share the contents of Garibaldi's Caprera library (on which see T. Olivari, 'I libri di Garibaldi': http://www.storiaefuturo.com/arretrati/2002/01/01/005.html).

For the present study, I have made extensive use of newspapers and patriotic 'ephemera' – cheaply produced biographies, pamphlets and published poems and songs. The main collections of these ephemera in Italy are in the Biblioteca di Storia Moderna e Contemporanea in Rome and the Museo del Risorgimento in Milan, although most public libraries in Italy have collections of published material relating to Garibaldi. The Società Siciliana per la Storia Patria in Palermo has a very large collection of nineteenth-century newspapers and pamphlets, with a substantial section dedicated to Garibaldi and the events of 1860. The general problem is choosing from the wealth of material on offer, and I have focused only on the ephemeral publications produced during Garibaldi's lifetime (and at his death), and have not considered, for example, the commemorative literature produced for the various Garibaldi anniversaries, or the Garibaldi literature produced under Fascism (a fascinating subject in itself). Outside Italy, the Bibliothèque Nationale de France in Paris has an extensive collection of newspapers, books and pamphlets, with a special emphasis on Garibaldi's role in Franco-Italian relations; and both the New York Public Library and the Anthony P. Campanella Collection at the University of South Carolina at Columbia have useful published material. In Berlin, the Ibero-Amerikanisches Institut has a substantial collection of Buenos Aires newspapers from the 1830s and 1840s. Scholars of Garibaldi are particularly well served by the British Library in London, which has a collection of Garibaldi material that in some respects is unparalleled, both in the volume and variety of printed material and in its geographical reach (including volumes and newspapers from Argentina, the USA, France, Germany, Spain and eastern Europe).

For the iconography of Garibaldi, the main collections are in the Museo Centrale del Risorgimento, Rome; the Museums of the Risorgimento in Milan and Genoa; and the Civica Raccolta delle Stampe A. Bertarelli, Milan, but most museums of the Risorgimento in Italy have a collection of Garibaldi art and/or 'relics'. Here too the amount of available material is overwhelming; a very detailed and helpful (if not entirely exhaustive) guide is *Garibaldi. Arte e Storia*, 2 vols, Florence, 1982. For photographs of Garibaldi, the most complete selection is W. Settimeli, *Garibaldi. L'album fotografico*, Florence, 1982.

Manuscripts and archives

Archivio Comunale, Palermo
Atti del Consiglio Comunale di Palermo, Deliberazioni Consiglio Comunale, Corrispondenza Finanza

Archivio di Stato, di Milan
Civica Raccolta della Stampe, A. Bertarelli

Archivio di Stato, Palermo
Ministero e Real Segretaria di Stato presso il Luogotenente Generale, Polizia, Miscellanea
Ministero e Real Segreteria di Stato presso il Luogotenente Generale, Interno (1818–1864)

British Library, London
Garibaldi's Englishman, performed 1859, Lord Chamberlain's plays, ADD52988U
Garibaldi, by Tom Taylor, performed 1859, Lord Chamberlain's plays, ADD52985H
Garibaldi the Italian liberator, performed 1860, Lord Chamberlain's plays, ADD52994K
Garibaldi's excursionists, by H. J. Byron, performed 1860, Lord Chamberlain's plays, ADD52997J

Museo del Risorgimento, Milan
Archivio Bertani
Archivio Garibaldi Curàtulo

Museo Centrale del Risorgimento, Rome

National Archives (PRO), London
Foreign Office Papers

Published documents

Il Carteggio Cavour-Nigra dal 1858 al 1861, 4 vols, Bologna, 1961
Cavour e l'Inghilterra. Carleggio con V. E. d'Azeglio, Bologna, 1933

Edizione nazionale degli scritti di Giuseppe Garibaldi, vols 4–6. Scritti e discorsi politici e militari, 3 vols, Bologna, 1934–7

Epistolario di Giuseppe Garibaldi, 11 vols, Rome, 1973–2002

Garibaldi in parlamento, 2 vols, Rome, 1982

D. Mack Smith (ed.), *The making of Italy, 1796–1866*, London, 1988 edn

I. Nievo, *Lettere garibaldine*, Turin, 1961

Scritti editi ed inediti di Giuseppe Mazzini, 106 vols, Imola, 1906–90

L. Valerio, *Carteggio (1825–1865)*, 4 vols, ed. A Viarengo, Turin, 1991–2003

E. Ximenes (ed.), *Epistolario di Giuseppe Garibaldi*, Milan, 1885

Newspapers and magazines

Apostolato Popolare
British Packet and Argentine News
La Civiltà Cattolica
La Concordia
Il Corriere Livornese
Il Diritto
Il Don Pirlone
L'Eco
Il Felsineo
Il Fischietto
Frank Leslie's Illustrated Newspaper
Gaçeta Mercantil
Die Gartenlaube
La Gazzetta di Milano
Il Gazzettino Rosa
Harper's Weekly
The Illustrated London News
L'Illustration
L'Italia del Popolo
Italia e Popolo
Journal pour tous
The Lady's Newspaper and Pictorial Times
The Liverpool Mail
Il Lampone
Il Legionario Italiano
Letture di Famiglia
Il Mondo Illustrato
Il Movimento
El Naçional
La Nazione
New York Daily Tribune
New York Evening Post
New York Herald
New York Times
The Northern Tribune
L'Osservatore Romano
La Patria
The Philadelphia Inquirer
Il Piccolo Corriere d'Italia
Punch

The Red Republican
Revue des Deux Mondes
Il Risorgimento
Le Siècle
The Times
L'Unità Italia

Palermo Newspapers (1860)
La Cicala Italiana
Il Corriere di Sicilia
La Costanza e la Supremazia d'Italia
La Forbice
La Frusta
Il Garibaldi
Gazzettino della Sera
Il Giornale di Sicilia
La Guerra
L'Italia Redenta
La Libertà
La Mola
Il Mondo Nuovo
Il Precursore
Il Predicatore Italiano
Il Pungolo
Tom Pouce
L'Unità Italiana
Il Vessillo Italiano

Contemporary books, memoirs and pamphlets

G. C. Abba, *The diary of one of Garibaldi's Thousand*, trans. E. R. Vincent, London, 1962 (1880)

G. Adamoli, *Da San Martino a Mentana. Ricordi di un volontario*, Milan, 1911 (1892)

E. Albanese, *La ferita di Garibaldi ad Aspromonte. Diario inedito della cura*, Milan, 1907

Album della guerra del 1866, Milan, 1866–7

Album storico–artistico. Garibaldi nelle due Sicilie ossia guerra d'Italia nel 1860. Scritta da B.G. con disegni dal vero, le barricate di Palermo, ritratti e battaglie, litografati da migliori artisti, Milan, 1862

Album storico–artistico delle guerre per l'indipendenza italiana. Pubblicato in due parti, Turin, 1860–1

Album storico–artistico. 1859 Guerra d'Italia. Scritta dal corrispondente del Times al campo Franco-Sardo con disegni dal vero di C. Bossoli. Lith. par les Frères Fd & Charles Perrin. Paris and Turin, 1860

A Giuseppe Garibaldi. Parole di cordoglio pronunziate il 17 giugno 1882 nella ricorrenza delle civile onoranze resegli in Pachino, Noto, 1882

A Giuseppe Garibaldi. Parole di Enrico Panzacchi dette alla Associazione Progressista Costituzionale delle Romagne nell'adunanza dell'11 Giugno 1882, Bologna and Conegliano, 1882

Alla venerata memoria del prode dei prodi Giuseppe Garibaldi, Messina, 1882

L'Âne et les trois voleurs. Proverbe garibaldien en un acte et en vile prose, Paris, 1860

A. Altadill, *Garibaldi en Sicilia ó la unidad italiana*, Madrid/Barcelona, 1860

L. von Alvensleben, *Garibaldi. Seine Jugend, sein Leben, seine Abenteuer und seine*

Kreigsthaten, Weimar, 1859

Anon, *Angelo. A romance of modern Rome*, London, 1854

Anon [H. Tuckerman], 'Garibaldi', *North American Review*, 92, 1861, pp. 15–56

Anon ['Fe. . .Gio. . .Gi'], *Garibaldi politico*, Rome and Florence, 1879

C. Arrivabene, *Italy under Victor Emmanuel. A personal narrative*, London, 1862

Aspromonte. Ricordi storico-militare, Turin, 1862

E. Atgier, *Garibaldi le Flibustier*, Rochefort-sur-mer, 1860

A. Azzi, *Garibaldi in Sicilia. Canto nazionale*, Ferrara, 1860

A. Balbiani, *Storia illustrata della vita di Garibaldi*, Milan, 1860

G. Bandi, *I Mille da Genova a Capua*, Milan, 1977 (1886)

M. Barthélemy, *Garibaldi ou le réveil du lion*, Paris, 1861

A. Bertani, *Resoconto della cassa centrale soccorso a Garibaldi, 1860*, Genoa, 1860

_____, *Le spedizioni per i volontari per Garibaldi*, Genoa, 1861

G. Bertoldi, *Alla legione Italiana in Montevideo ed al colonello Giuseppe Garibaldi*, Lugano, 1847

J. R. Beste, *Modern Society in Rome*, 3 vols, Rome, 1856

C. Bianchi, *I martiri d'Aspromonte, cenni storici*, Milan, 2nd edn, 1863

A. Bizzoni, *Impressioni di un volontario all'esercito dei Vosgi*, Milan, 1871

P. G. Boggio, *Cavour o Garibaldi?*, Turin, 1860

_____, *Da Montevideo a Palermo. Vita di Giuseppe Garibaldi*, Turin, 1860

F. de Boni, *Così la penso. Cronaca*, 1, Lugano, 1846, pp. 365–84

A. Bresciani, *Lionello*, Rome, 1852

A. Brofferio, *Garibaldi o Cavour?*, Genoa, 1860

W. B. Brooke, *Out with Garibaldi: or from Milazzo to Capua*, London, 1860

A. S. Bucknell, *In the tracks of the Garibaldians through Italy and Sicily*, London, 1861

J. Butler, *In memoriam Harriet Meuricoffre*, London, 1901

F. Cavallotti, *L'insurrezione di Roma dai sui primordi fino alla esecuzione di Monti e Tognetti*, Milan, 1869–70

G. Cadolini, *Memorie del Risorgimento dal 1848 al 1862*, Milan, 1911

M. du Camp, *Expédition des Deux-Siciles: souvenirs personnels*, Paris, 1861

L. Capuana, *Garibaldi, leggenda drammatica in tre canti*, Catania, 1861

Father V. Cardella, *Julian Watts Russell, pontifical zouave*, London, 1868

T. Carlyle, *On heroes, hero-worship and the heroic in history*, Lincoln, NB, and London, 1966 (1841)

F. Carrano, *I Cacciatori delle Alpi comandati dal generale Garibaldi nella guerra del 1859*, Turin, 1860

H. Castille, *Garibaldi*, Paris, 1859

G. la Cecilia, *Storia della insurrezione siciliana, dei successivi avvenimenti per l'indipendenza ed unione d'Italia e delle gloriose geste di Giuseppe Garibaldi compilata su note e documenti trasmessi dai luoghi ove accadono*, 2 vols, Milan, 1860

Colonel Chambers, *Garibaldi and Italian unity*, London, 1864

E. Checchi, *Memorie di un Garibaldino*, Livorno, 1866

P. Chiara, *Garibaldi dall'Italia alla gran giornata della Sicilia già mossa*, Palermo, 1860

Cinque giorni in Calabria o la catastrofe d'Aspromonte per un volontario garibaldino, Palermo[?], 1862

W. G. Clark, 'Naples and Garibaldi', in F. Galton (ed.), *Vacation tourists and notes of travel in 1860*, Cambridge, 1861

A. H. Clough, *The poems and prose remains of Arthur Clough with a selection from his letters and a memoir*, 2 vols, London, 1869

R. J. Cooper, *Three letters to the conservatives of England . . . on the subject of Garibaldi and Revolution*, London, 1864

S. Corleo, *Garibaldi e i Mille a Salemi*, Rome, 1886

G. B. Cuneo, *Biografia di Giuseppe Garibaldi*, Turin, 1850, and Rome, 1932

E. Dandolo, *I volontari ed i bersaglieri lombardi*, Turin, 1849

A. Delvau, *G. Garibaldi. Vie et aventures, 1807–1859*, Paris, 1859

S. Devine, 'A new song on the capture of Garibaldi', Dublin [?], 1871

A. Dumas, *Les garibaldiens. Révolution de Sicile et de Naples*, Paris, 1861

_____, *Montevideo ou une nouvelle Troie*, Paris, 1850

F. Dupanloup, *Lettre a M. Ratazzi . . . sur les entreprises de Garibaldi* [*sic*], Paris, 1867

P. Dupont, *Sicilienne à Garibaldi*, Paris, 1860

P. Dupont and A. d'Aunay (eds), *Mémoires sur J. Garibaldi*, Paris, 1860

H. Durand-Brager, *Quatre mois de l'expédition de Garibaldi en Sicile et en Italie*, Paris, 1861

T. Dwight, *The Roman Republic of 1849; with accounts of the Inquisition and the siege of Rome*, New York, 1851

H. Elliot, *Some revolutions and other diplomatic experiences*, London, 1922

Colonel Exalbion, *Garibaldi: his life, exploits and the Italian campaigns*, London, 1859

O. Féré & R. Hyenne, *Garibaldi. Aventures, expéditions, voyages. Amérique, Rome, Piémont, Sicile, Naples. 1834–1848–1859–1860*, Paris, 1861

U. de Fonvielle, *Souvenirs d'une chemise rouge*, Paris, 1861

C. S. Forbes, *The campaign of Garibaldi in the Two Sicilies. A personal narrative*, Edinburgh and London, 1861

A. de la Forge, *Histoire du Géneral Garibaldi*, Paris, 1859

A. B. Fuller (ed.), *At home and abroad. Or things and thoughts in America and Europe*, Boston, MA, 1874

C. Garibaldi, *Mio padre*, Florence, 1948

G. Garibaldi, *Edizione nazionale degli scritti di Garibaldi, vol 1. Le memorie di Garibaldi in una delle redazioni anteriori alla definitiva del 1872*, Bologna, 1932

_____, *Edizione nazionale degli scritti di Garibaldi, vol 2. Le memorie di Garibaldi nella redazione definitiva del 1872*, Bologna, 1932

_____, *I Mille*, Bologna, 1874

_____, *Cantoni il volontario*, Milan, 1870

_____, *Clelia, ovvero il governo del monaco (Roma nel secolo XIX)*, Milan, 1870

_____, *Garibaldi's Denkwürdigkeiten nach handschriftlichen Aufzeichnungen desselben und nach authentischen Quellen bearbeitet und herausgegeben von Elpis Melena*, Hamburg, 1861

_____, *Mémoires de Garibaldi*, Paris, 1860

_____, *The life of General Garibaldi written by himself with the sketches of his companions in arms*, New York, 1859

Garibaldi. Eine biographische Darstellung nach bisher unbekannten Documenten, Berlin 1859

Garibaldi et la civilisation. La rédemption – les puissants – le Pape – mensonges de la civilisation – l'avenir, Turin, 1862

Garibaldi et ses hommes rouges, Paris, 1860

Giuseppe Garibaldi da Caprera ad Aspromonte, 1860–61–62. Memorie storiche raccolta da Felice Venosta, Milan, n.d

Glorieuse victoire de Mentana . . . par les troupes du Saint-Père, Paris, 1868

L. Goethe, *Garibaldi, sa vie, son enfance, ses moeurs, ses exploits militaires*, Paris, 1859

G. Guerzoni, *Garibaldi*, 2 vols, Florence, 1882

Halte-là Garibaldi!, Paris, 1860

C. G. Hamilton, *The Exiles of Italy, or Garibaldi's miraculous escapes. A novel*, London, 1857

P. Harro-Harring, *Dolores. A historical novel. With an introduction to Mazzini*, New York and London, 3rd edn, 1853

A. Herzen, *My past and thoughts*, 3 vols, London, 1968

G. von Hoffstetter, *Giornale delle cose di Roma nel 1851*, Turin, 1851

Hommes du Jour, L'empereur Francois-Joseph, Garibaldi, Lord Palmerston, Le prince Schwarzenberg . . . Le général Filangieri, Le roi Ferdinand II, Le duc de Modène, Le prince régent de Prusse, Madame la princesse de Prusse, Le maréchal Canrobet, Paris, 1859

R. Huguet, *Les victoires de Pie IX sur les garibaldiens en 1867 et les soldats du pape devant l'histoire*, Paris and Brussels, 1868

H. d'Ideville, *Journal d'un diplomate en Italie*, Paris, 1871

Il 19 luglio 1860. Festa popolare in Palermo pel giorno natalizio del generale Giuseppe Garibaldi, Palermo, 1860

L'Italia e i suoi difensori. Album storico-biografico dell'avv'Giuseppe Pistelli, ornato da ritratti e stampe litografiche, Florence, 1860

Generale Kanzler, *Rapporto alla santità di nostro signor Papa Pio IX. Felicemente regnante ... sulla invasione dello Stato Pontificio nell'autunno 1867*, Rome, 1867

J. C. P., *Les pontificaux et les Garibaldiens ou histoire anecdotique d'après les documents officiels et les correspondances*, Paris, 1868

J. P. Koelman, *Memorie romane*, 2 vols, Rome, 1963 (1863)

La libera parola. Foglio estraordinario pel giorno onomastico del Generale Garibaldi, Catania, 19 March, 1861

E. Lockroy, *Au hasard de la vie. Notes et souvenirs*, Paris, 1913

C. MacGrigor, *Garibaldi at home. Notes of a visit to Caprera*, London, 1866

E. Maison, *Journal d'un volontaire de Garibaldi*, Paris, 1861

————, *Caprera. Les loisirs de Garibaldi*, Paris, 1861

H. E. Manning, *The visit of Garibaldi to England. A letter to the Right Hon. Edward Cardwell, M.P.*, London, 1864

D. Manuel Gil de Salcedo, *Garibaldi y Procida, ó las Pasquas Sangrientas de Sicilia. Novela histórica contemporánea*, Madrid, 1860

A. Mario, *The red shirt. Episodes*, London, 1865

L. Mariotti [A. Gallenga], *Latest news from Italy*, London, 1847

E. Melena [Esperanza von Schwartz], *Hundert und ein Tag auf meinem Pferde und ein Ausflug nach der Insel Maddalena*, Hamburg, 1860

P. Mencacci, *La mano di Dio nell'ultima invasione contro Roma. Memorie storiche*, 3 vols, Rome, 1868

M. Menghini (ed.), *La spedizione garibaldina di Sicilia e di Napoli nei proclami, nelle corrispondenze, nei diarii del tempo*, Turin, 1907

J. la Messine, *Garibaldi*, Paris, 1859

F. Mistrali, *Storia popolare della rivoluzione di Sicilia e dell'impresa di Giuseppe Garibaldi*, Milan, 2nd edn, 1862

B. Mitre, *Ricordi dell'assedio di Montevideo (1843–1851)*, Florence, 1882

M. Monnier, *Garibaldi. Histoire de la conquête des deux Siciles. Notes prises sur place au jour le jour*, Paris, 1861

R. Mundy, *H.M.S. 'Hannibal' at Palermo and Naples during the Italian Revolution, 1859–1861*, London, 1863

I. Nievo, *Gli amori garibaldini. Con poesie e introduzione*, Como, 1911

V. Navarro di Ribera, *Il Garibaldi*, Palermo, 1860

G. Nuvolari, *Come la penso*, Milan, 1881 (1861)

G. Oddo, *I Mille di Marsala. Scene rivoluzionarie*, Milan, 1863

L. Oliphant, *Episodes in a life of adventure*, Edinburgh and London, 1887

F. dell'Ongaro, *É Garibaldi. Canzone*, Florence, 1859

V. Ottolini, *Cacciatori delle Alpi (1848–59). Scene storico-militari*, Milan, 1860

C. Pardi, *Pel primo anniversario del 4 aprile. Orazione*, Palermo, 1861

————, *A Giuseppe Garibaldi. Ode*, Palermo, 1860

C. Paya, *Histoire de la guerre d'Italie. Garibaldi*, Paris, 1860

C. Pisacane, *Guerra combattuta in Italia negli anni 1848–49*, Genoa, 1851

C. Pita, *Biographie du Général Garibaldi*, Paris, 1859

W. Raible, *Leben und Abenteuer des berühmten Freischaarenführers Joseph Garibaldi, General der sardinischen Armee und der italienischen Liga*, Munich, n.d. but 1859

'Rendicion de Capua y triunfal entrada de S.M. el Rey Victor Manuel y el Garibaldi',

Barcelona, 1860

F. Ribeyre, *Histoire de la seconde expédition française à Rome*, Paris, 1868

G. Ricciardi, *Vita di G. Garibaldi narrata al popolo ... e continuata sino al suo ritiro nell'Isola di Caprera [9 novembre, 1860]*, Florence, 1860

M. Roget, *Les diplomates italiens et Garibaldi devant l'Europe*, Paris, 1868

J. Sadler, 'The Pope's trumph over Garibaldi', Dublin, 1871

T. Salzillo, *I fatti d'arme delle prodi legioni pontificie nella invasione garibaldesca di ottobre e novembre 1867 del patrimonio di S. Pietro*, Rome, 1868

G. Sand, *Garibaldi*, Paris, 1859

M. Smith, *A wreath for Garibaldi*, London, 1864

E. Socci, *Da Firenze a Digione. Impressioni di un reduce garibaldino*, Prato, 1871

Souvenirs de la guerre d'Italie. Chants guerriers par messieurs Auguste Barbier, Pierre Dupont, Fernand Denoyers, Gustave Mathieu, Charles Vincent. Musique et accompagnement de piano par MM. Darcier, Pierre Dupont, Hector Salmon et Mme Mélanie Dentu, Paris, n.d. but 1859

R. Tosi, *Da Venezia a Mentana (1848–1867)*, Forlì, 1910

Il tributo all'immortale Giuseppe Garibaldi o sia catechismo politico–costituzionale italiano per la necessaria istruzione del popolo, Naples, 2nd edn, 1861

L. de la Varenne, *Vita del General Garibaldi*, Bologna, 1860

G. della Valle, *Varese, Garibaldi ed Urban nel 1859 durante la guerra per l'indipendenza italiana*, Varese, 1863

La verità sul fatto di Aspromonte, per un testimonio oculare, Milan, 1862

O. J. Victor, *Life of Joseph Garibaldi. The Liberator of Italy. Complete up to the withdrawal of Garibaldi to his island home after the Neapolitan campaign, 1860*, New York, 1860

G. Visconti Venosta, *Ricordi di gioventù: cose vedute o sapute (1847–1860)*, Milan, 1904

A. Vitali, *Le dieci giornate di Monterotondo. Racconto Storico*, Rome, 1868

Una voce dalle prigioni. Il fatto d'Aspromonte, Lugano, 1862

A. Vuilletet, *Garibaldi en France*, Paris, 1876

Comte Eugène de Walincourt, *Les Héros de Mentana*, Paris and Lille, 1868

J. White Mario, *Garibaldi e i suoi tempi*, Milan, 1884

H. F. Winnington-Ingram, *Hearts of oak*, London, 1889

E. Zasio, *Da Marsala al Volturno. Ricordi*, Padova, 1868

Secondary works

M. Agulhon, 'Le Mythe de Garibaldi en France de 1882 à nos jours', in idem, *Histoire vagabonde, vol II. Idéologie et politique dans la France du XIXe siècle*, Paris, 1988, pp. 85–131

W. Altgeld, 'Giuseppe Garibaldi in zeitgenössischer Sicht von der Verteidigung Roms bis zur Niederlage bei Mentana (1848–1867)', *Risorgimento*, 1982–3, pp. 169–99

B. Anderson, *Imagined communities*, London, 1991 edn

P. Anderson, *The printed image and the transformation of popular culture, 1790–1860*, Oxford 1991

A. M. Banti, *Il Risorgimento italiano*, Rome and Bari, 2004

C. Barr, 'Giuseppe Mazzini and Irish nationalism', *Proceedings of the British Academy*, forthcoming

G. Batticuore, K. Gallo and J. Myers (eds), *Resonancias románticas. Ensayos sobre historia de la cultura argentina (1820–1890)*, Buenos Aires, 2005

D. Beales, 'Garibaldi in England. The politics of Italian enthusiasm', in J. A. Davis and P. Ginsborg (eds), *Society and politics in the age of the Risorgimento. Essays in honour of Denis Mack Smith*, Cambridge, 1991, pp. 184–216

J. Belchem and J. Epstein, 'The nineteenth-century gentleman leader revisited', *Social*

History, 22/2, 1997, pp. 174–93

C. di Biase, *L'arresto di Garibaldi nel settembre 1849*, Florence, 1941

F. Brancato, 'La partecipazione del clero alla rivoluzione siciliana del 1860', in *La Sicilia verso l'unità d'Italia*, Palermo, 1960, pp. 7–33

A. Boldrini, 'Il mito di Garibaldi nella letteratura del Rio Grande do Sul', *Quaderni Storiografici dell'Istituto internazionale di studi Giuseppe Garibaldi*, 8, 1993, pp. 3–25

M. Bonsanti, 'Una generazione democratica: amore familiare, amore romantico e amor di patria', in A. M. Banti and P. Ginsborg (eds), *Il Risorgimento*, Turin, forthcoming

F. Boyer, 'Les Volontaires français avec Garibaldi en 1860', *Revue d'Histoire Moderne et Contemporaine*, 7, 1960, pp. 123–49

P. Brantlinger and W. B. Thesing (eds), *A companion to the Victorian novel*, Oxford, 2002

S. Candido, *La rivoluzione riograndese nel carteggio inedito di due giornalisti mazziniani: Luigi Rossetti e G.B. Cuneo (1837–1840). Contributo alla storia del giornalismo politico di ispirazione italiana nei paesi latinoamericani*, Florence, 1973

_____, *Giuseppe Garibaldi nel Rio della Plata, 1841–1848*, Florence, 1972

_____, *Giuseppe Garibaldi. Corsaro riograndese (1837–1838)*, Rome, 1964

A. Cavaciocchi, 'Le prime gesta di Garibaldi in Italia', *Rivista Militare Italiana*, 6, 1907, pp. 5–87

O. Chadwick, *A history of the Popes, 1830–1914*, Oxford, 1998

G. Cingari (ed.), *Garibaldi e il socialismo*, Rome and Bari, 1984

G. Claeys, 'Mazzini, Kossuth and British radicalism, 1848–1854', *Journal of British Studies*, 28/2, 1989, pp. 225–61

R. Chartier and H.-J. Martin (eds), *Histoire de l'édition française. Vol 3. Le temps des éditeurs, du romantisme à la belle époque*, Paris, 1990 edn

C. Clark and W. Kaiser (eds), *Culture wars. Secular–Catholic conflict in nineteenth-century Europe*, Cambridge, 2003

F. Conti, *L'Italia dei democratici. Sinistra risorgimentale, massoneria e associazionismo fra '800 e '900*, Milan, 2000

G. Cubitt, 'Introduction: heroic reputations and exemplary lives', in idem and A. Warren (eds), *Heroic reputations and exemplary lives*, Manchester, 2000, pp. 1–26

G. Curàtulo, *Il dissidio tra Mazzini e Garibaldi. La storia senza veli*, Milan, 1928

_____, *Garibaldi e le donne*, Rome, 1913

J. A. Davis, 'Introduction: Antonio Gramsci and Italy's passive revolution', in idem (ed.), *Gramsci and Italy's passive revolution*, London, 1979, pp. 11–30

_____ (ed.), *Italy in the nineteenth century*, Oxford, 2000

G. Dawson, *Soldier heroes. British adventure, empire and the imagining of masculinities*, London, 1994

C. Dipper, 'Helden überkreuz oder das Kreuz mit den Helden', *Jahrbuch des Historischen Kollegs*, Oldenbourg, 1999, pp. 91–130

F. Dolci, 'L'editoria d'occasione del secondo Ottocento nella Biblioteca di Storia Moderna e Contemporanea di Roma,' in *Il mito del Risorgimento nell'Italia unita*, Milan, 1995, pp. 124–48

_____ (ed.), *Effemeridi pattriotiche*, Rome, 1984

C. Duggan, *Francesco Crispi. From nation to nationalism*, Oxford, 2002, pp. 426–50

G. Eley, 'Nations, publics, and political cultures: placing Habermas in the nineteenth century', in C. Calhoun (ed.), *Habermas and the public sphere*, Boston, MA, 1994, pp. 289–339

E. Feraboli, 'Il primo esilio di Garibaldi in America, 1833–1848', *Rassegna Storica del Risorgimento*, 19/2, 1932, pp. 251–82

M. Finn, *After Chartism. Class and nation in English radical politics*, Cambridge, 1993

L. G. Fossati and N. Tranfaglia, *La stampa italiana nell'età liberale*, Rome and Bari, 1979

S. Freitag (ed.), *Exiles from European revolutions. Refugees in mid-Victorian England*, Oxford, 2003

N. Frye, *The anatomy of criticism*, Princeton, NJ, 1957

F. Furet, *Interpreting the French Revolution*, Cambridge, 1981

A. Galante Garrone, *I radicali in Italia, 1849–1925*, Milan, 1973

A. Galante Garrone and F. della Peruta, *La stampa italiana del Risorgimento*, Bari, 1976

Garibaldi. Arte e storia, 2 vols, Florence, 1982

E. Gellner, *Nations and nationalism*, Oxford, 1983

E. Gentile, *Le religioni della politica. Fra democrazia e totalitarismi*, Rome and Bari, 2001

R. Gerwarth, *The Bismarck myth. Weimar Germany and the legacy of the Iron Chancellor*, Oxford, 2005

A. M. Ghisalberti, *Momenti e figure del Risorgimento romano*, Milan, 1965

L. Giampolo and M. Bertolone, *La prima campagna di Garibaldi in Italia (da Luino a Morazzone) e gli avvenimenti militari e politici nel Varesotto 1848–1849*, Varese, 1950

S. Gilley, 'The Garibaldi riots of 1862', *The Historical Journal*, 16/4, 1973, pp. 697–732

P. Ginsborg, 'Il mito del Risorgimento nel mondo britannico: "la vera poesia della politica"', in *Il mito del Risorgimento*, pp. 384–99

————, 'Risorgimento rivoluzionario: mito e realtà di una guerra di popolo', *Storia e Dossier*, 47, 1991, pp. 61–97

————, *Daniele Manin and the Venetian revolution of 1848–49*, Cambridge, 1979

————, 'Gramsci and the era of the bourgeois revolution in Italy', in J. A. Davis (ed.), *Gramsci and Italy's passive revolution*, London, 1979, pp. 31–66

E. Goffman, *The presentation of self in everyday life*, London, 1969

A. Gramsci, *Selections from prison notebooks*, ed. and trans. Q. Hoare and G. Nowell Smith, London, 1971

————, *Il Risorgimento*, Turin, 1949

J. Grévy, *Garibaldi*, Paris, 2001

R. Grew, *A sterner plan for Italian unity. The Italian National Society in the Risorgimento*, Princeton, NJ, 1963

C. E. J. Griffiths, 'The novels of Garibaldi', *Italian Studies* 30, 1975, pp. 86–98

L. Guidi, 'Patriottismo femminile e travestimenti sulla scena risorgimentale', *Studi Storici*, 41/2, 2000, pp. 571–87

P. Gut, 'Garibaldi et la France, 1848–1882. Naissance d'un mythe', *Rassegna Storica del Risorgimento*, 74/3, 1987, pp. 299–328

B. Hamnett, 'Fictitious histories: the dilemma of fact and imagination in the nineteenth-century historical novel', *European History Quarterly*, 36/1, 2006, pp. 31–60

I. Haywood, *The revolution in popular literature. Print, politics and the people, 1790–1860*, Cambridge, 2004

S. Hazareesingh, *The legend of Napoleon*, London, 1994

E. Hobsbawm, *Nations and nationalism since 1780*, London, 1990

————, 'Introduction, inventing traditions', in idem and T. Ranger, *The invention of tradition*, Cambridge, 1983, pp. 1–14

L. Hunt, *The family romance of the French Revolution*, London, 1992

M. Isabella, 'Exile and nationalism: the case of the *Risorgimento*', *European History Quarterly*, 36/4, 2006, pp. 493–520

M. Isnenghi, 'Garibaldi', in idem (ed.), *I luoghi della memoria. Personaggi e date dell'Italia unita*, Rome and Bari, 1997, pp. 25–45

————, 'I due volti dell'eroe. Garibaldi vincitore–vinto e vinto–vincitore', in S. Bertelli and G. Clemente (eds), *Tracce dei vinti*, Florence, 1994, pp. 265–300

————, *Le guerre degli italiani*, Milan, 1989

A. M. Isastia, *Il volontario militare nel Risorgimento. La partecipazione alla guerra del 1859*, Rome, 1990

C. Jean, 'Garibaldi e il volontariato nel Risorgimento', *Rassegna Storica del Risorgimento*, 69/4, 1982, pp. 399–419

A. Jourdan, *Napoléon. Héros, imperator, mécène*, Paris, 1998

I. Kershaw, *The 'Hitler myth'. Image and reality in the Third Reich*, Oxford, 1987

D. Kertzer, *Rituals, politics and power*, New Haven, CT, 1988

D. Laven, 'Italy: The idea of the nation in the Risorgimento and liberal era', in T. Baycroft and M. Hewitson (eds), *What is a nation? Europe 1789–1914*, Oxford, 2006, pp. 255–71

————, 'Mazzini, Mazzinian conspiracy and British politics in the 1850s', *Bollettino Storico Mantovano*, nuova serie, 2, 2003, pp. 267–82

U. Levra, *Fare gli italiani. Memoria e celebrazione del Risorgimento*, Turin, 1992

J. Lynch, *Argentine caudillo. Juan Manuel de Rosas*, Wilmington, DE, 2001

————, *Caudillos in Spanish America, 1800–1850*, Oxford, 1992

A. Lyttelton, 'Creating a national past: history, myth and image in the Risorgimento', in A. Russell Ascoli and K. von Henneberg (eds), *Making and remaking Italy. The cultivation of national identity around the Risorgimento*, Oxford, 2001, pp. 27–74

D. McLean, 'Garibaldi in Uruguay: a reputation reconsidered', *English Historical Review*, 113, April 1998, pp. 351–66

D. Mack Smith, *Mazzini*, London, 1994

————, *Cavour and Garibaldi. A study in political conflict*, Cambridge, 2nd edn, 1985

————, *Victor Emanuel, Cavour and the Risorgimento*, London, 1971

————, *Garibaldi. A great life in brief*, London, 1957

———— (ed.), *Garibaldi. Great lives observed*, Englewood Cliffs, NJ, 1969

E. Mana, 'La "democrazia" italiana. Forme e linguaggi della propaganda politica tra Ottocento e Novocento', in M. Ridolfi (ed.), *Propaganda e comunicazione politica*, Milan, 2004, pp. 147–65

H. R. Marraro, *American opinion on the unification of Italy, 1846–1861*, New York, 1932

M. Martenengo, 'Garibaldi narratore. Vicende editoriali e stato attuale dei manoscritti', *Il Risorgimento*, 55/1, 1996, pp. 89–112

L. Mascilli Migliorini, *Il mito dell'eroe*, Naples, 1984

M. Milan, 'Opinione pubblica e antigaribaldinismo in Francia: la querelle sull'unità d'Italia (1860–66)', *Rassegna Storica del Risorgimento*, 70/2 1983, pp. 141–66

D. Mengozzi, *La morte e l'immortale. La morte laica da Garibaldi a Costa*, Manduria, 2000

G. Monsagrati, 'Garibaldi e il culto vittoriano dell'eroe', *Studi Storici*, 42/1, 2001, pp. 165–80

————, 'Garibaldi Giuseppe', *Dizionario biografico degli italiani*, 52, Rome, 1999, pp. 315–31

G. Mosse, *The image of man. The creation of modern masculinity*, New York, 1996

————, *The nationalisation of the masses. Political symbolism and mass movements in Germany from the Napoleonic wars through the Third Reich*, New York, 1975

M. Mulinacci, *La bella figlia del lago. Cronaca intima del matrimonio fallito di Giuseppe Garibaldi con la marchesina Raimondi*, Milan, 1978

H. Nelson Gay, 'Il secondo esilio di Garibaldi (1849–1854)', in idem, *Scritti sul Risorgimento*, Rome, 1937, pp. 193–213

P. Nora, 'Memoirs of men of state: from Commynes to De Gaulle', in idem (ed.), *Rethinking France. Les lieux de mémoire. Vol 1, The State*, Chicago, 2001, pp. 401–51

M. O'Connor, *The romance of Italy and the English political imagination*, London, 1998

T. Olivari, 'I libri di Garibaldi', *Storia e Futuro*, 1, 2002, pp. 1–16, www.storiaefuturo.com

D. Outram, *The body and the French Revolution. Sex, class and political culture*, New Haven, CT, and London, 1989

M. Ozouf, *Festivals and the French Revolution*, Cambridge, MA, 1988

N. W. Painter, 'Representing Truth: Sojourner Truth's knowing and becoming known', *The Journal of American History*, 81/2, 1994, pp. 461–92

F. della Peruta, 'Il mito del Risorgimento e l'estrema sinistra dall'Unità al 1914', in *Il mito del Risorgimento*, pp. 39–70

————, 'Garibaldi fra mito e politica', *Studi Storici*, 23/1, 1982, pp. 5–22

S. Patriarca, 'Indolence and regeneration: tropes and tensions of Risorgimento patriotism',

American Historical Review, 110/2, 2005, pp. 380–408

S. di Paola, 'Il mito di Garibaldi nella poesia italiana', in F. Mazzonis (ed.), *Garibaldi condottiero. Storia, teoria, prassi*, Milan, 1984, pp. 507–21

N. Petiteau, *Napoléon, de la mythologie à l'histoire*, Paris, 1999

D. Pick, *Rome or death. The obsessions of General Garibaldi*, London, 2005

P. Pieri, *Storia militare del Risorgimento*, Turin, 1962

J. Plunkett, *Queen Victoria. First media monarch*, Oxford, 2003

I. Porciani, 'Der Krieg als ambivalenter italienischer Gründungsmythos – Siege und Niederlagen', in N. Buschmann and D. Langewiesche (eds), *Der Krieg in den Gründungsmythen europäischer Nationen und der USA*, Frankfurt and New York, 2003, pp. 193–212

_____, *La festa della nazione*, Bologna, 1997

M. Praz, *The romantic agony*, London, 1933

C. Prendergast, *Napoleon and history painting. Antoine-Jean Gros's La bataille d'Eylau*, Oxford, 1997

L. Riall, 'Eroi maschili, virilità e forme della guerra', in A. M. Banti and P. Ginsborg (eds), *Il Risorgimento*, Turin, forthcoming

_____, 'Elites in search of authority: political power and social order in nineteenth-century Sicily', *History Workshop Journal*, 55, 2003, pp. 25–46

_____, *Sicily and the unification of Italy. Liberal policy and local power, 1859–1866*, Oxford, 1998

_____, *The Italian Risorgimento. State, society and national unification*, London, 1994

J. Ridley, *Garibaldi*, London, 1974

M. Ridolfi, C. Brice and F. de Giorgi, 'Religione civile e identità nazionale nella storia d'Italia: per una discussione', *Memoria e Ricerca*, 13, 2003, pp. 133–52

T. Roberts, 'The United States and the European revolutions of 1848', in G. Thomson (ed.), *The European revolutions of 1848 and the Americas*, London, 2002, pp. 76–99

R. Romeo, *Cavour e il suo tempo*, 3 vols, Rome and Bari, 1969–84

S. Salomone-Marino, 'Garibaldi e le tradizioni popolari', in *Archivio per lo studio delle tradizioni popolari*, 1, 1882

_____, *Leggende popolari siciliane in poesia*, Palermo, 1880

M. Samuels, *The spectacular past. Popular history and the novel in nineteenth-century France*, Ithaca, NY, 2004

R. Sarti, 'La democrazia radicale: uno sguardo reciproco tra Stati Uniti e Italia', in M. Ridolfi (ed.), *La democrazia radicale nell'ottocento europeo*, Milan, 2005, pp. 133–57

_____, *Mazzini: a life for the religion of politics*, Westport, CT, 1997

G. Schöpflin, 'The function of myth and a taxonomy of myths', in G. Hosking and G. Schöpflin (eds), *Myths and nationhood*, London, 1997, pp. 19–35

B. Schwartz, *George Washington. The making of an American symbol*, New York, 1987

M. Schwegman, 'In love with Garibaldi: romancing the Risorgimento', *European Review of History – Révue européenne d'histoire*, 12/2, 2005, pp. 363–81

A. Scirocco, *Garibaldi. Battaglie, amori, ideali di un cittadino del mondo*, Bari and Rome, 2001

W. Settimelli, *Garibaldi. L'album fotografico*, Florence, 1982

E. Shils, 'Charisma, order and status', *American Sociological Review*, April 1965, pp. 199–213

A. D. Smith, 'National identity and myths of ethnic descent', in idem, *Myths and memories of the nation*, Oxford, 1999, pp. 57–95

J. Smith Allen, *Popular French romanticism. Authors, readers and books in the nineteenth century*, Syracuse, NY, 1981

A. Soboul, 'Religious feeling and popular cults during the French Revolution: "patriot saints" and martyrs for liberty', in S. Wilson (ed.), *Saints and their cults. Studies in religious sociology, folklore and history*, Cambridge, 1983, pp. 220–44

C. Sorba, *Teatri. L'Italia del melodrama nell'età del Risorgimento*, Bologna, 2001

J. Sperber, *The European revolutions, 1848–1851*, Cambridge, 1994

G. Spini, *Risorgimento e Protestanti*, Naples, 1956

V. Titone, 'Garibaldi', *Quaderni Storici*, 2, 1963, pp. 52–65

B. Tobia, *Una patria per gli italiani. Spazi, itinerari, monumenti nell'Italia unita*, Rome and Bari, 1991

G. M. Trevelyan, *Garibaldi and the making of Italy*, London, 1911

_____, *Garibaldi and the Thousand*, London, 1909

_____, *Garibaldi's defence of the Roman Republic*, London, 1907

G. Tricoli, 'Il mito di Garibaldi in Sicilia', *Archivio Storico Siciliano*, serie 4, 9, 1983, pp. 79–106

R. Ugolini, *Garibaldi. Genesi di un mito*, Rome, 1982

W. L. Vance, *America's Rome*, 2 vols, New Haven, CT, and London, 1989

Colonel Vecchi, *Garibaldi at Caprera*, trans. Mrs Gaskell, London, 1862

J. Vernon, *Politics and the people: a study in English political culture, c.1815–1867*, Cambridge, 1993

R. Villari, 'La prefigurazione politica del giudizio storico su Garibaldi', *Studi Storici*, 23/2, 1982, pp. 261–4.

M. Weber, *Economy and society*, 2 vols, Berkeley, CA, 1978

Unpublished theses and papers

M. Bernardi, 'Garibaldi et l'opinion publique française de 1860 à 1882', Université de Paris, I, Centre de Recherches en Histoire des XIX–XXe Siècles, Mémoire de Maîtrise, 1982

N. Blakiston, 'Garibaldi's visit to London in 1864', unpublished paper, British Library

INDEX